As a creative medium, ancient Greek tragedy has had an extraordinarily wide influence: many of the surviving plays are still part of the theatrical repertoire, and texts like *Agamemnon, Antigone,* and *Medea* have had a profound effect on Western culture. This *Companion* is not a conventional introductory textbook but an attempt, by seven distinguished scholars, to present the familiar corpus in the context of modern reading, criticism, and performance of Greek tragedy. There are three main emphases: on tragedy as an institution in the civic life of ancient Athens, on a range of different critical interpretations arising from fresh readings of the texts, and on changing patterns of reception, adaptation, and performance from antiquity to the present. Each chapter can be read independently, but each is linked with the others in different ways, and most examples are drawn from the same selection of plays.

THE CAMBRIDGE
COMPANION TO
GREEK TRAGEDY

CAMBRIDGE COMPANIONS TO LITERATURE

The Cambridge Companion to Old English Literature
edited by Malcolm Godden and Michael Lapidge

The Cambridge Companion to Dante
edited by Rachel Jacoff

The Cambridge Chaucer Companion
edited by Piero Boitani and Jill Mann

The Cambridge Companion to Medieval English Theatre
edited by Richard Beadle

The Cambridge Companion to Shakespeare Studies
edited by Stanley Wells

The Cambridge Companion to English Renaissance Drama
edited by A. R. Braunmuller and Michael Hattaway

The Cambridge Companion to English Poetry, Donne to Marvell
edited by Thomas N. Corns

The Cambridge Companion to Milton
edited by Dennis Danielson

The Cambridge Companion to British Romanticism
edited by Stuart Curran

The Cambridge Companion to James Joyce
edited by Derek Attridge

The Cambridge Companion to Ibsen
edited by James McFarlane

The Cambridge Companion to Brecht
edited by Peter Thomson and Glendyr Sacks

The Cambridge Companion to Beckett
edited by John Pilling

The Cambridge Companion to T. S. Eliot
edited by A. David Moody

The Cambridge Companion to Renaissance Humanism
edited by Jill Kraye

The Cambridge Companion to Conrad
edited by J. H. Stape

The Cambridge Companion to the Eighteenth-Century Novel
edited by John Richetti

The Cambridge Companion to Faulkner
edited by Philip M. Weinstein

The Cambridge Companion to Thoreau
edited by Joel Myerson

The Cambridge Companion to Edith Wharton
edited by Millicent Bell

The Cambridge Companion to Realism and Naturalism
edited by Donald Pizer

The Cambridge Companion to Twain
edited by Forrest G. Robinson

The Cambridge Companion to Whitman
edited by Ezra Greenspan

The Cambridge Companion to Hemingway
edited by Scott Donaldson

THE CAMBRIDGE
COMPANION TO
GREEK TRAGEDY

EDITED BY
P. E. EASTERLING
Regius Professor of Greek in the University of Cambridge

CAMBRIDGE
UNIVERSITY PRESS

PUBLISHED BY THE PRESS SYNDICATE OF THE UNIVERSITY OF CAMBRIDGE
The Pitt Building, Trumpington Street, Cambridge CB2 1RP, United Kingdom

CAMBRIDGE UNIVERSITY PRESS
The Edinburgh Building, Cambridge CB2 2RU, United Kingdom
40 West 20th Street, New York, NY 10011–4211, USA
10 Stamford Road, Oakleigh, Melbourne 3166, Australia

© Cambridge University Press 1997

First published 1997
Reprinted 1999

Printed in the United Kingdom at the University Press, Cambridge

Typeset in Sabon

A catalogue record for this book is available from the British Library

Library of Congress cataloguing in publication data
Easterling, P. E.
The Cambridge companion to Greek tragedy / edited by P. E. Easterling.
      p.   cm.
Includes bibliographical references (p. 359).
ISBN 0 521 41245 5 (hardcover). – ISBN 0 521 42351 1 (paperback)
    1. Greek drama (Tragedy) – History and criticism.
        2. Theatre – Greece – History.
            I. Title
          PA3131.E28   1997
    882'.0109–dc21   96-37392 CIP

ISBN 0 521 41245 5 hardback
ISBN 0 521 42351 1 paperback

CE

CONTENTS

List of illustrations   *page* ix
List of contributors   xiii
Preface   xv
Plan of the city of Athens   xvii

Part I: Tragedy as an institution: the historical context

1   'Deep plays': theatre as process in Greek civic life   3
    PAUL CARTLEDGE

2   A show for Dionysus   36
    P. E. EASTERLING

3   The audience of Athenian tragedy   54
    SIMON GOLDHILL

4   The pictorial record   69
    OLIVER TAPLIN

Part II: The plays

5   The sociology of Athenian tragedy   93
    EDITH HALL

6   The language of tragedy: rhetoric and communication   127
    SIMON GOLDHILL

7   Form and performance   151
    P.E. EASTERLING

8 Myth into *muthos*: the shaping of tragic plot   178
   PETER BURIAN

Part III: Reception

9 From repertoire to canon   211
   P. E. EASTERLING

10 Tragedy adapted for stages and screens: the Renaissance to the present   228
   PETER BURIAN

11 Tragedy in performance: nineteenth- and twentieth-century productions   284
   FIONA MACINTOSH

12 Modern critical approaches to Greek tragedy   324
   SIMON GOLDHILL

   Glossary   348
   Chronology   352
   Texts, commentaries and translations   355
   Works cited   359
   Index   380

ILLUSTRATIONS

page

1 *Stēlē* from Aixone, in honour of two *chorēgoi*. *Photo*: Epigraphical Museum, Athens; reproduced by courtesy of the Ministry of Culture and Science, Archaeological Receipts Fund, Athens — 7

2 Attic calyx-crater with *aulos*-player and chorus members or actors. Malibu, Collections of the J. Paul Getty Museum 82.AE.83 — 12

3 Sculptured base from Delos. *Photo*: Wim Swaan — 50

4 Attic crater with 'Basle Dancers'. Basle, Antikenmuseum und Skulpturhalle BS 415 — 70

5 Fragments of Attic jar. Corinth Museum T114. *Photo*: American School of Classical Studies, Athens, Corinth Excavations — 71

6 Fifth-century representation of Aeschylus' *Libation-Bearers*. Copenhagen, National Museum of Denmark, Department of Near Eastern and Classical Antiquities inv. no. 597 — 72

7 The 'Pronomos Vase', showing a team of tragic actors costumed for the satyr play. Naples, Museo Nazionale 3240 inv. no. 81673. *Photo*: François Lissarrague — 73

8 Crater from Apulia, South Italy, probably depicting Dionysus. New York, Metropolitan Museum of Art L.1988.81.4, Collection of Jan Mitchell & Sons — 75

9 Apulian vase with comic actors. New York, Fleischman Collection F56 — 75

10 Fourth-century Attic vase with scene derived from Euripides' *Iphigeneia among the Taurians*. Ferrara, Museo Archeologico Nazionale di Spina T1145 inv. no. 3032 — 77

11 Jar from Heraclea with Medea escaping in her dragon chariot. Policoro, Museo Nazionale Della Siritide 35302 — 78

12 Early fourth-century South Italian crater with a more elaborate representation of Medea's escape. Cleveland, Museum of Art, Leonard C. Hanna Jr Fund 91.1 — 79

13 Apulian volute-crater depicting a different version of the Medea story. Munich, Staatliche Antikensammungen und Glyptothek 3297   81

14 Vase with scene inspired by Euripides' *Hippolytus*. British Museum BM F279. *Photo*: copyright, British Museum   83

15 Apulian calyx-crater with scene inspired by Sophocles' *Oedipus at Colonus*. Melbourne, Geddes Collection A5:3. *Photo*: by courtesy of Graham Geddes   84

16 Apulian jug depicting blind man and king. Basle, Antikenmuseum und Skulpturhalle BS 473. *Photo*: Claire Niggli   86

17 Sicilian crater with scene inspired by Sophocles' *Oedipus the King*. Syracuse, MusArchReg 66557   87

18 Scene from the 1968 Santa Fe Opera production of Hans Werner Henze's opera *The Bassarids*. *Photo*: New York Public Library for the Performing Arts, Research Division; by courtesy of the Santa Fe Opera   270

19 Electra Catselli as Clytemnestra in Michael Cacoyannis' film *Electra*, 1961. *Photo*: Museum of Modern Art, Film Stills Archive, New York   277

20 Melina Mercouri as Phaedra in Jules Dassin's film *Phaedra*, 1961. *Photo*: Museum of Modern Art, Film Stills Archive, New York   278

21 Franco Citti as Oedipus in Pier Paolo Pasolini's film *Edipo Re*, 1967. *Photo*: Museum of Modern Art, Film Stills Archive, New York   280

22 Scene from *Antigone* at Covent Garden, 1845. From *The Illustrated London News*, 18 January 1845. *Photo*: by permission of the Syndics of Cambridge University Library   287

23 Jean Mounet-Sully in *Oedipus* at the Comédie Française, 1881   290

24 The chorus of *Ajax*, the first Cambridge Greek play, 1882. From centenary programme, 'A hundred years of the Cambridge Greek play', 1983, reproduced by courtesy of the Cambridge Greek Play Committee   293

25 *Helena in Troas* at Hengler's Circus, London, 1886. From *The Graphic*, 5 June 1886. *Photo*: by permission of the Syndics of Cambridge University Library   295

26 Max Reinhardt's production of *Oedipus Rex* at Covent Garden, 1912. *Photo*: from the Collections of the Theatre Museum, reproduced by courtesy of the Trustees of the Victoria and Albert Museum   300

27 Lillah McCarthy as Iphigeneia at the Kingsway Theatre, London, 1912. *Photo*: from the Collections of the Theatre Museum, reproduced by courtesy of the Trustees of the Victoria and Albert Museum   303

28 *Prometheus Bound* at the Delphic Festival, 1930. *Photo*: Athens, Benaki Museum, Photographic Archive   307

29 Laurence Olivier in the Old Vic production of *Oedipus Rex*, 1945. *Photo*: John Vickers   310

30 Douglas Campbell in the Stratford (Ontario) Festival's production of *Oedipus Rex*, directed by Tyrone Guthrie, 1955. *Photo*: McKague, Toronto 311

31 Tokusaburo Arashi playing the lead in Yukio Ninagawa's *Medea*, at the National Theatre, London, 1987. *Photo*: John Haynes 314

32 Karolos Koun's production of the *Oresteia*, 1982. *Photo*: Argyropoulos Photopress 315

33 The Furies from Peter Hall's production of the *Oresteia* at the National Theatre, London. *Photo*: Nobby Clark; from the Collections of the Theatre Museum, reproduced by courtesy of the Trustees of the Victoria and Albert Museum 317

CONTRIBUTORS

PETER BURIAN is Professor of Classical and Comparative Literatures at Duke University. He has published a number of critical essays on the three extant Greek tragedians as well as translations from Aeschylus and Euripides. He was the editor of *Directions in Euripidean Criticism* (Duke University Press 1985).

PAUL CARTLEDGE is Reader in Greek History in the University of Cambridge and Fellow and Director of Studies in Classics at Clare College. His publications include *Aristophanes and his Theatre of the Absurd* (Duckworth/Bristol Classical Press, revised edition 1995) and the forthcoming *The Cambridge Illustrated History of Ancient Greece*.

PAT EASTERLING is Regius Professor of Greek in the University of Cambridge and Fellow of Newnham College. She was one of the editors of *The Cambridge History of Classical Literature* and is a General Editor of Cambridge Greek and Latin Classics, in which series she has published a commentary on Sophocles, *Trachiniae* (1982). She is currently writing a commentary on Sophocles, *Oedipus at Colonus*, also for the series.

SIMON GOLDHILL is Lecturer in Classics in the University of Cambridge and Fellow of King's College. Among his publications are *Reading Greek Tragedy* (1986), *The Poet's Voice: Essays on Poetics and Greek Literature* (1991) and, most recently, *Foucault's Virginity: Ancient Erotic Fiction and the History of Sexuality* (1995) (all published by Cambridge University Press).

EDITH HALL is Lecturer in Classics in the University of Oxford and Fellow of Somerville College. Her publications include *Inventing the Barbarian: Greek Self-Definition through Tragedy* (Oxford University Press 1989) and an edition of Aeschylus' *Persians* (Aris & Phillips 1996).

FIONA MACINTOSH is Lecturer in English at Goldsmith's College, University of London. She is the author of *Dying Acts: Death in Ancient Greek and Modern Irish Tragic Drama* (Cork University Press 1994), *Sophocles' Oedipus Rex: A Production History* (Cambridge University Press, forthcoming) and co-author with Edith Hall of *Hellas Rehearsed: Greek Drama on the British Stage 1660–1914* (Oxford University Press, forthcoming).

OLIVER TAPLIN is Professor of Classical Languages and Literature in the University of Oxford, and Fellow and Tutor of Magdalen College. His most recent book is *Comic Angels – and Other Approaches to Greek Drama through Vase-Paintings* (Oxford University Press 1993).

PREFACE

The study of Greek tragedy can be described as a constant dialogue between two approaches, one that sees Greek culture as alien and remote, and emphasises the paramount need to decode the historical context, and another that reads the plays as part of its own tradition, as works in the 'classic repertoire' of theatre and culture. This book tries to do justice to both, in the spirit of Clifford Geertz's question, 'How is it that other people's creations can be so utterly their own and so deeply part of us?' Its aim is to present ancient Greek tragedy in the context of late twentieth-century reading, criticism, and performance, and it has three main objectives: to study the plays in relation to the society that created and developed tragic theatre, to make practical use of strategies of interpretation that have yielded interesting results in recent years, and to take note of changing patterns of reception, from antiquity to the present. All the contributors share these objectives, but it would have been wrong to try to arrive at any kind of critical consensus, and each chapter needs to be taken as an independent and personal view.

Each chapter can be read separately from the rest of the volume, but there are several ways in which each is linked with the others, particularly through recurrent discussion of a limited selection of primary texts (*Oresteia, Antigone, Oedipus the King, Philoctetes*, the Electra plays, *Bacchae, The Children of Heracles, Hecuba, Helen, Hippolytus, Ion, Medea, Trojan Women*). Suggestions for further reading are given at the end of each chapter, except in the case of Chapter 1: this offers more extensive footnotes on each paragraph, which are designed to give a survey of the background work on Athenian society. All footnotes are keyed to the list of Works Cited (pp. 359–79). In recent years much of the new work on tragedy has been presented at conferences; a good way of catching the flavour of the current critical debate is to sample the publications that have followed these events, especially Winkler and Zeitlin (1990); Sommerstein et al. (1993); Scodel (1993); Silk (1996); and B. Goff, ed., *Tragedy, History, Theory* (Austin

1996) and C. Pelling, ed., *Greek Tragedy and the Historian* (Oxford 1997), which appeared too late to be cited by contributors to this volume. Some issues of journals are also relevant: *BICS* 34 (1987); *Métis* 3.1–2 (1988); *Arion* 3rd series 3.1 (1995).

For information on texts, commentaries, fragments and translations the reader is referred to vol. 1 of *The Cambridge History of Classical Literature* and to pp. 355–8 below. Abbreviations of titles of Greek plays can be found in the lists on pp. 355–7, and there is a Glossary of transliterated Greek words on pp. 348–51.

This is a truly collaborative work which owes much to the generosity of all contributors in finding time to make detailed criticisms and suggestions. I am grateful, too, for comments on my own material to Eric Handley (Ch. 2) and to Joyce Reynolds and Charlotte Roueché (Ch. 9). Fiona Macintosh has shared some of the editorial responsibility; her help, along with that of three colleagues at the Press, has been vital to the cohesion of the whole volume. Nancy-Jane Thompson had the original idea for a *Cambridge Companion to Greek Tragedy* and put a great deal of energy into its planning, Pauline Hire has guided us through the complicated later phases with her usual wisdom and thoughtful attention to detail, and Susan Moore's copyediting, as always, has been matchless. Finally, it is a pleasure to thank Jennifer Potter for her vigilant proof-reading.

Part of the credit for the vigorous state of contemporary critical work on tragedy is due to the influence of a Cambridge author, R. P. Winnington-Ingram, a modest, witty and formidable scholar who died in 1993, after a distinguished career in the University of London. This *Companion* is gratefully dedicated to his memory.

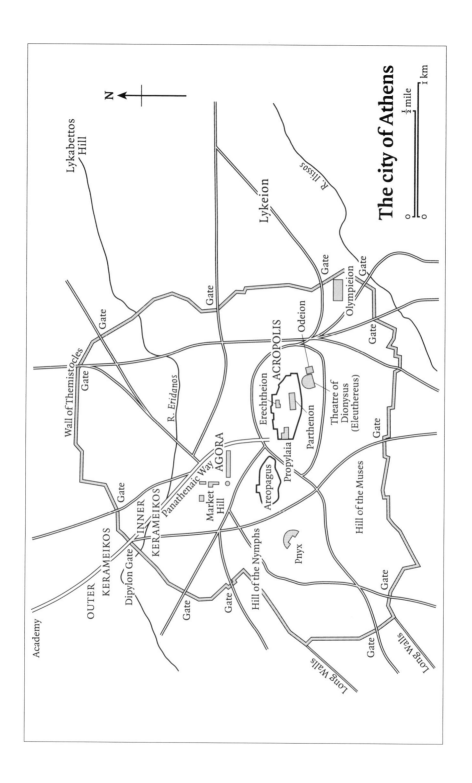

The city of Athens

N

$\frac{1}{2}$ mile

1 km

Lykabettos Hill

Lykeion

R. Ilissos

Wall of Themistocles

R. Eridanos

Gate

Gate

Gate

Gate

Gate

Gate

Gate

Gate

Gate

Gate

Gate

Gate

Gate

ACROPOLIS

Erechtheion

Parthenon

Propylaia

Odeion

Theatre of Dionysus (Eleuthereus)

Olympieion

Hill of the Muses

Areopagus

Panathenaic Way

AGORA

Market Hill

Pnyx

Hill of the Nymphs

INNER KERAMEIKOS

OUTER KERAMEIKOS

Dipylon Gate

Academy

Long Walls

Long Walls

I

TRAGEDY AS AN INSTITUTION: THE HISTORICAL CONTEXT

I

PAUL CARTLEDGE

'Deep plays': theatre as process in Greek civic life

LIFE IMITATES ART?

Theatre as we understand it in the West today was invented in all essentials in ancient Greece, and more specifically in classical Athens. In Athens, however, theatre was always a mass social phenomenon, considered too important to be left solely to theatrical specialists or even confined to the theatres to be found both in the centre of Athens itself and in some of the constituent demes (villages or wards) of the surrounding civic territory of Attica. Athenian tragic drama did not have merely a political background, a passive setting within the polis, or city, of the Athenians. Tragedy, rather, was itself an active ingredient, and a major one, of the political foreground, featuring in the everyday consciousness and even the nocturnal dreams of the Athenian citizen.

This was especially the case after the establishment of an early form of democracy at Athens, the world's first such polity, towards the end of the sixth century BC, although some kind of tragic drama seems to have been developed and officially recognised several decades earlier during the relatively benign and populist rule of the aristocratic dictator Peisistratus (c. 545–528). Indeed, democratic Athenian political life in the fifth and fourth centuries was also deeply theatrical outside the formally designated theatrical spaces. Not only did the Athenians theatricalise their ordinary experience through ritual dramas of everyday life, in the manner of the African Ndembu studied by Victor Turner. There was a formal analogy or even identity between their experience inside and that outside the theatre, most notably in the performance of the constitutive communal ritual of animal blood-sacrifice. The latter serves also to remind us that Greek tragedy,

For their unstinting help with this chapter I am indebted to my friends and fellow-*choreutai* Simon Goldhill, Edith Hall, and Oliver Taplin, but above all to our general editor (both *koruphaios* and *chorēgos*) Pat Easterling. For the defects that remain, even those due to some heaven-sent *hamartia*, I accept full responsibility. My title is adapted from a famous article by the doyen of cultural anthropologists, Clifford Geertz, 'Deep play: notes on the Balinese cockfight' (see list of Works Cited).

although as an art-form it developed its own professionally theatrical ethos and conventions, as a communal ritual never broke completely free of its originary cultic moorings.[1]

Athens was not the whole of classical Greece. It was just one among more than a thousand separate political communities stretching from Spain in the far west to Georgia on the Black Sea in the east, communities that collectively made up the cultural entity 'Hellas'. Yet in several ways, most notably its size and social complexity but chiefly its radically democratic way of life, and for economic and military as well as political and aesthetic reasons, Athens was both an exceptional and an exceptionally influential Greek city. This exceptionalism embraced a peculiarly intense devotion to the practice and dissemination of the visual, literary and performing arts. Already in the fifth century Athens had attracted to itself the flower of Greek intellectual life from all around the Mediterranean basin, including several tragic poets (Ion from Chios, Pratinas and Aristion from Phlius, Achaeus from Eretria, Spintharus from Heraclea on the Black Sea, and possibly Hippias from Elis and Acestor from Thrace). Throughout most of the fifth and fourth centuries, indeed, Athens was the undisputed cultural epicentre of all Hellas, its 'City Hall of Wisdom' in Plato's patriotic phrase.[2]

Thus defeat of Athens by its arch-rival and cultural antipode Sparta in the unhappily prolonged Peloponnesian War (431–404 BC) did nothing to alter its focal cultural status. The local Attic dialect of Greek along with other markedly Athenian cultural forms (including tragedy) became the basis of that wider Hellenism which in the wake of the conquests of Alexander the Great of Macedon (334–323) spread eastwards through Asia as far as Afghanistan and the Punjab, and embedded itself more firmly nearer to home, in Egypt and the Levant as well as in Turkey, where Greek communities had been established along the Aegean coast since the turn of the last millennium BC. The newly founded or revitalised cities of Alexandria, Berytus and Pergamum bear eloquent witness to this novel, Hellenistic culture of the last three centuries BC, and it was principally through them, besides Athens itself, that the Greek heritage as a whole was transmitted to Rome and so eventually to contemporary Western civilisation.[3]

Central to this heritage is the idea of the theatre that was Athens' peculiar original invention and is still today a vital and vibrant part of the wider

[1] Origins/democratisation of tragedy: see final section of this chapter, and n. 31. Peisistratus and drama: Shapiro (1989) ch. 5. Ndembu: Turner (1973). Sacrifice: Detienne & Vernant (1989). Tragedy and religion: see nn. 7, 19.
[2] Greek world: Hornblower (1993); Jones et al. (1984). Athens as capital city of culture (Plato, *Protag.* 337d): Ostwald (1992).
[3] Alexander and Hellenism: Lane Fox (1980).

Hellenic legacy. To judge by our scattered and anecdotal literary evidence, and the more substantial testimony of archaeology in the shape of theatrical scenes depicted on vases, Athenian theatre struck a notably resonant chord in Sicily and South Italy (known later to the Romans as Magna Graecia or 'Great Greece'). Aeschylus, one of the founding fathers of developed Athenian tragedy, not only produced or re-produced his tragedies in Sicily but also met his death there, in *c.* 456. Some forty years later, a number of the Athenians held prisoner in Syracuse's stone quarries after the catastrophic failure of imperial Athens' attempt to conquer Sicily were said to have been reprieved in exchange for the recital of some verses of Euripides. It was immediately from Magna Graecia that Greek theatre moved house to Rome, as part of the process whereby in Horace's neat phrase 'captive Greece captivated its fierce conqueror and introduced the arts to rustic Latium'.[4]

The experience of Greek Sicily and South Italy, however, was just the most vivid illustration of a universal Greek theatrical phenomenon, whereby following the Athenian model a purpose-built stone theatre came to be as much of a fixture in Hellenic civic architecture as the *agora*. Equally interesting in its way, unless the anecdotal evidence is deceiving us, was the migration of Athenian playwrights to the Macedonian court of King Archelaus towards the end of the Peloponnesian War: both Euripides and his fellow-tragedian Agathon (whose maiden victory at the Great Dionysia festival of 416 provides the dramatic occasion for Plato's *Symposium*) beat a path to Pella and royal rather than democratic patronage. In other words, unlike some of the finest vintage wines, Athenian tragedy could travel, and in this we see the ultimate origins of the process through which Aeschylus, Sophocles and Euripides have become 'classics' of the tragedians' art. But in this opening chapter it is the local and original quality of Greek tragedy, its Athenian bloom and quintessence, that provide the dominant themes and topics for discussion.[5]

THE ATHENIANNESS OF FESTIVAL HISTRIONICS

Clifford Geertz used the phrase 'the theater state' in the subtitle of his study of Bali in the nineteenth century. That description would be at least as apt for classical Athens. Alternatively, the culture of Athens may be viewed

[4] Idea of theatre: Finley (1980). Spread of Athenian theatre to South Italy: Taplin (1992) and (1993). Illustrations: Green & Handley (1995); Trendall & Webster (1971); and Ch. 4 below. Syracuse anecdote: Plutarch, *Nicias* 29. Fourth-century and later reception of fifth-century tragedy: Ch. 9 below.

[5] Civic architecture: Kolb (1979), (1981) and (1989); Whitehead (1995). Macedon's cultural attraction: Hatzopoulos & Loukopoulos (1981); cf. Easterling (1994).

fruitfully as a 'performance culture' (cf. Ch. 3 below). The city celebrated more statewide religious festivals (in Attica as well as in Athens proper) than any other Greek polis. These included the two annual city play-festivals in honour of Dionysus, together with an unknown number of local festivals in the 140 or so demes. At least one of the local festivals, the Rural Dionysia, which all the demes celebrated, also served as a vehicle for formal theatrical performance, and it is possible that plays staged originally in one of the two 'national' festivals subsequently 'transferred' to one or other Attic venue. Deme inscriptions ([1] is an example) bear witness to a system of elite sponsorship modelled on that used for the central celebrations, and among the several known deme theatres that of Thorikos is a particularly impressive extant example.[6]

On one level, which we might be tempted to label secular, these festivals were an occasion for rest, relaxation and recuperation from the back-breaking round of manual labour that fell to the lot of the vast majority of the 200,000–250,000 inhabitants of Attica, male and female, citizen and non-citizen, slave and free, who in this radically pre-industrial society earned their living typically from farming Attica's not especially fertile terrain. But the festivals were also religious and political, or rather political because they were religious, since in ancient pre-Christian Greece the religious and the political were fabrics of thought and behaviour woven from the same threads. Thus they, and the play-festivals of Dionysus not least among them, served further as a device for defining Athenian civic identity, which meant exploring and confirming but also questioning what it was to be a citizen of a democracy, this brand-new form of popular self-government. The use of rituals – standardised, repeated events of symbolic character, symbolic statements about the social order – and especially the ritual of collective animal-sacrifice helped to sustain and reinforce that internalised Athenian civic identity.[7]

All Athenian tragedy was performed within the context of religious rituals in honour of one or other manifestation of that 'elusive but

[6] Phrase 'theater-state': Geertz (1980). 'Performance culture': Rehm (1992) ch. 1. Tragedy in context: Csapo & Slater (1995) (sources); Green (1994); Longo (1990); Scodel (1993); Vernant & Vidal-Naquet (1988); Walcot (1976); Wilson (1993); Winkler & Zeitlin (1990). Festivals (Rural Dionysia: Plato, *Rep.* 475d): Mikalson (1975); Parke (1977); Parker (1987); Whitehead (1986a) ch. 7 and (1986b).

[7] Nature of festival: Mikalson (1982); Cartledge (1985). Democracy: Hansen (1991). Slavery: see Ch. 5 below. Religion and politics: Bruit Zaidman & Schmitt Pantel (1992). Rituals: Osborne in Osborne & Hornblower (1994); Strauss (1985). Tragedy and ritual: Easterling (1993b); Rehm (1994); Seaford (1994); Sourvinou-Inwood (1994). Sacrifice and tragedy: Burkert (1966); Henrichs (1995) 97 n. 44. Identity: Boegehold & Scafuro (1994); Loraux (1986), (1993).

[1] Honorific *stēlē* from the Attic deme Aixone, set up in the theatre in the second half of the fourth century BC on behalf of two prizewinning *chorēgoi*. The relief depicts a satyr bringing a jug to fill Dionysus' wine-cup; on the fascia above are incised five comic masks.

compelling god' Dionysus. The Great or City Dionysia was a spring festival celebrated annually towards the end of March or beginning of April in terms of our calendar. The Dionysus honoured here was the local patron god of Eleutherae, a village on the border between Attica and the region of Boeotia (of which the principal city was Athens' regular enemy, Thebes). This was a more grandiose and international affair than the older and more inward-looking Lenaea festival held during the depths of winter in January–February time. The Rural Dionysia, thirdly, honoured Dionysus 'in the fields'. Different demes celebrated this on different days but at the same time of the agricultural year, during the dead, rainy season of December–January a few weeks before the Lenaea.[8]

Dionysus' cult-title Lenaeus may have been derived from one of the artefacts essential for creating his *spécialité de la maison*, the fermented juice of the wine grape, namely the wine-vat. But the god's significance comprehended much more than vinous intoxication or agricultural fertility more generally. Quite why all tragedy, indeed all drama, at Athens was performed under the sign of Dionysus is still found problematic, although his association with illusion, transgression and metamorphosis was obviously germane to his theatrical status. The quintessential outsider, he was entirely appropriately worshipped in the form of a mask, which could both figure his absent presence and provide actors and chorus with the alibi and means of alienation required for the dramatic representation of others (and otherness). Nevertheless, Dionysiac devotion and religious experience, which could be personal and private as well as communal and civic, extended well beyond the formalised performance of drama and might carry very different implications and aspirations according to context. For instance, some aspects or forms of Dionysiac worship outside the theatre were notably, or notoriously, attractive to women, yet women were certainly excluded from active roles in dramatic representations and possibly also from spectating, which the Greeks regarded as an integral part of the performance. There is reason, moreover, for supposing that the Dionysus routinely worshipped in the Attic countryside was not the disturbing, even potentially lethal deity who periodically held sway in his theatre at the foot of the Athenian Acropolis.[9]

It is one of the paradoxes of our evidence for ancient Athenian democracy that the most articulate contemporary theorists and commentators were

---

[8] Quotation from Nagy in Carpenter & Faraone (1993) vii. All aspects of the Great/City Dionysia and the Lenaea: Pickard-Cambridge (1988). Archaeology: Simon (1983).

[9] See Ch. 2 for full bibliography. Masks, literal: Frontisi-Ducroux & Vernant (1983): Frontisi-Ducroux (1989), (1991) and (1995); Vernant & Vidal-Naquet (1988) 189–206; cf. Brook (1988) 217–31; Soyinka (1976) 38. Masks, metaphorical: Carpenter & Faraone (1993).

almost to a man deeply hostile to it on principle – on the grounds that it constituted the dictatorship of the ignorant and poor many, the proletariat as it were, over their social and intellectual betters, the elite few (such as themselves). Perhaps the foremost of these diehard critics, or implacable foes, was Plato, who found himself unable to avoid paying grudging and veiled tributes to the importance of Athenian democratic theatre, so central was it to Athenian civic and cultural life. The dialogue form with which his name is inseparably linked may well have owed much to his first-hand experience of Athenian dramatic exchanges. One of his best-known dialogues, as we have seen, has an explicitly tragic connection. And in his final work of extreme old age, the *Laws*, which he called ironically the 'best' sort of tragedy, he coined the punning term 'theatrokratia', meaning literally the sovereign rule of the theatre-audience, to refer to the dictatorship of the mass (or mob) of poor Athenian citizens who formed the majority of the spectatorship, as they formed the ruling majority of the Athenian democratic state as a whole.[10]

Further testimony to the perceived importance of the theatre in Plato's day (*c.* 428–347) is the long-running public controversy that raged over the best use of the city's Theoric or Festival Fund, from which a small 'dole' was given to enable even – or especially – the poorest citizens to pay their theatre entrance-fee. Financially, in terms of the public assets of the state as a whole, the Theoric Fund was no doubt 'very small beer'. But that merely corroborates its enormous symbolic significance as a token of democratic ideology. As Thucydides' Pericles famously observed during a performance of the city's annual grand and solemn ritual of state funeral for its war dead, no Athenian should be debarred by simple poverty from playing his full part in democratic debate and action. And such debate and action took place in the theatre no less than in the other democratic arenas to be considered below. This explains how the Theoric payments could be colourfully but not fantastically labelled by one prominent fourth-century politician as 'the glue of the democracy'; and how, fantastically, the hero of Aristophanes' *Peace*, which was staged in 421 just as a real peace was about to be concluded with Sparta, could make a present to the Council, the Athenians' chief administrative body, of Theoria, the personified goddess of Festival.[11]

---

[10] Critics of democracy: Jones (1957) ch. 3; Roberts (1994). Plato's politics: Finley (1977b). His 'theatrokratia': *Laws* 701b; cf. *Rep.* 492b–c (theatre as a characteristically mass gathering on a par with the Assembly, People's Court and military camp). Spectating: Segal (1995). Plato's 'anti-tragic theater' (esp. *Laws* 817a – the 'best' tragedy): Nussbaum (1986) 122–35; Euben (1990).

[11] Theoric Fund as 'very small beer': Jones (1957) 34. Theoric Fund as 'glue of the democracy':

It is not certain that the Theoric Fund was already in existence in the fifth century. But the principle of payment from public funds for political participation was firmly established in the 450s, when Pericles introduced a small *per diem* payment for jurors serving in the People's Court, and a similar grant began to be made to Athenian infantrymen on active duty. On the other hand, the semi-private, semi-public 'liturgical' system of financing the choral and dramatic festivals was certainly in place by the time of Pericles' death in 429, indeed well before, since he had himself as a young man performed this official function for Aeschylus in 472. A liturgy was literally a work performed on behalf of the people; under the Athenian democratic regime of public taxation, it became a legally enforceable obligation. It was imposed on wealthy citizens (and in some cases resident aliens) possessing a certain, very high, minimum value of property to compel them to contribute from their own pockets to the expense of running the state. Liturgies, of which there could be over a hundred in any one year, were of two main kinds: military, that is naval (the upkeep of a state warship for a year), and festival. Of the latter, the one that concerns us particularly here is the tragic *chorēgia*, payment for a tragic (and satyric) chorus at the Dionysia or Lenaea.[12]

About the time of Pericles' death, which coincided approximately with the birth of Plato, another extreme if idiosyncratic anti-democrat penned a splenetic pamphlet that is our earliest surviving Attic prose composition. The anonymous author, fondly if probably inaccurately known as the 'Old Oligarch' (he was certainly an oligarch), fulminates against this Athenian liturgy system of sponsorship of the arts, which he represents as a sort of gigantic confidence trick to redistribute the wealth of the elite compulsorily to the differential benefit of the poor mass of the Athenian citizen body. To which a committed democrat such as Pericles would surely have replied, no less vehemently and with rather better justification, that, as the favour of the gods was likely to be won by lavish expenditure on religious display, private funds ought to be channelled into the magnification of the state's religious festivals no less unstintingly than the public expenditure that was then being poured into public religious buildings, most conspicuously those on the Acropolis. Besides, super-rich liturgy-payers who fulfilled their obligations with gusto stood to gain at best enormous public good will and political

Demades *ap.* Plutarch, *Moral Essays* 1011b. Theoric payments generally: Buchanan (1962). Periclean Funeral Speech: Thuc. 2.35-46, at 38; state funeral: Loraux (1986).

[12] Jury-courts: Hansen (1991) ch. 8; Cartledge, Millett & Todd (1990). Liturgies, general: Davies (1967), (1971) and (1981). Liturgies, naval: Gabrielsen (1994). (A comparable work on festival liturgies as a whole is desiderated.) Tragic *chorēgia*: Wilson (1993) and (forthcoming). Minimum age of *chorēgos*: Golden (1990) 65-7. See further below, pp. 18-19.

support, at worst some protection against an accusation in the courts of anti-democratic prejudice and subversion.[13]

Somewhat less acrimonious witness to the all-pervasive cultural influence of tragedy is borne by the pioneer historians of the fifth and fourth centuries. Herodotus, who was not himself an Athenian citizen but had close connections both with Athens itself and with the South Italian colony of Thurii sponsored chiefly by Athens, betrays a strong bond of shared moral, theological and indeed tragic outlook with both Aeschylus (they had common subject matter in the Persian Wars) and Sophocles (tradition spoke of a personal friendship between them). As for Thucydides, the whole intellectual cast of his historiography has been seen as generically tragic and specifically Euripidean in both approach and tone. From the world of lived experience rather than theoretical reflection comes a suggestive anecdote preserved by Diodorus of Sicily, the first-century BC Greek author of a 'universal' history. Immediately before one of the crucial Peloponnesian War sea-battles, off the Arginousai islands in 406, the Athenian admiral (and later democratic hero) Thrasybulus dreamed that he and six of his fellow-admirals were in a packed theatre playing the roles of the Seven against Thebes in Euripides' *Phoenician Women* (first staged at Athens a few years previously). Against them he saw ranged the enemy commanders, in a different play but by the same author, the *Suppliant Women* (of the 420s), and from this vision he is said to have inferred, correctly, that the Athenians would win the naval battle, but only just.[14]

THE MENTALITY OF *AGONIA*

That anecdote may be evidence for the dissemination of tragedy in Thrasybulus' day by private means, either through written texts or by dramatised readings at upper-class symposia perhaps. It is certainly evidence for competition between plays at Athens, though in real waking life that occurred between plays by different authors. The ancient Greek word for competitiveness is *agōnia*, from which comes English 'agony', and 'agony' in our sense aptly enough captures the awfulness of the internecine and fratricidal Peloponnesian War. But for the Greeks that ruinous struggle was also literally an *agōn* or contest, animated by *agōnia* in its primary Greek

[13] 'Old Oligarch' = Pseudo-Xenophon, *Constitution of the Athenians* 1.13. Practicality (and rhetoric) of liturgy-payment: Ober (1989); Wilson (1991) and (1993). Acropolis building programme: Wycherley (1978) chs. 4–5.
[14] Herodotus: Waters (1985) 21. Thucydides: Finley (1967); Macleod (1983) ch. 13. Thrasybulus' dream: Diodorus 13.97.6. Dreams generally: Kyrtatas (1993) (esp. essay by K. Valakas). Athenocentrism of tragedy: see further Ch. 5 below.

[2] This small, late-fifth-century Attic red-figure calyx-crater depicts on its main surface a theatrically costumed *aulos*-player flanked by what seem to be two chorus members dressed as fighting cocks. Any identification of the scene must remain speculative.

signification of fight-to-the-death, zero-sum competitiveness. As one anonymous fifth-century philosopher (not necessarily an Athenian) observed, 'people do not find it pleasant to honour someone else, for they suppose that they themselves are being deprived of something'.

Perhaps the sharpest illustration of this Greek competitive attitude is to be seen in the cock-fight. The Athenians were typically Greek in their passion for cock-fighting, and they used it also as a metaphor for masculine rivalry, erotic or otherwise, in life as in art. Aristophanes, for instance, is said to have portrayed Right and Wrong Arguments as two fighting cocks in the original staged version of *Clouds* (423), and a contemporary vase-painting may actually depict that theatrical scene [2]. In a real cock-fight the defeated bird, if not actually slaughtered, was given the derogatory tag of 'slave', recalling a famous dictum of Heraclitus of Ephesus (*c.* 500) concerning human war, that it 'is the king and father of all: some it makes free, others slaves'.[15]

Cock-fighting, though, was a continuation of human warfare by other, avian means, not an alternative to or substitute for the real thing. The true site for the display of Greek manhood and masculine prowess was always the battlefield, the ancient Greek term for pugnacious bravery being precisely 'manliness' (*andreia*). War was to a Greek man, it has been justly remarked, what marriage was to a Greek woman: in each sphere they respectively fulfilled what their culture deemed to be their essential natures. The ancient Athenians, who in the fifth and fourth centuries were at war – usually from choice – by both land and sea for on average three years in every four, found plenty of opportunity to put their virility to the test. A particularly graphic witness to this relentless bellicosity is provided by the official casualty-list set up in about 460 BC by one of the ten Athenian tribes (artificial political-geographical divisions of the citizenry); this proudly enumerates its 177 dead, including two generals, who had been killed during a single year and in battlegrounds stretching from the Greek main-land to Cyprus. If that figure were to have been reproduced across all ten tribes, something approaching three per cent of the entire Athenian citizen body would have died in battle in that one year. Perhaps it is not altogether surprising that obsession with the destructiveness of war comes across so strongly as a theme and subject for debate in tragedy, in *Agamemnon*, *Ajax*, *Hecuba* and *Trojan Women*, among many other plays.[16]

War, however, although archetypal, was not by any means the only kind of *agōn* known to and lovingly practised by the Athenians. Competitive athletic sports or games, also a Greek invention within an originary religious framework, were another field of peculiarly masculine valour, sometimes indeed, in the case of the combat sports, almost a paramilitary exercise. The Athenians' Panathenaic Games held every fourth year since 566 were easily the largest such celebration staged by an individual Greek city and fell not far short in magnificence of the 'Circuit' of Panhellenic Games, also quadrennial, held at Olympia, Delphi, Isthmia and Nemea. Hippolytus,

---

[15] Symposia: Murray (1990). Greek 'contest-system': Gouldner (1965). Fifth-century philoso-pher = Anon. Iamblichi (? = Democritus of Abdera), *Fragmente der Vorsokratiker* 2: 400. Cock-fighting: Csapo (1993); Hoffmann (1974). See also n. 6, above.

[16] Nature of Greek warfare by land: Hanson (1989), (1991), (1995). By sea: Morrison & Coates (1986). Brief survey of Athens at war: Jones et al. (1984) ch. 6. War/marriage analogy: Vernant & Vidal-Naquet (1988) 23. Erechtheid casualty-list: Fornara (1983) no. 78.

eponymous subject of two tragedies by Euripides, was a conspicuously keen sportsman.

The idea of war and athletics as essentially competitive does not strike us as odd. Nor do we seem to find anything especially strange in competition between motion pictures at film 'festivals' such as the annual jamboree at Cannes. The Greeks, however, saw nothing odd in theatrical competition either, in which they engaged to the hilt. In the Dionysia and Lenaea festivals there was competition both between the plays or rather groups of plays (and playwrights, actors and liturgist-impresarios) and within the plays (between the leading characters or themes or ideas), and their idea of a one-off performance of a play or group of plays corresponded exactly to the one-off, everything-at-stake character of a Greek pitched battle by land or sea. Occasionally the connection between theatre and war (a connection that we but not they exploit metaphorically) could be made even more dramatically concrete, as when in 403, during the brief but bloody civil war between an oligarchic pro-Spartan junta and the democratic Resistance organised by Thrasybulus, the democrats mustered for battle in the theatre of the port district of Piraeus. The ceremony held to celebrate the restoration of democracy later that same year was a classic instance of the Athenians making a ritualised drama out of a political crisis.[17]

In a city peculiarly governed (in both senses) by use of the spoken word in public arenas, Athenian theatre was perhaps predictably dominated by antagonistic debate. *Hupokritēs*, literally 'answerer', was the standard word for actor, and *hupokrisis* was also used to mean non-theatrical rhetorical debate. Antagonistic debate was of the essence, too, in the democratic People's Court, which convened in several different spaces within the Agora, in the court of Areopagus, and in various other courts, before which lawsuits, another sort of *agōn*, were played out in dramatised adversarial format. The Athenians indeed, like the modern Americans, had a formidable, and not wholly undeserved, reputation for litigiousness to rival their reputation as theatregoers, and their experience in one sphere was easily transferable to the other, not least through the practice of creating a hubbub (*thorubos*) to influence the verdict.

The first of the ten canonical Attic orators, Antiphon of the deme Rhamnous, is said quite plausibly to have written tragedies, as well as speeches for his – usually oligarchic – clients in the lawcourts; pupils of

[17] Panathenaic Games: Neils et al. (1992). Olympics: Cartledge (1985) 103–13. Athenian athletics: Kyle (1987). Combat sports: Poliakoff (1987). Dionysia and Lenaea as competitive festivals: Osborne (1993). *Agōn* within tragedy: Duchemin (1968); Lloyd (1992). 403 BC civil war: Xenophon, *Hellenica* 2.4. Post-civil war reconciliation ritual: Strauss (1985) 69–72. Civic ceremonial and political manipulation: Connor (1987).

Isocrates, founder of Athens' first institute of advanced rhetoric in the early fourth century (not long before Plato opened his Academy), are credited with the same feat. The speech Antiphon gave in his own defence on a charge of oligarchic high treason did not get him acquitted but it did earn the highest praise from Thucydides, no mean critic. Composing pleas to suit the ethos of a client, who had to appear to act on his own behalf, was after all not that far removed from writing a script for characters in a staged dialogue. Some forensic speechwriters, moreover, were also regular prot-agonists in legal actions, seemingly fancying themselves as actors in the process. Aeschines, indeed, the principal political opponent of Demosthenes, had actually started in public life as a tragic actor, anticipating the more recent and rather more successful careers of President Ronald Reagan and Pope John Paul II.[18]

Besides a structure of competitive performance in front of lay citizen 'judges' representing the People of Athens, tragic drama also shared with litigation such significant subject-matter as wrongdoing towards both gods and men and its punishment, including debate over what punishment best fitted the criminal. In their role as civic teachers (cf. p. 21 below), tragedians were expected to contribute to popular understanding of the ways in which the gods sought to impose or foster justice among men. Moreover, the tragedians' dramatic exploitation of technical legal language and ideas underlines the affinity between the theatre and the courts. We have become perhaps too familiar through the medium of television with the notion of staged courtroom drama, but it was a bold, imaginative and above all original stroke on the part of Aeschylus in his *Eumenides* to stage a trial scene with a jury and an enacted vote, a genuine *coup de théâtre* not apparently emulated by his successors.

In short, a good case can be made for there having been a productively dialectical relationship between Athenian drama and lawcourt procedure. Conversely, it came naturally to Athenian forensic speechwriters to draw on tragedy in order to dramatise and strengthen their case. Thus Demosthenes in 343, when prosecuting Aeschines for alleged misconduct of an embassy to King Philip of Macedon, quoted from a speech of Creon in Sophocles' *Antigone*. Half a dozen years later Lycurgus, the leading statesman of the 330s and 320s who was responsible for having the first all-stone theatre of

---

[18] Athens as 'city of words': Goldhill (1986) ch. 3; O'Regan (1992) ch. 1. Interplay between theatre and courtroom: Ober & Strauss (1990); Bers (1994); Hall (1995). See further Ch. 6 below. Litigation as *agōn*: Chaniotis (1993); Faraone (1991). Antiphon: Cartledge (1990). Praise of Antiphon's last speech by Thucydides: 8.68.1. People's Court and litigiousness: see n. 12. Adjudication in Dionysia: Pope (1986). Isocrates: Too (1995). Aeschines: Lane Fox (1994).

Dionysus constructed and papyrus copy-texts of plays by the three 'classic' fifth-century tragedians committed to the public archives, elected to perform Praxithea's famous patriotic speech from Euripides' (mainly lost) *Erechtheus* as an integral part of his successful public prosecution of Leocrates in 336.[19]

THE MENTALITY OF PARTICIPATION

After much lucubration Aristotle in his *Politics* ended by defining the Greek citizen as the person relevantly qualified by gender (male), age (adult), and social status (free, legitimate, of citizen descent) who had an active share in public decision-taking (including the giving of judicial verdicts) and office-holding. In practical reality, he added with some reluctance (since, ethically and ideologically, he was not a democrat), such a theoretical definition applied most closely to the citizen of a democratic state. Athens was the most radical Greek democracy on offer. Here there was no property qualification for the holding and exercise of democratic citizenship, and official governmental functions were performed routinely by a remarkably high percentage of the normally 30,000 or so citizens. Yet even in egalitarian Athens there was a palpable gap between the theory and the practice. Although every citizen counted for one and no one for more than one when voting in the Assembly, it was easier for the wealthier, leisure-class Athenians to attend meetings if they wished; and there were certain vital military and financial officers elected by the Assembly who by law or in practice were drawn only from the wealthiest citizens. Birth too continued to be a factor of discrimination, as is amply attested by Euripides' dramatic questioning and subverting of its claims, for example in *Electra*. On the other side, it was apparently the poorer (and perhaps older) citizens who predominated among the jurymen of the People's Court. In warfare too there were important social-class divisions between the most opulent, who could serve as cavalrymen, the moderately wealthy who could provide their own heavy equipment and serve as hoplite infantrymen, and the poor majority of the citizens who served as rowers of the trireme warfleet. The latter was the basis of Athens' external power, including in the fifth century an overseas empire, yet a public social stigma seems still to have been attached to the oar-pulling 'thetes' (whose ancient name meant literally 'dependent labourers').[20]

---

[19] Tragedy and punishment: Fisher (1992); Williams (1993). Tragedy as theodicy: Mikalson (1991); Yunis (1988). Trial-scene in *Eumenides*: Goldhill (1992) 89–92. Demosthenes and Creon: Dem. 19.247. Lycurgus' career: Humphreys (1985a). Lycurgus and Praxithea: Lyc. 1.100. (On Eur. *Erechtheus* see also below, p. 19.)

[20] Aristotle's citizen: *Politics* 1274b31–78b5, with Cartledge (1993) 108–11. Participatoriness of Athenian democracy: Sinclair (1988).

The tragic theatre, characteristically, both confirmed and questioned the participatoriness of Athenian democracy. With the Assembly tragedy shared the common features of being a ritualised performance partaking of the sacred (every Assembly meeting began with a blood-sacrifice and prayers) that served to construct and reinforce a strong sense of the Athenians as a religious and political community. Yet, from the point of view of democratic participation, experience in the Assembly and experience in the tragic theatre also differed in important respects. Whereas a normal attendance at the Assembly in the fourth century, bolstered by the introduction of pay for attendance in *c.* 400, amounted to about a quarter of the qualified citizenry, a performance of tragedy at the Great Dionysia might attract a figure nearer to fifty per cent. Moreover, whereas the number of active 'performers' at an Assembly meeting could be counted on the fingers of not many more than two hands, there were some 1,200 needed annually at the Dionysia festival, if one includes the ten competing tribal choirs of men and ten of boys singing dithyrambs. Speakers in the Assembly, who tended in the main to come from those known semi-officially as 'the public speakers (*rhētores*) and politicians', were normally of elite social status, but citizens even from relatively humble backgrounds might as actors impersonate kings or gods. In all these ways tragedy was if anything even more democratic than the Assembly.[21]

On the other hand, the discourse of tragedy as often fractured as it confirmed that comforting corporate identity. Consider first the elevated social status of most stage characters in tragedy. It would have been hard for the average citizen, however strongly he might have considered himself to be a lineal descendant, morally speaking, of the noble Homeric heroes, to identify himself with these larger-than-life characters – in those cases, that is, where they were represented as figures worthy of admiration or imitation. Most Athenians, as we have seen, were trireme oarsmen, not cavalrymen or hoplites, yet despite the regular use of nautical imagery and metaphors from rowing in tragic verse, it was very rare for the majority in the audience to see themselves – or vaguely kindred mythological prototypes of themselves – represented on the tragic stage, as in the sailor-choruses of the Sophoclean *Ajax* and *Philoctetes*. The *Persians* of Aeschylus, therefore, which ends with a reference to triremes, was doubly exceptional in actually describing the Salamis sea-battle fought and won by real Athenians, including members of the audience, just eight years before. Normally and normatively, on the tragic stage as off, the hoplites' ideology of solidary

---

[21] Assembly, 'orators', etc.: Hansen (1987) and (1991) ch. 11. Numbers attending tragedy: see Ch. 3 below.

service and unflinching fortitude was assumed to be dominant. Yet not even the hoplites escaped entirely unscathed. Medea's famously unfavourable comparison of the terrors and pains of a woman's childbirth to the frontline battle experience of a male hoplite was no doubt undercut somewhat by her status as a woman, barbarian and sorceress, in short, an outsider. But the chorus of Euripides' *Helen* are presented wholly sympathetically when they declaim 'Madmen are you who seek glory in combat, among the spearshafts of war, thinking in ignorance to find a cure for human misery there.'[22]

A POLITICAL THEATRE?

In a straightforward and broad sense all Athenian tragedy was political, in that it was staged by and for the polis of the Athenians, through its regular public organs of government, as a fixed item in the state's religious calendar. The Great or City Dionysia, being a comparatively recent creation, was in the charge of the senior member (sometimes known as the Eponymous, since the civil year was named after him) of the board of nine annually appointed Archons. The Lenaea, on the other hand, as a more ancient and 'traditional' festival, was under the management of the Archon known as the 'King', the city's chief religious official (though he had no special religious vocation or qualifications). Organising a civic festival was regarded as on a par with organising the state's war-effort, so the Eponymous, just as he oversaw the financing of the fleet through the trierarchic liturgy-system, was likewise responsible for appointing the six *chorēgoi* who would undertake the festival liturgy of funding the choruses for each of three tragedians and three comic dramatists. That indeed was apparently his first official task on assuming office in the summer. He it was too who 'gave a chorus to' the tragedians whose work would be staged in the coming spring: that is, he selected the successful applicants, formally at any rate. And he was also somehow responsible for assigning a principal actor to each playwright, whose services were remunerated from public funds. These actors had to be citizens, since they were considered to be performing a properly civic function – in sharp contrast to the theatre in Rome, where acting was rather despised as something foreign, effeminate, fake, licentious, in short illegitimate and un-Roman.[23]

For the Dionysia, the *chorēgoi* also had to be citizens, but that rule was

---

[22] Homeric nobility: Gernet (1981) 333–43. Dominant hoplite ideology: Loraux (1986). Medea: Hall (1989a) index s.v. Outsiders and tragedy: Vidal-Naquet (1992). *Helen* chorus: 1151–4.

[23] Civic officials: Develin (1989). Civic organisation: Pickard-Cambridge (1988). Roman theatre (e.g. Livy 24.24): Rawson (1985) and (1987).

relaxed somewhat for the Lenaea, where wealthy resident aliens too might be summoned to choregic liturgy duty and, if successful, have their victory commemorated publicly and permanently in stone. Further significant differences were that at the Lenaea tragedy and comedy were late insertions in an ancient festival, whereas drama and the Dionysia had come together much sooner, if not indeed from the outset; and, secondly, that the Dionysia was much more of an international affair than the Lenaea, with the city putting itself on show for the sake of the effect on others no less than for internal consumption. During the Dionysia, indeed, no effort was spared to impress on all participants, Athenian or foreign, from the outset that this was a ritual of the city as a city: not only through the prior strictly religious ceremonies of procession and sacrifice but also through the more narrowly political ceremonies performed within the theatre before the plays began. In the unlikely case of all this ceremonial proving insufficient, the point would have been made incontrovertibly by the theatre's physical setting up against the Acropolis citadel. The temple ruins (caused by Persian sack in 480 and 479) meeting the eye of any backwards-glancing spectator during the staging of *Persians* in 472 would have delivered a no less potent political message than the astonishing plenitude of civic and imperial architecture to which the audience's eyes were directed fifty years later by Euripides in the *Erechtheus*.[24]

Athenian tragedy was also 'political' in several other, more or less informal, senses. At its widest outreach, the Athenian democratic way of life could be represented as 'an education for all Hellas' (the famous phrase of Thucydides' Pericles in the Funeral Speech). But in the first instance participation in the democratic process, including being present to hear such a public civic oration, was conceived primarily as an education for Athenian citizens, most of whom had received no formal schooling during childhood beyond the inculcation (perhaps) of basic literacy, numeracy and musical appreciation. For such average citizens, tragic theatre was an important part of their learning to be active participants in self-government by mass meeting and open debate between peers. Only occasionally and generically were Athenian citizens themselves represented on the tragic stage, as for instance in Sophocles' *Oedipus at Colonus*, where the chorus consisted of citizens from the deme of Colonus situated just outside the city of Athens – the deme of the playwright himself. Tragedy's characteristic method of instruction was analogical, allusive and indirect. Sophocles' *Philoctetes*, for example, is in a sense a play about education, or more specifically about the

---

[24] Exclusion of metics as *choregoi* at Dionysia: Hall (1989a) 163–4. Pre-play ceremonial at Dionysia: Goldhill (1990a). Erechtheus and rebuilt Erechtheum temple: Calder (1969).

initiation of an ephebe (an adolescent on the verge of manhood) into full membership of adult male citizen society; other tragedies (e.g. *Hippolytus*) play variations on the ephebic theme. Among the many competing solutions to the problem of tragedy's origins is the suggestion that it developed somehow out of adolescent initiation ritual.[25]

Also politically educational in a broad sense was the urgency with which the highly charged theme of words and persuasion was played out again and again on the Athenian democratic stage both inside and outside the tragic theatre. Thucydides, for example, represents the leading democratic politician Cleon as lambasting the Assembly in 427 for being mere 'spectators of words, auditors of deeds', although this accusation was surely itself double-edged, given Cleon's own sharply honed rhetorical skills. In tragic drama Euripides makes Eteocles in the *Phoenician Women* lament the 'strife of warring words among mortals', and characters in many others of his plays comment adversely on the deleterious moral content and political impact of honeyed words and well-turned speeches, none more bitterly so than Hecuba in her name-play. In the innovative scenario of the concluding play of Aeschylus' *Oresteia* trilogy, where he puts the courtroom on stage, he uses emphatically marked religious language in pitting 'Holy Persuasion', the power that induced the retributive, kindred murder-avenging Furies to become the propitious, city-benefiting Eumenides, against the unholy persuasion through which first Agamemnon and then his murderous widow Clytemnestra are led or rather seduced to their unpropitious deaths.[26]

The other side of the coin, however, was the pragmatic necessity, not just the ideological desirability, of freedom, equality and openness of political speech in a system of direct participatory democracy such as that of Athens. This too receives its due tragic recognition. Democratic voters' hands were raised in the Athenian Assembly only after speeches had been delivered on either side of an issue, speeches which were indeed often their only source of reasonably authentic information on the subject literally in hand. (To save time, it would seem, the numbers of hands were usually assessed by tellers rather than counted individually.) The earliest known reference to democratic assembly voting is to be found in the *Suppliant Women* of Aeschylus (probably 463 BC), where King Pelasgus refers metonymically and of course

---

[25] Pericles quotation: Thuc. 2.40.1; cf. Ostwald (1992). Popular literacy: Harris (1989) ch. 4 (too negative); Harvey (1966) (perhaps too optimistic); Thomas (1992) ch. 7 (balanced). Music: West (1992); Storr (1992). Tragedy and ephebes: Vernant & Vidal-Naquet (1988) 161–80; Winkler (1990b).

[26] Thuc. on Cleon: 3.38.4, with Macleod (1983) ch. 10. Eteocles: Eur. *Phoen.* 499; cf. *Hipp.* 486–7, 983–5; *Medea* 576–8; *Or.* 907–8; *Ba.* 266–7; and esp. Hecuba's denunciation of Odysseus in her name-play. Persuasion, esp. in tragedy: Buxton (1982); Bers (1994); Meier (1990) ch. 5. See further Ch. 6 below.

anachronistically to 'the sovereign hand of the People' of Argos. A similar procedure of antagonistic formal debate obtained in the People's Court, though usually before a much smaller audience of 500 or so; but the voting here was by secret ballot. Through Assembly and Court the sovereign People of Athens wielded direct political power, and for the informed and wise exercise of their near-limitless authority the tragic poet's function as civic teacher – confirmed by Aristophanes' not entirely unserious parody of it in the *Frogs* – was no less valuable in its way than that of either orator or advocate.[27]

The Athenian tragic poet might therefore be described, adapting Shelley, as an acknowledged legislator of the word. Yet as with even the most perspicacious and farsighted of lawgivers, his teaching could be mightily and consciously controversial. Somewhat in the manner of the English theatre of the 1630s, for example, Athenian tragedies did not always merely reflect pre-formed moral and political ideas but moved ahead of contemporary thinking, exploring or problematising the practical and theoretical possibilities. Alternatively, they might remain within the usual bounds of received wisdom and conventional pieties, but do so in order the more deeply to explore and question them. For this genuinely was a theatre of ideas, within a culture not the least remarkable attribute of which was a capacity to encompass the most radical critiques of social mores and cultural norms in a stable institutional framework. It would be quite wrong therefore to see such questioning tragedy as necessarily the product and symptom of a culture in crisis. Nor, on the other hand (to correct any possible misunderstanding of what follows), was the fundamentally questioning, risk-taking sort of tragedy by any means the only sort staged, even in the undoubted crisis of the Peloponnesian War. The *Antigone* of Euripides, for example, was a very different exercise from the Sophoclean play of the same title, being a melodrama of disguise, recognition, capture and intercession, rather than a tragedy of civic and familial self-destruction. However, it is the problematic sort of tragedy that provides the best forum for understanding the tragedians' public pedagogical function as civic teachers.[28]

In his *Oresteia* trilogy, for example, Aeschylus does not merely celebrate the triumph of human civic justice, with crucial help from Athens' divine

[27] Equal freedom of public speech (*isēgoria, parrhēsia*): Hansen (1991) 83. Dating of Aesch. *Suppl.*: see edition of H. Friis Johansen and E. W. Whittle (1980) vol. I, 21–9. Aeschylus' 'sovereign hand' (*Suppliant Women* 604): Easterling (1985); Meier (1993) 93. Tragedians as public teachers: Croally (1994); Gregory (1991); Meier (1993); Nagy (1990) 409ff.

[28] 'Theatre of ideas': Arrowsmith (1963). Scholarly disagreements on how to read tragedy as social and political comment or critique: see n. 29 and 40, and Ch. 13, below.

patron. He chooses instead to problematise the nature of 'justice' itself. Although a strong preference for due legal procedures of dispute-resolution over the pursuit of private blood-feud emerges clearly enough from the plays' internal movement and final plot-resolution, it is surely among other things a tribute to Aeschylus' subtlety and indirection that scholars are still divided over the playwright's own political attitude to the major constitutional changes of the late 460s and to the politically motivated assassination of one of their principal authors, Ephialtes. Or take Sophocles' *Antigone*. Here two in principle compatible and indeed mutually supportive public norms – the unwritten laws of the gods and the man-made laws of the polis – are so construed by the principal antagonists that they inevitably clash head-on, with no serious possibility of harmonious and practical resolution as long as the terms of the argument are understood conventionally. Finally and most starkly, in Euripides' *Medea* Greek confronts Barbarian, and Man confronts Woman, while in his *Bacchae* the two faces of Dionysus – creative euphoria and lethal retribution – confront each other: no single right answer is offered or advocated. In short, tragic experience of this probing and unsettling kind was considered conducive to the formation of a better informed and more deeply self-aware community, and to its periodical political re-creation. For that reason no less than from considerations of recreation in another sense it was supported publicly and wholeheartedly.[29]

TRAGIC POLITICS IN CHRONOLOGICAL PERSPECTIVE

To put that and the other selected aspects of tragedy discussed above in a more precise developmental context, this chapter ends with an abbreviated chronological narrative attempting to relate the history of tragedy as a theatrical genre to that of the other formal institutions of the Athenian polity over the two centuries from the tyranny of Peisistratus (*c.* 545–528) to the forcible end of the democracy in 322.

As an artistic medium, tragedy antedates by some way the Cleisthenic reforms of 508/7 that ushered in the world's first democracy. Tragedy's antecedents, moreover, most conspicuously choral lyric, were not all endogenous to Athens. There is probably something to the tradition that credited the Athenian Thespis with the decisive innovation of dramatic dialogue between himself and a chorus and dated it to the 530s, when Athens was ruled by the fairly benign dictator Peisistratus. However, there

---

[29] Reading tragedy politically: contrast Podlecki (1966b); and Zuntz (1963); with Meier (1993); Rose (1992) e.g. 327. *Oresteia*: esp. Dodds (1966); Goldhill (1992). *Antigone*, various readings of: Steiner (1984). *Medea*: Hall (1989a) index s.v. *Bacchae*: Segal (1986) ch. 9; Vernant & Vidal-Naquet (1988) 381–412.

is also much to be said for the modern view that the Great or City Dionysia did not become formalised as a theatre festival of tragic (and satyric) drama until about 500 BC; on this view, the festival in its new guise was a strictly democratic creation. Although some notion and definition of citizenship had existed at Athens since at least the reforms of Solon in about 600, the Cleisthenic reforms embodied a new, positive conception of active, democratic citizenship. Tragedy as we know it, which may have differed considerably from that pioneered by Thespis, could plausibly have come into being as a consequence of the re-scrutiny of traditional myth through the new democratic lens. This has been called tragedy's 'moment'.[30]

The fledgeling democracy depended on a twofold liberation: from dictatorship at home, and from foreign control. The myth that served as the political charter myth of the democracy was that of the Tyrannicides – historically false, in that Harmodius and Aristogiton had probably not killed a reigning tyrant and certainly were not democrats, but none the less authoritative, since democracy was conceived ideologically as the antithesis of dictatorship. On the foreign relations front, Sparta had briefly but ominously occupied Athens in 508, and in 507–505 sought to reverse Cleisthenes' reforms; and behind Sparta stood Athens' neighbours and enemies in Thebes and Chalcis, and possibly even the looming threat of the mighty Persian Empire.

The Dionysus who was worshipped at the Great Dionysia took his epithet from the border village of Eleutherae, originally Boeotian but now brought firmly within the ambit of Athens. The adoption – or nationalisation – of his cult was intended among other things to safeguard Athens' frontier against Boeotian encroachment. But Dionysus was also himself a god of liberation (another of his epithets, Lysios, meant precisely 'the liberator'), and the verbal similarity of Eleutherae to *eleutheria*, the Greek word for 'freedom', was too obvious to be missed. It might not therefore be stretching the imagination or the evidence too far to see the newly institutionalised theatre-festival of the Dionysia as a festival of democratic liberation. Archaeologists date the first, purpose-built theatre of Dionysus at the foot of the Acropolis to about 500 BC, so it would be economical of hypothesis to suggest that it was then too that dramatic performances were first transferred here from their previous venue, the Agora. Some Attic demes – notably Icarion, whose local traditions included associations with Dionysus' first arrival in Attica and with the beginnings of tragedy and comedy – may

---

[30] Thespis: Pickard-Cambridge (1988) 130–1. Reforms of Cleisthenes: Lévêque & Vidal-Naquet (1996); Ostwald (1988). Tragedy's 'moment': Vernant in Vernant & Vidal-Naquet (1988) 23–8.

also have begun staging tragedy less officially soon after 500 BC, for example during the Rural Dionysia.[31]

If the institutionalisation of the Great Dionysia as a tragedy-festival was indeed post-democratic, a transitional, experimental phase might be expected, during which playwrights, officials and the People as audience alike worked out what was and what was not suitable material for tragic representation. Such at any rate is what seems to have occurred, during roughly the first quarter of the fifth century. The principal issue then would seem to have centred upon the legitimacy of making tragic drama out of contemporary political experience as opposed to the traditional tales of myth and legend. Thespis reportedly had staged tragedies on traditional mythical themes – among them the stories of Pelias, Phorbas, and Pentheus – though we cannot of course say how he had handled or reworked the traditional material. So too did the leading tragedian of the first post-democratic generation, Phrynichus, to whose name are credited among others an *Actaeon*, *Alcestis*, *Antaeus*, *Daughters of Danaus*, and *Tantalus*. Twice at least, however, Phrynichus abandoned the ancient for the modern, indeed the absolutely contemporary, in what turned out to be a dangerously contentious move.

In the later 490s his *Capture of Miletus* took for its subject the traditional, indeed epic, theme of the sack of a city, but the city and sack in question in this tragedy were much closer to home than those of the Trojan cycle, since the play was about the annihilation by the Persians in 494 of Miletus, an Ionian Greek city with which Athens had both pragmatic and sentimental ties. The drama proved all too successfully affecting, and in accordance with democratic notions of legal responsibility it was the unfortunate author, not the Eponymous Archon who had granted him a chorus, who was saddled with a heavy fine. This was presumably imposed at the meeting of the Assembly that was regularly held in the theatre of Dionysus – not, as was otherwise usual, on the Pnyx hill – at the end of the Dionysia to review the festival's conduct. After a perhaps tactful interval of fifteen years or so, and emboldened no doubt by the Athenians' astonishing successes over the Persians in 480–79, Phrynichus returned to the contemporary mode with a group of tragedies including *Phoenician Women*, which made direct reference to the Persian Wars and for which the war-hero Themistocles may have acted as *chorēgos*.[32]

[31] Tyrannicides myth: Cartledge (1993) 32–3. Sparta and Athens: Cartledge (1979) 146–7. Theme of liberty in tragedy: de Romilly (1982). Great Dionysia as democratic liberation festival: Connor (1989); but see Osborne (1993) 27, 37–8. Archaeology of theatre: Wycherley (1978) 203–15. Icarion: Whitehead (1986a) 215–18.
[32] Early experimentation: Herington (1985) ch. 1. Phrynichus' *Miletou Halosis*: Hdt. 6.21. Themistocles as *chorēgos* for *Phoenissae*: Pickard-Cambridge (1988) 90, 236.

Some four years after Phrynichus' *Phoenician Women* Aeschylus followed suit with our earliest extant tragedy, the *Persians*, one of a group for which the barely adult Pericles served as *chorēgos*. Themistocles is never mentioned by name, and the action is set not in Greece but at the defeated Persian court in Susa. Yet there is no mistaking the play's direct contemporary reference and relevance. Salamis, the battle that both set Athens on her imperial course and solidly established the democratic constitution as the rule of the poor, trireme-rowing majority, is even explicitly described. The Athenian most responsible for the deeply controversial policy culminating in that famous and much celebrated victory was Themistocles, who at the time of the play's performance was embroiled again in a bitter political faction-fight that resulted soon after in his being at last ostracised (honourably exiled for ten years thanks to a majority vote against him of the 6,000-plus Athenians casting a ballot in the Agora). No known Greek tragedy after the *Persians* dealt with a contemporary theme centred on an actual event and a real political actor in quite the same way. Of course the Salamis affair is mythicised by Aeschylus (himself a participant), and tragic pathos is achieved by requiring the Athenian audience to sympathise somewhat, if not empathise, with their former – but also very much present – Persian enemies. Nevertheless, the audience, or Aeschylus, may well have felt that in this case tragic distancing and alienation had not been carried far enough, or conversely that the danger of blunting the cutting edge of tragedy's peculiar contribution to democracy by eliding the distinction between the theatre and the city's other public political spaces had not been clearly enough avoided.[33]

The original stated purpose of ostracism (from the Greek for 'potsherd', *ostrakon*, on which the names of 'candidates' were written or painted) may well have been to prevent the recurrence of tyranny; as such, it could have formed part of the Cleisthenic reform package. In practice, however, the device functioned to abort the outbreak of *stasis*, civil strife, or rather to stop civil strife spilling over into outright civil war (also called *stasis*). This it certainly helped to do, until its last recorded use at Athens in 417 or 416, whereafter it was superseded by other political instruments, chiefly involving use of the People's Court. But Athenian democratic politics were always a high-tension, high-risk business, and the threat of *stasis* was rarely all that far beneath the surface of everyday events. In the five years or so after 461, following the assassination of the democratic reformer Ephialtes, civil war came as close to erupting outright at Athens as at any time before the final phase of the Peloponnesian War. Hence, surely, the remarkably

[33] *Persians*: Hall (1989a) index s.v.; and (1996).

urgent plea for avoidance of *stasis* at all costs that Aeschylus in his *Eumenides* (458) placed paradoxically in the mouths of the traditionally vengeance-driven Erinyes (Furies) and caused Athena to echo. Not that Aeschylus offered any specific political solution or nailed his colours to any personally identifiable political mast: a middle way between tyranny and anarchy, and 'great advantage for the city from their terrifying faces' (as Athena remarks of the Erinyes/Eumenides), were almost the limit of his detailed prescriptions.[34]

The democratic reforms of Ephialtes were abetted and, despite or thanks to his murder, extended by Pericles, most significantly by the introduction of political pay to compensate those citizens selected by lot to serve on the mass juries of the People's Court. In the 450s, thanks mainly to the Empire but also to a variety of internal sources of revenue, Athens' public coffers were unusually full, and the notion of payment for political service was both ideologically democratic, in that it enabled poor citizens as well as rich to participate actively in politics, and economically attractive. A further application of the same principle affected the tragic theatre, by way of the introduction of payment for actors and a cash prize for the best actor at the Dionysia in about 450. A few years later, such was its growing popularity, tragedy was introduced also on the same conditions alongside comedy at the more ancestral and Athenocentric Lenaea festival, although comedy seems to have continued to rank relatively higher here than at the Great Dionysia, where it had been formally recognised only in 486.[35]

So far, most of this chapter has been men-only and male-ordered, but mention of *Eumenides* with its prominent, indeed decisive, female protagonists (played of course by male actors) prompts separate reflection on the role and status within the democracy and its tragic theatre of the other half of the Athenian citizen population, women. The two ablest philosophers of Classical Athens, Plato and Aristotle, were also teacher and pupil. Yet in their attitude to women they differed markedly and between them covered almost the entire spectrum of possible male attitudes to the female Other. Plato has sometimes been hailed as a feminist, or proto-feminist, for his treatment of some, very few, women as the intellectual peers of some, also very few, men in his *Republic*. But the *Republic* was only a sketch of a political utopia, not necessarily a blueprint for some pragmatically realisable

---

[34] Ostracism: Vanderpool (1970). *Stasis*: Lintott (1982); Ste Croix (1983) 78–9, ch. 5. Athenian democratic politics: Finley (1985) esp. ch. 2. *Eumenides* references: 696–7, 987–9; cf. Meier (1990) ch. 5.

[35] Political pay for People's Court: Markle (1985). Pay for actors: Ghiron-Bistagne (1976) 179ff.

polity, and it is doubtful whether his representation of the women partners of the ruling Guardian class would have been taken as implying much if anything for male Greek attitudes to their real-life female dependants (never partners). Aristotle, on the other hand, in his philosophical sociology of Greek political life was ever the prophet of things as they are, and he began from and returned to what he took to be the received and reputable opinions held by reasonable men (males). His considered sociobiological view that women were deformed, incomplete males and therefore designed by nature to be subservient to men may strike us as extreme, distasteful, even absurd, but we may be sure that it far more accurately reflected the gendered images of the average Greek citizen male than did Plato's utopian vision. If corroboration be sought, we need look no further than the theatre of Dionysus, to the absurdist comic fantasies of Aristophanes. To get some idea of how life really was outside the theatre, we might profitably start by turning right side up the upside-down worlds of his *Lysistrata*, *Women Celebrating the Thesmophoria* and *Women in Assembly*. The fictive women of tragedy were a different, and as usual far more ambivalent and complex, matter.[36]

Athenian women, in the sense of the mothers, sisters, wives, and daughters of Athenian citizen men, were 'citizens' only by courtesy, in all respects but one – religion. The feminine form of 'citizen' was rarely used, and Athenian women were usually referred to either as 'female inhabitants of Attica' or, more puzzlingly, as 'townswomen'. They were never granted the full rights and corresponding duties of active political citizenship that they would have required to participate in the governmental arenas of Assembly or People's Court. There, in part, lies the black humour of Aristophanes' *Women in Assembly*, which has probably mistakenly been seen as partaking of the same 'feminist' tendency as Plato's *Republic*. In this comic fantasy (or nightmare scenario) formerly respectable citizen wives in male-citizen disguise 'pack' an Assembly meeting in order to outvote the relatively few male citizens so far present and carry a motion handing over the governance of Athens to women. But this Aristophanic brave new world is no Platonic or any other sort of utopia; rather it is a dystopian feminocracy in which the horrors of enforced economic communalism are exceeded only by the outrageous legislation passed to enable the women to gratify their naturally voracious and uncontrollable sexual appetites. Perhaps at the time the play was staged (in about 392) proto-feminist ideas

---

[36] Plato on women: Kraut (1992) 44–5 n. 49. Aristotle on women: Cartledge (1993) 66–70; Lloyd (1983) 94–105. Aristophanes on women: Cartledge (1995) ch. 4. Tragedy and women: n. 40, and Chs. 3 and 5 below.

were in the air at Athens, but if so, this play was calculated to bring them back down to earth with a resounding crash.[37]

In the real world, religion was the one public activity in which Athenian women might achieve parity or even superiority of esteem *vis-à-vis* their menfolk. The annual Thesmophoria festival, for example, which Aristophanes gently sent up in one of his women-plays, was the most important of several women-only public festivals celebrated throughout Greece, not only in Athens; and in the sphere of death, burial and mourning the women of Greece had traditionally taken the more active and more publicly demonstrative religious role. Correspondingly, the one civic function approximating to the holding of public political office by men that Greek citizen women might legitimately perform, indeed were required to perform, was to serve as priestess of an officially recognised city cult, usually of a female divinity. The most ancient Athenian priestesshoods, notably that of the city's divine patron Athena Polias, were tied to families of the hereditary nobility who styled themselves Eupatrids (literally, 'lineal descendants of good fathers'). But as with all other public offices at Athens, the rule of exclusive aristocratic prerogative was gradually relaxed, and it was a sure sign of the triumph of democracy that in about 450 BC a new priestesshood of Athena of Victory (Nike) was created – by the men, admittedly – on expressly democratic lines. All Athenian women were deemed eligible for the post, without discrimination on grounds of birth or wealth or even capacity, and the selection was to be carried out by the maximally egalitarian procedure of the lottery.[38]

Another measure passed in the Assembly at about the same time affected even more directly and vitally the life-chances and social status of all Athenian women. In 451/0, on a motion proposed by Pericles from factional as well as statesmanlike motives, the Athenians voted a law providing that citizenship was henceforth to be based on double-descent; a (male, adult) citizen, in other words, would have to have been born of an Athenian mother as well as – what had hitherto been sufficient – an Athenian father. In the absence of birth certificates and blood tests, the sworn testimony of kin and friends was now required to prove against challenge not only that the father who put his son forward for acceptance by his fellow-demesmen was indeed his natural or adoptive father but also that his natural mother was of Athenian citizen status and, probably, that the son had been conceived or born in legitimate wedlock. Given that respectable Athenian

---

[37] Terminology of citizen women: Patterson (1986). Religion: see next paragraph. Assembly pay: see below, p. 33.

[38] Women and religion: Bruit (1992). Thesmophoria: Winkler (1990a) 188–209. Athena Nike: Fornara (1983) no. 93; cf. Jameson (1994).

women were expected for ideological reasons to remain as invisible as was deemed compatible with the authentication of their male offspring's status, such proof was not always easily forthcoming.

Precisely what motives and aims lay behind this momentous new double-descent law is unclear, although several of its possible, likely or certain effects can be specified. By reducing the number of potential mothers of Athenian citizens – for example, it is likely to have made it more difficult at least for a man to pass off his son by a slave woman as his legitimate Athenian son – the law could perhaps have slowed the rate of growth of the citizen body. It will also have penalised Athenian aristocrats who had formerly been accustomed to contracting marriage alliances for dynastic and diplomatic reasons with Greek or foreign women from families of comparable social status in other cities or countries. (Ironically, had Pericles' law been in force in the sixth century, Cleisthenes, the founder of the democracy, and some other exceptional Athenians would have been disqualified from Athenian citizenship.) But the one unambiguous effect of its passage, as long as it was enforced, will have been to enhance the marriageability of Athenian-status women at the expense of the ever-increasing numbers of foreign-born women in Athens, both free and slave. For they and only they could confer the gift of citizenship, an increasingly precious commodity – especially for the poor – with the growth of democracy and the influx of imperial wealth. On the other hand, they could confer this gift only with the acquiescence of the male kinsman, father, husband, even adult son, in whose legal power they firmly remained, or were perhaps now even more firmly retained.[39]

It is unthinkable that so momentous a development should not have had an impact in the theatre, especially as Dionysus was a god whose rituals of worship and cultic attributes had such specifically feminine associations. But what exactly that impact was, and how we should assess its significance, are controversial issues. No less controversial is the debate as to whether Athenian women might watch, or rather be permitted or encouraged to watch, the plays themselves, which often allocated crucial dramatic roles to female characters. To be schematic, one line of modern criticism detects an increasingly sympathetic portrayal of women in tragedy, including the presentation of a specifically 'women's viewpoint' on both practical and civic ideals – roughly from the Clytemnestra, Niobe and daughters of Danaus of Aeschylus, through the Antigone, Procne and Deianeira of Sophocles, to the Medea, Melanippe, Creusa, Phaedra and Stheneboea

---

[39] Citizenship law: Patterson (1981); Boegehold (1994). Status of women in law: Just (1989) Foxhall in Foxhall & Lewis (1996) 133–152.

of Euripides. (Lack of extant plays prevents our prolonging the series in detail into the fourth century.)

The contrary line of interpretation stresses that all performers in tragedy, not to mention the dramatists, were citizen males, and notes the almost formulaic consistency of plot-development, whereby it is women, whenever they are for any reason not adequately controlled by their relevant male relatives, who typically and predictably engender social and political dislocation, disharmony or destruction. Thus at the close of Aeschylus' *Seven Against Thebes*, although this scene falls within the characteristically female sphere of mourning, the sisters Antigone and Ismene are presented as virtual faction-leaders. [In Sophocles' *Antigone* (produced perhaps about the time that he served as one of the ten elected generals of the Athenian empire) the eponymous heroine is clearly on the side of the gods, but she is equally clearly a menace (in a different way from her uncle Creon) to the smooth running of the male-ordered city.] In a more extreme variation on the theme of the danger of women and the paramount need to control them, Euripides' Hippolytus (like Aeschylus' Eteocles) bitterly laments the physical necessity of women for human reproduction, and seeks to live without them, yet in the end is compelled to learn by suffering that the force of Aphrodite, goddess of sex as well as sex goddess, cannot be denied. In the words of the first (not the extant) *Hippolytus*, 'those who exceed in shunning Kypris [Aphrodite] are as sick as those who exceed in hunting her'.[40]

Yet perhaps the most extreme instance of Athenian citizen males' would-be social control of women through dominant ideology is to be seen in their use of myth. According to the aboriginal Athenian charter-myth, the myth of autochthony, the founding mother of the Athenian citizen body was not an animate being, human or divine, but 'mother' Earth, the very soil of Attica. Human female reproduction was thereby finessed, or suppressed, in official civic ideology. The evidence we have would seem to indicate that in its most developed form the foundational myth of autochthony crystallised round about the middle of the fifth century – too close to the passage of the Periclean citizenship law for sheer or mere coincidence. Euripides pointedly explores this autochthony myth in *Ion*, but although here as elsewhere in his work Athens' most basic gender norms are seriously questioned, *Ion* does not convey the suggestion that the autochthony myth should be

---

[40] Femininity of Dionysus, and of tragedy: see Ch. 5 below. Women attending the theatre?: Goldhill (1994a); Podlecki (1990); also Ch. 3. Contrary readings of tragic women: des Bouvrie (1990); Easterling (1987b); Foley (1992); Henderson (1991); Katz (1994); Loraux (1987); Pomeroy (1975) 93–115; Rabinowicz (1992) and (1993); Zeitlin (1990). (First) *Hippolytus* quotation: F 428 Nauck.

scrapped as so much masculinist bunkum and balderdash. What the Athenian men gave with one hand they appear to have taken away with the other.[41]

However, for all the social cohesion that the myth of autochthony and other applications of ideological cement may have engendered in the male citizens as distinct from or in opposition to their women, no amount of symbolic mythmaking could prevent a recrudescence of the class-based political *stasis* within the citizenry that had briefly afflicted Athens in the late 460s and early 450s and increasingly convulsed the entire Greek world during the course of the Peloponnesian War. Most of our surviving tragedies were composed during this war, by Sophocles and his younger contemporary Euripides (Aeschylus having died in Sicily in 456). I select just one play of each in order to illustrate the strains and tensions to which the Athenians were increasingly subjected and also the remarkable quality of the dramatists' reflection on and response to them: in short, the interplay between tragedy in the non-theatrical sense and tragic drama.

Sophocles' *Oedipus the King* was probably performed around the time of the war's outbreak in *c.* 430 and set in the city of one of Athens' principal enemies, the Thebans, who indeed as allies of Sparta were responsible for initiating the hostilities. Of course the *Iliad* too begins with a plague, but that afflicted an army at war in some corner of a foreign field, whereas the plague in Sophocles' Thebes was an urban phenomenon, affecting a great city precisely as the Great Plague blighted Athens from 430 onwards. Of course, Sophocles' Thebes was not in any simple sense a mere surrogate or allegory of Athens, any more than Oedipus was of Pericles. All the same, it would have been a peculiarly obtuse Athenian spectator who was not sharply stabbed by a prick of transhistorical and cross-cultural recognition as he watched *Oedipus the King* unfold – or unravel. Were Athens and Pericles, he might well have mused, also riding for a fall, having misread the divine signals? It is not irrelevant that even Thucydides' ultra-rationalist Pericles is made to refer to the Plague as something 'heaven-sent' – beyond the power, or ken, of mere mortal men.[42]

Some fifteen years later, in spring 415, Euripides staged a Trojan War trilogy, including the extant *Trojan Women*. This was possibly written during and certainly performed immediately after the Athenians' massacre of the adult males and enslavement of the women and children of the small

---

[41] Autochthony myth: Loraux (1986) index s.v. and (1993) 37–71. In *Ion*: Loraux (1993) 147–236 ('dark face', 220–4); Zeitlin (1989). Crystallisation of the myth: Rosivach (1987).

[42] Spread of *stasis*: Thuc. 3.82.1. Soph. *O.T.*: Knox (1979) chs. 8–10; Segal (1993a). Tragic Thebes as 'anti-Athens': Zeitlin (1986) and (1993). Pericles on Plague as *daimonion*: Thuc. 2.64.2; cf. Cartledge (1993) 168.

Cycladic island-state of Melos (better, and more happily, known today under its Venetian name of Milo). Of course, as was noted in connection with Phrynichus' *Capture of Miletus*, the epic cycle also was focused on the capture and sack of a city, with its attendant atrocities, but it was surely not only or even primarily of Homer's Troy that Euripides intended his audience to think, except perhaps to draw the contrast between little Greek Melos and mighty barbarian Troy. To convey the flavour of Euripides' almost recklessly daring démarche, and the depth of self-scrutiny to which he was inviting the audience to proceed, we might perhaps imagine a British playwright of known radical political persuasion composing a tragedy in response to the bombing of Baghdad during the Gulf War of 1991 and equating it by implication with the Nazi German air-raids on London during the Second World War. The processual dramatisation of Athenian political life could scarcely be taken further.[43]

Four years after the Melos massacre, during which time Athens suffered the comprehensive and largely self-inflicted defeat in Sicily remarked upon above, a group of extreme oligarchs led by Antiphon and supported somewhat naively by a large section of the economically and ideologically middling citizenry (including, perhaps, Sophocles and Euripides) succeeded in overthrowing the democracy in 411. A combination of internal squabbling among the oligarchs and consequent inefficiency in their conduct of the war, the unwavering loyalty of the fleet to the old regime, and a residual fondness among the middling citizens for democracy as the devil they knew soon brought about the full restoration of democratic government. But it proved an uneasy restoration, notably reflected on the tragic stage by Euripides' *Orestes* (408), and defeat in the Peloponnesian War was merely postponed not avoided. The defeat of 404 brought with it a second abrogation of democratic government, directly imposed this time by the Spartan victors. The very narrow and extremist oligarchy behaved so savagely, however, that it earned itself the sobriquet of the 'Thirty Tyrants'. Even the Spartans found it politic to abandon their puppets and permit the restoration of democracy – at their ultimate discretion – in 403. Retrospectively, the civil year 404/3 was treated as a null year of 'anarchy' in the Athenian calendar, and the new era of restored democracy was signalled both by immediate celebrations of reconciliation and by the establishment for the future of a revised law-code publicly inscribed on marble walls within the official residence of the Basileus or 'King' Archon.[44]

The new code naturally embraced the Athenian religious calendar, within

[43] Eur. *Tro.*: Croally (1994).
[44] Antiphon: above, n. 18. Eur. *Orestes*: Hall (1993b). Thirty Tyrants: Krentz (1982). Restored democracy celebration: Strauss (1985). Law-code: Hansen (1991) 162–5.

which the Dionysia and Lenaea play-festivals retained their honoured places. Thus Sophocles' *Oedipus at Colonus*, for example, was first produced posthumously (Sophocles had died in 406/5) by his grandson in 402/1, a critical moment in the process of post-war reconstruction. This is also probably our latest surviving whole tragedy (unless *Rhesus* is post-400; cf. Ch. 9, p. 211 below), but that chronological datum must not be allowed to obscure the continued, indeed in some senses augmented, vitality of tragedy during what is to us, but not of course the Athenians, the fourth century BC. Although fourth-century Athenians came to judge Aeschylus, Sophocles and Euripides as the nonpareils of the genre, and regularly honoured their plays with revivals, tragedy itself was not merely a fifth-century phenomenon, the product of a short-lived golden age. If not attaining the quality and stature of the fifth-century 'classics', original tragedies nevertheless continued to be written and produced and competed with in large numbers throughout the remaining life of the democracy – and beyond it. Indeed, in so far as the genius of fourth-century playwrights was palpably humbler than that of the fifth-century holy trinity, their works perhaps mirrored or reflected the audience's concerns even more faithfully.[45]

The restored and restabilised post-403 democracy lasted until its suppression by Macedon in 322. It was possibly less ideologically and institutionally radical than its predecessor, though it was if anything even more participatory (the introduction of pay for Assembly attendance in *c.* 400 enabled a higher proportion of citizens to attend regularly, for example), and Aristotle properly classified it as belonging to the 'ultimate' or most extreme of the several types of Greek democracy known to him in the third quarter of the fourth century. Certainly it had to be more self-consciously pragmatic, because with the loss of power and income from an overseas empire economic problems bulked larger even than heretofore. The importation of wheat to Athens from the Ukraine and Crimea, for example, could no longer be guaranteed by Athenian warfleets, nor could the grain be purchased at source by Athens-based traders at the previous favourably discounted prices. It was symptomatic that the grain-supply became a staple item on the agenda of the 'principal' Assembly meeting of each month. In the fourth century, too, financial acumen became as important a qualification for political leadership as diplomatic or military skills, if not more so. Hence the rise to prominence of a 'technocrat' such as Lycurgus in the 330s. But hence, also, the ever more intense debate about the proper use of the

---

[45] Soph. O.C.: Vernant & Vidal-Naquet (1988) 329–59. Fourth-century tragedy: Xanthakis-Karamanos (1980); Easterling (1993a).

Theoric or Festival Fund mentioned above, a sure sign of the continued significance of the theatre to the functioning of democratic politics in the widest sense.[46]

In the good old days, lamented the crypto-oligarchic pamphleteer Isocrates, 'many of the common people never visited Athens even for festivals' – allegedly. By implication, at the time of Isocrates' writing (the 350s) they regularly poured in from the Attic countryside to take their perhaps tribally apportioned seats alongside their urban brethren in the theatre of Dionysus. There were of course few other mass entertainment media at Athens, if theatre-going within the context of a religious festival may be so described. But money too was tighter, and the prospect of state-subsidised entertainment (and instruction) coupled with a beef supper liberally lubricated by Dionysus' special juice might have been a very attractive proposition indeed. Nor were the celebrations conspicuously less lavish in the fourth century than in the more opulent fifth. In 333/2, for instance, possibly as many as 240 bulls were sacrificed in the central ritual of that year's Great Dionysia, and that was despite – or maybe as partial compensation for – the economic, military and political crisis that had beset Athens since her catastrophic defeat by Philip of Macedon at Chaeronea in Boeotia in 338, which threatened to deprive her of her independent existence as well as her democracy and grain-supply.

So lavish a supply of sacrificial animals depended on the continued willingness of the wealthy to act as civic benefactors, but not all of these were democratically minded and motivated, or not at least to the same extent as Demosthenes, the People's champion and leader of the anti-Macedonian resistance. Demosthenes knew exactly what he was doing when he made a litigating client claim that his opponent was spending money hand over fist like a *chorēgos*. For Demosthenes himself had been involved in a notorious lawsuit with Meidias, a rival *chorēgos* (in the men's tribal dithyramb), who he claimed had openly struck him actually within the theatre of Dionysus. His extant prosecution speech, even if not delivered as such, is a compendious vade-mecum of the democratic rhetoric of theatricality, and of the theatricality of fourth-century democratic rhetoric. In Aeschines, the actor turned politician, Demosthenes found an entirely suitable opponent, but when Athens proved to be insufficiently big for the two of them, it was Aeschines who, having gambled and lost all on a political prosecution of 330, was forced to make a hasty and final exit, in accordance with the usual rules of Greek zero-sum competition.[47]

[46] Fourth-century democracy: Hansen (1987) and (1991). Grain-supply: ?Aristotle, *Constitution of the Athenians* 43.4; cf. Garnsey (1988) Part III. Theoric Fund: above, n. 11.
[47] Isocrates quotation: 7 (*Areop.*).52. Dionysia of 333/2: Parke (1977) 127; but see Jameson

By then, though, Lycurgus not Demosthenes was Athens' number one man, credited with turning around Athens' finances and fortunes alike. Two of his pet projects of public expenditure, as we have already noted, concerned the tragic theatre directly: the commissioning of authoritative copies for the state archives of the still extant plays of Aeschylus, Sophocles and Euripides; and the construction of the first all-stone theatre of Dionysus, ancestor of the Roman remodelling visible to visitors today. The former measure is testimony both to the establishment of a fixed repertoire of 'classics' and to the extent to which actors – an increasingly mobile, cosmopolitan and perhaps professionally jealous crew – had been taking liberties with their scripts. Even more significantly, perhaps, it breathes the spirit of an incipient movement of scholarship that was soon to receive physical embodiment in the Museum and Library established by the Ptolemaic rulers of Egypt at Alexandria, their great Hellenistic capital founded by and named after Alexander the Great.[48]

The building of a monumental theatre in stone bespeaks a determined conviction of the likely central importance of drama to Athens (as to the rest of Greece) for the foreseeable future. That future, however, was not destined to be a democratic one. In 322, the year after Alexander's death in Babylon, the new Macedonian overlord of Greece forcibly replaced Athens' existing constitution with an oligarchy, and notwithstanding increasingly desperate attempts to restore it democracy remained for ever after but a dream of past glories. Spatially, the locus of formal political decision-making shifted symbolically from the Pnyx to the theatre of Dionysus, since Athens like any other Hellenistic Greek polis was able to muster only the show rather than the substance of politics. So far as theatre in the narrower sense was concerned, the most influential form of Athenian drama now went under the sign of the muse of (situation) comedy. Tragedy – though by no means a dead art form – proved less capable of evolution or mutation outside a democratic environment. So when the conquering Romans introduced the arts of captive Greece to Latium, it was not Aeschylus, Sophocles or Euripides who provided the chief source of popular dramatic inspiration (though political tragedy modelled on Euripides was not unknown in Rome), but Menander. *Sic transit gloria mundi tragici?*[49]

(1994) 316 n. 13. Demosthenes' *chorēgos* image: 40.51. Demosthenes as *chorēgos* (*Against Meidias*): Wilson (1991). Aeschines: Lane Fox (1994).

[48] Lycurgus: above, n. 19. Actors' mobility: Pickard-Cambridge (1988) 279. Ptolemaic scholarship: Fraser (1972).

[49] Destruction of democracy in Athens (and Greece): Ste Croix (1981) 300–15. Menander: Green & Handley (1995) ch. 7.

2

P. E. EASTERLING

A show for Dionysus

Since Nietzsche published *The Birth of Tragedy* in 1872 Dionysus has been the dominant Greek deity in the imaginations of scholars. His glamorous and ambiguous personality has stimulated a great deal of research and interpretation, recently intensified by the discovery of new evidence for Dionysiac mystery cult.[1] Not all the factors at work have been academic and intellectual; in the 1930s, for example, the power of Dionysus could be strongly felt in the rallies orchestrated by Hitler and Mussolini (R. P. Winnington-Ingram wrote his pioneering *Euripides and Dionysus* under the influence of his response to fascism).[2] Since the Second World War Dionysus has found a new place in theatrical life, largely because *Bacchae* has seemed to actors, directors and audiences to need so little mediation as a play for the times, in which drug culture, rock music, sex and violence, the many varieties of modern ecstatic cult, and even football hysteria all find recognisable analogues.[3]

Yet despite the intensive and brilliant work devoted to Dionysus in his ancient context[4] we still have to face some obstinate puzzles. If tragedy at

---

[1] For reception see Henrichs (1984), (1993), (1994); Bierl (1991) 13–20. For a review of recent findings on mystery cult see Bremmer (1994) 84–97.

[2] Cf. p. 269 below, on Auden and Kallman. On Winnington-Ingram see M. L. West's account (1994) 584–5: 'There is no explicit reference in *Euripides and Dionysus* to the events of the thirties. But in his [unpublished] memoir he states outright that the book was haunted by the Nuremberg rallies. Euripides' view of Dionysus, as he portrays it, is in some degree the counterpart of his own view of Hitler.' As West points out, Winnington-Ingram and E. R. Dodds were in close touch, and each influenced the other's work; Dodds's commentary on *Bacchae* (first published in 1944) and his *The Greeks and the Irrational* (1951) have both contributed powerfully to the reading of Dionysus in the second half of the twentieth century. Cf. Lloyd-Jones (1982) 174–5.

[3] Cf. Cartledge (1993) 176: 'Euripides' *Bacchae* has been presented as a hymn of counter-cultural liberationist rebellion' (on a production at the Berliner Schaubühne in 1974); an article in *The Independent on Sunday* for 27 August 1995 compares the 'hysterical atmosphere' described by participants in the 'Charismatic' Nine O'Clock Service in Sheffield with accounts of Dionysiac worship.

[4] See Bibliographical Note for surveys, esp. by Bremmer (1994) and Henrichs (1996).

Athens was originally and essentially under the sign of Dionysus, though other deities would appropriate drama for their own festivals in due course (see Ch. 9, pp. 223–4), what was it about this art form that was particularly Dionysiac? Was there a logic in the Athenian construction of Dionysus that made him uniquely appropriate as god of the drama, and especially of tragic drama? (Comedy has seemed to pose less acute problems because of its more obvious appropriateness for performance at festivals in honour of the wine-god.) Was it a matter of stories about Dionysus shaping the mythological groundwork and plot patterns of tragedy, as used to be the standard view,[5] or of the god's symbolic characteristics – as the Other, the outsider, sexually ambivalent, transformative, elusive[6] – making him good to think with, or of the distinctively dramatic features of his rituals (the mask, ecstatic possession, mystic initiation)?[7] These factors are not easily separable and cannot safely be treated as strict alternatives to one another in any explanatory model. All must be relevant in some way, but there is something to be said for trying to put the old questions in a new perspective, by thinking first of what made Dionysus good to perform with (and through). In this chapter I discuss two questions, first, what was common to the different performance elements at the City Dionysia,[8] and second, whether Dionysus offered something that no other deity did, or could have done.

DIONYSIAC PERFORMANCE

The Great or City Dionysia at Athens, the most fully developed and ambitious concentration of Dionysiac performance known to the fifth century, had a great deal to do with dithyramb, a poetic composition sung and danced in honour of Dionysus by choruses of fifty men or boys,[9] as well as with tragedy, and in due course (from 486) comedy was prominent, too, with a day of the festival devoted to comic competition. As for tragedy itself, at any rate all through this early period, it was inseparable from satyr drama, with the same playwrights competing in the same event with tragedies and a satyr play. The common denominator in all these lyric and dramatic performances was song and dance, and among them it was satyr play that was the most obviously Dionysiac element, since the chorus of

---

[5] Cf. e.g. Pickard-Cambridge (1927) 165–6, restated by Seaford (1994) 272 with n. 165. For discussion see pp. 46–7 below.

[6] Discussed below, pp. 44–53. Cf. also Chs. 1 and 10.

[7] Discussed below, pp. 47–53. Cf. also Chs. 1 and 10.

[8] For the arrangements at the City Dionysia see Chs. 1 and 3; much less is known about the Lenaea, where tragedy was in any case a late arrival.

[9] See Zimmermann (1992) for details.

satyrs, far more than any other choral group, was explicitly and by definition part of the god's entourage, and satyrs of various types, as we know from vase-paintings, had been associated with Dionysus well before the dramatic festivals were established.[10] The meaning of tragic performance – its place in the festival, in democratic ideology, in the teaching of the citizens – needs therefore to be approached with satyr play in mind. Each set of three tragedies, whether or not they were thematically linked, was followed by a (culminating?) short play in which the chorus was made up of Dionysus' devoted followers, the playful, violent, sensual creatures, part-human, part-animal, whose dancing and singing were in vehement contrast with the tone, style, music and costume of the choruses of tragedy. But what is important is that the *same performers* provided the show:[11] it was not a question of a few clowns or unattached music-makers offering incidental entertainment as a relief from the seriousness of tragedy.

A favourite way of defining satyr play is to call it an 'after-piece',[12] but perhaps any term which suggests that satyr play was some kind of addition is misleading, and the readier we are to think of it as a *culmination* of each tragedian's competitive entry the more sense we may be able to make of the fact that these plays were in some ways so like tragedy – in range of vocabulary, metrical style, cast of characters and so on. The chorus might indeed be made up of entertainingly uninhibited creatures of the wild, but the heroes themselves were allowed to retain their heroic dignity, and there was nothing of the hilarious obscenity and grotesquerie of comedy in the way they were made to behave.

What then was satyr play for? To give the big popular audience a light and enjoyable performance to look forward to, with plenty of opportunities for the display of virtuoso skills? To 'bring them back to their senses', to adapt a phrase from Tony Harrison, the only modern writer to use satyr play as a model for live drama of his own,[13] and thereby to make the audience strongly aware of their own animal spirits, their interest in food

---

[10] See Buschor (1943); Brommer (1959); Bérard & Bron (1989); Lissarrague (1990); Hedreen (1994); Green (1994) 38–46 with n. 43.

[11] The implication of the ancient didascalic record is that each set of tragedies and satyr play (*tragikē didaskalia*) constituted a single entry, with the same chorusmen taking part throughout. This is certainly the view of most scholars: see e.g. Winkler (1990b) 44. Seaford (1984) 4 speculates that different choruses may have performed the tragedies and the satyr play, but he cites no evidence, and his argument is mainly designed to explain why the Pronomos Vase [7] shows only eleven chorusmen plus Silenus, on which see Pickard-Cambridge (1988) 236. Green (1994) 10, with n. 23, also considers the possibility that different choruses performed tragedy and satyr play, but on no stronger grounds than a guess as to the stamina of the performers.

[12] E.g. Seaford (1984) 1. Cf. Nagy (1990) 391: 'a subordinated attachment of tragedy'.

[13] *The Trackers of Oxyrhynchus*, first performed at Delphi in 1988, followed by performances

and drink, sex, jokes, as well as hard political or moral or existential problems? To worship Dionysus? That is, to enact the success of the followers of Dionysus in escaping the wicked ogre, or whatever power has kept them in servitude, and in celebrating the freedom to dance for their god in the band of devotees (*thiasos*)?[14]

Audience expectation, as Peter Burian points out (Ch. 8 below), will shape perceptions. When ancient Athenian audiences saw *Oresteia*, or *Trojan Women* and the plays that went with it, they knew that a satyr play was still to come *with the same chorus and actors performing*, and the total meaning of the show must have been construed in the light of that knowledge. Tony Harrison puts it more eloquently: 'With the loss of these [satyr] plays we are lacking important clues to the wholeness of the Greek imagination, and its ability to absorb and yet not be defeated by the tragic. In the satyr play, that spirit of celebration, held in the dark solution of tragedy, is precipitated into release, and a release into the worship of Dionysus who presided over the whole dramatic festival.'[15] The only difficulty with this attractive formulation, which rightly stresses the interconnexion between the different elements, is that its image of 'release' leaves us guessing about the tragic parts of the *tragikē didaskalia* (the total set of plays offered by each tragedian): in what sense may *they* have been felt to be 'worship of Dionysus'?

The early history of performance at the Dionysia cannot be used to throw light on the question because it is a notoriously unclear and disputed area, with almost no reliable evidence to work from.[16] One of the few facts that is definitely known is that satyrs in Dionysiac cult comfortably predate the introduction of plays of any kind into the Dionysia,[17] but there is no record of the process whereby the tragic competition came to be defined as a contest of three tragedies and one satyr play. A famous passage in ch. 4 of Aristotle's *Poetics* (1449a20) implies that tragic plays of the kind that have survived were the successors of humbler dramas with small plots and ridiculous diction, having developed from something[18] vaguely described as *saturikon*, 'relating to satyrs' (i.e. less elevated, more boisterous?), but the same chapter also traces the origin of tragedy to those who 'led off the dithyramb' (1449a1), and other sources, especially Horace (*Ars poetica*

---

of an adapted version in 1990 at the National Theatre in London and at Salts Mill in Yorkshire; revived in 1991. See Harrison (1991) and Astley (1991).

[14] See Seaford (1984) 33–44 for an account of the typical themes of satyric drama; Simon (1982a) for vase-paintings.

[15] Harrison (1991) xi.

[16] For details see Pickard-Cambridge (1988) ch. 2; Csapo and Slater (1995) ch. 2 with pp. 412–13.

[17] For bibliography see n. 10 above; Seaford (1984) 5–10.

[18] The vagueness is due to the absence of a noun for *saturikon* to agree with.

220–4), claim that satyr play was added to the competition *after* tragedy had become established at the Dionysia. As scholars have suggested,[19] there may be ways of reconciling these traditions, but for our purposes what matters is that in the fifth century, at any rate, satyr play was treated as an intrinsic element of the *tragikē didaskalia*. Perhaps there is a clue to this kind of thinking in Plutarch's comment about Ion of Chios and his criticism of the social manner of his contemporary Pericles: 'Ion apparently expects that virtue, like a complete *tragikē didaskalia*, should not be without a satyric element' (*Pericles* 5).

But this pattern did not last: satyr play began to detach itself from the 'three-plus-one' formula, and at some point in the fourth century a new arrangement was introduced, with a single satyr play starting off the tragic performances but not itself forming part of the contest.[20] Already in the fifth century there had been pointers in the same direction: when tragedy was introduced at the Lenaea in the 430s satyr plays were not included in the contest, and when Euripides staged *Alcestis* in 438 in the place of a satyr play this perhaps reflected a perception on the part of performers and audiences that the old tradition was not inviolable.[21] It is hard not to link this trend with the development of an acting repertoire and with an interest on the part of actors in staging revivals at the rural festivals of plays that had had a particular success at the City Dionysia (cf. Ch. 9 below, p. 213). By the time revivals of 'classics' were established at the city festival itself, as part of the competition (from 386), these were performances of single tragedies, prompted, it seems, by the professional concerns and aspirations of actors. There is no reason why we should think that such changes came about because satyr play was perceived to be a 'quaint', 'primitive' survival from some folk tradition: the surviving samples are in fact extremely sophisticated pieces of writing, and the form did not go wholly out of fashion: experiments were made later with new kinds of satyr play and separate competitions.[22] But once the 'three-plus-one' pattern had been superseded, the definition of tragedy must have been significantly affected. Certainly the classical canon that evolved in late antiquity did not include satyr play as an automatic concomitant of tragedy, and notions of the tragic in more modern times have normally been unaffected by the satyric element. This makes it all the harder for us to test the idea that this might be the piece of the jigsaw that tells most about Dionysus.

[19] For recent suggestions see Seaford (1984) 11–12; Nagy (1990) 384–5.
[20] Cf. Pickard-Cambridge (1988) 123–5, 291; Csapo and Slater (1995) 41–2.
[21] Cf. Green (1994) 38, 45–8, with n. 43.
[22] Seaford (1984) 25–6. The development of comedy must have had some bearing on these changes.

For the modern reader, trying to understand how performance at the Dionysia communicated itself to contemporary audiences, it is peculiarly frustrating to have no surviving satyr play known to have been composed for the same year's Dionysia as a surviving tragedy; Euripides' *Cyclops*, for all we know, may not even have been meant for performance at Athens at all,[23] and no other play survives in complete form or with a date. But there must be something to be teased out from the few fragmentary texts that have come down from antiquity.

François Lissarrague[24] has interpreted this evidence in the light of what vase-paintings from the sixth and fifth centuries have to tell about the satyrs and their world ('an imaginary world, which is constellated around Dionysos' ... 'satyrs reproduce the "normal" values and activities of Greek males by transforming them, according to a set of rules that are never random'). He points out that satyric drama works on the same lines:

> The location is often rural, pastoral, or exotic, a liminal territory far from cities or royal palaces. The themes seem to have been quite conventional. We find all kinds of ogres, monsters, or magicians, and the satyrs are often their captives. Sometimes they try to pass for athletes. Frequently the subject of the play is tied to a discovery or an invention: of wine, for example, or music, metallurgy, fire, or the first woman, Pandora. That is, everything takes place as if satyrs were a means to explore human culture through a fun-house mirror; the satyrs are antitypes of the Athenian male citizenry and present us with an inverted anthropology (or andrology) of the ancient city-state.

Lissarrague argues persuasively that the dynamic interplay between satyr play and tragedy depends on the presence of satyrs, required by the nature of the chorus, in the serious world of the heroes:

> The recipe is as follows: take one myth, add satyrs, observe the result. The joke is one of incongruity, which generates a series of surprises. Euripides' *Kyklops*, for example, depicts the progressive rediscovery of wine and the rituals for drinking which were so basic to Athenian culture ... the presence of satyrs within the myth subverts tragedy by shattering its cohesiveness. Tragedy poses fundamental questions about the relations between mortals and gods, or it reflects on such serious issues as sacrifice, war, marriage, or law. Satyric drama, by contrast, plays with culture first by distancing it and then reconstructing it through its antitypes, the satyrs. It does not seek to settle a controversy, nor to bring man face to face with his fate or the gods. It plays in a different key, with the displacement, distortion and reversal of what

---

[23] Easterling (1994) 79–80. The popularity of satyr plays on vases from Sicily and South Italy in the early fourth century is worth noting.

[24] Lissarrague (1990) 233–6.

constitutes the world and culture of men; it reintroduces distance and reinserts Dionysos in the center of the theater.

A more holistic view based on the strong likelihood that the same performers participated in these different kinds of show might suggest that tragedy and satyr play, taken together, offer a model for holding contradiction in some kind of equipoise: if satyr play works through distancing and displacement so too does tragedy, with its heroic – and marginal – settings and characters (cf. Part II below). The point might be not so much to contrast 'serious' and 'distorted' as to juxtapose two fields or worlds of experience, neither literally represented but each enacted through performance in such a way as to make sense for Dionysus as well as for his worshippers. ('Playing in a different key' is perhaps the most helpful of Lissarrague's metaphors.) This might be another way of putting what Harrison means by 'the wholeness of the Greek imagination' (p. 39 above).

Albert Henrichs[25] has recently stressed the enormous importance of the dance, or rather of *choreia*, the combination of song and dance performed by a *choros*, for an understanding of the Dionysiac element and ambience of tragedy. His study of the way in which choruses draw attention to their own performance is extremely suggestive for the argument that I am presenting here, if we explore its implications when applied to satyr choruses. The basic premise of Henrichs' discussion is that

> choral dancing in ancient Greek culture always constitutes a form of ritual performance, whether the dance is performed in the context of the dramatic festival or in other cultic and festive settings. The external setting in the sanctuary of Dionysos Eleuthereus and in the distinctly cultic ambience of the City Dionysia reinforces the ritual function of the choral dances in tragedy.

When choruses comment self-referentially on their own performance as dancers Henrichs argues that they do so

> not only in their capacity as characters in the drama but also as performers: while emphasising their choral identity, they temporarily expand their role as dramatic characters. In fact they acquire a more complex dramatic identity as they perceive their choral dance as an emotional reaction to the event onstage and assume a ritual posture which functions as a link between the cultic reality of the City Dionysia and the imaginary religious world of the tragedies.[26]

Henrichs mentions in passing a couple of examples from satyr play which can be compared with the phenomenon that he studies in detail for tragedy,[27] but the comparison can be taken further. A closer look at some

[25] Henrichs (1995) 56–111.   [26] Henrichs (1995) 59; cf. Easterling (1993a).
[27] Henrichs (1995) 92, n. 14.

passages might help us to see that here too the choral references have a ritual function, and that there is an understandable logic in making the final play of each set the one in which the performers are most identifiably Dionysiac.[28]

In Sophocles' *Trackers* the satyrs, alarmed and mystified by the sounds that turn out later to be the music of the newly-invented lyre, do a lot of kicking and jumping to rouse up whoever is making the noise (217–20), probably drawing attention with their 'I'll make the ground ring with my jumps and kicks' to the fact that they are performing the special satyr dance, the *sikinnis*.[29] The commotion brings out the nymph Cyllene, who contrasts the row they are making with the proper Dionysiac atmosphere:

> Wild creatures, why have you come rushing so noisily to this green and wooded hill, haunt of wild beasts? What are these tricks? What a change from the way you used to serve your master – when clad in fawnskin and holding high the thyrsus you used to follow along with the nymphs and a crowd of goatherds, singing the holy song as you escorted the god!

This is analogous to *Cyclops* 35ff., where Silenus introduces the satyr chorus by drawing attention to their performance. He has been describing the miserable and degrading life that he and the satyrs live as captives of Polyphemus: he has to sweep out the Cyclops' cave, while the satyrs look after his flocks. And now they are arriving with the sheep: 'What's this? Surely not the same beat of the *sikinnis* – not the beat you used to dance to when you went along to Althaea's place, Bacchus' band of supporters, sexily swaying to the lyre-songs?' This sets the tone for a typical satyrs' entrance, but instead of a cheery, drunken or lecherous song-and-dance we get the Chorus first preoccupied with driving the straying sheep then gloomily contrasting their present state with the true Dionysiac life-style: 'No Bromios here, no choral dancing, no bacchants with their thyrsuses, no rhythm of the drums, no freshly bubbling wine by flowing springs! I'm not on Nysa with the Nymphs, singing "Iacchos! Iacchos!" for Aphrodite, flying after her with the white-footed bacchants as I used to do.'

In each case the action of the play moves towards liberation and ultimate triumph or celebration. In *Cyclops* the satyrs will at last resume the service of their true master Dionysus (709); the ending of *Trackers* is not preserved, but we can guess, from Apollo's promise that Silenus and the satyrs will be

---

[28] Aristotle, *Poetics* 1449a2–3 says that the (tragic) *poiēsis* in early times was *saturikē* and *orchēstikōtera* 'satyric and more dependent on dance'.

[29] On this dance see Seaford on Eur. *Cyclops* 37. There is a further reference to kicking at Soph. *Trackers* 237.

'freed' if they find his lost cattle (164–5), that they are in a typical state of enslavement to the wrong master and are longing to return to Dionysus.

There are other fragments that seem to show the same preoccupation with performance: in a lyric attributed by scholars to Aeschylus' play *Prometheus the Fire-Kindler* the playful references to dancing and singing by nymphs celebrating Prometheus' discovery of fire may well be part of a satyr chorus (fr. 204b Radt, especially vv. 4–5: 'often shall one of the Naiads, hearing me tell this tale, pursue me by the blazing hearth'); and there is a well-known song ascribed to Pratinas, a contemporary of Aeschylus who was celebrated for his satyr plays, which is all about choral dancing and the right kind of musical accompaniment, and is best understood as part of a satyr play on the strength of lines like these:

> Mine, mine is Bromios: it's for me to shout and stamp, racing over the mountains with the Naiads ...[30]

If we now go back to Henrichs' discussion of choral self-referentiality in tragedy we can see more clearly that there is a functional similarity between the choruses of tragedy and of satyr play in the references both make to their own performance. And the implication of this similarity is that the satyr play, by virtue of its placing at the end of the sequence of four plays, its typical plot pattern, and the identity of its chorus, represents the performers ultimately getting nearest to their 'true' cultic role of Dionysus-worshippers.[31]

THE UNIQUENESS OF DIONYSUS

The introduction of a specifically dramatic element into some of the festivals of Dionysus was an event of incalculable significance for Western culture, and thence for the history of culture in general. Not surprisingly, scholars have been attracted by the idea that there must have been something – if only we could put our finger on it – about the way Dionysus was understood by the Athenians of the late sixth and early fifth centuries that would account for this extraordinary happening. But Dionysus, known from the *Homeric Hymns* onwards as a god of outstanding elusiveness, tends to resist scholarly capture. It may be salutary to enumerate his main qualities

[30] *PMG* I (708) = Athenaeus XIV 6176b–f. This fragment has been variously understood, and its date is disputed. Cf. Campbell (1991) 321–3 for text and bibliography; Zimmermann (1992) 124–5. Another relevant text is the fragment from an Oeneus play, printed by Radt in the *dubia et spuria* of Sophocles (= fr. 1130); cf. Lloyd-Jones (1996) 418–21. Here the satyrs advertise themselvs as skilled in 'songs' (12) and 'dancing' (15).

[31] Could this help to explain why satyr plays are more often represented on vases than tragedies?

and spheres of influence, and to see if any of this evidence will help to elucidate his patronage of drama.

From literature, art, cult titles and records of cult practice it is clear that Dionysus was identified by Athenians as (i) god of wine and wine miracles, who gave them the vine and taught them how to make wine; (ii) god of wild nature, particularly associated with luxuriant plant growth and with some wild animals (lion, snake, bull), and in cult honoured by phallophoric processions displaying the god's power over sexuality; (iii) god of ecstatic possession, characterised by the behaviour of women worshippers taking on the role of maenads; (iv) god of the dance, in company with satyrs and nymphs and/or maenads; (v) god of masking and disguise, often represented on vases by a mask as the object of worship; (vi) god of mystic initiation, who offers his worshippers the possibility of blessing in an afterlife. These categories of course overlap, and all are relevant for a discussion of Dionysus as theatre god. We also have to pay attention to the myths of Dionysus, some of which emphasised his 'otherness', his supposed arrival from outside Greece and the introduction of his rites in the face of opposition from god-fighters like Pentheus and Lycurgus, while others associated his gift of the vine and wine-making with madness and destructiveness as well as with liberation, and another (secret) category told the stories of dismemberment and rebirth that 'explained' the Dionysiac mysteries. Then there is the historical evidence for the development in importance of his festivals as the democracy became firmly established, and the seemingly strong link between the worship of Dionysus and the self-definition of the polis.

Given this wealth of possibly relevant material can we hope to identify what (if anything) made Dionysus uniquely appropriate as god of drama? He was not, after all, the only dancing god, or the only god of ecstatic possession, and not the only one associated with the mask or with mysteries.[32] The best we can do is to set out the considerations that any plausible explanation must take into account.

1. Scholars used to approach tragedy with an interest in origins high on their agenda, undeterred by the fact that the scraps of evidence surviving from antiquity and the Byzantine period are quite untestable as authentic record of the earliest phases in the history of tragedy. Even Aristotle's

---

[32] Dancing is associated with (e.g.): Pan, Artemis, Apollo; ecstatic possession with Pan and Cybele; masking with Artemis; mysteries with Demeter. Dionysus' powers of self-transformation did not set him apart, either: other divinities from Zeus downwards were believed to have the habit of taking on different disguises and are often so represented in myth. And boundary-crossing was a speciality of Hermes as well as of Dionysus.

famous pronouncements in *Poetics*, which cannot be ignored, can hardly go
back to documentary evidence from the late sixth century.[33] And in any
case, there is no reason why a complex and continuously developing
institution should be best explained in terms of an account of its origins.
Theatre was a dynamic phenomenon, and we should expect its ritual, social,
political and artistic functions to change rapidly during a period of intense
activity and experimentation like the fifth and early fourth centuries.[34]

The plays themselves, supplemented by what we know from titles and
fragments of lost plays and from vase-paintings, are always going to be the
major source of evidence. Here too it is important not to look for too neat a
model. The surviving complete plays (with the probable exception of
Rhesus; see Ch. 9 below) cover a period of only about seventy years (from
472, the date of *Persians*), representing only a small fraction of the output
of those years, and even though the supplementary evidence takes us back a
little earlier, as well as onward into later generations,[35] we can hardly
expect to construct a perfectly balanced story about the relation between
ritual, myth and the changing structures of the polis.[36]

The theory, for example, which makes the sacred history of Dionysus the
original subject matter of the plays put on in his honour,[37] is in danger of
being too restrictive in this way. Nor is it based on ancient authority.[38]
There is plenty of evidence, of course, that the Greeks composed hymns for
performance on ritual occasions which celebrated the attributes and achievements of particular gods or told cautionary tales of their wrongful treatment
by men (always duly punished), but so far as we know the plays composed

[33] For discussion of such evidence as there is see Pickard-Cambridge (1927); Else (1967);
Privitera (1991); Csapo and Slater (1995).
[34] Cf. Green (1994) 12 and 42; Bierl (1991) 20.
[35] Texts in *TrGF* i–iv of fragments of lost plays other than those by Euripides. For Euripides
see Nauck²; Austin (1968); Collard, Cropp and Lee (1995).
[36] See Seaford (1994) for an ambitious attempt; Griffith (1995) takes a very different view of
the political structures.
[37] See most recently Seaford (1994) 272.
[38] None of the ancient sources discussed by scholars explicitly says that the plots of early
tragedies were Dionysiac. The passage from Zenobius (5.40) which discusses the proverb
'Nothing to do with Dionysus' refers explicitly to dithyramb, not tragedy, in giving examples
of non-Dionysiac subject-matter, while the Suda entry, which mentions the Peripatetic
scholar Chameleon, and so takes us back to an earlier period of scholarship, sketches a
gradual process of 'turning to plots and stories [and] no longer making reference to
Dionysus'. This seems to imply a contrast between the use of plot and something formally
different, such as direct invocation of the god. Cf. Plutarch's wording at *Symp.* 1.1.5, 615a:
'People said "What has this to do with Dionysus?" when Phrynichus and Aeschylus
developed tragedy in the direction of plots and sufferings (*muthous kai pathē*).' For the
history of the debate see Bierl (1991) 5–17 with n. 13; Silk and Stern (1981) 142–50;
Henrichs (1984) 222 n. 35.

for competition at the drama festivals always took their subjects from a wider range of myths than just stories about Dionysus. And even allowing for some original link between drama and dithyramb, as most scholars would accept, there is no reason to see the plays as direct developments from cult hymns to Dionysus or as elaborations of liturgical patterns specifically relating to his worship. As John Herington remarks, 'The more one surveys Attic tragedy *as a whole*, including the titles and fragments of the lost dramas, the more one is struck by the catholicity of the art form, both in content and in tone, especially in its earlier phases.'[39] Even Aeschylus, who was evidently more interested than any other known dramatist in plots directly relating to Dionysus, devoted only about one-tenth of his output to such stories.[40] It is perhaps not irrelevant to draw a contrast with the biblical plays of medieval Europe, where there seems to be a much clearer link, in terms of plot and subject matter, with a liturgical context: these plays typically dramatise a biblical episode to fit a relevant point in the performance of an office, or in a procession, on a particular festival day.[41]

2. The (entirely proper and understandable) search for a detectable logic in Dionysus' association with the theatre has tended to make scholars look for a hermeneutic model which will match the god with what one might loosely call the ideology of Attic drama, in its social, political, psychological and religious aspects. The temptation here, as Henrichs has pointed out, is to use the *Bacchae* as the key text for understanding the Dionysiac in drama, which is liable to be reductive, threatening to 'obscure the regional and functional diversity of Dionysus, and the fundamental difference between his mythical and cultic manifestations',[42] just as exclusive definitions of Dionysus as 'the outsider', 'the Other', the god who confuses boundaries, risk imposing a too abstract pattern on the extremely rich and diverse evidence of the texts.

Perhaps the best model will be a capacious one which allows us to see the interplay[43] between Dionysus' different aspects as providing a particularly

---

[39] Herington (1985) 69.
[40] See Herington (1985) 266, nn. 34 and 35, and Bierl (1991) 10–13 for details of plays with Dionysiac plots.
[41] See Muir (1995).
[42] Henrichs (1990), especially 257–60, 269. Cf. Schlesier (1993) 90–3 for an interesting discussion of the issues raised by recent work. On the important differences between myth and cult see also Buxton (1994) 152–5, and on the difficulty of 'pinning down' Greek gods see Silk and Stern (1981) 167.
[43] Cf. Goldhill (1990a) 126–7, who looks for a similarly complex model to express the relation between the ritual events at the City Dionysia and the content of the dramas that followed them; see also Osborne (1993), especially 37, and Zeitlin (1993).

strong stimulus to mimetic performance. If we try to avoid telling a story of *how* or *why* drama developed, and concentrate our attention on what sort of phenomenon it was, we may find many hints in the surviving texts that what was performed was intended specifically for the god and associated in distinctive detail with his worship. As Steven Lonsdale has pointed out in a chapter on Dionysus and the dance, the god is 'present in the particular – in wine, in the siffle of the *aulos*, in the mask, in the dances of the maenads, and in his cult hymn, the dithyramb. The divine shape-shifter is portrayed as *chorēgos* and dancer in poetry, and with great frequency in art, especially on vessels used for storing, mixing, and drinking the god's wine.'[44] For drama, too, this combination of associations must be significant, even if no single aspect can be treated as decisive.

The power of wine both to liberate and to madden is brought out in many ways: in stories like that of *Cyclops* or Sophocles' lost satyr play *Dionysiscus*, on the invention of wine-making, or in more disturbing tales like that of Icarius and Erigone.[45] Whether the effects of the wine are presented as positive or negative or both at once, they must always have been closely linked with the wild state of the Dionysiac performers, itself an ambiguous phenomenon evoking both natural instinct and behaviour and the culture of the city and its rituals. Archilochus, poet of dithyramb, gave the idea a memorable expression: 'I know how to lead off the lovely song of lord Dionysus when my wits are struck by the lightning-bolt of wine' (fr. 120 W).

Wildness, indeed, is always an essential element of these shows for Dionysus, suggested most of all by the appearance of the satyrs, who as Oliver Taplin puts it 'belong in the wild, and are always threatening to turn animal',[46] and by the rest of the *thiasos*, particularly the maenads, who do not appear on stage with such regularity as the satyrs, but powerfully influence the imagery of tragedy. Their state of ecstatic possession is often used as a metaphor for the violent actions and experiences of tragic characters and choruses[47] even in plays with plots in which Dionysus plays no direct part. And the god's own closeness to wild nature was always strongly represented at the Dionysia, both at the city festival and at the Rural Dionysia in the demes, when huge model *phalloi* were carried in procession through the streets by his worshippers[48] – a benign cultic

---

[44] Lonsdale (1993) 81; cf. Frontisi-Ducroux (1989) 152.
[45] Cf. Seaford (1994) 301–6 for similar stories.
[46] In Astley (1991) 461. On other aspects of the wild see e.g. Gould (1987) and Segal (1982).
[47] See especially Schlesier (1993), Seaford (1994) 257–62, Henrichs (1994) 57; also Ch. 5 below (p. 106).
[48] See Cole (1993).

representation of an element of the god's power that could never be treated as safe or tamed (and cf. [3] from Delos). Dionysus' presence, like that of the other gods, was always potentially dangerous, but his sexuality could be generative[49] as well as violent, just as his madness could be cathartic and conducive of communal participation in the mythical world.

It is an interesting feature of the Dionysiac *thiasos* that the main players, the satyrs and maenads (or nymphs), are not found in the 'real world' in the form that they take in art and drama: the animal ears and tails of the satyrs, and the maenads' characteristic habits, like wearing snakes in their hair, taking part in the *sparagmos* and eating raw flesh,[50] set them apart from ordinary human worshippers, making them ideally suited to mimetic performance and able to carry metaphorical meaning with ease. One way in which they do this is through the blurring of 'normal' social boundaries: for example, the way the satyrs and maenads share the dance is not representative of historical patterns: as Lonsdale has pointed out, there is little evidence for mixed dancing in the traditions of the Greek cities, but the gender demarcations of everyday life are not observed in the choreography of the *thiasos*.[51] Symbolic detachment of this kind gives a particular piquancy to the passage preserved from Aeschylus' *Theoroi* or *Isthmiastae* (*Spectators at the Isthmian Games*) in which satyrs describe 'portraits' of themselves: 'Look and see if this image – this likeness by Daedalus – could be more like me! All it needs is a voice' (fr. 78a Radt). In performance the 'portraits' could only be masks, identical to the ones worn by the chorusmen playing the parts of the satyrs, without which their very existence as satyrs would be impossible. So the reference to these 'images' and 'likenesses' works in the same way as the references to choral dancing, as a reminder of the theatrical and ritual nature of the performance.[52]

The use of the mask, both in the worship of Dionysus – familiar, though still mysterious, from vase-paintings[53] – and in the dramatic competitions, must be one of the most important clues for anyone trying to understand 'the Dionysiac'. But it is an interestingly multivalent and elusive sort of clue. As worn in drama, the mask enables individual performers to assume multiple identities: each actor will play different roles from one drama to the

---

[49] Plutarch (*Moral Essays* 365a) says that the Greeks regard Dionysus as 'lord and master not only of wine but of the whole wet element in nature'; (cf. Eur. *Ba.* 284 for the idea that Dionysus is 'poured out' in libations). Silk and Stern (1981) 172 suggest that we should think of sap, semen and blood as well as of wine.

[50] Cf. Henrichs (1978) 121–60 and (1982); Hedreen (1994) 54–8.

[51] Lonsdale (1993) 94; cf. Bérard and Bron (1989) 130–5; Seaford (1994) 272.

[52] Green (1994) 45–6.

[53] On the so-called 'Lenaean' vases see Frontisi-Ducroux (1989), (1991); Seaford (1994) 264–6.

[3] One of two sculptured bases flanking a shrine of Dionysus on Delos, set up to commemorate his *chorēgia* by the local man Carystius, *c.* 300 BC. Pride of place is given to the relief of a cock, whose phalloid head and neck point upwards to the giant human phallus surmounting the base. The cock symbolised both fighting competitiveness and rampant male sexuality, and hence was thought a peculiarly appropriate Dionysiac symbol.

next, and often enough within a single play, and each chorusman will have four different identities, one for each tragedy and one for the satyr play. So Pentheus is also Agave, and the Furies of *Eumenides* are also satyrs. While the performers take on these different roles the masks themselves, fixed and unchangeable, are a visible reminder to the audience of the fictive nature of the dramatic events.[54] Yet paradoxically the mask in performance may create the illusion of facial movement and fluidity of expression, as viewers have often noticed in modern performances of masked drama. This exciting complexity perhaps helps to explain the reverence that performers evidently felt for their masks, shown, for example by the fact that the masks were dedicated to the god after the performance was over and hung from the temple in his sanctuary. As J. R. Green suggests, there may have been a felt need 'to leave behind with the god in his sanctuary the "otherness" created in his honour, and not to take it out into normal society. The beings represented by the masks were potentially dangerous and disruptive things.'[55]

The influential image of Dionysus as performer with his *thiasos* – leader of the dance, master of disguise, controller of the action – has to be balanced by that of Dionysus as spectator, the supreme *theātēs*[56] for whom the shows are put on. This duality suggests that the drama was felt to have power to generate interactive response between players and audience, and there may be a significant link here with the way the Dionysiac mysteries functioned. It seems to have been important for the achievement of mystic communion that the worshippers should be viewers, *theātai*, of sights forbidden to the uninitiated, and if Dionysus was a model of the viewer, as well as of the power that made possible the mystic experience, one can see how theatre and mysteries might share the same logic.[57] This is very different from tracing the origin or development of the drama from patterns of mystic cult, an approach which would have to explain why Dionysus was so closely associated with theatre while Demeter was not (although Eleusinian mystic practice has been thought to be deeply implicated in the language of some plays).[58]

---

[54] On the dramatic function of the masks see p. 153 below; also Calame (1986) 141, who stresses the power of the mask in effecting 'not only safe passage from the Same to the Other, but from the Other to the Same as well'; Schlesier (1993) 94–7.

[55] Green (1994) 79. Even in the commercialised culture of contemporary Bali, actors still make offerings to their masks as supernatural powers (*The Times*, 21 June 1995).

[56] Though not, of course, the only one: the gods more generally had a crucial role as spectators; cf. Lonsdale (193) 52–68; Osborne (1993) on their liking for competitive events. Nor was Dionysus the only impresario: cf. the control over the action of a particular play by e.g. Athena in *Ajax* or Aphrodite and Artemis in *Hippolytus*.

[57] Cf. Segal (1982).

[58] Notably the *Oresteia*, for which see Bowie (1993) with earlier bibliography. For Sophocles see Seaford (1994) 395–402.

Scholars these days are much readier to see references in drama to Dionysiac mystery cult, to Dionysus in his association with death and the afterlife and with the means whereby 'salvation' may be achieved. This is thanks to the discovery of evidence for fifth-century initiation with a much wider geographical spread than used to be thought probable.[59] For under-standing drama the implications are quite far-reaching, and not just in relation to *Bacchae*, although this is the play that (naturally enough) has attracted most attention. In his recent book Seaford goes some way in the direction of the Nietzschean view that the mystic sufferings of Dionysus are at the centre of tragic patterns of action,[60] but this approach is open to the objection that surviving Attic tragedy is not easily understood in relation to any master plot-pattern (cf. pp. 46–7 above). Maybe we should be content to see the secret story of Dionysus' dismemberment, death and rebirth,[61] and the pattern of mystic initiation for which the story served as *aition*, as one of several powerful myths about the relations between gods and men that offered the dramatists particular scope – subjects which were multi-valent enough to be used for the dramatisation of a range of possible issues, political, social, moral or existential, without imposing a narrowly limiting interpretation on any of them.

This last section leads on naturally to larger questions about content. What is the connexion between tragic meditation on violence and suffering, guilt, punishment, mortality, human limitations etc. if what Dionysus is believed to offer is 'salvation' rather than a manifestation of divine power to help and harm? It is not enough to say that tragedy explores one side of the picture and satyr play (and comedy) the other, because there seems to be a more coherent pattern to which they all conform, and to which dithyramb too can be seen to belong. Maybe we should go back to the wisdom of Silenus, the elderly leader or 'father' of the satyrs, the figure used by Plato as an analogy for Socrates. According to the story (which goes back at least to the archaic period; cf. Theognis 425), the rich king Midas caused Silenus to be captured (by being made drunk), and the drunken satyr in response to the question 'What is best?' answered 'Not to be born at all', adding that the second-best, if one has the misfortune to be born, is to go back where one came from as quickly as possible. This insight into mortality and its sorrows is explicitly linked to the drunken old satyr, and the image has the advantage of combining the different strands of Dionysiac thinking that this chapter has briefly reviewed. The satyr is by definition a Dionysiac performer, a leading member of the *thiasos* of the god and therefore a dancer and mask-

---

[59] See Burkert (1987); Bremmer (1994) 84–97.
[60] Seaford (1994), especially ch. 8.
[61] Cf. Detienne (1979); Burkert (1987).

wearer, who will adopt different disguises. He is also a creature of wild nature with the appetites of the wild, but he is in contact with the god's gift of wine, and it is the power of the wine that enables him to be caught and questioned. His message, it turns out, is not about performance, still less about celebration, but about death.[62] The most radical way to escape mortality and the cycle of change is never to be born; is this perhaps a way of expressing some of the aspirations and anxieties of the mystic initiant, who seeks the rebirth that abolishes death but at the same time knows that death itself has to be experienced? Death never ceased to be a defining feature of tragedy as understood in Greek tradition; it is perhaps not an accident that the presiding deity of the festivals which included tragedy should have had strong connexions with the world of the dead.[63]

All Greek gods resist easy categorisation, but Dionysus' multiform and elusive nature seems to have lent itself to the development of performance traditions of exceptional sophistication and complexity. As time went on, and as the regular instantiation of myth at the dramatic festivals contributed in influential ways to the imaginative life of successive audiences, Dionysus took on a specifically theatrical persona. He had of course been the object of cult and the subject of myth long before drama came into being, but it should not surprise us if the dramatic performances came to be seen as reflecting every aspect of his unique personality – as if he had always been the god of theatre.

BIBLIOGRAPHICAL NOTE

For recent work on Dionysus, with reference to earlier bibliography, see a series of papers by Henrichs (1982, 1984, 1990, 1993, 1995) and particularly his entry in the *Oxford Classical Dictionary*, 3rd edn 1996; also H. S. Versnel, *Ter Unus (Inconsistencies in Greek and Roman Religion* I), Leiden (1990) ch. 2; R. Friedrich, 'Everything to do with Dionysos?' with R. Seaford's reply in Silk (1996) 257–94. Bremmer (1994) surveys work on Greek religion generally; Burkert (1987) discusses mystery cults. On Dionysus and theatre see most recently Winkler and Zeitlin (1990); Bierl (1991); Carpenter and Faraone (1993); Seaford (1994); Sourvinou-Inwood (1994).

Iconography: Bérard and Bron (1989); C. Gasparri, 'Dionysos', *LIMC* III.1, 414–566 and III.2, 296–456.

---

[62] Nietzsche, *The Birth of Tragedy* ch. 3, sees great significance in this story, but he uses it to construct a metaphysical view of Dionysus which is hard to sustain. Cf. Silk and Stern (1981) 148, 178 for a critique, which perhaps draws too sharp a distinction between Silenus and the satyrs.

[63] Cf. Heraclitus, fr. 22B15, 27 D–K: 'Dionysus and Hades are the same.' Cf. Segal (1990) 418; but there is no need to take the mystic Dionysus as necessarily 'softening' the meaning of tragic stories.

3

SIMON GOLDHILL

The audience of Athenian tragedy

The culture of classical Greece was a performance culture. It valorised competitive public display across a vast range of social institutions and spheres of behaviour. The gymnasium with its competitions in manliness, the symposium with its performances of songs and speeches, and the theatre become – with the spreading of Greek culture throughout the Mediterranean world in the wake of Alexander the Great – the key signs of Greekness itself. The dominant culture of Athens in the fifth century is particularly influential in the development of these institutions, and can be said to have invented the theatre. Yet in this, as in most respects, Athens is not a typical Greek city. For the unique institutions of Athenian democracy constitute a special type of performance culture. The lawcourts and the Assembly are the major political institutions of democracy, the city's major sites of conflict and debate, its citizens' major route to positions of power. Both lawcourts and Assembly involve large citizen audiences, public performance by speakers, and voting to achieve a decision and a result. Democracy made public debate, collective decision-making and the shared duties of participatory citizenship central elements of its political practice. To be in an audience was not just a thread in the city's social fabric, it was a fundamental political act. The historian Thucydides has Cleon, a leading politician of the fifth century, refer dismissively to the Athenians as *theātai tōn logōn*, 'spectators of speeches' (Thuc. 3.38); Athenian political ideology proudly highlighted democracy's special commitment to putting things *es meson*, 'in the public domain to be contested'. A discussion of the audience of Greek tragedy must take as its frame not modern theatrical experience but both the pervasiveness of the values of performance in Greek culture and in particular the special context of democracy and its institutions, where to be in an audience is above all *to play the role of democratic citizen.*

SOCIAL DRAMA AND AUDIENCE PARTICIPATION

Drama was a major political event in the Athenian calendar. I call it 'political' not in the narrow sense that 'political' is often used today but in the wide sense of 'pertaining to the public life of the polis' that Paul Cartledge has already outlined in this volume: the drama festivals were institutions in which civic identity was displayed, defined, explored, contested. This can be seen in the arrangements for the festival, the ceremonial performances by which the plays are framed and by the plays themselves. The most important festival for drama is the Great Dionysia, and I will focus first on different types of festival activity to show how widely diffused a sense of audience participation was at the Great Dionysia.

The calendar of events on the days before the plays were performed is not quite certain.[1] It included however: (a) the procession of the Statue of Dionysus to a temple on the road to Eleutherae, a village near Athens, and then back to the theatre precinct in Athens, where sacrifices and hymns were performed. In the second century BC, ephebes – young males on the point of the formal status of adult and full citizen duties – played a major role in this, and many scholars have assumed that this class of Athenians also performed this role in the fifth century. (b) There was, at least from 444 BC, a *proagōn*, a ceremony in which the playwrights and performers were presented in public and the subject of the plays announced. It is not clear what audience there was here, but Plato does describe the event as nerve-racking for the playwright Agathon (*Symp.* 194a). (c) The *proagōn* was followed by the spectacle of a massive ceremonial procession (called a *pompē*), which led to the sacrifice of bulls in the sanctuary of Dionysus. This *pompē* was particularly grand. The procession included a variety of sacred objects and offerings carried by various representatives. For example, a young girl of noble birth was chosen to carry a golden basket of offerings; ritual loaves of bread were carried, as were phalluses, which are often associated with Dionysiac worship (cf. Ch. 2 above). Resident aliens as well as citizens marched in special robes. So too citizens without any special role in the festivals could process. (d) The *pompē* may have been followed by a *kōmos*, a celebratory revel, though it is unclear if this is different from the *pompē*, or merely a description of the less formal conclusion of the procession and sacrifice.

These opening events thus engaged many Athenians either as selected representatives of particular classes or groups within the city, or more generally, as residents of Athens. The boundary between audience and

---

[1] For details of and sources for the following ceremonies, see Pickard-Cambridge (1988).

participants as the *pompē* progressed towards the sacrifice and its feast (and the *kōmos*) must have been increasingly indistinct. The festival is for – and participated in by – the Athenians as a body.

In the theatre itself, this process of participation and display continues. Before the plays themselves, at least from the middle of the fifth century, four ceremonials of evident importance took place:[2] (*a*) The ten generals, the leading military and political figures of the state, poured a libation. Only very rarely indeed in the calendar did these elected officials act as a group together in such a ritual. This emphasises the power and organisation of the polis under whose aegis the festival is mounted. (*b*) There was an announcement by a herald of the names of citizens who had benefited the state in particular ways and been awarded a crown for their services. According to the orator Aeschines, other announcements were once made at this time, such as proclamations of the freeing of slaves or honorific awards from foreign cities, until a law was passed limiting such announcements to those who had been honoured publicly by the polis itself (Aeschines 3.41–7). Again, the political frame of the polis is clearly highlighted. (*c*) There was a display of tribute from the states of the Athenian empire, where all the monies were paraded around the theatre – a ceremony that glorifies Athens as a military and political power. (*d*) There was a parade of ephebes whose fathers had been killed fighting for the state. These orphans were brought up and educated at state expense, and when they reached the age of manhood they were presented in the theatre, in full military panoply, and they took an oath promising to fight and die for the state as their fathers had before them. The duty of the citizen towards the military state is ceremonially displayed.

Each of these ceremonials in different ways promotes and projects an idea and ideal of citizen participation in the state and an image of the power of the polis of Athens. It uses the civic occasion to glorify the polis. The audience of the plays included those singled out by the pre-play ceremonials, and this special time in the theatre had the potential to become a highly charged moment in the political life of the city. The bitterly contested political row between Demosthenes and Aeschines in 330 was ostensibly on the subject of the presentation of a crown to Demosthenes in the theatre in 336 (Dem. *On the Crown*; Aeschines, *Against Ctesiphon*) and Demosthenes' speech *Against Meidias* is predicated on the fact that Meidias punched Demosthenes in the theatre (cf. Ch. 1 above, p. 34). Demosthenes' account of Meidias' appearance at the Dionysia shows well the sense of personal honour at stake before the citizen body: 'Those of you who were spectators

---

[2] For details of and sources for these ceremonies see Goldhill (1990a).

at the Dionysia hissed and booed him as he entered the theatre, and you did everything that showed loathing of him …' The orator's description of the scene is full of theatrical language, as the social drama of Meidias in the theatre becomes the subject of further debate on the stage of the lawcourt. The theatre was a space in which all the citizens were actors – as the city itself and its leading citizens were put on display.

The role of the *chorēgos* is represented in many ways in Greek writing – sometimes as merely a form of taxation on the rich to benefit the poor, sometimes as the perfect opportunity for the rich to benefit the city, as all good citizens should – but it is clear that being a *chorēgos* offered a special chance to glory in the full light of the citizens' gaze.[3] (It is as a *chorēgos* for his tribe's dithyrambic chorus that Demosthenes was hit by Meidias; hence the highly charged and public effect of the blow.)[4] The conspicuous expense of the lavish costumes, the possibility of victory in the context and thus its celebration, a grand personal appearance before the assembled city, presented the *chorēgos* with a magnificent occasion for self-promotion. So – inevitably – we hear about Alcibiades, the fifth-century citizen who was most prominent in the citizens' gaze, marching in purple before the amazed citizens, and also (from his enemies) about his outrageous arrogance towards the judges and other citizens in the competition (Dem. 21.143; Athen. 12 534c; Andocides, *Against Alcibiades* 20–4). The Great Dionysia was a festival in which men competed, not merely in plays or in dithyrambic choruses, but also as *chorēgoi* in the contests of status within the city.

The major festival at which drama takes place, then, is also itself a social drama. The audience participates in this drama as the body before whom and by whom prominent citizens' standing is constructed as prominent. As the city and its citizens are ceremonially on display on stage at the Great Dionysia, so the audience constitutes what may be called 'the civic gaze'.

THE AUDIENCE AS CITY

The size of this civic audience is estimated by scholars according to the size of the theatre – a task made more difficult since the theatre was rebuilt in stone by Lycurgus between 338 and 330 BC. A figure between 14,000 and 17,000 spectators is usually and plausibly given. Plato in the *Symposium* (175e) says that Agathon's victory in the tragic competition was gained 'before the witnesses of more than 30,000 Greeks'. This statement indicates more about the prestige and public glory of the Great Dionysia than the possible number of spectators. Plato's exaggeration is likely to come in part

---

[3] Peter Wilson's forthcoming work analyses this fully.   [4] See Wilson (1991).

at least from the use of 30,000 as a conventional – and not wholly improbable – figure for the number of citizens in Athens. For whatever the actuality of numbers and constitution of the audience, it was repeatedly said that 'the whole city' was in the theatre, or, more grandly, 'all Greece'.

A formal collection of even 14,000 citizens, however, makes the Great Dionysia the largest single body of citizens gathered together not only in the Athenian calendar but also throughout the Greek world, except perhaps for the Olympic games (for which figures are not readily available) or for certain major battles. The Assembly in the fifth century held around 6,000 citizens – also often termed 'the city', 'the whole city' – and the lawcourts had juries chosen from a panel of 6,000 citizens: numbers of the jurors varied from court to court and from case to case, but were certainly larger than present-day juries – the lowest figure we have is 200, the highest 6,000.[5] The only event to come close to the Great Dionysia in scale and grandeur is the Great Panathenaea, a festival held every four years. The Panathenaea was, as the name suggests, a festival for all Athens, where the central event was a huge procession (pompē) to the Parthenon, in which all groups of the city were represented. This procession is pictured on the frieze of the Parthenon.[6] The pompē was followed by athletic games and musical and poetic competitions in which competitors from across Greece competed. (There is a Panhellenic element in the Panathenaea too.) This remarkable spectacle, like the Great Dionysia, projected and promoted a glorious image of the polis of Athens as a polis – it displayed the city as a city to the outside world and to itself.[7] Yet even in the Panathenaea there was not the focused attention provided by the stage and the huge audience of citizens. The sheer scale of the Great Dionysia invests the social drama with an immense importance.

It is certain that a very large majority of this huge audience was made up of Athenian citizens – adult enfranchised males. Many texts treat the 'proper or intended' audience of tragedy as the collectivity of citizens. I will discuss the implications of this when I consider questions of audience response and tragic teaching. Here I shall look first at how the citizen body is organised within the theatre, and secondly at the other members of the audience.

In Greek theatres, seating is divided into wedges of seats called *kerkides*, and even before Lycurgus rebuilt the theatre, the seating was divided in a fascinating way.[8] There was a block of seats called the *bouleutikon* which was reserved for members of the *boulē*, the executive council of 500 citizens

[5] See MacDowell (1978) 36–40.   [6] See Osborne (1986).
[7] For discussion and bibliography see Goldhill (1991) 171–85.
[8] For an interesting if overstated discussion see Winkler (1990b) 37–42.

who prepared and enacted the business of the policy-making Assembly (Aristophanes, *Birds* 794, with schol.; *Peace* 887). These 500 citizens were appointed by lot, as were most officials in democratic Athens, and there was a compulsory geographical spread of councillors, since each of the ten tribes provided fifty councillors. It is worth recalling here that the dithyrambic competitions are between choruses of fifty from each tribe, and also that each tribe was required to provide a list of names from which the judges of the competition were selected – one from each tribe, by lot. These organisational principles, and in particular the special seats of the *boulē*, highlight the authority of officials of the democratic state on the one hand, and, on the other, the formal socio-political organisation of the *dēmos*.

It is also clear that the ephebes who were paraded as war orphans had special honorific seats (Aeschines 3.154); and the scholia to Aristophanes and Pollux – both very late sources – tell us that the ephebes as a class had special seating (Pollux, *Lexicon* 4.122 (see also Hesychius s.v. *bouleutikos*); schol. to Aristophanes, *Birds* 794). This conforms with the ephebes' special role at the Dionysia in the transfer of the statue of the god and the opening sacrifice, which, as I have already mentioned, is also attested only in late inscriptional evidence. The changing nature of the formal institutions of the ephebes, however, makes it unwise to assume that what was true of the second century BC was true for the fifth century. So it cannot be assumed with certainty that the whole class of ephebes had special seating. None the less, at the very least it is clear that the special seats allotted to the war orphan ephebes distinguish – ceremonially and spatially – a group of those who are about to assume their full duties as citizens.

There is also reason to suppose that each block of seats was reserved for a particular tribe. There are three pieces of evidence for this hypothesis.[9] First, there is (once again) very late inscriptional evidence that shows that in Hadrian's time – over five hundred years after the death of Sophocles – the *kerkides* were allotted to particular tribes. It is often assumed that this may reflect earlier practice also. Second and most importantly, tickets for the theatre have survived, lead tokens dated to the fourth century or earlier, which are inscribed with tribal names.[10] This may imply that tribal affiliation was important in seating arrangements and from an early date. Third, and of least use, a fragment of a comedy called *Female Power* by Alexis, which has its woman speaker complain of having to 'sit in the last of the *kerkides*, like foreigners' (Alexis fr. 41), seems to suggest that foreigners had a special block of seats. This may imply that particularised blocks of

[9] See Winkler (1990b) 39–41, following Pickard-Cambridge (1988) 270.
[10] See Pickard-Cambridge (1968) 270–2.

seats did exist, but without a context the fragment remains tantalising. While again no certainty is possible, the hypothesis of tribal seating reflects strikingly both the other tribal aspects of organisation in the festival, and the festival's spatial representation of socio-political division.

There were also honorific seats – *prohedriai* – in the front rows of each block. These were reserved for particular priests, notably priests of Dionysus himself, and for particular dignitaries. In democratic Athens, there was a marked tension between on the one hand collective endeavour, the ideology of citizen equality, and the pre-eminence of the state over the individual, and, on the other, the desire for individual honour, conspicuous personal display and familial pride. The spatial dynamics of the audience – with blocks of citizens, and certain authoritative or representative groups or individuals distinguished by honorific seats – dramatises this central dynamic of Athenian social life. As the audience of the Great Dionysia constitutes 'the civic gaze', so the audience is seated in ways which map the constitution of the citizen body. The Great Dionysia, ceremonially and spatially, puts the city on display.

What, then, of non-citizens? Which and how many non-citizens attended the theatre? Some of the answers to these questions are straightforward, others involve great controversy. There are four groups to be considered, foreigners (*xenoi*), resident aliens (metics), slaves, and women. I will look at each in order.

Foreigners were certainly present at the Great Dionysia, and it is likely that there were increasing numbers, particularly from neighbouring states, as the fame of the festival spread and theatre began to have great cultural capital (cf. Ch. 1 above). There is, however, no substantial evidence for the numbers of foreigners – certainly the rhetoric which proclaims events at the Dionysia happening 'before all Greece' cannot be taken as an indication of very large numbers of foreigners. Whether there was a separate section for foreigners (as suggested by the fragment of Alexis) or not, we have no notion of how admission was organised. However many foreigners in general were present, the Dionysia was also used in particular to honour foreign dignitaries[11] or benefactors of the state – which in some cases meant the honour of foreign ambassadors, in the *prohedriai*, watching the tribute they themselves had been compelled to bring, as it was paraded in the theatre. This sense of the city on display internationally at the Dionysia is contrasted by Aristophanes with the Lenaea, a secondary drama festival,[12] where, as one of his characters put it, 'there are no foreigners present yet . . .

---

[11] See Aeschines 3.76, where Demosthenes is said to have been hissed by the audience for his servility towards the Macedonian ambassadors.

[12] For details of the Lenaea see Pickard-Cambridge (1988) 25–42; cf. Ch. 1 above.

we are just ourselves' (*Acharnians* 502–7). This statement of the complete absence of foreigners at the Lenaea need not be taken literally; but it does indicate how at the Great Dionysia the heightened awareness of the presence of foreigners in the audience, particularly the official representatives of foreign states, increased the sense of the festival as an arena of maximum public self-awareness and self-promotion for the city and the citizens.

Metics – non-citizen resident aliens – were also present, both at the Dionysia and at the Lenaea. It is not known if they had special seats, but, as at the Great Panathenaea and at the *pompē* of the Dionysia, where they probably marched in special robes,[13] they are singled out by Athenian writers specifically as being present as a group. Again, we have no evidence of how admission was organised or how many metics attended.

With slaves and women we enter more contested waters. It is often said that slaves definitely could attend the Dionysia (though it is also always assumed that not many did). An inscription indicates that the 'assistants to the Council' – eight slaves in public service – had special seats in the theatre, presumably with the *boulē*.[14] There are, however, only three pieces of evidence for other slaves, all far from compelling, though each is from the fourth century BC. The first is also used for the case of women at the Dionysia. In Plato's *Gorgias* (501e–502d), Socrates argues that music and poetry, unlike philosophy, aim at the pleasure of an audience rather than its education; and that even tragedy, the most serious art form, is a type of 'demagoguery'. This is part of an extremely rhetorical attack on 'rhetoric', where poetry and drama are assimilated to rhetoric. Socrates concludes his critique of the arts: 'Therefore we have now found a type of rhetoric aimed at a populace (*dēmos*) such as is composed of children and men and women together, slave and free, a rhetoric I do not much admire; for we have said it is a type of fawning (*kolakikēn*).' Although tragedy has been Socrates' last and most difficult example, his conclusion is not solely about tragedy (and does not mention any performance context at all); rather, he is concerned with all arts as types of demagoguery. His conclusion does not imply an audience of slaves (or women) for tragedy; rather, Socrates is denigrating the promiscuity and amorality (*kolakeia*) of a rhetoric which can only pleasure its audience; the failure of this type of (democratic) rhetoric to distinguish properly between audiences or to recognise how an audience may be bettered is expressed in a typically (aristocratic) Greek way by

---

[13] See Suda s.v. '*askophorein*'.
[14] See Pickard-Cambridge (1946) 20; a stone from the late fifth-century theatre is inscribed ΒΟΛΗΣ ΥΠΗΡΕΤΟΝ, 'servants of the council'. This inscription is surprisingly not quoted in the standard discussions of the presence of slaves in the theatre.

suggesting that such rhetoric mixes hierarchical, social categories normally kept separate (adult/child, male/female, slave/free).

The second piece of evidence is from Theophrastus, who in his work *The Characters* (9.5) characterises the 'Shameless Man' as a figure who would buy tickets for foreigners (*xenoi*) but then take 'his own sons and their tutor' to the plays. Taking a slave to the theatre here, however, may be part of the character's 'shamelessness' – '*and* their *tutor*!' – a transgression rather than a norm of Athenian practice. The third and least telling passage comes from Aeschines, who claims that in earlier years the time before the plays was used by citizens to announce the manumission of slaves. So, it may be inferred, slaves may have been present for this announcement (though, of course, slaves who are in the process of being freed). There is no other evidence for the presence of slaves in the audience of the theatre. The invisibility of slaves is a well-known problem in ancient sources; conversely, there are several occasions where slaves are explicitly said to attend religious events, such as the Anthesteria. It is hard from this evidence to come to a certain conclusion about the presence of slaves, except the public officials, at the Dionysia. If they did attend, they were not described by any available Athenian writer as part of the 'intended or proper' audience. The invisibility of slaves is a social and not just a historiographical factor.

The presence of women at the Great Dionysia is a hotly contested subject, with more extensive implications for our understanding of the audience and the nature of the dramatic performance (cf. Ch. 1 above, pp. 29–30). Unfortunately, there is no single piece of evidence that can offer a clear and direct answer to the problem. Consequently, the debate has tended to rely on analogies with other Athenian festivals, general suppositions about the role of women in Athenian culture, oversimplified interpretation of difficult and ambiguous sources, and, all too often, mere hypothesis – 'gut feeling'. I shall not be able here to deal with all the material that has been brought to bear on the issue.[15] I will outline first the very few uncontested 'facts of the case'; second, I will look at the passages in ancient writers which those who believe women were present argue to be the strongest evidence; third, I will look at the arguments from analogy with other festivals and from the position of women in Athens. Finally, I will look at the implications of this debate for our understanding of the audience of tragedy.

Let me begin, then, with what I take to be uncontested facts. No women participated directly in the writing, production, performance or judging of the plays. No women could claim money from the funds which assisted

---

[15] I have considered the arguments in fuller detail in Goldhill (1994a).

Athenian citizens to attend the plays (the Theoric Fund, discussed below). At least one female took part in the *pompē*: the sacred basket was carried by a specially chosen, well-born – i.e. citizen – unmarried female (*parthenos*). Beyond this, however, each piece of material that has been brought to bear is open to question.

The most important texts that have been utilised to demonstrate the presence of women in the theatre in the classical period come from Aristophanes and from Plato. (Late anecdotes – such as the famous story that women had miscarriages at the first sight of Aeschylus' Furies entering the theatre – are of most dubious value, since there is no doubt that women did attend the theatre in these much later periods, and these stories are often invented from the cultural perspective of the late writers in response to particular passages in the plays themselves.) In Aristophanes' play *Peace*, the hero and his servant are throwing barley into the audience (962–7): 'Has everyone got some barley?' asks the hero; 'There's no one among these spectators who hasn't got barley', says the slave; 'But the women haven't got any', says his master; 'Well, their husbands will give it to them tonight', replies the slave. The word for barley grains (*krithai*) is the same word in the plural as a slang term for penis (*krithē*). So the joke can easily be understood (though not translated) as saying 'all the spectators have their barley / a penis', 'women don't have barley / a penis', 'their husbands will "give it to them" tonight'. This humour does not depend on the presence of the women in the theatre at all. Conversely, it has been assumed that the women sit too far back to be thrown the barley; thus the joke has a spatial as well as a bawdy point. Both readings of the line are acceptable. Critics have found it possible to decide between them only by claiming that one reading gives a 'better joke' than the other. It is not easy to see how this could be adequate for proving or disproving the presence or absence of women in the theatre.

The other major passages come from Plato. I have already looked at Socrates' dismissal of tragedy and the other arts as a rhetoric aimed at a *dēmos* made up of children, women, men, free and slave. The *Laws* is also regularly quoted as saying 'tragedy is a form of rhetoric addressed to "boys, women and the whole crowd" '.[16] This quotation is extracted from a speech of 'The Athenian Stranger', the *Laws*' leading figure, who in setting up his imaginary constitution is dismissing some imaginary tragic poets from the city. He says (*Laws* VII 817b–c) that 'since we too are poets' – but the law is our art – 'do not suppose that we will casually allow you into our midst to set up your stages/pavilions (*skēnai*) in the market place and bring in your

---

[16] Henderson (1991) 138. This, together with Podlecki (1990), forms the fullest defence of the presence of women.

actors with their fine voices (much louder than ours) and permit you to declaim before children, women and the whole throng'. This tells us nothing about the audience of the Great Dionysia, though much about Plato's rhetoric of denigration. These travelling players (with their louder voices than the 'poets of law', the philosophers) are not allowed to set up in the market place and have an influence over those most likely to be influenced by such people – children, women, the throng (*okhlos*). Similarly, at *Laws* II 658, where Plato is again attacking the associations of pleasure and art, the Athenian stranger specifies tragedy as the pleasure of 'educated women, young men and perhaps almost all the general public'. Leaving aside the customary Platonic denigration of tragedy by associating it with women, youth, and the masses, does the specification of '*educated* women' imply that *only* educated women knew tragedy, and if so, does it imply a theatrical audience or an (educated, and thus small) reading public? So – a passage less commonly quoted – at *Laws* VII 816e the Athenian stranger warns against letting any free person, man or woman, *learn* (*manthanein*) comedy, although they must watch it to learn the difference between 'the serious' and 'the ridiculous'. Plato's interest here is in the training of the 'wise person' (*phronimos*) and in the dangers of the seductions of literature. He advises that only slaves or foreigners should be allowed to perform comedy. Hence, it must not even be taken seriously or learnt by a free person. The education in the Athenian Stranger's utopia clearly does not tell us much about the Great Dionysia, but the idea of a free woman 'learning comedy' may help in understanding the contact of 'educated women' with tragedy.

These are the passages that are taken as the strongest positive evidence for women's attendance at the Great Dionysia, and they are not compelling. There are also no addresses to women as audience, though many addresses in comedy to all classes of men. We are told many details of women's attendance and practice at other festivals; none of women at the theatre. So, the general questions can be framed as follows: is the absence of mention of women at the Great Dionysia a chance effect of our lacunose sources? Or, since women's presence in male company is surrounded by many taboos in Athenian culture, is there an Athenian protocol of invisibility for women on this most public of occasions? Or is the silence a significant indication of the difference between the Great Dionysia and, say, the Great Panathenaea, at which women processed as representatives of women as a group within the city? This is, in other words, not just the usual difficulty of constructing an argument from silence, but rather a more specific and significant problem of the 'conspiracy of silence' with which women's history is particularly concerned.

Can analogies with other festivals or what we know about women's roles in Athens help us? (Cf. Ch. 1 above, pp. 28ff.) Women no doubt were excluded from certain major political institutions such as the Assembly. Nor could citizen women, it appears, attend the lawcourt as witnesses, even when they were principals of the case, and any presence of women in the court is hard to prove.[17] They could not sit in the court as jurors; and there were clearly strong taboos associated with any appearance – even in the speech of others – in such a public arena.[18] At the Great Panathenaea, however, a festival for the whole city, women as a group within the city were publicly represented in the *pompē*. Indeed, in many religious spheres women's participation was fundamental. So, is the theatre to be thought of as more like the Assembly or more like the Great Panathenaea?

Let us start from one of the uncontested facts and consider female presence in the *pompē*. 'It is hard to believe', writes Jeffrey Henderson, 'that the basket carrier who led the procession of the Great Dionysia was the only female present or was barred from watching the plays.'[19] He offers in support of this claim the evidently important role of women in religion and the relaxation at times of festival of the normal restrictions on female mobility. Yet there are many other elements of the *pompē* and women's roles in religion that would need to be taken into account before we can assent to Henderson's appeal to likelihood. First, the basket-carrier is a *parthenos*, a category in Greek thought surrounded by particular taboos, one who would appear before male eyes only when protected by ritual – as here.[20] But what of the other *parthenoi*? Are we to assume that they too processed? Is it further to be assumed that this high-born *parthenos* and other citizens' wives and daughters took part in the *kōmos* at the end of the *pompē* (when they could not attend a symposium)? Why is there no consideration of other cults where individual or selected *parthenoi* are mentioned? But even if women did process in the *pompē*, does this imply anything for the theatre itself? For it is hard to see what cultic role women could be said to perform here, or how the wives and daughters of citizens could appear before the citizens' gaze without the formal protection of ritual. The theatrical performances were on different days, and less involved with obviously cultic activity. If women were present, where did they sit and how did they get there? Henderson assumes that there was special seating at the rear for women (on the highly dubious basis of the passage of Aristophanes' *Peace* and the Alexis fragment, both quoted above); and also

[17] Todd (1990) 26. Todd, like Bonner (1905), wrongly assumes women's regular presence in court: see Goldhill (1994a) 357–8, following Fernandes.
[18] See Schaps (1977).   [19] Henderson (1991) 136.
[20] On the *parthenos*, see e.g. King (1983); Lloyd (1983) 58–111; Sissa (1990a); Dean-Jones (1994).

that women 'attended in the company of other women' since 'the husbands would be unlikely to have come to the theatre or departed from the theatre with their wives.[21] It is hard to believe – to use Henderson's argumentation – that well-born women wandered to and from the theatre with their friends. What this exchange of rhetorical appeals makes clear, however, is that it is only on the basis of a general understanding of women's roles in Athens and in Athens' different festivals that a view of the likelihood of female attendance at the theatre can be asserted; but also that the very variety of possible ways of constructing such analogies makes it hard to offer the certain conclusion – for or against the presence of women – that most scholars do.

One reason why scholars have been unwilling to admit that the evidence is so inconclusive is that the presence or absence of women in the theatre has important implications for the festival as a whole.[22] The frame of drama is determined by its audience. If there are only men and predominantly Athenian citizens present, then the plays' evident concerns with gender politics and with social debate and with the practice of deliberative life within the city become questions addressed to the citizen body as a body: it is as citizens that an audience may be expected to respond. The issues of the play are focused firmly through the male, adult, enfranchised perspective. If there are women present, although the 'proper or intended' audience may remain the citizen body, there is a different view of the city on display, and while the citizen perspective remains dominant, it is in the gaze of citizens and their wives that the plays are enacted. So, Henderson can write 'some passages in Aristophanes virtually call out for partisan cheers from such [indecorous or unruly] women', as if the tensions on the stage are to be rehearsed within the audience.[23] It remains intensely frustrating, then, that a question of such importance in the understanding of Greek drama cannot be securely answered, even though some of the implications of an answer can be sketched.

The social drama of theatre finds a map of the city in the audience: whether women are to be thought of as a silenced presence on the map or an absent sign, the audience represents the body politic.

TEACHING THE CITY

There was a fund called the Theoric Fund, established by the city probably under Pericles, which made payments to the citizens to enable them to

[21] Henderson (1991) 142.
[22] See e.g. Goldhill (1986) 57–167; Zeitlin (1990); Winkler (1990b); Henderson (1991) 144–7.
[23] Henderson (1991) 146. He does not make the same case for the slaves and foreigners and metics...

attend the theatre (cf. Ch. 1 above, pp. 9–10). Any citizen inscribed on a deme roll – the deme was the local organisational and residential unit of the polis in which every citizen had to register – could claim the price of a ticket (usually taken to be two obols, the wages of an unskilled working man for a day). This fund was protected by law: it was a prosecutable offence even to propose changes to the fund. It is easy to infer that attendance at the theatre was regarded as a citizen's duty, privilege and requirement. This sense of theatre as a civic act is enforced by repeated statements that poets are 'the teachers of the people'. Indeed, Plato's attacks on tragedy as dangerous demagoguery are in part at least precisely because of the position of tragic theatre within the discourses of the polis. The playwright was a *sophos*, a privileged and authoritative voice, who spoke to the city. Tragedy indeed rapidly entered the formal and informal teaching institutions: it was learnt for performance at symposia, read and studied, and from the fourth century on widely disseminated throughout the Greek world. Plato and Aristotle – our two most extensive, written audience responses to the teaching of tragedy – differ greatly in their appreciation of tragedy's didactic mode. Both, however, recognise its power over an audience. Both treat it as making a serious contribution to the construction of a citizen.

We also have a few late anecdotes of wild or unruly audience response, and of fiercely partisan crowds – the educational aspect of tragedy certainly did not efface its competition or its spectacle. The theatre's semi-circular form with its scenes of debate and deliberation clearly invite audience engagement. So too the plays themselves offer a fascinating insight into a dynamic between the plays and audience, as the collective on the stage – the chorus – repeatedly dramatises a response to the action, as the collective in the theatre – the audience – itself makes a response. Neither partisan engagement, nor unruliness, nor even the plays' spectacle, are to be contrasted with the educational force of tragedy. If tragedy teaches, it is certainly not only in its pronouncements or dramatic engagements. For what this study of the audience of Greek tragedy has tried to show is that it is by participating in the festival at all its levels that the Athenian citizen demon- strated his citizenship, and it is by staging the festival that the city promoted and projected itself as a city. That Athenian tragedies can provoke, question and explore this sense of citizenship and of the city remains testimony of the remarkable power and openness of this democratic institution.

BIBLIOGRAPHICAL NOTE

Although there are many scattered comments on the audience of Greek tragedy, the most stimulating of which are to be found in Winkler (1990b), there is no full discussion in English. On the question of women's presence see Henderson (1991), Goldhill (1994a) and the collection of testimonia in Podlecki (1990). On the dynamics of collectivity, individuality and display, see Wilson (forthcoming). On the festival as a festival, see Connor (1989); Goldhill (1990a); Sourvinou-Inwood (1994).

4

OLIVER TAPLIN

The pictorial record

By 300 BC or so Athenian tragedy had become the property of every Greek city, performed in its local theatre and reflected in its visual arts. This iconic prominence was sustained throughout the Graeco-Roman world for the next 600 years and more. That is why, for example, many of the wall-paintings discovered at Pompeii and Herculaneum show tragic subjects, and even more include the motif of the tragic mask. These provide their own interest, but this chapter will concentrate on the period from 500 to 300 BC, the era when Athens was still the active centre of drama. It will also concentrate mainly on painted pottery, if only because very little that is relevant survives of the wall-paintings, sculpture, metal-work or other art-forms.

As is amply shown throughout this *Companion*, tragedy was a major prestigious event within the cultural and political life of classical Athens. Pottery-painting was, by comparison, a humble and domestic art-form. Detailed paintings in the red-figure techniques were, none the less, an especially Athenian achievement; and, like drama, this Attic product was disseminated to all corners of the Hellenic world. While many of the vessels were standard and mass-produced, many others display elaborate work-manship, and must have been objects which expected individual attention. A fair number, furthermore, represent mythological and heroic scenes; and they do so in a dignified and serious style – at first glance not unlike that of tragedy.

Throughout the world's museums and galleries there must be something of the order of 100,000 Athenian decorated vases from the canonical 'golden age' of tragedy (say 499 to 406 BC) – and those presumably represent well under 1 per cent of the total produced. We might, then, expect quite a few illustrations or reflections of that peculiarly fashionable and Athenian form of heroic narrative, tragedy. This expectation turns out to be drastically unjustified.

I know, in fact, of only two fifth-century paintings that can plausibly be

[4] 'Basle Dancers' (Attic, *c.* 490): it may be that the figure on the left is a ghost summoned up from his tomb by the chorus of young soldiers.

claimed to show a play in performance. Both are early, from the era of Aeschylus. The 'Basle Dancers' [4] (*c.* 490, found probably in Italy) dance in unison and have indecipherable lettering issuing from their open mouths: so they definitely represent a *choros*, a group in performance.[1] Their identical hair, head-dresses and features are suggestive of masks, though there is no decisive indicator. And their military costumes, with some indications of ornate decoration, appear to be a signal of their mimetic role as soldiers (bare feet seem to be standard for choruses). So tragedy is likely, though not finally certain. In that case, we have two lines out of four or five (depending on whether the chorus had 12 or 15 members).[2] Whatever the interpretation of the scene, the chief interest of the vase is for choral formation, costume and choreography.

Secondly five fragments of Attic pottery of *c.* 460s, found at Corinth, though only a small part of the whole picture, are remarkably informative

---

[1] See Schmidt (1967) 70ff.

[2] The structure they are dancing before seems to be a tomb rather than an altar; and the facing figure may be rising from the tomb rather than standing behind it. In that case we would have a ghost-raising scene, as, for example, in Aeschylus' (lost) *Psychopompoi*, where Odysseus' men summoned the dead prophet Teiresias.

[5] Fragments of an Attic jar (c. 460s): Oriental king on his pyre? Note the *aulos*-player (top left).

[5].[3] There are at least two figures in flapped caps and decorated costume, and at least one has a trouser-leg, indicating orientals. There is another figure in the same costume, but even more elaborate, half in and half out of a burning pyre. Lastly there is an *aulos*-player (pipes-player) with *phorbeia* (cheek-band), and decorated outfit. It is hard to see what this can be other than a picture based on a particular scene in a tragedy – even though it is unclear how the pyre would have been staged.[4]

In between these two misleadingly promising pieces and the end of the century, there are meagre pickings – a boy holding a mask, two actors putting on *kothornoi* (the characteristic boots), an *aulos*-player in full regalia but accompanied by a 'real' maenad. There *may* be all sorts of other tragedy-related paintings, but, if so, they do not seem to call on the viewer to bring to bear on them an acquaintance with a tragedy; and they do not seem to include signals of their connection with drama. It is none the less still worth exploring the issues raised by these possible connections.

It has been claimed, for example, that inscriptions of 'X is handsome' (in the masculine) written alongside a female figure show that this is an actor impersonating a female part.[5] But since there is no other indicator of any kind of connection with tragedy, it is hard to see how the viewer can take

---

[3] See Beazley (1955) 305–19.

[4] Some have thought of Aeschylus' *Persians* as the inspiration for this painting, but the flaming pyre (as opposed to a tomb) is an objection. The pyre would better fit a play about Croesus.

[5] E.g. Padel (1992) 4–5.

[6] Apparently an early reflection of Aeschylus' *Libation-Bearers* (Attic, *c.* 440). On one side two women at a tomb inscribed 'AGAMEM'; on the other, presumably, Orestes and Pylades.

advantage of acquaintance with any particular dramatisation. There are, more specifically, three such inscriptions saying 'Euaion is handsome', one adding 'son of Aeschylus'.[6] As Euaion is known to have acted, it is proposed that he performed in the play of the myth in question. Again there are no detectable theatrical signals; though, admittedly, one of the scenes could be associated with Sophocles' tragedy *Andromeda*, and the binding of Andromeda is found on later, more evidently theatre-related vases (after Euripides' celebrated play of *c.* 412, however). So this might be a picture of the actual performer in a role, although the iconography and outfit have nothing specifically theatrical about them.

It has also been claimed that the impact of a particular play has changed the iconography of the myth in question. Again, it is difficult to confirm this when the paintings flag no overt signals. Without an *aulos*-player or costume or masks or something, how are we to know whether the viewer is expected to bring any theatrical associations to bear? For example, we find paintings from about 440 BC onwards, though mostly of the fourth century, showing a young woman mourning with offerings at a tomb, as two young men stand by. There is no example of this before Aeschylus' *Oresteia* of 458 BC. While it is obvious that such a scene would have a general appeal for the market for funerary offerings, and that it is appropriate enough without invoking the opening scenes of *Libation-Bearers*, two Attic examples (dated to about 440 [6] and 390) actually label the tomb as Agamemnon's. Even so, there is nothing that particularly relates to the actual theatre performance of *Libation-Bearers*.[7]

---

[6] These are most easily found in Trendall & Webster (1971) numbered III.1, 28; III.2, 1; III.2, 9.

[7] For this and other possible examples see Prag (1985).

[7] The 'Pronomos Vase' (Attic, *c.* 400): the most important single representation of Athenian drama. It celebrates a team of tragic actors, with costumes and masks, *aulos*-player, playwright, and chorus, costumed for the satyr play. Dionysus and 'friend' (Tragedy? Muse? Festival?) dominate.

After this dearth of an explicitly theatrical record, there comes a group of vases, painted about the end of the fifth century, which undoubtedly do show actors. They are, however, expressly *not* in performance; they are 'off-stage', but in costume and holding their masks. The best preserved and most important by far is the 'Pronomos Vase' [7], found in northern Apulia (South Italy) and now in Naples. It shows the actors and chorus-members (each inscribed with his real-life name), costumed for a satyr play, quite likely because it was painted in celebration of a victory and shows the cast after their last play. The masks and costumes of the three main actors show no signs of being different from those of tragedy. Without going into details of interpretation (which include a fascinating blurring of the worlds of actors and play, of satyrs and myth), we have here good evidence for masks and costumes from Athens in about 400. It is also evidence for the celebrity of the Theban *aulos*-player, Pronomos, and for the individual pride taken by members of the chorus in their

73

collective achievement.[8] The vase is interesting evidence of South Italian Greek interest in Athenian drama productions – perhaps a visitor to Athens commissioned the painting to recall a performance that had particularly impressed him?

As can be seen from [7], the tragic mask at this period was relatively plain and representational, without obvious distortion or stylisation. This might be suggestive for methods of acting and representation in general. It looks as though the 'neutrality' of the mask was ready to take its 'expression' from the tragedy rather than imposing a certain tone upon it. The costumes, on the other hand, are highly ornamented with patterns and with figures of people and animals (indeed they are so ornate that an element of virtuosic miniature-painting should not be ruled out). They also display two particular features which seem to be derived from theatrical costume rather than from 'real' life outside the theatre: the tight patterned sleeves, and the *kothornoi* (decorated boots). The fact that three male actors played all the parts, young and old, men and women, may largely explain the sleeves, which conceal the age and gender of the actor's arms; the boots, however, seem to have been emblematic of tragedy, as well as being practical. For, far from the high platform soles which are to be seen on monuments of Roman times, the *kothornoi* of this early period had thin soft soles and turned-up toes that would make for easy mobility. There does often seem to have been also some elaborate lacing up the front and ornamented tops or flaps below the knee.

These highly ornate costumes with sleeves and boots became the typical heroic garb on many of the mythological vases which were painted in large numbers by and for the Greeks in cities in South Italy (Magna Graecia) during the next century. Between about 425 and 390 there was a decline in the production of Athenian vase-paintings, especially for export to the west; and there was complementarily a great increase in home-produced fine ware, especially in the area of Taras and Metapontion (on the high 'instep' of the boot of Italy).[9] Reflections of the theatre, both tragedy and comedy, are clear on these so-called 'South Italian' vases from 400 BC or even earlier. There are, for example, figures (whether Dionysus or actors) holding masks in their hands – and it is worth noting that these masks are indistinguishable from those on Athenian vases [8].[10] It is not at all implausible that Athenian

---

[8] The *aulos*-player, unlike the dramatist and actors, was not necessarily Athenian. Note also the relatively secondary and textual role of the playwright, Demetrius, who sits to one side holding a roll of papyrus. For some other related vases see Green (1982) 237–48.

[9] The best account of all this is Trendall (1989). The Athenian-led colony of Thurii, founded in 444/3, may have been the channel for the art of red-figure pottery – and indeed for the theatre as well.

[10] See Trendall (1988) 137–54.

[8] Wine-mixing bowl painted in a Greek city in Apulia, South Italy, in about 400. The left-hand figure, probably Dionysus, is holding a tragic mask which is indistinguishable from those on the Pronomos and other Attic vases.

[9] 'The Choregoi' or 'Comic Angels', painted in Apulia not long after 400 BC. Uniquely among the many South Italian *comic* vases, this one has a full-fledged 'tragic' figure, Aegisthus, on the same stage. There may be a contest between him and the typically comic Pyrrhias, who is standing on a wool-basket.

tragedy should be known and appreciated in Magna Graecia by 400 or even earlier: there is a consistent scatter of evidence for the popularity of Athenian tragedy outside Athens, for travelling players, and for the construction of theatres – indeed every leading city acquired one during the course of the fourth century.

There is also an important painting, first published in 1992, showing a tragic costume in an explicitly theatrical context. The 'Choregos Vase' [9], painted in Taras or nearby in the period 400–380, shows the performance of a comedy on stage, but the comedy – unprecedentedly – includes a figure (labelled 'Aigisthos') in the full outfit of tragedy. His face is mask-like, but with closed lips (perhaps it was a silent role?); and he wears the decorated robe, tight sleeves, and laced *kothornoi*. It seems likely that Aegisthus somehow 'represents' tragedy within the comedy, and that his costume is a marker of this.[11]

Closely comparable outfits are to be seen in many paintings, often in scenes of highly theatrical events. The problem – and the challenge – is to ask *to what degree* any particular painting reflects the theatre. Is this or that picture enhanced by bringing to it the knowledge of a specific tragedy? Does it call for acquaintance with a play in order to be understood or fully appreciated? My view is that there is a great range of theatrical reference, all the way from slight and distant influence to essential references without which the painting loses much of its point for the viewer. It may be best to explore some test cases, focusing especially on Euripides' *Medea* and Sophocles' *Oedipus* plays.

By way of approach, let us consider first *Iphigeneia among the Taurians*. The legend was that Iphigeneia was whisked off by Artemis to a remote area of the Crimea to rescue her from sacrifice at Aulis. It is, however, virtually certain that Euripides' play (about 414 BC) first added the complication of having Orestes and Pylades washed up there and almost sacrificed by Iphigeneia, who has become the priestess of Artemis under the command of a Greek-hating local king. Euripides' play is made round the recognition of brother and sister by means of a letter, and their exciting escape from this barbarian tyrant, making use of the cult-image. There are no signs of any of this in the literary or artistic sources before Euripides' play. From the early fourth century, however, there is a whole series of South Italian paintings (and one Attic example), including the characteristic ornate costumes, which pick out scenes from within this narrative. The favourite, known now in eight representations, shows Iphigeneia handing over the crucial letter to Pylades.[12]

[11] For discussions see Trendall & Cambitoglou (1992) 7–8; Taplin (1993) ch. 6.
[12] See *LIMC* Iphigeneia (L. Kahil) nos. 19–25. For some examples see Trendall & Webster III.3, 27–30.

[10] An unusual Attic fourth-century vase (c. 375): like many South Italian examples, this is inspired more or less directly by tragedy. The story of Iphigeneia's reunion with her brother through a letter addressed to him (in her right hand) must have been derived from Euripides' *Iphigeneia among the Taurians*.

Other features shown by most or all of these eight paintings are the temple, the image of Artemis, the temple-key carried by Iphigeneia and, of course, Orestes himself. Otherwise, however, there is a great variety: some include gods, others not, some include token barbarians, others not – the single Attic representative [10] also shows the local tyrant, Thoas, seated at the side. Clearly these paintings are, in no sense, representations or 'production photos' of any actual performance of the play: they include figures from different scenes, and even some who do not appear in the play at all; Orestes and Pylades are usually shown naked, which they would never have been on stage; the cult-image is visible instead of being inside, and so on. But, once it is granted that this incident of Iphigeneia's letter to Orestes was Euripides' creation, and that the play must, therefore, at some stage have inspired the vase-painters, the interesting question becomes this: to what extent, and in what ways, does the viewing of these paintings reflect or relate to the viewing of the play? The difficulty of answering this does not invalidate the question. The centrality of the temple-statue, for instance, may be suggestive both for performance and interpretation; and so may be the prominence of

[11] Medea escapes in her dragon chariot on this locally painted jar (c. 400) from Heraclea, on the border of Apulia and Lucania. The helplessness of Jason below, accentuated by the shape of the pot, is reminiscent of the ending of Euripides' play of some 30 years earlier.

Iphigeneia's heavy temple-key on one arm, while she holds the small, fragile letter in the other hand.

It is much disputed whether it was an innovation of Euripides in his *Medea* of 431 BC to have Medea deliberately kill her own sons, as opposed to their accidental death or to their slaughter at the hands of the Corinthians, a version which is known to have pre-existed Euripides. Either way, it is more than likely that Euripides invented Medea's escape from the revenge of Jason in the chariot of her grandfather the Sun. This scene is found on four South Italian vase-paintings.[13] The earliest two, both Lucanian, date from about 400 BC; and they show some interesting features in relation to each other and to Euripides. They are [11] the hydria (water-pot) found at Policoro (ancient Heraclea) in 1963, and [12] the much more elaborate calyx-crater (wine-mixing vessel), first exhibited in 1983 and now in the Cleveland Museum of Art. In both Medea wears theatrical costume with sleeves and oriental headgear, as she holds a whip over the dragon 'steeds' of her chariot (which in [12] are painted as glowing within a kind of sun-burst). Her two sons lie dead below – in [11] lamented by their 'tutor'

[13] See *LIMC* Medeia (M. Schmidt) 35–8. Those Medea vases known at the time were well discussed by Simon (1954) 203–27.

[12] A more elaborate and spectacular version of the same iconography, painted around the same time and place. Again the children are lamented below, and are not, as they were in Euripides' play, in the chariot.

(*paidagōgos*), and in [12] lying over an altar mourned by him and their more prominent old 'nurse'. In [11] the corners are occupied by Eros (or a Fury?) and Aphrodite, and in [12] by winged, female demons, presumably Erinyes (i.e. Furies).

Clearly neither of these directly reproduces the final scene of Euripides' play. Apart from the nakedness of Jason, the variety of divine figures, and the presence of the tutor and nurse, the sons lie apart from Medea, while in Euripides it is important, and emphasised, that she has their bodies with her in the chariot.[14] Despite this significant difference, it is hard to see how this composition could have been conceived of in the first place without the influence of Euripides' play. And there is one feature which has its point seriously weakened, I suggest, for those who do not know the play, and enhanced for those who do: the spatial positioning of Jason and Medea and its implication for their relative power. In the tragedy Medea appears above

---

[14] There is a Faliscan (Etruscan) vase of the second half of the fourth century showing Medea in her chariot carrying the bodies of her sons – but no barbarian outfit, and no Jason.

('from the machine') triumphant, and scornful of Jason's appeals, while he is humiliated, helpless and crushed. This is vividly reflected in both paintings – so much so that (I propose) they presuppose and expect the viewer's acquaintance with the particular, celebrated play.

It is increasingly often claimed, to the contrary, that vases such as these simply present 'the myth', and that the tragedy (or, indeed, any other 'literary' version) is irrelevant. But this is to react too far against the old over-literary approach. There was no single or definitive version of 'the myth', only a multiplicity of narrations, some literary and some not. Painters display different versions of myths, and *some* may well have been developed without any literary inspiration or influence – but that does not mean that they *all* were. In the particular case of Medea, there is at least one other painting which goes out of its way to signal that it reflects another tragic narrative, not the celebrated Euripidean version. On the monumental volute-crater [13] from Canosa, painted in Apulia, perhaps as late as the 320s BC, it is the dreadful death of King Creon and his daughter that is central. Lower down, Medea (in highly 'tragic' costume) kills one of her sons, while the other escapes under the care of a young man (his *paidagōgos*?). Jason rushes up, as on the earlier vases, but on the same level as Medea, and separated from her by a dragon-chariot manned by the torch-bearing figure of '*Oistros*' ('frenzy'). There are other labelled figures who play no part in Euripides, such as Merope and Hippotes, on either side of the death-tableau; and, above all, there is to the right the elaborately costumed 'ghost of Aeetes', Medea's father, who might well have delivered the prologue. It seems obvious (to me, at least) that this is based on a tragedy, and that it is overtly signalled as *not* that of Euripides.

Another character in this crowded composition who is worth further attention is the bent, white-haired man to the left of the middle register. A figure like him appears on well over thirty vase-paintings which have likely tragic connections, most of them painted in Apulia in the middle third of the fourth century.[15] Generally speaking, he is short and aged, his costume relatively undecorated, his sleeves plain, often white; and he usually carries a crooked staff. Yet he nearly always wears (as in [13]) ornate *kothornoi* with prominent and fancy flaps. We might have taken him to be an unnamed old servant, even without the three examples which are labelled *botēr* (cowherd), *tropheus* (child-servant), and *paidagōgos* (tutor).[16] Why should the painter have included this figure, who is seldom essential to 'the myth', except to allude to the old servants who are so common in tragedy?

---

[15] For a good account of this figure see Chamay & Cambitoglou (1980) 40–3.
[16] Two recently published examples are illustrated in Taplin (1993) pl. 5.109 and 110.

[13] A substantially different version of the Medea story, also evidently tragic in inspiration, is reflected in this monumental funerary vase, painted in Apulia some 75 years later. At bottom left one son escapes Medea's sword; note the old 'messenger' figure (middle left) and the ghost of Aeetes (middle right).

Some such character often delivers the characteristic eyewitness report which we know as a 'messenger-speech'; and sometimes this figure on the vases may signal that the events of the messenger-speech are actually included, as in the *Hippolytus* scene in the British Museum [14], which shows Hippolytus in his chariot confronted by a Fury and by the bull emerging from the sea. The old man's alarmed gesture may recall the old man who warns Hippolytus in the prologue of Euripides' play; but it may also suggest an analogy between his position as an eyewitness within the tragedy and the position of the viewer in relation to the painting – a kind of signal of the theatrical perspective.

Might there, then, be other indicators to alert the viewer that acquaintance with a tragedy is part of the point of a painting? The inclusion of Furies, as in the BM Hippolytus [14] and Cleveland Medea [12], might be one. They are found most of all in pictures of the Orestes-myth, especially in the several vases which show Orestes at Delphi, as at the beginning of *Eumenides*. But they turn up occasionally in quite a range of stories, most of them with plausible tragic connections and involving themes of vengeance.[17]

Another possible signal might be the inclusion of a prominent doorway, which would reflect the importance of the *skēnē*-doors and of the indoors/ outdoors division in many Greek tragedies. It is worth recalling that the *skēnē*-door is painted to one side of the stage in quite a few comedy-related vases, including the Choregos Vase [9]. This crops up in some tragedy-related pictures, but not many; and the same is true of the kind of rocky arch that occasionally figures, especially in *Andromeda* paintings.[18] Some other vases, mainly Paestan and from the mid-to-late fourth century, have windows, ceilings, porticos and other architectural features which may refer to stage-settings; but the general absence of such theatrical indicators is more striking than their occurrence. This may mirror a basic characteristic of the genre: Athenian tragedy, in extreme contrast with Athenian comedy, is not overtly metatheatrical – it does not explicitly remind the spectator that it is 'only a play' (though there may be other kinds of non-explicit metatheatrical elements – see pp. 161–71; 193–8 below). So it is telling that the many vase-paintings which reflect comedy do so explicitly with overt representations of staging, costume and comic 'business' – unlike those under discussion here.[19]

For a viewer, faced with any particular painting – and given no decisive indicators – it is initially an open question whether it has any theatrical

---

[17] See *LIMC* Erinyes (H. Sarian).
[18] See briefly Taplin (1993) 25; more fully on stage decoration see Gogos (1983) 59–86; for Andromeda see *LIMC* (K. Schauenburg).
[19] See Green (1991) for the development of this distinction.

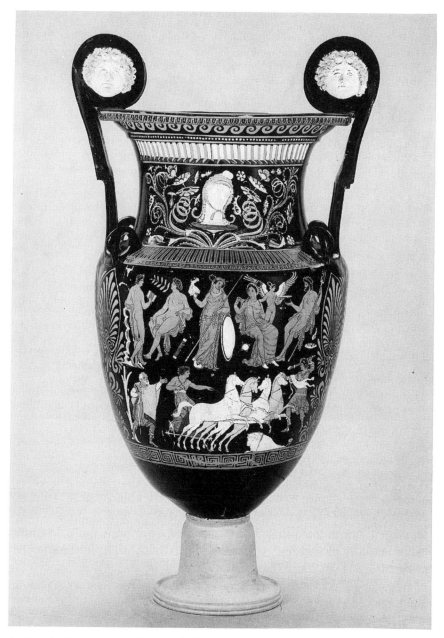

[14] A similar vase to [13], inspired this time by Euripides' *Hippolytus*, especially the messenger-speech.

[15] Unprecedentedly, this recently discovered mixing-bowl (Apulian, *c.* 340s) reflects Sophocles' *Oedipus at Colonus.* The placing of Creon and Polyneices on either side brings out well the structure of the action.

connections; and, once having taken the step of supposing that it has, there are still questions of how much and in what ways it is related to a particular tragedy. It may even be that the posing of such questions was part of the experience and pleasure for a viewer. I believe that the case made so far shows that at least *some* vase-paintings had *some* productive connections with tragedies. And so the questions, however difficult for us with our limited evidence, are worth posing.

My last examples of these intriguing issues are concerned with the myth of Oedipus, as dramatised by Sophocles. Up until 1969 there was, so far as I know, not one single vase which could be claimed at all plausibly to have any connection. Now there are three, though each is very different, illustrating the wide range of possible relations between painting and theatre.

On a large calyx-crater [15], in a private collection in Australia, painted in *c.* 340s, an old man sits on an altar with two young women.[20] The old man's eyes are painted as closed, so he is evidently blind; his costume is simple, and so is that of the woman he is closer to, while the other is more fancily clothed. There is surely a case to be made that the viewer's appreciation would be enhanced by reference to Sophocles' *Oedipus at Colonus*, and that without that reference the point of the painting would be significantly diminished. It is doubtful whether any other story would fit; and the combination of Oedipus along with his two daughters taking refuge is likely to have been Sophocles' invention. Furthermore the Fury in the top right is a general indicator (see above), and is particularly apt here since in *Oedipus at Colonus* Oedipus comes to a grove of the Erinyes, where the play is set. And once a knowledge of Sophocles' play is brought to bear, then the other two figures in the picture, otherwise unexplained, make immediate sense. The beardless youth on the right, with his diffident stance, must be Oedipus' son Polyneices; and the older, more confident man on the left is Creon, his brother-in-law and senior statesman in Thebes. Their relative placing reflects the contrast and opposition set up between them within the play.

The Apulian jug [16], painted *c.* 330s, and acquired by the Museum in Basel in 1978, is not so specific in its reference, and arguably has only a distant relationship to Sophocles.[21] The blind old man (closed eyes again), who wears 'tragic' costume and is led by a boy, is clearly reminiscent of Teiresias. The mature man with the stick and sword has been taken to be Oedipus, and the painting thus associated with the scene at Sophocles' *Oedipus the King* 300ff. But the scene might just as well (so far as I can see) be associated with *Antigone* 988ff., where Teiresias confronts Creon (in fact there is more reference there than in *Oedipus the King* to the boy-guide and to the tyrant's military power). So the acquaintance with tragedy identifies Teiresias, but is otherwise less informative in this case.

The third and final piece is different again: the now well-known fragments of a calyx-crater found at Syracuse in 1969 [17], and attributed to a Sicilian artist of *c.* 330, known as the Capodarso Painter.[22] This shows four figures on a kind of platform, though it is not explicitly a stage; and they conspicuously include on the left the figure of the 'little old man' (see

[20] Geddes Collection, Melbourne A5:3. The only previous publications that I am aware of are *LIMC* Ismene I (I. Krauskopf) 2, Trendall (1989) 200, and Trendall & Cambitoglou (1992) Supp. III p. 136 with pl. xxxiii, 4.
[21] Published by Schmidt (1982) 236–43, and not, so far as I know, reproduced anywhere else since.
[22] This is Trendall & Webster (1971) III.2, 8 = Trendall (1989) 429, cf. Taplin (1993) 27–9.

[16] The meeting of the blind man with the king on this relatively simple jug (Apulian, *c.* 330s) may be inspired by the Teiresias scene in *Oedipus the King*.

above). They are divided by columns (and, in front of two of the three, little girls); but the right-hand young woman is turned away (unfortunately the pot beyond her is broken). It is significant that the only other vase attributed to the Capodarso Painter uniquely shows a tragic scene on a stage (like the comedy-related scenes), including three women, one kneeling, and the 'little

[17] This fragmentary mixing-bowl (painted in Sicily, *c.* 330s) is highly unusual and interesting because it is closely evocative, not just of a tragic narrative, but of a particular moment in performance. This is the scene in *Oedipus the King*, where Jocasta (half covering her face) first sees the truth. The mask-like face of the Old Corinthian is theatrically turned to the audience.

old man' again.[23] But the situation there does not readily fit any known tragedy, and so the painting remains impenetrable as long as we are ignorant about which scene of which play is reflected in it. In the case of [17], however, a scene has been proposed which does indeed seem to make sense of the composition – in other words, a knowledge of the tragedy interprets and enhances the iconography.

[23] Trendall & Webster (1971) III.6, 1 = Taplin (1993) 6.111.

In his *Poetics* (1452a24), which dates from about the same period, Aristotle picks out an instance of how events in a tragedy can take an unexpected turn (peripeteia): 'for example in the *Oedipus*, where the man came and it seemed that he would comfort Oedipus and free him from fear about his mother, but in fact, by revealing who he was, he does the opposite'. In the dialogue of *Oedipus the King* at 924ff. the old man from Corinth (a former shepherd for the king) reveals his link with Oedipus' past: far from being the son of the king and queen of Corinth, Oedipus was given to them as a baby by this very man. In the painting the demeanour and gestures of the old man and of the 'hero' suit this sequence well. Jocasta remains silent through the dialogue, but the detail that the Corinthian was given the baby by a servant of the house of Laius (1042) is enough to enable her to reconstruct Oedipus' life-story – this also suits the woman's gesture of undemonstrative distress in the painting. Yet it is not a totally exact illustration of a performance: the two little daughters have been brought in from the final scene, and the fourth figure remains unexplained. None the less the picture makes *such* good sense in connection with this particular juncture of *Oedipus the King* that it seems perverse to resist this explication.

So although this vase was painted not in Athens but in Sicily (where Syracuse was the place keenest on theatre), and although it was painted about 100 years after Sophocles' original production, it still gives a fascinating glimpse of how the play was perceived there and then. There is the great importance of gesture, for instance, and the way that the faces, while mask-like, are also conceived as taking expression from the context. There is the reminder of the pathos of the two incest-born girls, the emphasis on the ominous reticence of Jocasta, and, above all perhaps, the irony of the way that the rather familiar manner and self-important 'gossip' of the old man (note his frontal gaze) are fraught with the most terrible implications for the main characters.

This vase, then, painted late in the fourth century by a minor craftsman, is probably as near to the representation of an actual performance of a tragedy as any we have – though another candidate, if only we had enough of it to tell, might have been the Corinth pyre [5], painted in Athens back in the days of Aeschylus. The big question that has to be faced, finally, is why Athenian tragedy is apparently reflected so *little* in contemporary vase-painting – or why, if it is reflected, that fact is so unsignalled and unemphasised. However problematic the relationship of the South Italian paintings to the tragic theatre, they stand in a striking contrast with the Attic norm. From 400 onwards there are plenty of South Italian vases that have *some* relation to the tragedies: in the half-century from 450 to 400 it is not clear whether one single surviving Attic painting has. The paintings of actors 'off-stage', such as [7], are another matter: their signal is the mask, usually taken off and held in the actor's hand.

This contrast suggests that the shortage of Attic theatre-related vase-paintings is not a coincidence or merely bad luck, but systematic abstinence. For some reason Athenian vase-painters positively *avoided* the theatre as subject matter – while those in South Italy positively took advantage of it. If we could only know why this was, that might tell us something important about the place of theatre in Athens.

The obvious starting-point is that for the Greeks in the west tragedy was an 'import', a form of narrative and spectacle pioneered by another polis back in mainland Hellas. Somehow this 'released' it for incorporation in the decoration of pottery, both for domestic use and for funeral, and in a way which was not acceptable at Athens, at least not in the fifth century (there are a few fourth-century exceptions, like [10] above). It might well be relevant that at Athens vase-painting had already been established as a medium for the representation of narratives set in the heroic era long before the time when the theatre was still developing as another quite different medium. In Magna Graecia, by contrast, the arts of drama and of red-figure vase-painting were both introduced from Athens at more or less the same time (possibly both through Thurii, see n. 9).[24]

But, while this must be part of the story, it hardly seems enough to explain the degree of exclusion, of inhibition against representing drama (both tragedy and comedy) in vase-painting at Athens. It strikes me that, more generally, the question of what subjects are and are *not* welcome in Athenian vase-paintings has not had the attention it deserves.[25] Restricting the question to representations of the life of the polis, it would seem to be roughly true to say that religious and domestic subjects were welcome, while more directly 'political' subjects were not. I am aware of very little, for example, that reflects – at least overtly – the Assembly or the Council, the two main executive gatherings of the democracy, or the highly impor-tant and active lawcourts. There is also remarkably little that alludes to the kinds of things that concern the histories of Herodotus and Thucydides – events, personalities, contemporary warfare, diplomacy, current affairs. The concrete manifestations of political life (as opposed to the 'X is handsome' inscriptions, which might have political undertones) were, then, not re-garded as suitable subject-matter for vase-painting. It might be that such

[24] It might be a further consideration that in Magna Graecia mystery cults of Dionysus were especially important for beliefs about the afterlife. Such cults also existed at Athens, and Dionysus was connected to the great cult of Demeter and her daughter at Eleusis; but he had a more direct association with death and afterlife in the Greek West.

[25] For a survey of some subjects that *are* found see Boardman (1989) ch. 7.

matters – and perhaps tragedy also – were acceptable in large-scale mural paintings (we know, for example, of the representation of recent battles in the Painted Stoa at Athens); but, if so, this did not extend to humble pottery. This leads me to the tentative thesis that tragedy (and comedy) was perceived as part of the 'political' life of Athens, political in the same sense as the lawcourts and executive meetings. So far as vase-painters were concerned, these were distinguished (it seems) from more 'ritualistic' activities such as religious cults, including, for example, the Panathenaic games.[26]

In conclusion, there is a lack of reflections of tragedy in Athenian vase-painting that is, on the most obvious level, disappointing; at the same time this may be revealing if it does indeed imply that vase-painters and their public perceived drama as being too close to the day-to-day political life of the city to be suitable subject-matter. On the other hand, there is a rich body of material from Greek South Italy, where the same inhibitions evidently did not apply. These supply valuable material on costumes, gestures and various other aspects of performance (and on the contents of lost plays). They can also be suggestive about the ways that the tragedies were perceived by viewers not far distant in time or place from the Athenian productions. This evidence may be full of problems, but it is far better than nothing.

BIBLIOGRAPHICAL NOTE

There is a large collection of material in Bieber (1961), but the discussion is unreliable; far superior is Trendall & Webster (1971), but this has long been out of print. The visual record as evidence for theatre-practice is well treated in Pickard-Cambridge (1988), Gould (1985) and Simon (1982a). The fifth-century material has been illuminatingly re-assessed by Green (1991), (1994) ch. 2. Changes in perspective on the fourth-century South Italian material, called for by new methods and new publications since 1971, are briefly indicated by Trendall (1991); but a thorough re-assessment is needed. Most of the new evidence is Apulian, and is to be found in Trendall & Cambitoglou (1978), (1983) and especially (1992). There is an accessible collection and good discussion of artefacts in the British Museum in Green & Handley (1995).

[26] It is not inconsistent with this thesis that dithyramb and, arguably, satyr-play were more admissible as ingredients for vase-painting. Their subject-matter was less directly 'political', i.e. less part of the business of the polis.

II
THE PLAYS

5

EDITH HALL

The sociology of Athenian tragedy

INTRODUCTION

In the modern sense of the word 'democracy' it is the tragic treatment of the *un*-democratic aspects of Athenian society which has been the focus of much recent scholarship. The Athenian democracy was a xenophobic, patriarchal, and imperialist community, economically dependent on slavery and imperial tribute, and tragedy has proved susceptible to interpretations disclosing its expression of ideas necessary to the system's perpetuation, ideas implying the inferiority of foreigners, women and slaves. This scholarly perspective is inseparable from its own social context, which has since the early 1960s been characterised by the unprecedented success of feminism and anti-racism.

This chapter suggests that through some recurrent types of plot-pattern tragedy affirmed in its citizen spectators' imaginations the social world in which they lived. The focus is on three types of pattern – plays in which male Athenian performers represented (i) mythical Athenians interacting with outsiders, (ii) women, (iii) significant slaves. Non-Athenians, women, and slaves were in reality excluded from the assembly and normally had to be represented by a citizen in the lawcourts (cf. Chs. 1 and 3 above, pp. 26–31; 61–6). Yet, paradoxically, the fictional representatives of these groups, silenced in the public discourse of the city, are permitted by the multivocal form of tragedy to address the public in the theatre as they never could in reality. Aristophanes seems prefiguratively to have sensed tragedy's claim to be 'democratic' in the more modern sense of the term: in an important passage of *Frogs* to be discussed below, the comic poet Euripides asserts that his tragedy is 'democratic' (*dēmokratikon*), on the precise ground that it gives voice to female and servile characters (949–52). The chapter therefore concludes that the ideological content dominant in Athenian tragic drama is simultaneously challenged by the inclusion through its multivocal form of otherwise excluded viewpoints.

The greatest innovation in the study of Greek tragedy over the last thirty years has been the excavation of its historical and topographical specificity. 'Classical Greek tragedy' is now more usually and more accurately called 'fifth-century Athenian tragedy'. For the notion of 'the Hellenic spirit', which informed criticism until the middle of this century, sprang from an anachronistic and idealist position. It emphasised the supposedly 'universal' significance of tragedy postulated by Aristotle in his *Poetics* (1451a36–1451b7), resuscitated by the Romantics, and perhaps given its definitive expression by Kierkegaard,[1] it presupposed an immutable human condition whose teleological imperative was suffering, and which somehow transcended transhistorical changes, and differences in culture and language. The 'eternal verities' contingent upon it were assumed to have been mysteriously encoded, by the 'genius' of the playwrights, in the tragic drama of the Greeks.

A scholarly project of the last three decades has been to undermine such universalising readings and to locate the plays within the historical conditions of their production. It is not that such attempts had not been made before.[2] But most earlier historicist readings of tragedy suffered from methodological crudity. Intentionalist and biographical interpretations tried to extract the playwrights' own political opinions from texts with no internal authorial voice and little external biographical evidence.[3] Others imposed reductive allegories, identifying characters in tragedy with contemporary politicians (e.g. Agamemnon in Aeschylus' *Agamemnon* with Cimon), or spotting direct references to contemporary events.[4] The difference between these and modern readings engaging with the socio-political background of tragedy, what Vernant calls its *under*-text,[5] is twofold. First, it is now stressed that tragedy offers no simple 'reflection' of the social processes of Athens: it transformed them while assimilating them into its own medium. Secondly, the focus is now less on the particularities of Athenian history than on the broader social tensions underpinning Athenian life.

While it is important to stress the plurality of plot-types in Athenian tragedy, a loose description could run along similar lines to Greenblatt's New Historicist formulation of Shakespearean drama, which he sees as 'centrally and repeatedly concerned with the production and containment of subversion and disorder'.[6] For the Athenian tragedies all enact the outbreak

[1] Kierkegaard (1987) 139–64.
[2] There are excellent insights in, for example, Flickinger (1918).
[3] On the unreliability of the ancient biographies of the tragedians see Lefkowitz (1981) 67–104.
[4] E.g. Delebecque (1951).   [5] Vernant and Vidal-Naquet (1988) 31.
[6] Greenblatt (1985) 18–47, 29.

and resolution of a crisis caused by imminent or actual death, adultery, exile, pleas for asylum, war, or the infringement of what Antigone calls the 'unwritten and unshakeable laws' of the gods (*Ant.* 454–5); these were traditional taboos proscribing kin-killing, incest, violation of oaths or the host–guest relationship, and disrespect towards parents, suppliants, and the dead.[7] Within this framework crises caused by the Athenian male's 'others', especially women and non-Athenian agents, insistently recur.

Indeed, the world represented in the tragic theatre of Athens is marked by extreme social heterogeneity and conflict. Some scholars now argue that it is the encounter with difference, with 'otherness', which constituted the Dionysiac dimension of the genre.[8] Tragedy offers a range of characters of all statuses from gods and kings to citizens and to slaves, all ethnicities from Athenian, Theban, and Argive Greeks to 'barbarians' (the generic term for non-Greeks) such as Persians and Egyptians, all age groups from babies to the very old, and an overwhelming insistence on the troubled relationships between women and men.

Any sociological reading of an artwork must address the relationship between its maker and its consumers. The relationship between the Athenian tragic poet and his audience was, formally, that of political equals. Tragedy is not the production of a hired poet for social superiors, like the songs of the bard Demodocus in the Homeric *Odyssey*; nor, however, is it the composition of an aristocratic leader talking down to his populace, like Solon's Athenian elegies. The three great Athenian tragedians were all Athenian citizens, albeit well-born ones (and in Sophocles' case prominent in political life); they composed their plays for an audience largely consisting of citizens, and the plays were performed at festivals defined by their nature as celebrations of Athenian citizenship (see Ch. 1). The texts were mediated through performance by agents likewise sharing Athenian citizenship: the chorus-members, actors, and sponsors.[9] Tragedy consequently defines the male citizen self,[10] and both produces and reproduces the ideology of the civic community.[11]

Aristophanes' *Women Celebrating the Thesmophoria* features an instructive central relationship between a maker and a consumer of tragedy. The heroes, both citizens, are Euripides and his kinsman by marriage. During their burlesques of Euripides' own tragedies they outwit both the women of

---

[7] See Ehrenberg (1954) 22–50, 167–72.

[8] Bibliography in Zeitlin (1993) 147–82, 152. Cf. Ch. 2 above.

[9] Metics, alien non-citizens resident in Athens, could act as sponsors (*chorēgoi*) at the smaller, almost exclusively Athenian, Lenaea festival, but not at the more international Dionysia when Athens was on display to the outside world (see Ch. 1, pp. 18–19).

[10] Zeitlin (1990) 63–96. Cf. Ch. 1 above.   [11] Citti (1978) 269–71.

Athens and a male, barbarian slave. These citizen heroes can participate together in the fantastic world of tragic parody ('paratragedy'), subjecting the texts to extended quotation, travesty, and interpolation, while the woman and the slave entrusted with guarding them cannot understand what they are doing. When the kinsman announces during the parody of Euripides' *Helen* that he is in Egypt, the female guard insists, quite rightly, that he is actually in the Athenian Thesmophorion (878–80); the barbarian slave similarly fails to be drawn into the paratragic experience of Euripides' Ethiopian *Andromeda*. The imaginative world of tragedy is therefore formulated by this comedy as an intellectual property, plaything and privilege of the citizen males, to the absolute exclusion of women and slaves.[12]

Social identity is a fluid phenomenon. Every individual partakes simultaneously in many distinct (though often overlapping) groups. Which particular group membership is temporarily predominant depends on immediate social context. At drama festivals the group identity depending on citizen status was paramount. Yet in democratic Athens group identity for the citizen male was complicated; within the post-Cleisthenic organisation of the polis the citizen was a member of a household, deme, tribe, phratry, and possibly an aristocratic *genos*, as well as a participant in the assembly and intermittently in other bodies such as juries and the council. Comedy is interested in the competing identities to which this internal civic organisation gave rise, but tragedy's examination of identity is more generalised. Human/divine, male/female, adult/child, free/slave, citizen/non-citizen, Athenian Greek/non-Athenian Greek, and Greek/barbarian are the most significant social boundaries negotiated by tragedy.

The answer to the sphinx's riddle, solved by Oedipus, is 'man'. A crucial frontier defined by tragedy is that between man and god. The Athenian was mortal, inhabiting a plane on earth below Olympus but above the underworld; although Aristotle briefly identifies a subspecies of tragedy 'set in the underworld' (*Poet.* 1456a2), *all* the extant tragedies – even the *Prometheus Bound*, whose cast is largely divine – are set in the terrestrial domain: Old Comedy made comparatively easy forays into Hades (Aristophanes' *Frogs*), into the upper air (*Birds*), or Olympus (*Peace*). But the earthly setting of surviving tragedy can nevertheless receive epiphanies from beyond. Gods from Olympus or the underworld mingle with mortals, as Apollo, Hermes, Athena, and the Erinyes do in Aeschylus' *Eumenides*, and the technical capacities of the theatre permitted ghosts to be seen to emerge from Hades, like Darius in Aeschylus' *Persians*.

---

[12] Hall (1989b) 38–54.

The Athenian citizen distinguished himself by his earthly habitat and mortality from the immortals (and death is omnipresent in tragedy, in contrast with the utopian tendency of the para-reality of Athenian comedy where it is hardly acknowledged as even a possibility). But the citizen also emphatically distinguished himself, as an inhabitant of a polis, from the primitive peoples and wild beasts without thought or language who lived in the untamed countryside beyond the boundaries of civilisation and the laws of the civic community. The barbarous Scythians are considered remarkable in *Prometheus Bound* because they do not live in settled communities, but are nomads, taking their caravans with them (709–10). The standard setting of tragedy came to be a house within a polis, or a house-surrogate within a polis-surrogate such as a tent in a military encampment (*Hecuba, Ajax*);[13] this contrasted with the wilder habitat of the semi-bestial satyrs of satyr drama, set on mountains (e.g. Sophocles' *Trackers*), or remote seashores (Aeschylus' *Net-Fishers*). The vision of the linear evolution of the human community from savagery to the city-state, formulated by the great fifth-century political theorist Protagoras, finds numerous expressions in tragedy. It informs Prometheus' speeches on the technologies he has given to humankind (*Prometheus Bound* 447–68, 476–506), the ode on human inventiveness in Sophocles' *Antigone* (322–75), Theseus' exposition of man's acquisition of intelligence, language, agriculture, navigation, and trade in Euripides' *Suppliant Women* (201–10), and certainly the means of survival to which the isolated cave-dwelling hero of Sophocles' *Philoctetes* has had to resort on the uninhabited island of Lemnos.

Philoctetes says that being without a polis is equivalent to being dead (1018). Tragedy's civic dimension is revealed in its repeated exploration of the theme of exile from the polis. The tragedy of the heroes' situations is consistently compounded by the hazard of being rendered, like Philoctetes, totally *apolis* – without a polis at all. It is a condition of the tragic Orestes' life, whether in the *Oresteia*, Sophocles' and Euripides' *Electra*-tragedies, or Euripides' *Iphigeneia among the Taurians* and *Orestes*, that he becomes an exile from his homeland; so are Jason and Medea in Euripides' *Medea*, Heracles and Deianeira in Sophocles' *Women of Trachis*, Oedipus, Antigone, and Polyneices in *Oedipus at Colonus*, and many others.

Tragic characters are forced to seek asylum or suffer captivity in alien cities for a variety of reasons: Danaus and his daughters in Aeschylus' *Suppliant Women*, Heracles' children in *Heracleidae*, Iphigeneia by the Black Sea in Euripides' *Iphigeneia among the Taurians*, and Helen in the Egypt of his *Helen*. War, the almost omnipresent background of tragedy as

[13] See Taplin (1977) 438–59.

it was a nearly continuous fact of Athenian life, displaces numerous females from their communities; this is feared by the chorus of Aeschylus' *Seven against Thebes*, and suffered by Cassandra in his *Agamemnon*, by the chorus of *Libation-Bearers*, by Euripides' Trojan Women in *Hecuba* and *Trojan Women* and his Andromache in her name-play. The Athenians' desperate dependence on recognised membership of the polis was expressed in the cultural production of these 'displacement' plots, in plots involving contested ethnicity and contested rights to citizenship,[14] and in the recurrence in tragic rhetoric of the themes of exile and loss of civic rights.

Since the civic consciousness central to the theatre defined an identity shared by only a small Athenian elite with the mass of ordinary citizens, it is an intriguing aspect of this democratic art-form that the crises it enacts afflict aristocrats. Minor roles could be taken by extraordinarily exotic characters of diverse status: a barbarian eunuch, Crimean cowherds, a muse, a semi-bovine maiden, and a god disguised as a dark-skinned Egyptian,[15] yet the democratic polis chose to represent itself through tragedies whose primary focus was on human royalty. Although in one experimental play, Agathon's *Antheus*, the characters were all 'invented' rather than familiar mythical figures (Aristotle, *Poet.* 1451b21), no tragedian seems to have attempted a tragedy in which the central figures were ordinary citizens. This was a privilege, apparently, of comedy, where none-too-wealthy Athenians can be heroes (Strepsiades in *Clouds*, Trygaeus in *Peace*, and Praxagora, a citizen's wife, in *Women in Assembly*).

The mythical legacy which the tragedians inherited from the poets of archaic epic and lyric, the 'forests of myths' as Herington, paraphrasing Baudelaire, calls it,[16] centred on the sufferings of kings. The tragedians' project was to reinterpret such myths for contemporary purposes, to use the authority of the past to dignify and legitimise the present. But another perspective can see the royalty of classical tragedy as operating at a high degree of abstraction from social reality, encoding the newly discovered political freedoms and aspirations of ordinary men in the symbolic language of pre-democratic political hierarchies. Frye observed in relation to Shakespeare, 'princes and princesses may be wish-fulfilment dreams as well as social facts'.[17] Every citizen, free and autonomous, subject to no individual and self-sufficient (Thuc. 2.41), saw himself in some sense as a 'monarch'.

---

[14] Hall (1989a) 172–81. Cf. also Ch. 8, pp. 188–9.

[15] In the Euripidean *Orestes*, *Iphigeneia among the Taurians*, and *Rhesus*, the Aeschylean *Prometheus Bound*, and Sophocles' lost *Inachus* respectively.

[16] Herington (1985) 64.   [17] Frye (1965) 146.

Aeschylus describes every citizen-sailor who rowed at Salamis, in defence of Athens' liberty and his own, as the 'king of his own oar' (*Pers.* 378).[18]

Real aristocrats in Athens had seen their rights considerably challenged, at least from the 480s onwards. Yet they remained disproportionately influential, maintaining their prominence not least through the regular enactment of their private dramas on the public stages of the lawcourts.[19] There lingered a belief that high birth was synonymous with virtue and intelligence, and the old and wealthy families who still held a near-monopoly on the higher offices of state continued to use the claim of *eugeneia*, or 'superior pedigree', to justify their pre-eminence: in fifth-century legal and political discourse, *eugeneia* appears as 'the wellspring of those qualities of mind and spirit that made a nobleman a superior person. Intellectual and moral proclivities are traced back to character, which, in the final analysis, is determined genetically.'[20] The contradiction between democratic ideals and the continuing respect for nobility produces frequent tragic discussions of the inheritability of virtue, but on balance the statements on nature versus nurture are surprisingly reactionary; in Euripides' *Children of Heracles*, for example, Iolaus compliments Demophon by saying that 'children have no finer endowment than to have been begotten by a noble and brave father' (287–8).[21]

Yet tragedy cannot be used as a document of the realities of life in Athens. It is essential to acknowledge the processes of artistic mediation: Athenian institutions and social relations are distorted by the genre. The tragic universe, an imaginative reconstruction of the mythical past, simultaneously idealised and dysfunctional, attempts to archaise but is often anachronistic.[22] Things could happen in the real life of Athens which were virtually unthinkable in tragedy, and vice versa. Thus, for example, in reality people could rise socially beyond birth-status (which is almost impossible in tragedy), and Athens was riven by factional in-fighting (but the idealised tragic Athens is virtually free from *stasis*). On the other hand, there is no historical record of any young woman flouting the authority of her male 'guardian' (*kurios*) in the 'real' life of Athens, in the manner of the challenges made by Antigone and Electra to the authority of Creon and Aegisthus. Yet *Antigone* and *Electra* are indisputably documents of the Athenian *imagination*. Sentiments expressed by tragic characters, even those apparently at odds with the dominant ideology (see pp. 118–24 below), are

[18] This is taking *Pers.* 374–83 as referring to the Greeks, rather than, with most editors, the Persians: see Hall (1996), note ad loc.
[19] Osborne (1985) 40–58; Hall (1995).   [20] Donlan (1980) 139.
[21] On this issue see Rose (1992), especially 266–30; Dover (1974) 88–95.
[22] Easterling (1985) 1–10.

clearly *imaginable* in the democratic polis. And the very plot-patterns of the genre itself, shaped by and shaping the Athenians' collective thought-world, testify to their social and emotional preoccupations.

ATHENS

The form of tragedy is Panhellenic. An inclusive genre, it absorbed multifarious metrical forms originating in places across the Greek-speaking world, such as Doric choral lyric and Aegean monody. This form has an equivalent in the casts of tragedy, which are almost always of mixed ethnicity. Every single tragic performance of which we know offered its audience the ethnically other, the non-Athenian, in the theatre.[23] A very few plays offer a cast confined to a single ethnic group if it is non-Athenian (in *Persians* everyone is Persian, and in *Antigone* everyone is Theban). But all the others represent interaction between characters of more than one provenance.

Yet despite tragedy's ethnic plurality, and its interest in heroes and communities spread over vast distances across the known world,[24] the Athenian focus, the 'Athenocentrism' of tragedy, is manifested in several ways. Many plays include explicit panegyrics of Athens, for example in Aeschylus' *Persians* (231–45) and Sophocles' *Oedipus at Colonus* (668–719);[25] the women of Troy, about to be sent off to slavery in Greece, hope that their destination is Athens (e.g. *Tro.* 208–9). Secondly, even plays with no obvious Athenian focus often include an *aition*, an explanation through myth, of the origins of an Athenian custom: Euripides' *Iphigeneia among the Taurians*, which portrays the escape of an Argive sister and brother from a barbarian community by the Black Sea, startlingly concludes with Athena ordering them to establish rituals at a cult-centre on Athenian territory, the sanctuary of Artemis at Brauron (1459–69). Thirdly, the tragedians used communities other than Athens as sites for ethnic *self-definition*; the barbarian world often functions in the tragic imagination as the home of vices (for example, Persian despotism, Thracian lawlessness, eastern effeminacy and cowardice) conceived as correlatives to the idealised Athenian democratic virtues of freedom of speech, equality before the law, and masculine courage.[26] Nearer home it can also be helpful to see other

---

[23] Hall (1989a); Vidal-Naquet (1992) 297–311.
[24] Easterling (1994) 73–80 has recently urged that scholarly attention to tragedy's undoubted Athenocentrism should not be allowed to obscure its interest in other places, and relevance to non-Athenian audiences elsewhere in the fifth century, for example in Italy.
[25] For others see Butts (1942).
[26] Hall (1989a) 121–33; on Asiatics in tragedy see also Hall (1993a) 108–33.

Greek cities, especially Thebes, as imagined communities whose negative characteristics are partly determined by their deviation from the Athenians' own positive *self*-representations. Democratic Athens was proud of its openness (Thuc. 2.39), while Thebes in tragedy is often closed in on itself, and its royalty susceptible to internecine conflict, incest, and tyrannical conduct.[27]

Fourthly, a subspecies of tragedy emerged enacting transparently 'patriotic' myths, concerned with the early mythical history of Athens and Attica, and stressing such vital components of the Athenians' identity as their claim to autochthony.[28] The repertoire included Euripides' *Suppliant Women, Ion*, and his *Erechtheus*, of which considerable fragments survive: *Erechtheus* was a patriotic piece dealing with the struggle over Athens between Athena and Poseidon. It also portrayed the self-immolation of Athenian princesses, and the death of King Erechtheus, during a patriotic war caused by the military aggression of Poseidon-worshipping Thracian barbarians (see fr. 50.46–9 Austin). The play, produced between 423 and 421 BC, celebrated the building of the Erechtheion on the Acropolis.

Even in plays set in Athenian territory, the Athenian characters always interact with representatives of other city-states. Some plots seek to display the superiority of Athenian democratic culture over other cities, especially Thebes or Argos, and imply that Athens is entitled to the imperial role of 'moral policeman' in Greece. In Euripides' *Suppliant Women* (almost certainly modelled on Aeschylus' lost *Eleusinians*) Theseus, the mythical founder of the Athenian democracy, is portrayed as a pious and egalitarian constitutional monarch of a democracy: he says, 'When I first assumed leadership, I gave my people freedom and an equal vote, and on this basis instituted monarchy' (352–3). He takes action against the despotic Thebans to impose the 'common law of Hellas' protecting the rights of the dead.

The Athenocentrism of tragedy is revealed when myths involving heroes from other cities are manipulated to serve Athenian interests. Until the sixth century Athens had enshrined little of its own local mythology in poetry and art; it had no hero equal in status to Heracles, Achilles, Orestes, Agamemnon, or Oedipus. There was an attempt in the late sixth and fifth centuries to develop a nexus of myths around the Athenian king Theseus, who appears in several tragedies; but the Argive, Theban, and other non-Athenian heroes from the old epic cycle, while remaining central to tragedy, are often appropriated to the *Athenian* past, in each case conferring on the city some special advantage.

---

[27] Zeitlin (1986); but see Easterling (1989) 1–17, who cautions against over-polarising Athens and Thebes.

[28] See Loraux (1993), especially 37–71. Cf. Ch. 1, pp. 30–1.

Orestes, for example, is brought to trial at Athens by Aeschylus in his *Eumenides*, and the myth is altered to make him, rather than Ares, the first figure to be tried for murder at the court of the Areopagus. Aeschylus has therefore to offer a reason why the Areopagus was named the 'hill (*pagos*) of Ares' rather than the 'Oresteopagus' (685–90). Orestes not only causes the foundation of the Athenians' court: he also benefits them by promising an eternal friendship between Argos and Athens (762–4), almost certainly an *aition* for the thirty-year alliance with Argos pledged by the Athenians in 460 BC (Thuc. 1.102.4). The play also provides an instance of Athens' fair treatment of suppliant strangers. It is a remarkable feature of *Eumenides* that the poet portrayed an Athens without a king, even in a play set only shortly after the Trojan war. As if to emphasise the democratic nature of the Athens of the heroic age, silent male characters appear on stage representing citizens, the first ever jurors at a trial for homicide at the court of the Areopagus. So the audience's direct forefathers mingled before their eyes with gods and heroes.

In Euripides' *Heracles* the greatest hero of Greek legend is similarly 'myth-napped' by the playwright and brought to spend the rest of his life at Athens. An ancient friendship between Theseus and Heracles, resting on the debt Theseus owes the great hero for rescuing him from the underworld (1169–70), is confirmed when Theseus dissuades Heracles from suicide and pledges to take him to Athens. There he will purify him, grant him land, and honour him after death with sacrifices and stone memorials (1322–33): these may offer an *aition* for the sculptures commemorating the famous deeds of both Theseus and Heracles on the 'Hephaesteion' in the Athenian agora, datable to between 450 and 440 BC.[29] The appropriation of Heracles to Athens was no small coup: as Theseus says, his citizens will win a fair crown of honour in the eyes of Greece for helping a man of such quality (1334–5). But friendship is one of the dominant themes in this fascinating play, and the mythical celebration of the friendship between Theseus and Heracles also acts as a moral or behavioural *aition* for the social institution of friendships between male citizens which were a central feature of Athenian democracy, and could even be used as a justificatory argument in Athenian law.[30]

In his *Oedipus at Colonus* Sophocles provides a mythical explanation for the near-permanent hostility between the 'real' city-states of Athens and Thebes in historical times; this is in the course of 'myth-napping' the Theban hero to a mystical death at the Athenian deme of Colonus (Sophocles' own birthplace). Oedipus is welcomed kindly, and formally

[29] Bond (1988) 396.   [30] Golden (1990) 52.

granted full citizen status by Theseus (636–7). Oedipus promises that if he is granted burial there, he will confer a great benefit on the city (576–8, 626–8). He explains that his body will always provide for the Athenians 'a defence, a bulwark stronger than many shields, than spears of massed allies' (1524–5). Theseus witnesses his death, and he is to communicate its secrets only to his heir (1530–2). Sophocles' tragedy thus not only attracts Oedipus into the Athenian mythical orbit: it actually transfers his allegiance from the city of his birth to the city of the play's production. Oedipus will lend posthumous assistance to the Athenians against the citizens of the much-hated city of Thebes.

This play offers as a speaking character a nameless Athenian citizen of the deme of Colonus. The mythical forefather of the citizens in the audience, he is the first speaking character after the exiles Oedipus and Antigone arrive at the grove of the Eumenides. He is distinguished by his pious regard for the sanctity of the grove, his fear lest it be defiled, and his exemplary respect for the processes of the Athenian democracy. He announces that he would never eject Oedipus from his seat without reporting his arrival to the other citizens, and taking his instructions from them (47–8).

Other Athenians in tragedy usually display virtue, piety, and respect for suppliants and the democratic principle of freedom of speech: this is a particularly revealing aspect of what might be called the Athenians' self-regarding use of tragedy as 'moral aetiology'. On the rare occasions when Athenians do misbehave or act foolishly in tragedy it is conspicuous that they are removed from their city for the duration of their misadventure. In Euripides' *Medea* the Athenian king Aegeus is no culprit but he is faintly ridiculous – credulous, and upset about his infertility. One of the reasons why *Medea* was so unsuccessful in the dramatic competition of 431 BC may have been that the audience did not appreciate hearing one of their own ancestral kings discussing his infertility on stage. But the play is set at Corinth. Likewise, it is at Delphi that Creusa, the daughter of Erechtheus in Euripides' *Ion*, plots the murder of the young man whom she believes to be her husband's illegitimate offspring. Even Theseus in *Hippolytus*, who although no bad man is precipitate in judgement and unfair to his son, is a resident of Trozen in the Peloponnese for the duration and purposes of the play.

GENDER

Although profoundly concerned with the Athenian's public, collective, identity as a citizen, tragedy came to be set not in the male arenas of civic discourse – the council, assembly or lawcourts – but in the marginal space immediately outside the door of the private home. The action takes place at the exact physical point where the veil is torn from the face of domestic crises, revealing them to public view, and disclosing their ramifications not only for the central figures but also for the wider community.

This domestic focus becomes less surprising if the relationship between the household and the city-state, no simple antithesis, is considered in its full complexity. The polis consisted of a multiplicity of households, and it was in the household that the citizen body reproduced itself; the Athenian's claim to the privileges of citizenship depended upon his ability to prove that he emanated from a legitimate union of two Athenians, at least after 451 BC (cf. Ch. 1 above, pp. 28–9). Any public man who wanted the confidence of the people or a generalship was certainly expected, and perhaps legally required, to father legitimate children.[31] In writings on political theory 'public' catastrophes – *stasis* and revolutions – are often traced to 'private' issues affecting eminent individuals, such as love affairs, marriages, and domestic lawsuits. Aristotle, who catalogues 'private' causes of public crisis in his *Politics*, says that 'even the smallest disputes are important when they occur at the centres of power', and 'conflicts between well-known people generally affect the whole community' (V 1303b19–20, 31–2).

A citizen's family life was a component of his political identity. It was important to be seen in the lawcourts as the responsible head of a well-ordered household; it was customary for a citizen involved in a trial to introduce his decorous children onto the rostrum in a public display. His 'private' conduct was seen as indicative of the manner in which he would exert political power: Demosthenes was criticised in court for dressing in white and performing public ceremonies only a week after his daughter's death (Aeschines 3.77). The speaker warns, 'The man who hates his child and is a bad father could never become a safe guide to the people ... the man who is wicked in his private relations would never be found trustworthy in public affairs.' Creon in Sophocles' *Antigone* fails both as a father and as civic leader, and the two failures are interdependent.

The tragic household is obsessed with its own perpetuation through legitimate male heirs. The institution of marriage necessary for the production of such heirs is a constant question for rhetorical examination, and it is a constant theme of tragic lamentation that the crises enacted will result in the extirpation of a family line. Childlessness itself is a concern of men in tragedy, leading both Aegeus in *Medea* and Xuthus in *Ion* to seek the advice of oracles. In reality one of the worst punishments which could be visited on

---

[31] παιδοποιεῖσθαι κατὰ τοὺς νόμους, Dinarchus 1.71; see also [Aristot.] *Ath. Pol.* 4.2. I am very grateful to Helene Foley for drawing my attention to these references.

a convicted criminal – usually for political crimes – was the overthrow, the physical razing to the ground of the house (*kataskaphē*), which was symbolically charged as the concrete manifestation of the whole kinship line through time. *Kataskaphē* involved the denial of burial, destruction of family altars and tombs, removal of ancestors' bones, confiscation of property, exile, and a curse applying even to offspring and descendants.[32] Heracles in his name-play by Euripides threatens to raze the house of the usurping tyrant Lycus to the ground in just this way (565–8).

The destruction of the kinship line is a major theme in tragedy. It provides the climax of Euripides' *Trojan Women*, where Astyanax, Priam's only surviving male descendant, is murdered: it is a reason why Medea chooses for Jason not his own death but the death of his new wife (on whom he could beget new heirs) and the deaths of his sons; it is the cause of Peleus' tragedy in Euripides' *Andromache*, when he hears the news of the death of his only son's only son: 'my family line (*genos*) is no more; no children remain to my household' (1177–8).

It was the reputation of his family which was the public man's greatest liability; political enemies might attack him by targeting his dependants, especially his wife, for litigation or ridicule. The convention that respectable women were not even to be named in public stems from the same ideal which led Thucydides' Pericles to proclaim that a woman's greatest glory was to be spoken of as little as possible, either in praise or blame (2.46). Eurydice, Creon's wife in Sophocles' *Antigone*, nearly conforms with this Periclean template of perfection, since she is never even mentioned, either in praise or blame, until nine-tenths of the way through the play. But most tragic women, by emerging from the door of the household into public view, run risks which Athenian citizens would have preferred their own womenfolk to avoid; idealised female characters, especially virgins, often apologise for their 'forwardness' when they appear (e.g. Eur. *Children of Heracles* 474–7).

In the second century AD the satirist Lucian remarked that 'there are more females than males' in these plays (*De Saltatione* 28); a character in a novel of similar date also comments on the large number of plots which women have contributed to the stage (Achilles Tatius, *Leucippe and Clitophon* 1.8). Only one extant tragedy, Sophocles' *Philoctetes*, contains no women, and female tragic choruses in the surviving plays outnumber male by twenty-one to ten. Since women were almost excluded from Athenian public life, their prominence in this most public of Athenian art-forms therefore constitutes a problematic paradox.

[32] Connor (1985) 79–102.

Death and killing are central to tragedy: women's role in religion, especially in funerary lamentation and in sacrifices, must partly explain their presence.[33] The Dionysiac origin of tragedy may illuminate its femininity: maenadic (and therefore female) frenzy often occurs in metaphors associated with kin-killing in tragedy, because of its affiliation with the cult of Dionysus.[34] The departure of women from the interior of the household, giving rise to its destruction, has also been seen as an originally maenadic motif.[35] Zeitlin refers us to the femininity of Dionysus, transvestism in his cult, and symbolic gender inversions in Greek ritual to help explain the role of women as the 'other' of the masculine identity defined in Athenian tragedy.[36] Drama required actors playing women apparently to change their gender; this helps to explain the playwrights' attraction to stories involving reversed gender roles (of which the most obvious example is that enacted in Aristophanes' *Lysistrata*), and therefore the 'masculinised' women of tragedy.[37] Anthropological symbolism shows that patriarchal cultures often use the figures and bodies of women to help them imagine abstractions and think about their social order.[38] Moreover, women were regarded as more susceptible to invasive passions than men, especially eros and daemonic possession;[39] women were thus both plausible instigators of tragic events, and effective generators of emotional responses.

The category 'women in Greek tragedy' is in itself problematic. It includes children and ageing widows, nubile virgins and multiple mothers, adulteresses and paragons of wifehood, murderesses and exemplars of virtue, lowly slaves and high priestesses, maenads, witches, and Io, the girl with a cow's head chased by a gadfly to the Scythian mountains. Yet there is undeniably a tendency towards plots with disruptive women: one generic pattern relating to male–female relations does draw together a large number of the plays and can be taken as an aesthetic expression of a defining feature of the Athenian male's world view. This plot-pattern can be formulated as follows: women in Athenian tragedy only become disruptive (that is, break one of the 'unwritten laws', act on an inappropriate erotic urge, or flout male authority) in the physical absence of a legitimate husband or *kurios*. This applies equally to unmarried virgins and to married women, who transgress only in the absence of their husbands. The converse does not always apply; husbandless women may behave with decorum (Chrysothemis, for example, in Sophocles' *Electra*, and Megara in *Heracles*). But every single transgres-

[33] Foley (1981) 127–68; cf. Ch. 1.　　[34] Schlesier (1993) 89–114.
[35] Seaford (1993) 115–46.　　[36] Zeitlin (1990).
[37] Gould (1980) 38–59, especially 56–9; Foley (1981) 156–9; Zeitlin (1984) 149–84.
[38] Ortner (1974) 66–87, especially 82–7; des Bouvrie (1990).
[39] See Padel (1983) 3–19 and (1992).

sive woman in tragedy is temporarily or permanently husbandless. This convention can be interpreted as a symptom of the Athenian citizen's anxiety about the crises which might afflict his household during his absence: as a character in a comic fragment said, 'there is no wall, nor fortune, nor anything as hard to keep guard on as a woman' (Alexis fr. 340 K–A).

The pattern is in turn dependent upon the prevalence of the type of plot in which the male head of the household enacts a homecoming (*nostos*) during the course of the play. The *nostos*-plot had an influential antecedent in the *Odyssey*, where chaos had also reigned in the king's absence, although his wife had not in that case been the culprit. More important archetypes were the *Nostoi*, the epic poems which told of the returns from Troy of heroes such as Agamemnon and Menelaus, and the difficulties (at best) they encountered on arrival. Many of the extant plays involve at least one male *nostos*: Xerxes in *Persians*, Agamemnon in his name-play, Orestes in *Libation-Bearers*, Aegisthus in Sophocles' *Electra*, Heracles in his *Women of Trachis*, Theseus in *Hippolytus*, Heracles in *Heracles*, Menelaus in *Orestes*, Pentheus in *Bacchae*, and Jason, back from the palace, in *Medea*. Even Euripides' *Andromache* is a distorted *nostos*-tragedy: the return from Delphi of the householder Neoptolemus is awaited throughout, but when he arrives it is as a corpse (1166).

A speech by Clytemnestra to her husband in Euripides' *Iphigeneia at Aulis* epitomises the position of women in the tragic universe. She argues that she has been a blameless wife, 'chaste with regard to sexual matters, increasing the prosperity of the household, so that joy attends you when you come home, and good fortune when you depart' (1159–61). There is an implicit acknowledgement that although women *were* transferred from household to household (by male consensus in the case of marriage and male violence in the case of war), they were essentially immobilised, in contrast with the unrestricted movements of men. [Greek tragedy generally portrays static household-bound women awaiting and reacting to the comings and goings of men.]

It is another tragedian's Clytemnestra, in Aeschylus' *Agamemnon*, who is arguably the most transgressive woman in extant tragedy. She has committed adultery, murders Agamemnon and Cassandra, and aspires to political power. But even she embarked on her transgressive career in the physical absence of her husband, who left her behind many years ago to fight for his brother's wife at Troy. There is no suggestion that Clytemnestra had transgressed her socially sanctioned role before her husband's departure. In extant tragedy the adulterous elopement of Clytemnestra's lovely sister Helen is never actually dramatised. But emphasis is often laid, in the passages which refer to it, on Menelaus' absence from home when the incident occurred. In Euripides' *Iphigeneia at Aulis* this is made quite explicit: Paris took Helen away from Sparta when 'Menelaus was out of town' (*ekdēmon*, 76–7). In *Trojan Women* it is said that the elopement could only occur because Menelaus went on a trip to Crete (943–4). The generic convention of the absent husband thus informs the construction of female transgression even in narratives of the past.

Deianeira, left alone for much of each year by her husband Heracles, does not kill him intentionally. But the *nostos*-plot of *Women of Trachis* under- lines the dangers inherent in leaving a wife alone, to make decisions without her husband's guidance. Deianeira's decision to try to win back her husband's love by using a potion of suspicious provenance is presented as the result of panic rather than malevolence, but it is an action she conceives in isolation from him. Similarly, Medea is living alone, abandoned by Jason, when she plans and executes the murders of his new wife and his children. It is also in the absence of Theseus that Phaedra embarks on the course of action which results in catastrophe (see pp. 116–18 below).

In Euripides' *Andromache* Neoptolemus' wife Hermione and concubine Andromache are living under the same roof when Hermione conceives her barbaric plan to murder her rival and her rival's child. Neoptolemus, typically, is removed from his household so that this crisis can occur: he is at the Delphic oracle. Hermione ultimately regrets her miscreant behaviour, blaming it on 'foul-minded women' who would visit her and endlessly gossip, asking her why she allowed a mere slave-woman to share her home and her husband (930–3). This exemplifies yet another generic pattern in Greek tragedy: while friendship between males of different households is consistently idealised, especially in the relationships between Orestes and Pylades, and Heracles and Theseus, no such relationship between two women from different households ever graces the tragic stage. Although great mutual affection is attributed to pairs of sisters like Antigone and Ismene and Electra and Chrysothemis, and female choruses express friendly sentiments to female characters, friendship between individual women is consistently portrayed as a dangerous phenomenon, disparaged even by (idealised) wives (e.g. by Andromache, *Tro.* 647–55).

Euripides' *Bacchae* portrays the return of the young King Pentheus of Thebes. Dionysus says in the prologue that he has maddened the sisters of Semele and sent them out to the mountains. The audience does not yet know the whereabouts of the king of Thebes or of the husbands of Agave and her sisters. When Pentheus arrives he reveals that he 'happens to have been out of town' (*ekdēmos*, 215). It becomes apparent that Agave, Autonoe, and Ino, the Theban royal sisters of whom the Dionysiac frenzy has taken hold, lack marital supervision. There are several references to Echion, Agave's husband and Pentheus' father, one of the original 'Spartoi' ('sown men') of Thebes, who sprang from the dragon's teeth (265, 507, 995, 1030, 1274). Although it is not stated that Echion is dead, he is certainly not present in Thebes. Autonoe's husband Aristaeus is also mentioned (1227); he seems to be living abroad. There is silence on the subject of Ino's husband, usually identified as the Boeotian king Athamas. Euripides has so structured his picture of the Theban royal house that the only male member present, Pentheus' grandfather Cadmus, is aged and infirm when Dionysus comes to wreak his vengeance through the fragile medium of the psyches of manless women.

Play after play, therefore, portrays the disastrous effects on households and the larger community of divinely inspired madness, anger, sexual desire, or jealousy in women unsupervised by men. This plot-pattern is illuminated by reference to the legal position of Athenian women, who were required to remain under the legal control of a male *kurios* throughout their lives, and also by the Greeks' view of the frailty of the female psyche. Aristotle said that the deliberative, decision-making faculty of the psyche is 'inoperative' in women: the word he uses is *akuron*, 'without command' or 'authority', literally, 'lacking a *kurios*' (*Pol.* 1 1260a). The psyches of women were thus perceived as analogous with their legal status.[40]

Medical ideas can provide further illumination. Virginity and chastity were viewed differently in the pagan ancient world: unmarried 'spinsters' were regarded as a social liability. Greek medical writings suggest that for a woman between menarche and menopause regular sexual intercourse was necessary to health; ideally she remained pregnant most of the time.[Indeed, enforced sexual continence after puberty was thought to make women liable to physical and psychic disorders.] The gynaecology of the Hippocratic corpus frequently prescribes intercourse as a cure for female diseases (*Nat. Puer.* 30.11, 82.6–12); to the Hippocratics, 'menstruation, intercourse, and childbirth are collectively essential to the health of the mature woman'.[41] Beliefs of this kind seem to be a contributory factor in the tragedians' portraits of transgressive wives: the sexual deprivation suffered by Medea is frequently stressed, and if Phaedra had consulted a doctor, it is likely that he would have prescribed sexual intercourse (with her husband, of course).[42]

The belief also informs the characterisations of the insubordinate virgins, Antigone and Electra. The author of the medical treatise *On the Diseases of*

---

[40] Just (1989) 188–93. [41] Hanson (1990) 309–37, 320.
[42] Hanson (1990) 320.

Young Women regards girls in and after puberty as prone to madness; marriage and childbirth are the recommended treatment.[43] In Sophocles' *Electra* stress is laid on her unmarried status; in Euripides' version Electra is so disturbed that she jointly wields the sword which murders her mother (1225). In this play she is married, but the poet seems to indicate that he is aware of the latent generic convention by making characters twice point out that the marriage has never been consummated (43–53, 253–7).[44]

Yet law, psychology, and medicine must be supplemented by an economic perspective. Male anxiety about female transgression, especially female infidelity, always has an underlying *economic* explanation in patrilineal societies where property is transmitted through the male bloodline. One of the ancient Athenian's worst nightmares was that his household would be extinguished by his heirlessness. Even worse was the idea that his household might be extinguished without his even knowing it – that is, by the infiltration of an heir he had not fathered himself: in Euripides' *Phoenician Women* the Corinthian adoptive mother of Oedipus tricked her husband Polybus in exactly this manner (28–31). Women could be challenged to take oaths in front of arbitrators affirming the paternity of children (Dem. 39.4, 40.10, see Aristot. *Rhet.* II 23.11). This preoccupation found expression in the mouth of Homer's Telemachus, who complains that he cannot be sure who his father is, whatever Penelope says (*Od.* 1.215–16). A Euripidean character in a lost play expressed the problem succinctly: 'A mother always loves a child more than a father does. She knows it is her own: he only thinks it is' (fr. 1015).

CLASS

Slavery was a central institution of the classical Athenian polis: only the most impoverished citizen could not afford a slave at all. Slavery affected the Athenians' conceptualisation of the universe at every level, a process reflected in their metaphors, for the citizen perceived analogies between his relationships with slaves and his relationships with women and children (see Aristotle's *Politics* book 1). He could use slavery to express the pressures on men in authority: in a rhetorical inversion of the real power structure,

---

[43] Sissa (1990b) 339–64, at 359.

[44] In Aeschylus' *Suppliant Women*, the first play of the *Danaids* trilogy, the fifty daughters of the Egyptian Danaus reject marriage with their cousins; in the lost second play they married them but killed them on their wedding night. It is highly likely that the murders took place before the marriage had been physically consummated. Unfortunately the fragmentary evidence for the remainder of the trilogy (on which see Garvie (1969) ch. 5) gives no explicit indication.

Agamemnon in *Iphigeneia at Aulis* reflects that low birth (*dusgeneia*) has its advantages, for the obligation of the high-born to preserve their public dignity means that they are metaphorically 'enslaved' to the crowd (*douleuomen*, 450). Slavery was even used to express the perception of fate: Heracles realises after his madness that men are 'enslaved' to fortune (*douleuteon*, *Her.* 1357; see also an anonymous tragic fragment, *TGF* II 374). And slavery, both literal and metaphorical, is a central focus of the tragic theatre.

One of the most frequent forms of peripeteia, or 'reversal', is actually peripeteia of status. Numerous characters, especially in plays treating the fall of Troy, lose previously aristocratic status and become slaves, a fate regarded in the tragic universe as particularly hard to bear (see e.g. *Tro.* 302–3). Enslavement was in reality the fate of women in the fifth century if their cities were sacked: when the islanders of Melos surrendered to Athens in 416/15 BC, the Athenians 'put to death all the men of military age whom they took, and sold the women and children as slaves' (Thuc. 5.116). Whether it is Cassandra in Aeschylus' *Agamemnon* and the chorus of *Libation-Bearers*, Tecmessa in Sophocles' *Ajax* and Iole in his *Women of Trachis*, or Hecuba, Cassandra, Andromache, and Polyxena in Euripides' *Hecuba*, *Trojan Women*, and *Andromache*, slave women, once royal but 'won by the spear', by their lamentations, their reflections, or just their silent presence, make their catastrophic fall in status a theme of tragedy.[45]

There is a crucial distinction to be drawn here. While heartbreaking descriptions of life in slavery are frequently rendered by tragic characters, for example by Hecuba in *Trojan Women* (190–6, 489–510), they are virtually all expressed by those once free who have lost their freedom. This seems to have been regarded by the free as considerably more 'tragic' than to have been born into a whole life in servitude: as Menelaus says in *Helen*, a person fallen from high estate finds his lot harder to bear than the long-time unfortunate (417–19). Deianeira can tell merely from the appearance of the enslaved Iole in *Women of Trachis* that the young woman is well-born, for she somehow stands out from the other captives (309). The very form of tragedy, while otherwise remarkably egalitarian (see pp. 118–26 below), does reinforce the distinction between the enslaved aristocrat and the slave from birth; the lyric medium is generally denied to characters of low birth status,[46] while enslaved aristocrats, in common with their free counterparts, can express their emotions in song.

---

[45] See Kuch (1974).

[46] See Maas (1952) 53–4. The only two exceptions, the Egyptian herald in Aeschylus' *Suppliant Women* and the Phrygian eunuch in Euripides' *Orestes*, are both non-Greeks, and the singing voice was especially associated with overwrought barbarians: see Hall (1989a)

The once-free, moreover, can regain their freedom. This happens to Andromache in her name-play, and to Sophocles' Electra, who is originally treated like a household slave, but has her status restored by her returning brother. Male characters who by accident of fortune lose high status also usually recover it, like Homer's Odysseus, for a time disguised as a beggar: in Euripides' *Alexander* a shepherd is revealed to be the son of the Trojan royal house, and in his *Ion* the servant-priest of Apollo at Delphi is upgraded to his birthright as heir to the Athenian throne. The disguised hero of Euripides' *Telephus* spent time in service as Clytemnestra's porter before he was proved to be the son of Heracles and an Arcadian princess.[47] While tragedy can *envisage* the opposite social movement, from seeming aristocratic to actual servile birth status, it never actually happens. Oedipus in *Oedipus the King* considers the possibility that his natural mother was 'a third-generation slave' (1062–3), and Ion fears that his mother was of servile or lowly birth (556, 1477), but in both cases their mothers turn out to have been aristocrats.

In the case, however, of the never-free, slaves from birth, the tragic texts everywhere assume that the slave/free boundary is as fixed, natural, and permanent as the boundary between man and god. It was necessary to the perpetuation of institutionalised slavery to foster a belief in the *natural* servility of those born into the slave class, and no character in tragedy proposes abolishing slavery. The majority of the theatrical audience probably agreed with the character in a fragment of Euripides' lost *Antiope*, who announced that 'a slave ought never to form an opinion becoming a free person, nor to covet leisure' (fr. 216); when slaves do express their own opinions in tragedy they often apologise for it, as Deianeira's nurse in *Women of Trachis* prefaces her advice to her mistress with the precautionary words, 'if it is right to advise the free with a slave's opinions' (52–3). In the tragic universe characters cannot improve upon the social status into which they were born. In Euripides' version of Electra's story, she is married to a free poor peasant whom Pylades is to make a wealthy man (1287), but even he was originally from an old Mycenean family. The sole exception to the inescapability of birth status is suggested by Alcmena's promise to grant freedom to the slave who reports the victory over Eurystheus in *Children of Heracles*, a promise of which he later reminds her (789–90, 888–90); but textual problems frustrate an exact understanding of the situation here.[48]

83–4, 119, 130–2. The nurse in Sophocles' *Women of Trachis* almost certainly does not sing: see Easterling (1982) 183.

[47] See Handley and Rea (1957); Webster (1967) 45.

[48] The text of this play almost certainly contains gaps (see below, n. 64); were it complete, the significance of this unique emancipation motif would presumably be clearer. It must be

Tragic characters of servile status perform various functions. Almost always nameless, frequently mute, they attend upon royalty and carry out menial tasks such as the carrying of Clytemnestra's carpet in *Agamemnon* (908–9), or the binding of the heroine on Menelaus' orders in Euripides' *Andromache* (425–6). The so-called 'messenger' is often a slave; his or her function is to report important incidents taking place within or away from the household. It is intriguing that tragedy should have granted such lowly figures these privileged speeches, especially since slaves could not even give evidence directly in Athenian courts. Although modern audiences can find them static, the frequency with which the scenes they describe appear on vases is an indication of their ancient popularity (cf. Ch. 4).[49]

Indeed slaves, although formally powerless, can wield enormous power in the world of tragedy through their access to dangerous knowledge.[50] Of peculiar interest is the Theban shepherd in *Oedipus the King*. He was a slave born into the Theban royal household, rather than bought in from outside (1123). This man with no name, identified variously as 'shepherd', 'peasant' and 'slave', is the only living person other than Tiresias who knows the truth concerning Oedipus. Mysterious parallels are drawn between the slave and the prophet; they are both reluctant to answer summonses to the palace. Tiresias was sent for twice, and Oedipus was surprised at how long it took for him to arrive (*palai*, 289): the slave who witnessed the murder of Laius was also summoned twice (see 118, 838, 861), and, when he finally arrives, Oedipus similarly comments on how long it took him to arrive (*palai*, 1112).

The ageing slave refuses to concede that he gave the baby Oedipus to the Corinthian messenger until he is threatened with the torture to which all slaves were subject at the discretion of the lawcourts of Athens. Indeed, slave evidence was regarded as inadmissible unless extracted under torture (Antiphon, *Tetralogies* 1.3.5).[51] Lying, seen as unbecoming to the free citizen (*Trach.* 453–4), was regarded as 'natural' in the slave. Oedipus first threatens the old man with pain (1152), and then actually orders his men to twist his arms behind his back, in preparation for torture (1154). Finally the old man breaks, and the truth is extracted from him. Thus perhaps the most famous *anagnōrisis* (recognition) in tragedy, Oedipus'

---

added that the play seems subsequently (esp. 961–82) to be critical of Alcmena's capacity for making sound ethical judgements!

[49] De Jong (1991) 118 and n. 5.

[50] Not only in tragedy: for evidence that slaves in reality had access to extensive information about their masters' families, see Hunter (1994), especially 70–89.

[51] DuBois (1991) 35–8; Hunter (1994) 89–95.

recognition of himself, is the direct result of the extorted testimony of a slave.

Critics have objected to so much dangerous knowledge residing in a single man, in particular finding it implausible that the same slave who was asked to expose the baby survived to be the only living witness of Laius' murder. 'This Theban is the man who took the infant Oedipus to "trackless Cithaeron", who witnessed the murder in the pass, who saw Oedipus married to Jocasta. In other words, astonishingly, wildly improbably, he has been keeping company with Oedipus all of Oedipus' life.'[52] But such criticisms fail to take into account the social structures which meant that slaves, especially those regarded as particularly trustworthy through having been born into the house, must often have known more about their masters and their families than their masters can have known themselves. Is it really so unlikely that a man sufficiently trusted by Jocasta to have been entrusted by her with the exposure of the infant would also have been selected to accompany Laius on his mission to Delphi? The invention of this slave-character in Sophocles' Oedipus the King expresses at an aesthetic level the ancient awareness that the dehumanised slaves who lived with the free, and were privy to their secrets, sometimes had knowledge with literally lethal potential. He also exemplifies the disastrous results of independent decision-making by slaves: if he had carried out his original order to expose the baby, the deaths of Laius and Jocasta, the incest, and the blinding of Oedipus, would all have been avoided.

An important category of tragic slave is comprised by the old female nurses and their male counterparts (paidagōgoi), who were appointed to care for aristocrats in their childhood, and remained with them in their maturity. In reality such figures must have known much about the households which they served, and the playwrights exploited this knowledge for dramatic purposes: in the opening scene of Euripides' Medea a nurse and a paidagōgos between them provide all the background information required by the audience.

The paidagōgos, appointed by a child's kurios, was in reality the kurios' agent in his absence, 'an instantiation of his interest and an extension of his authority'.[53] In the two Electra tragedies by Sophocles and Euripides, the paidagōgos is indeed a symbolic extension of the authority of the master who had appointed him, even beyond the grave. In Sophocles' version Electra significantly wants to call Orestes' paidagōgos 'father' (1361), when in reality even elderly male slaves could be insultingly addressed as 'boy' (pai).[54] This

[52] Cameron (1968) 22.   [53] Golden (1990) 62.
[54] See Golden (1985) 91–104. At Aesch. Cho. 653 Clytemnestra's doorman is addressed as 'boy'.

slave is an authoritative figure obsessed with avenging Agamemnon's death. He urges on the two siblings to matricide, rebukes them for time-wasting, and facilitates the murder by his brilliant 'false' messenger-speech, reporting the fictional death of Orestes. Euripides, typically, takes convention to extremes: his *paidagōgos* had reared not only Orestes, but also Agamemnon.[55] Thus his authority stretches far back into the past; he is the appointee of Atreus himself.

Nurses and *paidagōgoi*, like other slaves, exhibit a profound 'vertical' allegiance to the households they serve, rather than to others of their class:[56] two Euripidean slaves, the nurse in *Medea* (54–5) and the second messenger in *Bacchae* (1027–8), express emotional attachment to their owners, saying that good slaves suffer along with their masters' fate. Even Orestes' old nurse Cilissa in *Libation-Bearers*, while hating Clytemnestra and Aegisthus, remains loyal to the household as represented by Agamemnon's memory and Orestes.

The influence of nurses and *paidagōgoi*, like the knowledge of Oedipus' Theban shepherd, can prove lethal. A driving force behind the plot of Euripides' *Ion* is cultural anxiety about the influence of slaves upon free members of the household, in particular women. If there is a crime in this tragedy it is the attempted murder of Ion, whom Creusa, at the time she agrees to it, believes to be an illegitimate child of her husband Xuthus.

Predictably, the dangerous dialogue between the slave and the woman occurs in the emphasised physical absence of her husband: Xuthus, who thinks he has discovered a long-lost son, has left to sacrifice on the 'twin peaks' of the mountain (749, 1122–7). Creusa now enters, with her old *paidagōgos*, long ago appointed by her father (725–7); the scene can be read as implying an unhealthy degree of cross-class intimacy. For Creusa insists that he is her friend although she is his mistress (730–4), helps him physically as he limps onto the stage (739–45), and affectionately hails the chorus as her 'slave-companions' in her weaving (747–8).

The plotting scene which ensues enacts the influence which trusted household slaves might be imagined by absent *kurioi* to wield over their mistresses. If women's deliberative capacity was thought by Aristotle to be 'inoperative', it was not present at all in natural slaves (*Pol.* 1 1260a12–13). The upshot of the scene, in which the two characters who both require the guidance of a free male are left to their own devices, is that the slave leaves to slip poison into Ion's drinking-cup. But it is important to see how the scene evolves psychologically. The Chorus transmits the necessary information (as slaves must often have had to do, 774–807). But it is the *paidagōgos*

[55] Bassi (1942–3) 80–7.   [56] Synodinou (1977) 62.

who suggests that Xuthus is planning to eject Creusa from her ancestral home in the house of Erechtheus (808–11). Xuthus, the slave suggests, has been breeding behind Creusa's back and intends to pass on her inheritance to his illegitimate child. He tells her to kill both Xuthus and Ion, and volunteers to stab Ion himself (844–56).

Creusa ignores the talk of murder, and spends over a hundred lines lyrically lamenting her fate (859–973). Once again the slave, who is almost preternaturally solicitous about the fate of the royal house, urges her to take action. Creusa does find the moral strength to withstand most of his suggestions. She wisely refuses to burn down Apollo's temple or to kill Xuthus (975, 977). But on the question of Ion's life she yields and provides the poison herself. It cannot, however, be sufficiently stressed that it was the slave who raised the question of murder. He encounters a slave's fate for his pains: he is tortured to extract Creusa's name (1214). But the plotting scene emanates from a social anxiety about the lethal effect of manipulative slaves on susceptible women lacking the judgement of a free male to steer their own.

In Euripides' *Hippolytus* the crisis is caused by a similar interaction between a slave with a dangerous degree of initiative and a psychically frail mistress, in the absence of her husband. The precise point, in human terms, at which the lethal machinery of this plot is set in motion, is when Phaedra breaks silence and confides her passion for her stepson to her nurse. For it would have damaged none but herself had it remained unspoken; Phaedra has, in fact, been in love with Hippolytus since before she and Theseus were required to leave Athens (24–40). Aphrodite says in the prologue that Phaedra has since been suffering the goads of *erōs* in silence, and adds the intriguing detail, the significance of which will only later become apparent, that 'not one of the household servants knows of her affliction' (40).

Theseus is away from Trozen: the nurse tells the anxious chorus that 'he happens to be out of town (*ekdēmos*), away from this land' (281). When he arrives it is clear that he has been on a pilgrimage to a cult centre or oracle (792, 806–7). It has been argued that Theseus' absence, and the reason for it, were invented for the present play, and that the author's motive was purely dramaturgical: it was to provide an 'effective contrast … with the disaster which greets him'.[57] But this is to overlook the ideological potency of the plot-pattern by which the *kurios* must be physically absent while the meddling slave and the emotionally susceptible mistress can jointly engender catastrophe.

[57] Barrett (1964) 313–14. In the Sophoclean version Theseus was in Hades, believed dead.

The nurse is solicitous towards Phaedra: she brought her up (698). She shares with the *paidagōgos* in *Ion* a loyal devotion to her mistress's position in the household, including Phaedra's two sons. Her emotional onslaught opens with the claim that Phaedra's death would betray them by allowing Hippolytus (an older son of Theseus by an Amazon) to share their patrimony (304–10). She applies more pressure (implying that the audience believed that slaves generally wanted access to their superiors' secrets (328)), and beseeches Phaedra with a formal act of supplication (310–33).[58] She persists despite the protests of her mistress, until Phaedra admits that she is in love. But at the climactic moment when Hippolytus is named as the object of her desire, it is, significantly, the nurse and not Phaedra who utters the name (352).

Uniquely for one of such low social status, the nurse is given the second largest part in the play. Her sinister instigation of the action on the human level would have been underscored in the likely event that she was played by the same actor who played Aphrodite, who instigates it on the superhuman level. The nurse is also dangerously well-educated. In the persuasive speech designed to make Phaedra act on her desire, the nurse marshals arguments from moral philosophy (pragmatism and expediency), and also from cosmogonic theory (447–50). Euripides ironically makes her cite mythical examples of the effects of *erōs* on the gods, whilst simultaneously signalling that such knowledge requires a full-time education in the liberal arts: such tales, she says, are known by those who study paintings and spend all their time with the muses (451–3).

To dangerous rhetorical proficiency the nurse adds excessive initiative. In direct disobedience to Phaedra, she decides to intervene with Hippolytus. An ideological premise of the tragic plot is that when slaves act independently as moral agents the results can be catastrophic. The moral boundary between slave and free is further underscored by the contrast between the nurse's breaking of her word to Phaedra, and Hippolytus' refusal to break the vow of silence imposed upon him by the nurse (657–60), even when his father curses him. Phaedra articulates the underlying premise of the first half of the play by excoriating the nurse for her untrustworthiness and meddling (712–14), before she departs to commit suicide.

The hazards involved in talking to servants, signalled so conspicuously in Aphrodite's prologue, are made quite explicit in Hippolytus' great invective. He says that women should be attended not by servants but by voiceless beasts, for it is communication between licentious women and their

---

[58] On the social ritual of formal supplication in tragedy and elsewhere, see Gould (1973) 74–103.

attendants which brings unchastity into the world (65–8).[59] What Hippolytus does not, however, articulate is the overall impression made on those
who have watched the foregoing scenes, that trusted slaves can manipulate
vulnerable women, and, given a little knowledge, manipulate them into
taking positions at which they would never have arrived alone: it is clear
from the fragments of Euripides' *Stheneboea*, another notorious tragedy
where an older woman developed a passion for a young man (in this case
her husband's guest), that it was not Stheneboea but her nurse who made
the approaches to the young Bellerophon.[60] It is no accident that the
'boorish man' amongst Theophrastus' *Characters* is recognisable by his
habit of confiding matters of utmost importance to his slaves while
distrusting his own friends and family (4.2): Aristotle recommends that
children, whose moral capacities he regards as undeveloped, 'spend very
little time in the company of slaves' (*Pol.* VII 1336a39–40).

POLYPHONY

The appreciation of the ideological potency of tragic plot-patterns, while an
important corrective to the romantic vision of democratic Athens and her
sublime drama, cannot, however, do full justice to the ideological complexity insinuated by the dramatic form itself. It has been one aim of this
chapter to demonstrate by an examination of some recurring plot-patterns
that, taken as a whole, tragedy legitimises the value-system necessary to the
glorification of Athens and the subordination of the slaves, women, and
other non-citizens who constituted the majority of her inhabitants. But it is
also important to the understanding of the 'sociology' of the plays to
remember that the polyphonic tragic form, which gives voice to characters
from all such groups, challenges the very notions which it simultaneously
legitimises. Some of the most thrilling moments in Athenian tragedy are
created when women and slaves are permitted, however briefly, to challenge
the hegemonic value-system, and tell us how it felt.

The multivocal form of tragedy, which allows diverse characters to speak
(and, more importantly, to disagree with each other), reflects the contemporary development of rhetoric in democratic Athens, itself a product of the
increased importance under the democracy of public debate in the assembly
and the lawcourts (see Ch. 6 below). Students of rhetoric were trained to
think antithetically, to be able to counter any one point of view or argument

[59] In Lysias' first oration the speaker, whose wife allegedly committed adultery, constructs his
narrative throughout so as to appeal to a similar assumption that transgressive wives
collaborate with their 'go-between' slaves.

[60] Webster (1967) 82.

with a speech in opposition. Some rhetorical exercises survive, including Gorgias' famous speech in defence of Helen of Troy, and Antiphon's *Tetralogies*, sets of two speeches in prosecution and two in defence in a hypothetical trial. Certainly by the second half of the fifth century the audiences of tragedy, like those of Shakespeare's day,[61] were trained to appreciate both arguments and counter-arguments and the defence of even seemingly indefensible positions and unconventional points of view. Their mindset, their imagination, was inherently dialogic. A character in a lost Euripidean play said, 'if one were good at speaking one could have a competition between two arguments in every case' (fr. 189 N²).

In later antiquity Plutarch complains that tragedy represented women as clever rhetoricians (*De Aud. Poet.* 28a), and the Christian writer Origen said that Euripides was mocked in comedy because he inappropriately made 'barbarian women and slaves' articulate philosophical opinions (*Contra Celsum* 7.36.34–6). The tragic actor Theodorus refused to allow any other actor to appear on stage before him because, he said, 'an audience always takes kindly to the first voice that meets their ears' (Aristot. *Pol.* VII 1336b27–31). This statement applies as much to the character being assumed as to the actor himself. It is striking, therefore, how often the audience's sympathies are first enlisted by female or servile characters, who appear before anyone else: Antigone, Helen, and Andromache open their name-plays, as Deianeira does *Women of Trachis*, and the prologue spoken by a low-class character seems to have been a regular feature (e.g. *Agamemnon* and *Medea*). And some classical Athenians were already aware of tragedy's dangerously radical potential for giving voice, and a sympathetic hearing, to the citizen's subordinates.

In tragedy, for example, even the most virtuous of women (e.g. Andromache) are often rebuked for speaking too freely and too antagonistically to men (Eur. *Andr.* 364–5). In Plato's *Republic* Socrates demonstrates that the main difference between drama and other kinds of poetry is that it consists entirely of speeches in the first person (that is in direct *mimēsis* or 'imitation' of characters), to the exclusion of narrative in the authorial voice. He says that the direct impersonation of 'inferiors' such as women and slaves, which drama entails, is profoundly harmful morally (III 394b3–e5); he is just as concerned about the ethical damage caused by the representation of 'womanish' emotions in tragedy (10.605c10–e6).

Tragedy consists of polyphony and antiphony. No genre is so definitively dialogic, nor conceals the authorial persona to such an extreme degree. Interestingly, *mythical* poets and bards figured much more as characters

---

[61] Altman (1978).

than the extant plays would lead us to suppose. Orpheus was a central character in Aeschylus' lost *Bassarids*; both Aeschylus and Sophocles composed plays named *Thamyris* dramatising the singing competition between this bard and the muses; Euripides' *Hypsipyle* portrayed the citharode Euneus, who founded an Athenian clan of musicians;[62] his *Antiope* featured a debate between Zethus and his lyre-playing brother Amphion about the benefits which poets confer on a community.[63] Yet the authorial voice of the tragic poet himself is more elusive in this genre than in any other ancient literary form, including comedy. The views of the speaking characters are thus subjected to no controlling moral evaluation, except by other characters and by the audience.

Even the laudatory tone with which democracy and Athens are usually discussed in tragedy is occasionally challenged. The polyphonic form even allows a Theban herald, in Euripides' *Suppliant Women*, to provide a critique of democratic constitutions, pointing out that they can lead to rule by an ignorant mob (410–25). In Euripides' *Medea* the whole plot-type by which non-Athenian heroic figures could bring honour to Athens is subverted by the addition to their ranks of Medea, the murderous barbarian sorceress; she ends the play, unpunished and unrepentant, flying off on the chariot of the Sun to Athens, 'to live with Aegeus son of Pandion' (1385). And the laudatory effect of the famous choral panegyric of Athens (824–45) is undercut by its occurrence after the scene in which Medea has dominated him completely.

Perhaps the best example is embodied in the figure of Demophon in Euripides' *Children of Heracles*. On a superficial reading the first half of the play seems to follow the standard lines of the 'patriotic' tragedies about Athens' own mythical past. The children of the deceased Heracles, persecuted by the Argive king Eurystheus, have arrived at the temple of Zeus (god of suppliants) in the Attic district of Marathon, a particularly patriotic site for the Athenians ever since the Persian wars. The suppliants are received by the old men of Marathon with politeness, pity, and pledges of protection. The play abounds in praise of Athenian democratic institutions, especially the rights to free speech, impartial judgements in the courts, and to sanctuary. Yet ambiguities suggest that in this play the Athenian king Demophon is not quite the exemplar of virtue the audience might have become accustomed to expect in an Athenian ruler in tragedy; he is made to threaten the herald Copreus with violence, an act of great impiety, as he is reminded (270–1). It is also implied that he is too susceptible to the advice of oracle-tellers (a group who were often the target of tragic criticism), when

<hr/>

[62] Plathhy (1985) 79. [63] Webster (1967) 207–8.

he heeds their admonition barbarically to sacrifice a high-born female virgin (399–409).[64]

Throughout the tragic corpus speakers disrupt the dominant ideological assumptions about women. Euripides even seems to have been aware that much of the blame for the bad reputation of women in myth must be laid at the feet of the male poets who had created them (*Med.* 420–30). His *Medea* includes a supremely negative portrait of a vituperative, vindictive, and murderous female, which could only be the product of a patriarchal society.[65] Yet by giving Medea a voice, and *imagining* the emotions of an abandoned wife, it allows her to deliver the most remarkable account of the second-class status of women to be found in ancient literature (214–66). She complains about the dowry system, about men's control over women's bodies, and about wives' lonely isolation in the home; she even asserts that giving birth to a single child is worse than standing three times in the front line of battle! This speech's explosive political potential caused it to be recited at meetings in Edwardian London in support of women's suffrage.[66]

Women's perspective on marriage was voiced in other plays: besides Medea's speech, the most striking example is Procne's denunciation of women's experience of marriage in Sophocles' famous *Tereus*. In this play Procne's husband had raped and mutilated her sister. Procne complains on behalf of women (fr. 583 Radt):[67]

> ... when we reach puberty and can understand, we are thrust out and sold, away from our ancestral gods and from our parents. Some go to strange men's houses, others to foreigners, some to joyless houses, some to hostile. And all this, once the first night has yoked us to our husband, we are forced to praise, and say that all is well.

Moreover, a reading sensitive to tragedy's portrayal of relations between men and women sees signs that male disrespect towards women in the sphere of the household met the same disapproval in the theatre as in reality. For however pervasive the sexual double standard in tragedy, as in Athenian life, which allowed men multiple sexual partners while severely

---

[64] Thereafter this fascinating play continues to confound expectations, as it develops from a suppliant drama into a revenge tragedy: Alcmena, Heracles' mother, vindictively demands the brutal execution of Eurystheus. His initial role as hostile invader of Attica then becomes transformed into its opposite: an oracle predicts that his grave will offer protection to Athens against the (Peloponnesian) descendants of Heracles, much as Orestes, Oedipus, and Heracles in other plays (discussed above) become allies of the city. But the textual problems which the play presents, especially the probable gaps after lines 629 and 1052 (concisely discussed by Wilkins (1993) xxvii–xxxi), make it difficult to draw conclusions about the overall presentation of Athens.

[65] See Rabinowitz (1993) 125–54.   [66] Murray (1913) 82.

[67] Translation taken from Lefkowitz and Fant (1992) 12–13.

punishing female adultery,[68] there is an immanent rule discernible in the genre by which the instalment of a concubine *in the marital home* is strictly censured. Every man who attempts it in tragedy suffers death shortly thereafter: Aeschylus' Agamemnon, who brings back Cassandra from Troy, Heracles in Sophocles' *Women of Trachis*, who does much the same with Iole, and Neoptolemus in Euripides' *Andromache*, who has outraged his wife by introducing Andromache to his marital home. As Orestes remarks in that play, it is a bad thing for a man to have two women he shares a bed with (*lechē*, 909); in the world of Greek tragedy it is apparently not only bad, but fatal. The ideology underlying this story pattern is a refraction through a mythical and poetic prism of the same culturally endorsed notion which leads the orator Apollodorus to praise Lysias for having refrained from bringing his girlfriends home out of respect for his wife and old mother ([Dem.] 59.2).

The recurring figure of the dignified priestess (especially those of Apollo at Delphi in *Eumenides* and *Ion*, and the high-minded Theonoe of Euripides' *Helen*) also reflects the importance of the one sphere in which women could achieve public authority in the city-state: it was women's central role in oracles and ritual to which Melanippe appealed in her famous defence of women in Euripides' lost *Melanippe Captive* (Eur. fr. 499 N²):[69]

> Men's criticism of women is worthless twanging of a bowstring and evil talk. Women are better than men, as I will show ... Consider their role in religion, for that, in my opinion, comes first. We women play the most important part, because women prophesy the will of Zeus in the oracles of Phoebus. And at the holy site of Dodona near the sacred oak, females convey the will of Zeus to inquirers from Greece. As for the sacred rituals for the Fates and the nameless Ones [i.e. the Erinyes], all these would not be holy if performed by men, but prosper in women's hands. In this way women have a rightful share in the service of the gods. Why is it, then, that women must have a bad reputation?

The speeches of Medea, Procne, and Melanippe were spoken by expert (male) actors in a poetic language enhanced by highly wrought rhetoric and elevated diction. Tragedy's medium of communication operates at a more heightened level than everyday speech, actually permitting Medea and the others to elicit responses beyond those achievable by mere communication of content.[70] Yet this same heightened language is shared by all the characters, whatever their ethnicity, gender, or class; there is little attempt

---

[68] See Cohen (1991).   [69] Translation from Lefkowitz and Fant (1992) 14.
[70] Coward and Ellis (1977) 79.

to differentiate even the speech of barbarians.[71] Tragic language is a democratic property owned collectively by all who use it; in the tragic theatre individuals whose ethnicity, gender, or status would absolutely debar them from public debate in democratic Athens can address the massed Athenian citizenry. It is clear, then, that only a bifurcated reading, sensitive both to latent ideological import and its patent verbalised subversion, can hope to do justice to texts of such complexity.

By giving voice to persons of lower social status than their aristocratic masters, tragedy also offers some remarkable, imaginative representations of the perspectives of the lower classes. The military life, and the ordinary soldier's personal experience of war, recur as topics of discussion. The experience may be displaced into the rhetoric of an upper-class figure: Peleus, for example, gives a fascinating speech in opposition to the militaristic Menelaus of *Andromache*. Despite Peleus' own personal high status the speech permits the audience to hear a grievance which must often have been felt by the ordinary citizen, that the glory for victory in battle goes always to the general and never to the thousands of soldiers who laboured under his command (693–8). Sometimes the lower-class characters themselves voice their own perspective on the leaders. The military chorus of the *Rhesus* attributed to Euripides (but see Ch. 9) criticise their leader Hector's decision, and state that they do not approve of generals who exercise power harshly and put their men in danger (132). In the same play there is a debate between Hector and a shepherd on the intellectual capacities of country people. Hector is contemptuous of the humble shepherd and his like (266–70), but the shepherd turns out to be both an acute observer of military matters and bilingual (284–316). And the herald in *Agamemnon* gives a unique account of what life was like for the common soldier in antiquity: the miserable quarters and inadequate bedding, the sensations of being rained on and infested with vermin, the unendurable cold of winter and the searing heat of summer-time (555–66).

Tragedy's fondness for portraying enslaved former aristocrats allows it to express some fascinating 'worm's-eye' views of slavery. The captive heroine of Euripides' *Andromache*, attacked by her mistress, laments that as a slave she cannot hope for a fair hearing, and that people hate to be worsted in argument by their social inferiors (186–90). A messenger, impressed by the virtues demonstrated by the sons of the (temporarily) captive Melanippe, remarks that even the children of slaves can prove nobler than free men with empty reputations (Eur. fr. 495 N², 41–3). Occasionally even slaves

---

[71] Although see Hall (1996) 40–1, for some possible exceptions. In comedy there was much greater exploitation of foreign accents: Hall (1989a) 117–21.

from birth are allowed to express something of their life experience. Menelaus' loyal slave in *Helen* proudly declares (728–31), 'Even though I was born to serve, I would like to be regarded as a noble slave. I may not have the title of a free man, but I have his mind.' Later in the play a slave of Theoclymenus offers to die instead of the priestess Theonoe, thus displaying virtues singularly lacking in his master; with heavy irony, Euripides makes him say that it is a great honour for 'noble slaves' to die on behalf of their masters (1640–1). And Cilissa, the nurse in *Libation-Bearers*, speaks with remarkable freshness across the centuries about the labour and responsibilities involved in child-care: her speech articulates the closest thing to an authentic first-hand account of the experiences of a servile nurse to survive from antiquity. The audience hears how as a baby Orestes disturbed her sleep with his urgent cries; she remembers his hunger, thirst, and even his 'call of nature', which often meant that she had to launder his linen (749–62). Unusually, Cilissa also expresses dislike for her mistress, a truly 'suppressed' voice released by the imaginative capacities of drama, for the grumbles of the real discontented slave women of Athens are for ever silent.[72]

The manner in which aristocrats treat their subordinates is an important means by which their characters are 'tested' in tragedy. Menelaus' clichés about the importance of the free not tolerating insolence from slaves in *Andromache* (433–4) are subverted by his own brutal cynicism. The central function of the guard in *Antigone*, besides bringing the news of the two burials of Polyneices, is to elicit responses from Creon suggesting his heavy-handedness and impetuosity. The guard fears that as simply a bringer of bad news he may be punished for a crime of which he is innocent (228), and his fear turns out to be justified: Creon threatens him with torture unless he and his fellow guards find the culprit. They are all to be strung up alive (308–9). The herdsman who delivers the first speech in *Bacchae* serves a similar function with respect to Pentheus' tyrannical tendencies. He asks Pentheus whether he can speak freely, or whether he should exercise caution, since he fears Pentheus' anger and royal power (670–1). Similar concern is expressed by the old female porter in Euripides' *Helen*, who is terrified to bring bad news to her savage master Theoclymenus (481–2).

CONCLUSION: TRAGEDY AND DEMOCRACY

It is customary in the late twentieth century to upbraid the ancient Athenian democracy for being far from democratic in the modern sense of the word.

---

[72] It is a realistic touch that Cilissa's name denotes her place of origin, Cilicia, which was a principal source of real slaves in fifth-century Athens.

Women, slaves, and foreigners were denied political power and silenced in the public discourse of Athens. The ideas and values which were necessary to the system's perpetuation permeated the tragic genre at every level: in just a few examples, we have seen how Athenian tragedy consistently manipulated myth to authorise Athens' claim to hegemony over other cities, and to provide enacted poetic justifications for the control of women by men and for the subordination of slaves. And yet the multivocal form of these documents of the collective Athenian imagination overleaps those narrowly restricted notions of democracy and right to free speech which mark our documents of Athenian reality, such as historiography and oratory.

Athenian tragedy is thus a supreme instantiation of what Marxists call art's 'utopian tendency'; this expression denotes art's potential for and inclination towards transcending in fictive unreality the social limitations and historical conditions of its own production.[73] To put it more simply: Greek tragedy does its thinking in a form which is vastly more politically advanced than the society which produced Greek tragedy. The human imagination has always been capable of creating egalitarian models of society even when they are inconceivable in practice, such as the communistic utopias of some 'golden age' myths; in tragedy the Athenians created a public dialogue marked by an egalitarian *form* beyond their imagination in actuality. Tragedy's multivocal form and socially heterogeneous casts suggest an implicit egalitarian vision whose implementation in the actual society which produced it was absolutely inconceivable.[74] Tragedy postulates in imagination a world rarely even hoped for in reality until very recently. It is a world which is 'democratic' in something akin to the modern, Western sense; it is a world in which characters of diverse ethnicity, gender, and status all have the same right to express their opinions and the same verbal ability with which to exercise that right.

Aristophanes, who was certainly aware that tragedy permitted publicly silenced voices to be publicly released, seems to have been prophetically aware of our more modern sense of the term 'democratic'; he gives his Euripides an extraordinary claim in his contest with Aeschylus in *Frogs*. Euripides says that he has made tragedy 'democratic' (*dēmokratikon*), precisely by keeping his women and slaves, young girls and crones, talking alongside 'the master of the house' (949–52).[75]

Although the Aristophanic Euripides here misrepresents Aeschylus and Sophocles in implying that it was he who first gave important tragic roles to women and slaves, this instance of the term 'democratic' deserves close

---

[73] On the 'utopian' tendency of art and its capacity for imaginative transcendence of social reality, see Jameson (1981) 290–1; Rose (1992) 36–42; Ryan (1989).

[74] Ryan (1989) 17.   [75] On this passage see also di Benedetto (1971) 213.

attention. Its inclusive meaning, extending to women and slaves, is unparalleled in Athenian discourse; the 'people' (*dēmos*) who exercised power (*kratos*) is elsewhere always exclusively defined as the collective male citizenry of the polis. But the context of the inclusive use is of course a discussion of *tragedy*. Despite the genre's prevalent authorisation of the social status quo, it does give voice to those debarred by their gender or class from what *we* would call their 'democratic right' to free speech. It grants them temporarily in imagination the 'equality in the right to public speaking' (*isēgoria*) and the freedom to express opinion (*parrhēsia*) in reality enjoyed solely by citizen males.

Athenian tragedy's claim to having been a truly democratic art-form is therefore, paradoxically, far greater than the claim to democracy of the Athenian state itself. The tension, even contradiction, between tragedy's egalitarian form and the dominantly hierarchical world-view of its content is the basis of its transhistorical vitality: it is certainly an important reason why it is proving so susceptible to constant political reinterpretation in the theatres of the modern world (see Ch. 11 below).

BIBLIOGRAPHICAL NOTE

For the Athenian and Athenocentric aspects of tragedy see Loraux (1993); Goldhill (1986) ch. 3; Hall (1989a) chs. 2–4; M. Whitlock-Blundell, 'The ideal of Athens in *Oedipus at Colonus*', in Sommerstein et al. (1993) 287–306.

The more important contributions to the study of gender issues in tragedy include Foley (1981) 127–68; Zeitlin (1984) 149–84, and (1990) 63–96. See also des Bouvrie (1990); Just (1989); Rehm (1994).

On issues of social class in tragedy generally there are important insights in di Benedetto (1971), Citti (1978), and Rose (1992) chs. 4–5. Slavery in tragedy has not prompted much work, except on Euripides, for whom see Synodinou (1977), and Kuch (1974).

6

SIMON GOLDHILL

The language of tragedy: rhetoric and communication

In Plato's *Republic*, when Socrates is describing the imperviousness to fear of the Guardians of his new Republic, he catches himself using rather grand metaphorical terms, and he immediately rebukes himself for speaking *tragikōs*, 'tragically', 'like a tragic character' (413b4). Demosthenes, the great orator, dismisses the rhetoric of Aeschines, his opponent, as bombast with the verb *tragōidein*, 'to play in a tragedy' (which is also a dig at his former career as an actor) (18.13; 19.189). The comic playwright Aristophanes, who repeatedly parodies the language of tragedy, has a character in his play *Peace* wonder why the hero didn't fly on Pegasus rather than a dung-beetle, and thus appear *tragikōteros*, 'more tragic', 'more like a tragic hero' (136). Already, in the classical polis, 'the tragic' has become synonymous with a certain grandeur of expression, high-flown periphrasis and even heroic posturing. Tragedy is – and was perceived to be – made up of a particular register of language: there is a style and vocabulary proper to the genre. So how is the language of tragedy to be characterised? There are several types of answer that can be given to this question, that take us far beyond generalisations about the grand and the heroic. What is more, the tragic texts themselves are deeply concerned with how language is (to be) used. This chapter will explore the questions of tragic language.

The first type of answer that can be developed is a formal one. One basic articulation of tragedy is the difference between scenes and choral odes. The scenes are conventionally divided into *rhēseis* and stichomythia. A *rhēsis* (plural *rhēseis*) is a set speech of varying length (rarely more than a hundred lines) in which a figure offers an exposition of his or her position, or a description of an event, or a reflection on events. Stichomythia is the rapid exchange of mostly single lines between two or more characters. Often the formal exchange of *rhēseis* breaks down into violent argument in stichomythia, and such a scene is known as an *agōn* (plural *agōnes*), 'contest'. Both *rhēsis* and stichomythia are almost invariably written in the iambic metre, which Aristotle calls the 'closest to human speech'; and in Attic dialect, that is, in the tongue of its audience, although, as we will see, with much heightening of expression. The choral odes, generally termed *stasima* (singular: *stasimon*), are strikingly different. First, they are sung by a group, not spoken by an individual, and they are accompanied by music and dancing. There is a large variety of metres, which can be associated with particular strong feelings or particular actions. (So, for example, the chorus' first entrance singing what is known as a *parodos*, or 'entrance song', is repeatedly written in 'marching anapaests', a rhythm fitted to the formal action of the chorus' entrance.) A *stasimon* is usually made up of one or more pairs of stanzas which have the same metrical form, and presumably would have had similarly corresponding music and dance. These are known as *strophē* and *antistrophē* (literally 'turn' and 'counterturn', dancing terms). The patterning of pairs of *strophē* and *antistrophē* may be preceded by an introduction and followed by an epode, a free-standing stanza. The language of the choral odes is not merely dense, heightened lyric poetry, but also is largely in a version – far from thorough-going – of Doric dialect. Doric is traditionally used for choral lyric throughout Greece (even in Attic-speaking regions like Athens). But it remains hard to judge exactly what the effect of such elements of Doric dialect would have been on an Athenian audience. In comedy, characters with strange accents and dialects are mocked; but the convention of choral lyric being composed in Doric is deeply institutionalised. Perhaps the Doric tones add to a Panhellenic grandeur of tragedy. Perhaps the special authority of the chorus in drama is reinforced by this dialectal shift which, along with other elements, distinguishes the choral odes from the utterances of the characters on stage.

The articulation of scene and choral ode and the resultant interplay of collective, sung lyric and individual, spoken exposition are basic to tragedy and its narrative technique, but there are many variations of form and interaction. For example, individual figures may perform solo lyrics, the chorus leader often contributes to spoken scenes, lyric exchanges take place between chorus and characters (cf. Ch. 7, pp. 157–61). It is always worth remembering that particularly in translation the fundamental shifts of dialect, verse rhythm, and speech and song, and collective and individual voices, are often very hard to appreciate – and to represent in English.

There is a second type of formal description of tragic language that can be developed, however. For the language of tragedy also incorporates many elements of the language of the city, as in its performance before the city it itself becomes a recognisable and key strand of public discourse. The language of tragedy is public, democratic, male talk (but cf. Ch. 5, pp. 118–24): that is, the language of tragedy is in all senses of the term *political*.

I want to trace here four elements that make particularly important contributions to the verbal texture of tragedy. The first is the tradition of literary language, and pre-eminently Homer. Homer holds a privileged place in Athenian cultural life. His epic poems, the *Iliad* and the *Odyssey*, played an integral role in the education, institutions and ideology of the polis. They were the main teaching texts in schools, and, like the bible in Victorian Britain, provided a resource of normative images of the world and ways to relate to the world that informed all aspects of Athenian culture. Homer's poetry was recited by bards or rhapsodes, and by less professional performers, not only at a host of social events – a figure in a Xenophon dialogue (*Symposium* 3.6) says he listens to a Homer recital every day – but also at grand civic occasions such as the festival of the Panathenaea, where the epics were recited in full before an audience of the polis by bards who were competing for prizes for their skills in recital.[1] Many of the stories of Greek tragedy are taken from Homer and the epic cycle (other epic poems often circulating under the name of Homer but already, in the fifth century, thought not to be by the author of the *Iliad* and the *Odyssey*). Aeschylus' *Oresteia*, for example, tells the story of Orestes' regaining of his property and proper place, a story which is rehearsed some dozen times in the *Odyssey*, and it would be hard indeed to appreciate the *Oresteia*'s narrative without seeing how it relates to and rewrites Homer's account.[2] The language of Homer is a particular literary construct that developed over many years of poetic performance, but seems to have been largely fixed by the seventh century BC – no one ever *spoke* 'Homeric Greek'. Its depiction of a heroic society, with its elaborate forms of address, intricate rituals, and extensive interactions with the divine, provides a privileged – and grand – vocabulary for key areas of tragic action. Homeric language also includes words, as well as grammatical and syntactical forms, that were already archaic and obscure to fifth-century audiences (a fragment of Aristophanes' earliest comedy displays a school-room with boys learning their Homeric vocabulary![3]). The willing adoption and adaptation of the epic timbre of Homer is central to the force of tragic language.

The archaic grandeur of Homeric language resounds throughout Greek tragedy. At one level, it can be heard in a very general sense: so, the opening line of *Philoctetes* is 'This is the shore of sea-girt Lemnos ...' 'Sea-girt', *perirrutos*, applied to Crete in Homer (*Od.* 19.173), is a compound adjective of a type very common in Homer and thus too in tragedy, as tragedy establishes its affiliations with the heroic world, and articulates its

---

[1] Plato, *Hipp.* 228b; Diogenes Laertius 1.57. On the Panathenaea's competitions, see Shapiro (1992) and Kyle (1992).

[2] See Goldhill (1986) 147–55.

[3] Fr. 222 K. For pictures of such study, see Beck (1975) esp. 14–15.

new representation of that heroic world. So, here at the beginning of the *Philoctetes*, where the topography of the play is being established in relation to a Homeric geography (as the play itself will traverse a space between Homeric and fifth-century obligations and duties), 'sea-girt' sets up a significant Homeric resonance. Unlike the Lemnos of Homer (and Aeschylus and Euripides) Sophocles' Lemnos is a desert island, and the opening adjective thus establishes a frame of expectation against and with which Sophocles works. At a more specific level, a Homeric inheritance can be heard in the epic associations of particular marked words. So, when Orestes at the beginning of Sophocles' grimmest masterpiece, the *Electra*, hopes he will win *kleos*, 'glory', by killing his mother, his comment inevitably recalls not only the commonly proclaimed purpose of epic heroes to win *kleos*, 'glory', but also the specific associations of Orestes in the *Odyssey*, where he is held up repeatedly to Telemachus, Odysseus' son, as an example of a young prince who has indeed won glory for himself. At a further level, there are precise and often extended literary allusions to the Homeric epics. So Tecmessa in Sophocles' *Ajax* tells Ajax that if he dies and she becomes a slave, 'someone of my masters will say "See the bedfellow of Ajax who was the mightiest of the host; see what menial tasks are hers, who once had such happiness." So someone will say ...' (500–4). This clearly echoes Hector's famous anticipation of his own death in *Iliad* 6, when he imagines his wife as a slave doing menial tasks for her new Greek masters: 'Someone may say ... "This is the wife of Hector who was the best at fighting of the horse-taming Trojans who fought around Troy." So someone will say' (459–62). The linguistic echoes between the representations of the two warriors and their women help reinforce the parallels between the encounter on stage and the epic scene – and stress the complex ways in which Sophocles develops his representation of Ajax through Homeric models of action and ideology.[4] Tragedy re-presents the tales of the Homeric, heroic past for the polis of the present: the way in which epic language constantly informs tragic language is integral to this process of rewriting, and this backward glance is a key element in the grandeur and heroic distance of tragic language.

A second area that provides a major influence on the language of tragedy is ritual and the world of religion. Tragedy is performed as part of a festival of Dionysus, and there has been extensive discussion about to what degree the Dionysiac frame affects the tragedies themselves.[5] But there is no doubt that many aspects of the religious life of the city are reflected on stage.

---

[4] See Knox (1961), criticised by Winnington-Ingram (1980) esp. 304–29, and Goldhill (1986) 155–61.

[5] See e.g. Henrichs (1984); Connor (1989); Winkler and Zeitlin (1990); Seaford (1994); Sourvinou-Inwood (1994); Ch. 2 above.

When Clytemnestra in the *Oresteia* describes how she killed Agamemnon, she says: 'I struck him twice, and with two groans his limbs went slack. I add a third blow as he falls, an offering to chthonian Zeus, the Saviour of corpses' (*Ag.* 1384–6). This moment is horrific because she is representing her three blows and spurts of blood as if they were the three libations that started every symposium or drinking-party at Athens. The libations in that domestic and celebratory ritual are to the Olympian gods, the chthonian gods, and, thirdly, to Zeus the Saviour. Clytemnestra with violently ironic blasphemy has made her third blow a libation to Zeus the Saviour ... of corpses – as she celebrates the spilling of blood rather than wine in the household. The perversion of norms that is this murder of husband and king is expressed as the perversion of the language of religious ritual. Indeed, the language of the rite of sacrifice in particular occurs throughout the *Oresteia* (and other Greek tragedy) to invest killing and other acts of violence with a sense of sacramental transgression.[6]

There are many other rituals which lend both vocabulary and a structure of action to the narrative of tragedy. So, the lengthy opening section of the *Libation-Bearers* is dominated first by Electra's pouring of libations at the tomb of her father, where she wonders what language of prayer to use, and secondly by the *kommos*, a ritual invocation of the dead Agamemnon that combines elements of a mourning song with a conjuration or raising of the spirit of the dead. As the language of sacrifice, ritual pouring and mourning recurs throughout the trilogy, so the action is here stated as ritual – in the progression towards the establishment of cult and the grand ritual procession with which the trilogy ends. The imbuing of the *Oresteia* with the language and performance of ritual is fundamental to its expressions of order and transgression in the polis. So, too, the *Bacchae*'s representation of the death of Pentheus is laced with the imagery both of a ritual initiation into the Dionysiac mysteries, and of other elements of Dionysiac religion: the collective dance of the *thiasos*, the ritual killing and dismemberment of an animal, the consumption of raw flesh.[7] The problem of recognising Dionysus in this drama – its central motif – is articulated in and by overlapping and distorted ritual models of worship of the god. So, the final scene of the *Oedipus at Colonus*, which stages the death of Oedipus and his transformation from blind exile to superhuman hero, a figure honoured with offerings by the Athenians at Colonus, mobilises the powerful religious feelings of hero cult.[8] The language and form of the religious institution are fundamental to the scene's sacral power and mystery.

[6] See e.g. Zeitlin (1965); Foley (1985); Seaford (1994).
[7] See e.g. Foley (1980); Seaford (1981); Segal (1982); Henrichs (1984).
[8] See e.g. Easterling (1967); Burian (1974); Segal (1981) 362–408.

A third major influence on the language of tragedy is the world of the democratic lawcourt and Assembly. In the democratic polis, the lawcourt and Assembly are analogous institutions to the theatre, and these three great public spaces for the performance of *logoi* – speeches, arguments, language as display – strikingly interrelate (cf. Ch. 1). Although there is an evident influence of tragedy and theatre in general on the lawcourt and Assembly, an influence that is beginning to be discussed by critics,[9] I will focus here on the legal and political language that runs through tragedy. The use of legal proceedings and a vote as a means of articulating the key matrix of conflict and choice finds its paradigmatic representation in the trial scene of the *Eumenides*. The *Eumenides*, the only extant tragedy to be set in the centre of Athens, is also the only extant tragedy to stage a courtroom scene (though other tragedies, such as Aeschylus' *Suppliant Women* and Euripides' *Orestes*, report trial or assembly votes, and Aristophanes' comedies, with their carnivalised versions of the institutions of the polis, offer both mock assemblies, such as in the *Acharnians* or *Women in Assembly*, and mock courts such as in the *Wasps*). None the less, the *Eumenides* has a profound influence on later tragedy, not least for the way that its staging of a trial is the final instantiation of a pattern of legal language that runs throughout the trilogy. The first mention of Menelaus as a military leader against Troy calls him an *antidikos*, 'adversary in law', and when Agamemnon returns in triumph, he announces that 'The Gods have heard the parties' pleas though not by spoken word, and in no uncertain fashion have they cast their votes in the urn of blood for the death of men and the destruction of Troy.'[10] The conflict and violent crises of tragedy are seen through the lawcourt's contest. So, Orestes, appearing over the bodies of Clytemnestra and Aegisthus, calls on 'the Sun to bear witness on the day of judgement that justly did I pursue this killing of my mother – Aegisthus' death I count for nothing; he has suffered the adulterer's just penalty, as is the law' (*Cho.* 987–90).[11] The *Oresteia* indeed explores how the role of law in the polis may be a means of resolving conflict, and Athena's establishment of the first court in the *Eumenides* and Orestes' trial – his 'day of judgement' – is prepared for by the constant use of the language of law to express the claims of the violent perpetrators of intrafamilial conflict.

Tragedy, as critics from Aristotle onwards have noted, is a genre fundamentally engaged with the complexities of responsibility, choice, causation and reasoning. The Greek word *aitios* which means 'responsible', 'cause of', also means 'guilty', and the verbal form *aitiasthai* means both 'to find

---

[9] See Eden (1986); Wilson (1991); Hall (1995); Ch. 1 above.
[10] *Ag.* 41; 810–17, analysed in Goldhill (1986) 41–2.
[11] For analysis, see below pp. 138–9.

responsible' and 'to prosecute' or 'charge'. There is in tragedy an integral association at the verbal level between the practice of law and the tragic world of conflicting responsibilities and decision-making. What is more, the political setting of many tragedies often requires its figures to engage in practical, political reasoning. So Creon in his first speech in the *Antigone* outlines an ideological position on duty and obligation in the polis. This position may be unravelled by the course of the drama, but it is also essential for the way it sets the political agenda of the play within a fifth-century framework: when Creon argues that 'no one who is hostile to the state can be treated as a friend of his' and that 'whoever shows good will to the state will be honoured' (187–91, 209–10), his argument finds many echoes in contemporary political rhetoric, where the Thucydidean Pericles famously could declare that 'We give our obedience to those we put in positions of authority, and we obey the laws themselves' (2.37) and that Athenians 'should fix their eyes on Athens ... and fall in love with her' (2.43). If the Homeric texts turn tragedy towards the heroic past, the constant use of the language of contemporary institutions sites tragedy integrally within the polis.

The fourth element, closely related to the third, is one which is more and more influential throughout the fifth century in all aspects of Athenian life, namely, the new interest in the formal training and analysis of speech-making – the art of rhetoric. While persuasive speech and scenes of formal argument are an essential part of the Homeric epics, where an ideal of heroism is to be not only a 'doer of deeds' but also a 'speaker of speeches' (as Phoenix puts it),[12] the democratic polis provides a quite different frame for the performance of winning words. The lawcourts and Assembly offer the citizen routes to political power, and both forums depend on verbal display. A citizen's authority and status are forged in the agonistic institutions of speech-making. Throughout the fifth century there is an increasing professionalisation of training in this process, and central figures in this development are the new intellectuals often, if misleadingly, known collectively as 'the Sophists'.[13] These new intellectuals studied and offered teaching in a vast variety of areas, and engaged in many areas of public life, but in the Athenian popular imagination – and in later Platonic propaganda – it was particularly as teachers of manipulative arguments that the Sophists featured. Protagoras, and by extension all sophists, were notoriously associated with the claim 'to make the weaker argument the stronger'. This outrageous claim is more than a strong or polemical version of the Sophists' well-known delight in paradox and arguments of reversal: it threatens the

---

[12] *Iliad* 9.443. See Martin (1989).
[13] See Kerferd (1981); Classen (1976); Goldhill (1986) 222–43; and the exemplary discussion of Rose (1992) 226–330.

very basis of the city's institutions of power, where the correct evaluation of the strength of competing arguments is the foundation of the democratic legal and political process. The arts of rhetoric were thus an integral but dangerous, even scandalous, element of the city's functioning, and as such were constantly set before the public gaze. Paradigmatically, in Aristophanes' comedy *Clouds*, not only does the hero send his son to a sophist (Socrates) in order to learn the arguments necessary to escape debts, but also the play stages an *agōn* between two figures called – with a strong nod towards Protagoras – 'Stronger Argument' and 'Weaker Argument'. The conclusion inevitably is a comically brilliant triumph for 'Weaker Argument'. The public *awareness* of the changing importance of verbal skills and changing methods of public speech-making establishes the *technē* of rhetoric as a focus of attention in the fifth-century polis.

The language of tragedy reflects this awareness, and, particularly in Euripides' plays, the influence of the formal training in rhetoric is strongly marked. It can be seen at several different levels. There is, first, an explicit vocabulary drawn from the speech-writers' handbook: the point-by-point articulation of argument ('first', 'second', 'my prologue', 'my summation'); the postulation of imaginary counter-cases ('Suppose', 'What if ...'); the declaration of proof and evidence ('I will demonstrate ...', 'It is clear that ...'). Second, there is the adoption of tropes and phraseology from the formal business of public argumentation ('Grant the opportunity of reply ...', 'Unaccustomed as I am to public speaking ...'). Third, and most importantly, *rhēseis* develop structures of argumentation that follow the lines of the new rhetoric. I have already mentioned, for example, the sophistic interest in arguments of paradoxical reversal: this is manipulated with extraordinary *élan* by Euripides. So, to mention a single exemplary case, Cassandra in the *Trojan Women* claims 'I will demonstrate that this my city is more blessed than the Greeks' (365–6). In the prisoner-of-war camp the defeated and raped princess sets out to perform a set piece of display oratory (her verb *deixō* connotes both 'demonstration' as a form of proof and a stylish public performance on a set theme, so-called epideictic rhetoric). And her speech consists precisely in taking a weaker argument and making it seem the stronger, namely, to demonstrate how the besieged and defeated Trojans are better off than the victorious Greeks. She offers an elaborate series of polarities ('The Greeks on the one hand ... The Trojans on the other ...') and paradoxes ('Hector would not have been a famous hero but for the war ...'), typical of the rhetorical style promoted by Gorgias, the leading rhetorician of the latter part of the fifth century.[14]

---

[14] See Croally (1994).

Cassandra is a prophetess who always tells the truth but is never believed, and this scenario is stretched and manipulated by Euripides when he gives Cassandra such a piece of self-conscious rhetorical posturing, such an argument of sophistic reversal. The rhetorical aim – and audience's suspicion – of persuasiveness is given a dizzying twist by this overlap of sophistic argumentation and the specific dynamics of truth and believability associated with Cassandra's prophecies.

The full integration of formal rhetorical argumentation into tragic language is especially evident in the *agōn*, and many examples could be chosen from Sophocles and Euripides in particular. I will look again and in more detail at the *Trojan Women* and its use of technical rhetorical forms at the end of this chapter. For the present, however, it is worth stating (against a commonplace of earlier criticism) that such a turn to the technique of rhetorical training on the tragic stage is not to be viewed as a piece of up-to-date posturing by the playwright seeking to please an audience used to the lawcourts, nor is it a regrettable fall from the purity and passion of a putative Aeschylean *Gesamtkunstwerk* (it is Aeschylus, after all, who stages the first trial). Indeed, the judgement 'mere rhetoric' is always a critical laziness. Rather, tragedians and sophists, who share the title of *sophos*, 'one publicly invested with authority for a special knowledge', share an intellectual environment. It is an environment in which changing attitudes – to the city, to justice, to responsibility, to rationalism itself – are being actively debated, and in which language itself – how to use it, how it functions, its dangers – is a central topic of discussion. Tragic drama and sophistic writing repeatedly turn to similar concerns and vocabulary: the relation of men and gods, of men and men in the city, of norm, transgression, punishment. That some sophists wrote tragedies and that tragedians manipulate sophistic rhetoric is not a casual overlap of interest. It testifies to the active, public debate about man, language and the polis in democratic Athens. Tragedy's use – and often critical exploration – of rhetoric in action is an integral part of its engagement with the public life of the contemporary city.

Tragic language, then, combines contemporary tropes and vocabulary of the public institutions of the city with elements of heroic grandeur which stem both from the epic poetry of the past and the sacral splendour of religious rite. Since tragedy is so concerned with retelling the stories of the past for the contemporary city, this pull between different registers is a highly significant dynamic of the genre. The different registers of tragic language mark the moment of tragedy's production as one of rapid cultural change, a sign and symptom of the fifth-century enlightenment's strongly felt awareness both of extreme social progressiveness and of an ancestral inheritance touched with glory. That tragedy critically explores the public languages it mobilises leads us, however, away from the formal approaches I have been pursuing so far. Indeed, the exploration of the political and mythic discourses of the city is one of the fundamental recurrent thematic focuses of tragedy, and it is with the thematic interest in how language is used that I will be concerned for the rest of this chapter.

I will begin with a well-known and highly influential general argument about the specificity of tragedy's view of language, developed most influentially by the French classicist Jean-Pierre Vernant. I will follow it with three case studies that show that for all the usefulness of the general model it requires considerable care and refinement if each individual play is to be adequately appreciated. Vernant begins from the different registers of language that I have been tracing: 'in the language of the tragic writers there is a multiplicity of different levels more or less distant from one another'.[15] But he adds the important qualification that the same term can 'belong to a number of different semantic fields depending on whether it is part of religious, legal, political or common vocabulary or of a particular sector of one of these'.[16] In the dialogues and debates that make up drama, words can take on opposed or different meanings according to who utters them and how they are deployed. The ambiguity or polysemy of central terms of the city's language is brought out by the way terms are used by different characters in such different and competing ways. Thus, 'the function of words used on stage is not so much to establish communication between the various characters as to indicate the blockage and barriers between them ... to locate the points of conflict'.[17] Indeed, it is an essential function of tragedy to display to its audience the polyvalence of words and the often destructive misunderstandings produced between the figures of the drama: 'the tragic message, when understood, is precisely that there are zones of opacity and incommunicability in the words that men exchange'.[18] One of Vernant's key examples is the word *kratos* (usually translated 'power' or 'force') as it occurs in Aeschylus' *Suppliant Women*:

> The idea of *kratos* can be seen to oscillate between two contrary accepted meanings, unable to settle for the one rather than the other. On the lips of King Pelasgus, *kratos*, associated with *kurios* ['figure of authority'], refers to legitimate authority, the control rightfully exercised by the guardian over whoever is legally dependent upon his power. On the lips of the Danaids [the Suppliant Maidens of the title] the same word, drawn into the semantic field of *bia* ['violence'], refers to brute force, constraint imposed by violence, in its aspect that is most opposed to justice and right.[19]

[15] Vernant & Vidal-Naquet (1988) 42.   [16] Vernant & Vidal-Naquet (1988) 42.
[17] Vernant & Vidal-Naquet (1988) 42.   [18] Vernant & Vidal-Naquet (1988) 43.
[19] Vernant & Vidal-Naquet (1988) 39.

The uncovering of this tension or ambiguity within a central term of political order constitutes a crucial factor in the play's thematic exploration of the nature of authority, its basis in consent, power and/or force (a question of immediate relevance to the emergent democracy). The fissure within the language of political control 'makes it possible to express as an enigma the problematic character of the bases of power exercised over others'.[20] For the audience therefore – the polis as a political entity – the nature of political and social power is opened to consideration through the narrative's articulation of the different and competing significances of the vocabulary, as well as the structures, of authority.

This view of a necessary and integral ambiguity and tension within tragic language has proved extremely stimulating for literary critics working on tragedy, not least because in paying due attention to the difficulties of tragic language it also tries to link such difficulties to the specificities of the fifth-century culture in which (almost all extant) tragedy is produced. (Textual play and cultural impact are not (to be) dissociated.) I want here, however, to investigate how three particular works engage with the 'ambiguities and tensions of language'. These three works (that span almost the whole period of our extant tragedies), Aeschylus' *Oresteia*, Sophocles' *Philoctetes*, and Euripides' *Trojan Women*, show how varied and how complex this engagement with what Euripides calls the 'strife of warring words' can be.

Aeschylus' *Oresteia* had more influence on other Greek writers than any other tragic work, and its treatment of language as a theme is significantly echoed by both Sophocles and Euripides. No adequate chapter on tragic language could ignore its importance. I want to focus on two particular ways this most intricate and involved of trilogies treats the use of language as a theme. First of all, its deployment of political language, as has been long recognised, is infused with a sense of the competing and contending comprehension of words. This is nowhere more striking than with one of the play's most evident thematic nexuses – the notion of *dikē*. *Dikē* is a central term of the public language of the fifth-century polis. Its range of sense runs from abstract ideas of 'justice' or 'right' through 'retribution', 'punishment', to the particular legal senses of 'lawcourt', and 'law case'. It is a fundamental term for the expression of social order in that it both indicates the proper organisation of society as a whole and delineates right action for individuals and the institutions through which order is to be maintained. It is a principle – and a practice – constantly appealed to in fifth-century discourse.

The word *dikē* and its derivatives are used obsessively in the *Oresteia*, where the plotting of revenge leads towards a resolution through the new institution of the lawcourt.[21] This has led to what is still a standard reading of the trilogy, namely, that the *Oresteia* traces a transformation from *dikē* as revenge to *dikē* as legal justice – a move from the bloody repetition of vendetta to the ordered world of the polis and its institutional resolution of conflict through the words of the court.[22] On this view, the *Oresteia* offers a sort of 'charter myth' for the institution of law, which is central to the development of democracy and to democracy's image of itself. The fissure within the term *dikē* – 'punishment' and/or 'revenge' and /or 'justice' and/or 'legal process' – with its competing senses of how transgression, violence and disagreement are to be negotiated in the household and the city, becomes thus part of a teleological progression towards the social order – the *dikē* – of the city of Athens. The trilogy's final symbolic procession represents the city of Athens to the city of Athens as the embodiment of social order: 'justice' triumphs over the uncontrollable violence of 'revenge'.

Although the teleology of this account has been extensively and rightly challenged and redefined,[23] the intricate opacity and contestation of the sense of the term *dikē* certainly demonstrates the refraction of the language of power that Vernant emphasises. I will give a single example here from lines I have already quoted, an example which is paradigmatic of this Aeschylean semantic violence. When Orestes appears over the bodies of his mother and her lover, Aegisthus, he calls upon the Sun to be his 'witness on the day of judgement (*dik-*) that justly (*-dik-*) I pursued this killing of my mother. Aegisthus' death I count for nothing: he suffered the adulterer's just penalty (*dik-*) as is the law'.[24] At this most paradoxical juncture of the trilogy where, in the pursuit of his rightful place, Orestes has committed the horrific act of matricide, and is here trying to justify it, the triple repetition of the language of *dikē* reveals the tension and ambiguity in the act of justification. He calls on the Sun to bear witness *en dikēi*, 'on the day of judgement', 'at my trial', 'in court'. Orestes will indeed appear before the court of the Areopagus in the *Eumenides*, and the use of the word 'witness' emphasises the technical legal aspect of Orestes' phraseology (although the audience – or Orestes – do not necessarily know of the coming trial). His claim, however, that he killed *endikōs*, 'justly', 'with right on my side', is an

---

[21] See for bibliography and discussion, Goldhill (1986) 33–56.
[22] For a strong version of this argument see Kitto (1961).
[23] For feminist, Marxist and other critiques, see Goldhill (1986) 33–56.
[24] *Cho.* 987–90:

> ὡς ἂν παρῆι μοι μάρτυς ἐν δίκηι ποτὲ
> ὡς τόνδ' ἐγὼ μετῆλθον ἐνδίκως φόνον
> τὸν μητρός · Αἰγίσθου γὰρ οὐ λέγω μόρον·
> ἔχει γὰρ αἰσχυντῆρος, ὡς νόμος, δίκην.

appeal to a generalised principle of justice, a moral right. But the case of Clytemnestra's death is immediately distinguished from that of Aegisthus, who has suffered the *dikēn*, 'penalty', of an adulterer. Here, the sense of 'revenge' and the sense of 'punishment' come to the fore. How, then, is Orestes' violence to be understood? Is it to be seen as violent revenge or as justice? What is the difference between such descriptions? How does his violent action relate to social order and the institutions of law? The questions raised by the matricide are articulated in the polyvalency of the terminology of its description. Orestes' justification – saying how it is just – is informed and exposed by the conflicts within his language of justice.

This fragmentation of the language of *dikē* reverberates throughout the trilogy and sets before the audience the complexities of the expressions of order within the polis. What is more, the work moves towards the establishment of the first Athenian lawcourt and Orestes' trial in it – the very constitution of legal process. As the trilogy ends with the assimilation of the Furies within the polis, and the final procession that represents the whole city and its celebration, the sense of *dikē* as social order seems to be strikingly embodied, enacted, envisioned, on stage. The play's search for an end to violence between the generations and between the genders has become the question of how *dikē* is to be defined – where and how right or justice or punishment or order are to be located, realised, determined. The exploration of the public language of the city is – inevitably? – part of an intense engagement with politics and gender.

The second particular way that language becomes a thematic focus of the trilogy is in the repeated dramatisation and investigation of the dangers and powers of words in action. The manipulation and failure of the process of communication is central to the plotting of the *Agamemnon*. The play opens with a watchman waiting for a beacon (which arrives), and the first scene consists of a discussion between the queen and the chorus about the beacon's message: Clytemnestra delivers two long speeches, the first of which explains how the beacon came from Troy, the second, what message it signifies. The second scene consists in the arrival of a human messenger from Agamemnon, with good and bad news, and the return of this messenger to the king with a false message, constructed and sent by the queen to lure her unsuspecting husband. The arrival of Agamemnon is thus prepared by two scenes that consist in, and discuss, different ways of sending and interpreting messages (with the queen central to both). This is significant, since the great dramatic moment of Agamemnon's return is the so-called Carpet Scene, in which Agamemnon is persuaded by Clytemnestra to enter his house along a path of tapestries. What is staged is not only an embodiment of Agamemnon's transgression, but also the queen's power of persuasion and deception. Her tricky language leads him to his death, and this is what she boasts of after his murder: 'I have said many things before to suit the occasion; now I will not be ashamed to say the opposite' (*Ag.* 1372–3): the queen is as shameless in her language as in her sexual behaviour. Between Clytemnestra's persuasion of her husband and this triumphing in – and of – her rhetoric comes the Cassandra scene. This scene is an extended dramatisation of the failure of communication, since the prophetess's gift from Apollo is always to tell the truth and never to be believed; and indeed the chorus fail to understand her repeated announcements of the danger to Agamemnon, even – especially – when they ironically claim to have understood her (1213). This lengthy exchange thus establishes a characteristically bold Aeschylean dramatic juxtaposition: between the woman who lies and persuades everyone, and the woman who tells the truth and persuades no one. As the fragmentation of the language of *dikē* led towards the dynamics of gender (and) politics, so too the thematic focus on language use – the failure of communication, the dangers of messages, the trickiness and deception of persuasiveness – leads towards a specific connection of language and gender. The *Agamemnon*, in other words, stages the powers and dangers of the exchange of words as a central thematic device in its plotting of conflict between king and queen.

Orestes is told by the Delphic oracle to take revenge in the same manner as Agamemnon was killed. Thus he arrives deceitfully dressed as a messenger, with a lying but persuasive tale of his own death. Aegisthus too is summoned with a message, carried by the Nurse, that is altered on stage by the chorus – the only time in extant tragedy when a chorus interferes in the action in quite so direct a manner. Tellingly, as he enters the palace the chorus pray for the assistance of *peithō dolia*, 'guileful persuasion' (726). For Orestes, like his mother before him, manipulating words is integral to his violence. Persuasion is also central to the *Eumenides*, not just in the trial scene itself, with its staging of rhetoric in action, but also as the heralded means by which Athena mollifies the Furies and brings them into her city. 'Persuasion', sings the goddess, 'I revere the eyes of Persuasion, because she oversees my mouth and tongue ...' (970–1). From the violent persuasion of Clytemnestra to the mollifying persuasion of Athena, from the deceptive woman at the centre of the house to the institution of the legal *agōn* at the centre of the city, the *Oresteia* charts the social function of language in the polis.

Both of these aspects of the *Oresteia*'s engagement with the public language of the city have an extended influence on tragedy.[25] I want here to

---

[25] For an overview of 'persuasion' in tragedy, see Buxton (1982).

look at two further plays which develop in particularly important ways the thematic concern with persuasion in action, persuasion as action, and which show the increasing effects of the formal training in rhetoric and the public discussion of rhetoric on tragic language and narrative.

Sophocles' *Philoctetes* is the only extant tragedy without a female character and is one of only very few plays not to be set within the physical frame of the polis itself. The island of Lemnos is, for this drama at least, deserted, and the play revolves around the attempt of Odysseus and Neoptolemus to persuade Philoctetes, who has been abandoned, sick and alone, in this wild space, to rejoin the Greek army, and to bring with him the bow of Heracles, which has enabled him to survive. Once again, the plot of the play depends on the staging of persuasion.[26] First, Odysseus persuades Neoptolemus to join in the enterprise; then Neoptolemus sets about deceitfully misleading Philoctetes. He spins a persuasive tale of how he has been deceived by Odysseus and has fled the Greeks. The one 'messenger scene' is the so-called False Merchant scene, where a sailor, disguised as a merchant, brings a false tale of the Greeks' pursuit of Neoptolemus in order to help convince Philoctetes of Neoptolemus' good faith (cf. Ch. 7, pp. 169–70). (Merchants, like messengers, have a patron in Hermes, who also presides over false communication: exchange and its corruptions are that god's sphere.) Neoptolemus, for all his persuasiveness, finds himself increasingly persuaded by the suffering and powerful feelings of Philoctetes. He breaks down and tells Philoctetes of the plot against him; but will not return the bow he has been given. Finally, he returns the bow – but cannot persuade Philoctetes to come to Troy. It is only the appearance of Heracles, a *deus ex machina*, that persuades Philoctetes to go to where mythic tradition requires he go. Deception, persuasion, and the morality of how language is to be used are constant subjects of discussion in the play: it is a key sign of how men interrelate. Significantly, Philoctetes' first delight in meeting Neoptolemus after many years of solitude is 'to hear a Greek voice again' (225): that this voice should be a lure in a deceptive plot is typical of the ironies, powers and deceptions of language in this play.

The status of language in the *Philoctetes* is closely bound up with a view of civilisation.[27] The contrast between the wild landscape of Lemnos, with its lack of any cultural institutions, and the hierarchical world of the Greek army, besieging Troy in the name of preserving the norms of society, is played out in a fascinating way at the level of communication. Odysseus, as we will see, is committed to an instrumental view of language, where

[26] See Podlecki (1966a); Segal (1981) 328–61; Rose (1992) 226–330.
[27] See Segal (1981) 292–327.

winning one's case is the only adequate criterion for speech-making. Neoptolemus, like his father Achilles, professes a strong distaste for verbal deceit, and wishes to maintain an upright, honest, straightforward rectitude in his dealings. Philoctetes is passionately committed to his moral stance: he will not listen to or be persuaded by the argument of an enemy, and insists on complete agreement and consistency from his friends (*philoi*).[28] Yet, Philoctetes is reduced by his illness to inarticulate cries of pain (which affect Neoptolemus as much as any argument). Between the civilised – trained – and amoral use of language to win a case, and the inarticulate cry of the anguished human on the margin of cultural life, a complex mapping of the politics and ethics of language as a sign and symptom of civilised life is developed.

A look at one brief dialogue will show how intricate this mapping is. Odysseus in the opening scene of the play has to persuade Neoptolemus to help deceive Philoctetes. Neoptolemus has stated his desire to fail in a proper way rather than succeed by immoral means, and Odysseus begins the process of persuasion with (96–9):

> Son of a noble father, when I myself was a young man
> I had a slow tongue and a hand ready for action.
> But as things are, from trial and proof, I see that for man
> The tongue, and not deeds, controls all.

Odysseus at once notes Neoptolemus' significant parentage. His father, the famously direct Achilles, passionately dismisses Odysseus in the *Iliad* with the famous declaration (9.312–13): 'I hate like the gates of Hell a man who says one thing and conceals another in his mind.' (The hero Philoctetes will describe Odysseus' plot as (1142) 'the concealed words of a guileful mind'.) It is this noble directness in Neoptolemus that Odysseus has to deflect (and to which Philoctetes appeals). The opposition of word and deed, however, is one of the central recurring polarities of fifth-century discourse: Odysseus, for his part, declares the absolute primacy of language, the tongue – it 'controls all', like a successful orator in the Assembly – and defends this position as something learnt by 'trial and proof': not just an appeal to experience but to experience formulated as a scientific or legal investigation, the keynote of enlightenment intellectualism. The scene of persuasion begins (as so often) with a comment on the role and power of language.

Words and how to use them remain the focus of the following sticho-mythia (100–22). Neoptolemus replies: 'What are you ordering me to do

---

[28] See Knox (1964) 117–42; Whitlock-Blundell (1989) 184–225.

except to tell lies?' The sign of his noble nature is to reject the manipulation of language as a willing adoption of the shameful practice of telling lies. For him, there is no economising with the truth. Odysseus, however, retorts with 'I am telling you to take Philoctetes by guile.' 'Guile', *dolos*, is a term closely associated with Odysseus as the hero of the *Odyssey*. He is offering – with guile – a positive gloss on his proposal. Not the corruption of lies but the flexibility of guile. 'But', asks Neoptolemus, 'why must it be by guile and not by persuasion?' 'Persuasion', *peithō*, so often opposed to 'force', *bia*, formulates *dolos*, 'guile', as the corruption of its own openness. It reglosses in a negative guise Odysseus' own gloss. 'He will never be persuaded', predicts Odysseus (with some justification). After Odysseus explains why force is also not an option (the arrows of the bow of Heracles are ineluctable and lethal), Neoptolemus returns to the status of deception: 'Do you really not think it is disgraceful to tell lies?' 'No', replies Odysseus, 'if safety is what the lie brings.' Odysseus, faced by the direct question of whether it is morally acceptable to lie, tries to set lying under the heading of self-preservation (as so often in the *Odyssey* he needs his verbal wits to survive). But Neoptolemus presses on: 'How could one have the face to speak these things?' 'When you do something for profit', replies Odysseus, 'it is unfitting to shrink back.' Lying for self-preservation has here tellingly become an expression of a sophistic agenda. First, it is 'profit' rather than self-preservation which is now the express motive – a different economics of truth-telling. Self-advancement at any cost, as well as taking payment – profit – from anyone for teaching, are common charges thrown at sophists. 'Profit' is a charged word in fifth-century debates about ethics and politics that, as here, focuses the discussion on the boundaries of proper action. Second, the neat sophistic twist of Odysseus' argument should not be missed. With knowing paradox, he dismisses Neoptolemus' ethical scruple with the assertion that, when lies bring profit, it is actually *improper* to shrink back (and fear is as commonly deprecated as lying for the upright man). The impropriety of lying is turned to the impropriety of fearful hesitation in the face of the enemy (or the sight of profit). Odysseus will indeed increasingly emphasise the moral duty of Neoptolemus to obey his military commanders and to act according to the army's requirements rather than his personal feelings. For Odysseus, the ends undoubtedly justify the means.

This opening discussion of how to evaluate – talk about – verbal deception is programmatic for the play as a whole. The figure of Odysseus draws both on his Homeric representation as heroic trickster and on models of sophistic verbal pragmatism. Neoptolemus echoes his father's epic stance, but also plays the role of a young man faced by an older, wily teacher of how to use language (like a pupil of Socrates). Indeed, as Neoptolemus is deceiving Philoctetes, he comments in generalising mode (387–8): 'Disorderly people in human society are made bad by the words of their teachers.' Neoptolemus, faced by Philoctetes and Odysseus, undergoes a painful lesson in the complexities of evaluating the words of those who wish to teach him – about duty to the collective authority of the army, duty to *philoi*, duty to a sense of personal integrity or nobility.

Indeed, when he decides to return the bow to Philoctetes, the boy is offered a harsh rebuttal which mirrors in reverse the opening scene of Odysseus' persuasiveness. 'Hear what words I bring', pleads Neoptolemus (1267). 'I am afraid', replies Philoctetes (1268–9); 'I fared ill before from your fair words, when I was persuaded by your words' (the triple repetition of *logoi*, 'words', is emphatic here). 'Is it not possible also to change one's mind?', asks Neoptolemus (1270), which Philoctetes rejects out of hand with (1271–2): 'You were like this too in your words when you stole my bow: "trustworthy" – but secretly ruinous.' Once trust has been removed by false speech, what can be *said* to reconstitute faith in language? How can words put back together the contract shattered by the deceptiveness of language? Philoctetes dismisses the boy's attempt to rediscover sincere expression, its persuasiveness, and Neoptolemus can only comment (1278–80): 'I would have wanted you to be persuaded by my words. But if I cannot say anything to hit the mark, I have done.' Language, he recognises, is failing him. Philoctetes expresses the problem succinctly (1280–1): 'You will say everything in vain. For you will never win my mind over to good will.' After deception, good will (*eunoia*) is lost; and with the loss of good will, the possibility of trust and persuasion is destroyed. But in response to this, Neoptolemus demands the right hand of Philoctetes (both the sign of strength and of the agreed contract) and gives him back his bow: 'There will be', he declares, 'a clear deed.' And this deed binds the men together. Where Odysseus had said the tongue and not the hand controls all, for Philoctetes it is a 'clear deed' – the action precisely of hands – which persuades, obligates, ties; which escapes the impasse of language's deceptions. And yet – with a typical Sophoclean extra twist of the plot towards the distortions of extreme commitment – for all the continuing and emphatic protestations of 'good will' (*eunoia*) between the two (e.g. 1322, cf. 1351), Philoctetes cannot let himself be persuaded by his newly trusted friend. His hatred of the Atreids and Odysseus, and his commitment to the principle of doing harm to his enemies, outweigh all else. 'Good will' can be only one of a set of criteria dominating and informing the process of communication and persuasion.

The *Philoctetes* thus displays to the audience the action of rhetoric in all its intricacy, irony and violence. Odysseus' sophistic pragmatism is one element in this exploration of language as process, an element that ties the play in a dialectic with the Homeric past and the city of the present. It is, however, also typical of the provocation of Sophoclean irony that for all that the play does not endorse Odysseus, by the end he does get exactly what he wants, namely, Philoctetes and the bow willingly travelling to Troy. His ends are – at whatever cost – achieved. Indeed, the anatomising of persuasiveness staged in the drama does not lead to a neat comprehensive conclusion, but leaves the audience thus with a problem of articulating its collective and several response to the play of language. In his 'profound reflection on the nature of man as a civilized being, on the bonds, needs and obligations that hold men together',[29] Sophocles gives a central place to the problem of communication between men, of words in action, words as action.

The staging of rhetoric in Euripides' *Trojan Women* is emblematic of the writing that led Nietzsche to blame Euripides for the 'death of tragedy'. Euripides' characters, drawn from the epics of Homer, do not merely show the signs of a sophistic training, but in the case of Helen in particular seem to have been reading the sophist Gorgias with especial care. I have already mentioned the prophetess Cassandra, and her argument that the Trojans fared better in defeat than the Greeks did in victory. That scene is one of three scenes around which the play is structured, each of which involves a debate between Hecuba, queen of defeated Troy, and one of her daughters or daughters-in-law – Cassandra, Andromache, Helen. In each case, the women debate a woman's role in a good marriage, what their suffering has been and means, and what part each has played and will play in the continuing saga of the families of Greece and Troy. In each scene, the signs of formal rhetorical training are strongly marked. In the space remaining I want to look briefly at the last of these *agōnes*. It will enable me to make some important points about the Euripidean staging of verbal contest.

The debate between Helen and Hecuba is set up in formal terms, with Menelaus as judge.[30] Helen's first words are (895–6) 'Menelaus, this is a *prologue* deserving of fear ...' and she asks (899–900): 'What *decision* have the Greeks and you arrived at ...?' When she hears of the death penalty, she begs for the right (903–4) 'to contend in argument that it would be an injustice to execute' her, and Hecuba agrees (907–10) that he should 'grant her the right of reply ... A full established debate will mean her inevitable

---

[29] Segal (1981) 361.
[30] For a good discussion of the *agōn*, see Croally (1994) 134–62.

death.' The argument is set up by this technical language as if it is a law-case.

Helen indeed shows at every level of her speech the deep influence of the professional training of the sophist. First, she articulates a precisely plotted and expressly signalled argument of defence: 'In relation to what your accusation will be if you enter into discussion with me, I will set my arguments point by point. First ... Second ... Listen to what followed next ... Consider the logical consequences which follow ... You will say I have not yet discussed one point in question ... At this point you may raise a specious objection ... I have witnesses ...' The stages of the argument are carefully articulated as such by the formal markers of trained argumentation. Second, Helen demonstrates the archetypal traits of fifth-century argumentation. On the one hand, she manipulates the paradoxical reversal so often associated with sophistic rhetoric: she claims, for example, that her adultery has benefited the Greeks since it enabled them to defeat the barbarians: 'but that which has given Greece happiness has ruined me. I was sold for my beauty and I am reviled by those who ought to have crowned my head.' The commonplace of the glorious triumph of the Greeks over the barbarian is by a neat twist made dependent on the transgression which started the war, as if her adultery was the source of Greek glory. On the other hand, she utilises one of the commonest tropes of fifth-century rhetoric, the appeal to plausibility, likelihood, probability with its dependence on a model of the natural. So, she argues for the overpowering influence of the gods on her action by asking a rhetorical question: 'What was I thinking of to follow the stranger from my home, and betray my home and country?' The question's implicit denial of a *plausible* reason for her action constitutes the argument for external compulsion for her behaviour.

Third, and perhaps most strikingly of all, Helen seems to follow the defence prepared for her by the sophist Gorgias in his famous work *The Encomium of Helen*. This short sophistic masterpiece is a speech which purports to exonerate the adulteress from any blame. He has four main, substantive arguments. First, that if Helen was raped – taken by force – she deserved pity not blame. Second, if the gods made her do it (as the standard accounts, utilised also by Helen, have it), then she cannot be blamed, since no one is stronger than a god. Third, if language made her do it, she cannot be blamed, since the power of words cannot be resisted. Fourth, if *erōs* made her do it, she cannot be blamed, since this external force has more than mortal power. This is not the place to discuss the intricacies of Gorgias' ideas of causality or the trickiness of his ideas about language. What is to be stressed is that Helen follows a very similar line of defence:

'Punish the goddess and become more powerful than Zeus', she scornfully declares, 'but I am to be forgiven' (949–50). And 'How would I die justly ... I whom Paris married by force ...? Wanting to get the better of the gods is an ignorant desire on your part' (961–5). That Helen should use the turns of the famous fifth-century rhetorician dramatises as starkly as possible the clash between the traditional heroic figures and the language and modes of the contemporary polis.

Hecuba's response (969–1032) shows an equal rhetorical polish and forcefulness. Hers too is a point-by-point response: 'You say ... but ... You declared ... but ... You said ... but ...' It too has the markers of professional argument: 'I will demonstrate that she is not speaking justly ... The conclusion of my speech is ...' Above all, she constructs an argument that repeatedly uses the principles of plausibility to attack Helen, and in particular Helen's argument about the divine and about her psychological motives. Why, she asks, would goddesses compete in beauty? 'Is it that Hera could possess a husband superior to Zeus?' Why would Aphrodite have come to Menelaus' palace? 'Could she not have transported you, and all of Amyclae too, to Troy, just remaining quiet in heaven?' Helen's psychological claims are similarly dismissed – with the typical sophistic delight in ludic etymology: Aphrodite is just a front for human transgression, claims Hecuba, 'rightly the name of the goddess [Aphrodite] begins with "folly" [aphrosunē]'. The barbarian queen even attacks Helen for wanting to luxuriate in barbarian wealth and have barbarians prostrate themselves to her. Hecuba's scorn is aimed at destroying Helen's claims to plausibility.

Menelaus as judge is clear that he has been persuaded by Hecuba's superior rationalistic argument, her more forceful use of the argument of plausibility in her attack on Helen's account of divine narrative. Yet it is typical of Euripides' ironic – sophistic – sense of reversal that this victory is undercut.[31] It is undercut first by the fact that for all Hecuba's rationalism about the improbability of the gods' direct intervention in human narratives of transgression, the opening scene of the play has shown us precisely such a *divina commedia* with Athena explaining to Poseidon, her brother, how she is now angry with the Greeks she previously supported and wants to destroy their fleet with a storm on their return home. Hecuba's treatment of divine narrative is framed by the play's own sense of the cause of things. Second, there is a strong literary tradition, headed by *Odyssey* 4, which asserts that Menelaus did not kill Helen, but returned and lived with her in Sparta. There is a story that when he approached her on board ship with a

[31] See Croally (1994) especially 157–62.

sword, she dropped her top, and at the sight of her breasts he was so taken by desire that all thoughts of punishment vanished from his mind. This, or similar tales, are strongly hinted at in the closing dialogue of the scene. Hecuba warns Menelaus not to let Helen on board his ship. He, with a wonderful lack of appreciation, replies (1050): 'Why? Has she put on so much weight?' 'No', replies Hecuba (1051); 'once a lover, always a lover.' Indeed, the desirability of Helen is made strikingly visible in this scene. Hecuba warns Menelaus as Helen enters not to look at her (891–4) 'in case you are seized with desire. For she captures the eyes of men, she ruins cities and she burns houses. Such is the power of her bewitching.' Helen, unlike the other women in the play, is dressed in all her finery and allure, as Hecuba points out at length (1022–8). So does it matter what Helen actually says? For what does persuade Menelaus? Or, more pointedly, since *peithō* is the normal Greek for 'seduction' (and as a personification is often accompanied by the figure of Eros in the artistic tradition[32]), what 'seduces' him? For all the superior rationalism of Hecuba, the literary tradition and the staging of the scene invite the audience to consider other factors than winning words in the scene of persuasion.

This wonderful *agōn*, then, lets us see three particularly important ways in which Euripides' mobilisation of the tropes of contemporary rhetoric engages with the thematic nexuses of his work. First, Euripides' deployment of different versions of the tales of the Trojan war, and different accounts of causality and different accounts of responsibility, is closely connected with the widely articulated fifth-century concerns with such issues (leading towards Aristotle's formalisation of the principle of 'the four causes'). The *agōn* dramatises and enacts this fragmentation and contestation of the language of causality and responsibility. If, as Vernant has argued, the moment of tragedy is to be located in the disjunction between legal, political, and traditional mythic modes of narrative and explanation, Euripides uses the rhetorical *agōn* – and its framing by the narrative of the play – to display and explore that disjunction. The *agōn* enacts the contests of explanation. The intellectualising rhetoric of Helen and Hecuba, with its evident links with sophistic argument, sets the play's concerns with the responsibilities, consequences and violence of war within a wide network of fifth-century intellectual discussions.

Second, the wilful manipulation of the stories of the past (in a festival which constantly retells the stories of the past for the present) is a constitutive dynamic of Euripides' often questioning stance towards the city's inherited tales and their influence. Euripides, like Sophocles and

---

[32] See Buxton (1982).

Aeschylus, charts the way in which the self-aware modernity of the demo-cratic polis is formulated in relation to Homeric and other narratives of the past. The sense that the traditional ethical stances are no longer sufficient for the life and attitudes of the polis is dramatised in a remarkable fashion by forcing the old characters and old stories into the modern form of a sophistic debate. The multiform relations between present and past are emphatically highlighted by the bold anachronism of the sophistic Helen and Hecuba.

Third, the question of what persuades Menelaus, which underlies the competing accounts of Helen's war, is to be linked to the more general question of how words relate to the world. The opposition of *logos* and *ergon* (word/deed, argument/reality, reason/fact) that I stressed with regard to Sophocles' *Philoctetes* is only one sign of the linguistic turn that the fifth century underwent. The way in which 'language is a sort of instructive instrument to organise reality'[33] is a shared fixation of the intellectual activity of the classical city; and, in the *Trojan Women*, Cassandra's prophecies, Andromache's mourning, and Hecuba's rationalism in different ways emphasise the insufficiency of words to deal with the violence and suffering of war, as much as the power of language to explain, define and control the narratives of war. Euripides' dramatisation of contemporary rhetoric in action is an integral aspect of his constant and profound exploration of the relation between words and the world, the (in)ability of contemporary public language to comprehend man's place in the city of words.

The contests of authoritative explanation, the relation between present and past, the relation between words and the world, are, then, three major concerns fascinatingly brought to the fore by Euripides' use of contem-porary, professionalised, rhetoric here – and in the rest of his corpus. This strongly marked turn to the art of rhetoric, however, only makes more evident questions which are shared with the other playwrights, sophists, and intellectuals of the city. Tragedy as a genre, tragic language, is in this way a fundamental element of the fifth-century enlightenment – an explora-tion of the developing public language of the city, performed before the city. Staging the *agōn*, dramatising the corruption and failures of communica-tion, displaying the conflicts of meaning within the public language of the city, provoke the audience of tragedy towards a recognition of language's powers and dangers, fissures and obligations. Democracy prided itself on putting matters *es meson*, 'into the public domain to be contested'. Tragedy

[33] Plato, *Cratylus* 388b13.

puts language itself *es meson*, on display and at risk in the glare of democratic scrutiny.

BIBLIOGRAPHICAL NOTE

There are many technical discussions of aspects of tragic language, though few are suitable for those reading tragedy in translation (see e.g. A. A. Long, *Language and Thought in Sophocles* (Cambridge 1968); H. Friis Johansen, *General Reflection in Tragic Rhesis* (Copenhagen 1959); M. Griffith, *The Authenticity of the 'Prometheus Bound'* (Cambridge 1977)). On the development of rhetoric in the polis, see G. A. Kennedy, *The Art of Persuasion in Greece* (Princeton 1963): the standard treatment, now updated and abridged in G. A. Kennedy, *A New History of Classical Rhetoric* (Princeton 1994); for a sense of what may be left out of the standard discussion, one may consult three different types of account of this history from a single year: J. Swearingen, *Rhetoric and Irony* (Oxford 1991); S. Jarratt, *Rereading the Sophists: Classical Rhetoric Refigured* (Carbondale and Edwardsville 1991); T. Cole, *The Origins of Rhetoric in Ancient Greece* (Baltimore 1991). For sophistic rhetoric and tragedy, see for an overview Goldhill (1986) 222–42, and for exemplary treatments, Rose (1992) 265–330; Croally (1994). For language as a theme in tragedy, see the seminal Vernant and Vidal-Naquet (1988) 1–28; Buxton (1982); Knox (1979) 205–30; Goldhill (1984), (1986) 1–32; Goff (1990); Segal (1981) especially chs. 7 and 10.

7

P. E. EASTERLING

Form and performance

The story of Greek tragedy in the fifth century BC is an extraordinarily difficult one to tell. On the one side there are thirty-two well-known plays transmitted from antiquity through the medieval tradition, plays that have exerted a profound, even immeasurable, influence on Western culture, while on the other there are fragmentary scraps of evidence, often enough distorted by the preconceptions of later times, from which scholars try to reconstruct a whole history of an institution. How Dionysiac festivals were organised, what the earliest theatres, masks and costumes looked like, how the music sounded, what sort of performance-styles and dramatic conventions developed, how far the surviving plays are typical of the hundreds, or thousands, that must have been composed during the period, and what tragedy meant for the contemporary Athenian – and non-Athenian – audiences that watched it: these are the questions that need answers. What is lacking is systematic documentation, surviving from the fifth century itself, of this new and extremely successful artistic and civic phenomenon, and there is no prospect that anything of the kind will ever be recovered.

The best that modern research can hope for is new fragments of evidence – a vase-painting or an inscription, a papyrus text of part of a lost play or of a scholar's introduction (*hypothesis*) – which will fill some of the gaps in the story. The most striking example was the publication in 1952[1] of a small papyrus scrap of a *hypothesis* which proved that Aeschylus' *Suppliant Women* was not the earliest surviving Greek tragedy but belonged to the 460s, and therefore to a late stage in the poet's career. This play, with its chorus of the daughters of Danaus (the myth said there were fifty of them), had previously been taken as a sample of the tragedy of the 490s and was thought to have a chorus of fifty like the dithyramb; it was read as a 'primitive' piece more akin to choral lyric poetry than to the true dialectic of drama. But once scholars recognised that the historical framework had to

---

[1] P.Oxy. 2256 fr. 3; for discussion see Garvie (1969) 1–28.

be dismantled they found it much easier to see how close the *Suppliant Women* is to the *Oresteia* in both form and subject-matter, and the early history of tragedy had to be re-imagined.

If so much of what we understand about Greek tragedy in its original context is a matter of construction, or reconstruction, from cryptic and elusive evidence, there is some point in looking at the process itself, trying to see how the basic data and the texts of the plays are continually being reassessed as critics try to fit them into a larger pattern (cf. Chs. 9–12 below).

RULES AND CONVENTIONS

A reader who studied only handbooks of Greek drama and made no direct contact with the plays themselves might be forgiven for being puzzled that what ought on the face of it to be a dynamic art-form was evidently so regimented. How could a genre as novel and sophisticated as tragedy have been hedged about by every kind of rule and restriction, with limits on the number of speaking actors, the showing of violent events on stage, the relation of the chorus to the stage action, the distribution of spoken and sung parts, and even, perhaps, the choice of subject-matter, which must surely have been a deterrent to creative talent?

The first questions to ask are what sort of limitations were imposed, and in what context. No set of rules for the conduct of the dramatic festivals survives, but we do know that they were overseen by presiding magistrates, that groups of plays were performed in competition with one another, and that a playwright who wished to compete had to be selected by the relevant magistrate (the Eponymous Archon in the case of the City Dionysia).[2] Because the festival entailed competitive performance at civic expense, the allocation of funds was regulated, through the direct payment of the leading actors (one protagonist for each dramatist) and through the appointment of *chorēgoi* to finance the choruses. Without regulation it would have been impossible to ensure that there was a fair basis for the competition and that expenditure was kept within reasonable bounds; even so, individual *chorēgoi* might be more or less lavish. But the rules of competition are not the same as the conventions of a genre; there is no evidence surviving from the fifth century which suggests that the dramatists were inhibited from experimentation, and plenty to indicate the opposite.

The number of speaking actors is a case in point.[3] One of the undisputed facts of Athenian dramatic history is that tragedy developed out of

---

[2] Pickard-Cambridge (1988) ch. 2; Cartledge (1985) 115–27 and Ch. 1 above.
[3] See Damen (1989) and Kaimio (1993).

performances by a chorus, in which one performer (the poet himself) was set apart from the rest of the group and took on a series of different roles. Aeschylus introduced a second performer to share the acting, and Sophocles later brought in a third.[4] The texts of nearly all the plays from the *Oresteia* onwards suggest that they were composed to be performed by a maximum of three speaking actors, and there is no external evidence for the regular use of more. How can this tradition be explained if not as some kind of restriction on the freedom of dramatists? In fact it makes best sense if it is understood in relation to performance in masks. The origins and symbolic significance of masked acting in the Greek tradition may be disputed, but there is no doubt that in the fifth century masks were worn by both actors and chorusmen, and vase-paintings show that they were masks with wigs attached, which covered the actors' heads completely.[5] In a theatre where such a masking convention is used, it is natural to confine the speaking in any one scene to a limited number of parts, so that audiences will not be in doubt as to where each voice is coming from; and since the masks also provide effective disguise, only a small number of virtuoso performers is needed to provide the cast of a whole play. It is easy, too, to see why a dramatist competing with a set of three tragedies and a satyr play should have used the same small team of actors throughout (cf. Ch. 2, p. 38). There must have been financial reasons for not creating large troupes, and the greater the versatility that was required the more highly trained the speaking actor needed to be. But there was plenty of scope for the dramatists to use non-speakers – attendants, bodyguards, trains of captives – and plenty of evidence that they did. Playing some of these roles may have been the first step on the theatrical ladder for young trainee actors, just as the very minor speaking or singing parts in the few plays that seem to need a fourth actor[6] may have given such beginners their first taste of making their voices heard before the assembled city.

At any rate there is nothing in the evidence as it has come down to us to suggest that the dramatists were prevented by an artificial 'three-actor rule' from doing anything they wanted; the main challenge to their freedom may indeed have come, not from any state-imposed regulations but from the emergence of leading actors as 'stars' who made their mark on the tradition in decisive ways. A prize for the best actor was instituted at the City Dionysia in *c.* 449; the surviving texts show that the leading actor, at any

---

[4] Ar. *Poet.* 1449a18; the ancient *Life* of Aeschylus (5) records a tradition which attributes the introduction of the third actor to him. Pickard-Cambridge (1988) 130–2.

[5] See [7] and [8]. For discussion see Frontisi-Ducroux & Vernant (1983) 56–69; Frontisi-Ducroux (1989); Calame (1995); Halliwell (1993) 195–211.

[6] *Oedipus at Colonus* is a striking example; cf. Pickard-Cambridge (1988) 142–4.

rate, was expected to be a skilled solo singer, with all the charismatic qualities that entails, and in the fourth century, when revivals of earlier plays became a regular fixture at the City Dionysia, it was actors (*tragōidoi*) who put them on. By the time Aristotle was writing, it was possible to take the view that the actors were altogether too influential.[7]

The notion that the dramatists were constricted by rules is no more helpful when we come to look at the presentation of stage action. Tragedy characteristically dealt with 'sad stories of the death of kings', but of the surviving plays only four show stage deaths: Ajax's suicide in Sophocles' play, and in Euripides the (non-violent) deaths of Alcestis and Hippolytus and the mysterious suicidal leap of Evadne in *Suppliant Women*,[8] by contrast with the many accounts of off-stage bloodshed given by messengers. Was this because dramatists were under constraint, inhibited by religious scruples or considerations of taste from showing what they would have liked to show, or aware, perhaps, that a brilliantly told (and mimed?) narrative might be more easily 'read' in a large open-air theatre than a piece of more realistic stage business? Messenger speeches are always very closely linked to what the audience are to see and hear: exits and entrances, including the return of killers and wounded victims, off-stage cries, and the display of corpses.[9] The intricacy with which the violent events are thus 'orchestrated' suggests that in avoiding direct presentation of the moment of killing or violent wounding the dramatists were making creative choices for positive reasons. Inhibitions, if any were felt, may have been related to what both actors and audiences believed to be dangerously ill-omened.

A couple of examples will illustrate the potential for innovation and experiment within a seemingly restrictive tradition. In Aeschylus' *Agamemnon* the murder of the king, to which all the foreboding and anxiety of the first thousand lines of the play have been directed, is 'played' three times, although never shown to the audience. First it is seen before it happens by Cassandra in her pre-visions (1100ff.); later Agamemnon's death cries are heard and the Chorus debate what they should do at the very moment of the murder (1343–72); and finally Clytemnestra displays the bodies of Agamemnon and Cassandra, and herself acts as newsbringer, telling in (mainly) present tenses exactly how she killed her husband: 'I swathe him in an endless wrapping, like a fishnet ... and I strike him twice. With two groans his limbs went slack, and on the fallen body I strike a third blow' (1382–6). In *Hecuba* Euripides uses not the perpetrator, but the major victim, to tell his own story: the Thracian king Polymestor, who is

---

[7] Ar. *Rhet.* III 1403b33; cf. *Poet.* 1451b35–9.
[8] See Arnott (1962) 137–8 and Rehm (1992) 129–31 for discussion of this scene.
[9] Bremer (1976) sets out the details.

blinded by Hecuba and the Trojan women after they have treacherously killed his children. Here too there is great elaboration: Hecuba formulates her plan to punish Polymestor (870–94) and lures him into the tent (968–1023); his cries ring out, and the Chorus respond (1035–43); Hecuba taunts her victim and announces his return to the stage (1044–55); he enters crawling 'like a wild beast', singing a desperate aria (1056–82), and when Agamemnon has arrived in response to his cries for help he makes a long speech which includes a detailed account of how the women trapped him, killed his children and then blinded him (1132–82) – a most unconventional messenger speech which does duty as the first half of a set debate (*agōn*) and is triumphantly countered by Hecuba's brutal response. This is arguably more theatrical, as well as more thought-provoking, than an on-stage scuffle between Polymestor and Hecuba and the women; as in *Agamemnon*, the effect is to draw all the attention to the problematic nature of the violent deeds.

MODELS OF DEVELOPMENT

Just as the 'rule-bound' approach can obscure the scope for experiment and innovation within a genre, so there is an historical model that is still liable to exert a restrictive influence on the way the plays are read. In its simplest outline this is the old notion of development from a primitive phase, which may or may not include Aeschylus, to the perfection of Sophoclean form, followed by Euripidean decadence and fourth-century decline.[10] Aristotle contributed to the influence of this model, at least to the extent that he often treats Sophocles as the norm, sometimes at the expense of Euripides, and he sketches a history of the tragic chorus in terms that have often been echoed (and misunderstood) in modern times.[11]

It is probably in relation to the chorus that this general approach needs to be considered most carefully. There are two complicating factors. First, the texts show quite plainly that in the fifth century there was a trend towards composing plays with a smaller proportion of choral song and a higher proportion of spoken dialogue; secondly, by the end of the century some dramatists, following the lead of Agathon, used what Aristotle (*Poetics* 1456a29–30) calls *embolima*, 'things thrown in', songs which could appropriately be performed in different plays and were not designed to fit one particular place in one particular drama. This has often been taken to mean

[10] This goes back at least as far as the ancient *Life* of Aeschylus (16); see Easterling (1993a) 559–60, and Ch. 9 below.
[11] Sophocles preferred to Euripides: *Poet.* 1456a27; history of the chorus: 1449a17; 1456a25–32. For helpful comments on Aristotle cf. Halliwell (1987) 9–17.

that the chorus was in decline and beginning to be perceived as unimportant or even as an embarrassment, no longer an organic part of the action and easily reducible to the status of incidental entertainment. But this reading does not square with any of the surviving plays (including *Rhesus*; see p. 211 below), and it does not account for the continuing prestige of the tragic *chorēgia* as an institution. Choral performances evidently went on being in demand, even if their style and function altered significantly; what we should be envisaging is a rather complex process of change and development. Drama at Athens was an outstandingly popular and successful medium, widely imitated in other cities, particularly from the late fifth century onwards; naturally enough, as its prestige grew so did the scope for professionalism, and this must have been one of the factors that contributed to rapid change. For example, actors were becoming virtuosi who claimed more attention for their own musical performances, and in some plays solo lyrics by actors encroached on time which would previously have been allocated to choral odes, while in others great prominence was given to lyric exchanges between actors and chorus. At the same time the sheer volume of dramatic activity was increasing: more occasions and locations were found for performances, at the Rural Dionysia in the deme theatres in Attica, for instance, where it became common to revive plays that had won acclaim at the city festivals. Thus it must have been possible for the same theatre-goer to see old plays revived with their traditional choral parts, new plays composed in the same style or with more emphasis on solo singing by actors or on lyric exchange between actors and chorus, and new plays put on with entirely unconnected choral elements. Against this background we can easily see that in addition to the chorusmen recruited by the *chorēgoi* for the city festivals there might be a developing need for professional musical troupes with an adaptable repertoire of song and dance.[12]

The fact that choruses danced as well as sang is of enormous importance for the understanding both of tragedy as an art-form and of its relation to the festivals and the community to which it belonged. The immediate sensuous appeal of the choral performance, the *thelxis*, or enchantment, of the costumes, masks, dancing, song and its musical accompaniment, must not be overlooked when we try to trace the history of the chorus in tragedy. This must be a major reason why the musical element did not vanish from Greek tragic plays as the spoken part became more complex and elaborate. Modern directors putting on ancient plays often make their choruses speak rather than sing and dance; this would presumably have struck an ancient audience as completely pointless and perverse. In the broader context of the

---

[12] Pickard-Cambridge (1988) 90; this is a guess, but an attractive one.

festival the factor uniting all the Dionysiac competitions was the group of singers and dancers: fifty for the dithyramb, twenty-four for comedy, and at first twelve, later (from the mid-fifth century) fifteen, for tragedy and satyr play. Nor was this just a Dionysiac phenomenon: long before tragedy was invented at Athens in the latter part of the sixth century BC, the Greeks in general had been familiar with groups of worshippers who expressed their devotion to particular deities and celebrated festal occasions through richly varied patterns of formal song and dance. It is no accident that the Muses themselves were imagined as a divine *choros* singing and dancing in honour of their father Zeus to the accompaniment of Apollo's lyre; this was the paradigm image for performance in the Greek polis.[13]

SCRIPTS FOR PLAYERS

Given a general willingness to look at the genre of tragedy less as an organism following the pattern of birth, flowering and decay, and more as a medium of festival performance, we can discover much from studying the texts themselves as scripts to be performed. This is not a matter of considering how an individual director might choose to stage a particular play – though that has its own interest (cf. Chs. 10 and 11 below) – but rather of looking at ways in which the plays offer guidance, or cues, as to how they are to be articulated, whether by the reader in imagination or by actors and chorus in the theatre.

1. Speech, song, dance

At the most basic level, the rhythmical patterns into which every tragedy falls were designed to give manifold cues to their original audiences: lyric metres for song and dance by chorus or solo performer, other rhythms, particularly anapaests, for sections of recitative, spoken iambic lines for most dialogue scenes. The fact that every performance included a fair proportion of singing, chanting and dancing by the chorus implies that the audience's attention must be focused on the activity of the anonymous group as they respond, in whatever way, to the actions and sufferings of the named individuals on whom the plot turns. But it does not have to imply 'interlude': the chorus members are physically at the centre of the theatre space, not on the periphery, as they perform in the *orchēstra*, and in their movements they can mime past and future events, thus contributing in a radical way to the stage action. This may well have been true of such

---

[13] Paradoxically enough, since the dramatic *choros*, like that of the dithyramb, was exclusively male. For influential images of the Muses' *choros* see Hesiod, *Theogony* 1–8, Hom. *Hymn to Apollo* 188–93 (cf. Ch. 2 above); Henrichs (1995), and Lonsdale (1993), (1995).

passages as the recall of the sacrifice of Iphigeneia in *Agamemnon* (218–47) or the 'preview' of the suicide of Phaedra in *Hippolytus* (764–75 'She will fix a noose to hang from the beams of her bedroom, and fit it around her white neck ...'). Song and dance performed by a chorus on its own, marking a break of some kind in the action, are quite different from sung exchanges, or exchanges of alternating speech and song, between an actor and the chorus:[14] act-dividing lyrics can cover any lapse of time in the action, even a period of days, whereas songs shared with actors belong to the same time-frame as the spoken dialogue. When an individual speaker breaks into song there is a change or intensification of mood, a release of energy or emotion – an extreme example is Polymestor's aria after his blinding (above, pp. 154–5) – just as the division of single iambic lines between two or occasionally even three speakers signals some kind of climax or moment of crisis. When a scene of spoken dialogue modulates into anapaestic recitative this is often a strong signal that a play is about to end and that a shift of perspective is being made.[15]

There can be no doubt that the Greeks associated heightened delivery and rhythmic movement with the power to arouse emotion, whether in the performance of tragedy or in other kinds of communal activity – cultic, celebratory, military – and the point needs no special demonstration here. But it is important to remind ourselves, as modern readers, of the danger of interpreting *any* aspect of the formalism of Greek tragedy as emotionally 'cold'. Even long scenes of spoken dialogue, particularly scenes using stichomythia, where a couple of speakers alternate symmetrically, each uttering a line or a pair of lines in turn, may rely on the close matching of the iambic rhythms to achieve effects of great intensity, especially when the pattern is suddenly broken.[16]

One of the basic functions of these formal patterns is to mark the difference between theatrical and ordinary discourse, reminding the specta-tors that they are *theātai* at a special event with its own established conventions and its own kind of artifice. As in modern opera, the audience understands from the formal signals of rhythm and delivery how to 'read' what is presented. Euripides' *Medea*, for example, opens with a sequence which in terms of action is fairly simple: the old Nurse expresses concern over Jason's abandonment of Medea; the Tutor, returning with the children, brings news that Creon is planning to send them into exile with their mother; Medea cries out in desolation from inside the house; the Nurse

[14] The most comprehensive term for these exchanges is *amoibaion*; the term *kommos* is also often used by scholars, particularly for shared lamentation. See Popp (1971) 221–4.

[15] See e.g. Soph. *Ajax* 1402ff., *Phil.* 1409ff.; Eur. *Med.* 1389ff.

[16] Cf. Seidensticker (1971) and Ch. 6 above, pp. 127–8.

sends the children indoors, warning them to avoid approaching her; a group of local women arrive in response to Medea's lamentations and offer sympathy, asking the Nurse to persuade Medea to come out and see them; Medea eventually appears and tells them about her situation. All this could be enacted in a more or less homogeneous and naturalistic style of delivery – and often is, in modern productions – but the metres and dialect forms used in the Greek text make clear that the action was differentiated in a highly elaborate way.[17]

The scheme is as follows:

1–95 Spoken iambics

1–48 Formal opening speech by the Nurse in high tragic style, delivered to an empty stage.

49–95 Relatively low-key conversation between the two slaves in more naturalistic style.

96–130 Anapaests for alternating voices; song and recitative

Medea sings from inside the house, and the Nurse chants in recitative. This happens twice over, and the focus is on the Nurse's fears for what Medea may do to the children; they are sent indoors, and the Nurse expresses some general thoughts on the dangers that threaten great and powerful families.

131–213 Choral song and dance; solo song; recitative

131–47 Enter the Chorus, singing and dancing in the same anapaestic metre, but soon modulating into more varied lyrics (131–8). They ask the Nurse anxiously about Medea, and (139–43) she responds in chanted anapaests.[18] (144–7) Medea, still off-stage, sings again in the same anapaestic rhythm, her sung delivery contrasting with the Nurse's recitative.

148–203 This part falls into two sections, each beginning with a metrically responding song by the Chorus (148–59, *strophē* = 173–84, *antistrophē*). The first is directly addressed to Medea, offering her words of comfort, although she is still out of sight; then (160–7) her voice is heard again, calling the gods to witness her suffering, and the

---

[17] The scene is discussed by Harder (1993) 62–3.

[18] If we follow Diggle's text (OCT), which gives the Nurse non-lyric dialect here as elsewhere in the exchange. Diggle is probably right to make the Nurse's utterances consistently recitative, rather than a mixture of recitative and lyric as implied in some of the manuscripts (manuscript evidence is notoriously erratic in such cases). This is not to say that there was necessarily a fixed 'rule' that characters of low social status were not given singing parts: the essential criterion seems to be dramatic prominence; see Maas (1973) 47–8; Dale (1968) 50–2. Cf. pp. 111–12 above, with n. 18

Nurse (168–72) summarises her song and comments on it. In their
antistrophē the Chorus ask the Nurse to fetch Medea out; this time
nothing is heard from Medea, and the Nurse has a longer passage of
recitative: she will try to persuade Medea, but is afraid of her ferocity.
Once again (as at 119–30), the Nurse ends with general reflections,
this time on poetry and its inability to cure the pain of human
troubles.

204–13   The Chorus round off the whole of this sung section with a
summary of what they have heard Medea singing. The alternation of
voices in 96–213 thus follows the pattern (M = Medea, N = Nurse,
C = Chorus):

M N M N C M N C M N C

There is an effect of ring-composition in the opening and closing
choral songs, and the Nurse's two passages of general reflection are
symmetrically placed.

214–66   Spoken iambics

Medea comes out of the house and makes a long speech to the women
in an orderly and analytical style which contrasts strikingly with the
passionate emotion of her songs.

Although Medea is off stage until 214 and has the fewest lines until this
point, she is at the centre of attention throughout, and everything that is
heard from her and about her is at the highest pitch of intensity (all her
utterances are in song, and most are exclamations, curses or despairing
questions). The Nurse has most lines, but her part is confined to speaking
and chanting. She also has the closest contact with Medea and the children
and can act as interpreter for the audience, and to a lesser extent for the
Chorus, commenting on Jason's behaviour, Medea's distress, and the threat
posed for the children, as well as offering thoughts on the nature of tragic
experience and the inability of poetry to deal with it. But though so
authoritative, and indeed prophetic, she is a subordinate figure – an old
female slave, after all – and her role is to present Medea and her tragedy,
not herself.[19] The use of recitative, by contrast with the songs of the Chorus
and Medea, is one way of underlining this subordination, but because the
Nurse's chants are in the same metre as Medea's songs there is a strong
sense, too, of an intimate link between them. The Chorus, a sympathetic
group of relative outsiders, can offer some sort of model for the audience in
the theatre, at least to the extent that they are sorry for Medea and want to

[19] On slaves cf. Ch. 5 above, pp. 110–18; 122–4.

know more about her situation, but they are also 'women of Corinth in the heroic age', and their dancing, singing, masks and costumes must mark them out as a distinctive part of this particular fiction. Far more is at work here, evidently, than a simple contrast of emotional register – the impassioned Medea followed by the coolly calculating Medea – on which critics have concentrated most of their attention.

What is important is that every surviving tragedy makes use in some way of such formal patterning (cf. Ch. 8 below, pp. 186–90); this needs to be remembered when claims are made for a development towards a more naturalistic style in the latter part of the fifth century.

2. Deixis

The precise effect of some of these rhythmical patterns is not easy to recapture across the centuries, particularly as our knowledge of musical traditions is so limited, but it is less difficult to recognise the many kinds of signal to audiences that are implicit in the words of the texts. Their function is simple but fundamental, to help an audience grasp what aspect of a scene or a situation is to be at the centre of their attention at any given moment.[20] In the passage of *Medea* discussed above, for example, the language of the Chorus leaves no doubt that the dramatic focus is the off-stage cries of Medea. Their first words are 'I heard the voice, I heard the cry, of the unhappy Colchian' (132–2) and a couple of lines later they repeat the idea: 'I heard the lamentation from inside the house.'[21] When Medea cries out again they respond with 'Did you hear?' (148), and after her next outburst it is the Nurse who asks the question of them: 'Do you hear?' (169).[22] Their final song, summing up the whole scene, stresses the Chorus's *hearing* and Medea's *crying out* and *calling on the gods* (205–8). There is a comparable example in *Oedipus the King* at the point when the Theban shepherd is finally forced to reveal Oedipus' identity to him, and all attention is directed to the *saying* and *hearing* of the unsayable (1169–70; cf. Ch. 8 below, pp. 200–1).

Similarly, when a character invites others to look at him or her the stage action and the words combine to direct the audience's attention to the spectacle and its meaning, as when Heracles in *The Women of Trachis*, fatally poisoned by the robe that is clinging to him, first tells his son Hyllus

---

[20] Cf. Segal (1996), with Easterling's response.
[21] Reading ἀμφιπύλου γὰρ ἔσω μελάθρου γόον | ἔκλυον at 135–6 with Diggle; the MSS have ἐπ' ἀμφιπύλου ... βοὰν | ἔκλυον. For the text see Diggle (1984) 54–5.
[22] Cf. e.g. Soph. *Trach.* 863–7; Eur. *Hipp.* 565–600 for emphasis on sounds from off stage. By contrast, Eur. *Tro.* 153–8, 65–7 and 176–81 draw attention to the on-stage cries of Hecuba heard from off stage by the Chorus.

to stand close to look at his ravaged body and then invites everyone present: 'See, everyone look at my wretched body; see me in my misery, what a pitiable state I am in' (1079–80).[23] Whether or not all the spectators can see the detail of the actor's costume when he throws back the coverings (1078) is immaterial: what they can certainly see and reflect on is a group of people witnessing the horrific sight that is being displayed to them, and what matters dramatically is that it is a publicly shared disaster.

A great many, in fact, of the appeals, commands and questions expressed by one character to another or to the chorus also function as cues to the audience. 'What am I to do?', Neoptolemus' insistent question in *Philoctetes* (755, 895, 908, 974, 1393; cf. 963), gives a clear signal to the spectators that his moral perplexity is a significant dramatic issue, while in *Oedipus at Colonus* there is an important and ultimately unresolved tension between the despairing questions of Antigone and Ismene as they lament the loss of their father ('What fate now waits for you and me, dear sister, left without a father?', 1715–17; cf. 1685–8, 1734–6, 1748–50)) and the exhortations of Theseus and the Chorus ('Stop your lamentations: it is wrong to mourn', 1751–3; cf. 1720–3, 1777–9). True enough, Oedipus' mysterious passing is not to be equated with an ordinary death, but the sense of loss remains for the daughters, and the question of what will happen to them when they go back to Thebes looms over the end of the play.

There are many other more obvious signals, often relating to a play's form and structure, from entrance announcements ('Here comes Ismene, in tears ...', *Antigone* 526–30) to the marking of endings ('Enough! The time has been long drawn out already ...', *Ajax* 1402–3; 'Farewell, sea-girt land of Lemnos, send me on a safe voyage', *Philoctetes* 1464–5). When messengers arrive with news they often emphasise, after giving a 'headline' ('Jocasta is dead', *Oedipus the King* 1235), that they are in a position to tell the 'whole story', thus preparing the audience for the long speech that is to come.[24] Sometimes a scene of debate is specifically announced, as in *Ajax*, when after the unresolved dispute between Teucer and Menelaus the Chorus say 'There will be a contest (*agōn*) of great strife' (1163), which soon follows when Agamemnon himself appears and carries on the argument. Similarly in Euripidean debates speakers often discuss the kind of speech they need to make, or the way they should set out their arguments (e.g. Jason at *Medea* 522–5, 545–50).[25] Even cues as seemingly formal as these may be loaded in some way for the audience's benefit, as when the Chorus in *Antigone*, introducing Haemon, ask whether he is coming in

[23] Cf. e.g. Eur. *Hec.* 807–11.
[24] Cf. e.g. Aesch. *Pers.* 254–5; Soph. *O.T.* 1239–40, *El.* 680, 892.
[25] See Lloyd (1992) 4–6 for the regular 'markers' used in *agōnes* and Ch. 6 above.

distress at the loss of his bride (626–30), a subject studiously avoided, at least for a start, by Haemon himself. And Jason's remarks about the need for skill as an orator are devalued by the Chorus of *Medea* when they remark that he has made a handsome speech but they disapprove of his behaviour (576–8).

Choruses, too, often draw attention to what they are doing in the theatre: 'I will sing a dirge', 'Let us join the dance', 'See, the ivy sends me whirling in the dance', 'I kneel on the ground and call to the dead below', 'Hush, go on tiptoe, make no noise'. Sometimes they participate in ritual actions which seem to invite the audience's endorsement, even though embedded in the fictive action of the play, as when they make prayers to the gods for blessings on 'the city', particularly if 'the city' is, or can be identified with, Athens itself.[26]

3. Witnesses

One of the major functions of the chorus, though, is to act as a group of 'built-in' witnesses, giving collective and usually normative responses to the events of the play. Of course this is very far from being an adequate definition of their activities: quite apart from their crucial role as performers, these groups are often represented as personally involved in the events they witness, like the old men of Argos in *Agamemnon*, who are physically threatened at the end of the play, or the women of Troy who are waiting to be allocated to Greek masters (Eur. *Tro.* 292–3), and in a few plays they have a specific identity as major participants in the plot, like the daughters of Danaus in the Aeschylean *Suppliant Women*. But it is broadly true, at least, that as choruses express their hope or fear, joy or sorrow for the characters, they offer possible models for the onlookers' emotional responses, pity for Cassandra, for example, or grief for the murdered king in *Agamemnon*. But they can also be witnesses without fully revealing their response: thus the old Argives display a respectful attitude to Clytemnestra which begins to seem more and more like veiled hostility, and in *Antigone* the Theban elders are said by Antigone to be afraid to speak their mind (509), a claim which directs the audience's attention to what they might 'really' be thinking. Again, in *Bacchae*, when the mad Agave displays the head of Pentheus as her hunting trophy, the women ask her questions which seem to imply mixed reactions on their part: revulsion at the same time as exultation (1169–201).

Thus the emotional range is immense, and the guidance offered by a

---

[26] Aesch. *Pers.* 947, *Eum.* 307; Soph. *Trach.* 218–20; Eur. *Tro.* 1305–9, *Or.* 140–1. Cf. Easterling (1993b) 17–18; Henrichs (1995); Ch. 2 above.

chorus may be quite elusive. The very fact that the tragic chorus is a group of twelve or fifteen people and not a single figure gives its behaviour more scope to fluctuate with fluctuating circumstances: it does not have to be as consistent as a single individual, and it speaks of itself in the plural just as freely as in the singular.[27] Its job is to help the audience *become involved in the process of responding*, which may be a matter of dealing with profoundly contradictory issues and impulses.

Often, indeed, the chorus combines witnessing with trying to understand, and its guidance is intellectual or even philosophical as well as emotional. *Agamemnon* illustrates this very well: the old men claim authority to speak of what happened when the Greeks were setting off on their expedition to Troy, but they repeatedly express their perplexity and the difficulty of making judgements, and in their struggle to decode what is happening to Agamemnon and his family they turn to the imagery of mantic interpretation (681–5, 975–83, 1112–13, 1130–5, 1366–7). Their language thus directs the audience to the problems of interpretation presented by the action, and paradoxically, despite the depth of some of their meditations, they are less able to 'see' than the audience itself. In the scene with Cassandra, for example, they fail to follow her reading of her visions, saying they have 'strayed from the track' (1245). This provokes Cassandra to spell out her message unambiguously: 'I say you will see the death of Agamemnon', a message which must by now have been plain to most of the spectators. Even then the old men cannot guess who the killer will be, and the language of their conversation with Cassandra makes ironic play with the difficulty of understanding prophecy (1251–5).

This kind of contradiction is the norm rather than the exception in tragedy: choruses typically fail to see what is clear to the audience, but at the same time they have the power to speak with authoritative wisdom, 'more truly than they know', and thus to offer guidance at the deepest level of understanding. In *Agamemnon*, for instance, the simple-seeming tale (717–36) of the lion cub, the lovable little creature that grows into a hideously destructive beast, encapsulates in a couple of brief stanzas the whole history of Helen and Troy and the House of Atreus.[28] Even in plays where the chorus is a group of inexperienced young girls rather than meditative elders, there are passages where they guide the audience's understanding in the same way, as at *Women of Trachis* 132–5: 'Neither glimmering night, nor misfortunes, nor prosperity stay with human beings, but suddenly they are gone, and it is someone else's turn to be happy and to be deprived of happiness.' The idea of alternating joy and sorrow, a

---

[27] Kaimio (1970) sets out the evidence.   [28] See Knox (1952).

traditional one in Greek thought, gives this play its basic structural pattern; here as often the Chorus's reflection is expressed in language hallowed by long proverbial use and makes an appeal to shared traditions of thought and feeling.

Sometimes a chorus draws explicit attention to its role as witness or spectator, as a model for the audience itself. In *Oedipus the King*, for example, the Chorus are caused to reflect on the fragility of all human success and happiness by their witnessing of Oedipus' discovery of the truth about himself:

> Ah generations of mortals! I count your life as nothing. What man is there, what man, who achieves more of happiness than seeming to be happy, and after the seeming, failure? With your destiny as my example, yours, unhappy Oedipus, I call nothing that is mortal blessed. (1186–96)

Or the prospect of witnessing a horrific situation may be so painful that the chorus wish they could avoid it altogether by flying away ('O for the wings of a dove!') or by being blown away by the wind; just occasionally they wish they could be transported elsewhere to see something desirable, like Theseus' hoped-for rescue of Antigone and Ismene in *Oedipus at Colonus*.[29] And there are times when the off-stage action becomes so absorbing that they threaten to desert their role as witness in the *orchēstra* and enter the stage-building, where choruses are not normally expected to go. In *Agamemnon* when the king cries out in his death agony the old men debate whether or not to enter the palace (1343–71), and there are similar scenes in *Medea* and *Hippolytus*, all of them pointedly referring to established theatrical convention and thus reminding the spectators that they are watching a play. This kind of subtle contact with the audience, through the reminder of the 'here and now' in the theatre, has often been achieved in drama from Elizabethan times onwards through the device of the stage audience and the play-within-the-play, but Greek tragedy with its ready-made group of witnesses within the dramatic action could operate more flexibly, a point that now needs to be put in a wider context.

'THE PLAY'S THE THING'

Until recently, critics used to resist the idea that Greek tragedies were designed in such a way as to remind their audiences of the theatrical event itself. Unlike comedy, which regularly addresses the spectators and refers to dramatic forms and stage business, tragedy does not openly refer to the

---

[29] O.C. 1081–4. For the wish to fly away from distress cf. e.g. Soph. *Trach.* 953–8; Eur. *Hipp.* 732–4, 1290–3 with Barrett's notes.

theatre, largely no doubt because in the heroic past in which the plays are set theatres did not exist – there are no theatres or plays in Homer, and the tragedians plainly took trouble to avoid introducing 'modern' detail that might lower the tragic tone.[30] But work in different areas of criticism – on the semiotics of drama, on intertextuality, irony and self-reflexiveness – has helped to bring about a shift in attitudes.[31] Given that drama in general depends on the paradox that everything presented to an audience is *both* real, in the sense that flesh-and-blood people are taking part in the enacting and witnessing of the event, *and* make-believe, in that the characters and situations presented to the audience are feigned, and given that audiences are generally capable of dealing with this paradox, we are forced to conclude that there is no such thing as a 'dramatic illusion' secure enough to be 'broken'. (Greek audiences evidently found no difficulty in weeping with Hecuba and Oedipus and at the same time taking an intense sporting interest in the outcome of the dramatic competition.) If 'dramatic illusion' is not an absolute the question becomes one of degree, whether a particular dramatic tradition actually seeks to remind audiences of the fictiveness of what they are seeing on stage or strives to draw their attention away from the medium itself.

An example often quoted of a major difference between Greek tragedy and comedy is direct address to the audience.[32] Tragedy has nothing to compare with the very common 'O Spectators' or 'Gentlemen' of comedy, even less with such extravagant outbursts as Strepsiades' in Aristophanes' *Clouds*: 'You poor things, why are you just sitting there stupidly for us clever people to exploit, you stones, mere numbers, useless sheep, rows and rows of jars?' (1201–3). But suppose we think away the conventions of naturalistic acting (as makes sense, since naturalistic acting is a development of the late nineteenth century), and imagine a tradition in which actors act with more overt acknowledgement of the audience: then the question of whether audiences are specifically addressed becomes less significant. There is nothing naturalistic about such play-openings as those of the Euripidean *Electra* or *Phoenician Women*, where a lone character talks in an expository way on an empty stage, or of Aeschylus' *Persians*, where the Chorus, as they march into the *orchēstra*, identify themselves as faithful guardians left behind by Xerxes and his army, and passages like these were surely designed to be played by actors and chorusmen who face out to the audience to give them necessary information. The tone is arguably more dignified – as befits tragedy – because the audience are not openly acknowledged, but this does

[30] Cf. Bain (1977) 209–10; Easterling (1985) 6.
[31] See e.g. Segal (1982); Goldhill (1986); Zeitlin (1989); Bierl (1991); Ch. 8 below, pp. 195–6.
[32] Cf. Bain (1987) for a recent discussion of the problem.

not mean that they are not to be reminded of their role as spectators. The opening line of *Persians*, for example, is quite closely modelled on the opening line of Phrynichus' *Phoenician Women*, in a scene evidently designed to recall that play and to appeal to their recent theatrical experience. In *Agamemnon*, too, when the Watchman says (39) 'I speak to those who understand', after making dark remarks about the state of the royal house, there is no one present to 'understand' except those members of the audience who can guess from their knowledge of earlier poetry what he is talking about.

Perhaps the main difference between tragedy and comedy lies not in their contact with the audience but in the tone of that contact. For the tragedian there is a paramount question of decorum, that is, of what is appropriate to the seriousness and dignity of the genre and to its setting in the time of the Homeric heroes (which could easily turn into burlesque). What is crucial is the mixture of past and present: the setting in heroic times in no way precludes reference to the contemporary world, and indeed depends on a multitude of ironic reminders to the audience that *they are in the present*, watching events that purport to be happening in another time and place. The more this tension can be exploited, the more powerfully should the play be able to enthrall its audience. A passage in *Eumenides* illustrates this point well. At 681 Athena begins the foundation-speech for the Areopagus with an appeal to the 'Attic people' to hear her ordinance. The next line makes it clear that her addressees are the citizens selected to be jurors at the trial of Orestes; there is thus no explicit address to the theatre audience as such. But if we take 'Attic people' as reminding the spectators of their own identity and prompting them to link themselves imaginatively with the citizens who long ago participated in that significant trial, we can see the force of J. L. Styan's description of spectators as 'self-conscious participants in the act of play making' and find the idea of *collaboration* or even *collusion* between play and audience more persuasive than that of 'breaking the illusion' or 'breaking the spell'.[33]

The placing of Athena's words to the 'Attic people' is important. The speech in which she announces the foundation of the Court of the Areopagus is an aetiological one, linking the events of the play with an institution known to the audience from their contemporary experience and recently the focus of violent political discord. Aetiology in drama must always function as a device for making the audience aware of more than one plane of reality – since the future predicted by a prophet or laid down by divine ordinance,

---

[33] Styan (1975) 158, cf. 153. For 'breaking the illusion' see Bain (1987) 10–14 and for 'breaking the spell' Taplin (1986) 164–5, 171.

as here, is guaranteed to be fulfilled because it is already the audience's past and present history. Such patterns are often established with great solemnity; they are certainly not to be seen as antiquarian oddities or signs of passing playfulness. Indeed, the 'collusion' between play and audience discussed so far is too pervasive to be seen as a matter of a little teasing of a rather marginal, even trivial, kind for the benefit of the *cognoscenti* among the spectators.[34] Nor is it confined to Euripides, the dramatist generally thought to be the most overt and witty in his use of 'metatheatrical' effects.

As an example of how one play might be designed to recall another through what was shown on stage and therefore make a reference that would be readily 'readable' by a large proportion of the spectators, one might choose the *Electra* plays by Sophocles and Euripides and their relation to Aeschylus' *Libation-Bearers*. In that play there is a scene which made a great impression on later vase-painters, and therefore, we may guess, on audiences: the scene in which Electra pours offerings and prays for vengeance at Agamemnon's tomb, before she sees the lock of hair and the footprints and is eventually reunited with her brother (84–263).[35] The visual focus is first on the urn carried by Electra and on the pouring of offerings, then on her discoveries at the tomb, the signs of Orestes' presence, which have to be interpreted before the recognition can take place. Electra with the urn – a memorable theatrical image – recurs in the Sophoclean play when Orestes gives her the bronze funerary vessel that he says contains the ashes of her dead brother. She holds it in her arms, making it the object of her most intense speech in the play (1125–70), and so long as she holds it she cannot be convinced that Orestes is alive after all: he has to force her to put it down before the truth can be understood (1205–29). Here the urn both represents the focus of Electra's affection and in its emptiness functions as the sign of deception. In the Euripidean play[36] the urn becomes the water-pot which is the emblem of Electra's humble life-style: as she enters the acting area (54) she is seen carrying it on her head like a slave; it is prominent, too, at the beginning of what 'ought' to be the recognition scene (107–9).[37] Each of the later dramatists seems to exploit the power of the stage picture to recall another play, and to suggest to those of the spectators

---

[34] Bain (1987) 13–14 with n. 64.

[35] For the vases see *LIMC* III.1, 709–14 (I. McPhee); Taplin (1993) 24 and n. 7 thinks that 'any recollection of *Choephoroi* must have been, at most, sporadic'; cf. p. 72 above.

[36] I deliberately refrain from attempting a relative dating of the two plays; for discussion see the bibliography cited by Zimmermann (1991) 138–9.

[37] Both Sophocles and Euripides postpone the recognition: cf. Soph. *El.* 80–5, 871–937; Eur. *El.* 107–11, 487–546.

who recall the famous scene in *Libation-Bearers* that what they are seeing now has a new kind of message to offer.

Sophocles' version of the story of Philoctetes is the only one to have survived; if we had those of Aeschylus and Euripides as well it might be possible to trace some scenic interconnexions like the ones with Electra's urn. As it is, there are interesting textual links in this exuberantly allusive and 'collusive' play both with what is known of the other plays and with earlier poetry, and there is strong theatrical self-consciousness in the use of a deception scene within a deception scene. This scene with the False Merchant (539–627) makes complex contact with the audience and in doing so raises some of the play's most fundamental issues.

At 539 the Chorus announce the approach of a member of Neoptolemus' crew along with a 'stranger', whom the audience must suspect to be Odysseus' scout in the disguise of a trader. In the prologue Odysseus promised to send this man to help Neoptolemus if he seemed to be taking a long time to trick Philoctetes into leaving the island, and he added the warning that the man would speak *poikilōs*, 'artfully', 'elaborately', 'speciously' (130–1) – a clear signal to the audience that the language would demand special attention. When he arrives the 'trader' (whose part, incidentally, must be played by the actor who plays Odysseus) explains that he has just happened to put in at Lemnos and by chance has come upon Neoptolemus' ship. He is sailing back from Troy to his home Peparethos, a good place for vines (548–9). For any member of the audience who recalls the passage at the end of *Iliad* 7 (467–75) describing the shipping of wine to the Greeks at Troy, this must imply that the 'trader' has been delivering a cargo of wine; what is particularly engaging is that the Iliadic passage makes the wine come from Lemnos, which in this play is a desert island. This is a Sophoclean innovation; Aeschylus and Euripides had each had a chorus of Lemnians, naturally enough, since Lemnos had plenty of epic associations as an inhabited place, but the Sophoclean Philoctetes must be totally isolated from humankind, and the delicate allusion to the play's own inventiveness has something of the flavour of the Paedagogus' lying tale in *Electra* (680–765), which draws on the story of the chariot race in *Iliad* 23.

The 'trader' now (553ff.) warns Neoptolemus that he is in danger from the Greeks, who want to fetch him back to Troy: Phoenix and the sons of Theseus are on his track. 'Why not Odysseus?' asks Neoptolemus, 'Why did he not come to be his own messenger? Surely he wasn't *afraid* ...?' (The audience might wonder how far Neoptolemus was playing his deceptive role, how far expressing doubts about Odysseus' behaviour in the present mission.) In the Cyclic epic version of his story Neoptolemus was fetched from his home on Scyros by Odysseus, while Diomedes went to Lemnos for Philoctetes, but in Euripides' play Diomedes accompanied Odysseus to Lemnos[38] – and this is the scenario suggested here by the False Merchant (570–2): 'Oh, when I left he and Diomedes were going off in pursuit of *someone else*.' Then in an elaborate aside he pretends to be anxious not to let Philoctetes overhear this little scene that is being played for his benefit.

There are other ways in which the scene refers to its own deceptiveness. At 575, in response to the 'trader', who asks 'Who is this man?' Neoptolemus, addressing his confederate as 'Stranger', makes a ceremonious introduction: 'This is the famous Philoctetes', which recalls the painful exchange earlier when Neoptolemus pretended never to have heard of him (248–53). Philoctetes' next words (578–9) offer a moral commentary on the whole passage: 'Why does he bargain with you about me in dark whispers?' *Diempolai*, 'treat as merchandise', is a good metaphor for both the False Merchant and for Odysseus his promoter.[39] Neoptolemus' answer to Philoctetes, 'I don't yet know what he is saying' suggests both that he is taking part in 'play-acting', because he goes on to tell the Merchant to speak openly for everyone to hear, and that he is not yet clear about what Odysseus' covert message might be. 'Speaking openly', too, is precisely what he has not been doing himself; similarly when he declares that Philoctetes is his 'greatest friend' the Merchant's reply (589, taking only half a line and breaking the run of stichomythia) is 'Watch what you are doing, boy' (ὅρα τί ποιεῖς, παῖ), which conveys at least three different signals at once. For Philoctetes as onlooker in the pretended situation it strengthens the sense of danger and of Neoptolemus' willingness to run risks on his behalf; for Neoptolemus it is a warning message from Odysseus to play his part in the deception carefully; for the audience, a suggestion that the young man must 'watch what he is doing' morally, and an invitation to savour the dramatic fiction itself. Neoptolemus completes the line with 'I have been doing that [sc. watching what I am doing] for a long time', which the audience may take, if they wish, as a hint that Neoptolemus has been feeling qualms about the propriety of deceiving the trusting Philoctetes. On the other hand, it could 'simply' mean 'Don't worry; I am carrying out Odysseus' orders and playing my part well.'

What is important here is that the ironic play with the dramatic medium is intimately related to the central issues of *Philoctetes*: truth and lies, loyalty and treachery, honour and self-interest, the conflicting needs, and the conflicting rhetoric, of individuals and groups. The collusion in which

---

[38] Proclus' summary of *Little Iliad* gives Philoctetes' story; cf. Dio Chrys. 52.14.

[39] Østerud (1973) 21–5.

the spectators are invited to participate has nothing in the least frivolous or trivial about it, but it may well contribute to the creation of that pleasure proper to tragedy on which Aristotle insists in the *Poetics* (1425b33; 1453a36).[40] One of the paradoxical features of the genre is precisely the fact that it gives pleasure while presenting material that is always sombre, often horrifying and frightening. It disturbs the audience's feelings, and forces them to confront problems that typically have no solutions. But people enjoy tragedy, and at the root of this enjoyment must be awareness of the medium itself, which through the distancing devices of form and convention is able to prevent the terror or despair or horror in the story from threatening the audience's capacity to remain an audience – or the reader's willingness to read on.

It remains true, however, that tragedy deals with extremely dangerous material. How, we might wonder, did a medium which attracted so much public notice and acquired so much prestige contrive to challenge its audiences in such radical ways about the nature and values of their community and their own sense of themselves? Or we could reverse the question and ask how drama of a specifically tragic kind came to acquire so central a position, exposed to the scrutiny, and inviting the empathetic response, of the assembled polis. Either way tragedy at Athens is almost unimaginable without the traditions of epic and lyric poetry as its context, traditions of story-telling and performance which had shaped a particular view of what was authentic in Greek life. From these, tragedy could take the habit of telling and enacting myths that dealt with threats to rationality and order, to the integrity of a family, or to the survival of a whole community, in language and artistic forms of extraordinary glamour (cf. Ch. 6, pp. 129–30).

Tragedy's high style, not only in the formally more elevated sections of song and recitative, but also in scenes of spoken dialogue and debate, is a crucial aspect of its meaning. Though very far from being Homeric pastiche, this style uses many words and forms that do not belong to the everyday spoken language of contemporary Athens, and even passages that use very little poetic colouring, like the passage from *Philoctetes* discussed above (pp. 169–70; cf. Ch. 6, pp. 141–5), are marked off from ordinary speech by the formality of their metrical patterns. All this implies a tacit understanding on the part of the community – the community that constitutes the audience, contributes to the funding, supplies the performers and controls the competition in which they compete – that heroic images of behaviour are appropriate to contemporary society as well as to an idealised past. The high language and noble persons of the plays belong not to 'period drama'

---

[40] Cf. Belfiore (1992) 44–82.

but to a form which offers images of behaviour such as contemporary society would like to see in its 'best' citizens, at the same time as finding ways of dramatising the danger to which they are always exposed: the transgressive desires of individuals, familial and civil discord, and existential factors like time and mortality.[41]

It is interesting that the essentially aristocratic bias of the Homeric poems and of much choral lyric poetry could so easily be reinterpreted to suit a democratic society. The notion of the 'best people' (as Louis Gernet pointed out)[42] could be transferred from one kind of elite, an aristocracy, to another, the citizen body, and whenever a *choros* performed on a ritual occasion, even if it was composed of some select group, it could always in some sense represent the wider community. Tragedy could therefore use these traditional elements – the hero and the chorus – to serve the needs of contemporary democratic society; the fact that both had a poetic pedigree, recognisable in their language and performance, may have served, like their masks and dignified costumes, to maintain the necessary distance between the audience and the events represented in the play. This notional distance is not, however, easily measured, particularly if it is true that the 'meta-theatrical' or ironic effects discussed above actually reinforce contact between play and audience through reminders of the play's fictionality. We must also remember that the same group of actors and chorusmen, after putting on three tragedies in succession, rounded off the day's events with a satyr play (cf. Ch. 2). The modulation, or constant renegotiation, of 'distance' is clearly something that needs to be taken into account.

In the end the most important point must be that the plays were about real issues,[43] however much the theatrical event involved displacement[44] – to another *time*, the heroic age, when gods might appear and make themselves known to mortals, to other *places*, whether Attic or foreign, but certainly not the Theatre of Dionysus on the Athenian Acropolis, to *persons* whose fictional status was emphasised by the fact that a single actor might play several of them, male or female, young or old, god or mortal, in one afternoon. The reason why all this elaboration was necessary and desirable was that the contradictions and problems explored in action in the theatre were fundamental to Greek religious and political thinking, and explosive enough to provoke violent reactions if audiences were not kept aware of the essentially metaphorical status of everything enacted before them. It is only because in some texts this metaphorical quality was so sustained that they

---

[41] See Griffith (1995).

[42] Gernet (1968) 333–43 (reprint of an article first published in 1938).

[43] For a fresh examination of some examples see Williams (1993).

[44] Cf. Zeitlin (1990) 65.

have survived as part of a living literary tradition inviting constant re-interpretation.

A SAMPLE: EURIPIDES' *TROJAN WOMEN*

This play deals with the worst that can happen to a city; Adrian Poole aptly called it 'Euripides' *Endgame*'.[45] It uses the events of the Trojan War, particularly the last hours before the ultimate firing of the ruins, when the men are already dead, the women waiting to be allocated to their new masters, and the victors preparing to sail home. The play was put on in 415 BC, when the possibility that a Greek city might be annihilated was not at all a remote one for the audience. Plataea, an allied city, hardly more than forty miles from Athens, had been utterly destroyed the year after it capitulated to the Peloponnesians in 427, and at Scione in Chalcidice in 421 and at Melos in 416 the Athenians themselves had put to death all the males of military age and enslaved the rest of the community. Euripides' play, the third in a group on related Trojan themes, must surely have been perceived as suggesting meanings relevant to its own times,[46] but the story of the fall of Troy had special advantages as a myth for all times. Troy was both the most 'real' of all ancient cities because of its vivid presence in the *Iliad* and, being non-Greek, the least obviously paradigmatic of a contemporary Greek polis. Even if there had been no risk of its being considered too painful or inflammatory, a play on the fall of a *Greek* city might have seemed intolerably ill-omened, whereas the whole point about Troy was that it fell. The distance in time and space and the cast of appropriate heroic characters in no way reduce the power of the text to challenge and disturb. It is worth looking at some ways in which the play prompts the audience's reactions.

The prologue at once suggests a strong sense of the desolation of the ruined city: Poseidon, the god who was its protector, is on the point of abandoning it: 'I am leaving famous Ilion and my altars, for when evil desolation takes hold of a city the things of the gods are sick and not given honour' (25-7). When gods appear on stage in Greek tragedy they always have a quasi-'directorial' role, establishing contact with the audience on a different level from that on which the human characters function, and thus offering ironic perspectives, often on the shape of the action to come, as in *Hippolytus* when Aphrodite, announcing to the audience the arrival of the doomed hero, says, 'He does not know that the gates of Hades have been opened for him, and that he looks on the daylight for the last time today' (56-7). Here the directorial role is divided between a pair of deities.

---

[45] Poole (1967) 257.   [46] Cf. Ch. 1 above, p. 31-2.

Poseidon first explains what has happened to Troy and the Trojan royal family, and introduces the stage picture: the figure of Hecuba, already in view of the audience, lying prostrate, overwhelmed by the extremity of her grief. 'And this unhappy woman, Hecuba, *if anyone wishes to see her*, here she is [lit. it is easy] lying in front of the gates, weeping many tears for many causes' (36–8). Then Athena extends the time reference to the future by asking Poseidon to help her take vengeance on the victorious Greeks. She was their champion in the past, but now they have insulted her by failing to punish the violence done to Cassandra by Ajax, son of Oileus. Zeus has promised to send a storm and lend her his thunderbolt; Poseidon is to help by stirring the sea and causing shipwrecks, 'so that the Greeks may know in future to respect my shrines and to honour the other gods' (85–6). Poseidon agrees at once; for the audience there ought to be no doubt that he means what he says. In the epic story (the Cyclic *Nostoi, Returns*) the Greek ships did get wrecked on their way back from Troy; a quite brief sketch of the horrors to come is enough to give the scene intertextual resonance. Thus the prologue creates an ironic framework within which the last hours of Troy are to be viewed.

Poseidon's parting words open out, as lines at ends of scenes often do, beyond the immediate situation: 'The man who destroys cities is a fool, and through making desolate temples and tombs, the sacred places of the dead, he himself later meets his ruin' (94–6). These lines give a clear signal that the coming action should be 'read' as a cautionary tale, an example for all times and places. But the message is not a simple one: the idea 'the winners are also to be losers' is given more weight than any detached assessment of the rights and wrongs of what the two sides have done, and at the end of the play no divine figure offers further explanation. This strongly suggests that no divine explanation exists for the suffering that constitutes the action of the rest of the play.

The role of Hecuba, the archetypal sufferer, is a magnificent one in theatrical terms.[47] From the prologue, where her prostrate figure is pointed out by Poseidon, to the last moment of the play, she is visible to the audience; after the gods' departure she is at the centre of the action, whether as prime singer or speaker or as the character most closely affected by all the other events – by what is happening to Cassandra, Andromache, Astyanax, the city itself. She speaks, chants or sings almost a quarter of the lines of the play; as well as solo song and recitative she takes part in lyric exchanges with the Chorus and Andromache, sings in response to Talthybius' spoken

---

[47] For comparable 'star' parts cf. Medea, Hecuba in her name-play, the Sophoclean Electra, and Oedipus in both *O.T.* and *O.C.*

lines, dominates the dialogue scenes and makes four big 'set-piece' speeches. She is also at the centre of the stage action: she begins her first chant as she lies on the ground and tries to raise herself (98–121); her first long speech is made from the ground after her collapse at 462; at the end of the play when she is being led off into captivity she tries to throw herself into the fire of the burning city (1282–3). But most often she is seen taking part in ritual: initiating lamentation (143–52), decorating the corpse of Astyanax (1209–34), beating the ground to make contact with the dead Trojans as she leaves the city (1305–7).[48]

The dramatic figure of Hecuba is thus one of power although she typifies weakness; this sense of authority is confirmed in her long speeches, each of which contributes something new to the audience's understanding. The first (466–510) is the most direct. Its theme is her change of fortune from regal state to bereavement and degradation; but it is not only her experience, or the Trojan experience: 'Call no successful person fortunate before he dies' (509–10). The second speech (686–708) is shorter and less climactic, placed between Andromache's two much longer ones. It is a brief attempt at consolation, ending with hopes for Troy's recovery through Astyanax, and it is immediately followed by the news that the child is to be thrown from the walls of the city. The whole scene charts the destruction of hope, but Hecuba's speech marks the need felt by sufferers to try to give strength to others. The third and longest of her speeches (969–1032) is her triumphant reply to Helen's self-defence. The second speaker in an *agōn* normally had the favoured position;[49] Hecuba seems to succeed in persuading Menelaus that Helen deserves a public stoning, but perhaps the triumph is hollow, as the references to future punishment with which the scene ends are contradicted by familiar scenes in the *Odyssey* of Menelaus and Helen happily settled back at home.[50] As in the prologue, there is an invitation to the audience to fill the gaps left by the text; even a spectator ignorant of the *Odyssey* could not feel certain that Menelaus would be able to resist his desire for Helen. The last speech (1156–206) shows Hecuba at her most authoritative as she pronounces a funeral oration over her grandson, concluding with lines that closely echo Poseidon's in the prologue, but this time the 'fool' is not the sacker of cities, but the person who feels complacent and secure in good fortune. Once more the equation between winners and losers is what comes out most strongly.

The most intense of all Hecuba's moments of understanding comes at the end of her obsequies for Astyanax: she suddenly stops her antiphonal

[48] Cf. Easterling (1993b) 19–20.   [49] But see Lloyd (1992) 17.
[50] *Od.* 4.1–305. Cf. Ch. 6 above, pp. 147–8 and Croally (1994).

singing with the Chorus, and prompted by their surprised questions she reflects on the meaning of her sorrows, the sorrows of Troy, 'of all cities the most hated by the gods', and the futility of the Trojans' piety, and concludes that without these disasters they would have perished without trace, without 'giving subjects of song to the poetry of future generations' (1240–5). These words raise questions about the function of poetry, and indeed of the play itself, all the more so as they are closely modelled on lines spoken by Helen in the *Iliad* (6.357–8).[51] As used by Helen the idea is a bitter one; she and Paris will be sung about to their shame; Hecuba's tone is less unambiguous, but there is no hint of easy consolation in her words, as she goes on to cast doubt on the meaning for the dead of the ritual she has just performed (1246–50).

The importance of the Chorus in this play is marked by Poseidon in the prologue: he explains that some of the Trojan women have already been allocated to Greek masters, but those who have not are 'in this building here, chosen for the leaders of the army' (32–5). So they are a significant group, although unlike the royal family they have no names, and it is never made clear what will happen to each of them individually. Their role is to provide a context for Hecuba's grief and to share in ritual with her; above all it is they who bring Troy into the play. The difference between actors and chorus is brought out very clearly right at the beginning of the play. Much is made in the first lyric exchange between Hecuba and the women about their anxieties for their own future: they are terrified at the sound of the queen's laments, fearing deportation or death, waiting for news from the herald, dreading being parted from their children, speculating about the Greek cities they may go to (153–229). But when Talthybius arrives with the news that each is to go to a separate master and tells Hecuba to ask for details one by one, the list is exhausted with the royal family: Cassandra, Polyxena, Andromache, Hecuba herself. At 292–93 the Chorus ask 'What about me?', but the herald has no reply; all that concerns him now is to have Cassandra fetched out, as Agamemnon's prize, so that he can then take the rest to their masters. No more is heard about the women's destinations until their song at 1089–99, and even then they know nothing further, but this is no marginal group of bystanders, and their presence is a constant reminder of the communal disaster.[52] When they sing about the Wooden Horse and the Greeks coming out of ambush (511–76), or about the sound of the lamentations at Troy (826–32), or about the neglect of worship at the old sacred sites (1059–80), they create for the audience a

---

[51] See Segal (1993b) 29–33.
[52] Cf. the function of the citizen chorus in *O.T.*, or that of the Elders in *Persians*.

more tangible sense of the city that has been destroyed than anything in any of the characters' speeches.

The song about the Wooden Horse begins, most unusually for a choral ode in tragedy, with an appeal to the Muse to sing them a new kind of song, a 'dirge accompanied by tears'. The newness, presumably, is not in the idea of lamentation itself, but in the idea of a dirge for a city.[53] The phrasing also draws attention to the text's own 'newness', another reminder of the play as performance, just as the extraordinary parody of a marriage song performed by the 'maenad' Cassandra turns into an invitation to Hecuba and the women to join the dance (308–40). For the Chorus and Hecuba her performance generates only horror; Hecuba tells the women to 'answer her wedding songs with tears' (350–1).

Finding the right kind of song to suit the terrible events at Troy is evidently a major issue. A similar question of perspectives is raised by the mad Cassandra, whose interpretation both of events in the Trojan War and of the future is closer to the vantage point of the prologue than anyone else's; but neither Hecuba nor the Chorus nor Talthybius can take the measure of what she says (cf. Ch. 6, pp. 134–5). The old proverbial sayings about the mutability of fortune take on new grimness when they are seen in the context of the destruction of a whole community and its culture, but Hecuba's words at 1240–5 have to be taken into account at the very end of the play, when she leads the women in a farewell ritual for the Trojan dead, beating the ground and calling out to children and husbands. The emphasis is all on loss and annihilation, but at least one statement can be understood differently by an audience brought up on epic poetry. When the Chorus sing that the 'name of the land will vanish' and 'Troy no longer exists' (1322–24) they are singing for an audience for whom Troy's name has survived.

BIBLIOGRAPHICAL NOTE

See Bibliographical Note to Chapter 8.

[53] Cf. Barlow (1986) *ad loc.*

8

PETER BURIAN

Myth into *muthos*: the shaping of tragic plot

TRAGEDY AS REPETITION AND INNOVATION

> Tragedie is to seyn a certyn storie
> as olde bookes maken us memorie
> of hym that stood in greet prosperitee
> and is yfallen out of heigh degree
> into miserie, and endeth ureccedly.[1]

In the Middle Ages, when tragedy as an enactment on stage had been all but forgotten, Chaucer still knew the right shape for a tragic tale. In such a scheme, only the names need be changed, for the form of the tale – and its meaning – always remain the same. Of course, Chaucer's definition is far too restrictive to describe the shapes that Greek tragic plots actually took, but even the much more knowing and differentiated analysis in Aristotle's *Poetics*, from which Chaucer's notion of tragedy ultimately derives,[2] appears to certify only some of the plots used by the tragedians as properly tragic. Still, it is clear that in practice not any subject was a tragic subject, not any plot-shape suitable to the requirements of the tragic stage. First, the plots of Greek tragedies were drawn largely from a limited repertoire of legends, the great cycles in which the Greeks came to terms with their own past – the stories of 'a few families', as Aristotle says, above all the legendary histories of Troy and Thebes.[3] Secondly, as we shall see, it appears that a

---

[1] Geoffrey Chaucer, *Canterbury Tales*: 'The Monk's Prologue' 85–9. That Chaucer is here thinking of epic is made clear from the next lines: 'And they ben versifyed comunly / Of six feet, which men clepe *exametron*.'

[2] For the development of the idea of tragedy from Aristotle through the Middle Ages, see Kelly (1993); for Chaucer's importance in the tradition, esp. 170–5.

[3] *Poetics* 1453a19. Aristotle is speaking of a restriction in subject matter that in his view characterises the best recent tragedies, but what we can learn of all but the earliest tragic practice suggests a similar concentration of subjects. Among the surviving thirty-two tragedies, fifteen deal with the 'matter of Troy', seven with Theban saga, and in addition four (all by Euripides) dramatise episodes in the legendary history of Athens. Of course these categories are not exclusive; Sophocles' *Oedipus at Colonus* brings Oedipus to his final

relatively few underlying plot-shapes ('story patterns') were found particularly congenial for use in the Theatre of Dionysus, and that the old tales were, from the earliest traceable stages in the development of the genre, made into tragic plots by being adapted to these patterns. Finally (and this is also true at least from the time of our first surviving examples), the plots of Greek tragedies are articulated through a limited but highly flexible repertoire of formal units, and we shall need to examine the ways in which the conventions of form create expectations and provide frames for interpretation (see also Ch. 7).

If, from the point of view of its plots, Greek tragedy constitutes a grandiose set of variations on a relatively few legendary and formal themes, forever repeating but never the same, it follows that tragedy is not casually or occasionally intertextual, but always and inherently so. Tragic praxis can be seen as a complex manipulation of legendary matter and generic convention, constituting elaborate networks of similarities and differences at every level of organisation. Such a praxis supplies the poet with constructive elements predisposed to favour certain actions, character types, issues, and outcomes, and provides the audience with a significant frame or control for the interpretation of what they are witnessing. The particular shape and emphases of a tragic plot, as the product of variation in the shape and emphases both of known legendary material and of familiar formal constituents, can forcefully direct or dislocate spectators' attention, confirm, modify, or even overturn their expectations. When this happens, a structure comes into being that depends upon a kind of complicity of the audience in order to be fully realised. Seen in this light, a tragic plot inheres not simply in a poetic text, but also in the dialectic between that text in performance and the responses of an informed audience to the performance as repetition and innovation.[4]

A useful principle can be inferred from observing this interaction between an ongoing series of tragic performances marked by sameness and difference and their reception by the 'interpretive community' (to use Stanley Fish's phrase)[5] of tragedy-goers. Where there is large-scale repetition, even small innovations and minor differences will be disproportionately prominent and emphatic. In comparing, for example, Aeschylus' *Libation-Bearers*, Sophocles' *Electra*, and Euripides' *Electra*, our only surviving group of plays on the same mythical subject by all three tragedians, it would be difficult to overestimate the consequences of the fact that the first

---

resting-place in Attic soil and Euripides' *Suppliant Women* shows the Athenians risking war to bury the Seven who fell at Thebes.

[4] It should be added that tragedy is not unique in this respect; something similar could be said of New Comedy and, e.g., Greek temple architecture, or the iconography of vase-painting.

[5] Fish (1980) esp. 171–2.

two are set, expectedly, before the palace at Argos, the last in the country-side at the house of a yeoman farmer. In the Euripidean version, self-conscious deviation from past presentations becomes the means of forcing the audience to rethink every facet of character, motivation, and the very meaning of the action.[6] The sufferings of Electra, who seems almost to luxuriate in her loss of status and privilege, ask to be understood as at least in part self-inflicted. Orestes, cautiously assessing his situation from the safety of the countryside, emerges as something less than the knight in shining armour Electra is awaiting. Clytemnestra and Aegisthus, away from the scene of their crime, do not seem to fit the vituperation of their enemies; and their deaths – he slaughtered like a sacrificial beast while himself sacrificing at a country altar, she lured to the farmer's house by the ruse of a grandchild's birth – undercut any easy sense of justice being done.

The vagaries of preservation have left the three Electra tragedies as a unique opportunity to observe the play of repetition and innovation at work. It is worth pointing out, however, that if we had more such groups of tragedies based on precisely the same subjects, these three plays would look much less like a special case.[7] Indeed, we should think of their relation as paradigmatic, since it points to the status of any given dramatisation of a segment of legend as one of a number of variations on a theme, to be understood from the outset as a version among other versions – supple-menting, challenging, displacing, but never simply replacing all the rest.

MYTH, NARRATIVE PATTERNS, AND THE SHAPING OF TRAGIC PLOTS

Traditionally, the criticism of tragedy has assumed that there is (or should be) something that can be called a 'true' tragic plot. The most widely accepted master narrative is an integral part of the Aristotelian tradition

---

[6] I assume that Euripides' *Electra* is later than that of Sophocles, although neither play can be dated with certainty, and the responsive relationship among the versions would be of equal interest and importance if the order were Aeschylus–Euripides–Sophocles. For arguments in favour of a relatively early dating of Euripides' *Electra*, see Zuntz (1955) 63–71, Newiger (1961), and Burkert (1990). For another important scenic link between the three plays, see Ch. 7, pp. 168–9.

[7] There is some further overlap in subject among existing plays which confirms this view: Euripides' *Phoenician Women* corresponds in subject – though hardly in treatment – to Aeschylus' *Seven against Thebes*; Euripides' *Orestes* may be said to open up a subject in the space between the end of *Libation-Bearers* and the beginning of *Eumenides*. A tantalising bit if evidence is provided by *Orations* 52 and 59 of Dio Chrysostom (first century AD), the first of which provides a comparison of Sophocles' *Philoctetes* and the lost Philoctetes plays of Aeschylus and Euripides, the second a prose version of the Euripidean prologue. See Bowersock (1994) 55–9.

that for centuries dominated tragic criticism and is still surprisingly resilient today. This schema emphasises *hamartia*, generally understood as the 'tragic flaw' of overweening pride, and its punishment.[8] The tragic hero, although caught in circumstances beyond his ken and control, is finally to be understood as destroyed by the gods (or fate) because of his own failings. Even cursory examination of the plots of extant tragedies will suggest some obvious ways in which this schema is inadequate and even irrelevant. After all, a play such as Euripides' *Trojan Women*, for example, makes its devastating effect without peripeteia or even a 'tragic hero' (though it certainly has a wonderful 'star' role; see Ch. 7, pp. 174–5.) It is perhaps more important to observe that the search for a master tragic narrative is itself problematic. It has at any rate created a situation in which the small corpus of surviving Greek tragedy has been further subdivided, leaving only a tiny group universally recognised as 'true' tragedies. The rest are treated as failed attempts at tragedy, relegated to mixed genres invented *ad hoc*, or left to the specialists. We should begin, then, by recognising that there is not a single tragic narrative, but rather a number of story patterns characteristic of tragedy, patterns that tragic practice from an early stage in its development was capable of mixing and even subverting.

1. Conflict

If there is one category that overarches these patterns, it is conflict, the starting-point of all storytelling. 'Conflict' has been a central term in criticism of tragedy only since Hegel's *Vorlesungen über die Ästhetik* of the 1820s,[9] surprisingly, since from our perspective it is in many ways the crucial one. Tragic narrative patterns can usefully be classified by their characteristic conflicts, and something can be said in general about the kinds of conflicts that tragic plots seem to require. The first and most obvious quality of tragic conflict is its extremity: it does not ordinarily admit of compromise or mediation. For Ajax to yield to his enemies, for Medea to accept Jason's new marriage, would be to deny or negate their very natures. Where reconciliation of enemies does occur in tragedy, it is generally the result of direct divine intervention, as when Heracles persuades Philoctetes to fight at Troy or Athena persuades the Furies (themselves divine) to drop their pursuit of Orestes in return for new civic honours at Athens. Odysseus, in *Ajax*, is an eloquent human spokesman for reconciliation, but he achieves only the limited goal of persuading Agamemnon to permit the burial of their old enemy. The other common pattern of

---

[8] On the traditions of interpreting *hamartia*, see Bremer (1969) 65–98.
[9] For the question of conflict in tragic theory and criticism, see Gellrich (1988).

reconciliation is that of 'late learning', after the tragic crisis has already and irrevocably occurred. Here, the scope for reconciliation is limited by the very fact that the learning comes too late. In *Antigone*, for example, Creon recognises his mistake only after he has caused Antigone's death, and Haemon and Eurydice have committed suicide. Theseus learns at the end of *Hippolytus* how unjustly he has condemned his son, and Hippolytus forgives him before he dies, but it is of course too late to call back the curse.

Secondly, conflict in tragedy ordinarily involves more than a clash of choices freely taken by human agents. We regularly find such elements as past actions that, whether recognised or not, determine the shape of present choices and even their outcome (e.g. the curse of Oedipus in the *Seven Against Thebes*); ignorance or misunderstanding on the part of the agents that produce or threaten catastrophe (e.g. Ion's and Creusa's mutual attempts at murder in *Ion*); and even the direct imposition of divine will (e.g. the maddening of Heracles in the play that bears his name).

Finally, conflict in tragedy is never limited to the opposition of individuals; the future of the royal house, the welfare of the community, even the ordering of human life itself may be at stake. Oedipus' downfall is not merely, in our common parlance, a personal tragedy. He became ruler of Thebes by saving the state from the ravages of the Sphinx, and now, if the oracles prove true, his undoing threatens Thebes with anarchy. Nevertheless, his citizens, and along with them the audience in the Theatre of Dionysus, cannot simply wish him to escape unscathed and prove prophecy false. 'Why should I dance?' (896) the chorus of *Oedipus the King* sings (and dances) in a famously self-referential moment when it seems that the oracles may fail. In this sense, the fundamental struggle is to wrest meaning from suffering, and the perennial question of tragic pleasure – the exaltation that accompanies the witnessing of awful events – can be related to tragedy's affirmation, despite everything, of both cosmic and social orders against the unknown and against all those 'others' that threaten stability. But tragedy, as a quintessentially dialogic form, is always raising questions about those very foundational assumptions, even as its form tends to their (at least formal) resolution. (See Ch. 5 for a sociological approach to this question; also Chs. 1 and 6.)

In introducing the concept of conflict, I have left unmentioned the element often given pride of place in discussions of tragic conflict: fate. Fate is omnipresent, at least in the sense that the outcome of the story is known, in broad terms, at any rate, and therefore the audience is aware of the overall patterning of events in a way that characteristically eludes the agents until the end. Fate describes the limits of the possible for the action as a whole, because it acts as a 'reality check' for spectators who know

that the Trojan War *did* take place, that Clytemnestra *did* kill Agamemnon when he returned home, and so on. The dramatist is, in effect,
relieved of the requirement of providing suspense at this level of the plot,
but instead he must find ways to make fate work for him as a tool for
building dramatic tension. Moreover, the fulfilment of fate can be an
essential part of the process of providing satisfaction for the expectations,
moral as well as aesthetic, of the community. Apart from such considerations, however, the notion that Greek tragedy is fate-ridden and its
characters essentially puppets in the hands of an angry destiny is very far
from the mark. I venture to say that in Greek tragedy fate never operates
in a simple, mechanical way apart from the characters and decisions of
human agents.

2. The legendary subjects

The fourth-century comic poet Antiphanes writes that

> tragedy is a blessed art in every way, since its plots are well known to the
> audience before anyone begins to speak. A poet need only remind. I have just
> to say, 'Oedipus', and they know all the rest: father, Laius; mother, Jocasta;
> their sons and daughters; what he will suffer; what he has done.[10]

Antiphanes' point is that tragedy is much easier to write than comedy, in
which everything has to be invented afresh. This is more than a little
disingenuous, as regards both comedy (which is of course a highly patterned
and conventional genre in its own right) and tragedy (which permits and
even encourages much more freedom of invention than Antiphanes allows);
but there is a kernel of truth in it. For our purposes, we may restate the
point by observing that the successful tragedian would have to vary
traditional stories to make new what had been seen before, perhaps many
times, in the Theatre of Dionysus. We might equally well speak of the
playwright's opportunity to give an individual, perhaps highly personal,
stamp to a tale whose outline was already thoroughly familiar to the
audience.

At any rate, on the basis of the surviving victory lists and lists of titles,[11]
we can say that the earliest history of Attic tragedy already shows subjects
repeated by later tragic poets. A late source attributes to the semi-legendary

[10] Fr. 191 Kock 1–8.
[11] Records of the dramatic competitions were systematically kept, and fragments of inscriptions that contain these *didaskaliai*, literary sources in which they are excerpted, and
comments appended to many of the surviving dramatic texts (*hypotheses* and scholia)
contain information concerning playwrights, titles, dates of production, and awarding of
prizes. The evidence (in Greek) is published most accessibly in Snell (1986); for full
publication of the sources for the *didaskaliai*, see Mette (1977).

Thespis a line taken from a *Pentheus*, presumably on the same subject as Euripides' *Bacchae*. The few surviving titles of Aeschylus' older competitors, Choerilus, Phrynichus, and Pratinas, all recur in the works of later tragedians.[12] Of the close to six hundred works[13] attributed by title to all the known tragic poets, there are a dozen different plays entitled *Oedipus* (at least six from the fifth century, including plays by all three surviving tragedians), eight plays named *Thyestes* (including versions by Sophocles and Euripides), and seven named *Medea* (Euripides' being the first). Six playwrights entered the lists with an *Alcmaeon*, a *Philoctetes*, and a *Telephus*; five with an *Alcmena*, an *Ixion*, and an *Orestes*. All in all, more than one hundred of the titles appear twice or more, and nearly half of the attested plays have repeated titles.[14] From the point of view of plot, the history of Greek tragedy is one of continuously recasting tales already known to the audience, already part of what we may call a system of tragic discourse.

In speaking, however, of tales already known, I want to avoid giving the impression that there was a fixed body of lore waiting patiently for the playwrights to give it dramatic form. In an important sense, poets were the mythmakers of Greece. At any rate, there was no mythological 'orthodoxy' in fifth-century Athens. A play whose plot has become canonical, Sophocles' *Antigone*, appears to have had little in the way of literary precedents.[15] Yet, even Sophocles cannot be said to have given the story its definitive form: we know that Euripides went on to write an *Antigone* in which the heroine

---

[12] Choerilus: *Alope* (also Euripides and Carcinus, fourth century); Pratinas: *Perseus* (presumably the same subject as the *Andromeda* tragedies of Sophocles, Euripides, and Lycophron, third century), *Tantalus* (Phrynichus, Sophocles, and his contemporaries Aristias, son of Pratinas, and Aristarchus); Phrynichus: *Actaeon* (also Iophon, son of Sophocles, and Cleophon, fourth century), *Sons of Aegyptus* and *Daughters of Danaus* (Aeschylus), *Alcestis* (Euripides), *Antaeus* (Aristias). For Phrynichus' tragedies on contemporary events, see Ch. 1, p. 24.

[13] Including numerous plays bearing the same title as well as titles that certainly or probably belong to satyr plays.

[14] I hasten to point out that these figures are meaningful only in an exemplary way. It is not possible to be sure that plays with shared titles actually share legendary subjects as well. Thus, for example, there are seven reported *Achilles* plays and an equal number of *Bacchae*, but they need not all have dealt with the same legendary episodes. On the other hand, different titles may well hide the same basic material (e.g. Euripides' *Phoenician Women* recasts the subject of Aeschylus' *Seven Against Thebes*).

[15] Unless, that is, one accepts the authenticity of the received ending of Aeschylus' *Seven Against Thebes*. It seems not unlikely that the nucleus of the story was known to the playwrights from a Theban tradition not fixed in literary form. A brief, judicious discussion in Kamerbeek (1978) 5 concludes that 'even if the core of the fable was to be found in epic tradition (or elsewhere) and even if the authenticity of the final scenes of the *Septem* deserves more belief than they are nowadays generally credited with, we may safely state that in the *Antigone* the handling of the story ... [is] as original as anything in Greek Tragedy'.

survived to marry Haemon and bear him a son.[16] This state of affairs is typical. As regards the actual structures and details of plot, there are few tragedies that retell a familiar story in a familiar way.[17] The very fact that the same material was dramatised again and again must have encouraged the impulse to vary and reshape so as to outmanoeuvre expectation. Evidently, it would make no more sense to show an Oedipus who did not kill his father and marry his mother than it would to show a Napoleon who triumphed at Waterloo.[18] That is to say, myth is subject to interpretation and revision, but not to complete overturn, because it is also history. But within the limits of a living, fluid, intensely local tradition, plot stood open to invention, most obviously in the areas of motivation and characterisation, but also in such features as location and sequence of events.

This invention could extend, in Euripides, at any rate, to the self-conscious highlighting of deviation from earlier tragic versions (e.g. the Euripidean Electra's rejection of the recognition tokens from Aeschylus' *Libation-Bearers*; cf. p. 196 below) and to the almost novelistic fleshing out of the received mythical tradition (e.g. the account of the events between Orestes' murder of his mother and his departure from Argos in *Orestes*). But with few exceptions, the tragic poets developed their plots within the framework of the legendary tradition, taking 'slices from Homer's great banquets', as Aeschylus is reported to have called his own plays.[19]

We know that fifth-century tragedians did experiment with plays based both on recent history and on entirely invented tales, but neither could find a firm foothold. The latter class is known to us from a reference in Aristotle's *Poetics* to Agathon's *Antheus*, a play 'in which the names and the happenings were made up, and [which] is none the less enjoyed' (1451b21–3). Aristotle, although urging poets of his own day to follow the example of this late fifth-century innovator, admits that they do not. We can, I believe, deduce that both the crucial civic functions of the dramatic festival and the literary traditions that inform the tragic text would make the purely 'fictional' plot appear at a disadvantage. It is not merely that the great cycles

---

[16] Sophocles' *Antigone*, Hypothesis 1 and schol. 1351; discussion in Webster (1967) 182. This process of adaptation continues of course to our own day: see Steiner (1984).

[17] On the transformation and criticism of myth in tragedy, see Vickers (1973) esp. 295–337.

[18] Euripides' *Helen*, whose heroine never went to Troy, comes close, but had precedents in earlier treatments. Poets can also play with overturn of the legendary tradition, as in Sophocles' *Philoctetes*, where the conclusion of the action itself, which would result in the indispensable man not going to Troy, is 'corrected' by Heracles' intervention as *deus ex machina*. But history is never simply overturned, as in the notorious modern example of Schiller's *Maid of Orleans*, in which Joan of Arc dies heroically on the field of battle.

[19] Athenaeus, *Deipnosophistae* VIII 347e.

of myth have a certain prestige; they have become an integral part of the system of tragic discourse.

As regards tragic plots based on recent history, the poets seem to have discovered at an early point that their ability to comment on civic life and the affairs of the Athenian state was impaired rather than enhanced by direct depiction of events from the immediate past (see Ch. 1, pp. 24–5, for further discussion of early tragedies based on contemporary themes). Aeschylus' *Persians*, the only such tragedy to survive, and as far as we know the last of its kind, dates from the 470s and dramatises the recent defeat of the Persian invader. It is fascinating, among other things, for the degree to which it has been accommodated to what we might call the mythic mode, with the full panoply of dreams, portents, and prophecy emphasising a pattern of divine punishment, while at the same time its focus on the hopes, fears, and sufferings of the Persians compels compassion for the vanquished foe.

3. Story patterns

By story pattern, I mean the shape of a narrative, constructed according to the rules of its own inner logic as storytelling rather than the probabilities of everyday life, and capable of generating indefinite numbers of variants.[20] To begin with a familiar example: romance, fairy tale, and legendary history offer a large number and variety of stories in which royal children are exposed, survive, and eventually return to claim their birthright. Notice first that the story pattern reverses ordinary expectations. Whereas exposure of children in real life must usually have ended in death, the logic of the story pattern demands the child's survival – no child, no story. Second, the logic of the plot coincides with clear moral and even social predispositions. We are invited to expect the child not only to live but to obtain what is rightfully his or hers by birth, and in particular to view the restitution of the birthright as an act not only of justice but of legitimation.[21]

Why might such a pattern appeal to a tragic poet? The answer, I suspect, is that both its narrative inevitabilities and its moral directionality can easily be made problematic. Since the inner logic of the story pattern inevitably sets up expectations that must be met or disappointed, the poet can direct our responses to the unfolding drama by meeting or disappointing them, or more precisely by controlling just how and to what extent the drama does

---

[20] I adopt the term from Lattimore (1964). Two studies of Euripides are of special interest for their treatment of typology of plot: Strohm (1957) and Burnett (1971), from which my pattern-categories are adapted.

[21] The pattern is thus at least as suited to comedy as to tragedy; we find a version of it in a fragmentary fourth-century comedy, Menander's *Epitrepontes (Arbitration)*.

so. And, since the outcome has moral and even social dimensions, more than just the aesthetic sensibilities of the audience can be engaged. Such patterns also participate in broader ritual paradigms. The pattern of the foundling's return, for example, clearly reflects the well-known *rite de passage* marked by separation from normal society and a period of liminality and testing, which, if successful, finally leads to reintegration into the social order at a new level. Patterning of this kind links the success or failure of tragic agents to the fate of the community as a whole.

We find characteristically complex adaptations of this story pattern in two surviving tragedies, Euripides' *Ion*, where it retains in a somewhat muted form the expected happy ending, and Sophocles' *Oedipus the King*, where it forms a crucial element in the irony for which the play is famous. In *Ion*, Creusa's attempt to murder her son, a young temple servant of Apollo at Delphi whom she believes to be her husband's bastard, is thwarted, and Ion, discovering that she is his mother and Apollo his father, at last assumes his destined role as prince of Athens and coloniser of Ionia. In *Oedipus*, the foundling plot reappears with ironic inversion, since Oedipus learns that he is hereditary king of Thebes only by discovering the double secret of his hideous pollution, and loses his kingship in the act of recovering his birthright.

In speaking of story patterns, I am not claiming to isolate a set of master plots to which all the narrative forms of tragedy can be referred; I am simply highlighting particular forms used repeatedly by the tragic poets in shaping their plots. Each involves a characteristic type of conflict, each presupposes a particular storytelling logic. We will examine a number of ways in which these patterns inflect spectator response, above all by forming frames of reference and what we might call frames of expectation for the experienced Athenian tragedy-goer. Even as story patterns are manipulated and combined to meet the needs of a particular tragic subject, they still retain sufficient identity as shared and even conventional elements to provide significant interpretative pointers. Their interest, then, lies largely in the ways they meet, deflect, or defeat the expectations that they themselves arouse. The commonest of these story patterns are those I shall refer to as retribution, sacrifice, supplication, rescue, and return–recognition. At the risk of making them seem far more mechanical and less problematical than they are as the tragedians deploy them – sometimes singly, but often in combinations and with surprising twists – to articulate their plots, let us take a brief look at each.

The *retribution* pattern is organised around punishment for past offences. It may involve conflict between gods and mortals, with the mortals' challenge to divine supremacy leading to their destruction. Aeschylus'

Persians, the sole surviving tragedy based on contemporary events, is such an action in its simplest form, but divine retribution also plays a central part in the more complex actions of Sophocles' *Ajax* and Euripides' *Hippolytus* and *Bacchae*. *Prometheus Bound* represents an interesting special case, since the punishment is inflicted by one god upon another over whom he has seized control, and since we know that his victim will not in the end be destroyed but reconciled to him. The other form of this pattern provides an analogous conflict between human agents, although divine interest and participation is by no means excluded. The Electra dramas of all three tragedians provide clear examples of plays whose plots are constructed around this form of retribution, as do Euripides' *Hecuba* and *Medea*. Aeschylus' *Seven against Thebes* shows retribution at work through Oedipus' curse of his sons, which they themselves bring to fruition by their own choices. In Sophocles' *Women of Trachis*, retribution takes the form of a malign trick: the centaur Nessus, as he was dying, gave Deianeira blood from the wounds made by Heracles' poisoned arrows, telling her to use it as a love charm if her husband should ever prefer another to her. The 'charm', of course, is deadly, and when Deianeira uses it, she unwittingly carries out the centaur's revenge against her husband.

The *sacrifice* pattern entails conflict between the needs and desires of the individual and those of a community in crisis, resolved in favour of the community through the willing participation of the sacrificial victim. Euripides' *Alcestis* and *Iphigeneia at Aulis* are organised around this pattern, more often in Euripides developed as a subsidiary motif (e.g. the self-sacrifice of Macaria in *Children of Heracles* or Menoeceus in *Phoenician Women*).

The *supplication* pattern involves a triangular confrontation: a suppliant or group of suppliants, pursued by an implacable enemy, seeks and obtains protection from a ruler who must then defend them, by force if necessary. There are four full-blown suppliant dramas in the corpus of extant tragedy: three involving suppliant bands, Aeschylus' and Euripides' *Suppliant Women*, whose choruses represent, respectively, the fifty daughters of Danaus and the mothers of the Seven who fell at Thebes, and Euripides' *Children of Heracles*; and one whose central figure is a lone suppliant, the aged Oedipus of Sophocles' *Oedipus at Colonus*. Supplication and rescue from an implacable and violent enemy are also primary plot elements of several other plays, notably Euripides' *Andromache* and *Heracles*. In *Orestes*, Euripides goes so far as to allow a suppliant action to fail when the intended saviour rejects the suppliant's suit.[22]

---

[22] See below, p. 190 and Burnett (1971) 184–7.

The *rescue* pattern enacts a struggle whereby the principals, unexpectedly reunited, defeat a common foe and work their own salvation. Here the type-plays are the closely related Euripidean *Iphigeneia among the Taurians* and *Helen*, in which pairs of clever Greeks (brother and sister in one case, husband and wife in the other) outwit barbarian oppressors and win freedom. Once again, the pattern can be used as one episode in a compound plot, as it is in Euripides' *Andromache*.

In the *return–recognition* pattern, conflict arises from the central character's ignorance of his own true identity. By labouring against inner and outer opposition to establish that identity, he is able to reclaim his proper inheritance. We have already noticed how the two chief surviving examples of return–recognition tragedy, *Ion* and *Oedipus the King*, illustrate the degree to which a given story pattern can be made to serve disparate dramatic ends. But the pattern is a variant of one of the most common plot elements in tragedy (and comedy and romance, for that matter): recognition of another, as in the three *Electra* plays, Euripides' *Helen*, and many others.

These tragic story patterns, of course, are special cases of narrative forms that are widely used in storytelling of many kinds. As story patterns, they control the overall shape of the tragedy, providing a satisfying logic for the adaptation of myths to the stage; and the same narrative forms are also deployed in tragedy as subsidiary elements and to articulate individual episodes. We cannot assume that the tragic poets inherited them already connected to the segments of heroic legend that they proposed to dramatise. In some cases, no doubt, the shape of the plot was largely given by the matter. In others, it seems clear that the poet has adapted a story pattern to a particular myth for specific dramatic ends. It is hard to imagine composing a *Medea* that is not structured as a drama of retribution, whereas the suppliant pattern of *Oedipus at Colonus* was presumably not part of the local legend of Oedipus' death in Attica, but rather Sophocles' means of giving it a suitable dramatic form.

Tragic plots often combine two or more underlying patterns in unexpected and disturbing ways. Sometimes it is a matter of an action adhering to one pattern but achieving its particular effect by the inherence of another. In Sophocles' *Electra*, for example, the revenge tragedy is modulated by an emphasis on the recognition of brother and sister and on the rescue of Electra effected by Orestes' return. In *Antigone*, a pattern of divine punishment involving Creon emerges from the action shaped by Antigone's self-sacrifice. In other cases, brief but complete actions based on one pattern may be inset into a central plot structure of a different kind: Euripides, for example, repeatedly constructs willing sacrifice actions as episodes within the larger plots of his dramas. The extreme cases are the Euripidean dramas that more or less abruptly allow patterns to succeed one another to form complex plots. There are three such patterns in *Heracles*: a suppliant action ending in the saving of Heracles' family, an action of divine punishment resulting in his destruction of that same family, and a rescue action, in which Theseus brings the abject hero to Athens.

Surprising and unsettling effects arise also from the deflection of expectations built into the story patterns themselves. Sophocles' *Philoctetes* is an extraordinary example of a rescue plot played, as it were, against type: Philoctetes, offered rescue from his agonised exile on Lemnos, does not wish it on the terms that are available and finally refuses it on any but his own, setting himself firmly against what we know to be the 'right' outcome of his story, his necessary part in the sack of Troy. And the drama is played out as if Philoctetes can indeed set his own terms – and thereby prevent Troy's fall – until Heracles intervenes *ex machina* to set the myth back on track. The effect is a double dislocation: Neoptolemus finally 'saves' the narrative form by offering to take Philoctetes home, but this alternative rescue must fail if the myth is to be saved. Something analogous happens in Euripides' *Suppliant Women*, in which Theseus, against all the expectations aroused by the suppliant pattern, initially rejects the plea for aid of the mothers of the Seven who fell at Thebes, until his own mother puts the plot back on track by persuading him to change his mind; and in *Orestes*, where the suppliant action actually fails when the suppliant's putative saviour, Menelaus, refuses to take any action on his nephew's behalf, and an entirely different rescue plot has to be substituted.

In cases such as these, the interesting thing is not just the flexibility of story patterns, but the tensions generated by gaps, real or potential, between the expectations raised by the patterns and their fulfilment in specific plots. The dissonance thus generated invites the audience to consider anew what the myth enacted before them really means. Breaches in the conventions of storytelling make the myths themselves problematic and open their religious and ethical, social and political meanings to question. In a system of production based on almost constant repetition of legends and story patterns, in which every version is a variant, the disruption of expectations is a crucial element of tragic plots.

4. The mythic megatext

This repertoire of narrative forms is part of what we might call the tragic matrix; some legendary subjects are congenial to these forms, while others require greater effort to adapt them for the tragic stage. Tragic plots, then, are not supplied ready-made in myth, but they are also not invented from scratch each time a poet composes a new drama. The intersection in tragedy of a relatively small number of well-known legendary subjects and a limited repertoire of narrative forms helps to clarify the way in which tragedy participates in what has been called the 'megatext' of Greek myth, the repertoire of legendary subjects seen not as a corpus of discrete narratives, but as a network of interconnections at every level, from overtly shared themes, codes, roles, and sequences of events to the unconscious patterns or deep structures that generate them.[23]

Myth functions as a system whose signifiers are closely aligned to the central values (and therefore the central conflicts) of a culture. It is engaged, among other things, in a struggle to validate cultural norms. Tragedy uses myth, and thus itself inflects the mythic megatext, through a specific complex of narrative forms that is hospitable to specific cultural issues, and those issues in turn become, as it were, canonical in tragedy. The obsessive way in which tragedy keeps reworking female threats to male power, whether figured as the murderous assault of a Clytemnestra or the political defiance of an Antigone, offers an obvious, and suitably complex, example of tragedy going about this cultural work (cf. Chs. 1 and 5 above). Tragedy in such instances acquires a particular valence as an intervention in the production of the mythic megatext, one which countenances a threat to order and reinscribes it in a larger affirmation of cultural values.

The fact that threats to order and its reaffirmation are at the centre of the tragic use of myth helps explain why we can and must read tragedy both as challenging and as justifying established power structures, practices and beliefs; neither challenge nor justification is unequivocally asserted to the exclusion of the other. Evidently, this observation is related to dramatic form as well, since tragedy lacks the single, authoritative voice of a bard, the authorised voice of truth, as it were. Rather, the multiple voices of tragedy can all claim their own truths, assert their own rights, and all – even divine voices – may be subject to doubt, contradiction, accusation of wrongs. The dramatic mode itself is particularly receptive to a dialectic of criticism and affirmation. Greek comedy, especially the political and cultural satire of Attic old comedy, shares this critical/affirmative stance.[24]

The cultural work of tragedy may be briefly illustrated with reference to the pattern of transition of the young male to adulthood found in many of the myths that it dramatises. This pattern encodes the marginality of adolescence in a series of narrative structures that express the underlying cultural values at stake. The rite of passage involves, among other things, wanderings outside the city (not fixed abode within it), virginity (not marriage), absence of the father (but presence – often baneful – of the

---

[23] Segal (1983) esp. 174–6.   [24] See Henderson (1990) and (1993).

mother). In other words, the liminality of the youth is figured precisely in the symbolic set of exclusions that he must overcome. But this set of structures is not itself a story pattern, for its shape is indeterminate. The passage may succeed (as it does, finally, for Orestes), or fail (as in the case of Pentheus), or even both succeed and fail (as happens with Oedipus), and therefore it is invested with both hope and danger. The rite of passage, like the rites of sacrifice and purification, is one of the narrative elements of tragedy that adumbrate the great rituals of communal propitiation and therefore evoke the welfare of the community. Just as initiation into adulthood entails the dangers of passage from one state to another, purification presupposes the threat of pollution, and sacrifice often implies a civic crisis. Tragedy as a genre accommodates both mythical narratives that show the threat realised in all its destructiveness and those that show it safely negotiated, but in either case the outcome is not to be understood simply as the fate of an individual. Its meaning for the continued life of the community is always part of tragedy's concern.

In Aeschylus' *Oresteia*, Orestes' plight is presented in terms suggestive of the initiation pattern not once but twice. Having been cast out of the city at the time of his father's murder, Orestes attempts to reclaim his patrimony and re-establish the primacy of the male line by returning as armed warrior and killing his mother. He is then driven out once again as a hunted victim of the Furies, who seek vengeance for his mother's blood; this time, however, with the intervention of Apollo and Athens, he wins his freedom and establishes his claim to his father's place in Argos. But the trial in which Orestes is absolved of guilt for his mother's death takes place in Athens, and its consequences for Orestes are given far less emphasis than those for the polis. These include, in the first instance, the reaffirmation of the primacy of the male in the structure of household and state, and secondly Athens' assurance of the Furies' favour as Eumenides, granted a new home and honours and a role in the democratic order of persuasion and law whose symbolic birth the trilogy has dramatised (cf. Ch. 1 above).

In Euripides' *Bacchae*, the same matrix of male transition yields an action of a very different shape, but concern for larger civic consequences can still be observed. Pentheus' initiation is marked as a failure in its every detail: he leaves the city disguised as a female worshipper of Dionysus, and instead of trials to prove his right to rule the city in patrilinear succession, he is hunted and defeated by women, dismembered and symbolically devoured by his own mother. But his horrifying death is also marked as a sacrifice on behalf of the community.[25] Before Pentheus leaves for the mountains, Dionysus

[25] On this element, as well as interpretation of the ritual elements, see Seaford (1994) 280–301.

tells him, 'alone you wear yourself out on behalf of this city, alone' (963) – and indeed his suffering does benefit the city, by deflecting punishment upon himself as a kind of scapegoat for the city's guilt, and by providing the starting-point for a communal cult of the god.

Pentheus' death is also a prime tragic example of the 'perverted sacrifice' that constitutes a prominent tragic theme. He is identified by his killers as an animal and explicitly described as a sacrificial victim (1246), adorned for the sacrifice, led in procession, and slaughtered in a sequence that reproduces the stages of animal sacrifice, with his mother as priestess (1114) making the kill.[26] The overt Dionysiac content of this sacrifice accounts for its detail and emphasis, but the representation of killing as sacrifice is a repeated tragic trope – in every case connected with the deformation and perversion of ritual practice.[27] The subversion and distortion of marriage ritual is similarly widespread.[28] Such elements have importance not only because of the intrinsic emotive power connected with the representation of religious ritual in distorted and aberrant forms, but also because such representations produce a sense of danger for the well-being of the community, a precarious imbalance that calls out for redress.

METATHEATRE AND THE PRESSURE OF PRECEDENTS

Given the character of the tragic corpus as a set of variations on mythological themes, we may expect to discover traces of both theatrical and non-theatrical (chiefly Homeric) antecedents inscribed in our tragic texts. The centrality of theatrical performance in Athenian civic and cultural life during the fifth century makes it equally likely that we will find reflections of theatrical practice. Such elements do not constitute primarily a form of literary allusion, but a resource for inflecting and extending the possible meanings of a given situation, a means of directing and modulating audience response. The traditions in (and also against) which the poets write do not constitute mere background, but a dialectic of assimilation and opposition out of which much of tragedy's social meaning is constituted.[29]

The mythological cross-references of tragedy are nothing new. The Greeks employed them constantly from Homer onwards – one need only

---

[26] Seidensticker (1979). It should perhaps be added that the reconstitution of the body in the last scene of the play may restore – or attempt to restore – Pentheus symbolically to the status of human being. On the complexity of the relation between tragedy and ritual, see Easterling (1988).

[27] For Aeschylus, see Zeitlin (1965); for Euripides, Foley (1985).

[28] See Seaford (1987); Rehm (1994).

[29] On this subject, see Goldhill (1986) esp. 138–67.

think of the sustained parallels in the *Odyssey* between the homecomings of Odysseus and Agamemnon, between what has already become of Clytemnestra, Orestes, and Agamemnon, and what may yet happen to Penelope, Telemachus, and Odysseus. Tragedy, especially in its choral lyrics, is full of such mythological comparisons and exempla, but for our purposes the interesting phenomenon is the covert or implicit cross-reference, such as is found, for example, in the well-known and striking use of *Iliad* book 6 in Sophocles' *Ajax*.[30] The memorable scene of Hector's farewell to Andromache serves as model for the episode in which Ajax takes leave of Tecmessa, though to call it a model is to understate the richness of Sophocles' allusive technique. His audience knew their Homer intimately, and he expects them to recognise his use of Homer and to use it in turn to interpret the scene they are witnessing. Hector, whose sword will kill Ajax, looms behind him as husband, father, warrior, and enemy; Andromache, whose husband is her all, conditions our perception of the despairing Tecmessa; even the child Astyanax informs the figure of Eurysaces (cf. Ch. 6 above).

It is not the parallels, however, but the differences that emerge once the parallels have been recognised that carry the interpretative burden, as in the striking contrast of the heroes' hopes for their sons. Hector, returning from the battlefield, only thinks to take off his helmet when it frightens his son. Gently lifting the child into his arms, he prays that Astyanax will grow to be as great and strong as he is, indeed better by far (*Iliad* 6.476–81). Ajax, emerging from his tent after his mad slaughter of the flocks, grasps his son in his bloody arms, saying that a child of his should be broken in to his own raw ways, and wishes for the boy to be in every way like himself – only luckier (*Ajax* 550–1). It is by such adaptation and inversion of Homeric situations and even locutions that Sophocles prompts his audience to compare characters, relationships, tones, outcomes. The allusion makes for a brooding richness hardly imaginable without it, appropriating Homer and at the same time inverting the Homeric value structure.

The fact that such cross-references can remain implicit and still be present for the spectator as interpretative frames suggests that they should be understood not with reference to the author, according to the traditional philological paradigm of source study, but with reference to the audience.

---

[30] See Easterling (1984c). Segal (1983) points out the interesting case of Sophocles' *Women of Trachis*, in which the central figures oscillate between Odyssean and Oresteian paradigms, Heracles appearing first as an Odysseus, then an Agamemnon, Hyllus as a Telemachus and then a kind of Orestes, Deianeira as a Penelope who becomes an inadvertent Clytemnestra. For discussion of this kind of intertextuality in Euripides, see Zeitlin (1980). For general discussion of allusion in Greek tragedy, see Garner (1990).

Allusions call on a cultural competence that the author counts on spectators to share. Implicit relations among texts can thus be understood as part of a formal design that depends for its full realisation upon an act of recognition – a form of audience complicity in the making of meaning.

Another form of intertextuality depends not so much upon recollection of parallel narratives as upon the evocation of prior theatrical experience. Here, the very conventions of tragedy are used to overturn audience expectations. As an example, let us look briefly at the end of Euripides' *Medea*, a sequence both powerful and disturbing. Medea's final entrance is not unexpected; on the contrary, everything has been pointing to a last confrontation with Jason, and he arrives to pound on the door of her house and demand it. But the manner of Medea's entrance – above the scene building, on a chariot provided by her grandfather Helios – is a carefully calculated and prepared surprise. Jason is told that Medea has killed their children. 'Open the door and you will see the corpses' (1313), says the chorus leader, and an audience of tragedy-goers knows what happens next. They have seen those doors swing open to reveal the bodies of Agamemnon and Cassandra, Clytemnestra and Aegisthus, and no doubt many equally terrible spectacles before the production of *Medea* in 431. So every eye is fixed on the doors – but they do not open. Instead, Medea swings into view on high, and her scornful words draw attention to the spectacular breach of expectations: 'Why do you batter and unbar these gates seeking the bodies and me, who did the deed?' (1317–18). This spine-chilling moment takes Medea literally out of range, but the point is not just in the scenic effect. Medea appears *ex machina* like a goddess, because, against all expectations, that is what she turns out to be, or something very like it. Her dreadful wrath has made her an elemental power, destroying everything in her wake and then flying from the ruin she has wrought.[31]

This example, in its grim play with the conventions of the tragic stage, introduces a note of metatheatricality that we find again and again in Euripides. Two passages that have traditionally been treated as cheap shots at Aeschylus are worth mentioning in this context. In the great central scene (369–685) of Aeschylus' *Seven against Thebes*, Eteocles carefully and elaborately chooses warriors to meet the challenge of the Argive captains attacking each of the city's gates, and finds in the end that he alone is left to defend the last gate against his own brother, thus fulfilling his father's curse. In the *Phoenician Women*, Eteocles simply agrees to Creon's suggestion that he should select a captain to stand at each gate, adding that it would be too time-consuming to name their names, but that he hopes to find his brother

---

[31] On Medea as daimon, see Knox (1977), esp. 206–11.

opposite him (748–55). Euripides marks his difference from his predecessor in no uncertain terms (and Aeschylus' play was evidently a famous one, since Aristophanes is still citing it in his *Frogs* in 405), but he does so not so much to score a stray critical point as to mark his vastly different purpose: his characters consciously pursue destructive and self-destructive ends rather than struggle with destiny.

The second 'critique' of Aeschylus, and the self-conscious outer limit of this form of intertextuality, is the notorious recognition scene of Euripides' *Electra*, in which the old servant trots out the tokens by which Aeschylus' Electra had recognised the return of Orestes, only to have Electra dismiss them with scorn. His hair would be a man's, not girlish curls like hers; his footprint would naturally be bigger than hers; he could not still be wearing some piece of weaving she made for him as a child (525–46). Commentators have tended to take this as a Euripidean critique of Aeschylus' lack of realism, but it is not simply an isolated bit of literary criticism. Euripides' mocking exposure of the incongruity of Aeschylus' tokens is also an exposure of the machinery of theatrical recognition, which only functions smoothly when it is hidden.[32] (Ironically, in the end, Orestes' identity is proved by the even hoarier, but incontestable, Odyssean token of the childhood scar – albeit one acquired in a fall in the courtyard while chasing a tame fawn!) Euripides is interested precisely in the arbitrary and theatrical character of the convention of recognition, because by highlighting it he can call its conventional satisfactions into question. The essential further irony is that the old man is right to deduce that Orestes has returned, and Electra is wrong. She impugns the tokens because she cannot believe that her high-hearted brother would cower in the countryside in fear of Aegisthus, and we immediately see how self-delusive that view is. Although this quintessentially Euripidean self-reflexiveness has traditionally been a sticking-point for critics, it is the logical conclusion of the intertextual development of the genre, an assertive response to the burden of tragic precedents.

The conventions of tragedy did not permit the overt breaking of the dramatic frame, direct audience address, or other forms of theatrical self-reference available to Old Comedy. Nevertheless, such theatrical elements as role-playing and disguise are commonplace, and by the time of Euripides' later plays, we occasionally find what amounts to tragic parody within the frame of tragedy itself. Already in Aeschylus' *Oresteia*, we find Clytemnestra shamelessly 'acting' her cunning welcome of the returning Agamemnon and Orestes' impersonation of a Daulian stranger announcing his own death to his mother. Sophocles' *Philoctetes* is organised around a kind of play-

---

[32] Goldhill (1986) 249.

within-a-play staged by Odysseus to bring Philoctetes to Troy. (On the most strikingly metatheatrical moment of this play, the scene involving a 'trader' whom the spectators know to be a sailor sent by Odysseus to aid the inexperienced Neoptolemus, see Chapter 7, pp. 169–70.)

Even more elaborate is the role-playing in Euripides' *Helen*, a drama that takes as its leitmotif the gap between appearance and reality. Helen stages the central intrigue in a way reminiscent of the Orestes story, by having Menelaus announce his own death. Here, however, that by now hackneyed device becomes not merely a way into the palace but the fulcrum of the whole escape plot, with the king, hoodwinked into helping with Menelaus' burial honours, providing the ship and resources needed. Euripides was notorious for bringing heroes on stage in rags, and in a number of plays, *Helen* among them, costuming becomes a major preoccupation. The ship-wrecked Menelaus' rags, at first a disconcerting symbol of his loss of place and power, become a useful element in Helen's scheme, since they add credibility to the tale that Menelaus is merely a sailor who survived his commander's disaster. Only when the escape plot has been set in motion does Menelaus reappear in the armour that suits his reputation; but we are made to see this, too, as a costume, designed first to make him seem a participant in the rites for the dead, and only then to serve his 'true' role as scourge of the barbarians who stand in the way of his and Helen's freedom.

Euripides' *Bacchae* constitutes the supreme example of tragic metatheatre, not surprisingly, perhaps, since its central character is the god of theatre.[33] The whole play is staged for us by Dionysus, who announces at the outset that he is playing the role of his own priest in order to punish Pentheus. He has already maddened the women of Thebes and sent them to the mountains as maenads. In his mortal disguise, he plays along with his own entrapment and then uses his divine powers to escape and to stage a horrible masque – the sacrificial procession to the mountains where Pentheus, attired as the god's surrogate, becomes surrogate victim of a mad sacrifice at the hands of his mother and the other Theban Bacchantes. In the end, he appears *ex machina* in his 'true' guise – one wishes it were possible to know just how this appearance of the god differed from that in his role of mortal priest. Altogether, costuming in this play has a far more complex function than in any other surviving tragedy. In a bleakly comic vein, Cadmus and Tiresias appear in maenadic costume, unsuccessfully trying to negotiate a Dionysiac deconstruction of the boundaries of age and gender. Pentheus mocks them but obviously feels threatened by the blurring of gender identity in the feminine garb and long hair of Dionysus. This feeling is intensified for

[33] See Segal (1982) 214–71 and Foley (1980).

us when the god breaks down the young ruler's last resistance by feminising him, robing him in full Bacchic regalia in a scene (912ff.) that endows the transvestitism of the theatre – men acting women's roles – with a real threat to sexual identity and male domination.[34]

TRAGIC FORM AND THE SHAPING OF TRAGIC PLOT

The conventions of the tragic stage form the matrix in which a given segment of legend takes shape on its way to becoming a plot. Chapter 7 examines conventions in detail, and I limit myself here to a few observations on the relation of plot and tragic form. Along with endless variations on a limited repertoire of heroic legends, the tragic poets generated enormously inventive permutations and combinations of a limited repertoire of closed forms, to some extent analogous to those of opera. From the formal point of view, the crucial fact is the alternation of speech and song, out of which each play makes its own distinctive musical patterns.[35] We should not think of these poetic forms as moulds into which a given story is poured, but rather as flexible and expressive devices for developing and articulating tragic plots out of the materials of the legendary tradition.

The choice of a chorus is one obvious way for the poet to articulate his approach to a legendary subject. The chorus, after all, constitutes not only a collective character standing in a defined relation to the other characters of the drama, but also an intermediary between the world of the play and the audience whose perspective it helps to shape. Thus, for example, Aeschylus' decision to use Theban women rather than elders for the chorus of the *Seven Against Thebes* permits him to give voice to desperate fears for the fate of the city against which we can measure the resolve of Eteocles, its defender. Sophocles' choice of Theban elders for the chorus of *Antigone*, rather than companions or servants of the heroine, initially furthers her isolation but then permits a dramatically crucial shift in their understanding and sympathy.[36]

---

[34] Even Pentheus' mask seems to play a special metatheatrical role in the equally chilling 'unmasking' of the horrible killing. Agave is made to see that the *prosōpon* ('face' or 'mask') that she carries is her own son's severed head, not the lion she has imagined.

[35] A detailed study of types and development of lyric exchange in tragedy can be found in Popp (1971). On the relation of lyric forms in tragedy to earlier Greek song traditions, see Herington (1985) esp. 103–50.

[36] This play provides one of the striking exceptions to the convention that choruses do not intervene directly in the action: after Teiresias has revealed that Creon's entombment of the living Antigone and failure to bury the dead Polyneices have caused ominous signs of divine anger, the leader of the chorus takes it upon himself to tell Creon in no uncertain terms that he must now try to undo his errors; Creon yields, but too late (1091–114).

From the parodos (entrance song) to the end of the play, the chorus is continually present in the orchestra, with rare and noteworthy exceptions, making palpable the communal and public character of tragic drama. One consequence of this convention is that, apart from prologue speeches that are in effect addressed to the audience to set the scene, there is practically no soliloquy in Greek tragedy, for at least the chorus is there to listen. (The great suicide speech in Sophocles' *Ajax*, 815–65, is one of the exceptions.)[37] The chorus does take part, through its leader, in the dramatic dialogue, as well as participating in lyric exchanges with other characters. The odes, however, stand apart from the action. Actors often remain on stage during the odes, but do not directly acknowledge their performance or contents. (The only exceptions constitute special cases.)[38] As moments of lyric reflection, choral odes draw the spectator away from the immediate concerns of the plot, while at the same time they inevitably have an effect on dramatic mood, providing a kind of objective correlative for the spectator's responses to the action.

Greek tragedy is essentially a drama of words. Characters enter, talk with each other, exit. Very little 'happens' on stage – no battles and no blindings as in Shakespeare. Physical action, though sometimes dramatically crucial, is usually limited in scope and relatively static – acts of supplication, gestures of affection or pity or lamentation. Violent events tend to be described in messenger-speeches, a convention that has often been interpreted as a matter of decorum, but more likely stems from the realisation that, within the conventions of the fifth-century theatre, such things can be made far more vivid through narration than through stage presentation (on this point, see Ch. 7, pp. 154–5). The confrontations of tragedy are also essentially verbal, although they very occasionally spill over into the physical, and when they do, the effect in context is shocking (for example, Creon's seizure and abduction of Antigone in Sophocles' *Oedipus at Colonus*, 818ff.). But the threat of physical violence is one of tragedy's important verbal tools, and in general what we may call verbal violence is a

---

[37] The earliest instance we have of a chorus exiting and re-entering involves the only scene change in an extant play, that from Delphi to Athens in Aeschylus' *Eumenides*. The chorus of *Ajax* leaves the *orchēstra* to search for Ajax, allowing him to enter an empty stage and die undisturbed. The other cases (in Euripides' *Alcestis* and *Helen* and the *Rhesus* attributed to Euripides) similarly serve to facilitate a scene that would be difficult or impossible to play in the presence of the chorus.

[38] In Aeschylus' *Suppliant Women*, Danaus, the father of the suppliant maidens who are both chorus and *de facto* protagonists, explicitly praises the song of thanks they sing when the Argive assembly has voted to accept their plea and protect them. In Sophocles' *Oedipus the King*, Oedipus appears to respond directly to the prayers of the choral parodos, and does so in language that claims oracular knowledge and power; see Knox (1957) 159–60.

regular feature of tragic discourse. Confrontation is not merely a matter of angry, emotional exchanges of insults. More often it is staged as a formal debate, with the whole panoply of opposing speeches and rancorous stichomythia, extended alternation between two speakers by single lines or pairs of lines (cf. Ch. 6 above, pp. 127–8).

The primacy of the word in tragedy is not, however, merely a function of the resources of the theatre or conventions of the genre. Words are tools of power in tragedy. Tragic discourse is still responsive to a notion of the ominous quality of language itself, as can clearly be seen, for example, in the constant etymologising of names like Ajax (from *aiai*, 'alas') or Pentheus (from *penthos*, 'grief'). The ominous refrain of the great opening chorus of *Agamemnon*, 'Sing sorrow, sorrow: but good win out in the end',[39] comes as the Argive elders discover that their song keeps turning unbidden to dark events in the recent past, which they try to counter with the power of positive speech. As the fifth century wore on, it might be argued, the discursive powers of speech, logical argument, sophisticated techniques of persuasion, came to have the upper hand over this archaic view of language. But, in whatever form, the power of words – intended or otherwise – remains one of tragedy's enduring themes in the form of prophecy, vow, curse, riddle, lie, and incantation.

The power of such words is not easily controlled, and it should come as no surprise that their effects are often diametrically opposed to what the speaker intended or the hearer understood. A familiar case is Oedipus' curse on the slayer of Laius, who turns out to be himself (*O.T.* 222–75). Even more arresting is the succession of speech-acts that produce the peripeteia of *Oedipus the King*: for Oedipus' downfall is constituted not by deeds, the killing of the father or wedding of the mother (outside the drama, as Aristotle would say), or even the self-blinding (after the fact and off stage), but by a dialogue sequence that puts special emphasis on the code of communication. I summarise the scene beginning at line 1146, with particular attention to the thematics of speech. The old shepherd, realising that the garrulous messenger from Corinth may inadvertently reveal the awful secret of Oedipus' origins, *orders* him to be silent. Oedipus *counter-mands* his order and *threatens* punishment. The shepherd *asks* how he has erred, and Oedipus *reproaches* him for *refusing to tell* about the child of which the messenger has *spoken*. The shepherd attempts to allay Oedipus' suspicion by *alleging* that the messenger is *speaking nonsense*. Oedipus again *threatens* torture, the old man *begs* to be spared, Oedipus *orders* his arms to be twisted. Again Oedipus *asks*, and this time the shepherd

---

[39] Lines 121, 139, 159; quoted in Lattimore's translation.

answers, adding the *wish* that he had died on the day he gave up the baby. Another round of *threats* and *laments* leads to the further *question*, 'Where did you get the child?', which the shepherd *evades* by the vague 'From someone.' To Oedipus' repeated *question*, the shepherd *answers* with a desperate *plea* to *ask* no more. But Oedipus *threatens* his destruction if he must be *asked* again, and he *admits* that the child was from the house of Laius. On the verge of the terrible recognition, Oedipus *asks* the final question, 'A slave, or one born of Laius' own race?' To the shepherd's *lament* that he is now about to *speak* the dread thing itself, Oedipus responds with one of the most memorable lines of the play (line 1170): 'And I to *hear* – but *hear* I must.' This is certainly an extraordinary passage, but in precisely the respects we have been attending to it is characteristic, even paradigmatic, for Greek tragedy in general. Discourse, verbal interaction, *is* the essential action, not a mere reference to or representation of the action. The issues of tragedy, lodged as they may be in political, moral, and/or personal conflicts, are enacted through speech-acts.

THE EXAMPLE OF EURIPIDES' *HIPPOLYTUS*

A closer look at one play may help to bring together some of the central themes of this chapter. I have chosen Euripides' *Hippolytus*, in part because of the many ways in which it typifies tragic practice and in part because of something that makes it unique. *Hippolytus* is the only known instance of a second dramatisation of the same subject by the same poet.[40] We know enough about the lost first version to trace two very different ways of telling the 'same' story, and by comparing them we can clarify the distinction between myth as the body of lore available to the tragic poet and *muthos*, Aristotle's term for plot as a structure of events embodied in a particular drama. The chief thing we know about the first *Hippolytus* is that in it Phaedra made a deliberate attempt to seduce Hippolytus, who responded by covering his head in horror (thus the lost play's distinguishing title of *Kalyptomenos*, 'Hippolytus Veiling Himself'). That is to say, this version conforms to the pattern of the biblical tale of Joseph and Potiphar's wife, in which a shameless advance by the woman was met with rebuff and followed by a false accusation of (attempted) rape. Our evidence permits us to deduce a few more things about the first *Hippolytus* with reasonable certainty. The scene of the play was probably Athens, not Trozen as in the surviving play. Phaedra's nurse may have tried to restrain her mistress's passion, rather

---

[40] There is also a *Phaedra* of Sophocles, which may well have intervened between the first and second *Hippolytus*. Discussion and fragments of both lost plays in Barrett (1964) 10–45.

than encourage its expression. After Phaedra made her accusation to her husband Theseus, there was a confrontation between him and Hippolytus, concluding as in the surviving play with the curse that Poseidon fulfilled by sending a bull from the sea to kill Hippolytus. The truth was revealed, perhaps through a confession on Phaedra's part, and she then killed herself.

This first version of *Hippolytus* apparently shocked and offended its audience through what our version's *hypothesis* (a brief synopsis and critique offered by the manuscript tradition) succinctly calls the 'unseemliness and blameworthiness' of its portrayal of woman's desire. Rethinking the subject, Euripides is able to present the same outline (approach – rebuff – accusation – double death) in a frame that 'saves' the character and motivation of Phaedra. He makes Phaedra a woman fighting to suppress and conquer her passion, who, when she finds that she cannot do so, is ready to die rather than bring dishonour upon herself and her children. The nurse in this version becomes the figure of seduction, at least vicariously, as she wheedles and supplicates in order to force her mistress to reveal the secret source of her 'illness', then betrays her by approaching Hippolytus in her stead. Hippolytus' shock is here answered by Phaedra's shame and the suicide with which she plots to salvage her reputation. Phaedra leaves a written accusation of rape against Hippolytus for Theseus to find, and on its strength the king curses his own son, only to discover his innocence as he lies dying.

No doubt there were many other changes from the first to the second *Hippolytus*, but even what little we can affirm with some assurance suffices to make clear that, within a frame that prescribes only the barest outline of the story, the poet is free to vary not only the place and the sequence of events, but the characters and motivations of the central figures. And precisely because not only the bare outline, but also previous versions theatrical and otherwise are known to all or most of the audience, he can gauge his effects in relation to that knowledge, and to expectations based on it as to how the story will be told. It is in playing with these expectations that new emphases, new centres of gravity, new meanings can emerge from the old myths. All of this seems to be at work in the second *Hippolytus*, where Phaedra's attempts to resist her passion and the nurse's betrayal emphasise the extremity of Hippolytus' scathing denunciation of Phaedra and change the emotional and moral balance between them, and where the new manner and timing of her death permit the final scenes of the drama to focus entirely on Hippolytus.

We can now turn to some of the ways in which this play typifies features of Greek tragedy that I have discussed in this chapter.[41] The first of these

---

[41] The following remarks are by no means intended to constitute even the sketchiest interpretation of *Hippolytus*, merely to show some elements of its construction. The English-language reader can consult a number of recent interpretative essays on this play, from which I single

involves an interesting and rather special case of metatheatricality. This is the introduction of Aphrodite herself as speaker of the prologue, matching the appearance at drama's end of Artemis. In all probability, we are dealing here with another change from the first to the second *Hippolytus*. Unlike the earlier play, this version insists on the secret nature of Phaedra's affliction, so that neither Phaedra nor anyone else at Trozen can reveal it, and Euripides brings on a god to set the scene. But theatrical convenience becomes metatheatrical coup; Euripides uses the occasion of the exposition to make the drama itself a kind of play-within-a-play staged by the goddess of love, just as Dionysus stages the action to come in the prologue of *Bacchae*. At the end of *Hippolytus*, Artemis foretells the next such divine drama when she promises to destroy one of Aphrodite's favourites in revenge for the loss of her own (1420–2). By such means is the plot drawn into the orbit of the pattern of divine retribution.

The plot of *Hippolytus* can also be seen in the light of an overriding ritual pattern, that of passage. The Potiphar's-wife story of attempted seduction here becomes symbolic of the failure of the male to reach sexual maturity through the transition to adulthood. This is accomplished in a number of ways, but is rooted in the feminisation of Hippolytus that accompanies his desire to remain a virgin, a status associated in Greece primarily with the female. Hippolytus' cultivation of the virginal Artemis to the exclusion of Aphrodite puts him in the position of the reluctant maiden, like Persephone, who must finally relinquish her maidenhood even against her will. In the end, ironically accused of the violation of his father's marriage bed, he sacrifices not his virginity but his life to his father's curse and Aphrodite's anger. But the refusal of adult sexuality is not merely destructive to Hippolytus; in its blurring of distinctions between male and female it represents a danger to the community, and in death Hippolytus partakes of another civic rite, that of the scapegoat, the liminal figure who is expelled from the polis to remove some threat to its safety. To the extent that the bull from the sea represents both the granting of Theseus' curse by Poseidon and the culmination of Aphrodite's wrath, responsibility for the violent death is transferred to the gods. To the extent that it also symbolises the passion that Phaedra recognised and resisted, Hippolytus denied and repressed, it expresses the human truth of the power of *erōs*. In a last ironic reversal, Hippolytus is associated for ever in Trozenian cult with Aphrodite (and the story of Phaedra's love) as the cult-figure to whom maidens on the eve of

out as particularly useful Segal (1965), Reckford (1972) and (1974), Zeitlin (1985), Goff (1990), and Mitchell (1991).

marriage dedicate locks of their hair. His heroic status corrects – tragically too late and for others, not himself – the imbalance of his life.

Finally, the nature of confrontation and conflict as verbal – the character of Greek tragedy as a drama of speech-acts – can nowhere be better illustrated than in *Hippolytus*. Bernard Knox's isolation of the choice between speech and silence as the motor of the plot provides a useful starting-point.[42] The drama proceeds as a series of encounters in which misguided estimations of the power of words successively produce omissions, repressions, indiscretions, irrational outbursts, and lies in a concatenation that brings destruction on all the parties. Phaedra and her old nurse, in very different ways, overvalue speech. In Phaedra's case, this verges on fetishisation when she can think of no way of speaking compatible with her honour and takes refuge in silence. The nurse, on the other hand, is a great believer in the ability of *logos* to solve any problem. Her mistress' silence exasperates her, and she wheedles a confession from her. Having ground down Phaedra's resistance with rhetorical cunning, she goes straight to Hippolytus, and when we next see her, she is begging the enraged youth to be silent about what she has told him (603). Yet, despite the disastrous failure of her speech, she does not lose faith in its power. Her final words to Phaedra are, amazingly, an offer of further machination, to which Phaedra replies by telling her one last time to stop talking and dismissing her with the tragic formula for sending an enemy packing, 'Get out of my way!' (708). Having fully grasped the extremity of her situation, Phaedra takes full charge, and her remaining speech-acts are decisive, efficient, indeed (in the case of her final written message, the indictment of Hippolytus) masterful and devastating. As she becomes Aphrodite's agent in the destruction of Hippolytus, she assimilates a divine ability to make her words achieve her ends.

Theseus and Hippolytus may be called, by contrast, men who undervalue the word, repeatedly misapprehending its relation to its conventional opposite, the deed. Hippolytus, comfortable only among the age-mates who share his values, leads them in hymning Artemis but refuses even the *pro forma* prayer to Aphrodite urged upon him by his old retainer. Unmindful of the danger of withholding honour from so powerful a god, a perfunctory 'fond farewell to your Cypris' (113) is all he can muster. His response to the nurse's pleading of Phaedra's suit is the opposite of reticent, however. He launches on an extraordinary tirade against all womankind, a heady mixture of absurd hyperbole, offended sensibilities, and assorted male anxieties (616–68). Theseus trusts the truth of Phaedra's written accusation

---

[42] Knox (1952b).

so much more than any word Hippolytus might speak that he launches his curse even before hearing what his son has to say (887–90). Ironically, Theseus appears to doubt the efficacy of his own curse, since he adds exile as the alternative punishment should it fail, and later tells Hippolytus that swift death would be too easy (1047). He displays a complete unwillingness to consider Hippolytus' solemn oath. Like his son, he knows what he knows and refuses to acknowledge that what he doesn't know is of any consequence. When Hippolytus suggests that he at least consult the utterances of soothsayers, the King replies, 'As for birds flying overhead, a fond farewell to them!' (1059). This is the very same phrase of dismissal with which, at the beginning of the play, Hippolytus 'greeted' Aphrodite.

In the end, only the gods can line up their words infallibly with the results they wish to achieve. (Even Phaedra's apparently authoritative writing can only destroy Hippolytus, not save her own reputation.) Both Aphrodite and Artemis assert, reveal, promise, predict, damn with a certainty unknown to mortals, while the mortals make the best they can of a world of uncertain meanings, broken promises, unrealisable wishes, ineffectual regrets. After Theseus' curse has mortally wounded his son and Artemis has arrived to instruct and rebuke him, the King can only wish that the curse had never come to his lips; it cannot be called back. The only effective human speech left comes from the dying Hippolytus, the words with which he frees his father from blood-guilt (1449). Like Phaedra, he finally makes the word do his bidding, but too late, when death is upon him.

CONCLUSION: MYTH, INNOVATION, AND THE DEATH OF TRAGEDY

The great period of Greek tragedy seems to have lasted less than a century. The extant plays date from a period of roughly seventy years (except for the *Rhesus* ascribed to Euripides, which may well be a fourth-century play), and it is admittedly risky to make guesses about what we have lost. Nevertheless, if it is true, as Aristotle tells us, that Aeschylus added the second actor, then tragedy in its fully developed form began with him and as far as we can tell the cultural dominance of tragedy did not survive Athens' loss of the Peloponnesian War. Of course, new tragedies continued to be produced, and we know that a number, such as the *Hector* of Astydamas (a great-grandson of Aeschylus!), had enormous success[43] but tragedy never again attained the centrality that it maintained in Athens through the fifth century.

---

[43] For a positive view of such successes and the state of tragedy in the early fourth century, see Easterling (1993a) 559–69 and Ch. 9 of this volume.

Nietzsche, in *The Birth of Tragedy*, offered perhaps the most influential explanation for tragedy's death: the poison of Socratic reason, administered by Euripides. The decline of tragedy as a creative force is, however, as complex a phenomenon as its meteoric rise. I want to suggest that the intertextual play of innovation and repetition that we have seen as an important feature of tragedy can help us understand both the intense flowering of the genre in the fifth century and its subsequent fading.

Recent scholarship has rightly emphasised the close relation between fifth-century tragedy and Athenian civic life (cf. Ch. 1 above). The rise of tragedy as an art-form gave Athens a powerful instrument for the celebration, criticism, and redefining of its institutions and ideals, for examining the tensions between heroic legend and democratic ideology, and for discussing political and moral questions. This civic role was intensified and focused by the continuity and concentration of tragic production. As we have seen, tragedy revolved around a restricted repertoire of subjects; it was embedded in the ritualised framework of the Dionysiac festivals and the resources of a particular theatre.[44] At the same time, both as the vehicle of an important competition and as a form of popular entertainment, tragedy had to meet a constant demand for novelty. The extent of this demand is made clear when we remember that each year saw the production of nine new tragedies, not allowing for the fact that earlier tragedies were occasionally revived, but also not counting satyr drama, formally and thematically linked so closely to tragedy (cf. Ch. 2 above). Furthermore, while tragedy enjoyed the highest civic prestige, it was also (as Aristophanes makes clear) the centre of passionate controversy. Intellectually, tragedy embodied the traditional wisdom of the culture at the same time as it lay open to the new languages of persuasion and philosophy that threatened the overturn of traditional values. Socially, it could be seen as validating the established political and religious order in its role as an institution charged with inculcating civic virtue, and equally as expressing the unresolved tensions within the polis and therefore breaching the armour of the establishment. Thus, tragedy's repetitions and innovations reveal themselves as symptomatic of a deeply rooted doubleness, bringing past into confrontation with present, staging in ever new guises the immemorial conflicts of male and female, of parent and child, of rival siblings, of individual and community, and of mortal and god. In this sense, innovation serves not only its obvious function of differentiation among repeated enactments of myth in the ritualised setting of tragic performance, but also pushes to the limit the

---

[44] However, the growing performance of tragedy outside Athens, both at the Rural Dionysia of Attica and in centres elsewhere in the Greek world, needs to be taken into account; see further Ch. 9 below.

search for truth in myth, for the authentic token of cultural identity and meaning.

So far as we know, the conditions of tragic performance in Athens remained essentially unchanged after the Peloponnesian War, but such evidence as we have suggests that even after the restoration of democracy the tragic theatre lost its intimate relation to public issues and political life (a process that can be much more fully documented for comedy by comparing Aristophanic 'old' comedy to the 'new' comedy of Menander). A typically laconic passage of Aristotle's *Poetics* informs us that the 'old' poets (i.e. the tragedians of the fifth century) had their characters speak 'politically', whereas the new poets make theirs speak 'rhetorically' (1450b7–8). The contrast implies a distinction between political discourse (the oratory of assembly and public ceremony) and the argumentation of the courtroom, with its litigation of personal disputes. In addition, the chorus, in many ways the voice of the community in fifth-century tragedy, is often removed from the action by the substitution of ready-made 'insert songs' (*embolima*) for the odes formerly composed for a particular dramatic context.

As long as it commanded the serious and thoughtful attention of the citizens of Athens by the solemnity of its production, the intensity of its poetry, and the expressiveness of its music and choreography, tragedy remained an important formative experience. It is all too easy to write off as insignificant the large body of tragedy from the fourth century that has not survived. But we can reasonably speculate that the concerns of the later tragedians were more private and psychological than those of their pre-decessors, and that they emphasised emotional effect over intellectual challenge. Freed from the expectation of comment on public affairs but caught in an increasingly complex interplay of repetition and innovation, involving both their own contemporaries and the classical repertoire of the preceding century, now regularly performed at the festivals, tragedians would inevitably gravitate to sensational situations and theatrical display. At the same time, the increased professionalisation of acting, about which we are reasonably well informed,[45] no doubt made its own demands on the tragic poets. Again, the evidence of Aristotle's *Poetics* is telling: good poets, he says, write in an episodic style 'for the benefit of actors; writing for the dramatic competitions, they often stretch a plot beyond its possibilities and are forced to dislocate the continuity of events' (1451b35–52a1).

To what extent might the very intensity of the repetition and innovation necessary to sustain tragedy be responsible for its ultimate decline? Charles Segal calls tragedy 'simultaneously a commentary on the megatext of the

[45] See Pickard-Cambridge (1988) 279–305.

mythic system and the final text of the system; simultaneously the culmination of the system and its dissolution'.[46] Culmination, certainly; but should we make tragedy, no matter how extreme the innovations to it or how frantic their pace, responsible for the dissolution of myth? That tragedy was inextricably wedded to myth seems clear from the failure of Agathon's attempt to free tragedy from the traditional tales; and by the end of the fifth century, powerful new forms of discourse were competing successfully with myth in the search for meaning. The opening of tragic discourse to sophistic rhetoric and Socratic rationalism may be seen not as the assault on myth that Nietzsche deplored but rather as a recognition that myth had already lost much of its prestige as a tool for the discovery of truth and the advancement of social dialogue. Once myth is in doubt, tragedy becomes marginal.

BIBLIOGRAPHICAL NOTE

Many general books on Greek tragedy deal with the subject matter of Chapters 7 and 8: earlier bibliography can be found in Lesky (1983); *CHCL* I; *Métis* 3.1–2 (1988). See also Goldhill (1986); Zimmermann (1991); Rehm (1992); and three collections of essays by Charles Segal: *Interpreting Greek Tragedy* (Ithaca 1986); *Euripides and the Poetics of Sorrow* (Durham, NC, 1993); *Sophocles' Tragic World* (Cambridge, MA, 1995). A new edition of Richard Buxton's *Sophocles* (*Greece & Rome* New Surveys in the Classics, no. 16) appeared in 1995. For tragedy's links with other artistic genres see Herington (1985); *Arion* 3rd series 3.1 (1995); Nagy (1996).

On performance criticism cf. Ch. 12, with bibliography, and O. Taplin, 'Opening performance: closing texts?', *Essays in Criticism* 45.2 (1995) 93–120.

On music in tragedy: W. C. Scott, *Musical Design in Aeschylean Theater* (Hanover and London 1984) and *Musical Design in Sophoclean Theater* (Hanover and London 1996); West (1992).

On myth and drama see Foley (1985); Buxton (1994); Seaford (1994).

[46] Segal (1983) 184–5.

III
RECEPTION

9

P. E. EASTERLING

From repertoire to canon

This is a chapter about change: the complex and largely irrecoverable process whereby Athenian tragedy transformed itself into an international art-form which became familiar and influential throughout the Greek-speaking world, was translated and imitated by Roman playwrights, mutated into various types of balletic and operatic performance, and as a select corpus of classical texts helped to shape the educational system, and inform the culture, of later antiquity. The small group of plays that survived into the Byzantine period and beyond have of course had a continuing history of reception, which in recent times has once more become a history of performance (see Chs. 10–12 below). But even for the history of tragedy in the ancient world, the range of space and time covered is too vast, the evidence too diverse and uneven, and the phenomenon itself too elusive for a comprehensive account of this momentous process to be written.[1] As one element in what became an elaborate entertainment industry, tragedy cannot easily be studied in isolation from other dramatic media: in terms of performance and organisation it needs to be considered alongside comedy and (increasingly) alongside musical performance and pantomime. And since the language and iconography of theatre in general invaded the life of later antiquity in innumerable ways, its deeper cultural influence is to be found almost anywhere one cares to look.

The best approach, perhaps, is to pick out some examples that will illustrate trends or at least suggest tendencies. The period of interest – between the dates of our latest surviving plays (last decade of the fifth century BC)[2] and the end of pagan antiquity[3] – is an unmanageably long

---

[1] For important surveys of different types of evidence see Green (1994) and Csapo & Slater (1995).

[2] The two plays transmitted from later times are *Rhesus*, traditionally attributed to Euripides but likely to date from the fourth century (see Fraenkel (1965) reviewing Ritchie (1964)), and the *Exagoge* of Ezekiel, a Hellenistic Jewish version of a tragedy on the story of Moses.

[3] Theatre as such had a longer life still: see Müller (1909) for the period between Constantine and Justinian.

one. Not surprisingly, we have to deal with changes of location, funding, organisation, artistic form, performance and ideology, but from the beginning to the end of this long period it is probably safe to assume that mention of a title like *Medea* or *Agamemnon* would prompt generic expectations that would have at least something in common. The terms 'tragedy' and 'tragic' may have been many times redefined, as the form itself went through progressive transformations, but they never disappeared from Greek or Latin usage, and certain stories, along with a certain stylistic range, both verbal and iconographic,[4] could be identified as belonging to this artistic domain. The ability to recognise such signals was no doubt one of the identifying features of Graeco-Roman culture; the presence of tragedians among the canonical 'best authors' is further proof that tragedy went on being important.

For the modern interpreter the picture is badly distorted by the almost total loss of play texts from later than the fifth century BC.[5] Everything we know about the Attic theatre down to the replacement of the democracy by Macedonian-influenced oligarchy in 322 suggests that the fourth century was a period of great dramatic activity and productivity. Very large sums continued to be spent, and valuable prestige to be won, by *chorēgoi* sponsoring events at the dramatic festivals, and there was no shortage of poets wishing to compete or winning favour with audiences. Some of them were famous enough to be mentioned by Aristotle in the same breath as the great 'classic' tragedians of the fifth century, and some of their works went on being copied and replayed in later generations.[6] Scholars have been too ready to take Aristophanes literally when at *Frogs* 71–2 (405 BC) he claims that all the good tragic poets are dead. If tragedy had simply 'wilted' at that stage, it would be much harder to explain the continuing importance attached to it in the fourth century,[7] and indeed later: competitions for new plays went on being organised throughout the Hellenistic period (with a single official, the *agōnothetēs*, rather than *chorēgoi* in charge after some time between 318 and 307 BC).[8] It is true that the fourth century was also

---

[4] Cf. Green (1994), esp. ch. 5, on the iconography of tragic and comic masks and its range of symbolic significance.

[5] There is no shortage of brief quotations (see *TrGF*) but what is missing is complete plays; New Comedy has been better served by papyrus finds.

[6] Astydamas' *Alcmeon*, Carcinus' *Thyestes*, and Theodectes' *Lynceus* and *Tydeus* are all mentioned in the *Poetics*. Cf. Xanthakis-Karamanos (1980) 18–20; p. 216 below on Astydamas. The inscription from Tegea mentioned below (n. 37) records third-century revivals of plays by Archestratus and Chaeremon as well as by Euripides.

[7] Cf. Easterling (1993a); 'wilting' is borrowed from Green (1994) 5, but later (50–1) he gives good evidence for thinking that scholars underestimate the popularity of fourth-century tragedy.

[8] See Pickard-Cambridge (1988) 91–3; Csapo & Slater (1995) 143, 156–7.

the time when the development of a 'classic' repertoire was given its most influential impetus, and there does seem to have been a significant shift in perceptions, reflected in the fact that remembrance of the great traditions of the past was now formally institutionalised. It may not be an exaggeration to suggest that the single most important date in the history of fourth-century tragedy was 386, the year when an official contest in revived 'old' plays was instituted at the City Dionysia, and the individuals responsible for the mounting of these productions were the tragic actors themselves (*tragōidoi*).[9] But the actors' interest in replaying old masterpieces need not be taken as a sign of artistic fatigue: it may rather be the confirmation of an important trend towards the formation of a repertoire.

This was a development, after all, of a habit that had already been establishing itself at the dramatic festivals in the demes of Attica, the Rural Dionysia,[10] and by the end of the fifth century it would not be surprising if actors were being invited to take successful productions to other cities. Other cities were certainly extremely interested in sharing the Athenian experience, as we know from the evidence for where playwrights and actors came from,[11] not to mention the vase-paintings showing scenes from drama, or the theatres that were built outside Attica, in the fourth century.[12]

That the Athenians were eager to keep their own festivals distinctively Athenian is shown by legislation forbidding non-citizens to perform as chorusmen or to serve (at the City Dionysia, at any rate) as *chorēgoi*.[13] But there was no ban on foreign playwrights or actors, and outside Athens the choregic system was not the only way of putting on shows: in the fifth century the tyrant Hiero of Syracuse had invited Aeschylus to compose plays for festivals under his patronage, and the same arrangement must have applied when Euripides wrote the *Archelaus* for the King of Macedon.[14] Any individual or group that could find the resources could invite a poet or artist to accept a commission, and if the system worked for lyric poets and sculptors why not for dramatists and actor-directors? Given the relative ease of travel and communications between the Greek-speaking communities, the opportunities opening up for enterprising leading actors

---

[9] Evidence in *TrGF* I (DID A I 201).
[10] Evidence in Pickard-Cambridge (1988) 42–56; Whitehead (1986a) 212–22.
[11] Playwrights from outside Athens: cf. Ch. 1 p. 4 above; for actors see Ghiron-Bistagne (1976) 306–64; Stephanis (1988).
[12] See Taplin (1993), esp. 1–39; Green (1994) ch. 3 and (1995).
[13] See MacDowell (1985); Csapo & Slater (1995) 351–2, 358–9. This suggests that there were other centres in which such performance skills were developing.
[14] Cf. Easterling (1994).

were immense, and the power of the theatre to influence mass audiences must have been a strong element in its appeal.[15]

A fragment of one of the most valuable inscriptions recording Athenian theatrical history, the so-called *didaskaliai*, which happens to survive for the years 341–339, can be used to illuminate some of the important trends of the times.[16] From what survives we can see that the pattern in the mid-fourth century was to list the year (by Eponymous Archon), and to give details as follows: first a satyr play by author and title, then the same information for an old tragedy, with the addition of the actor who put it on, then the three poets who competed with new tragedies, giving their names, the titles of their plays, and the names of the protagonists who acted in them, concluding with the name of the winner of the prize for the best actor. Although many lines of the text are preserved only in part, scholars have been able to supply some of the missing names from other sources.

Here is the restored text for the years 341 and 340 (the text for 339 is much more damaged):

341 [The *archōn*'s name and the record of the satyr play are missing; the *archōn* is known to have been Sosigenes.]
With old <tragedy>: Neoptolemus with *Iphigeneia* of Euripides
Poet <victor>: Astydamas

with *Achilles*	Thettalus acted
with *Athamas*	Neoptolemus acted
with *Antigone*	Athenodorus acted

Euaretus second

with *Teucer*	Athenodorus acted
with *Achilles*	Thettalus acted
with [title missing]	Neoptolemus acted

Aphareus third

with *Peliades*	Neoptolemus acted
with *Orestes*	Athenodorus acted
with *Auge*	Thettalus acted

Actor: Neoptolemus was victorious

340 In the archonship of Nicomachus
With satyr <play>: Timocles with *Lycurgus*
With old <tragedy>: Neoptolemus with *Orestes* of Euripides

---

[15] Cf. ps.-Plato, *Minos* 320f, in which tragedy is described as the branch of poetry 'most delightful to the mass of the people and most powerful in its appeal to the emotions' (*dēmoterpestaton* and *psuchagōgikōtaton*).

[16] For the whole inscription (*IG* II^2 2319–23) see Pickard-Cambridge (1988) 107–20; Csapo & Slater (1995) 41–2.

```
Poet <victor>:  Astydamas
                    with Parthenopaeus    Thettalus acted
                    with Lycaon           Neoptolemus acted
              Timocles [or Philocles?] second
                    with Phrixus          Thettalus acted
                    with Oedipus          Neoptolemus acted
              Euaretus third
                    with Alcmeon          Thettalus acted
                    with [title missing]  Neoptolemus acted

        Actor: Thettalus was victorious
```

This is a richly informative inscription, though we are not always certain how to interpret its implications. First, it clarifies the programme of events. Evidently by the mid-fourth century there was no longer a competition for three tragedies plus satyr play as in the early days (see Ch. 2 above, pp. 39–40); the proceedings began with the performance of a single satyr play, which was followed by a revival of an old tragedy put on by one of the leading actors (*tragōidoi*), and then came the competition for new plays. The significance of the new order may have been that it suggested continuity with old tradition while actually offering something different: a satyr play to start with might recall the style and atmosphere of the contests of earlier times, and the revived tragedy would have the appeal of a classic favourite as well as providing a well-tried vehicle for the display of talent.[17] That Euripides was the chosen playwright for the revival (also in 339, though the title is missing) is not surprising for the period; there is plenty of other evidence which shows that he was posthumously one of the most popular and influential of the fifth-century tragedians. The titles of the new tragedies are typical, too, of what we know of fourth-century plays in that they still deal with heroic subjects and (probably) familiar myths. There is certainly no suggestion here that the traditional source-material was felt to be exhausted; but with only the titles surviving we can do no more than guess at the kinds of meanings now given to the old stories.[18]

Secondly, the text brings out the importance of the actors. By this date[19] the competition was so regulated that each playwright was allocated a different actor for each tragedy and thus competed on exactly equal terms

---

[17] The leading actors who are identified as 'acting a play' are always to be understood (at any rate in the context of the Athenian dramatic contests) along with their supporting troupe, two speaking actors and a number of mutes. Cf. Sifakis (1995).

[18] See Xanthakis-Karamanos (1980) for a review of surviving fragments from fourth-century tragedies.

[19] Sifakis (1995) 17 implies that this had been the practice since the competition for best actor was instituted; see Pickard-Cambridge (1988) 93–5 for a different view.

with his rivals. Actors now played on an international circuit, and it is tempting to guess that the reason why there were three playwrights competing in 340 but only two actors is that a third (Athenodorus?) had broken his contract in favour of a better offer from elsewhere. We know from contemporary evidence (e.g. Aeschines, *Embassy* 19) that fines were levied 'by the cities' on actors who failed to keep to their commitments, a rule which would not have been needed if there had not been serious competition between festival organisers and patrons in different places.

Most of the individuals named in the inscription are interesting for one reason or another. The winning dramatist Astydamas the younger was highly popular in the fourth century (he composed 240 plays and had a good record of first prizes);[20] he is mentioned familiarly by Aristotle and is one of the few tragedians whose dates are recorded on the *Marmor Parium* (*FGrHist* 239). His *Parthenopaeus* in 340 was so much admired that the Athenians put up a statue of the poet in the theatre (which is recorded because it occasioned a notoriously arrogant reaction on his part).[21] Some of his plays seem to have had lasting fame: an 'old' satyr play put on at the Lenaea in 254, the *Hermes*, was probably his, and scholars believe that his *Hector* was still being read in the third and second centuries BC.[22] One very telling fact about Astydamas is that he was a relative of Aeschylus and therefore a member of one of the most remarkable theatrical families in Attic history (his father Astydamas the elder, his grandfather Morsimus, and his great-grandfather Philocles, nephew of Aeschylus, were all trage-dians, as was his brother Philocles the younger). Family networks – often (as in this case) including actors as well as dramatists – were an important aspect of the whole system, particularly before it became thoroughly professional, and *xenia* (long-distance guest-friendship) networks, too, must have been significant as poets and actors became more and more mobile, and before they had their own international organisation (for the actors' 'trade union', the Artists of Dionysus, see p. 224 below). It seems very likely that the actual preservation of the scripts of plays depended a great deal on family archives in the early days; the best evidence for this is the fact that dramatists' descendants are known to have competed with productions of plays left unperformed at their relatives' deaths (Sophocles' *Oedipus at*

---

[20] He is credited with 15 victories, several of them at the Dionysia and at least one at the Lenaea: we cannot compute the exact number of tragedies involved, but he may have been victorious with *c.* 40. For testimonia on Astydamas see *TrGF* 1 60.

[21] The statue base has been found (*TrGF* 1 60 T 8b); for his boastful epigram see *TrGF* 1 60 T2a and b.

[22] See *TrGF* 1 210–14 for the evidence.

Colonus, for example, was put on in 401 by his grandson, about five years after he died).

Of the three actors involved in the events of 341–340, Neoptolemus and Thettalus were especially famous and successful. Star status guaranteed actors invitations from powerful people – to perform, to visit as guests, and to use their speaking skills as diplomats. There was also a great deal of money to be earned: lavish dedications by actors, on a scale normally outside the range of private individuals, are attested by inscriptions.[23] For wealth and glamour actors could now be compared with famous performers of other kinds: athletes, rhapsodes and musicians, who had long been able to count on lucrative commissions and appearances all over the Greek-speaking world.[24]

Neoptolemus, who was responsible for the revivals of Euripidean plays in 341 and 340 and won the prize for best actor in 341, was an incomer to Athens from Scyros[25] – hence, no doubt, his stage name, after the son of Achilles who was brought up on the island – and he must either have been granted Athenian citizenship or at any rate have enjoyed high standing at Athens, where he became extremely wealthy: according to Demosthenes (18.114) he was honoured for his donations when overseer of public works, and he claimed (5.8) that he expected to have to perform further liturgies there. He had enormous popularity as an actor (5.7) and acquired influential friends, particularly Philip of Macedon. Like his colleague Aristodemus of Metapontum, who was actually appointed an ambassador by the Athenians along with Demosthenes and Aeschines, he reported very favourably to the Athenians on Philip's policy towards them after the fall of Olynthus in 348 (Dem. 19.315), and they liked what he said, though Demosthenes saw him as positively injuring Athens by acting as Philip's agent. After the peace settlement in 346 he sold his Athenian property and went to live in Macedonia (Dem. 6.8).[26]

As well as illustrating the scope for actors to acquire wealth and influence along with their fame, some of the stories told about Neoptolemus have great symbolic interest, bringing out the particularly close analogies between theatrical and political power and the way in which drama and life, particularly the lives of famous people, were felt to interact and to shape one another.

---

[23] Examples in Csapo & Slater (1995) 237–8; cf. Athenaeus 472c for Neoptolemus' dedication of gold-plated cups on the Acropolis.

[24] See Kurke (1991).

[25] Demosthenes 5.6 with schol. 2.

[26] See Ghiron-Bistagne (1976) 156–7, 345 for the ancient sources.

Diodorus' account (16.92–3) of the assassination of Philip in 336 is worth quoting in full:

> Great numbers of people came pouring from all directions to the festival, and the games and the marriage were celebrated at Aegae in Macedonia [Philip's daughter Cleopatra was being married to her maternal uncle, Alexander of Epirus]. Philip was crowned with golden wreaths by individual persons of note and also by most of the important cities, including Athens. When the award of the Athenian crown was announced, the herald ended by saying that if anyone were to plot against Philip and take refuge in Athens he would be liable to extradition. It was as if the routine expression was being used by divine providence to give a sign of the imminent plot against Philip. There were other remarks giving advance warning of the king's death which seemed to be similarly inspired. For example, at the royal banquet Philip ordered the *tragōidos* Neoptolemus, outstanding for his vocal power and popularity, to perform some successful pieces from his repertoire, particularly anything relevant to the campaign against the Persians [Philip had already begun the preparations for this campaign, as elected leader of the Greeks; 89ff.]. Neoptolemus chose a piece which he thought would be taken as appropriate to Philip's crossing [to Asia]; he had in mind to belittle the wealth of the Persian king and suggest that, although now it was notoriously vast, chance could obliterate it one day. This is how he began:

> > Your thoughts now reach higher than the air
> > You dream of farm lands in great plains
> > You plan buildings, surpassing the buildings <of the past?>
> > Foolishly projecting your life into the future.
> > But there is a swift-footed one who captures <travellers>:
> > He goes by a dark path
> > But suddenly, unseen, he catches up,
> > And makes away with the far-reaching hopes
> > Of mortal men: he is Hades, source of woe.[27]

> He continued with the rest of the song, all of it relating to the same theme. Philip was delighted with what it said and was totally absorbed by the idea of its relevance to the defeat of the Persian king. He also recalled the Pythian oracle,[28] which (he thought) bore a similar meaning to the words quoted by the *tragōidos*.

> In due course the drinking was over, and as the games were due to start the following day the crowd hurried to the theatre while it was still dark. At daybreak the procession began. Philip's display was lavish in all its details,

---

27 Text in *TrGF* II 127; The last three lines are quoted in a slightly different form by Philodemus (*De morte* 4) as 'well known', but the author's name is not given. For textual problems see Gigante (1983) 206–8.

28 Diodorus (16.91) reports Philip's favourable interpretation of the ambiguous oracle.

including statues of the twelve gods, which were artefacts of outstanding workmanship decorated with dazzlingly rich adornment. Along with these a thirteenth statue was paraded, representing Philip himself in a style befitting a god – so the king displayed himself as a throned companion of the twelve gods.

When the theatre was full Philip came in wearing a white cloak; he had given orders to his bodyguard to stand back and follow at a distance, eager to demonstrate to the public that he was protected by the goodwill of all the Greeks and had no need of a bodyguard. At such a high point in his success, when everyone was praising and congratulating him, the unexpected happened: the revelation of a completely unforeseen plot against the king, a plot that meant death. [Diodorus then interrupts his narrative to sketch in the events that led up to the plot, resuming at 94 with an account of the assassin, Pausanias, rushing at Philip as he entered the theatre unprotected, and stabbing him to death.]

So Philip, as presenter of a spectacle, playing – in the theatre itself – the role of beloved leader of the Greeks, even the role of a divine power, ultimately becomes the central figure in a new and typically 'tragic' spectacle, the fall of a tyrant. The theatrical emphasis in this narrative is matched by an interest in the way the actor's words, intended by him to have a layer of meaning other than that of their original context and to be heard as a flattering prediction of success for Philip against the Persians, turn out to have another layer again, a true prediction, this time, of an event which the spectators watch instead of a dramatic show, the assassination of their king.

The story seems to have become emblematic of the vulnerability of rulers and the theatrical character of their power. Many centuries later Neoptolemus is quoted in the *Florilegium* of John of Stobi (in a section on the brevity and anxiety of life) as replying to someone who asked what he admired in the works of Aeschylus, Sophocles or Euripides, 'Not anything of theirs, but what he himself had witnessed on a greater stage: Philip in procession at the wedding of his daughter Cleopatra and hailed as thirteenth god, and the next day murdered in the theatre and thrown out' (98.70). When the Emperor Gaius was murdered on leaving the theatre at Rome in AD 41, the story of Philip and Neoptolemus was recalled: according to Suetonius (*Caligula* 57), one of the 'omens' seen in retrospect as marking the approach of his death was the fact that on that very day the pantomime Mnester 'danced the tragedy which the actor Neoptolemus had once acted at the games at which Philip, King of the Macedonians, was killed'. Josephus, writing a generation before Suetonius, has a version which differs in interesting details: for him (*Jewish Antiquities* 19.90–104) the day was the anniversary of Philip's murder (95), and Gaius saw two shows which entailed the shedding of a great quantity of artificial blood, a mime in which a chieftain was caught and crucified, and a performance by a dancer of 'a drama *Cinyras*, in which Cinyras himself and his daughter Myrrha were killed' (95). By combining these two pieces of evidence scholars have concluded, perhaps too readily, that *Cinyras* was the play put on at Philip's theatrical games at Aegae in 336; but there is no means of telling whether it has any connexion, either with the aria sung by Neoptolemus at the banquet or with the play that he and his troupe would have acted if Philip had not been assassinated.[29] What is interesting here is the way in which theatre and life become metaphors for one another: the words and actions of plays could prefigure (or seem to evaluate) events, and rulers were only as 'real' as the roles played by actors. Philip on the 'greater stage' was playing the part of the thirteenth god, but his fall was more like that of a tragedy tyrant.

There are other questions that these stories help us to explore. The actor becoming more prominent or carrying more weight than the poet – Diodorus names Neoptolemus, but not the author of the piece he performs – this is a trend that Aristotle already mentions in the *Rhetoric* (1403b), and it should not surprise us. Once actors had their own individual repertoires and did not have to rely on the poets chosen for a particular dramatic festival to provide them with new material, there was plenty of scope for change and development. One kind of change was clearly formal: if the actor could be invited to perform at a patron's drinking party as well as in the theatre, and if all he needed was his expertise as a soloist, it becomes easier to understand how the artistic medium could diversify, and how actors could have greater influence over it. Much of the evidence for 'tragedy' in later antiquity is for solo performances of one sort or another: in addition to full-scale productions of plays old and new, with chorusmen and troupes of actors, we hear more and more of solo performances by *tragōidoi*, particularly of sung performances. Here in Diodorus, it is clear from the metre of the passage quoted that Neoptolemus is singing. By the time of Caligula in the first century AD at Rome there is no doubt that 'performing a tragedy' typically meant solo performance either by a singer (*cantor*) or by a dancer (*saltator, pantomimus*). Mnester is described as a *pantomimus*: he 'danced (*saltavit*) the tragedy which Neoptolemus had acted (*egerat*)'.[30] Once the performance of the pantomime could be described as 'tragedy', a crucial artistic move had been made, since this was

---

[29] Csapo & Slater (1995) 235 wrongly attribute to Josephus (94) the remark that Philip was murdered when he was entering the theatre to see a play called *Cinyras*.

[30] Suetonius, *Caligula* 57. This medium seems to have become dominant despite the long and distinguished tradition of full-scale tragedy performance at Rome in the Republican and

an essentially balletic and musical performance in which the soloist danced and mimed the dramatic action while a chorus or musicians provided backing. The common elements between this and traditional tragic drama might be no more than the mythological story and perhaps some features of verbal style.

It thus becomes extremely difficult to be precise when we look at references to performance in later antiquity.[31] But even allowing for great heterogeneity of form we can find something of interest in the continuity of subject matter. One of the reasons, surely, for the persistence of performances based on the stories of Thyestes or Medea or Hector was their potential multivalence: if songs or speeches composed for one dramatic situation could be made to apply tellingly to another, the medium could be used politically, for flattery, for subversion, for both at once, and the close link between theatre and power was not lost on patrons and performers. It is a pity we know nothing about *Cinyras*, except the myth from which it presumably came, the story of a king who was tricked into committing incest with his daughter. (One can see why incest on the part of a ruler might be a good subject for a show in Caligula's time; but in Philip's the marriage, for dynastic reasons, of a niece to her uncle would hardly have raised eyebrows.) Tacitus[32] is full of anecdotes which can be compared with that of Diodorus; but perhaps the best known of all is Plutarch's account of the performance of part of the *Bacchae* (or lyrics from the play) for the Parthian king, with the defeated Crassus' head substituted for Pentheus' (*Crassus* 32–3). The fact that this is most unlikely to be a true story only enhances its significance: it brings out yet again the sense in which drama and life are felt to interconnect. (Cf. Ch. 1, p. 11.)[33]

Plutarch sets the story in the context of celebrations in Armenia marking the engagement of the daughter of Artavasdes the king of Armenia to the son of Hyrodes (Orodes) the king of Parthia, explaining that both these monarchs were familiar with Greek culture, and Artavasdes 'was actually the author of tragedies, speeches, and histories, some of which have been preserved'. He continues, 'At the moment when Crassus' head was brought to the door, the dining tables had just been removed, and an actor of tragedies named Jason, from Tralles, was singing the Agave scene [lit. 'the

---

Augustan periods: cf. Rawson (1985); Beacham (1991) ch. 5. On pantomime see Kokolakis (1959); Jones (1991).

[31] There is some help to be got from papyri which seem to provide actual scripts for performance. See Turner (1963); Di Gregorio (1976).

[32] See esp. Bartsch (1994) ch. 3 for the interaction between actors and audiences in Republican and Imperial Rome.

[33] See also Polyaenus 7.41. For the motif of the severed head displaced at a banquet see Paul (1991).

things about Agave'] in the *Bacchae* of Euripides.' This is not unlike the context described by Diodorus for Neoptolemus and Philip, but here Plutarch includes a chorus, one of whose members is given the dummy head (i.e. the mask) of Pentheus to hold when the actor picks up Crassus' real one and sings some of Agave's frenzied lines. There is a scuffle over the head when one of the spectators, Pomaxathres, the soldier who killed Crassus, intervenes on hearing the chorus's question, 'Who killed him?' and Agave's response, 'The prize is mine.'[34] Plutarch rounds off the story with a comment that brings out the point, the way in which the life of Crassus mimicked art: 'The king, who was delighted, presented Pomaxathres with the traditional Parthian decorations and gave Jason a talent, and such, it is said, was the finale (*exodion*) with which Crassus' Asiatic command ended, just like a tragedy.'[35]

Plutarch's reference to the dummy head takes us back to the 'artificial blood' mentioned by Josephus and Suetonius in their accounts of the shows preceding the assassination of Caligula (in Suetonius the blood is a special feature only of the supporting mime). There is plenty of other evidence for a more explicit display of violence in Hellenistic and later theatre than in earlier times, which scholars have usually interpreted as sensationalism and therefore as a symptom of artistic decline. But we should allow for the possibility that such changes were perceived as marks of modern sophistication, like ever more ambitious effects in film and television nowadays, and reports of performers who were noted for their brilliant expertise, like the actor Timotheus of Zacynthus who specialised in the role of Ajax falling on his sword[36] or the athlete-actor from Tegea who was admired for his strong-man parts,[37] might even be evidence for theatrical vitality. The ancient sources for the story of post-classical dramatic production, particularly from the imperial period, tend to be influenced by moralists or satirists, and there are real difficulties in trying to capture the style and reception of performances that went under the heading 'tragic' in later antiquity.[38]

A passage from a late pagan author, the sophist Eunapius of Sardis

---

[34] This is a loose quotation of *Ba.* 1179.

[35] Plutarch's use of theatrical language and motifs is interesting: cf. de Lacy (1952); Mossman (1988); Jones (1991).

[36] See schol. on *Ajax* 864: 'The audience must believe that he falls on his sword, and the actor must be strongly built so as to make them imagine Ajax, as is said of Timotheus of Zacynthus, who so captivated and enthralled the spectators with his acting that they called him Sphageus [the Slayer].' This was the word used by Ajax of his sword (815). For the use of stage swords with retractable blades cf. Achilles Tatius 3.20.

[37] *SIG*[3] 1080 (= *TrGF* I DID B 11); cf. Csapo & Slater (1995) 200.

[38] For discussion of different types of evidence see Beacham (1991) ch. 5; Jones (1993); Rouché (1993); Bartsch (1994).

(fourth century AD), might give some sense of what a *tragōidos* might hope his performance would achieve, though this comes out only incidentally, and the larger context of our fragment is unclear.[39] Eunapius tells the story of an unnamed *tragōidos* in the time of Nero, who decided to leave Rome and go on tour because at Rome he was the object of the emperor's professional jealousy. He went 'to display his vocal powers' to half-barbarian audiences, to a city which had a theatre but evidently had not had visits from tragic performers before. At first the spectators were terrified at the sight of him, but he took aside some of the local elite and explained the nature of the mask and the platform-soled boots that increased his height,[40] and then tried another performance. The role he was acting was that of Euripides' Andromeda. This time he gradually accustomed the audience to his vocal range, but the weather was extremely hot, and he suggested they should wait till the cool of the evening. By now, however, they were wildly enthusiastic for him to carry on, and he let himself go in a passionate rendering of his part. 'This untrained audience was unable to respond to most of the features of tragedy: the majesty and grandeur of the language and style, the charm of the metre, the clarity of the character-drawing, most finely and compellingly designed to move the hearer, and in addition they were unfamiliar with the plot, but even stripped of all these advantages he enthralled them with the beauty of his enunciation and his singing.' The story ends with a grotesque scene: a week later the city was hit by an epidemic, and the whole population lay in the streets suffering from violent diarrhoea, 'singing (or 'crying out') as best each one could the melody [presumably of Andromeda's famous monody] without managing a very clear rendering of the words: Andromeda had had a dire effect on them'. As well as telling us something about the aspirations of a performing artist the passage suggests the way in which tragedy might be seen as a defining feature of Greek culture, even if its effects were not always beneficial.

One very important development illustrated by the games at Aegae, as by many other pieces of evidence, is that even as early as the fourth century BC the religious context of drama was changing fast. No difficulty, it seems, was felt in attaching dramatic shows to festivals in honour of other gods than Dionysus or to more personal celebrations. The Macedonian kings were particularly influential here, but there must always have

---

[39] Eunapius fr. 54 in *Historici graeci minores*. There is a suspiciously similar story in Lucian, *How to Write History* 1, set in 'Abdera at the time of King Lysimachus'; cf. Philostratus, *Vita Apoll.* 5.9, set at 'Ipola' in Baetica, but with no mention in Philostratus' case of *Andromeda* or the epidemic.

[40] For the high boots and exaggeratedly stylised masks of Hellenistic and later theatre see Bieber (1961); Green (1994).

been scope for local variations: the theatre at Syracuse, for example, which goes back to the early fifth century, was in a precinct of Apollo. The Tegean inscription mentioned above (p. 222 and n. 37), which records the victories of the actor who specialised in strong-man roles, illustrates the range of festivals and presiding deities familiar in the third century BC: the Great Dionysia at Athens, the Soteria at Delphi (Apollo), the Ptolemaia at Alexandria (though here the actor was competing as a boxer), the Heraia at Argos, the Naia at Dodona (Zeus), 'and 88 victories at the dramatic contests in the cities, at festivals of Dionysus or whatever other festivals the cities celebrated'.[41] Although the Dionysiac iconography of masks, satyrs and maenads remained definitive for drama in visual terms, the occasions themselves had a far more diverse religious character than in the early days at Athens. This too must have had a profound effect on perceptions.

Yet the Dionysiac connexion always persisted, through a new type of organisation, the exceptionally powerful actors' unions, based in many different centres, which represented the performers' interests wherever they travelled.[42] The name these groups gave themselves was *technitai Dionusou*, which is usually rendered 'Artists of Dionysus', though 'craftsmen' might be more inclusive. Alongside lead actors for tragedy and comedy we find supporting actors and chorusmen, musicians of different kinds, rhapsodes, and also poets, suggesting that professional troupes with their own script-writers were now being formed. These official organisations, with centres in different parts of the Greek world, are well attested from the third century BC onwards by inscriptions which demonstrate the wealth and prestige of the performers and the extraordinary privileges that went with their status. The fact that performance (including tragedy in its different guises) was so elaborately institutionalised at an international level shows just how tenacious its hold was on audiences all over the ancient world; in this sense Dionysus triumphantly transcended the specific context of his cult, in which tragedy had first been generated.

TEXTS

If the process of change in terms of performance was as complex and elaborate as this sketch has tried to suggest, it is hardly conceivable that any complete tragedies from the early days could have survived to be trans-

[41] For festival locations see e.g. Csapo & Slater (1995) 186–206.
[42] See Pickard-Cambridge (1988) ch. 7; Stephanis (1988); Roueché (1993) ch. 4; Csapo & Slater (1995) 239–55, 418. Places especially associated with the Artists were Athens, Corinth, Thespiae, and the island of Teos.

mitted to the Middle Ages and beyond through the performance tradition alone. Clearly some works acquired canonical status, and out of the thousands of new plays produced from the fifth century onwards a (fluctuating) selection became classics with a book life of their own. The popularity of particular plays must have been influenced by their familiarity in the repertoire, and the demand for texts must often have been related to the demand for revivals, but it is hard to see the transmission of whole plays continuing as it did without the intervention of scholars.[43]

An unbroken history of scholarly interest in tragedy can be traced from the time of Aristotle and his pupils at Athens to the Alexandrian researchers who took over the methodology of the Peripatetics and collected, emended, classified and analysed texts on a heroic scale.[44] These scholars set a pattern of commentary writing which was to be carried on for centuries, giving the plays that were singled out for such attention a much greater chance of long-term survival. There are many things to be learned from the remnants of these commentaries that survive in the marginal scholia of a fair number of the manuscripts of Aeschylus, Sophocles and Euripides. Typically these are only a brief sample of notes picked out at different times in late antiquity from much more extensive commentaries, but they help us to understand the process of canon formation, which had been officially recognised in 386 BC (see p. 213 above), showing how 'the ancients' became paradigms of tragic excellence. Even Euripides, who had been much ridiculed, as well as much appreciated, in his own time and was quite often criticised by scholars,[45] was still one of the essentially unassailable masters, and indeed it was he who was more often revived in performance, more often used as a model by later imitators (or Roman translators), and more often quoted, than any other tragic dramatist.

The evidence of the scholia does not stand alone: there are papyrus fragments of passages from new and old plays and of schoolboys' exercises in tragic style, which along with quotations from tragedy in anthologies and rhetorical handbooks make clear how much the educational system itself used and imitated tragic texts. A group of inscriptions from Aphrodisias in Asia Minor, dating from the second century AD and reporting honours given to C. Julius Longianus, a tragic poet, shows that we must allow for repeated cross-fertilisation between performance and the production of texts. One of the inscriptions, a copy of an honorary decree

---

[43] There is a famous piece of evidence for legislation in the fourth century to guard against the wholesale alteration of texts by actors (Plutarch, *Lycurgus* 841f). On interpolation see Hamilton (1974); Csapo & Slater (1995).

[44] See Pfeiffer (1968) and for a brief survey *CHCL* I, ch. 1.

[45] Hostile comments crop up regularly in the scholia; cf. e.g. on *Hec.* 254; *Phoen.* 388.

probably issued at Halicarnassus,[46] includes the following revealing details: Longianus had evidently made a visit to the city in the course of which he had given

> demonstrations of poems of every citizen among us without payment, being both a good man and the best poet of our times.

Bronze statues of Longianus were to be put up

> both in the most notable places of the city and in the precinct of the Muses and in the gymnasium of the ephebes next to the ancient Herodotus; it has also been voted that there should be public presentation of his books in the libraries of our city, so that the young men may be educated in these also, in the same way as in the writings of the ancients.   (trans. C. M. Roueché)

If we take this example as a cue to ask questions about the wider impact of Greek tragedy on the culture of antiquity, there is an immensely complex story waiting to be told which can only be adumbrated here under the most provisional headings.[47] The fact that in the Latin-speaking world Greek tragedy had a new lease of life in translation and adaptation is hugely important, both for the culture of Republican Rome, which was deeply influenced by the plays of Ennius and Accius and others, and for the long-term impact of Seneca's tragedies, one of the most significant of all literary legacies. Greek literature of the Roman period, too, shows many traces of the 'theatricalisation' of ancient culture: historians like Diodorus and Plutarch, novel writers like Heliodorus, and essayists like Lucian use the imagery of the theatre, including tragedy, to express views of human experience that they could expect their readers to recognise and share. This intense penetration of the language and literature of antiquity gave tragedy a special imaginative status that did not ultimately depend on performance traditions for its survival. The task of capturing in detail the reverberations of tragedy in later antiquity is one of the most interesting challenges for contemporary critics.

BIBLIOGRAPHICAL NOTE

Two recent publications have made the whole field of ancient dramatic history more accessible. These are: (i) Green (1994), which makes systematic use of the visual evidence, such as theatre buildings, vase-paintings, terracottas and mosaics, taking account of their distribution at different periods and in different parts of the Graeco-

[46] For text, discussion and translation see Roueché (1993) 223–7.
[47] See Bibliographical Note for references.

Roman world, and considering the more general contexts in which theatrical iconography was used. This work builds on the evidence set out in T. B. L. Webster, *Monuments Illustrating Tragedy and Satyr Play*, 2nd edn, *BICS* Suppl. 20 (London 1967). Green is also responsible for a detailed bibliographical survey (1989) 7–95 and 273–8. (ii) Csapo & Slater (1995) provides translations, with analysis, discussion and detailed bibliography, of much of the ancient epigraphic and literary evidence for drama, its origins, organisation and performance. This can be used as a companion to Pickard-Cambridge (1988). Further documentation in Mette (1977) and *TrGF* I.

For the spread of Attic drama outside Athens see Taplin (1993). On actors: Ghiron-Bistagne (1976), and (for the Artists of Dionysus) Stephanis (1988) and Roueché (1993). For theatre in the Hellenistic and Roman periods see G. Sifakis, *Studies in the History of Hellenistic Drama* (London 1967); B. Gentili, *Theatrical Performances in the Ancient World: Hellenistic and Early Roman Theatre* (London 1979); C. P. Jones, 'Greek drama in the Roman Empire' in Scodel (1993) 39–52; J. Blänsdorf (ed.), *Theater und Gesellschaft im Imperium Romanum* (Tübingen 1990); B. Le Guen, 'Théâtre et cités à l'époque hellénistique', *REG* 108 (1995) 59–90. The Roman tragedians' relations with the Greek tradition are discussed by Jocelyn (1969). For Seneca see R. J. Tarrant, 'Senecan drama and its antecedents', *HSCP* 82 (1978) 213–63. On pantomime: Kokolakis (1959) 1–56.

On the 'theatricalisation' of culture in later antiquity see e.g. P. de Lacy, 'Biography and tragedy in Plutarch', *AJP* 73 (1952) 159–71; F. Fuhrmann, *Les images de Plutarque* (Paris 1964) 45, 228–9, 241–4; F. W. Walbank, 'Tragedy and history', *Historia* 9 (1960) 216–34; M. Kokolakis, 'Lucian and the tragic performances of his time', *Platon* 12 (1960) 67–109 and *The Tragic Simile of Life* (Athens 1960); A. S. L. Farquarson, ed., *Marcus Aurelius, Meditations* (Oxford 1944) on 11.6 and 12.36; J. W. H. Walden, 'Stage-terms in Heliodorus' *Aethiopica*' (*HSCP* 5) (1894) 1–43; T. Paulson, *Inszenierung des Schicksals: Tragödie und Komödie im Roman des Heliodor* (Trier 1992); S. Bartsch, *Actors in the Audience* (Cambridge, MA, and London 1994).

10

PETER BURIAN

Tragedy adapted for stages and screens: the Renaissance to the present

A history of the influence of Greek tragedy on later Western literature and thought, if it could be written at all, would be not only enormously long but also extremely complicated.[1] Given the cultural prestige of tragedy, however, it is striking how rarely the plays themselves were brought to the stage until relatively recent times. The extraordinary beginning made with the production of Sophocles' *Oedipus the King* at Vicenza in 1585 remained a more or less isolated event until the end of the eighteenth century, and indeed it is only in the last few decades that productions of Greek tragedy have become common occurrences (see Ch. 11). What did happen, and on a large scale, was the adaptation of tragic plots to create a new corpus of dramatic texts, more often than not the product of 'contamination' with Senecan tragedy,[2] and drawing on historical and mythological lore from non-tragic sources as well as current religious, philosophical, and political ideas.[3]

---

[1] No such history has in fact been written, to my knowledge. There are of course a number of extremely valuable partial accounts, among which I have found Mueller (1980) of greatest value. For a selective survey of adaptations of Greek tragic themes, with emphasis on the modern period, see Hamburger (1969). Three important studies are in German: von Fritz (1962), Friedrich (1967), and Flashar (1991). The last is largely devoted to modern productions, particularly in German-speaking lands, but contains valuable observations on the earlier history of adaptation. Of course a full treatment of the influence of Greek tragedy would have to go beyond the translation and adaptation of extant Greek tragic texts and even the grand project of developing new tragic subjects and forms. It would need to treat many vexed and sometimes ideologically charged issues, such as the relation of tragedy and epic (a question that goes back at least as far as book 4 of Virgil's *Aeneid*) and the possibility of adapting tragedy to Christian themes. Moreover, the influence of Greek tragedy on thinkers as varied as Freud and Nietzsche, and their influence in turn on playwrights and producers, would need to be investigated in far more detail than is possible here.

[2] Senecan tragedy was known earlier and better, and in many ways was equated with Greek tragedy, by the early adapters of tragedy to the stage. See Charlton (1946).

[3] Another element that goes beyond the scope of this chapter is the influence on dramatic practice of the lively and often polemical traditions of interpreting Aristotle's *Poetics* (sparked by J. C. Scaliger's *Poetices libri septem* of 1561 and Luigi Castelvetro's translation and

228

This chapter confronts some of the intellectual and aesthetic issues involved in the process of coming to terms with Greek tragedy over the last five centuries. I limit myself largely to plays and operas (and, in the final paragraphs, films and television) that are clearly based on extant Greek originals, not because these plays are necessarily of the highest literary or cultural importance in and of themselves (though no doubt a number are), but because they suggest in obvious ways the challenge that adapters from the Renaissance onwards faced in assimilating a particularly prestigious but in many ways intractable heritage. At the same time, it is important to recognise that there may be a deeper inner connection to Greek tragedy in plays that are not direct translations or adaptations than in those that claim to be. It would not, for example, be meaningless to assert that there is more of Sophocles in Milton's *Samson Agonistes* than in all the English versions of *Oedipus* or *Antigone* produced before or since.[4]

THE RE-EMERGENCE OF GREEK TRAGEDY

The texts of the extant Greek tragedies began to be available to Western Europe, along with the other central texts of the Greek heritage, in Italy in the fifteenth century.[5] Early Latin translations helped to propagate the direct knowledge of Greek tragic theatre. Erasmus himself produced Latin translations of *Hecuba* and *Iphigeneia at Aulis* and was followed by the greatest Scottish humanist, George Buchanan, with translations of *Alcestis* and *Medea*. Translation into the European vernaculars was patchier and less frequent, Aeschylus in particular being almost entirely neglected, but by the time of the Vicenza *Oedipus*, there were translations into Spanish, French, and English,[6] as well as Italian, of tragedies by both Sophocles and

commentary *Poetica d'Aristotele*, 1570), which sometimes seem to overshadow the ancient dramas themselves as the repository of the essential lessons to be learned from the Greek theatre. See Weinberg (1961) chs. 9–12.

[4] Cf. Goethe's remark to Eckermann on 31 January 1830: 'I read [Milton's] *Samson* not long ago, and it is in the spirit of the ancients like no other play of any modern writer.' Milton himself, in the Preface to *Samson*, invites comparison with the practice of the Greek tragic poets: 'Of the style and uniformity, and that commonly call'd the Plot ... they only will judge best who are not unacquainted with *Aeschylus, Sophocles*, and *Euripides*, the three Tragic Poets unequall'd yet by any, and the best rule to all who endeavour to write Tragedy.'

[5] See Bolgar (1954) 494–504 for manuscripts of the Greek tragedians in Italy in the fifteenth century. The first printed edition of Greek tragic texts, a volume containing Euripides' *Medea, Hippolytus, Alcestis*, and *Andromache*, was published in Florence around 1495. The *editio princeps* of Sophocles was printed by Aldus Manutius (Venice 1502), followed almost immediately by eighteen plays of Euripides (1503) and, somewhat later (1518), six of Aeschylus.

[6] The case of England is, however, rather different from that of France, Italy, or Spain. The existence in England of a great tragic tradition that develops prior to the full onset of

Euripides.[7] This makes all the more surprising the fact that the Vicenza *Oedipus* was not only the first public performance of a Greek tragedy[8] but (making exception for school productions) the only such performance on a public stage until late in the eighteenth century.

Certainly, the Vicenza production, which on 3 March 1585 inaugurated the Teatro Olimpico designed by Palladio and completed after his death by his pupil Scamozzi, was as auspicious an occasion for the formal re-emergence of Greek tragedy on the European stage as may be imagined.[9] In many ways, it can be seen as a kind of *summa* of Humanism: the play itself was chosen by the Accademia Olimpica, after long discussions, primarily because the *Poetics* of Aristotle treated it as the ideal example of what the Renaissance regarded as the most elevated of all literary genres. The Venetian scholar Orsatto Giustiniani was chosen to produce a translation 'in lingua volgare' – a translation of remarkable fidelity, it should be said. The theatre itself was designed on the pattern of an ancient theatre, and its fixed scenery (still in place today) closely followed the specifications of Vitruvius for the Roman *scaenae frons*, though the perspective behind its three openings showed the streets of a Thebes imagined as a Palladian Vicenza. The music for the choral odes was specially composed by the famed Venetian composer Andrea Gabrieli. The production, directed by Italy's best known man of the theatre Angelo Ingegneri, was kept as faithful as possible to what was known about the conventions of Greek tragic performance.[10] The chorus, for example, was made up of fifteen men (fourteen choreuts and a chorus leader) as attested by the ancient 'Life of Sophocles', deployed for their songs in five rows of three or three of five. The audience included the politically and socially prominent from the entire

---

Hellenism sets up a dialectic, often expressed in the form of an antithesis between nature (Milton, for example, has Shakespeare 'warble his native wood-notes wild') and learning (understood primarily as respect for the 'classical' unities and decorum), that will have profound importance for the history of British and indeed European drama.

[7] See Bolgar (1954) 508–25 for a list of vernacular translations of Greek authors before 1600. The only German translation of a Greek tragedy known to Bolgar is that of Euripides' *Iphigeneia in Aulis* by H. Bebst, 1584. There are no vernacular versions of Aeschylus before the seventeenth century.

[8] Though not the first translation into Italian: there was an *Oreste* by Giovanni Rucellai (d. 1525), an *Antigone* by Luigi Alamanni (1533), and an *Edipo* by Giovanni Andrea del'Anguillara (1556).

[9] The fundamental treatment of this well-documented event is Schrade (1960), which includes the text of Giustiniani's translation and the music of Gabrieli. See also Vidal-Naquet in Vernant and Vidal-Naquet (1988) 361–71.

[10] Ingegneri later published the first practical handbook of theatrical production, *Il Modo di Rapprenetare le Favole Sceniche*, 1598, drawing his examples wherever possible from the *Oedipus*.

region, and the performance was judged in all the contemporary accounts to have been an enormous success.

Despite all that, further such loving revivals of ancient plays were not to follow. The response to ancient tragedy was to be both more creative and more complex. An earlier performance in Vicenza, in Palladio's Basilica and under Palladio's direction, turns out to be a better gauge of the future influence of Greek tragedy than the 1585 *Oedipus*. This was the belated première of the first original drama self-consciously modelled on Greek tragedy, Giangiorgio Trissino's *Sofonisba*, completed in 1515, published in 1524, but not performed until 1562. The hybrid character of Trissino's play is immediately clear in its attempt to graft onto explicitly Greek theatrical practice as it was then understood (respect for the unities, no more than three characters on stage at one time, continuous presence of the chorus) a subject from Roman history, using Virgil's account of the death of Dido in *Aeneid*, book 4, itself already a kind of hybrid of epic and tragedy, as a primary model. The plot, based on Livy, involves a sister of Hannibal, betrothed to Masinissa of Numidia, but married for political reasons to his rival Siface (Syphax). Masinissa defeats Siface, claims Sofonisba, but is forced to give her up to the Romans. Rather than endure this fate, Sofonisba takes the poison offered to her by Masinissa.[11]

Sofonisba showed the path that humanist tragedy would take by its choice of subject, for it is to history and to the Bible that the early tragedians most often turn, and indeed most serious drama until the nineteenth century follows suit. There are a number of possible reasons why this is so,[12] not least of which is the humanists' understanding of tragedy as the genre *par excellence* of great public themes. For both playwrights and audiences, the Bible[13] and history – usually, as with *Sofonisba*, Roman history, but also later and more local events[14] – offered a vast store of widely known and deeply resonant stories of the fates of noble men and women. The Greek plots are also available as subjects, of course, but since they are remote and therefore timeless, they tend to be deployed as paradigms for the uncertain-

---

[11] The theme became quite popular, spawning, among others, plays by Marston, Corneille, Voltaire, and Alfieri, and operas by Caldara, Leo, and Gluck. An exhaustive list may be found in Cremante (1988) 18–20.

[12] See the brief but interesting discussion in Mueller (1980) 6–11.

[13] For example, the earliest play composed according to the conventions of ancient tragedy but based on a scripture, Buchanan's *Jephtha* (first published in 1544, but written about a decade earlier), is based on the story of Jephthah's vow from Judges and uses Euripides' *Iphigeneia at Aulis* as a model, along with elements from the *Hecuba*, and even a scene adapted from Plautus' *Amphitryo*.

[14] The best known example of the latter is Giovanni Rucellai's *Rosamunda* (first published in 1525, and written as much as a decade before), based on the history of the sixth-century Lombard invasion and patterned closely on Sophocles' *Antigone*.

ties and tribulations of the day. The stories of the fall of Troy and the destruction of the royal house of Thebes have enormous prestige precisely because they can be invoked as emblems of tragic overturn. A character such as Hecuba, widowed and bereft of her children and her country, is the very figure of changeable human fortunes, and events such as the killing of Antigone or the mutual fratricide of Eteocles and Polyneices can easily be made to stand for the internecine wars of religion that split families, communities, and states in the sixteenth and seventeenth centuries.

Humanist sources are unanimous in rehearsing the view, derived from the Latin grammarians Donatus and Diomedes, that the primary function of tragedy is to show the instability of human affairs through a reversal of fortune in the lives of the great. That being so, it is not surprising that contemporary definitions of tragedy all include – indeed at times become – lists of the various atrocities, sufferings, and outrages appropriate to the genre.[15] There is a marked tendency to regard the power of tragedy as increasing in proportion to the accumulation of incident and high emotion. Not surprisingly then, Euripides' *Phoenician Women*, a Greek tragedy that until recently has been mostly neglected or treated with contempt, was one of the most admired in the sixteenth. Like the lists of tragic sufferings, the plot of the *Phoenician Women* piles sorrow upon sorrow. And its subject is not merely the downfall of an individual, but the fall of Thebes' royal house.

The terms in which the *Phoenician Women* is praised provide another crucial clue to the Humanist conception of tragedy. Stiblinus, in the preface to his Latin translation of 1562, calls the play 'most tragic and full of vehement passions'; Grotius, some seventy years later, included in the dedicatory epistle to his translation a more elaborate commendation: '... poetry excels within the whole art of speech [*in omni dicendi opere*], tragedy undoubtedly within poetry, Euripides, by agreement of the philosophers, within tragedy, and among his plays the *Phoenician Women*, because, in the judgement also of the ancient grammarians, its structure is so artful, its events so various, its commonplaces so copious, and in particular its description and praise of justice are handled with such wisdom ...'[16] Tragedy here is construed as a branch of rhetoric; its structure is understood as an arrangement of passionate discourses filled with

---

[15] Discussion and quotation of a number of these definitions in Stone (1974) 9–29. Perhaps the most inclusive is that of Scaliger in *Poetices libri septem*, bk 3, ch. 97: 'The events of tragedy are great, terrible, the commands of kings, murders, lamentations, hangings, exiles, bereavements, parricides, incests, fires, battles, blindings, wailings, shriekings, complaints, funerals, eulogies, and dirges.'

[16] Both Stiblinus and Grotius are quoted by Mueller (1980) 21 and 253, n. 39.

appropriate and ennobling sentiments. Sixteenth-century rhetoric attempt to codify precepts that applied to all serious use of language. Tragedy was at the pinnacle of rhetorical art, because in it could be embodied the greatest dignity and elevation of diction. Not least, it could be seen as the vehicle for imparting lessons in eloquence and morality through its maxims, the *sententiae* that Scaliger compared to the 'columns or basic pillars, so to speak' of the tragic edifice.[17] And indeed, tragedy in the sixteenth century had a far more important role in the teaching of rhetoric and morality than in theatrical praxis.[18]

Antigone ou la piété, by the magistrate-poet Robert Garnier (1580), provides an excellent example of the strengths and limitations of humanist tragedy. Its structure seems additive rather than intrinsically dramatic. Garnier strings together his ancient sources (chiefly Statius and Seneca for the first three acts, Sophocles for the final two) to produce a panorama that begins before the duel of Polyneices and Eteocles and includes the matter of two or three Greek tragedies. The first act, 467 lines of dialogue and debate between Antigone and Edipe, focuses on Edipe's desire to die, with Antigone urging him to overcome his grief and live. Only two-thirds of the way through the act, after a debate over Edipe's responsibility for his crimes, do we learn of the impending struggle between the brothers with which the action proper begins. But Garnier's seemingly deficient dramaturgy is a corollary of his thematic concerns; he has let an essentially rhetorical strategy govern his formal choices. The play is articulated as a series of confrontations – the main ones after that of Antigone and Edipe in Act I are between Iocaste and Polynice (Act II), Antigone and Iocaste (Act III), and of course Antigone and Creon (Act IV) – in which the central themes of the play are set out by the juxtaposition of opposing views. Antigone's *piété*, which gives the drama its subtitle, is of the essence here. Each of her confrontations displays heroic determination and a self-sacrificial concern for others. In this light, her plea to her father to live in order to bring peace to Thebes, and even more her departure for the city at the end of Act I, are not at all irrelevant.[19]

Above all, Garnier's *Antigone* reflects the tendency of humanist tragedy to treat its dramatic subjects, whether classical or biblical, as *exempla* transcending time and place to speak with immediacy to the here and now. Civil war, good government, the constancy of human suffering and the need for sacrifice, these are all public themes through which the myth of Thebes can be made to address directly the France of Garnier's own day. The confrontation of Antigone and Creon provides Garnier with the opportu-

---

[17] *Poetices libri septem*, bk 3, ch. 96.   [18] See Stone (1974) 29–45.
[19] See Stone (1974) 94. Steiner (1984) offers a sympathetic view of the *piété* of Antigone (139–40) and a brief account of the play's influence (195–6).

nity to stage the conflict of religious and civil authority; his heroine's *piété* is opposed to the tyranny of Creon explicitly and in the language of current political thought. Antigone dies a martyr for her virtue, Creon suffers horrible retribution for what he himself calls the *crime detestable* of a bad ruler (2626). Living in the midst of civil and religious strife, Garnier's audience would have found the application of his drama to their own day all too clear. As if to underline it, laments for Thebes' misfortunes resound through the play with unmistakable relevance:

> Mars dedans la campagne bruit,
> Nostre beau terroir est destruit:
> Le vigneron quitte la vigne,
> Le courbe laboreur ses boeus,
> Le berger ses pastis herbeus,
> Et le morne pescheur sa ligne.   (978–83)[20]

Whatever its limitations as drama, Garnier's *Antigone* embodies a deeply felt vision of communal suffering. The French classical theatre of the seventeenth century went on to develop a far more sophisticated drama-turgy but at the cost of turning away from the great public themes of the best humanist plays. (Ironically, this thematic move from public to private coincided with the rise of the public stage as a venue for serious drama.) The *Antigone* of Jean de Rotrou (1638), though closely related to Garnier's, clearly points in a new direction.[21] Rotrou is more concerned than Garnier to unify the plot by carefully integrating all its elements. As is the norm in the seventeenth century, he dispenses with the chorus so as not to interrupt the continuity of action. That action itself is more tightly interwoven; the first part of his drama develops above all a special intimacy, bordering on the erotic, between Antigone and Polyneice, which then comes into conflict with the love of Antigone and Hémon, so that the crisis of the play is felt less as a matter of Antigone's defiance of Creon's decree than of her need to choose between loyalty to brother and fiancé. The play ends as a tragedy of star-crossed lovers, Antigone's death leading to Hémon's suicide on stage in the presence of his father. The emphasis on themes of love and personal loyalty in Rotrou's *Antigone* illustrates the focus on individual subjectivity

---

[20] 'Mars roars in the fields, our beautiful countryside is destroyed; the vine-dresser leaves his vineyard, the bent labourer his cattle, the shepherd his grassy pasture, and the sad fisher his line.' See further Jondorf (1969); these lines are quoted on p. 87.
[21] See Mueller (1980) 33–8, where this comparison is elaborated. Mueller points out that, as so often in the history of the European theatre, the development of French neoclassical tragedy was a conscious attempt to restore the dignity of an art corrupted by popular entertainment (in this case early seventeenth-century tragicomedy) by looking to ancient models.

that will increasingly dominate European drama. In practice, this comes to mean the introduction of a love interest, often in the form of a subplot interwoven with the main action, which opens up dramaturgical possibilities for suspense and for more fully psychologised treatments of motivation and reaction. But the interest in individual psychology often threatens the integrity of the tragic theme, and that too is illustrated by Rotrou's play. In attempting to make Antigone a more believable character, the playwright recentres the action from her refusal to obey an iniquitous decree to an inner conflict caused by her competing loves.

It was not easy to integrate the amatory subplot fully into the thematics of tragedy, but the positive possibilities of a psychologised and eroticised rereading of tragic myth can be seen in the enduring masterpiece of French classical theatre, Jean Racine's *Phèdre* (1677). Racine himself, in the Preface to *Phèdre*, explains the changes he has made to his Euripidean source[22] in terms of the *vraisemblance* and *bienséance* that constitute what might be called the ideology of seventeenth-century classicism:

> I have ... taken care to make [Phaedra] somewhat less odious than she is in the tragedies of the Ancients, where she herself resolves to accuse Hippolytus. I felt that the calumny was rather too base and foul to be put into the mouth of a princess whose sentiments were otherwise so noble and so virtuous. Such baseness seemed to me more suitable to a nurse ... The blameless Hippolytus is accused, in Euripides and in Seneca, with having in fact violated his stepmother ... but in this play he is accused only of having had the intention to do so. I wished to spare Theseus a degree of violent feeling which might have made him less sympathetic to the audience. As for the figure of Hippolytus, ... I thought it best to give him some frailty which would render him slightly guilty toward his father, without however detracting in any way from that greatness of soul which leads him to spare Phaedra's honour ...[23]

The 'frailty' of course is Hippolyte's love for Aricie, daughter and sister of Theseus' mortal enemies. Euripides and Seneca (and for that matter Garnier in his *Hippolyte*) make Hippolytus reject love. Racine, perhaps feeling that both verisimilitude and decorum would be violated by a prince who shied away from women, introduces the requisite amatory subplot (and his chief innovation on the ancient sources) into a dramatic situation already suffused with *erōs*. But Racine's own accounting does little to reveal the

[22] Racine's Preface insists on the direct descent of *Phèdre* from Euripides' *Hippolytus*, but as Knight (1974) and others have demonstrated, his plays are much less purely Greek in inspiration than he likes to admit. In the case of *Phèdre*, such elements as the Queen's confession of love to her stepson and the management of her suicide owe little or nothing to Euripides and much to Seneca.

[23] Quoted from the excellent translation by Richard Wilbur (1986).

235

sources of the greatness of this play. I am not arguing that Racine's attention to reason and proportion are irrelevant, merely that in this play formal balance and elegance do not supplant unreason and obsession, but rather concentrate them and allow the full mythic and psychological dimensions of a legend of mad love to find expression. Even the Aricie subplot bears its fruit in the searing sequence of Phèdre's jealousy, anger, and remorse after Thésée has revealed the young prince's love for the captive princess (Act 4, Scenes 5 and 6) rather than by fulfilling its announced purpose of giving Hippolyte the flaw that will keep his death from eliciting indignation rather than pity.

The world of *Phèdre* is a world in which unreason is a given, in which 'the daughter of Minos and of Pasiphaë' (as Hippolyte calls her in the play's first scene) fulfils her cruel destiny pursued by an unexplained, implacable anger of the gods. Blood and fire are her images; the Sun is her ancestor. She erupts onto the orderly seventeenth-century French stage as a barbaric, monstrous, and deeply irrational force. Indeed, she is the embodiment of the mythical monsters who wait off stage to be fought once more. Racine manages to suspend Phèdre between a mythical realm made palpable and the psychology of passion that at some level it represents. And all this is accomplished within the solemnity of a theatrical language that seems intent on suppressing the wildness she represents with the counterforce of discipline and rigour. As often happens in great classical art, the tension between conceptual abandon and formal control reveals itself in the smallest touches: for example, in Phèdre's famous and even shocking shift from the formal *vous* to the intimate *tu* when at last she drops all pretence and confesses her love to Hippolyte.[24] Committed to a discourse deeply imbued with the particular forms of reason implied (or imposed) by *vraisemblance* and *bienséance*, Racine discovered in *Phèdre* that myth can express what otherwise there would be no way to say. It can be made to convey a vision of the terrifying, irrational workings of the soul.

Paradoxically, however, to function as a representation of inner drama, myth must be transformed from metaphor to reality. Racine achieves this not by convincing his audience that the pagan tale embodies literal truth, but by embodying the tale itself in the language of his drama. What might at the outset seem merely to be mythological periphrasis comes more and more to represent the reality of myth, the factual world of the play. When Phèdre herself reaches the point of contemplating suicide and conjures up the terrifying vision of her soul appearing for judgement before her father in the

---

[24] See Steiner (1961) 103, who also points out (88) the significance of Phaedra's apparently simple and natural gesture of sitting down at her first entrance.

world below, what her words make us see is hardly mythology as decor and certainly no mere *façon de parler*:

> Où me cacher? Fuyons dans la nuit infernale.
> Mais que dis-je? Mon père y tient l'urne fatale;
> Le sort, dit-on, l'a mise en ses sévères mains:
> Minos juge aux enfers tous les pâles humaines. (1277–80)[25]

Through such poetry a world that seemed to be governed by the comforting conventions of theatrical decorum is engulfed by the terror of myth.

That terror belongs in the soul and in the cosmos; it is not part of the polis. There is of course a good deal of politics in *Phèdre*, but it concerns only the mechanics of the plot.[26] Garnier's tragedy of the city has been entirely supplanted by the tragedy of individuals. But how are we to understand that tragedy? Racine himself, at the end of his Preface, claims that *Phèdre* offers a clear moral lesson:

> The least faults here are severely punished. The mere thought of crime is seen with as much horror as the crime itself. Weaknesses begot by love are treated here as real weaknesses; the passions are here represented only to show all the disorder which they bring about; and vice is everywhere painted in colours which make one know and hate its deformity. To do thus is the proper end which every man who writes for the public should propose to himself; and this is what, above all, the earliest tragic poets had in view.

If Racine believed this, one would be tempted to call him a great tragic poet *malgré lui*, but like so much in his prefaces, it seems designed to confuse rather than clarify. Crimes are punished but so is innocence. The passions that cause disaster are also shown to be beyond the control of those who suffer them. Phèdre would escape her monsters but cannot. Hippolyte longs to escape and prove himself worthy of his father, but he finally leaves under his father's curse and is slain by the monster his father has sent against him. Thésée, slayer of monsters far and wide, is helpless against the monstrous passions that await him at home; in the end, he must face responsibility for slaying his own son. Heroism is of no use in *Phèdre* and escape is impossible. The cosmos seems not so much evil as inscrutable in its demands and indifferent to human suffering.

With *Phèdre*, Greek tragedy is again at the centre of the European stage, but a hundred years will pass before another play appears that is as complex in its response to a Greek original and as convincing in its use of

---

[25] 'Where shall I hide? Let us flee to infernal night. But what am I saying? There my father holds the fatal urn; destiny, it is said, placed it in his stern hands: Minos passes judgement in the underworld on all the pallid humans.'

[26] See Pocock (1973) 257–8.

myth as a metaphor for the passions of the soul. Johann Wolfgang von Goethe's *Iphigenie auf Tauris* (1779 in prose, 1787 in its final verse version), in many ways the conceptual antithesis of *Phèdre*, remains the only adaptation of Greek tragedy from its century compelling enough to be widely read and performed today, at least in German-speaking lands. *Iphigenie* comes at the end of a process of refining ideal images of Greek antiquity that led, in eighteenth-century versions of Greek tragedy, to simpler plots and the mitigation of tragic horror.[27] Goethe is fully in tune with these developments and turns them to great advantage in the moral economy of *Iphigenie*. Simplicity of plot is thematised as a choice made by the protagonist to reject duplicity and intrigue; mitigation of horror is achieved as the characters free themselves from the grip of tragic necessity that is their heritage.

A clear indication of the change in tonality that Goethe has made in his Euripidean original is that his Iphigenie has persuaded Thoas, the Taurian king, to abolish the old custom whereby all wanderers who set foot in the land were sacrificed to placate Diana (Euripides' Artemis). This Iphigenie is the luminous embodiment of enlightened humanity, recognised by all, and she has in some sense remade the world around her. Thoas, who decides to offer Orest and Pylades to Diana as a sacrifice he has come to feel is long overdue, is no longer simply a barbarian, but a man whose inner wounds – the death of his son and the rejection of his suit by Iphigenie – have driven him to regress from the civilised world he has come to know to an older, barbarous dispensation. Orest, on the other hand, finds that he cannot flee his crime and the burden of the family curse until out of respect for her greatness of spirit he reveals himself to Iphigenie:

> Ich kann nicht leiden, daß du große Seele
> Mit einem Wort betrogen werdest.
> Ein lügenhaft Gewebe knüpf ein Fremder
> Dem Fremden, sinnreich und der List gewohnt,
> Zur Falle vor die Füße, zwischen uns
> Sei Wahrheit!   (1076–81)[28]

This truth-telling begins the process that sets Orest free. He learns in turn that the noble priestess is the sister he thought he had lost, but this seems

---

[27] For discussion of this development, see Mueller (1980) 64–92; Mueller also helpfully points to the inherence of a version of the *Electra* embedded in the first three acts of Goethe's play and points to Voltaire's *Oreste* (1750), which he certainly knew at least in translation, as perhaps having suggested the connection.

[28] 'I cannot bear that you, great soul, should be deceived by my words. Let a stranger, clever and accustomed to deceit, weave a web of lies for another stranger, a trap laid at his feet. Between us let there be truth!'

only to intensify his longing for death as the way to assuage his guilt and break the cycle of crime. He succumbs once more to madness. At last, however, Iphigenie dispels the clouds from her brother's soul with a prayer to the divine brother and sister Apollo and Diana, and Orest knows that his curse is ended.

It is often said that the gods invoked in *Iphigenie* are no more than images of humanity, but that oversimplifies the evocation of the mythical world made so vivid both by Iphigenie and by Orest.[29] Iphigenie's prayer reminds us that, if the gods represent a human ideal, humans feel the need to give that ideal, that potentiality, transcendent expression. When Iphigenie herself reaches a moral crisis, she casts it in terms of the hatred felt by the old gods of the Titan generation for the Olympians:

> O daß in meiner Busen nicht zuletzt
> Ein Widerwillen keime! der Titanen,
> Der alten Götter tiefer Haß auf euch,
> Olympier, nicht auch die zarte Brust
> mit Geierklauen fasse! Rettet mich
> Und rettet euer Bild in meiner Seele!   (1712–17)[30]

The Titans represent the old world of curse and mutual hatred. The new generation of gods represents a new moral dispensation in which Iphigenie has placed her hope 'with pure hand and pure heart one day to redeem the house so deeply defiled' (1701–2). Her salvation is one and the same as the salvation of the image of these new gods in her soul. Pylades' plan for escape (the Euripidean intrigue plot) asks her to compromise that purity by practising deceit. For the Goethean Iphigenie, tricking Thoas would represent not a triumph over the barbarian but the destruction of a moral ideal. She recognises that the pragmatic necessity with which Pylades justifies his scheme is no other than the necessity that binds her house to its curse. And so she proceeds to test whether the curse has really been broken, the image of the new gods saved, by continuing to practise her radical honesty and trust. Iphigenie places her fate in the hands of the king she was meant to deceive and prevails upon him with the truth. And she does not stop when she has won his permission to leave, but only when he has spoken in friendship the simple word 'Farewell' (*Lebt wohl!*) with which the play ends.

Iphigenie auf Tauris may be seen as an attempt to rewrite the myth of the

---

[29] See, for example, the helpful remarks in Manasse (1952).
[30] 'Let opposition not grow at last in my bosom, let the deep hatred of the Titans, the old gods, for you, Olympians, not fix its vulture's claws upon my breast! Save me and save your image in my soul!'

House of Atreus in a way which confronts its central moral dilemma to produce a reconciliation that fulfils the highest human aspirations.[31] The characters, with their gentleness, nobility, and consideration for others, seem far removed indeed from the world of Greek tragedy, but they do not lack passion or depth of feeling. Goethe himself later described his play as rich in inner life but poor in action,[32] and it is hard to disagree with that judgement. What this points to is Goethe's decision to recast the essential conflicts as internal to the individual characters, and to include them all – Orest the matricide, Thoas the barbarian king, Pylades the advocate of trickery – in the overarching human sympathy for which Iphigenie stands as a kind of emblem. One may feel that *Iphigenie auf Tauris* is finally unsatisfactory as drama while still admiring the deep seriousness with which its author has sought to rethink the meaning of Greek tragedy for his own time.

OEDIPUS FROM CLASSICISM TO COCTEAU

Oedipus plays a crucial role in our culture in more than one way. Since the recovery of the *Poetics* in the Renaissance, *Oedipus the King* has had unique prestige as the paradigm of Greek tragedy. Freud in our own century raised the Oedipus myth to the status of master discourse of the unconscious. One way, then, to get a sense of how tragedy has been reshaped is to look at a group of Oedipus plays written over the last four centuries. The first thing we will discover, paradoxically, is how unsatisfactory a drama this Aristotelian play of plays proved to its adapters to be. Looking at a group of versions from the seventeenth and eighteenth centuries, we find a concerted effort to improve what seems implausible or repugnant in Sophocles' treatment of the subject.[33] Pierre Corneille's *Œdipe* (1659), the *Oedipus* of John Dryden and Nathaniel Lee (1678), and Voltaire's *Œdipe* (1718), although they share a number of neoclassical features (for example, a notable reduction in the role of supernatural and ritual elements), have very different emphases. Corneille attempts to revive a subject uncomfortably burdened with fatality by surrounding it with a love plot and a struggle for power. Dryden and Lee, whose subplot is even more elaborate, turn fate into a psychological datum by emphasising the mutual attraction of mother and son. Voltaire is interested above all in rationalising plot and motivation, in short, in the process of recognition rather than in its meaning.

---

[31] See Trevelyan (1941) 99–103.   [32] Conversation with Eckermann, 1 April 1827.

[33] As in the case of *Phèdre* (see n. 22), we must reckon also with the influence of Seneca's very different *Oedipus*.

Corneille's rewriting of the *Oedipus* has been understood in terms of alignment to ideals of *vraisemblance* and *bienséance* for the purpose of removing some Sophoclean improbabilities and making the play acceptable to a French audience.[34] Thus, for example, where Sophocles offers no explanation of the surviving eyewitness's false claim that Laius was murdered by a band of robbers, Corneille supplies the motive of shame. Corneille explains the failure to find and punish the supposed culprits during the intervening years by Œdipe's belief that his attack *was* punishment of the robbers. And since Œdipe has not, as in Sophocles, received the fateful oracle or been accused by Tiresias, his failure to understand his own guilt seems less incongruous. Furthermore, Corneille's chief innovation, the love of Dircé (daughter of Laius and Jocaste) and Thésée (king of Athens) is used to give what Sophocles presents as conspiracy fantasies on Oedipus' part a far more plausible basis. Dircé, who in effect replaces Sophocles' Creon, feels that she has been denied her rightful position by the usurper Œdipe, and Thésée is himself an ambitious ruler whose marriage to Dircé might threaten Œdipe's throne. Far more is at stake here, however, than harmonising Sophoclean matter with seventeenth-century French taste. Corneille rewrites the relation of fate and will by dividing his Œdipe in two: first a tyrant who wilfully thwarts a noble love in order to ensure his own power, then an innocent victim of fate worthy of pity. The relation of these two aspects of Œdipe is never fully clarified in Corneille's text, but their coexistence testifies to the strength of his impulse to turn the Sophoclean drama of knowledge into a drama of conflicting wills.

The central struggle of the play shifts from the search for Œdipe's origin to the defence of his power against the alliance of Dircé and Thésée. In this new context, the revelation of the horrible truth of Œdipe's fated crimes comes as a kind of resolution that redeems him and frees the lovers to marry at last. Perhaps the most curious aspect of Corneille's version is his treatment of Dircé and Thésée as competitors in a contest of nobility. Œdipe wants Dircé to marry Hémon, which would end her claim to the throne, and Thésée to marry Antigone or Ismène, which would strengthen his own hold on power. The lovers refuse to co-operate. This stems from their mutual love (this is the Corneillian tragedy most suffused with erotic feeling) but also, in Dircé's case, from the need for self-assertion. She refuses to accept marriage to Hémon because 'he is not the king' (404) and asserts her own will in the matter with complete self-assurance. She tells Œdipe:

---

[34] Yarrow (1978) 125–8.

Seigneur, quoi qu'il soit, j'ai fait choix de Thésée;
Je me suis à ce choix moi-même autorisée. $(425-6)^{35}$

The situation is thus in stalemate when the ghost of Laius reveals that 'the blood of my race' must expiate his murder. This appears to point to his daughter, who embraces her own sacrifice as a way of showing Thebes how great a queen she could have been, and, since she cannot marry Thésée, of proving to him that her generosity and magnanimity matches his. Now Thésée springs into action. Dircé had criticised his readiness to abandon everything for love:

Il faut qu'en vos pareils les belles passions
Ne soient que l'ornement des grandes actions. $(67-8)^{36}$

But love moves him to the noble gesture of proclaiming himself Laius' long-lost son, ready to be sacrificed for the good of all. Jocaste, who doubts his claim, points out to him that as Laius' child he must also be Laius' killer, 'since that was the black fate of my son' (1133). Thésée responds with the play's best-known speech, a denial cast as a stirring defence of free will (1149–85), symptomatic of how much Corneille has changed the themes of his ancient sources. In the end, of course, fate finds its way and the Oedipus plot is quickly completed with the requisite account of the blinding and of the suicides of Jocaste and Phorbas, the servant who saved the exposed child. Yet the fall of Œdipe seems less the culmination of the action than a subsidiary element in the contest of nobility. Dircé and Thésée, overtopped by Œdipe in his generous acceptance of his responsibility, join in admiring his 'rare constancy amidst such misfortunes' (1881). Œdipe, shouldering his fate with almost wilful indifference, removes the plague from Thebes and leaves Dircé and Thésée to find their happiness at last.

Corneille's seeming subordination of the Oedipus theme to his erotic and dynastic subplot might be dismissed as simply perverse, but it stems from serious reflection on the nature of the myth and the requirements of tragedy. Rereading the ancient tragedies, Corneille finds no fault in Oedipus that could justify his fate; he is too attached to the moral calculus of the *Poetics* to show the fall of a wholly good man and too honest to procure a fault mechanically. His solution, separating the essentially innocent parricide from the flawed tyrant, fails in the end because it entails subordinating the discovery of Oedipus' hidden sins and the depiction of his fall to an action that lacks tragic resonance.

---

35 'Sir, whatever may come of it, I have chosen Theseus; and I have made that choice on my own authority.'

36 'Sweet passions in the likes of you must be but the ornament of great deeds.'

The Preface to Dryden and Lee's *Oedipus* offers the following critique of Corneille's *Œdipe*:

> A judicious Reader will easily observe, how much the Copy is inferiour to the Original. He tells you himself, that he owes a great part of his success to the happy Episode of Theseus and Dirce; which is the same thing, as if we should acknowledge that we are indebted for our good fortune to the under-plot of Adrastus, Euridice, and Creon. The truth is, he miserably failed in the Character of his Hero; if he desired that Oedipus should be pitied, he shou'd have made him a better man.

In fact, although Dryden and Lee[37] take an almost diametrically opposed approach to the character of Oedipus, their version is even more indebted to its 'under-plot' than is Corneille's. This play is an extraordinary farrago of elements taken more or less directly from Sophocles and from Seneca (the conjuring of Laius' ghost), to which are added a subplot inspired by that of Corneille and, for good measure, a Jacobean ending that leaves corpses littering the stage.

The interweaving of dynastic and amorous interests in Dryden and Lee's subplot beggars anything in Corneille. Creon returns as villain of the piece, cast in the mould of Shakespeare's Richard III, a deformed and monstrous figure who aspires in fact to Oedipus' royal power, and is introduced at the outset of the play using the plague and Oedipus' absence at war to foment rebellion among the rabble, 'citizens' like those in *Coriolanus*. Furthermore Creon loves Eurydice, in this version the daughter of Laius and Jocasta, who was betrothed to him as a child. But Eurydice scorns him; she loves the noble Argive prince Adrastus, and Oedipus, having defeated him in battle, consents to their marriage. When Tiresias accuses 'the first of Lajus blood' of murdering the old king, Creon accuses Eurydice and Adrastus of the crime, and the scene in which Tiresias raises Laius' ghost is framed as a kind of trial for the lovers. When Tiresias goes on to accuse Oedipus directly, Creon manages to turn Oedipus' anger against Adrastus as well as the old seer, then goes before the citizens to denounce Oedipus and Jocasta in a further attempt to gain the throne for himself. Having failed in this, Creon resolves to wed Eurydice or kill her, and does battle with Adrastus. His capture of the princess opens a final scene that out-Hamlets *Hamlet*. Creon kills Eurydice, Adrastus kills him and in turn is killed by Creon's soldiers. Only then is Jocasta revealed, 'stabbed in many places of her bosom, her hair dishevel'd, her Children lain upon the Bed' to lament her fate and die. Oedipus, who has been confined to a tower for protection against Creon's attack, appears at its windows, bemoans Jocasta, who 'has out-done me, in Revenge and Murder', and throws himself to his death.

As regards the fall of Oedipus, nothing is spared that might add piquancy to the much-told tale. The treatment of the incest theme is telling. At the end of Act I, when Oedipus has pronounced his curse on the murderer of Laius, Dryden has Jocasta enter and, seeing Oedipus and the Thebans 'at your devotions', add her wish to 'bring th' effect of these your pius pray'rs / on you, and me, and all'. Reproached for these words of ill omen, she tells Oedipus, 'My former Lord / Thought me his blessing: be thou like my Laius.' This leads to a declaration of love between the two that culminates in this exchange:

> OEDIPUS: No pius son e'er loved his Mother more
>   Than I my dear Jocasta.
> JOCASTA: I love you too
>   The self same way: and when you chid, me thought
>   A Mother's love start up in your defence,
>   And bad me not be angry: be not you:
>   For I love Lajus still as wives should love:
>   But you more tenderly; as part of me:
>   And when I have you in my arms, methinks
>   I lull my child asleep.

In such a context, Oedipus, even if a 'better man' than in Corneille, seems not so much tragically lacking in self-knowledge as simply clueless. Jocasta goes on to press for Oedipus' consent to her brother's marriage to Eurydice, but Oedipus abhors the very thought of uncle marrying niece. 'They are too near, my Love', he tells Jocasta, who presses her brother's suit, ' 'Tis too like Incest: 'tis offence to Kind.' Even in Act V, after all has been revealed, Lee does not scruple to return to the bonds of love between husband-son and mother-wife:

> JOCASTA: In spite of all those Crimes the cruel Gods
>   Can charge me with, I know my Innocence;
>   Know yours: 'tis Fate alone that makes us wretched,
>   For you are still my Husband.
> OEDIPUS: Swear I am,
>   And I'll believe thee; steal into thy Arms,
>   Renew endearments, think 'em no pollutions,
>   But chaste as spirit joys: gently I'll come,
>   Thus weeping blind, like dewy Night, upon thee,
>   And fold thee softly in my Arms to slumber.

In the end, Dryden's and Lee's response to the horror of the truth now revealed is a combination of melodrama and prurience that only reinforces the sense of artifice that besets the whole production.

Artifice is an issue, too, for Voltaire's Œdipe, despite its fundamental difference of approach. Voltaire seems intent on reducing the myth as much as possible to what can be encompassed by reason. His efforts to rationalise what he takes to be the chief irrationalities of the Sophoclean plot produce in the end an elegant piece of dramatic machinery rather than a gripping drama. The third of Voltaire's Lettres sur Œdipe, written in 1719 to accompany the first publication of the play, is a critique of Sophocles, directed almost entirely to the mechanics of the search for Laius' murderer.[38] For Voltaire, it is all but unthinkable that the crime of regicide should have gone uninvestigated for so long, and at best improbable that Oedipus should be so slow to understand what the oracles pronounce so clearly. He sees here a series of lapses in vraisemblance for the sake of theatrical effect. The first he attempts to fix by reducing the time between the murder and the discovery to four years, postponing his Œdipe's arrival in Thebes until two years after the murder, and then making him hesitate to reopen his wife's still recent wound. The second problem he resolves with a series of changes designed to make Œdipe more self-aware and at the same time more rational in his pursuit of truth than the Sophoclean hero. In Voltaire's version, for example, Œdipe is left more shaken than angered by the accusation of the High Priest (a conflation of Tiresias and the priest of the Sophoclean prologue). In Act IV, filled with foreboding, he interrogates Jocaste about the circumstances of Laius' murder. When her account only increases his suspicions of his own guilt, she tries to discredit prophecy by telling him about her lost child, but he sees instead how her story dovetails with his own. Phorbas (Laius' servant) arrives merely to confirm what Œdipe has already deduced about the death of the old king.

Since this Œdipe is more perspicacious and less easily distracted than his Sophoclean forebear, it requires some effort to postpone the revelation that he killed Laius until the fourth act. The requisite delay is provided by a subplot involving the love of Jocaste and the hero Philoctète, who arrives in Thebes after the death of his companion Heracles to find Laius dead but his beloved already remarried to Œdipe and again unattainable. Philoctète serves Voltaire's needs by adding a suitably chaste and ennobling amour, though one with so little bearing on the main plot that Philoctète disappears after Act III. He also assumes the Creon-like role of attracting false suspicion; in this case, however, it is not Œdipe but the people of Thebes

---

[38] The Lettres are conveniently printed with the play itself in the Œuvres complètes edited by Louis Moland, vol. II (Paris 1877), 11–46. See also Mueller (1980) 108–15.

who believe Philoctète to be the murderer and demand his death. Philoctète is a figure of exemplary nobility, ready to sacrifice his life if he can thus protect Jocaste, sure of Œdipe's innocence when he in turn is accused, even though Œdipe had reserved judgement about him and preferred to await the arrival of Phorbas. Yet it is hard to feel that Philoctète's greater magnanimity or his thwarted love serve any real function in the economy of the drama other than to permit it to reach the proper length. And casting Jocaste as a long-suffering woman who has put duty before true love in both her marriages, for all that it makes her an even greater victim, can only render the central tragic relation to son and husband more diffuse.

Perhaps the most remarkable change in Voltaire's version is the separation of the civic crisis from the discovery of the hero's identity. In Sophocles, the investigation of Laius' death yields to the search for Oedipus' parentage that will uncover the full horror of his parricide and incest. In Voltaire, Œdipe's search leads to the knowledge that he killed the king before the question of his identity is more than tangentially engaged. This is part of what seems to be a conscious downplaying of the incest theme in order to make Œdipe as sympathetic as possible, as much as possible the victim of malign gods. But it also means that the investigation proper reaches its climax in Act IV, with Œdipe preparing to leave Thebes. The final act, with the arrival of the Corinthian messenger and the revelation of the terrible truth, no longer functions as the ineluctable goal of the whole action, but rather as a kind of melodramatic tail-piece. At its conclusion, the High Priest returns to assure us that Œdipe's departure will put an end to the city's sufferings. Voltaire, taking a hint from Seneca and Corneille, formally connects plague and hero's fall at last, in a way that is as far as possible from Sophocles' tragic conception but may be thought to give the suffering that the gods inflicted on Œdipe some semblance of human meaning. The last words belong to Jocaste, dying of a self-inflicted wound but sure of her nobility and essential innocence:

> Prêtres, et vous Thébains, qui fûtes mes sujets,
> Honorez mon bûcher, et songez à jamais
> Qu'au milieu des horreurs du destin qui m'opprime
> J'ai fait rougir les dieux qui m'ont forcée au crime.[39]

Every version of Oedipus is an interpretation, and Sophocles' version can

[39] 'Priests, and you Thebans who were my subjects, honour my pyre, and think always that amidst the horrors of the destiny that oppresses me, I have made the gods blush, who forced me to my crime.' On Voltaire's Œdipe as the first of a series of at least seventeen adaptations whose starting-point was the widely read translation by André Dacier (1692), see Vidal-Naquet in Vernant and Vidal-Naquet (1988) 372–80.

no more exhaust the possibilities of the subject than can any other. Why then do these neoclassical dramas seem arbitrary and artificial in comparison with his? It is not that they are derivative, but that they are in some sense reductive, that they offer to explain in terms of will or passion or morality what in Sophocles exists prior to rationalisation and remains finally immune to explanation. Myth, no longer a representation of reality but merely an illustration of what must be explained otherwise, is subjected to alien categories, conveniences, conventions. Inevitably, the resulting choices appear as evasions or substitutions of the tragic issue. One might suppose that this would be even truer of versions made in our own century, and in certain ways it is, but, as we shall see, more recent texts do not constitute themselves to the same extent as rewritings and rivals, but rather as self-conscious and ludic variations. Dryden's critique of Corneille, 'how much the Copy is inferiour to the Original', does not apply, for these 'copies' do not ask to be measured by the same standard, do not inhabit the same tragic realm.

A sly but serious comedy by Heinrich von Kleist, *Der Zerbrochene Krug* (*The Broken Jug*, 1806), provides an early example of playful adaptation of the Sophoclean *Oedipus*.[40] At the centre of Kleist's drama is a sustained and knowing parody of Oedipus' search for the truth, in which the guilty party is a judge who does everything he can to obscure his own responsibility but in the end is forced to convict himself. The situation is in the tradition of Roman comedy. Adam, an old village magistrate, has attempted to seduce the innocent young Eva. When her fiancé Ruprecht discovers the two together, he beats Adam, who manages to escape unrecognised, breaking a jug and losing his wig as he flees. Eva's mother, Frau Marthe, assumes that Ruprecht has broken the jug, and Eva does not dispute the notion, since to reveal the identity of her assailant would only endanger Ruprecht. Her behaviour confirms Ruprecht's suspicion that Eva is unfaithful. As the play itself begins, Frau Marthe has hauled Ruprecht into court to answer for the loss of her beloved jug. The parallels to the *Oedipus* now become precise and inescapable. Most obviously, the clubfooted Judge must adjudicate his own crime in his own court. Although he schemes to hide the truth with an ever-expanding web of lies, the search for the criminal leads back to the investigator just as inexorably as in Sophocles. Licht, the clerk of court, is the play's Creon figure, wrongly suspected by Adam of trying to supplant him, which in the end, like Creon, Licht does. The force of destiny is embodied not in an oracle but by Court Inspector Walter, who, in the very

---

[40] See Schadewaldt (1970) and Mueller (1980) 115–28, who argues persuasively that Kleist conflates in this play the myth of Adam with that of Oedipus.

kind of chance by which necessity reveals itself in Sophocles' plot, happens
to visit the court to assess the justice rendered there on the very day that the
case of the broken jug is being heard. There is even a 'messenger'
corresponding to the Theban and Corinthian herdsmen in Sophocles, a
certain Frau Brigitte, who arrives bearing the incriminating wig and tells of
seeing 'a bald-headed fellow rush past me with a misshapen foot'. She
believes she has seen the devil, and Adam seizes on the suggestion in one
final, futile attempt to stave off the revelation of the truth. In the end, like
Oedipus, Judge Adam attempts to exile himself, only to be brought back
from the hills, and Licht is appointed to succeed him on the bench.

All this might amount to no more than a clever though empty spoof of
the Sophoclean tragedy, except that the discovery of truth is as central to
Kleist's play as it is to the *Oedipus*. Adam's unlimited capacity for lies
makes him a mirror image of Oedipus, for his conscious and wilful
opposition to the discovery of truth is equal and opposite to Oedipus'
unwitting and delusive resistance. But the crucial truth turns out not to be
about Judge Adam's bad character, for he gains no self-knowledge by his
failure to evade the truth; rather it concerns Eva's virtue. Her innocence and
Ruprecht's doubt about it give the drama its moral seriousness. Adam
literally blinds Ruprecht by throwing sand in his eyes during their struggle;
figuratively, however, *Sand ins Auge werfen* is the German equivalent of
pulling the wool over one's eyes, and Ruprecht must come to understand
that he has been blinded by what he thought he saw. He convicts his
beloved of betrayal with Oedipus-like haste, only to learn that things may
not be what they seem and that real recognition of truth must proceed from
inner assurance not outward appearances.

Moving closer to our own time, two French Oedipus plays from the
1930s, André Gide's *Œdipe* and Jean Cocteau's *La Machine Infernale*,
provide good examples of what may be called paratragic adaptation,
making direct use of the ancient tragic tradition while self-consciously
undermining the traditional tragic emotions with wit, irreverence, and
ironic detachment. Gide, in a journal entry dated 2 January 1933, is quite
clear about his intentions in regard to *Œdipe*:

There is in the pleasantries, trivialities, and incongruities of my play something
like a constant need to alert the public: you have Sophocles' play and I do not
set myself up as a rival; I leave pathos to him; but here is what he, Sophocles,
could not see or understand, and which nevertheless was offered by his theme;
and which I do understand, not because I am more intelligent, but because I
belong to another era; and I intend to make you see the reverse of the stage-
set, at the risk of hurting your feelings, for it is not they which matter to me or

to which I address myself. I intend, not to make you shiver or weep, but to make you think.[41]

Although Œdipe (written in 1930) follows the Sophoclean outline rather closely in many respects, crucial differences establish Gide's particular stance. To begin with matters of style and tone, Gide's prose, parodic of tragedy and humorously colloquial by turns, creates an almost Brechtian distance. Consider, for example, Créon's reaction to the news that Œdipe is the child of Laius:

> Ah! par exemple! ... Comment! Qu'apprends-je? Ma sœur serait sa mère.
> Œdipe, à qui je m'attachais! Se peut-il rien imaginer de plus abominable? Ne
> plus savoir s'il est ou mon beau-frère ou mon neveu! (Act III)[42]

There is much more in this vein, not only from Créon but from the chorus, who declare at their first entrance that their job is to represent the opinion of the majority. But these are not isolated satirical thrusts. Gide is carefully building a set of contrasts between the existential authenticity of Œdipe and the evasions, compromises, pieties, and conformities of other characters in the play.

Gide's Œdipe knows from the outset that he is a foundling, and he glories in that knowledge:

> Enfant perdu, trouvé, sans état civil, sans papiers, je suis surtout heureux de ne
> devoir rien qu'à moi-même. Le bonheur ne me fut pas donné; je l'ai conquis.
> (Act I)[43]

He stains his hands with a man's blood on his way to consult the oracle at Delphi, not after; at that moment he decides to change direction and takes the road that leads to the Sphinx, preferring to remain ignorant of his parentage. Jocaste, on the other hand, has apparently known who he was from the moment he appeared in Thebes and has willingly suppressed the truth for the sake of bourgeois contentment. Tirésias, who embodies the religious orthodoxy that Œdipe rejects, goads him from the happy torpor of his ignorance to terrible self-knowledge but cannot make him submit to the power of God. Créon is merely self-serving and shallow, the chorus utterly conventional.

No doubt there is smugness, as well as the pride against which Tirésias

[41] Quoted from Steiner (1984) 163.
[42] 'Well, my word! Dear me, what do I hear? My sister would be his mother! Oedipus, to whom I've become so attached. Can one imagine anything more horrible? Not to know whether he is my brother-in-law or my nephew!'
[43] 'A lost child, a foundling, without civil status, I rejoice above all that I owe nothing to anyone but myself. Happiness was not given me; I conquered it.'

rails, in Œdipe's mistaken claim of self-sufficiency, but his authenticity is vindicated precisely in his response to learning his true identity. Œdipe figures it out without having to question a shepherd or Corinthian messenger and then laments not so much the deed as the state of ignorance and torpor in which God could trick him. Œdipe recognises the hand of God, but angrily, not in submission. To Tirésias, who offers repentance and divine forgiveness of his crime, Œdipe replies angrily that God ambushed him, 'for either your oracle lied or I could not save myself. I was trapped.' Œdipe seeks some way to escape the God who has betrayed him and finds it precisely in the traditional gesture of putting out his own eyes – a new act of pride more than one of atonement, and above all a refusal to submit to Tirésias and his God. Groping his way from the palace, he seeks out Tirésias to tell him that he now equals him in blindness, and that even if self-blinding was part of his destiny, he has chosen it willingly. In his blindness, Œdipe reclaims autonomy from the God of Tirésias and announces that he will follow his own inner vision. Having refused the happiness based on ignoring truth with which Jocaste was content to live (and thereby driven her to death), Œdipe becomes 'a nameless traveller who renounces his possessions, his glory, himself' in order, precisely, to be true to himself.

One of the most interesting aspects of this play is Gide's treatment of the children of Oedipus as adolescent reflections of their father. Ismène, the youngest, shares his unfettered enjoyment of life. Polynice and Etéocle share their father's questing nature and his incestuous desire. Indeed they share everything, an ironic foreshadowing of the mutual destruction that awaits them. Overhearing them converse, Œdipe recognises their affinity to him; not shocked to hear that each longs for one of his sisters, he advises them that 'what touches us too nearly never makes a profitable conquest. To grow up, one must look far beyond oneself.' Ironic advice from one whose own conquest has been so very near! But it is Antigone who most fully shapes Œdipe's quest for authenticity and comes to achieve it by sharing his fate. At the outset of the play, Antigone is very much under the sway of Tirésias and wants to become a nun. By the end, her religiosity has undergone what might be thought of as a kind of Protestant revolt against Tirésias' Catholic orthodoxy. She offers to lead her father into exile, telling Tirésias that she has not broken her vows but is now listening not to him but to her own reason and her own heart.

Gide's Œdipe is not perhaps a great play, and certainly not a tragedy, but it remains an interesting drama of ideas, at whose heart is a serious conceit. For Gide, each true individual has an idiosyncrasy or anomaly that is both a distinguishing mark and source of strength. Individualism is threatened when one rejects or succumbs entirely to the anomaly; it triumphs when one accepts the anomaly and makes it fully part of oneself, whatever sacrifice that entails. If that means forfeiting fortune, happiness, the figure one cuts in the world, so be it. Œdipe, by appropriating his destiny and becoming the 'nameless wanderer' who renounces himself to be true to himself, embodies the nobility of the true individual.[44]

Cocteau's *La Machine Infernale* (completed in 1932) is more inventive theatrically but conceptually less coherent than Gide's *Œdipe*. The action that corresponds to *Oedipus the King* occupies only the final (and by far the shortest) act, the first three acts being inventions on the themes of Oedipus' conquest of the Sphinx and marriage to Jocasta. Cocteau moves freely from the seriousness of high myth (in the device of 'The Voice' with which each act begins, reminding the audience of the workings of the infernal machinery that fate has constructed for 'the mathematical annihilation of a mortal') to language and situations freely drawn from *comédie de boulevard* and designed to mock tragic pomposity and even to flout conventional decency. In the first act, Cocteau (following in the footsteps of Seneca, Corneille, and Dryden) introduces the ghost of Laius, but stages his appearance as a kind of send-up of the ghost scene from *Hamlet*. Two soldiers doing sentry duty on the city walls have seen the ghost, who tries in vain to warn of the impending catastrophe. Jocaste, a good-natured but spoiled café-society queen, arrives with Tirésias, whom she calls Zizi and treats as a sort of family retainer, but the ghost cannot make himself seen or heard when they are present, no matter how hard he tries. Even the symbolism of fate is deployed with comic insouciance. For example, the instrument of Jocaste's suicide will be a long scarf, on which both Tirésias and the younger of the soldiers step and almost choke her already in the opening scene. Jocaste makes advances to this soldier and leaves, entirely oblivious to the meaning of what has taken place.

Act II is a sparkling staging of the encounter of Oedipus and the Sphinx, who, in the form of a beautiful young woman, falls in love with the dashing hero and gives him the answer to the riddle, but reveals herself as the terrible goddess Nemesis when Œdipe runs off without a word of gratitude or affection. When Œdipe rushes back, the Sphinx again hopes for his love but discovers that he only wants her corpse as proof of his victory. She co-operates in Œdipe's destruction by fitting her body with the jackal head of her companion, Anubis, and letting him carry it off. Something of the attitude toward tragedy that informs *La Machine Infernale* is suggested by Œdipe's decision to fling the body over his shoulder like Heracles' lion skin rather than carry it in his arms:

---

[44] See O'Brien (1953) esp. 159–60, 204.

Pas ainsi! Je rassemblerais à ce tragédien de Corinthe que j'ai vu jouer un roi et porter le corps de son fils. La pose était pompeuse et n'émouvait personne.[45]

This self-reflexive deflation of tragic effect extends even to the moment in Act IV when Œdipe discovers that he has killed his father: 'Voilà de quoi fabriquer une magnifique catastrophe. Ce voyageur devait être mon père. "Ciel mon père!" '[46] That 'Heavens, my father' in inverted commas replaces Sophoclean horror with a deliberate parody of 'Heavens, my husband' from bedroom farce.[47]

Cocteau's shock tactics reach their limit in Act III, which he sets on the night of Oedipus' and Jocasta's wedding, in the bedroom they are to share with the cradle of her lost child. The Freudian element here is given its head: Jocaste and Œdipe both awake from nightmares, and as she begins to undress her 'big baby' for a better rest, he calls her 'my little mother dear'. Œdipe finally falls asleep across the marriage bed, his head resting on the empty cradle, which Jocaste, terrified for reasons she cannot quite understand, keeps rocking. At the very end of the play, Cocteau brings Jocaste back as a ghost, visible only to Œdipe and to us. Purified by death, Jocaste returns as mother, not as wife, to reclaim her child and to guide him (through Antigone) to the fulfilment of his fate. Tirésias forbids Créon to interfere with their departure, saying that they no longer come under his authority, but belong 'to the people, to the poets, to the pure of heart.' After the brittle comedy of Cocteau's treatment of the myth, this ending may seem incongruous. How seriously are we to take it? As one critic has said, 'the general impression is that Cocteau has always something to do, if not always something to say.'[48] Yet, even if Cocteau's presentation seems to emphasise theatrical fireworks, cleverness, and verve, one can argue that the ending of La Machine Infernale lends it a certain aesthetic and even moral weight. The Voice that introduces the final act announces that we shall see the 'playing-card king' at last become a man. Given the inexorable workings of the infernal machine, the man is his myth, and stands fully revealed only by escaping the world of petty and ironic delusions, by the suffering and acceptance of fate that elevates him to the 'glory' that Tirésias says now awaits Œdipe.

The plays of Gide and Cocteau typify in their different ways the witty mixing of tragic and comic elements that characterises most French versions of Greek tragic subjects in our century. The very fact that there are so many

[45] 'Not that way! I'd look like that tragic actor I saw from Corinth playing a king and carrying the body of his son. The pose was pompous and moved nobody.'
[46] 'There's just the thing from which to make a magnificent catastrophe. That traveller must have been my father. "Heavens, my father!"'
[47] Norrish (1988) 20. [48] Guicharnaud (1967) 46.

such versions testifies to a continued need for the powerful myths that spring from the roots of our culture, but the distanced and often ironic treatment that the myths receive points to a realisation that in the shadow of the Enlightenment their meaning is ours to remake. Many modern writers seem to suggest that the old stories can continue to hold meanings for us only when viewed through the distancing filters of psychoanalysis or anthropology. For others, an ironic stance offers the possibility of directing myth toward modern ideology.

Tragic form itself is the subject of a particular irony directed toward that supposedly essential ingredient of tragedy, the concept of a fate that governs human affairs. The paradoxical title of Jean Giraudoux's *La Guerre de Troie n'aura pas Lieu* (1935) suggests its theme of a destiny that defeats and devalues human will. Hector does everything he can to prevent the Trojan War from happening, even persuading Paris and Helen to part. When the poet Démokos seizes on the drunken insults of a Greek soldier to foment war, Hector kills him; but as Démokos dies, he blames a Greek; the Trojan War will take place after all. The *machine infernale* of Cocteau's title refers to just such a notion of fate, and the Chorus of one of the best known of the French adaptations of Greek tragedy, Jean Anouilh's *Antigone* (1944), develops a similar metaphor for tragedy: 'Cela roule tout seul. C'est minutieux, bien huilé depuis toujours.' ('The thing runs by itself; it's in perfect shape, well oiled ever since time began.') Armed with a conception of tragedy in which things roll along of their own accord to their destined end, Anouilh is at liberty to play as much as he likes with character and motivation. The result is a set of virtuoso variations on Sophoclean themes. For example, at the climax of their confrontation, Créon undercuts the existential ground of Antigone's action by revealing to her that the remains of Etéocle and Polynice have been so badly mangled that there is no way of distinguishing between them. Antigone yields at first to an argument that seems to rob her gesture of all meaning, but decides almost immediately to defy Créon nevertheless. This second rebellion has nothing to do with the gods' will, or moral imperatives, or even sisterly love. Antigone is repelled by Créon's evocation of a happiness to come that she can only understand as mundane and mediocre. On that basis Anouilh's Antigone embraces her destiny, in the process rejecting reason, politics, maturity, and bourgeois compromise.[49] Fate, here and elsewhere, has no explanatory function or value; it serves primarily to create a metatragic irony, a counterforce that outweighs rational choice and defeats good intentions.

---

[49] Steiner (1984) 193. For the political context of Anouilh's drama and the ideological thrust of this scene, see Witt (1993).

ORESTES AND ELECTRA IN THE TWENTIETH CENTURY

The preceding section looked diachronically at the adaptation of Sophocles' *Oedipus* in four different periods. In this section, I turn the reader's attention to roughly contemporary versions of the myth of the house of Atreus: Eugene O'Neill's *Mourning Becomes Electra* (1931), T. S. Eliot's *The Family Reunion* (1939), and Jean-Paul Sartre's *Les Mouches* (*The Flies*, 1943). These examples make clear how directly Greek tragic form and matter may be adapted to particular ideological ends. O'Neill's sprawling trilogy is an *Oresteia* set in New England at the end of the Civil War, and is at least superficially 'Freudian' in its themes of love and hate within the family. Eliot's verse drama is a brittle drawing-room version of Aeschylus' *Eumenides* with a specifically Christian eschatological slant. Sartre's play, the only one with the traditional characters in a more or less traditional Greek setting, is at once an exposition of the existentialist ethics of freedom and a covert call to political resistance in occupied France. All three works have intelligence and skill on their side; all three already seem very dated.

In contrast to the ironic 'metatragedy' being produced at the same time in France, O'Neill's drama approaches the task of modernising Greek tragedy with unrelieved seriousness. Beginning with its trilogic structure, *Mourning Becomes Electra* finds equivalents for the major narrative elements of Aeschylus' *Oresteia*. In the first play, a general (Ezra Mannon / Agamemnon) returns home from war and is killed by his adulterous wife (Christine / Clytemnestra), in league with her husband's dispossessed cousin (Adam Brant / Aegisthus), whom she has taken as her lover. In the second play, the son (Orin / Orestes) returns and joins the daughter (Lavinia / Electra) in vengeance by killing the lover, thus driving their mother to suicide. The final play varies most radically from Aeschylus, for reasons that we shall briefly explore: when Orin, verging on madness and totally dependent on Lavinia, prevents her from marrying, she drives him to suicide and then, overcome by remorse, immures herself with her ghosts in the family mansion.

Perhaps the most Aeschylean element in O'Neill's drama is use of a history of lust and hatred in the previous generation to suggest a curse on the Mannons, just as the family curse in the *Oresteia* is linked to past crimes in the house of Atreus. Like Atreus and Thyestes, Ezra's father Abe and Adam's father David are rivals in love for the serving-girl Marie Brantôme; when David marries her, Abe cuts his brother off and effectively destroys a branch of his own family. However, the curse that works the ruin of this family is not determined by divine retribution for the crimes that have been committed, but rather by the blind replication of psychological compulsions through the generations. O'Neill substitutes the determinism of psycho-logical complexes within the family for that of fate from without. This is the 'Freudian' element in *Mourning Becomes Electra*, but as has often been pointed out, it is a highly irregular version of Freud. The interlocking Oedipal attractions and repulsions within this family are so explicitly voiced as almost to exclude self-deception and the sublimation of desires, motives and fantasies; characters often, and embarrassingly, seem to have stepped out of the pages of a textbook of Freudian psychoanalysis.[50] It is quite characteristic, for example, that when Lavinia threatens to betray Christine's adultery to the returning Ezra, Christine blurts out:

> I know you Vinnie! I've watched you ever since you were little, trying to do exactly what you're doing now! You've tried to become the wife of your father and the mother of Orin! You've always schemed to steal my place!
>
> ('Homecoming', Act II)

In this manner, O'Neill gives us a 'peculiarly non-Freudian version of the Oedipus complex' that 'lacks the most important elements of Freud's, ambivalence and unconsciousness'.[51]

Two immediate consequences of this curious explicitness are a loss of verisimilitude and a lowering of the tone traditionally expected of tragic discourse. George Steiner memorably commented that 'O'Neill commits inner vandalism by sheer inadequacy of style. In the morass of his language the high griefs of the house of Atreus dwindle to a case of adultery and murder in some provincial rathole.'[52] This is no doubt unfair. O'Neill is at pains to find a setting as close to that of ancient Argos at the end of the Trojan War as American history can offer. Contemporary readers are likely to be more impressed by this drama's stylisation, visual and verbal, than by its naturalism. And yet, Steiner's comment rings true in the sense that O'Neill's approach is inevitably reductive and restrictive. The passions of the characters are reduced to an endlessly repeated, implausibly symmetrical set of attractions and repulsions, self-consciously and relentlessly enacted. And the world of the play is very largely restricted to this private psychopathology; despite the attempt at a 'chorus' of townspeople and the backdrop of the civil war, there is very little sense of connection to a larger social order, to a public reality. The great Aeschylean theme of justice is not absent from *Mourning Becomes Electra*, but it only appears, ironically, as a

---

[50] Nugent (1988) 41, who makes a convincing case for reading the trilogy as displacing sexuality by textuality in order to confront and master feminine desire.

[51] Alexander (1953) 928, quoted by Nugent (1988) 41.

[52] Steiner (1961) 327. This might be more accurately applied to Thomas Berger's recent novelistic version of the *Oresteia*, *Orrie's Story* (1990).

form of special pleading. At the end of the second play, 'The Hunted', for example, Lavinia keeps insisting that Adam Brant, whom Orin has just killed, 'paid the just penalty for his crime. You know it was justice. It was the only way true justice could be done.' But we have seen all too clearly the jealous rage that has been her central motivation, and we now witness Orin's paroxysms of remorse as he discovers that his murder of Adam has caused Christine to kill herself.

Whereas Aeschylus' trilogy ends with Orestes restored to his inheritance and public role in Argos, and with the Furies installed as Eumenides in the soil of Attica, O'Neill concludes his trilogy with Lavinia shutting herself up for ever in the living tomb of her family home. Lavinia had resisted Orin's suggestion that she herself could only escape retribution by confession and atonement, until Orin, too, killed himself. She ends the play by announcing that she will now punish herself for the rest of her life:

> Don't be afraid, I'm not going the way Mother and Orin went. That's escaping punishment. And there's no one left to punish me. I'm the last Mannon. I've got to punish myself! Living alone here is a worse act of justice than death or prison! ('The Haunted', Act IV)

Lavinia has become, at last and in her own case, the stern Judge that her father was in years long past. There is no way out of this curse, only a path endlessly inward to plumb the unsatisfied desires and unresolved conflicts of the individual psyche. An Aeschylean ending would require some agency beyond the self, some belief in the possibility of transformation. For all its reminiscences of the *Oresteia*, *Mourning Becomes Electra* in the end feels more Euripidean.

Eliot's verse drama *The Family Reunion* shares Aeschylean roots and a modern setting with *Mourning Becomes Electra*, but its orientation to Greek tragedy is almost the inverse of O'Neill's play. As we shall see, it is specifically the reconciliation of the *Eumenides*, useless to O'Neill, that inspires Eliot's strongest response. On the other hand, the structure of the Greek drama and even the outline of the legend have been largely abandoned. Eliot's setting is Wishwood, a country house in the north of England, specifically a drawing room and library such as have appeared in countless comedies and melodramas since Victorian times. On the surface, very little happens. Harry, Lord Monchensey, has come back to the ancestral home on his mother's birthday, after an absence of eight years. Amy, the Dowager Lady Monchensey, is eager for Harry to assume his position as head of the family, but he is evidently under a great strain and eventually decides to leave again for an as yet unknown destination. Amy dies from the shock of Harry's departure.

Eliot himself, in a lecture first published in 1951, judged *The Family Reunion* harshly, describing its 'deepest flaw' as 'a failure of adjustment between the Greek story and the modern situation'.[53] Initially, there is little to link the drawing room to the world of the *Oresteia*, unless we notice that the unsettling figures that Harry alone seems to see as he enters Wishwood correspond to Orestes' private vision of the Furies at the end of the *Libation-Bearers*. Gradually, however, the presence of Aeschylus begins to loom ever more unmistakably behind the civilised conversation of the assembled party. At the culmination of a crucial scene between Harry and his cousin Mary, the curtains part and the Furies appear, although Mary does not yet see them. Later she and others will. In his lecture, Eliot singles out the appearance of the Furies as a symptom of the failed synthesis: 'They never succeed in being either Greek goddesses or modern spooks.' The problem is not just one of stage technique or theatrical conviction. The appearance of the Furies makes incongruously literal what the powerful language of the play presents in symbolic terms; their presence defies our habits of belief. And yet, their presence seems central to Eliot's conception.

The chief contribution of the *Oresteia* to Eliot's drama of guilt and redemption is the transformation of the Furies from tormenting pursuers to the 'bright angels' that Harry understands he must follow to his own salvation. This transformation happens in Harry's mind, but if it is not to seem a merely psychological process, we must accede to the objective reality of the Furies as agents of grace. Indeed, Eliot's text emphasises not only their real presence but the recognition of their reality as essential to healing. As Harry says,

> The things I thought were real are shadows, and the real
> Are what I thought were private shadows. O that awful privacy
> Of the insane mind! Now I can live in public.
> Liberty is a different kind of pain from prison. (Act II, Scene 2)

Why have the Furies been pursuing Harry? Harry himself is conscious above all of what he calls his filthiness:

> What matters is the filthiness. I can clean my skin,
> Purify my life, void my mind,
> But always the filthiness that lies a little deeper ...
> (Act II, Scene 1)

His sense of guilt is associated primarily with the death of his wife, whether, as he at first asserts, he pushed her overboard during a sea voyage or, as later seems likelier, she jumped to her death. In the course of the play,

[53] Eliot (1957) 84.

however, he learns about the guilty relations of the previous generation that constitute Eliot's version of the curse on the house. From his Aunt Agatha, a kind of Cassandra, he discovers the pattern of the past: his parents' bleak marriage, his father's love for Agatha and plan to kill his wife, which Agatha foiled in order to save Harry, still in Amy's womb. Liberation comes with recognition of the shadows of sin – real even if merely willed – that have darkened his life. When Harry tells Agatha that he may only have dreamt he pushed his wife to her death, she replies:

> So I had supposed. What of it?
> What we have written is not a story of detection,
> Of crime and punishment, but of sin and expiation.
> It is possible that you have not known what sin
> You shall expiate, or whose, or why. It is certain
> That the knowledge of it must precede the expiation.
>
> (Act II, Scene 2)

By such means, the *Oresteia*'s theme of communal absolution is transformed into a tale of personal salvation. As in *Mourning Becomes Electra*, the larger community is entirely overshadowed by the dynamics of family, but Eliot's Christian eschatology offers a means to purge at last the neuroses and psychoses. Whether the result is a successful drama, whether it manages to meld secular and religious, ancient and modern, is open to question. By the time of his lecture, Eliot was willing to declare that his 'sympathies now have come to be all with the mother, ... and my hero now strikes me as an insufferable prig'. Certainly, *The Family Reunion* is long on explanation and symbol and short on theatrical event. For our purposes, at any rate, the play's chief interest lies in its ability to find in the *Oresteia* and Orestes a figure for the Christian concept of salvation.

Sartre's *Les Mouches*, produced in Paris during the German occupation, also transforms Orestes into a figure of salvation, but within an entirely different ideological framework. Sartre makes explicit use of elements from Aeschylus (e.g. a chorus of Furies, here imagined as gigantic flies), Sophocles (e.g. Orestes' tutor, here the teacher of a cultured and finally frivolous disengagement), and Euripides (e.g. Electra's notorious entrance carrying her water jug, reprised here with her dumping of an ash-can at the shrine of Zeus). All this serves, however, to underline the difference in spirit between his play and the ancient tragedies. In Sartre's play, myth serves as a vehicle for confronting contemporary political realities and illustrating his own philosophy of freedom. Freedom, indeed, is the theme that links the political and the philosophical in *Les Mouches*. On the political side, the Orestes myth offers the possibility of oblique commentary on the occupation and the encouragement of resistance. It is, for example, no great leap from the policy of public repentance promulgated in Argos by Sartre's Egisthe to the French trials of those held 'guilty' of declaring war against Germany.[54] *Les Mouches* holds out the prize of freedom to those willing to seize it; what such willingness means is the play's philosophical problem. Sartre uses the Orestes myth to embody his view that freedom lies in the choice of being rather than merely existing. His Oreste must pull himself painfully but definitively loose from all fatality, all authority, to the point that he becomes his freedom ('Je *suis* ma liberté', Act III, Scene 2).

Les Mouches begins with the arrival of Oreste at an Argos whose obsession with guilt and remorse is symbolised by thick swarms of flies and manifested in a fear of strangers and of the dead. Oreste returns to the homeland from which he was exiled as a baby out of a vague, inchoate need to find real attachments, but the arguments of his tutor and his first encounter with the plague-ridden town, mediated by a sardonic Jupiter disguised as a traveller, bring him to the verge of leaving again. At this point, Oreste seems ready to renounce attachments in favour of a false freedom of non-belonging: 'Moi, je suis libre, Dieu merci. Ah! comme je suis libre. Et quelle superbe absence que mon âme.'[55] The bitterness of this formulation, however, testifies to Oreste's doubts about a freedom that he cannot use to any purpose. He senses that only an action could bring the attachment he is seeking:

> Ah! s'il était un acte, vois-tu, un acte que me donnât droit de cité parmi eux; si je pouvais m'emparer, fût-ce par un crime, de leurs mémoires, de leur terreur et de leurs espérances pour combler le vide de mon cœur, dussé-je tuer ma propre mère ...   (Act I, Scene 2)[56]

His encounter with Electre, whose rebellious spirit remains unbroken, convinces him to stay, but after a futile rebellion, in which she refuses to appear at the annual ceremony of repentance, and, when she can no longer refuse, wears white rather than mourning, she suggests flight. Oreste feels

---

[54] Sartre himself emphasises the political element in his comments on *Les Mouches* collected in Sartre (1976) 186–97. He also makes clear that, unlike many of his French contemporaries, he found dramatising Greek myth to be at best a useful expedient: 'Why stage declamatory Greeks ... unless to disguise what one was thinking under a fascist regime?' (p. 188). De Beauvoir (1962) 386 remarks that the Orestes myth met Sartre's need for a subject 'both technically unobjectionable and transparent in its implications'. See further McCall (1969) 9–24.

[55] 'I am free, thank God. Ah, how free I am! And what a proud absence is my soul.'

[56] 'Ah, if there were an act, you see, an act that would give me the freedom of the city among them; if I could acquire, even by a crime, their memories, their fear, and their hopes to fill the void in my heart, even if I had to kill my own mother ...'

that he should remain and prays to Zeus[57] for a sign. The sign comes: light blazes around a stone. The sign tells Oreste to submit, to accept authority, but Oreste understands that this is for the good not of him but of others ('*leur* Bien'), and he refuses the sign. He will stay.

This is, in effect, the moment when Oreste chooses to make himself free. The transformation is sudden and radical, and it leads Oreste to kill Egisthe and then his own mother, without remorse but assuming full responsibility for his deeds. This existential freedom is almost unbearable, as is shown by another transformation – the transformation of Electre from defiant rebel to frightened conformist. For Oreste, who can bear it, however, freedom from the power of Jupiter is absolute as soon as he seizes it. 'Qui donc t'a créé?' asks the angry god. 'Toi', responds Oreste. 'Mais il ne fallait pas me créer libre' (Act III, Scene 2).[58] Oreste then turns to the deliverance of his people, something that might seem to contradict the logic of a freedom that can only be freely assumed. Oreste, however, as a rebel against all authority, paradoxically aspires to use his own authority as king to free the Argives from subjugation to fear. When Jupiter objects that, by opening the eyes of his people, Oreste will force them to see the futility of their lives, Oreste replies, 'ils sont libres, et la vie humaine commence de l'autre côté du désespoir' (Act III, Scene 2).[59] In the final scene, Oreste faces the angry people with exhortations to live without fear. Now that Jupiter wishes him to stay, he chooses to leave Argos, drawing behind him all the avenging flies that have infested the city. Oreste becomes a Pied Piper, like the rat catcher of Scyros whose story he tells as he departs, but what the consequences of his act will be for the Argives is not clear. Electre has proved unable to accept her freedom, and we do not learn whether the Argives fare any better. Oreste, however, crowns his revolt against the will of Jupiter by refusing remorse, claiming responsibility, and continuing to use his freedom.

In the Greek versions of the myth, Orestes acts on orders from Apollo to avenge the slain Agamemnon. Oreste in *Les Mouches*, although he regards the continued rule of Egisthe and Clytemnestre as unjust, never speaks of vengeance, and his primary goal seems to be to disobey the gods, not to follow their orders. Indeed, the murder of Clytemnestre is particularly unmotivated in this version and therefore emphatically Oreste's chosen

[57] Sartre consistently calls the god by his Latin name, so Oreste's invocation of him by his Greek name is presumably significant. Jeanson (1955) 15 suggests that whereas Jupiter is merely a figure of coercion in the name of what is proper, Zeus represents the Good that Oreste still seeks. Oreste's response suggests, then, that he understands that his prayer to Zeus has been answered by one of Jupiter's cheap tricks.
[58] 'Who then made you?' 'You. But you should not have made me free.'
[59] 'They are free, and human life begins on the other side of despair.'

act.[60] For Oreste, his own freedom and that of Argos depends on over-turning the order to which Jupiter has given his blessing; that makes the murder of Egisthe and Clytemnestre a necessary act of defiance. Destiny and divine plan have no part to play, and neither do psychological dynamics or ethical quandaries. On such grounds as these, one might describe *Les Mouches* as antitragic, rather than merely untragic. At any rate, its design denies reality to the order beyond human control and understanding that has traditionally formed the backdrop for tragic conflict. Moreover, there is an almost allegorical quality to Sartre's characters, and a concomitant lack of the emotions, the tensions, the hesitations that traditionally give 'human' depth to deeds as extreme as assassination and matricide. Now that the immediacy of Sartre's political commentary has faded, what remains of *Les Mouches* is chiefly its philosophical message.

Beyond their roots in the Orestes myth, there seems to be little common ground among the plays of O'Neill, Eliot, and Sartre. O'Neill employs myth and trilogic structure to weave a drama of a family's self-destruction; Eliot and Sartre offer allegories of redemption, one specifically Christian and the other fiercely antireligious. O'Neill and Eliot modernise the settings of their plays, Sartre retains a version of ancient Greece for his. O'Neill presents a rather rigid conception of fate in terms of the most mechanistic kind of psychological determinism; Eliot shows the overcoming of destiny in the form of a family curse; and Sartre denies the relevance of destiny in any form to his version of the myth. In the diversity of their ideological perspectives and dramatic techniques, these plays suggest the variety of purposes to which Greek tragedy has been adapted in our age. In their relative lack of success with public and critics alike, they illustrate how hard a task such adaptation is.

OPERA

Greek tragedy plays perhaps no greater role in furnishing subjects for opera than for the spoken theatre of the seventeenth century and beyond, but it does have a far more central place in opera's development. When Sophocles' *Oedipus* was staged in 1585 at Vicenza to inaugurate the Teatro Olimpico, Andrea Gabrieli set only the choruses to music. By the end of the century, however, the view that in ancient times the entire tragedy was sung[61] had

---

[60] McCall (1969) 16 argues cogently that, in the political context in which Sartre wrote, Oreste as unrepentant matricide upholds the necessity for the Resistance to kill French as well as German Nazis.

[61] Associated especially with Francesco Patrici's *Della poetica* of 1586; see Schrade (1964) 53–4.

assisted the birth of the new form of music drama that we have come to call opera. The 'inventors' of opera quite self-consciously took upon themselves the task of reviving something unknown since antiquity: the fusion of music and drama in a continuous and unified work of art. Ottavio Rinuccini asserts in the preface to his libretto for the first surviving opera, Jacopo Peri's *Euridice* (1600), that 'the ancient Greeks and Romans, in representing their tragedies on stage, sang them throughout. But until now this noble manner of recitation has been neither revived nor (to my knowledge) even attempted by anyone . . .'[62]

In this statement, and in many others by members of the Florentine *camerata* of Count Giovanni de' Bardi (the group of musicians, scholars, and poets whose discussions provided theoretical and practical foundations for the beginnings of opera), the problematic term may be thought to be 'tragedy'. This is not, of course, because they were wrong (as they were) in assuming that Greek tragedies were entirely sung – an historical error with the most fruitful consequences – but because neither the Christian/Neoplatonic ideas that underlay their speculations nor the ceremonial occasions for which the entertainments themselves were regularly devised lent themselves to the full realisation of a revived tragedy. Heroic struggle in a world of hostile gods or indifferent destiny could only with difficulty be made to serve the purposes either of princely festival or of popular entertainment.

The immediate literary model of the earliest operas is the pastoral drama begun by Poliziano's *Favola di Orfeo* (1471) and given special prestige by the success of Guarini's *Pastor fido* (early 1580s), a genre that unites Ovidian myth with a setting derived from Virgil's *Eclogues*. Early subjects of serious opera were as likely to be derived from Ovid (e.g. Claudio Monteverdi's *Arianna*, 1608), Virgil (e.g. Francesco Cavalli's *Didone*, 1641), or Roman history (e.g. Monteverdi's *L'incoronazione di Poppea*, 1642) as from tragedy. When subjects drawn from Greek tragedy appear, they tend to do so in elaborations that fully deserve the epithet *baroque*, as in the case of Cavalli's great festival opera *Ercole amante*, composed for the wedding of Louis XIV (1662). Here, the central plot – the *Women of Trachis* story of Heracles' love for Iole and his death from the poison of Nessus, with which Deianeira hopes to regain his love – is combined with a sub-plot involving the love of Hyllus and Iole and Hyllus' apparent death at sea. A scene in Hades in which all the victims of Heracles' valour plot vengeance provides a Senecan twist. The opera concludes with an epiphany in which the newly deified Heracles foretells . . . the marriage of Louis XIV.

Of course, to speak only of the plot of these early operas is to miss the

[62] Quoted from Strunk (1952) 367–8.

point that in opera 'the imaginative articulation for the drama is provided by music'.[63] From that perspective, the culmination of the work of the *camerata* came not in Florence, but in Mantua and Venice in the operas of Monteverdi, who achieved the unity of drama and music of which the Florentines only dreamed. Monteverdi's recitative gives reality to his characters' passions and conflicts, responding to the affect of their words with an unprecedented variety and flexibility of style. A famous example is 'Possente Spirto', Orpheus' plea to Charon for admission to the Underworld in *Orfeo* (1607). The passage begins with a formal lament, five stanzas of recitative sung with varying degrees of ornamental elaboration and virtuosity; these are punctuated by instrumental *ritornelli* (refrains), each calling for different instrumentation to heighten the solemnity. Significantly, the moments of greatest intensity are those of greatest directness and simplicity in the recitative, and Orpheus follows the formal lament, whose beauty delights Charon but does not succeed in arousing his pity, with the simplest and most intense of his recitatives, each phrase lowered by a tone until the final phrase, *Rendetemi il mio ben, Tartarei Numi!* ('Give back my love, gods of Tartarus!'), which is sung in an imploring ascent of the chromatic scale. It is by such means that Monteverdi's music attains the resonance and intensity of great tragedy.

The French *tragédie en musique* of the late seventeenth and early eighteenth centuries, which develops under the influence of French classical tragedy, frequently turns to Greek tragic subjects and tends to be more 'regular' (i.e. Aristotelian) in its dramatic practice than earlier opera. Thus, Jean Baptiste Lully's *Alceste* (1674), his only venture into the realm of Greek tragedy, is the last of his serious operas to contain a comic scene (Charon refusing to ferry to the Underworld shades who cannot pay), since decorum now comes to demand a separation of tragic and comic. Charpentier's superb *Médée* (1693), to a libretto by Corneille's younger brother Thomas Corneille, shows all the musical strengths of the genre, including choruses and dances in a variety of musical forms, and effective realisations of by now conventional situations such as Creon's mad scene and Medea's incantation. What distinguishes *Médée* is a dramatic concentration that can be seen especially in the detailed characterisation of Medea provided by the music of her monologues, charged with a wide range of powerful emotions. While Corneille's libretto turns the Euripidean love triangle into a quadrangle by adding the figure of Oronte, Prince of Argos, as Creusa's spurned suitor, it does not mitigate the horror of the myth with the usual happy ending. In the fifth act, we learn that Creon in his madness has killed

---

[63] Kerman (1988) 8.

Oronte and committed suicide; Medea's poisoned robe kills Creusa; and Medea reveals to Jason that she has killed their children before departing on her dragon chariot as flames destroy the palace.

Perhaps the greatest *tragédie en musique* based on a Greek tragic subject is Jean-Philippe Rameau's first, *Hippolyte et Aricie* (1733), whose very title suggests its close relation to Racine's *Phèdre*, in which the figure of Aricia is introduced to provide the love interest felt to be necessary for Hippolytus. Over against Racine, however, the tragic figure of Theseus is given greater depth, especially through a second act devoted to his attempt to rescue his friend Peirithous from Hades. Phaedra's role is smaller than in Racine, but the scenes in which she reveals her love to Hippolytus and reacts to the report of his death by admitting her guilt are given a musical development that makes them comparable to Racine in power. As we have come to expect, Pellegrin's libretto offers a happy ending: through the intervention of Diana, Hippolytus has been rescued, and in the final scene he is reunited with the disconsolate Aricia in a kind of inversion of the restoration of Alcestis to Admetus.

Despite these examples, it should be said that in the first half of the eighteenth century Greek tragedy appears to lose rather than gain importance as an influence on opera. It is worth noting that the greatest composer of *opera seria*, George Frideric Handel, wrote only one opera based on a Greek tragic source (*Admeto*, 1727), and that was in fact based partly on Euripides' *Alcestis* and partly on a convoluted tale in which the heroine disguises herself after her return to life in order to test her husband's fidelity.[64]

Greek tragedy returns to the centre of the operatic stage with the famous reform operas of Christoph Wilibald Gluck. In the first of these works, *Orfeo ed Euridice* (1762; French version 1774), Gluck and his librettist, Ranieri de' Calzabigi, return to the subject of the first great opera to stunning effect. The plot is kept as simple and uncluttered as possible and the music is directed to the powerful passions and conflicts engendered in it – the expression and the sublimation in musical form of monumental emotion. This was followed by three operas based closely on Euripides: *Alceste* (1767; the much expanded French version 1776), *Iphigénie en Aulide* (1774), and *Iphigénie en Tauride* (1779). Gluck's preface to the

---

[64] Handel's *Teseo* (1713), which Dean (1969) 83 describes as 'a hybrid between the classical-heroic and magic types' of opera, has a wonderfully realised tragic Medea; and in 1734 Handel presented an *Orestes*, a *pasticcio* whose score was largely drawn from his own earlier works. *Hercules* (1744), although usually classified as a secular oratorio, is an extremely powerful dramatic setting of a libretto closely modelled on *Women of Trachis*.

printed score of *Alceste* makes clear his attitude toward the tradition against which he was rebelling:

> When I undertook to write the music for *Alceste*, I resolved to divest it entirely of all those abuses, introduced into it either by the mistaken vanity of singers or by the too great complaisance of composers, which have so long disfigured Italian opera … I have striven to restrict music to its true office of serving poetry by means of expression and by following the situations of the story, without interrupting the action or stifling it with a useless superfluity of ornaments.[65]

But Gluck's achievement is not merely the negative one of stripping away excess; it lies in a renewal of the idea with which opera began, the expression of emotion on an heroic scale in drama through the collaboration of word and music. Alcestis' love and self-sacrifice, for example, are given a musical life that contrasts them sharply with the callousness of others; and when Admetus learns the price of his survival, the complex and conflicting emotions are fully realised (and contained) in a musical continuum of aching purity.

It is perhaps worth noting that the three Greek tragedies adapted by Gluck all end happily; for that matter, so does his version of the Orpheus legend, a feature inherited from earlier versions beginning with Peri and Monteverdi but already criticised during Gluck's lifetime. In fairness, neither opera as a social institution in the eighteenth century, nor Gluck as the artist *par excellence* of emotional control, nor for that matter the rationalist spirit of the Enlightenment could easily accommodate patterns that ended with surrender to or defiance of final disaster.

Luigi Cherubini's Médée (1797), perhaps the last major monument of classical opera, does insist with savage emphasis on the horrible consequences of Medea's revenge. It carries the concentration on emotion that lies at the heart of Gluck's reform to a new pitch of intensity. François Benoit Hoffman's libretto offers characters drawn in considerable depth, and the score focuses unswervingly on their destructive passions. The opera's many ensembles brilliantly follow those passions and their conflicts. Altogether, Cherubini's music not only manages, within the frame of its classical idiom, to produce effects of stark horror but sustains dramatic intensity from the first chords of the overture to Medea's final outburst, a promise of still more revenge in the world below. It is not surprising that Beethoven and Brahms admired it.

Cherubini carried the neoclassical recovery of Greek tragic passion as far as it was to go. By the time Gluck's greatest nineteenth-century follower,

---

[65] Quoted from Strunk (1952) 673–4.

Hector Berlioz, composed *Les Troyens* (1856–8), direct adaptation of Greek tragedy had come to seem hopelessly old-fashioned and the classical style had given way to romanticism. This grandiose *tragédie lyrique*, however, demonstrates a sensibility attuned to classical tragedy as well as to romantic abandon. Berlioz reaches back to antiquity for his subject, organising his own adaptation of the *Aeneid* around the fall of Troy (Acts I and II) and the tragedy of Dido (Acts III–V). Only the second part was staged in Berlioz's lifetime, and the two sections were not performed together more or less whole until the late 1950s,[66] but they form a single grand design, united by dramatic as well as purely musical motifs. The central idea reflects the romantic understanding of tragedy by exalting fate – the majestic yet destructive destiny of Rome – above the sufferings of individuals; and yet the music fully engages the anguish of Dido and Cassandra, who live and die proudly and tragically in fate's embrace. Berlioz reaches beyond the conventions of the grand opera of his day to establish an astonishing evocation of the spiritual climate of tragedy.

Les Troyens is exceptional in every way, and later nineteenth-century opera only rarely drew its subjects from classical mythology. Nevertheless, Greek tragedy is centrally important for the chief mythological operas of the age, those of Richard Wagner, and above all *Der Ring der Niebelungen* (1853–74). Michael Ewans has carefully shown how Wagner's engagement with the *Oresteia*, beginning at the time he began working out his ideas for a drama based on the story of the Nibelungs, led to profound affinities at many levels between the two great dramatic cycles.[67] Indeed, the decision to construct the *Ring* as a trilogy with prologue, reached as early as 1851, is an indication of Wagner's sense of himself as continuator of the Aeschylean tradition, as are the subtitle *Bühnenfestspiel* ('stage festival play') and the goal of uniting poetry, music, dance, and spectacle in a *Gesamtkunstwerk*. The interplay of gods and heroes within the frame of a brooding fatality owes much to a romantic understanding of the Greek tragic spirit, mediated by assimilation to Feuerbach's vision of nature and Schopenhauer's conception of renunciation. The overt mythology of the *Ring* is Germanic and the central preoccupation, as in so much of Wagner's work, is with Judaeo-Christian themes of temptation, betrayal, and redemption; its inner life evolved in continuous dialogue with the form and subject-matter of the *Oresteia*. Wagner's way of approaching Aeschylus was as remote as possible from the procedures of neo-classicism; his aim was renewal, not restoration. By the time he had completed its music – the orchestra functioning, as he

---

[66] Indeed the first staging of the complete score in the original language appears to have been mounted at the Royal Opera House, Covent Garden in 1969.

[67] Ewans (1982).

claimed, in the role of a Greek chorus – he had indeed renewed the form and manner of Aeschylus with a power unequalled before or since.

A Greek tragic subject gets Wagnerian garb at last in Richard Strauss's *Elektra* (1906–8), a setting of Hugo von Hofmannsthal's free adaptation of Sophocles, with Euripidean and even Aeschylean touches and an ending all his own – Elektra's manic dance of triumph and collapse in death. The music, appropriately expressionistic and requiring the largest forces of any opera in the repertoire, is fraught with what one critic has called 'its period's mod. cons. of psychology and decadence'.[68] One is tempted to call this opera a child of the marriage of Wagner and Freud. Certainly, the character of Elektra has been rethought in both text and music as a study in obsession, and the Greek world of the opera owes far more to Bachofen and Nietzsche than to Winckelmann and Goethe. Strauss and Hofmannsthal returned once more to Greek tragedy and post-Wagnerian style in a strange and idiosyncratic revisiting of Euripides' *Helen* (*Die Ägyptische Helena*, 1928), but in general the use of Greek tragedy in twentieth-century opera seems to constitute a declaration of independence from Wagner.

Indeed, the renewal of interest in Greek tragic subjects is part of a larger, many-sided effort to free the lyric theatre from Wagner's hegemony. Three pairs of settings of tragic subjects provide an idea of the range of possible operatic responses to Greek tragedy in the late nineteenth and early twentieth centuries. The *Oresteia* of Aeschylus inspired the monumental but rather static *Oresteia* (1887–94) of Sergei Ivanovich Tanayev, based on an extremely schematic libretto by A. Wenckstern. Tanayev's lucid and harmonically conservative idiom wraps the story of murder, revenge, and resolution in beautifully controlled and accomplished lyrical tableaux. The result is a kind of dramatic pageant, statuesque in its mythic impersonality, a reassertion of classical measure in the face of late romantic excess. Darius Milhaud, drawn to the *Oresteia* through the translation of Paul Claudel, successively produced incidental music for *Agamemnon* (1913), a more extended score for *Les Choéphores* (1915), and a three-act operatic setting of *Les Eumenides* (1917–22).[69] The entire trilogy was finally given its stage première in 1935. Milhaud's harmonic and metrical experimentation produces settings of remarkable expressiveness and dramatic conviction. Generous lyricism combines with a willingness to extend tonal resources to include what the composer described as an 'orchestration of stage noises', employing unusual combinations of percussion instruments with whistles, groans, cries. Polytonality, as Milhaud practises it beginning with

[68] R. Holloway, in Puffett (1989) 145.
[69] Milhaud also wrote a score (1913–19) for Claudel's *Protée*, an imaginative reconstruction of the lost satyr play that concluded the Aeschylean *Oresteia*.

Choéphores, permits the superimposition of melodies that remain distinct because they are in different keys but produce a range of harmonic effects ranging from great sweetness to violent power.

The *Antigone* of Arthur Honegger (1927; a setting of Jean Cocteau's fast-moving, colloquial version of the myth) is generally agreed to be the composer's most severe and challenging score. Honegger's unorthodox prosody, designed to align musical stress with word accent, and his harmonic and melodic language, 'created by the word itself', as he puts it in the preface to the vocal score, achieve a stylistic complexity and consistency that give the drama enormous force. Carl Orff's *Antigonae* (1949), like Honegger's, reflects a departure from the lushness of his more popular work, but its austerity has little of Honegger's refinement. Orff seems to be visualising the ancient tragic theatre through the medium of Hölderlin's great translation, which he employs unaltered and uncut. A sense of reversion to origins is produced by a deliberately 'primitive' vocal line, moving from recitative to melismatic arioso against pulsating ostinato patterns from an orchestra of four pianos, brass, double basses, and fifty-nine percussion instruments. Heard today, however, the score seems to foreshadow minimalism as much as it evokes a distant past.[70]

The Oedipus myth spawned two almost contemporary but utterly different musical settings. Igor Stravinsky's opera-oratorio *Oedipus Rex* (1927) is a standard-bearer of musical neoclassicism. The composer had Cocteau's brief, straightforward treatment of the myth translated into an artificial basic Latin, deliberately chosen as stylised, impersonal, 'not dead but turned to stone'. The music is equally impersonal and lapidary, and its relentlessness conveys the idea of destiny with great directness. The whole work reads like an embodiment of the artistic credo Stravinsky was to enunciate in his 1939–40 Norton Lectures at Harvard:

> What is important for the lucid ordering of the work … is that all the Dionysian elements which set the imagination of the artist in motion and make the life-sap rise must be properly subjugated before they intoxicate us, and must finally be made to submit to the law: Apollo demands it.[71]

A less well-known, but more ambitious and perhaps greater work is the *Œdipe* of George Enescu, conceived, composed, and revised over a period of more than twenty years and first performed in 1936. This, too, is an opera liberated from Wagnerism, but through a highly individual combination of the modal chromaticism of the East with the subtlety of declamation

---

[70] Orff later composed an *Oedipus*, also to Hölderlin's translation, and a setting of the Greek text of *Prometheus Bound*.
[71] Stravinsky (1970) 105.

and clarity of orchestration of the French school. Enescu was first inspired to attempt an Oedipus opera in 1910, when he saw Mounet-Sully in the role at the Comédie Française (see Ch. 11). His librettist, Edmond Fleg, supplied a libretto in four acts, of which the first two deal with the birth of Oedipus and his defeat of the Sphinx (a scene of great musical power); and the third and fourth parallel the two Sophoclean Oedipus plays. Enescu's most recent biographer gives a terse explanation of the opera's neglect: 'There are no love-duets in Œdipe.'[72] But it is a work whose originality and dramatic intensity can be compared to Berlioz's Les Troyens.

Wagner exerts a complicated and ambiguous influence in Hans Werner Henze's The Bassarids (1966) [18], a version of Euripides' Bacchae with a libretto by W. H. Auden and Chester Kallman. This powerful opera is of particular interest for the differing views of Dionysus that coexist within it. Called an 'Opera Seria with Intermezzo in One Act', it is also divided into four movements that constitute a dramatic symphony in which the explosively Wagnerian music of Dionysus assaults, as it were, and finally overpowers the music of Pentheus. Auden and Kallman seem deeply suspicious of the Dionysiac, identifying it with the Götterdämmerung of Nazism: in their introduction to the opera, they describe Dionysus as 'a heartless monster ... impossible to admire', and warn that 'whole societies can be seized by demonic forces'. Henze, on the other hand, is far more receptive to Dionysus, understanding the basic theme of the opera as a 'conflict ... between social repression and sexual liberation, ... the intoxicating liberation of people who suddenly discover themselves, who release the Dionysus within themselves'. The seductive and powerful Wagnerism of Henze's score might be invoked to support either view of Dionysus, depending on the proclivities of the listener. The opera's final tableau symbolises its deep ambivalence. Against 'a sky of dazzling Mediterranean blue', we see the ruined wall of Pentheus' palace; two primitive fertility idols, the male daubed with red, adorn Semele's tomb. As the Bassarids repeat 'A ... do ... re, A ... do ... re', vines 'sprout everywhere, wreathing the columns, covering the blackened wall'. The triumph of unreason and superstition is at the same time the promise of burgeoning new life.[73]

---

[72] Malcolm (1990) 159.

[73] Not surprisingly, the Bacchae myth has been one of the most prominent tragic themes in twentieth-century opera. Other versions include Karol Szymanowski's masterpiece, Król Roger (King Roger, 1926), in which the mediaeval Sicilian king Roger II, a nobler Pentheus, resists the allure of the Shepherd, for whom Queen and courtiers have deserted him, but is finally reconciled to the force he represents; and Harry Partch's Revelation in the Courthouse Park (1961), interspersing episodes from Euripides with scenes in which Dionysus is the rock star Dion, the Bacchantes are groupies, and Agave is Mom. John Buller's opera Bakhai, sung in ancient Greek (with some English), was produced in 1992.

[18] Agave with the head of Pentheus in a staging by the Santa Fe Opera in 1968 of *The Bassarids*, an opera after Euripides' *Bacchae* (text by W. H. Auden and Chester Kallman, music by Hans Werner Henze (1966).

The opposition of Apollonian and Dionysiac in *The Bassarids*, so fundamental a part of the conceptual history of opera as well as of the post-Nietzschean conception of tragedy, provides an appropriate end-point for this brief survey. One thing seems certain, however: as long as operas continue to be written, that opposition, and the tragic myths that embody it, will be among their central preoccupations.[74]

TRANSLATION YESTERDAY AND TODAY

We have been looking at examples of the adaptation of Greek tragedy in a number of European languages and cultural traditions. This brief examination of direct translation will of necessity have to be limited to English, and for the most part to recent times. Translations, like adaptations, can serve more than one purpose; some of the most useful are plain prose aids to understanding an original text.[75] Rarely, a writer of real genius finds just the right text and makes a version that stands on its own as a lasting work of art. Most translations fall somewhere between these extremes, attempting to offer reasonably reliable guidance to the primary meaning of the source text as well as some approximation of the literary values the translator finds in it. The availability of serviceable and attractive translations is now more than ever an indispensable tool in the breaking-down of cultural boundaries and the expanding of cultural horizons.

It cannot be said that English readers were especially well served by translators of Greek tragedy for the first four centuries after the restoration of the texts to currency in Western Europe. No major poet before Browning turned his hand to translating Greek tragedy; there is nothing to set against Pope's Homer or even the powerful Elizabethan versions of Seneca. The first English translations of Greek tragedy were of individual plays of Euripides.

---

[74] An interesting recent example is *Greek* by Mark-Anthony Turnage (1988), a jazzy, musically eclectic adaptation of Steven Berkoff's play of the same name. *Greek* is an irreverent and provocative version of *Oedipus the King* set in the contemporary East End of London. Violence, intolerance, and unemployment are the plague in the background of the story of Eddy, a skinhead who moves from the raw culture of the pubs to material success – and unknowing parricide and incest. The self-knowledge of this version, however, constitutes a rejection of the myth. In the end, after an attempt to tear his eyes out and a mock funeral procession, Eddy revives to declare his unabashed, undying love for the Mum that he has married.

[75] In this respect, readers of Greek tragedy have been served reasonably well. The widely diffused Loeb series (Greek text and translation) offers the still useful Aeschylus of Smyth and a new (1994) Sophocles by Sir Hugh Lloyd-Jones. A much-needed new Euripides is being prepared by David Kovacs; the first two volumes appeared in 1995. Well-annotated versions of individual plays have been made available in the series published by Aris & Phillips (with Greek text), Prentice Hall, and Focus Classical Press. Cf. pp. 355–8 below.

The only one published in the sixteenth century was *Jocasta*, a version of
The Phoenician Women from Lodovico Dolce's Italian by Francis Kinwelmersh and George Gascoigne, but it appears to have been preceded by a
version of *Iphigeneia at Aulis* by Lady Jane Lumley.[76] Aeschylus, however,
was not available in English at all until the 1770s. Thomas Morell,
remembered as Handel's librettist, published a *Prometheus Bound* in 1773,
and Robert Potter's verse translation of all seven plays followed in 1777.
Potter held the field into the nineteenth century, but by its end readers could
choose among some two dozen rival versions of *Agamemnon*.[77] Indeed, the
nineteenth century saw an explosion of translation that has hardly abated
since.

Potter was typical of the earlier translators, largely clerics and school-
masters of some learning and literary ambition. His success was based in no
small measure on his ability to speak fluently in the voice of his time – in
Potter's case, with the accents of Dryden and Gray. Here, for example, is his
rendering of *Agamemnon*, lines 773–81:

> But Justice bids her ray divine
> E'en on the low-roof'd cottage shine;
> And beams her glories on the life,
> That knows not fraud, nor ruffian strife.
> The gorgeous glare of gold, obtain'd
> By foul polluted hands, disdain'd
> She leaves, and with averted eyes
> To humbler, holier mansions flies;
> And looking through the times to come
> Assigns each deed its righteous doom.[78]

A sense of decorum and elegance is at work here that today seems foreign to
Aeschylus, but that helps to explain Potter's considerable popularity in his
time. Translation in general reflects accepted poetic practice at the time of
its writing. Thus, nineteenth-century translations tend to sound like somewhat etiolated Shelley or Tennyson, and those at the beginning of our own
to be reminiscent of Swinburne, Morris, and their epigones. Here is the
same passage in Gilbert Murray's best mock-archaic manner:

> But Justice shineth in a house low-wrought
> With smoke-stained wall,

[76] Date uncertain, but most likely in the 1550s; first published in 1909 in an edition prepared
by H. H. Child for the Malone Society. In his preface, Child mentions a lost translation of a
play of Euripides by no less a personage than Princess (later Queen) Elizabeth, and there is
also evidence for a lost version of one of the Iphigeneia plays by George Peele.
[77] Green (1960) 191.
[78] These lines are quoted and analysed by Brower (1974) 182–3.

> And honoureth him who filleth his own lot;
> But the unclean hand upon the golden stair
> With eyes averse she flieth, seeking where
>   Things innocent are; and heeding not the power
> Of wealth by man misgloried, guideth all
>   To her own destined hour.[79]

T. S. Eliot memorably castigated Murray for having 'simply interposed between Euripides and ourselves a barrier more impenetrable than the Greek language' by dressing Euripides in 'a vulgar debasement of the eminently personal idiom of Swinburne'.[80] For all that, the large audience for Murray's work serves to remind us that the great majority of theatre-goers and readers in the period between the World Wars remained to be convinced of the triumph of modernism (cf. Ch. 11, pp. 302–4). And Murray's audience was large indeed; his translations of the complete Aeschylus and about half of the other surviving tragedies sold extraordinary numbers of copies and gave many thousands their notion of what Greek tragedy is like. Still, Eliot's objection carries weight today, when most translations of Murray's vintage have become almost unreadable. This suggests why any poetic author worth translating is worth translating anew for each new generation.

Even allowing for historical near-sightedness, the picture has changed for the better since Eliot wrote his essay on Murray (or rather, was already changing as he wrote). There are a number of reasons for the improvement. The first is that several of the most important British and American poets have devoted themselves to translations of Greek tragic texts. Perhaps this is because few poets now aspire to write tragedies of their own, as in earlier generations many of them did. At any rate, a case can be made that we are in, if not a golden, at least a silver age of translation. This age may be thought to have begun some decades before Murray's efforts with two translations by Robert Browning: Euripides' *Heracles* (in *Aristophanes' Apology*, 1875) and *The Agamemnon of Æschylus* (1877).[81] Browning's Euripides has the virtues of much of his poetry – including language and rhythms that reflect real speech – but the hyperliteral *Agamemnon* is a strange performance indeed. Declared 'a somewhat toilsome and perhaps fruitless adventure' by Browning himself, it remains a curiosity, but a magnificent one, a version in the spirit of Hölderlin's Sophocles that pushes English expression to its limits to accommodate the expressiveness of the

---

[79] First published in 1920; here quoted from *The Complete Plays of Aeschylus* (1952).

[80] Eliot (1950) 48–9; the essay was first published in 1920 and refers specifically to a performance of *Medea* in Murray's translation.

[81] To these we may add the *Alcestis* narrated complete in *Balaustion's Adventure* (1871).

Greek.[82] In a very different vein, W. B. Yeats produced 'versions for the modern stage' of *Oedipus the King* and *Oedipus at Colonus*, with the dialogue, considerably compressed, in rhythmic prose and the choral odes, considerably rewritten, in verse. The effect is often pure Yeats, but has the splendour of Sophocles ever been rendered more palpable?

> Never to have lived is best, ancient writers say;
> Never to have drawn the breath of life, never to have looked
>   into the eye of day
> The second best's a gay good night and quickly turn away.[83]

Louis MacNeice's *Agamemnon* (1936), the work of a poet who was also a Greek scholar, rightly won acclaim for both accuracy and masterful control of diction and rhythm and is perhaps the first fully 'modern' verse translation of Greek tragedy in English.

Two American poets achieved notable successes with Euripides in the 1930s and 1940s. There are stunning passages from Euripides by H. D. (Hilda Doolittle), and in her *Ion* (1937), she realised a Euripidean voice of great lyrical, if not dramatic, intensity. Here, for example, is a portion of Creusa's reproach of Apollo, whom she still believes to have abandoned her after she bore his child:

> why did you seek me out,
> brilliant, with gold hair? vibrant
> you seized my wrists,
> while the flowers fell from my lap,
> the gold and the pale-gold crocus,
> while you fulfilled your wish;
> what did it help, my shout
> of mother,
> mother?
> no help
> came to me
> in the rocks;
> O, mother,
> O, white hands caught;
> O, mother,
> O, gold flowers lost.[84]

---

[82] Sympathetic but not uncritical appraisal in Brower (1974) 172–5 and Steiner (1992) 329–32.

[83] Yeats' *King Oedipus* was published as a separate volume in 1928; *Oedipus at Colonus* first appeared in *Collected Plays* (1934); the lines quoted had already appeared in *The Tower* (1928) in 'From "Oedipus at Colonus"'. For the genesis of Yeats' *King Oedipus*, see Clark & McGuire (1989); for an appraisal of both Sophoclean versions, see Arkins (1990).

H. D. called *Ion* 'a play after Euripides'; similarly, Robinson Jeffers' *Medea* (1946) is identified on the title page as 'freely adapted' from Euripides. Coarser in language than H. D.'s play, but theatrically quite effective, it was written as a vehicle for the actress Judith Anderson, who brought it to thousands of spectators in repeated tours (cf. Ch. 11, p. 312).

Late in his career, Ezra Pound did a controversial but lively version of Sophocles' *Women of Trachis* (1954). Dismissed by more than one classicist as an arrogant and vulgar travesty, it alternates moments of great eloquence with language of slangy directness. Although there is much to admire here, it is hard to feel that Sophocles is well served by the glaring inconsistencies of tone. A brief sample will show something of its strength and oddness. As the dying Herakles enters, the Chorus sing:

> These strangers lift him home,
> with shuffling feet, and love that keeps them still.
> The great weight silent
> for no man can say
> if sleep but feign
> or Death reign instantly.

And Herakles speaks:

> Holy Kanea, where they build holy altars,
> done yourself proud, you have,
> nice return for a sacrifice:
> messing me up.
> I could have done without these advantages
> And the spectacle of madness in flower,
> incurable, oh yes.
> Get someone to make a song for it,
> Or some chiropractor to cure it.
> A dirty pest,
> take God a'mighty to cure it and
> I'd be surprised to see Him
> coming this far ...[85]

[84] This passage, taken from the 1986 republication of *Ion* with H. D.'s revisions pp. 68–9, corresponds to lines 887–96 in the Greek text. *Ion* was not H. D.'s only version from Euripides; it was preceded by a free reworking of *Hippolytus* called *Hippolytus Temporizes* (1927) as well as lyrics from *Iphigeneia in Aulis* and *Hippolytus* (1919), and from *Bacchae* and *Hecuba* (1931).

[85] Adapted from lines 964–70 and 993–1003 of the Greek text; taken from the book publication (New York 1957) 42. For the controversy surrounding *Women of Trachis*, see Davie (1964) 233–9; for a sympathetic critique, see Mason (1969). Pound also wrote a version of Sophocles' *Electra* (1949, in collaboration with Rudd Fleming), which was published only in 1989.

Robert Lowell, a poet with abiding interests both in theatre and translation, produced a prose *Prometheus Bound* (1967), and one of his last projects (posthumously published in 1978) was a spare, eloquent verse rendering of the *Oresteia* meant for performance in a single evening. Similarly, Stephen Spender's *Oedipus Trilogy* (1985) is a version, mixing verse and prose, that is intended primarily for the stage. Both poets had some knowledge of Greek; both worked primarily from translations. Perhaps the most noteworthy recent translation for the stage, Tony Harrison's *Oresteia* (1981), achieved its prominence as part of Peter Hall's successful London production (see Ch. 11, pp. 314–17).

None of these versions is definitive for our time or an unqualified masterpiece; all have genuine virtues. And the fact that figures of such stature have published translations of Greek tragedy has no doubt encouraged younger poets to labour in the same vineyard. One as yet unfinished project, the Oxford Greek Tragedy in New Translations, has specialised in bringing together poets and scholars in collaborations; the results have been mixed, but the best of these volumes are excellent. The founder of that series, the late William Arrowsmith, was himself a poet-scholar of a rare order, as was Richmond Lattimore, coeditor of the Chicago series, a complete Greek tragedy that still constitutes the American vulgate in this field. Penguin Books, widely distributed wherever English is spoken, have published the praiseworthy verse translations of Aeschylus' *Oresteia* and Sophocles' Theban plays by Robert Fagles, and a number of fine individual versions by British and American poets are also available. One can only hope that the most promising younger poets can be encouraged to devote the enormous energy that serious translating requires to provide the next generation with a living body of Greek drama. As Eliot reminds us, it is too delicate a task to be left solely to the professors.

GREEK TRAGEDY FOR TOMORROW

Tragedy returned to the European stage with a special prestige conferred by its antiquity and its status as the loftiest form of poetic discourse. That prestige was still felt intensely by Goethe and Schiller, Byron and Shelley. Keats hoped that his reputation would at last be made by producing a tragedy. More recently, O'Neill and Arthur Miller staked a good part of their reputations on the possibility of a tragedy of the down and out. It would perhaps be hard to find a playwright today for whom tragedy still has that kind of appeal, but there is nevertheless plenty of evidence that the old bones still live. Much of the work of adaptation and interpretation has now been assumed by the directors of new and experimental productions

[19] Clytemnestra (Electra Catselli), lured from the palace by Electra (Irene Papas), descends from her carriage; from Michael Cacoyannis' film *Electra* (Greece, 1961).

(see Ch. 11). In addition, Greek tragedy has begun to reach vast audiences through film and television. Kenneth MacKinnon's *Greek Tragedy into Film* lists eighteen cinematic versions of twelve tragedies filmed between 1927 and 1978. The first records brief excerpts from the historically significant Delphi production of *Prometheus Bound* (Ch. 11, pp. 305–6), and a number of films of stage productions. Several more, notably the three Euripidean films of Michael Cacoyannis that constitute his 'Trojan Trilogy' – *Electra* (1961) [19], *The Trojan Women* (1971), and *Iphigenia* (1976) – are fully cinematic adaptations that use ancient sites and costumes to evoke a Greek atmosphere.[86] Their freedom from the constraints of the stage makes possible effective realisations on film of things only reported or alluded to in the plays. For example, *Iphigenia* (based on *Iphigeneia at Aulis*) begins with a very effective sequence that 'translates' the play's choral catalogue of ships into cinematic terms by showing the beached ships, then hundreds of idle, restless soldiers, and Agamemnon's appearance in the

---

[86] On the Cacoyannis films and others based on plays of Euripides, see McDonald (1983) and McDonald and MacKinnon (1993).

[20] Phaedra (Melina Mercouri) amidst the 'Greek chorus' of women who have lost their men in the sinking of the SS *Phaedra*, from Jules Dassin's *Phaedra* (USA/Greece, 1961).

camp marred by a soldier fainting as he passes. This evocation of the expedition in crisis is followed by a scene that makes visible the background that Euripides simply assumes – the killing of a deer sacred to Artemis and Calchas' announcement that the goddess demands the sacrifice of Iphigenia if the fleet is to sail. The ending of the film, on the other hand, is made deliberately enigmatic. There is no suggestion of the last-minute substitution of a deer for Iphigenia that may or may not have been part of the original Euripidean conception, and the sacrifice itself is presented only through Agamemnon's reaction as he watches. The mounting wind as Iphigenia climbs toward the altar raises other kinds of questions. Feeling the wind, Odysseus orders the soldiers to the ships; Agamemnon alone turns back, shouting 'Iphigenia'; and she turns around and screams as Calchas swoops down on her. Is the sacrifice truly necessary? Has Artemis anticipated its completion and sent the winds, or are we meant to doubt Calchas' prophecy?

Jules Dassin's *Phaedra* (1962) represents another possible approach to filming Greek tragedy [20]. Like several of the more recent plays we have examined, Dassin modernises his subject, making Theseus into a wealthy

Greek shipping magnate named Thanos; the Hippolytus figure is his son by a previous marriage, a half-English innocent named Alexis, whose sexual diffidence comes not so much from a rejection of carnality as from inexperience and timidity. Dassin dramatises a conflict between erotic passion and the claims of family set among a self-absorbed and fundamentally irresponsible elite. In his version, Phaedra's seduction of Alexis is consummated in a love scene in which the rain outside and flames from the fireplace come to symbolise the meeting of innocence and passion. When it becomes clear to Alexis that Phaedra has no intention of breaking with Thanos to live with him, he decides to remain in England, but Thanos insists that he come to Greece, and lures him with the Aston Martin car that he has introduced to Phaedra in a showroom as his 'best girl'. Eventually, Phaedra, in desperation at her rejection by Alexis, confesses to Thanos that she loves his son. Thanos orders Alexis to leave Greece with his curse. The young man dies in his Aston Martin, colliding with a truck as he speeds along a cliff road. Phaedra's trusted maid Anna permits her to die of an overdose of sleeping pills, as if in recognition that her death has been ordained by forces beyond human resistance. (This bald summary elides the element of social criticism prominent in this film. For example, when Phaedra comes to Thanos's office to confess her love for Alexis, she must push her way, dressed in white, through a crowd of women dressed in black who await word of their loved ones aboard the SS *Phaedra*, which has just sunk. As Alexis and Phaedra are dying, Thanos reads the names of the dead in the shipwreck to the women in black. Thus is the reckless self-destruction of the rich put into perspective.)

Medea (1967) and *Edipo Re* (1970) [21], both by Pier Paolo Pasolini, illustrate yet another tendency in the filming of Greek tragedy. MacKinnon refers to this as 'metatragedy', but we might also call it the 'mythic' mode, in which the setting is neither specifically Greek nor modern, but shifting and cross-cultural, to suggest the universality of mythic experience. Both films use locales, decors and costumes, and music eclectically and in ways deliberately designed to defamiliarise the Sophoclean and Euripidean originals. Similarly, both include their versions of the ancient dramas within a larger narrative framework. Let us look briefly at how Pasolini's *Edipo Re* employs and elaborates its source text. The film has a prologue and epilogue set in modern Italy. The prologue takes place in what seems to be an Italian town of the 1920s or 1930s, and gives a rather Freudian account of a baby's birth, his mother's attachment, and his father's antipathy, symbolised by his lifting the baby by the ankles and squeezing hard. The epilogue, which clearly alludes to *Oedipus at Colonus*, takes place in contemporary Italy, but includes the same town square, meadow, and country house as in

[21] The self-blinded Oedipus (Franco Citti) with Angelo, messenger and companion (Ninetto Davoli), from Pier Paolo Pasolini's film *Edipo Re* (Italy, 1967).

the prologue. The blind Edipo wanders, accompanied by Angelo (the messenger of the central section; the Oedipus of this version has no children), to the place where he began. The central section takes place in a different world, one that seems at once primitive and exotic (these sections were filmed in Morocco). It takes up, as it were, where the prologue left off, with a servant carrying the baby away, his ankles bound to a pole, and it brings Edipo to Corinth, Delphi, and finally Thebes. There follows a fairly faithful enactment of the Sophoclean *Oedipus*.

Pasolini's most jarring departure is to deprive Edipo of the intellectualism that is Oedipus' hallmark in Sophocles, to make him a creature of impulse and unreason throughout, rather than a thinker and a seeker of knowledge.[87] Recognition of this strategy helps to clarify many details. For example, Edipo, when he has heard his doom, chooses the road for Thebes not once but twice, and both times without thought, by whirling around at random with his eyes closed. The encounter with Laio, protracted and brutal, is also entirely unmotivated. It is as if father and son are obeying

---

[87] MacKinnon (1986) 137–9.

some impulse that they recognise and do not need to understand. Similarly, the Sphinx in Pasolini does not set a riddle, but rather tells him that there is an enigma in his life. 'I do not want to know', replies Edipo, and forces her to her death. In this context, the wilful primitivism of setting can be understood as the evocation of a prerational world, non-Greek and decidedly unclassical. The plot, of course, requires Edipo to be a seeker, to a point. What he resists is the knowledge that he carries within himself.

Whatever one's opinion of films such as these, they show that the cinema is a legitimate medium for the interpretation of Greek tragic themes. Television, too, offers almost unlimited possibilities for the diffusion of tragedy. Enormous audiences worldwide have already had the opportunity to see the BBC productions of the *Oresteia* and the Oedipus cycle. Indeed, it is possible to speculate that more people have seen these plays on television in a few short years than have seen them in any other form in all previous performances. These BBC productions command respect. The *Oresteia* was presented in a translation by Frederic Raphael and Kenneth McLeish,[88] directed by Bill Hays. The Oedipus plays were translated and directed by Don Taylor. Both featured starry casts, including such well-known actors as Claire Bloom, Diana Rigg, John Gielgud, and Cyril Cusack. They illustrate both the strengths and the limitations of a filmed stage production: in the case of the Oedipus plays, that the combination of an abstract set and nineteenth-century costume already seems dated, arbitrary rather than provocative, and one wishes for a more imaginative treatment of the (admittedly intractable) choruses. Nevertheless, the emotional force of the presentation will surely have given many new spectators a sense of the power that still resides in these ancient plays. A far less likely medium for displaying the power of Greek tragedy is the Broadway musical, but Bob Telson and Lee Breuer successfully adapted *Oedipus at Colonus* as *The Gospel at Colonus*, 'an oratorio set in a black Pentecostal service, in which Greek myth replaces Bible story'.[89] First presented at the Brooklyn Academy of Music's Next Wave Festival in 1983, *Gospel* toured extensively and arrived for a run of several months on Broadway in 1988. Television broadcast, sound and video recordings have added to its fame. Its linkage of two cultures is full of energy and deeply felt.

Through film and television, Greek tragedy is becoming part of a new global culture, and its adaptations to the new media show that a tradition begun so locally in the Theatre of Dionysus has a broad appeal and need no longer be the exclusive property of a Western elite. In the end, the question

---

[88] Published in book form under the title *The Serpent Son* (1979).
[89] 'Note on Production' from the published play (1989).

of whether and in what ways this inheritance from fifth-century Athens can remain part of a living tradition depends not so much on the toil of scholars as on the discovery by playwrights and public of ways in which tragedy can speak to their own lives. There are many signs that this is continuing to happen. Consider, for example, the frequent revivals of Euripides' *Trojan Women*. The major translations and adaptations are closely connected to the sense that this drama speaks to the horrors of war in our own time as well as its own. Thus, Franz Werfel's *Die Troerinnen* (1915) was produced amidst the horrors of World War I; Sartre wrote his adaptation, *Les Troyennes* (1964), in response to the French war in Algeria;[90] Cacoyannis made his striking film version (following on an enormously successful stage run of over 650 performances in New York) during the Vietnam War. A more recent instance is Seamus Heaney's splendid version of Sophocles' *Philoctetes*, *The Cure at Troy*, first performed in Derry in 1990 and clearly crafted to urge reconciliation between the warring sides in Ireland. In the words of his Chorus:

> So hope for a great sea-change
> on the far side of revenge.
> Believe that a further shore
> is reachable from here.[91]

I conclude with mention of two adaptations, both by Africans, that suggest the ability of Greek tragedy to bridge cultures and to serve as a living element in contemporary consciousness. One was commissioned by a great Nigerian writer for the National Theatre in London; the other was written by a white South African playwright and two black collaborators in a theatre that operated on the margins of Apartheid legality. The first is Wole Soyinka's extraordinary adaptation of *The Bacchae* (1973). Subtitled 'A Communion Rite', Soyinka's play combines a translation of Euripides with elements derived from African culture and experience, and at one point even a mimed version of Christ's miracle of turning water into wine. Although Dionysus' vengeance is no less implacable here than in Euripides, Soyinka insists on a different and celebratory ending that appears to have two convergent sources. One is his emphasis on the tyrannical nature of

---

[90] Sartre (1976) 313. For the 1915 production of Murray's *Trojan Women* that toured in the US under the auspices of the Women's Peace Party and a 1974 Japanese production that represents the Trojan women as Japanese victims of merciless American soldiers, see Ch. 11, pp. 302–4 and 313.

[91] Marianne McDonald, in an unpublished paper that she has kindly sent me, points out that Heaney's play is one of ten treatments of Greek tragic subjects by Irish poets since 1984, all of which bear in one way or another on the Irish question, suggesting the way in which such translations and adaptations can become part of a contemporary debate.

Pentheus and his regime. The stage setting includes 'a road lined by the bodies of crucified slaves': Pentheus' rule is based on slavery and propped up by military force. Soyinka suggests that his tyrannical nature is the result of his refusal to come to terms with the part of his nature represented by Dionysus. The second source of Soyinka's new ending is his identification of Dionysus with the Yoruba deity Ogun, 'god of metals, creativity, the road, wine and war', as Soyinka describes him in his Introduction. Dionysus–Ogun represents a force that encompasses the cyclical nature of life and death, the destruction that is part of creation. In Soyinka's play, when Kadmos asks, 'Why us?' Agave answers, 'Why not?' At this point, Pentheus' impaled head spurts wine, becoming a fountain at which the entire community can take communion.

The Island, which Athol Fugard wrote together with John Kani and Winston Ntshona in 1973, takes place in the notorious Robben Island prison. John and Winston are political prisoners who improvise a two-man production of *Antigone* for a prison concert and discover that it is about *their* lives. The final scene of the play is their performance of 'The Trial and Punishment of Antigone', with the audience becoming the prisoners for whom they perform. John, who has earlier learned that he will soon be released, plays Creon as the people's protector against 'subversive elements'. He cross-examines Antigone (Winston in a wig and falsies), who pleads guilty, but claims obedience to a higher law. After the inevitable sentence to be immured for life – 'Take her from where she stands, straight to the Island' – Winston, the lifer, tears off the wig and speaks Antigone's last words in his own persona: 'I go now to my living death, because I honoured those things to which honour belongs.' It is a powerful moment of recognition: Winston will no more be freed than was Antigone, but he has not been broken. Examples such as Soyinka's version of *The Bacchae* and Fugard's *The Island* show one thing for certain: the tragedies themselves are not exhausted, have not yet yielded all their potential meanings. The question is, will they still find their poets and their audiences, and what kind of poets and audiences will they be?

BIBLIOGRAPHICAL NOTE

Most of the relevant references are given in the footnotes to this chapter. For background information see G. Highet, *The Classical Tradition* (New York 1949); R. R. Bolgar, *The Classical Heritage and its Beneficiaries* (Cambridge 1954); T. J. Rosenmeyer, 'Drama' in M. I. Finley, ed., *The Legacy of Greece: a New Appraisal* (Oxford 1981) 120–54.

11

FIONA MACINTOSH

Tragedy in performance: nineteenth- and twentieth-century productions

Greek tragedy has enjoyed a vigorous afterlife on the modern stage both in the original Greek and in translation. Yet whilst the production history of, say, Shakespeare has long been the subject of academic inquiry, it is only very recently that classical scholars have appreciated both the value and the importance of charting the fortunes of Greek drama in the modern period. It is not simply that classicists need to be aware of the extent to which their own area of study has shaped major dramatic trends in Europe from at least the 1880s onwards. It is not even that a general lack of interest in such matters has meant that classical scholars have remained unaware of the (by no means insignificant) fact that Sophocles' *Oedipus the King* was banned from the professional stage in Britain until 1910. What a survey of modern productions of Greek plays does, above all, is provide us with a salutary reminder that contemporary investigations into Greek drama are no less time-bound than those of previous periods. Indeed, every encounter with artworks of the past is really an exploration of current concerns and needs; and nowhere is this better illustrated than through a study of the performance histories of Greek tragedies.

Yet the tendency of classical scholarship to ignore the fortunes of Greek tragedy on the modern stage is somewhat surprising. For the production histories of these plays reveal that close ties have, in fact, existed between the professional theatre and the world of scholarship since at least the nineteenth century. The row that followed Nietzsche's capitulation to Wagner and Bayreuth at the end of the nineteenth century may well be notorious (cf. Ch. 12, pp. 324–5), but it is the exceptional nature of the episode that has guaranteed its notoriety. The relations between the two worlds have generally been fruitful rather than stormy. And the fact that the plays of the fifth century BC have finally been incorporated into the classical repertoire of the London theatres is surely ample testimony to the success and the significance of those relations.

ANTIGONE IN THE NINETEENTH CENTURY

In the modern world, Greek drama was rarely enjoyed at first hand on the stage until the nineteenth century. The famous production of *Oedipus the King* in a vernacular translation in Vicenza in 1585, mounted to mark the occasion of the completion of Palladio's Teatro Olimpico, was exceptional (cf. Ch. 10, pp. 229–31); and there were no other Greek plays at Vicenza until 1847. When the members of the Camerata gathered together towards the end of the sixteenth century in Florence to discuss how to create a form of musical drama based on the example of Greek tragedy, they paradoxically guaranteed that their paradigm would remain unknown for even longer. For although the form of Greek tragedy was recalled in early opera, it was the mythological handbooks rather than the Greek plays themselves that provided the subjects for the new musical dramas until the late eighteenth century.

It was only in school and university theatres in Germany and England in the sixteenth and seventeenth centuries, and in school productions in Ireland and England in the eighteenth century in particular, that anything like authenticity was aimed at in the productions of the Greek tragedies that were staged in the original Greek. Elsewhere on the public stage, Greek tragedy competed alongside the tragedies of Seneca as source material in the enormously influential French neoclassical adaptations of Racine and Corneille (cf. Ch. 10 above). But adaptation, *per se*, need not rule out familiarity with the original, as the eighteenth-century English versions of Greek tragedies clearly demonstrate. In plays such as James Thomson's *Agamemnon* (1738) and William Shirley's *Electra* (1762), an intimate acquaintance with the Greek model is a prerequisite for an understanding of the political subtext that provided – as the Lord Chamberlain was quick to appreciate – the rationale behind the adaptations in the first place.[1]

However, it was not until resentment against the pre-eminence enjoyed by the French neoclassical adaptations built up in Germany that any public staging of the Greek plays themselves became possible. For in Germany in the late eighteenth century, nationalist fervour combined with developments in both classical scholarship and in the theatre, and led eventually to a revival of Greek tragedy that was to spread throughout the whole of Europe. When German classical scholarship first sought to encompass all aspects of the ancient world within its range of study, it found a keen audience amongst members of an intelligentsia in search of a model upon which to base their own ideas. And since many German cities were able to

[1] Macintosh (1995).

enjoy permanent, standing theatres from the late eighteenth century onwards (long before any comparable institutions existed elsewhere in Europe), the stability of the profession entailed an unprecedented respectability and an increasing vitality. Goethe took over the Hoftheater in Weimar in 1791, giving Europe for the first time a theatre which was, generally speaking, free from the whims of public taste and able to experiment in the staging of Greek tragedy in verse translations.

Whilst the French plays had been designed primarily to improve on the Greek originals by extending the emotional range of the material, and the English adaptations had provided clear comment on contemporary political events, the productions at the Hoftheater sought to capture the universal in Greek tragedy and usher it into the world of Goethe's Weimar. Goethe's own enthusiasms were evidently not shared by all: August Schlegel's adaptation of Euripides' *Ion* (produced early in 1802) failed to satisfy the Weimar audiences; and Rochlitz's abbreviated and inelegant adaptation of Sophocles' *Antigone* (early in 1809) was strongly criticised by classical scholars. But the Weimar experiment is still of some (albeit indirect) significance. For even if Schlegel's version of the *Ion* proved unsuccessful, it was his lectures on Greek tragedy between 1809 and 1811 that first established the high status accorded to the Greek plays throughout Europe in the nineteenth century. Moreover, by staging the Rochlitz version of the *Antigone* – its infelicities notwithstanding – Goethe had introduced the public to the Greek tragedy that was to remain pre-eminent in the German-speaking theatre, and indeed in the European theatre as a whole, throughout the second part of the nineteenth century.

It was the production of Sophocles' *Antigone* that opened at the Hoftheater in the Neuen Palais in Potsdam on 28 October 1841 that secured the pre-eminence of Sophocles' play in the nineteenth-century European repertoire. Although generally referred to as the 'Mendelssohn *Antigone*' on account of the orchestral introduction and the choral settings that were composed by Felix Mendelssohn-Bartholdy, the production was in fact a collaborative undertaking overseen by Friedrich Wilhelm IV. The translation, which was by Johann Jakob Christian Donner, was both accurate and lucid as well as being metrically complex; and August Böckh was called in from Berlin University as the philological adviser. The play was performed in the Vitruvian theatre in the palace, and the responsibility for the staging fell largely to Ludwig Tieck, who sought to avoid all illusionist techniques that had predominated on Goethe's Weimar stage.

The choice of Sophocles' *Antigone* was by no means fortuitous, since Hegel's pupils had already applied to contemporary politics their master's ideas of the 'moral community' (*sittliche Gemeinschaft*) that for Hegel

[22] Scene from *Antigone*, at Covent Garden in 1845. From *The Illustrated London News* of 18 January 1845.

constituted the Greek polis. And here, in the new liberalism of Friedrich Wilhelm IV's Prussia, there was to be no better illustration of that 'moral community'. This is not to imply, however, that a Hegelian interpretation of the play was adopted *tout court* and that the production was simply an apology for Creon, as has sometimes been claimed.[2] For not only were the collaborators in the production themselves of diverse political persuasions, but the Potsdam audience's liberal outlook would have made them most likely to have been in sympathy with Antigone rather than with Creon.[3]

It was clearly not any contemporary political message that led to the *Antigone*'s continued success when it was seen in Paris at the Odéon in 1844 and in London at Covent Garden at the beginning of 1845. It was the authenticity of the staging and the costumes, together with the use of speech

[2] Steiner (1984) 182.
[3] See Steinberg (1991) 141–2; Flashar (1991) 74–5.

and song in serious drama, that captured the audiences' imaginations [22]. Mendelssohn's music was not immediately appreciated by the English reviewers, and the fact that the chorus of sixty male members was poorly rehearsed undoubtedly contributed to their misgivings.[4] But the performances of George Vandenhoff and his daughter as Creon and Antigone respectively were highly praised; and the audiences' appreciation of the production, which even included a ballet to accompany the dance ode to Dionysus (1115–54), led to an extension of the run for an additional month.

The play continued to capture the public imagination long after the production was transferred from London to Edinburgh. And just as the *Antigone* had been parodied in Berlin after its transfer there by Brennglass, so too in London E. L. Blanchard's burlesque, *Antigone*, appeared at the Strand Theatre in February 1845. That the *Antigone* had become a byword for serious theatre in Britain is amply illustrated by the fact that in 1867 when Albert Joseph Moore was commissioned to paint a frieze to go above the proscenium at the new Queen's Theatre, in Long Acre, the subject he chose was 'An Ancient Greek Audience watching a performance of "Antigone" by Sophocles'.[5]

In 1850 the English Ambassador in Athens asked for the 'Mendelssohn *Antigone*' to be staged on Sophocles' native soil, but it was not until December 1867 that the play was finally performed in the translation of Rangabis in the Herodes Atticus Theatre in Athens. Despite the fact that early audiences had found Mendelssohn's music both baffling and disappointing by turns, it was the music that was to remain popular the longest and was the main attraction in revivals towards the end of the century.[6] It was not uncommon to find new productions using Mendelssohn's score; and even when Stanislavsky mounted a production of the *Antigone* in 1899 at the Moscow Art Theatre, he chose Mendelssohn's music to complement the naturalistic details of the actors' performances.

AMATEUR REVIVALS

There were other productions of Greek plays under the patronage of Friedrich Wilhelm IV at Potsdam, such as the *Oedipus at Colonus* with Mendelssohn's music that opened on 1 November 1845, but none enjoyed

---

[4] *The Illustrated London News*, 18 January 1845. A cartoon of the Chorus appeared in *Punch*, 18 January 1845 and is reproduced in Grove (1880) vol. II, s.v. Mendelssohn.

[5] Ashton (1992) 61–4.

[6] Cf. Campbell (1891) 318; and Jebb (1900) xlii: 'To most lovers of music Mendelssohn's *Antigone* is too familiar to permit any word of comment here.'

the same success as the *Antigone*. Elsewhere in Germany the Saxe-Meiningen Company – which was to prove so influential in shaping the naturalistic theories of Antoine and Stanislavsky – staged Sophocles' three Theban plays in 1867, and then an adaptation of Aeschylus' *Libation-Bearers* in 1868. Not surprisingly, however, having perilously exchanged Greek tragedy's ritual for domestic realism on these two occasions, the Meiningen Company never made any further experiments with the Greek tragedies.

Generally speaking, there were few new productions of Greek plays in Germany as a whole towards the end of the nineteenth century; and this dearth was as much due to the influence of Richard Wagner as it was to the rise of theatrical naturalism. Although Wagner's prejudices against Mendelssohn's *Antigone* – which cannot be divorced from his deep-seated anti-semitism – had little impact on public opinion, his views on the impossibility of reviving Greek drama in the modern world, on the other hand, clearly held sway.

Instead, it was in France that a significant professional production of *Oedipus the King* was staged, which laid the foundations for the eventual pre-eminence of the figure of Oedipus in Europe in the first half of the twentieth century. In a rhymed translation by Jules Lacroix, the French production opened on 18 September 1858 at the Théâtre Français and was regularly revived to great acclaim; and in 1881 when the famous French tragic actor Jean Mounet-Sully took over the part of Oedipus, the production achieved international renown [23]. In marked contrast to the 'Mendelssohn *Antigone*', the Chorus had a purely incidental role and the focus was on Oedipus, a man of great suffering, who when played by Mounet-Sully moved those in the pit as readily as those in the circle;[7] and amongst them was Oedipus' most significant modern exponent, Sigmund Freud.[8] What astonished one reviewer was Mounet-Sully's ability to convey the deepest woe after the self-blinding through body movements and tone of voice alone.[9] When the classical scholar Lewis Campbell saw the production, he asked himself: 'Why can we not have the like of this in England?'[10] And even if it was to be some years before a professional company would mount a similarly successful production in England, other highly significant steps had already been taken in Britain that were to make such a production possible.

Campbell himself had been involved in one (generally forgotten) experiment in Edinburgh as a member, together with the novelist Robert Louis Stevenson, of Fleeming Jenkin's private theatre. Jenkin was a professor of

---

[7] Campbell (1891) 328.   [8] Jones (1953) 194.
[9] *Saturday Review*, 19 November 1881.   [10] Campbell (1891) 329.

[23] Jean Mounet-Sully in *Oedipus*, at the Comédie Française 1881.

engineering at the University, with a passion for ancient Greece and for the theatre; and from 1873 onwards he staged a number of Greek plays in translation in his theatre at number 3 Great Stuart Street. In 1877 Sophocles' *Trachiniae* was performed in Campbell's translation, and it was played again that year in the Town Hall in St Andrews. In May of 1880, six hundred people saw the same company perform Aeschylus' *Agamemnon* in English, just one month before the famous production of the *Agamemnon* in ancient Greek that was staged in the hall of Balliol College at the University of Oxford.

The Oxford production of the *Agamemnon*, which took place on 3 June 1880, is of enormous importance, not only because it was the first production of a Greek tragedy in modern times in the original language to receive serious critical attention, but also because the personalities involved continued to promote Greek drama in England long after they had left Oxford. The undergraduate Frank Benson (who went on to become a famous actor-manager) joined with the young philosophy don W. L. Courtney (later drama critic of the *Daily Telegraph*), and they managed with the help of the Hon. W. N. Bruce to persuade Benjamin Jowett, Master of Balliol, to let them use Balliol's hall for their production.

Benson took the part of Clytemnestra, Courtney the watchman, and Bruce was Agamemnon. The play was performed on an open stage, against a set that was made by Burne-Jones and painted by Professor W. B. Richmond. Music for the beginning of the parodos was composed by the organist of Magdalen, Walter Parratt, and consisted of a few austere bars.[11] The choral delivery was controversial, and the alternation between monotone recitation and dialogue between the Chorus members was not deemed a success. The production as a whole, however, was much acclaimed by leading figures of the day. On the first night Robert Browning was in the audience as Jowett's guest; and after further performances at Eton, Harrow and Winchester, it was performed for three nights at St George's Hall in London, where it was seen by an enthusiastic George Eliot, and no lesser luminaries than Henry Irving and Ellen Terry, who were eventually to become Benson's employers at the Lyceum Theatre in 1882.

Before joining the Lyceum, however, Benson was invited in 1881 by the newly appointed Headmaster of Bradfield College, the Revd Herbert Branston Gray, to stage a performance of Euripides' *Alcestis* at the school. Benson took the part of Apollo, Courtney was Heracles, and Gray played Admetus. The Bradfield production was particularly significant because it led eventually to the establishment of regular productions of Greek plays at the school from 1890 onwards, when the open-air Greek theatre, modelled on the theatre at Epidaurus, was completed. For the next twenty or so years, in particular, the Bradfield plays were to provide members of the professional theatre with new and challenging ideas, not only for staging Greek plays but also for finding antidotes to the naturalistic techniques that held sway on the professional stage.[12]

Although Oxford was the first university in recent times to stage a play in the original Greek, the fact that the distinction was only narrowly won must not be overlooked. In America, Professor Goodwin at Harvard had planned to stage the *Antigone* in the newly constructed Sander's Theatre in 1876; and the University of Notre Dame had planned to perform *Oedipus the King* in 1879. In the event both projects were postponed and it was not until 1881 and 1882 respectively that both Harvard and Notre Dame were able to stage *Oedipus the King* in the original Greek.

The Harvard production of *Oedipus* was lavishly set (having benefited

---

[11] Mackinnon (1910) 61.

[12] Cf. Gilbert Murray's letter to William Archer early in 1906: 'The phrase about the superiority of Bradfield [in comparison with professional productions of his own translations] seems to be running like the measles through cultural circles ... Of course, if this point of view is right, my whole work as scholar and translator is useless ...', cited by Wilson (1987) 107. Bradfield productions, of course, continue to this day on a triennial basis.

from seven months' preparation), and ran for five nights to great acclaim. However, when the New York theatre director Daniel Frohman transferred the production to the Booth Theatre in New York in the winter of 1882, the reception was somewhat different. Although the new audience's general ignorance of the Greek language dictated (of necessity) a different approach, the method selected to overcome the language barrier clearly militated against the production's success. Here members of the supporting cast responded in English to the Greek pronouncements of Oedipus, resulting in a stilted performance which no doubt destroyed all sense of suspense and urgency in the second half of the play. But it was not simply the production that the American audiences found objectionable – they found little sympathy with a Greek myth that ran counter to the ethos of the American dream.[13]

In Britain, however, the interchange between amateur and professional circles in the staging of Greek plays at this time was rather more fruitful. When the University of Cambridge mounted a production of Sophocles' *Ajax* in the original Greek in 1882 [24], the occasion marked the inauguration of the Cambridge Greek Play – a tradition which continues to this day. The early Cambridge productions were closely associated with the study of classical archaeology, and so extreme care and attention were devoted to the construction of the sets.[14] The Cambridge Greek Play became – as was to be the case with Bradfield some years later – an important event in the calendar for those in the professional theatre who were planning to bring Greek drama to the commercial stage. But however successful the staging, it was the music, in particular, which seems to have attracted wide publicity, and to have drawn the crowds from London in the special trains that the Great Northern Railway Company laid on from King's Cross.[15]

The productions in British and American universities established a trend throughout the English-speaking academic world, with the University of Sydney following suit when it staged the *Agamemnon* in 1886. The Edinburgh, Oxford, and Cambridge productions, however, were not simply isolated, academic experiments: they were both a cause and a symptom of a rush of philhellenism that was particularly marked in Britain towards the end of the nineteenth century.

In 1883 a private production of George Warr's *Tale of Troy, or Scenes and Tableaux from Homer* was staged over four evenings in both Greek and English in the Odeon of Cromwell House in London. This seemingly marginal event was of sufficient importance to attract the Prime Minister, William Gladstone, to one of its Greek performances. It illustrates, more-

---

[13] Hartigan (1995) 9–10.   [14] Easterling (1984b) 90–1.   [15] Easterling (1984b) 91–2.

[24] The first chorus of *Ajax*, from the first Cambridge Greek play in 1882.

over, the extent to which academic and what might be termed 'social' philhellenism coalesced at this time. As Professor of Classics at King's College, London, Warr was particularly committed to the higher education of women, and the *Tale of Troy* was staged to raise funds for the foundation of the Women's Department at the College.[16] With a cast that included Sir Herbert and Mrs Beerbohm Tree, Mrs Andrew Lang and Jane Harrison, and set designs by Lord Leighton, Sir E. Poynter, Walter Crane and Henry Holiday, Warr's Greek play became a major cultural and social event. Furthermore, had the original proposal to perform in King's College itself not been scotched by the Council's prohibition against women acting, the tradition of King's annual Greek play (dating from 1953) would have had a particularly illustrious ancestry.[17]

In May of 1886 Warr's highly condensed version of the *Oresteia* was staged at the Prince's Hall in Piccadilly. In the same week John Todhunter's imitation of a Greek tragedy entitled *Helena in Troas* opened at Hengler's Circus, causing one drama critic to assert: 'Since the year 1845, when the "Antigone" was played, London has seldom been so Greek before.'[18] The production of Todhunter's play is important not simply as another illustration of the general philhellenic tendency; what it added to the growing understanding of Greek drama was an authentic performance space. In Hengler's Circus, in Argyll Street, the late E. W. Godwin had designed a Greek theatre with a raised *skēnē* (according to the Vitruvian model which was to prevail until the publication of Dörpfeld and Reisch's discoveries in 1896), an *orchēstra* with a *thumelē* in the middle, and tiered seats for the audience; and the proceeds of the performances significantly went to the newly established British School of Archaeology in Athens. That we have to wait for the next generation – for the theatrical ideas of Godwin's son, Gordon Craig, for example – for a complete departure from the confines of the proscenium stage, however, is best illustrated by the fact that London's 'Greek theatre' in 1886 had curtains draped round the front of the *skēnē* building [25].

OEDIPUS AND THE EDWARDIAN SUMMER

Other contradictions formed a part of this *fin de siècle* philhellenism in Britain. In 1887 Sophocles' *Oedipus the King* was performed at Cambridge

---

[16] Hearnshaw (1929) 318.
[17] The King's annual play in Greek is now part of the London Festival of Greek Drama which began in 1988, and includes a play in translation by University College's Classical Society and lectures and workshops at the British Museum and elsewhere.
[18] The *Daily Telegraph*, 18 May 1886.

[25] *Helena in Troas* at Hengler's Circus, London, 1886. From *The Graphic*, 5 June 1886.

in the original Greek; but, despite the Cambridge precedent, a professional production of Sophocles' play was not permissible at this time in Britain. If New York audiences had been offended by the crushing blows inflicted on the hero of Sophocles' tragedy, members of the British establishment were convinced, in the words of a leading actor-manager of the time, that granting a licence for *Oedipus the King* might 'prove injurious' and 'lead to a great number of plays being written ... appealing to a vitiated public taste solely in the cause of indecency'.[19] That the Lord Chamberlain's Office had reduced the Sophoclean original to a play about incest *tout court* is clear from the official correspondence, where it is explained that a new version of Sophocles' play would most probably fall foul of the censor 'on the ground that it [is] ... impossible to put on the stage in England a play dealing with incest'.[20]

The linking of *Oedipus the King* to Shelley's controversial play involving incest and parricide, *The Cenci*, when it received its first staging in 1886 (some seventy years after it was written) meant that Sophocles' play became

---

[19] Sir John Hare, Member of the Advisory Board on Stage Plays, in a letter to the Lord Chamberlain, November 1910. Lord Chamberlain's Plays Correspondence File: *Oedipus Rex* 1910/814 (British Library).

[20] Letter from Douglas Dawson to Sir Edward Carson, 11 November 1910. Lord Chamberlain's Plays Correspondence File: *Oedipus Rex* 1910/814 (British Library).

embroiled in the campaign to abolish theatre censorship in Britain that was gathering momentum at this time. And from 1886 until 1910, when *Oedipus the King* was finally granted a licence after much public pressure (*The Cenci* had to wait until 1922 to receive a licence), the fates of the two plays are inextricably linked, and they feature prominently in almost every important debate concerning theatrical censorship. By 1909 when the playwright Henry Arthur Jones issued his vitriolic pamphlet against the Censor, Sophocles and Shelley had become bywords for the absurdity of the licensing system. Jones concludes: 'Thus the rule of Censorship is "Gag Shelley! Gag Sophocles! License Mr Smellfilth! License Mr Slangwheezy!" '[21]

As efforts had been made to stage Shelley's play, attempts were similarly under way to stage *Oedipus the King* in London. The first attempt seems initially, at least, to have been unrelated to any political campaigning. In 1904 the distinguished actor-manager, Sir Herbert Beerbohm Tree, who had taken part in both Warr's and Todhunter's plays, was sufficiently inspired by Mounet-Sully's performance in the role of Oedipus in the version of Jules Lacroix to make an informal inquiry to the Lord Chamberlain's Office about the possibility of staging the play in London. Tree was told that a London performance was impossible.[22]

Tree's informal inquiry led to a flurry of activity. W. B. Yeats had heard about the production of *Oedipus the King* at the University of Notre Dame, and now, learning about the British proscription, was determined to stage Sophocles' play at the Abbey Theatre in Dublin shortly after it opened at the end of the year. The Lord Chamberlain's Office had no jurisdiction in Dublin; and it was recognised by the founders of the Abbey that there could be no more effective beginning to a national theatre's career than to stage a play which would enable the theatre to go down in history as the champion of intellectual freedom – Ireland would liberate the classics from English tyranny. Almost immediately Yeats wrote to Gilbert Murray – who had recently resigned the Chair of Greek at the University of Glasgow on the grounds of ill health – asking him to write a translation of Sophocles' play for the newly founded Irish theatre.[23] Murray had already seen his translation of Euripides' *Hippolytus* being successfully performed in two London theatres in 1904, but he declined Yeats' invitation to turn his hand to

[21] Henry Arthur Jones' pamphlet, written in the form of a letter to Herbert Samuel, Chairman of the Joint Select Committee on Censorship and Licensing, is reprinted in *Censorship and Licensing (Joint Select Committee) Verbatim Report of the Proceedings and Full Text of the Recommendations* (London 1909).

[22] *Censorship and Licensing* (1909) 74.

[23] 24 January 1905 in the Bodleian Library, reprinted in Clark & McGuire (1989) 8–9.

Sophocles' *Oedipus the King*.[24] But not only did Yeats still have to search for a suitable version of the play, he also had to contend with the fact that plans in London to mount a production looked as if they would upstage those at the Abbey.[25] And it was not until 1926, after Yeats had completed his own version, that the Abbey Theatre finally staged Sophocles' *Oedipus the King*.

Mounet-Sully's performance as Oedipus had also made a deep impression on the actor-manager John Martin-Harvey. Harvey invited W. L. Courtney, who had appeared in the Oxford production of the *Agamemnon* and was now drama critic of the *Daily Telegraph*, to write a free version of *Oedipus the King*.[26] Courtney's free version of Sophocles' tragedy was refused a licence, and so significant was the ban that the rejected play was submitted as evidence before the Joint Select Committee on Censorship in 1909, where its presence guaranteed that a high profile was granted to Greek tragedy in general and Sophocles' play in particular throughout the proceedings of the Committee. Robert Harcourt, the Member of Parliament who had introduced the Theatres and Music Halls Bill designed to abolish censorship, was determined to keep the Sophoclean scandal at the forefront of the Committee's concerns. When the 500,000-word report on the Committee's findings and recommendations appeared in November 1909, the frequency with which references to Sophocles' play occurred made it inevitable that a production would be mounted in London before long.

Two leading theatre managers were indeed planning to stage *Oedipus the King* by the middle of 1910.[27] Sir Herbert Tree, undeterred by the previously negative response of the Examiner of Plays, was again hoping to mount a production at His Majesty's Theatre. And Herbert Trench, the new Manager of the Theatre Royal in the Haymarket, had approached Murray for his almost completed translation of Sophocles' play.[28] Murray's involvement in the 1909 campaign had undoubtedly led him to a temporary rejection of Euripides in favour of a translation of Sophocles' now notorious tragedy. Murray had clearly been particularly concerned on first hearing of the ban from Yeats' letter in 1905 and had replied: 'I am really distressed that the Censor objected to it. It ought to be played not perhaps at His Majesty's by Tree, but by Irving at the Lyceum, with a lecture before ... and after. And a public dinner. With speeches. By Cabinet Ministers.'[29] The

---

[24] 27 January 1905 in Finneran, Mill Harper & Murphy (edd.) (1977) 145–6.
[25] Clark & McGuire (1989) 17–18.   [26] Martin-Harvey (1933) 391–403.
[27] See the correspondence between Granville-Barker and Gilbert Murray in Purdom (1955) 99–102.
[28] See Murray to Granville-Barker, 6 August 1910 in Purdom (1955) 112.
[29] 27 January 1905 in Finneran et al. (1977) 145.

banning of such a significant play, according to Murray, should be taken to the heart of the British establishment; and there was no person better equipped to do that than the man who was now Regius Professor of Greek at Oxford.

When Trench sent Murray's translation to the Lord Chamberlain's Office, the Examiner of Plays added the significant *caveat* in his correspondence with the Lord Chamberlain that 'Mr Trench and Dr Gilbert Murray are opponents of the office, and no doubt desire to make capital out of a prohibition of an ancient Greek classic so familiar to every school boy etc. etc.'[30] The *caveat* was clearly heeded because the play was placed under review; and Murray's translation was granted the dubious distinction of being the first play to be referred to the newly appointed Advisory Board.[31] The members of the Board felt that a ban would be hard to sustain in the face of mounting public pressure, and Murray's translation of Sophocles' play, entitled *Oedipus, King of Thebes*, was finally granted a licence on 29 November 1910. Not only had the greatest barrier to a performance of Sophocles' play now been removed, but news from Germany of an exciting new production of *Oedipus the King* in the Zirkus Schumann in Berlin by the celebrated Austrian theatre director Max Reinhardt provided an even greater impetus to the British campaign.

Reinhardt's *Oedipus Rex* in Hugo von Hofmannsthal's version had opened at the Musikfesthalle in Munich in September 1910. It was not Reinhardt's first attempt at staging a Greek play – he had turned his considerable talents to the *Medea* with mixed fortune in 1904, and to Aristophanes' *Lysistrata* with great success in 1908 – but it remained his outstanding achievement, and secured his status as Europe's leading theatre director at the beginning of the twentieth century. Reinhardt was already renowned for his direction of crowd scenes, but in the *Oedipus Rex* he put those skills to a severe test by directing a crowd of three hundred extras who represented the citizens of Thebes, together with a chorus of twenty-seven Theban Elders (there were fewer members of the chorus in the London production). But it is misleading to focus on the monumental aspects of the production because the naturalistic acting was particularly noteworthy – Reinhardt himself had trained at the Deutsches Theater under the so-called father of stage naturalism, Otto Brahm; and Hofmannsthal's version, no

---

[30] Letter from Redford to Lord Spencer 10 November 1910. Lord Chamberlain's Plays Correspondence File: *Oedipus Rex* 1910/814 (British Library).

[31] Letter from Dawson to Redford 11 November 1910; and from Dawson to Sir Edward Carson 11 November 1910. Lord Chamberlain's Plays Correspondence File: *Oedipus Rex* 1910/814 (British Library).

less than the version of Jules Lacroix, focused on the individual suffering of Oedipus.

There were three performance levels in Reinhardt's production – the space at the front of the auditorium for the crowd, the palace steps for the chorus and the front of the palace itself for the actors – and the infringements of those separate performance levels at points of high tension were particularly noteworthy. Most striking was the opening of the play, which broke with the conventional relationship between performers and spectators absolutely when the vast crowd surged through the darkened auditorium, reminding the *Times* critic of 'some huge living organism'.[32] A murky blue light broke through the darkness, partially revealing the chanting, groaning crowd; and after a strong yellow light had been cast over the altar and steps, the entry of Oedipus from the central doors, dressed in a brilliant white gown, was captured in spotlight. If the Mounet-Sully production had downplayed the Theban context in order to highlight the sufferings of Oedipus in his relations with the gods, Reinhardt's Nietzschean-inspired production emphasised the extent to which those individual (Apolline) sufferings had to be seen against a background of the general (Dionysiac) suffering of the Chorus. The highly spectacular (Nietzschean in spirit and strictly non-Sophoclean) ending, when Oedipus made his cathartic exit from Thebes groping his way through the audience, was deemed so effective that it led some members of the audience to avert their gaze as he passed them by. Certainly, there were aspects of the staging that came in for criticism – most notably the dumb show that surrounded the messenger-speech – but few who saw the production failed to be impressed by the sheer scale and grandeur of the formal patterns of movement.[33]

The attention of British directors, actors, and theatrical impresarios alike towards the end of 1910 was fixed on this Reinhardt production which went on to be produced in almost every major European city over the next few years. In October 1910, the British producer Harley Granville-Barker went to Berlin to see the production shortly after it had transferred from Munich, and wrote enthusiastically to Murray about what he had seen.[34] Murray was frustrated by Herbert Trench's dilatoriness at the Haymarket Theatre, which meant that the chances of a production there looked increasingly remote.[35] Reinhardt's emissary, Ordynski, came to London in mid-February 1911, saying that Reinhardt himself wanted to stage a London production using Murray's translation.[36] The plans for a London

[32] *The Times*, 16 January 1912.
[33] For the production's reception in Germany, see Beacham in Walton (1987) 309–10.
[34] Granville-Barker to Murray in Purdom (1954) 114–15.   [35] Purdom (1954) 116.
[36] Wilson (1987) 165.

[26] Max Reinhardt's production of *Oedipus Rex* at Covent Garden in 1912.

production at the Kingsway Theatre in 1911 fell through with the death of the financier, but by the end of July there were firm plans for a production of the *Oedipus Rex* in January 1912 at Covent Garden, with Martin-Harvey in the leading role and Granville-Barker's wife Lillah McCarthy as Jocasta. In order to incorporate the interpolations of the Hofmannsthal version, Murray's translation had to be slightly adapted by Courtney; and in order to accommodate the vast crowd, a number of rows of seats had to be removed from the stalls in the Theatre Royal, Covent Garden [26].

When the production opened it was hailed as 'the first performance of the play in England since the seventeenth century',[37] a clear allusion to Dryden and Lee's *Oedipus* written in 1679. Despite the highly exaggerated nature of this claim – it ignores, for example, all eighteenth-century revivals of the Dryden and Lee play, as well as the Cambridge Greek production of 1887 – it is not without some foundation. English audiences were overwhelmed by what they saw, and although certain aspects of the production came in for criticism, the performances of Martin-Harvey and Lillah McCarthy were unanimously praised; and Martin-Harvey continued to tour with the play for many years after the event, winning for himself the same distinction as his hero Mounet-Sully of being a truly great Oedipus.

Amongst the criticisms levelled at the production was that audiences were being offered undiluted Reinhardt rather than pure Sophocles, and this particular barb led Gilbert Murray to make a spirited defence of Reinhardt and his production in a letter to *The Times* on 23 January 1912:

> After all Professor Reinhardt knows ten times as much about the theatre as I do. His production has proved itself: it stands on its own feet, something vital, magnificent, unforgettable. And who knows if the more Hellenic production I dream of would be any of these?[38]

Sadly, the *Oedipus Rex* was the only production of a Greek tragedy that Reinhardt was able to render 'magnificent, unforgettable'. The *Oresteia* that he directed in the translation of Karl Volmoeller at the Munich Musik-festhalle in 1911 – which failed to include the *Eumenides* when it transferred to Berlin – was unable to capture the audiences' imaginations because the *Oedipus* model was followed too rigidly and too soon. Even when Reinhardt revived the production in 1919 in the Grosses Schauspielhaus that was built on the site of the Zirkus Schumann, the production was not a success – this time because the monumentality of the stage architecture dwarfed the actors.

---

[37] A copy of the programme is in the Production File to the *Oedipus Rex* in The Theatre Museum, Covent Garden. The note was written by F. B. O'Neill.

[38] *The Times*, 23 January 1912.

TRAGEDY AND THE WORLD CRISIS

Despite, or even because of, the domineering presence of Europe's first modern theatre director, it is important not to overlook Murray's own contribution to the 1912 *Oedipus Rex* – both to the events leading up to the production and to the production itself. Not only had Murray taken an active part in the campaign against censorship, it is also largely on his account that Greek tragedy did not remain the exclusive preserve of the private theatres in the English-speaking world. Murray's translations of Euripides' plays had already been produced with some success by Granville-Barker in the professional theatre – *Hippolytus, Trojan Women, Electra* and *Bacchae* (the latter being directed by William Poel) had been staged at the Royal Court Theatre between 1904 and 1908, and the *Medea* at the Savoy Theatre in 1907. As Murray's letter to the *Times* reveals, he felt honoured to have been associated with the Reinhardt production, even though Reinhardt's ideas about Greek tragedy differed so markedly from his own.

Murray had always argued for the primacy of the word in the staging of Greek tragedy, and so it was inevitable that some of the 'stage business' of the Reinhardt production should not have been to his taste. But it was nothing new for Murray to find that his translation was to be used in a production that was not entirely to his liking; and it was the handling of the chorus that usually troubled him the most, where his own preference was for a speaking, rather than a singing chorus. Murray had already had reservations, for example, about the experiments with the Chorus in the *Bacchae* at the Royal Court Theatre, where Florence Farr as Choral Leader chanted to the psaltery; and he felt that the Hebridean antiphonal chants used by Lewis Casson in his production of the *Trojan Women* at the Gaiety Theatre in Manchester should probably have been avoided altogether in favour of the spoken word. But when Granville-Barker's (otherwise Reinhardt-inspired) production of the *Iphigenia in Tauris* opened at the Kingsway Theatre in March 1912, the handling of the Chorus was much more in line with his thinking, with individual, as well as unison, chanting being combined with spoken recitative [27].[39]

Despite Murray's own misgivings about the Manchester production of the *Trojan Women*, however, it is probably his translation of this Euripidean play that was the most widely performed and became the most popular as events in Europe made it increasingly topical. In 1915 Maurice Browne of the Chicago Little Theatre took the *Trojan Women* in Murray's

[39] See Kennedy (1985) 118–22 for details of the production.

[27] Lillah McCarthy as Iphigeneia at the Kingsway Theatre, London, in 1912.

translation across the midwest of the United States on a tour sponsored by the Women's Peace Party. Murray did not want it to be inferred from his co-operation with the tour that he advocated peace with Germany on any terms; but he hoped that the British would 'scrutinize earnestly, though I hope generously, the proposed terms of Peace'.[40] The same year Barker took the *Trojan Women* and the *Iphigenia in Tauris* on a tour to America.

[40] Cited by Thorndike (1960) 163 n. 1.

The *Trojan Women* was performed in the open air at Harvard, Princeton, the University of Pennsylvania, and at the College of the City of New York, and it became the first professional production of a Greek play in America to be critically acclaimed. With Lillah McCarthy (who had played Jocasta in the London production of *Oedipus Rex*) as Hecuba and a chorus that chanted to music, which had been especially composed for the tour by Professor David Stanley of Yale University, the play was considered to emerge 'living, with the glory of a drama that has never, at any time, been dead'.[41]

So clearly could Euripides' play articulate the concerns of the war-weary western world that it was decided in 1919, when the Versailles negotiations were taking place, to mount a production in a cinema in the Cowley Road in Oxford (directed by Lewis Casson) to coincide with the Oxford Conference of the League of Nations. And in the immediate post-war period, there were a number of matinée performances of the play at the Old Vic, where the spirit of despair of the Trojan women struck a deep chord in the war-torn nation's psyche. There was also one performance at the Alhambra Theatre in 1920 to mark the formation of the League of Nations Union, over which Murray himself presided as chairman. When the playwright was called for at the end of the performance, Murray rose from his seat and exclaimed: 'The Author is not here, he has been dead for many centuries, but I am sure that he will be gratified by your reception of his great tragedy.'[42] However much it became fashionable later to follow T. S. Eliot in his famous dismissal of Murray's Swinburnian language,[43] the episode neatly conveys the ethos of Murray and an aspect of his work that should not be forgotten: he was a great communicator, and it was through his efforts that Greek tragedy became accessible, and above all alive, to the English-speaking world for the first time.

By the 1920s, however, the style of Murray's translations was indeed outmoded; and when Yeats completed his own version of Sophocles' *King Oedipus* in 1926, it superseded Murray's as the popular translation for performance. Yeats' translation is eminently speakable, but it also radically departs from the original in certain respects, notably in its rendering of Oedipus into the isolated modern tragic hero. But it was not simply Yeats' own concerns that dictated this transformation; the restricted space at the Abbey Theatre where it was first performed on 7 December 1926 meant that a chorus of six Theban Elders alone could be accommodated in the narrow area usually reserved for the orchestra. When Yeats' version of

---

[41] *New York Mirror*, 2 June 1915 cited by Hartigan (1995) 16.
[42] Cited by Thorndike (1960) 166.   [43] Eliot (1951) 59–64.

Oedipus at Colonus was staged in 1927, there was an even greater decline in the role of the chorus and for broadly similar reasons.

The productions of Greek drama that emanated from the Cambridge Festival Theatre at about this time, however, had no such constraints in terms of stage space. Terence Gray's Festival Theatre was the first permanent indoor theatre to be based on a Greek theatre. Gray was heavily influenced by Reinhardt's English counterpart, Gordon Craig, and when the theatre opened with a production of the *Oresteia* on 22 November 1926 the set consisted of a series of Craig-style screens and rostra. The choreography was by the distinguished Irish dancer Ninette de Valois, who had trained with the Ballets Russes and was shortly to go and work with Yeats at the Abbey (and much later, of course, was to go on to found the Royal Ballet). Though often dismissed as a dilettante, Gray should be remembered as the first director to show the English-speaking theatre how masks and highly stylised sets and costumes could be combined with formal patterns of movement to intensify the effect of Greek tragedy in performance. Moreover, his commitment to performing Greek drama did not stop with the *Oresteia*; over the next seven years, he produced two Aristophanic comedies and five other Greek tragedies – most notably mounting the first English production of Aeschylus' *Suppliant Women* in February 1933.

Whilst Gray sought to re-create the experience of Greek theatre through production style and stage architecture at his Festival Theatre, he also hoped 'ultimately to make Cambridge the centre of an annual dramatic festival'.[44] There were a number of other serious attempts elsewhere in Europe during the inter-war period to mount genuine festivals of theatre along the lines of the fifth-century Athenians. A highly significant experiment occurred in Greece in the 1920s, when the apparent failure of the League of Nations led the poet Angelos Sikelianos and his American wife Eva Palmer to plan an international gathering of intellectuals at Delphi with the aim of working towards world peace. The first cultural festival took place in 1927, after some three years' preparations, with a genuinely broad programme of events. The festival included sport, folk-dancing and demonstrations of weaving and other popular arts and crafts, as well as a lecture by the distinguished classical archaeologist, Wilhelm Dörpfeld, and a production of the *Prometheus Bound* directed by Eva Palmer with music by K. Psachos. Over one thousand spectators watched the performance, which was an attempt to re-create the ancient Greek theatre through extensive archaising, with the costumes and movements of the Chorus being taken directly from vase-paintings. Eva Palmer's earlier tutelage at the hands of

---

[44] *Cambridge Chronicle and University Journal*, 21 April 1926, 3.

Isadora Duncan meant that the choreography had a distinctly modern feel despite the near-geometric formations. But there was no attempt to re-create the fifth-century *skēnē*, with the vast rock upon which Prometheus was pinioned owing more to the monumental sets of early Hollywood epics than to any ancient Greek precedent.

In 1930 another festival was organised by Sikelianos and his wife with the help of wealthy benefactors and a state grant, which included a revival of *Prometheus Bound* (with a considerably diminished set) [28] and a new production of Aeschylus' *Suppliant Women*, again under the direction of Eva Palmer and with music by Psachos. But on this occasion popular tastes seem to have changed and audiences were left puzzled and alienated by the archaising tendencies. In some quarters, aesthetic tendencies were deemed inseparable from political preferences, and the festival was vilified as the cultural expression of a reactionary elite. But it was financial constraint rather than political pressure that prevented any further attempts to revive the ancient Delphic Festival. However short-lived, the memory of the festivals none the less persists with the recent annual symposia of the European Culture Centre of Delphi (that were most successful during the 1980s) clearly taking their cues from Sikelianos and his experiment.

The longest-running of these festivals, however, is the Festival at Syracuse which flourished in the inter-war period and continues to this day. It began in the spring of 1914, when Count Mario Tomas Gargallo decided to organise a production of the *Agamemnon* on the grounds that tradition maintained that Aeschylus himself had staged his plays in Syracuse. The director was Ettore Romagnoli and the designer Duilio Cambelotti, and together with the composer Giuseppe Mule who joined them in 1921 (when the second festival took place), they worked for the next twenty-five years staging Greek plays in Italian translations on the first professional outdoor stage in the ancient theatre at Syracuse.

At first the production styles were largely inspired by archaeological evidence, but in time innovative stage techniques from the indoor theatre were adopted. The festival, however, soon became a useful tool in Mussolini's propaganda machine; and after the success of the *Seven Against Thebes* and the *Antigone* in 1924, it was put under the 'National Institute for Ancient Drama', which became an official government organ of the Ministry of Education in 1929 and came under the Ministry of Propaganda in 1935. From the late 1920s onwards the productions inevitably sought to reflect and promote military and imperial values; and at the last festival before the war in 1939, Sophocles' *Ajax* was played out against a vast teutonic set by Pietro Aschieri chillingly reminiscent of Nuremberg's stadium.

[28] *Prometheus Bound* performed at the Delphic Festival in 1930.

But Syracuse does not appear to have mounted any production to rival the blatantly Nazi production of the *Oresteia* in the State Theatre, Gendarmenmarkt, in Berlin (1936), which was directed by Lothal Müthel, during the Olympic Games. In the Berlin production, it was not simply military and imperial prowess that was extolled; Wilamowitz's translation – Wilamowitz himself had died in 1931 – was so seriously distorted that Aeschylus' play about the path towards an enlightened democracy was reduced to a struggle between the Aryans and the *Untermenschen*. It may well be because Syracuse never produced such grotesque distortions that it was able to rid itself successfully of its sordid pre-war associations in the post-war period. The success of the Festival at Syracuse can be measured both by its longevity and the size of its audiences: it continues to stage two Greek plays every second year over a 2–3 week run, attracting as many as eighty thousand spectators over the festival period.

That Paris during the inter-war period became the site of at least one attempt to create an Athenian-style festival is hardly surprising. For it was here, above all, that Greek tragedy was to yield the most promising material for the avant-garde adaptations of Cocteau, Gide and Giraudoux in the 1920s and 1930s. In 1919 a monumental production of *Oedipe, roi de Thèbes*, in a version by Saint-Georges de Bouhélier, was mounted by the actor and director Firmin Gémier at the Cirque d'Hiver in Paris. Both the scope and setting owed much to the Reinhardt example of 1910, but Gémier's decision to accompany the tragedy with athletic displays by some two hundred athletes was part of his own long-cherished vision of creating a genuinely popular theatre. Inspired by ancient precedent, where athletic and literary prowess could be celebrated at one and the same time, Gémier realised that by seeking to re-create the aesthetic conditions of the Athenian theatre, he could also go some way towards replicating its mixed social base: the Cirque d'Hiver could attract audiences that the proscenium Parisian theatre could never hope to court.

Gémier's experiment was not repeated, and it was not until 1936, when 'le groupe de théâtre antique de la Sorbonne' performed Aeschylus' *Persians* in the courtyard of the University, that a revival of a Greek tragedy made a similar impact in France. The production toured the provinces in the summer of 1936 and was seen in Belgium and Greece the following year, where the play's topicality (the defence of a nation against a more powerful aggressor) guaranteed its popularity.[45]

Festivals continued to be founded after the war as well. The most significant of these occurred in Greece, with the foundation of the Festival

[45] Burgaud (1984) 78.

of Ancient Greek Drama at Epidaurus in 1954, followed by the Festival in Athens at the Herodes Atticus Theatre the following year. The festivals were launched by the director Dimitris Rondiris, who had been a pupil of Max Reinhardt. Reinhardt's influence on Rondiris was particularly noticeable in his ensemble productions where the chorus functioned as a closely knit group with recitation rather than dialogue as the preferred mode of delivery. But however strong an influence German and French theatrical traditions have exerted on the revivals of tragedy in Greece, it is equally important not to overstate that influence and deflect from the contribution of popular native traditions. It is, moreover, choral performances in modern Greek productions that have been most instructive to directors from the rest of Europe; and here, it is modern Greek rituals (rather than Reinhardt) that are understood to inform those performances. When London audiences were able to enjoy the Theatro Technis production of Aeschylus' *Persians* directed by Karolos Koun at the Aldwych Theatre in 1965, for example, it was the chorus that was a revelation to those who had come to conceive of the Greek tragic chorus as an archaic encumbrance.[46]

TOWARDS AN INTERNATIONAL STAGE

Immediately after the war, *Oedipus the King* again became the Greek tragedy most responsive to current concerns and needs. At the Deutsches Theater in Berlin at the end of 1946, under the direction of Karl Heinz Stroux and in the translation of Heinrich Weinstock, the play reflected the contemporary questions of guilt and responsibility. In marked contrast, the London production at the Old Vic in 1945 (in the same month that the war ended) used the Yeats translation to highlight the sufferings of an isolated tragic hero [29]. To counter the bleakness of the Sophoclean ending, the *Oedipus* was staged as part of a double bill with Sheridan's *The Critic*. It is hardly surprising that this odd collocation of Athenian tragedy and Restoration comedy did not yield much praise, except for the actors, whose versatility was put to a severe test. Directed by Michel Saint-Denis, with Laurence Olivier in the part of Oedipus and Sybil Thorndike as Jocasta, the only aspect of the production to receive unanimous acclaim was the performance of Olivier himself, whose rendering of Oedipus' two cries on discovering the truth about himself has gone down in the annals of British theatre history – Oedipus' piercing cries can be seen as the forerunners of the Beckettian scream.

---

[46] E.g. the *Sunday Telegraph*, 25 April 1965; the *Daily Mail*, 21 April 1965; *The Times*, 21 April 1965.

[29] Laurence Olivier (with Chorus) as Oedipus in the Old Vic production of *Oedipus Rex*
in 1945.

The Irish director Tyrone Guthrie had originally recommended the Yeats
version to Saint-Denis, and Guthrie used it himself when he mounted his
own production of the *Oedipus Rex* in 1955 at the New Shakespeare
Festival in Stratford, Ontario [30]. Guthrie's production, initially intended
as a minor event, was the highlight of the Festival. His conception of an
Oedipus who has attained mythopoeic status is clearly indebted to Yeats'
own ideas about the Greek hero. In Guthrie's production, Oedipus had

[30] Douglas Campbell as Oedipus in the Stratford (Ontario) Festival's production of *Oedipus Rex* directed by Tyrone Guthrie in 1955.

ceased to be a man; instead, he was the Freudian symbol that the early twentieth century had made of him, and his larger-than-life golden mask (designed by Tanya Moisewitsch) served to reinforce that status. Guthrie's adaptation of the *Oresteia*, *The House of Atreus*, in 1966 was equally monumental. Even if many theatre critics deplored Guthrie's textual and conceptual infidelities when it toured the United States in the late 1960s, the production consolidated Guthrie's reputation as the first major interpreter of the Greek tragedies in North America – a distinction which the Guthrie Theater in Minneapolis appears to commemorate with a production of a Greek tragedy each decade since its inauguration.[47]

Guthrie's production of *Oedipus Rex*, in particular, remains significant not least because it marks a watershed in the history of revivals of Greek tragedy. Before the 1950s, the main centres for professional productions were all in Europe (in Germany, France, Britain, Italy and Greece in

---

[47] Guthrie's second production of the *Oedipus Rex* in 1972 (in Anthony Burgess's translation) was mounted just after his death at the Guthrie Theater, Minneapolis. *The Bacchae* was produced at the theatre in 1984, *Medea* in 1991 and the 'Clytemnestra Project' in 1992.

particular), with only tours and College productions providing the opportunity to see Greek tragedies elsewhere. Since the Second World War, however, the interest in Greek tragedy has become a world-wide phenomenon. The enormously popular adaptation of *Medea* by Robinson Jeffers that opened in October 1947 in New York and ran for 214 performances over three years is another example of the increasingly international nature of Greek revivals: although it was a star vehicle for the Australian-born actress Judith Anderson, and although the English actor John Gielgud was both Jason and director at the beginning of the run, the Jeffers *Medea* was the first American-born production of a Greek tragedy to be brought to Europe when it went on tour in 1951. However, it is Guthrie's *Oedipus Rex* that may be said, in retrospect, to have provided the most significant turning-point: like the Gielgud/Anderson *Medea*, as a North American production by a European theatre director it stands at the crossroads; but when it became the first major production of a Greek tragedy to be recorded on film in 1956, it guaranteed that Greek tragedy's strictly European ties would be loosened indefinitely (see Ch. 10 above, pp. 277–81).

It is undoubtedly the post-war Japanese productions that celebrate this internationalism most fruitfully. The student productions mounted at Tokyo University during the late 1950s and 1960s were directly informed by Japan's war experiences. Parallels between Greek and Noh drama had been traced as far back as the late nineteenth century, when the American orientalist Ernest Fenollosa began his study of Noh plays, which Ezra Pound was to edit in 1916. These Greek and Noh parallels were then successfully explored by Yeats in his cycle of Dance Plays at the Abbey Theatre from 1914 onwards.[48] Europeans in search of an alternative to Western stage naturalism delighted in these parallels; but to the Japanese at this stage they were of little concern. Following the Second World War, however, a generation of students at Tokyo University turned deliberately towards Greek tragedy as the fountainhead of the Western humanist tradition, in their search for the values of freedom and democracy (tinged with Marx and Weber) that had eluded their own culture.[49] They performed a number of Greek tragedies in translation in front of large audiences, and formally cemented, from an Eastern perspective, those ties that Fenollosa himself first detected.

Even if the political concerns of those early student productions have not been widely shared in the affluent climate of the following decades, the

[48] Taylor (1976); Macintosh (1994) 62–3.
[49] I am indebted to Pat Easterling for allowing me to see her correspondence with Shigenari Kawashima (Professor of Greek, International Christian University in Tokyo), who himself performed in the student productions in the 1960s.

aesthetic affinities between the Japanese performance traditions of Noh and Kabuki and those of Greek drama have guaranteed the continuing interest in the Greek plays.[50] In Tadashi Suzuki's Noh- and Kabuki-inspired adaptations, the traditional Japanese view of the creative role of the actor is given priority over the (modern Western) notion of the primacy of the text. The result is that deviations from the Greek originals abound in Suzuki's versions, and that the performance text itself is not fixed. In the case of the *Bacchae*, which was first seen in Tokyo in 1978, there are numerous versions. In his *Trojan Women* (first seen in Tokyo in 1974) – in which the Trojan victims represent the Japanese at the hands of overweening, merciless American victors at the end of the Second World War – Andromache is raped before the audience's eyes, and Astyanax, represented by a doll, is killed by sword on-stage. In 1982 Suzuki organised the first of his annual international theatre festivals which are held in his open-air Toga Theatre modelled on Greek lines, in the mountain village of Togamura. And when Suzuki was invited to perform his *Trojan Women* at the Los Angeles Olympic Games in 1984, his international reputation was confirmed.

The other distinguished Japanese director to have successfully illuminated Greek tragedy for Western audiences is Yukio Ninagawa, whose all-male production of *Medea* (which was first seen in Tokyo in 1978) remained, by contrast with Suzuki's adaptations, remarkably faithful to Euripides' text. Ninagawa's production showed the extent to which a chorus trained in Kabuki dance techniques could amplify the emotional range of the action. When the Toho Company (later known as the Ninagawa Company) performed Euripides' *Medea* in the Courtyard of the Old College of the University of Edinburgh during the Festival in 1986 – at a time when the *Medea* was enjoying a number of feminist and anti-racist revivals in London[51] – it was the mystical and irrational dimensions to the play that the Japanese production emphasised.

A chorus of sixteen members, in blue-black cloaks and wide-brimmed hats with veils, entered in groups of four from both sides of the Courtyard vigorously plucking the strings of their shamisens and intersecting along the diagonals of the orchestra. At moments of high tension, they tossed back their cloaks to reveal a vibrant red lining, sometimes wheeling around Medea, sometimes surging towards the doors of the house with astonishing

---

[50] See the full-length comparative study by Smethurst (1989).
[51] In 1986 there were three productions of the *Medea* in London: Gate Theatre (trans. D. Wiles, dir. Marina Caldarone) in March; Theatre Clwyd at the Young Vic (trans. J. Brooke, dir. Toby Robertson) in April, with a white woman exiled among blacks; Lyric, Hammersmith (trans. P. Vellacott, dir. Mary McMurray) from May to July, with Madhur Jaffrey as Medea.

[31] Yukio Ninagawa's *Medea* with Tokusaburo Arashi in the title role.

rapidity. The most powerful moment of the Edinburgh production, however, occurred at the end of the play, when the terrifying figure of Medea in her golden chariot drawn by dragons loomed out of the night sky above the roof of the neoclassical building. It is doubtful whether Medea had ever received such an astonishing apotheosis before; and when the production was staged indoors at the National Theatre in September 1987 [31], it became obvious that the Edinburgh finale was unlikely to be matched again.

That audiences should have turned out in their thousands in Edinburgh in 1986 to see an open-air production of a Greek tragedy being performed in Japanese was not as surprising as it may first appear. At the very beginning of the 1980s, there had been a sharp change in attitudes towards revivals of Greek plays in Western Europe. Indeed, during the last fifteen or so years Greek tragedies have been performed with such increasing regularity (both in amateur and professional productions) around the world that it becomes impossible to give anything like a comprehensive survey.

It was undoubtedly the three professional productions of the *Oresteia* between 1980 and 1982 by the influential directors Karolos Koun, Peter Hall and Peter Stein that proved the turning-point in the new trend towards regular, and international, revivals of Greek tragedy. Some eighteen months after John Barton's hugely popular cycle of Greek myth drawn from Homer and nine Greek tragedies entitled *The Greeks* appeared at the Aldwych Theatre in London in 1980, we find that it is the daring nature of Peter

[32] Karolos Koun's production of the *Oresteia*, in 1982.

Hall's undertaking at the National Theatre that is emphasised in the previews – it is simply unknown for a straight revival of a Greek tragedy to appear in the repertoire of a London theatre at this time.[52] Indeed, these three productions of the *Oresteia* demonstrated to audiences around the world that Greek drama need not be confined to academic institutions, or marginalised in specialised festivals, but could just as readily be incorporated into the classical repertoire of any modern theatre.

Karolos Koun's Theatro Technis performed the *Oresteia* (1980, 1982) to great acclaim in Greece [32], breaking with the rather conservative traditions that had led to a period of stagnation in Greek productions of the classics throughout the 1970s. With the rule of the Junta in very recent memory, and the possibility of great changes in the political system becoming increasingly likely (Papandreou's ticket of 'Change' won him the election in 1981), the production was acclaimed for its creation of a lugubrious primeval world (in the designs of Dionysis Fotopoulos) from which the trilogy eventually escapes.

When Peter Hall chose a cast of sixteen male actors for his production [33] that opened at the National Theatre in London on 28 November 1981, he justified his choice on the grounds that he wished to emphasise the extent to which the trilogy traced the emergence of male supremacy. This theme was forcefully conveyed by the translation of Tony Harrison which used compound, Anglo-Saxon inspired, neologisms like 'she-god' and 'he-god'. The initial intended run of twenty performances was extended to sixty-five following public demand, and yet the only aspect to receive unanimous critical acclaim was the music by Harrison Birtwhistle, which became an inseparable part of the production. The full masks clearly affected the audibility of Harrison's highly alliterative (and often extremely inventive) translation, and the cumulative effect of the persistent trochaic base was to diminish rather than reflect the complexity of Aeschylus' verse. But the production's success with London audiences and its appearance at Epidaurus in 1982 – making it the first non-Greek production to have been performed in the ancient theatre – clearly confirm Hall's considerable achievements.

Peter Hall's production was predicated on the assumption that only by stylising every aspect of the theatrical experience can the essence of Greek tragedy be conveyed. Many critics clearly disagreed, and felt that they had been considerably more moved by Peter Stein's Berlin production of the *Oresteia*, which opened on 18 October 1980 at the Schaubühne am Halleschen Ufer (and was revived in 1994) in a prose translation by the

---

[52] See, e.g., *The Times*, 25 January 1981.

[33] The Furies from Peter Hall's production of the *Oresteia* at the National Theatre, London, in 1981.

director, and employed no musical accompaniment.[53] Having benefited
from eighteen months of rehearsals, the production lasted some seven
hours, broken up by two one-hour intervals. In many respects the scale and
magnitude of the production place it firmly in the tradition of Reinhardt's
Oedipus Rex. Stein sought to challenge the traditional relations between
actors and audience (as Reinhardt had done earlier) by having his audience
seated on the ground and having a central corridor that was largely used by
the Chorus. The palace at one end also recalled the Reinhardt set, albeit
scaled down, and the intensity of the acting (notably from Edith Clever as
Clytemnestra) guaranteed that the production received similar critical
acclaim.

If Stein's 1980 production of the *Oresteia* was to some extent a highly
successful return to the staging traditions of the past, it was very much a
production of the moment in terms of its handling of the trilogy's political
message. As the Eumenides put on clothes at the end of the play in the same
purple cloth that had entwined the dead bodies in the previous plays, he
appeared to be highlighting the extent to which the emergent democracy
was by no means unsullied: Bonn was coming under sharp scrutiny from the
gloomy prospect of a divided Berlin.

By turning to Greek tragedy in order to explore the ideological polarities
in Europe attendant on the outcome of the Second World War, Stein was
doing what his colleagues in the East had been doing for some time. In
Eastern Europe, with Brecht's 1948 version of the *Antigone* (in which
Creon was equated with Adolf Hitler) as the obvious paradigm, playwrights
and directors frequently turned to Greek tragedies as a safe vehicle for
exploring forbidden ideas closer to home.[54] The East German playwright
Heiner Müller, for example, wrote versions of *Philoctetes* and the *Medea* in
the 1960s and 1970s. And when the Polish director Andrej Wajda set his
1984 production of *Antigone* in a Gdansk shipyard and aligned Antigone's
cause with that of Solidarity, he too was following the Brechtian example.

Three major productions of Greek tragedies in the late 1980s and early
1990s reflected the more recent political changes in Eastern Europe. Even
the Royal Shakespeare Company's production of *The Thebans*, directed by
Adrian Noble at Stratford in 1991 and the Barbican in 1992, was in many
respects a product of these changing circumstances. Although the production did not seek to address the current political developments directly, its
fidelity to the Sophoclean originals (in a new lucid translation by Timberlake Wertenbaker) meant that the moral and emotional issues in the plays

[53] See John Barber in the *Daily Telegraph*, 30 November 1981.
[54] For a recent survey, see Seidensticker (1992) 347–67.

318

were of primary concern. Moreover, the unusual juxtapositions afforded by its grouping of Sophocles' *Oedipus the King*, *Oedipus at Colonus* and the *Antigone* in a $6\frac{1}{2}$-hour programme meant that revenge and its consequences, rather than the question of guilt and responsibility or secular and divine law, became the controlling motif of the trilogy.

The most widely seen, and probably the most controversial of these productions, was Ariane Mnouchkine's extremely powerful *Les Atrides*. In a 10-hour, four-play cycle that included Euripides' *Iphigeneia at Aulis* and Aeschylus' *Oresteia*, Mnouchkine's company, Théâtre du Soleil, drew on the performance styles of Indian Kathakali theatre, Kabuki and Noh. Originally mounted at Mnouchkine's theatre, La Cartoucherie, on the outskirts of Paris, the tetralogy slowly evolved over a couple of years (*Iphigeneia at Aulis* and *Agamemnon* opened in November 1990, *Libation-Bearers* in February 1991 and *Eumenides* in May 1992). This gradual evolution may well account for the apparent disjunction in artistic and conceptual styles between the first three plays and the *Eumenides*. In the early plays the strengths of the collaboration of Eastern and Western theatrical traditions were embodied in the Kathakali-inspired vigorous dancing and the voluminous costumes of the Choruses. And although the Choruses eschewed both singing and unison delivery – the Chorus leader chanted alone in between the dance sequences – the overwhelming impact of the choreography gave audiences the impression, if not the reality, of the Wagnerian *Gesamtkunstwerk*. In the *Eumenides*, however, a depleted Chorus of three bag-ladies and a pack of dogs, who were (oddly) excluded from the stage during Athena's speech, meant that the final play was both an aesthetic and an intellectual puzzle. According to Mnouchkine, the production was concerned no less with the Furies unleashed in Eastern Europe than it was with those of the fifth century BC.[55] But by dressing the chief Furies as bag-ladies from the urban wastelands of Europe, Mnouchkine finally offered audiences an unsettling fusion of East and West that lingered in the mind way beyond the point when the seemingly implacable demons had been ultimately appeased.

Whilst *The Thebans* and *Les Atrides* cast an oblique light on current political events, Andrei Serban's *An Ancient Trilogy* is both a direct product of those events and a direct encounter with them. Serban's production began life in Ellen Stewart's Café La Mama in New York, where his versions of the *Trojan Women* (*Fragments of a Greek Tragedy*) and the *Agamemnon* had evolved in the 1970s. *An Ancient Trilogy* only reached its final form in 1989 after Serban was invited to return home as director of the National

[55] Mnouchkine in conversation with Jack Kroll, *Newsweek*, 5 October 1992, 51.

Theatre of Romania following the overthrow of the Ceausescu regime. Serban has very often paid little more than lip-service to the originals with the trilogy consisting of Euripides' *Medea*, the *Trojan Women* and the *Electra* of Sophocles translated into a Grotowski-esque saga of the Ceausescu family. When the production was staged at the National Theatre in Bucharest, the ancient and modern worlds collided as Clytemnestra was struck down in the box in the theatre that had formerly been reserved for Romania's leading family.

The performances of Greek tragedies in the nineteenth and twentieth centuries include the scenic disasters no less than the milestones of modern theatre history. Having once been confined to amateur or matinée productions for the cognoscenti, the Greek plays are seen on the stage today in countries where the classics have never traditionally had a stronghold. The path taken by Diana Rigg's *Medea* (directed by Jonathan Kent) from the Almeida Theatre, Islington, in 1992, to the Wyndham's Theatre in the West End in 1993, and finally to Broadway in 1994 (with *Evening Standard* and Tony Awards gathered en route) is ample testimony to the centrality of the Greek tragedies within the traditional repertoire of the English-speaking theatre. Moreover, the tragedies have proved catalysts for combining the strengths of the markedly separate theatrical traditions that have developed in the East and West. And the most notable and encouraging development as the millennium approaches is the broadening of the performance repertoire, with Euripides' *Hecuba*, *Ion*, *Orestes* and *Phoenician Women* being seen for the first time on the professional English stage.[56]

The tragedies have always been turned to for commentary on prevailing political questions; occasionally, as with *Oedipus the King* in Britain, they have become embroiled in contemporary controversies. When Peter Stein's 1980 production of the *Oresteia* was substantially revived in Moscow in 1994, the trial scene was clearly intended as a biting satire on contemporary Russian politics, with the Athenian jury behaving like members of the Kremlin.[57] And when the production toured Europe (East and West), Aeschylus' play was again being called upon to urge a reconciliation of opposing forces within an enlightened democracy. Just as Andrei Serban has enlisted Euripides' support in an examination of his country's recent

---

[56] *Hecuba* at the Gate Theatre, dir. by Laurence Boswell, September 1992; RSC's *Ion* at the Pit, dir. by Nicholas Wright in September 1994; Actors' Touring Company's *Ion*, Oct./Dec. 1994, dir. Nick Philippou; *Agamemnon's Children* (Euripides' *Electra*, *Orestes* and *Iphigeneia among the Taurians*) at the Gate Theatre, dir. Laurence Boswell, in March 1995; RSC's *Phoenician Women* at The Other Place, Stratford-upon-Avon, dir. by Katie Mitchell in November 1995.

[57] See Arkady Ostrovsky in the *Financial Times*, 2 February 1994.

turbulent events, it is most probable that the Greek tragedians will continue to be sought in the future to illuminate the problems attendant on emergent democracies.

The controversial production of the *Persians* in 1993 by the American director Peter Sellars aligned the defeated Persians with the Iraqis during the Gulf War; whilst a far less publicised production of the *Antigone*, subtitled 'A Cry For Peace', was directed early in 1994 by Nikos Koundouros in no man's land between northern Greece and the former Republic of Yugoslavia, with armoured personnel carriers, soldiers and log fires providing the backdrop. Indeed, the frequent adoption of Serbo-Croat chants in the delivery of choral lyrics in recent British productions[58] underlines the fact that the Balkans may well provide the most appropriate late twentieth-century setting for the staging of Greek drama. Moreover, the tragedies of Bosnia and the horrors of ethnic cleansing are, like the other dark and catastrophic events of this century, perhaps, only to be broached through the medium of Greek tragedy.

BIBLIOGRAPHICAL NOTE

General

Flashar (1991) is the only full-length study of productions of Greek drama on the modern stage. Best on revivals in the German-speaking world, it none the less makes references to Greek, Italian, French and English productions and contains an excellent appendix; Walton (1987) contains essays on revivals in Greece (A. Bakopoulou Halls), Europe (R. Beacham), England (J. M. Walton) and America (P. D. Arnott). See too the essays in *Le théâtre antique de nos jours: Symposium International à Delphes 18–22 août 1981* (Athens 1984) which include university productions in Paris (A. Burgaud) and Cambridge (P. E. Easterling); the productions at Syracuse (G. Monaco), and those on television (K. McLeish), and on film (M. Cacoyannis). For the USA see now K. V. Hartigan, *Greek Tragedy on the American Stage: Ancient Drama in the Commercial Theater, 1882–1994* (Westpoint, CT, 1995). Excellent photos of early productions can be found in *Thespis* 4–5 (1966), the journal of the Greek Centre of the International Theatre Institute; and for more recent productions, see O. Taplin, *Greek Fire* (London 1989), and the electronic journal, *Didaskalia* (distributed from the University of Warwick, ISSN 1321-4853), which contains advance listings of productions. For further reading on particular areas covered within the chapter, see the bibliographical details below.

Early revivals and Antigone in the nineteenth century

B. R. Smith, *Ancient Scripts and Modern Experiences on the English Stage 1500–*

---

[58] E.g. *Women of Troy* at the National Theatre, dir. by Annie Casteldine in March 1995, and RSC's *Phoenician Women*, dir. by Katie Mitchell in November 1995.

1700 (Princeton 1988); G. C. Moore Smith, *College Plays Performed in the University of Cambridge* (Cambridge 1923); L. V. Gofflot, *Le théâtre au collège du moyen âge à nos jours* (Paris 1907); Flashar (1991) 35–109; Macintosh (1995); Vernant in Vernant and Vidal-Naquet (1988) 361–80; Steiner (1984).

Amateur revivals at the end of the nineteenth century

Campbell (1891); F. Jenkin, *Papers, Literary, Scientific etc, by the Late F. Jenkin with a Memoir by R. L. Stevenson* (London 1887); J. Stokes, *Resistible Theatres: Enterprise and Experiment in the Late Nineteenth Century* (London 1972); A. McKinnon, *The Oxford Amateurs: a Short History of Theatricals at the University* (London 1910); H. Carter, *OUDS: a Centenary History of the Oxford University Dramatic Society 1885–1985* (Oxford 1985); J. C. Trewin, *Benson and the Bensonians* (London 1960); D. E. Pluggé, *History of Greek Play Production in American Colleges and Universities from 1881–1936* (New York 1938).

Oedipus and the Edwardian era

Purdom (1955); Kennedy (1985); Martin-Harvey (1933); *Censorship and Licensing (Joint Select Committee) Verbatim Report of the Proceedings and Full Text of the Recommendations* (London 1909); J. L. Styan, *Max Reinhardt* (Cambridge 1982); R. Beacham, 'Revivals: Europe' in Walton (1987) 304–14.

Tragedy and two world wars

Thorndike (1960); West (1984); Wilson (1887); Eliot (1951); Clark & McGuire (1989); R. Cave, *Terence Gray and the Cambridge Festival Theatre* (Cambridge 1980); Special issues of ΗΩΣ 98–102 (1966), and 103–7 (1967), in honour of Eva Sikelianou; D. Whitton, *Stage Directions in Modern France* (Manchester 1987).

The post-war period

L. Olivier, *Confessions of an Actor* (London 1982); T. Guthrie, R. Davies & G. Macdonald, *Twice Have the Trumpets Sounded: a Record of the Stratford Shakespearean Festival in Canada 1954* (London 1955); O. Taplin, *Greek Fire* (London 1989) 36–61; M. McDonald, *Ancient Sun, Modern Light: Greek Drama on the Modern Stage* (New York 1992); J. Chioles, 'The Oresteia and the Avant Garde: Three Decades of Discourse', *Performing Arts Journal* 45 (September 1993) 1–28; A. Kiernander, *Ariane Mnouchkine and the Théâtre du Soleil* (Cambridge 1993).

Unpublished sources

Cambridge Greek Play Archive; The Todhunter Collection in the Library of the University of Reading; the Lord Chamberlain's Correspondence in the British Library; Production Files in the Theatre Museum, Covent Garden.

Acknowledgements

Special thanks for details of productions abroad, not all of which could be incorporated here, are owed to Kevin Lee and Michael Ewans (Australia), Robin

Bond (New Zealand), Platon Mavromoustakos and Christina Symroulidou (Greece), Shigenari Kawashima (Japan) and Karelisa Hartigan (USA). Paul Cartledge, Pat Easterling, Edith Hall, David Ricks, Chris Stray and Oliver Taplin have also given help of various kinds.

12

SIMON GOLDHILL

Modern critical approaches to Greek tragedy

How are the texts of ancient drama to be understood by modern interpreters – separated as we are by so great a distance of time and difference of culture? This problem has been treated in many ways in this century, as the study of ancient literature, like the study of other literatures, has undergone rapid institutional and intellectual changes. There are many paths and genealogies that could be traced through this history, and not only do many different methodological approaches overlap and interrelate in a variety of complex ways, but also there is great variety within any one broad heading (such as 'structuralism'). In this chapter I shall try to unravel some of the main threads that make up the texture of contemporary debate about critical methodology with regard to Greek tragedy. The methodology of each critic who works on Greek tragedy – myself included, for sure – is not the application of a ready-made theory so much as the product of (at least) teachers' and colleagues' influence, reading and study within classical scholarship and other fields, institutional pressures, laziness, acumen ... In attempting to trace some of the main lines of enquiry, it is inevitable that the siting of each scholar within the intellectual and social institutions of classical scholarship cannot be finely nuanced. What is more, the teleology of a history that ends with a necessarily partial view of the here and now must distort the picture of the critical developments to be traced. None the less, some lines on the map – however tentatively drawn – will help an appreciation of how contemporary understandings of Greek tragedy have developed.

PHILOLOGY AND ITS DISCONTENTS

Let me begin with a book that has been massively influential in the twentieth century and with a nineteenth-century row between former schoolfellows, the echoes of which are still reverberating. When Nietzsche published *The Birth of Tragedy*, one of its earliest reviews was a 28-page pamphlet of

324

vitriolic abuse by Ulrich von Wilamowitz-Moellendorff.[1] Wilamowitz attacked Nietzsche, a professor of Classics at Basle, for betraying the principles of classical philology (though the motives for the attack can be traced back to their time at school together at Pforta).[2] This attack led to a series of pamphlets – including Nietzsche's deeply ironic 'We philologists', which contrasts the wonders of ancient Greece with the desiccated world of philological scholarship[3] – and to a set of battlelines being drawn up between 'philology' and 'modernism' (the sarcastic title of Wilamowitz's pamphlet was 'Philology of the future!', '*Zukunftsphilologie!*'). Wilamowitz indeed has become an icon for the tradition of classical philological scholarship, just as Nietzsche is established as a founding father of much modernist criticism. To understand modern critical approaches to tragedy, one must first attempt to outline the place of philology. For although the vitriol and violent polarisation of the clash of Wilamowitz and Nietzsche have only rarely been repeated, modern criticism of tragedy inevitably and often passionately articulates its affiliations and challenges to the traditions of philology.

The texts of tragedy were transmitted from the fifth century to the Renaissance in a manuscript tradition, the first thousand years of which is almost completely lost (cf. Ch. 9 above). On the one hand, since errors inevitably enter when difficult texts are copied by hand, there is an evident need to establish each tragic text as accurately as possible by collating the different manuscripts of the play, by investigating the history of the text's transmission, and by comparing and contrasting the language of the play with the other plays of our corpus. On the other hand, the language of tragedy is a literary construct of great complexity that needs careful semantic and grammatical analysis both diachronically within the history of Greek literature and synchronically within other types of Greek writing of the fifth century. These two projects are the work of classical philology.

The history of this field goes back at least to Hellenistic Alexandria, where in the third century BC the institutions of critical annotation were set in place in the great library of the Ptolemies with its assembly of scholars and avid collecting and annotating of the texts of the past.[4] But for present purposes it is the influence of a largely German scholarship of the nineteenth century that needs emphasising. For throughout the nineteenth century Classics and in particular classical philology constituted the privileged

---

[1] See Silk & Stern (1981) 95–125 for a fine account of the row and its effects.

[2] See Silk & Stern (1981) 103–5.

[3] An unfinished work, now conveniently translated, and still showing its polemical force, in *Arion* n.s. 1 (1973).

[4] See Pfeiffer (1968) for an excellent introduction to this history.

SIMON GOLDHILL

intellectual pursuit in the German educational system, and German scholarship took what had often been an amateur study of the ancient world to new heights of professionalism with the exhaustive collection of evidence and the extensive discussion of technical problems. (The importance of the row between Nietzsche and Wilamowitz stems partly from the position of classical philology in German culture at the time.) The weight of this scholarship is still strongly felt in Classics as a discipline. A landmark in this history – and in the development of British Classics – was the publication in 1950 of Eduard Fraenkel's three-volume edition of Aeschylus' *Agamemnon*. Its 860 densely packed pages contain a text of Aeschylus' play with a facing translation, and with a line-by-line commentary that treats problem after problem in this most difficult work with a magisterial deployment of scholarship. Fraenkel not only mobilises an astonishingly extensive reading of ancient sources to explicate the text but also traces the history of the recognition of problems and their attempted solutions throughout the scholarly tradition. The process of how scholarly understanding is produced is thus strikingly articulated on every page. Although he is interested in formal questions of dramaturgy and writes with strong feelings about many aspects of the play, it is primarily on the questions of the establishment and semantics of the text that Fraenkel focuses; it is the model of the recognition and solution of philological problems that Fraenkel's work repeatedly and paradigmatically demonstrates. Indeed, Fraenkel sets exemplary standards for the philological approach to Greek tragedy. Many scholars continue to work within this tradition (though rarely with the scope or authority of a Fraenkel), extending and developing its insights: papyrology has provided many new texts from the sands of Egypt, particularly texts of comedy; the understanding of the history of texts and their interpretation itself has been deepened by studies of the Renaissance contribution to manuscript transmission and of the history of scholarship back to the scholia, the ancient annotation of texts;[5] above all, new editions continue in different ways to guide the readings of tragedy for a range of different audiences. Reading Greek tragedy always involves *reading through* such a scholarly history of the text and its glosses, and a serious understanding of ancient theatre cannot hope to dispense with an immersion in this philological world. A close, historically aware, reading of the language of ancient texts, and an understanding of how the language of these texts is transmitted to the modern era, is an essential part of the discipline of Classics, and a necessary element of any serious study of ancient drama.

Yet the debt to nineteenth-century scholarship is also still evident in a

[5] See e.g. Reynolds & Wilson (1991).

more negative guise. For its painstaking analysis of ancient language is often dependent not only on a positivism common to much nineteenth-century intellectual effort but also on a set of assumptions about language that have rarely received the critical attention they need. The study of literary language – the role of ambiguity and irony, the role of the reader in the production of meaning, the ways meaning is constructed with a text – has moved far beyond the certainties of Victorian annotation. The study of linguistics as a discipline, of the philosophy of language and of the sociology of criticism, has enabled recent critics to explore nineteenth-century scholarship (and its heirs) not merely as it would see itself – as a progressive science – but rather as a historically based and theory-laden activity. What is more, contemporary criticism has found it easy to see both how the cultural categories of nineteenth-century thought have been anachronistically applied to ancient texts and how this affects the interpretation of the language and action of Greek drama. (It is, of course, harder for contemporary criticism to see where its own tacit knowledge is being dangerously ignored or unthinkingly deployed.) So – to return to 1950 – the most quoted and most ridiculed judgement in Fraenkel's monumental edition of the *Agamemnon* is his statement that Agamemnon steps on the tapestries spread for him by Clytemnestra because 'in his reluctance to get the better of a woman ... he proves a great gentleman' – a view which says far more about Fraenkel's ideas of social interaction than about Greek ideas of gender or persuasion. Similarly, since many decisions that are taken in the name of philology depend on an understanding of a play – its thematic structures, say – or on a more general comprehension of the religion, sociology and ideology of ancient culture, it is important that such understanding too is developed in as sophisticated and self-aware a manner as possible.

As we shall see, there are many ways scholars have negotiated the claims and practices of philology and other branches of classical learning. Sometimes, in the agonistic world of contemporary critical debate, as if rehearsing the clash of Wilamowitz and Nietzsche, philology – constructed as 'traditional' Classics – is set in opposition to literary criticism or to the researches of historical anthropology, which are constructed as 'modern' Classics. While this opposition may represent the working practice of some scholars today – and many more in the past – it does not do justice either to the majority of classicists who are not so naively affiliated, or to the inevitable interdependence of these different spheres of classical learning. For on the one hand, the language and transmission of a play cannot be understood in a (cultural, historical, intellectual) vacuum, nor can an adequate philology hope to ignore its theoretical underpinnings in a theory of language and of culture. On the other hand, any attempt to read an ancient play must broach the difficult questions of the (philological) constitution and comprehension of the text. Classicists will continue to produce editions of plays, and students will continue to read tragedy through such editions and thus through a history and sociology of the academic production and glossing of meaning. But neither a philology that fails to question its debt to a Victorian tradition of positivism nor a Classics that hopes to do without philology can be adequate to the study of Greek tragedy.

Much of what would now be recognisable to many readers as 'mainstream' literary criticism in the Classics was developed explicitly as a polemical reaction against the critical edition on the one hand and against the types of reading it encourages on the other. The traditional format of a critical edition morselises a text, dividing a work into a series of discrete problems for analysis. This has extensive implications for the way meaning is viewed. Although, as I have already said, many decisions taken under the rubric of philology depend on a wider understanding of a play or a culture, and although critical editions vary greatly in their conception of the relation between wider and more local elements of commentary, modern criticism has often constituted itself as a reaction against a narrowly conceived philology that separates the business of linguistic analysis from the wider interpretative concerns of a play and avoids the sorts of issue which require a more synthetic or thematic approach. So Karl Reinhardt – to start suitably in Germany – opens his highly influential study of Sophocles (published in 1933 with new editions in 1941 and 1947) with a programmatic statement that is, like most methodological claims of the period, brief but telling. His book is to be 'an attempt to examine [Sophocles'] work by means of comparisons, in order to rescue it from certain prevalent methods of interpretation which succeed only in obscuring it'.[6] His study is made up of a series of chapters on each of Sophocles' plays, read to uncover 'Sophoclean *situations*', by which is meant 'the relationship between god and man, and between man and man ... as it develops scene by scene and play by play'.[7]

Reinhardt's intense and close thematic reading was both novel and powerfully influential on those writing about Greek tragedy. Yet it is interesting to see how many striking similarities there are between his work and the critical schools in English literature developing over the same period before and after the Second World War. For at this time in England and America the so-called 'New Criticism' – with its luminaries I. A. Richards, T. S. Eliot, John Crowe Ransome, W. K. Wimsatt, Cleanth Brooks – was

---

[6] Reinhardt (1979) ix.   [7] Reinhardt (1979) 1.

reaching a position of intellectual and social dominance in academic institutions.[8] The watchwords of New Criticism were 'coherence' and 'integration' – terms which clearly could easily be aimed against the practices of the philological edition, New Criticism famously regarded a poem as a self-sufficient object in itself – 'as solid and material as an urn or an icon'.[9] Rather than read a work through its author's biography or through readers' sentiments, New Criticism typically aimed to uncover a poem's structure – its objective form. The New Critics looked at the tensions or ambivalences within a poem and tried to explore through 'close reading' how such tensions were integrated or resolved in the poem's structure. The principles and methods of New Criticism which were developed as a bold and excitingly revolutionary method have become so widely naturalised in our education system that to value 'close reading' or to talk of a 'tension between ideas' in a poem has long since lost its radical edge. None the less, the historical specificity of this development – and its ideological and social impact – must not be forgotten.

Reinhardt, like the New Critics, shows an almost formalist concern with the structure of a work, and a marked interest in irony and conflict within the plays – and how these shifting effects of the writing are resolved and integrated in the play's dramatic structure. Like the New Critics, Reinhardt allows literature to escape the confines of history – in the case of Sophocles by 'the portrayal of universal types ... Mortality, outlined and defined against the background of the divine by the contours of its mortal quality.'[10] Reinhardt was influential among classicists in part at least because, in adopting and adapting his play-by-play, scene-by-scene reading and his liberal humanist perspective, classicists were also adopting and adapting the critical practices dominant in contemporary literary departments. So – to trace the development of this critical tradition in the study of Sophocles in particular, where it is especially marked – H. D. F. Kitto in his widely read study (published first in 1936, with new editions in 1950 and 1961) writes: 'A book on Greek tragedy may be a work of historical scholarship or of literary criticism; this book professes to be a work of criticism. Criticism is of two kinds: the critic may tell the reader what he so beautifully thinks about it all, or he may try to explain the form in which the literature is written. This book attempts the latter.'[11]

Kitto's injunction to 'consider the form'[12] is explicitly here also a rejection of the specifically philological enterprise of 'historical scholarship' and of

[8] On 'New Criticism' and its influence, see Lentricchia (1980); Eagleton (1983) 17–53; Culler (1988) 3–40; and on the relation of Classics and New Criticism, Baldick (1988).
[9] Eagleton (1983) 48.   [10] Reinhardt (1979) 2.   [11] Kitto (1961) v.
[12] Kitto (1956) vii.

criticism from the sentiments. So Maurice Bowra, although he disagrees with Kitto about the place of a historical background in interpreting tragedy, none the less writes in 1941 'drama seems to follow patterns, and at the end of a play we have found an idea of what its pattern is, of what the play "means" or is "about"'.[13] Bowra, like Kitto and Reinhardt before him, finds much of this meaning in the relation between man and god. Cedric Whitman (1951) in America (who also stresses a historical dimension of tragedy more than Kitto or Reinhardt) lays emphasis rather on 'the metaphysics of humanism' in Sophocles and explores further Reinhardt's portrayal of human beings suffering and striving to transcend the contours of humanity – an idea which also looks back to the Romantic ideals of artistic achievement. B. M. W. Knox, in one of the most influential books on Sophocles since the war (1964), develops this sense of the tragic hero in a more nuanced manner, and sees the Sophoclean play as the perfect form to express the paradoxical figure of the transgressive yet transcendent hero – a figure to be traced in a 'recurrent pattern of character, situation and language'.[14] More recently (1980 – but collecting material written over many years), firmly within the same tradition, R. P. Winnington-Ingram begins his study of Sophocles with the claim that 'the main function of criticism is the interpretation of individual works of art ... each in its own unique form, quality and theme'.[15] As he criticises Knox for an insufficient attention to the role of Homer in the representation of the hero, so he names Reinhardt, Bowra, Kitto and Knox among the scholars who have most influenced him. The tradition that appeals to integral form and thematic unity as keynotes of criticism, along with the focus on the human being contoured against the divine, stretches thus over fifty years of Sophoclean criticism – a series of highly influential scholars, each aware of his place in a tradition and writing through it in an active debate with other critics. And, for all that each of these scholars explicitly *contrasts* his work with a tradition of philology, each also *affiliates* himself with such a tradition and draws on it, both in technical footnotes and articles, and, most strikingly, in the repeated return to the authority of the greatest of Victorian Sophoclean scholars, Sir Richard Jebb, whose editions of Sophocles justifiably continue to hold a privileged position in the literary and philological study of these plays, and whose reading of the plays embodied in his commentary (if not his introductions) continues to have a massive influence. (And his facing-page prose translations are also still the most reliable and nuanced English translations of Sophocles.) Such an interweaving of dependence on and

---

[13] Bowra (1944) 6.   [14] Knox (1964) 9.
[15] Winnington-Ingram (1980) vii.

resistance to the scholarly traditions of the past remains a typical dynamic of the study of tragedy, a dynamic that the polemical antithesis of a Wilamowitz to a Nietzsche fails adequately to represent.

I have sketched this best known tradition of Sophoclean scholarship in this briefest of ways not merely to name (*honoris causa*) some central figures in the history of twentieth-century criticism; rather, by bringing what may fairly be called 'mainstream' classical criticism close to the more explicit methodological arguments of New Criticism and by stressing that such writers work in response to each other and to the traditions of philological scholarship, I want to underline that there is no natural, self-evident or obvious way of reading – but always only approaches, each with its history, its set of presuppositions and its own ideological commitments. The approaches I am going to discuss in the rest of this chapter cannot profitably be set in contrast either with a *'natural'* reading (even if many critics claim their work is to be contrasted with the *norms* of reading), or with an absence of methodology, that greatest of all critical fictions. All readers of tragedy read from a position, a position that is indebted to a range of influences, intellectual and otherwise. The question is how explicit, how sophisticated and how self-aware the discussion of that position is to be.

ANTHROPOLOGY AND STRUCTURALISM

The relationship between anthropology and the Classics has been long and turbulent. As much as classical myth and religion were a fundamental factor in the development of anthropology as a discipline, so anthropology has frequently highlighted classical examples and revitalised areas of classical scholarship.[16] This is nowhere more evident than in the study of tragedy.

The most profitable place to start is a much-reviled group whose international influence in the early part of this century was once immense and can still be seen in surprising ways – the so-called Cambridge Ritualists, a group of anthropologists and classicists centred in Cambridge.[17] A theory was developed that attempted to explain the performance of tragedy *as ritual*. This is usually known as the 'year spirit' or *eniautos daimon* theory. It proposes that magic, and in particular the attempt to control nature and vegetation by a form of sacral kingship, lies at the root of religion. The annual cycle in nature of budding, flowering, fruitfulness and death must be re-enacted in the ritual of the sacrifice of the sacral king (or 'year spirit') and

16 See e.g. Detienne (1981); Humphreys (1978).
17 See e.g. Ackerman (1987); Fraser (1990); Calder (1991); Beard (1992); Versnel (1990).

represented in myth. Gilbert Murray saw Greek tragedy as arising from a
dancing ritual around the year spirit Dionysus. In tragedy, he claims, the
following pattern may be perceived. A conflict between the year spirit and
his enemy; the year spirit's sacrificial death; the messenger's report of the
death; the mourning of the death; the resurrection and epiphany of the god.
Since most of Greek tragedy scarcely conforms to this pattern, much effort
was required to show how this pattern 'disintegrated' and yet could be
'reconstructed' from the extant plays.

This particular approach has been completely discredited in this form,
and the Cambridge Ritualists are studied now almost exclusively as figures
of interest in twentieth-century intellectual history. Their influence,
however, can be seen in surprising ways: Harrison, for example, who
proclaimed herself a 'disciple of Nietzsche',[18] was instrumental also in
bringing to the attention of classicists the work of Durkheim, van Gennep
and Mauss, which has been so very profitable in the study of ancient ritual;
and Murray is the apt dedicatee of his successor's most influential study,
namely, E. R. Dodds' *The Greeks and the Irrational*. This is a book whose
theses were also crucial to Dodds' edition of the *Bacchae*, an edition which
shows well how a developed reading of a play and a view of Greek culture
can permeate a philological commentary on it. (Thus we circle from
Nietzsche back to philology ...) In particular, the belief of the Cambridge
Ritualists that tragedy must be studied as ritual – a view which Nietzsche
also influentially promoted – has far from disappeared. Most influentially,
Walter Burkert and René Girard have developed theories of sacrifice as a
social process that take tragedy as a key example.[19] For Girard, sacrifice –
the central ritual of Greek religion – is to be seen as an institution that
works to direct and control violence within the social group. In sacrifice,
violence – both the need to kill to provide meat and the threat posed to
social order by undifferentiated violence – is sacralised and thus bounded by
the rituals of religious observation. A surrogate, that is, a figure like the
scapegoat which takes on itself the violence from within the group, is
chosen as victim and is killed *ritually*; the crisis, the disorder of violence, is
avoided by such transference and such control. Tragedy, Girard argues, is a
dramatisation – and thus ritualisation – of the force of threatening,
undifferentiated violence, a representation which displays the threat of
disorder to expiate it. 'To know violence is to experience it', writes Girard,
'tragedy ... is the child of sacrificial crisis.'[20] Tragedy works to turn aside
violence from the city: hence its social purpose as ritual. Thus, for Girard,

[18] Harrison (1912) viii.   [19] Burkert (1983); Girard (1977).
[20] Girard (1977) 65.

Oedipus represents a surrogate victim whose sacrifice removes his polluting presence – the sign of violence and the collapse of differentiation – from the city, so that the city can continue. Like the Cambridge Ritualists before him, Girard finds the basis of tragedy in 'apotropaic' ritual – ritual designed to turn away (*apotrepein*) disaster.

Although Girard has been widely and sharply criticised by classicists and others (and followed by many, too),[21] apotropaic theories of tragedy – motivated in part by these anthropologically based interpretations – have proved extremely productive. At one level, scholars interested in the psychology of tragedy have stressed the value of the emotional release involved in watching the representation of such transgressive stories. Such approaches find classical support in Aristotle, who under the famous rubric of *katharsis* argues that the pity and fear of an audience faced by such horrors can be beneficial in the training of the *phronimos*, the wise citizen. In this he argues against his teacher Plato, who repeatedly attacks the dangerous psychological and moral effects on actors and audience of acting and watching such scenes of transgression. So, too, more recent critics who have discussed the political discourse of the city have stressed how important it is that tragedy is normally set in other cities, at other times, and involves those other than (Athenian) citizens.[22] By setting the tragic world of disorder elsewhere, the city can face its own dangerous instabilities and control them through the ritualisation of staging. By these explorations of the apotropaic functions of tragedy an answer is being sought to the puzzling and fundamental question of why in the midst of a civic festival and before the whole city again and again there are staged such tragic narratives of violence, disorder and transgression. This central question has been tellingly illuminated by anthropological criticism which has brought to bear cross-cultural studies of 'rituals of reversal' and the sociology of festivals to explain tragedy's position within the cultural order of the polis.[23]

The Cambridge Ritualists, Girard, and Burkert have been especially criticised for their commitment to 'grand theory', that is, universal models of myth and ritual violence, for which tragedy and Greek society provide but one, albeit important, example. There is also a largely French tradition that utilises anthropology and in particular structuralist anthropology to understand specifically Greek culture and its festival of tragedy. The founding father of this group is Louis Gernet, who worked with the famous

---

[21] See e.g. Gordon (1979) for a sharp critique of Girard, and Henrichs (1984).

[22] See e.g. Zeitlin (1990).

[23] On rituals of reversal see Stallybrass & White (1986); Babcock (1978); Turner (1969); and for an overview of such material on Greek drama, see Goldhill (1992) 176–88 and (1990a).

sociologists Durkheim and Mauss, and published a series of articles from 1909 onwards on Greek culture.[24] In his lifetime, Gernet's work on law and religion – he published almost nothing on tragedy – was read primarily by specialists, and he taught for many years in Algiers.[25] But when he returned to Paris in 1948, his seminar included Jean-Pierre Vernant (amongst others) whose work has become the touchstone of this group. It is important to realise the place of Gernet as Vernant's teacher, however, not least because it shows the roots in sociology, linguistics, law and cultural studies that, together with what has become known as structural anthropology, dominate Vernant's approach to tragedy.

Vernant's work maps many areas of Greek culture – social institutions, intellectual history, ideological formations, the function and meaning of myth – and his writing on tragedy, published with the work of Pierre Vidal-Naquet, draws on this full cultural picture. He aims to take account of three interlocking historical aspects of tragedy.[26] First, he analyses tragedy as an institution of the democratic polis; second, as a particular and new genre of aesthetic production; third, he is concerned with what tragedy tells of a new sense of the self – tragedy's contribution to a history of notions of the will, responsibility, mental states. Vernant tries to show that tragedy – for all its rhetoric of universal messages – takes place at a specific historical juncture, a specific *moment*. He sees this moment as integrally linked to the growth of democracy. If Homer offers a view of the individual hero, prey to external divine forces, fighting for individual glory, in democracy the commitment to personal responsibility, to collective endeavour, and to the city's law offers a different frame for action. Tragedy takes place, argues Vernant, at a crucial moment of conflict between the archaic religious system, with its view of human action, and the democratic legal and political system, with its very different sense of behaviour, authority, and causation. The tragic moment

> thus occurs when a gap develops at the heart of the social experience. It is wide enough for the oppositions between legal and political thought on the one hand and the mythical and heroic traditions on the other to stand out quite clearly. Yet it is narrow enough for the conflict in values still to be a painful one and for the clash to continue to take place.[27]

The institution of tragedy thus enables the city publicly to express and

[24] Gernet (1981).

[25] For an account of Gernet, see Humphreys (1978).

[26] For Vernant and tragedy see Vernant and Vidal-Naquet (1988); for an introduction to the range of Vernant's work, see Vernant (1991); for the influence of Vernant, see e.g. *Arethusa* 16 (1983).

[27] Vernant and Vidal-Naquet (1988) 27.

explore the tensions and ambiguities in its rapidly developing social system. Here we see a more subtle development of an apotropaic principle.

The form of tragedy, with its interrelation of hero and chorus, on the one hand, and its structural basis in the *agōn*, on the other, is uniquely suited to the expression not merely of conflict within a system of ideas, but also, more specifically, of conflict that stems from a tension between individual and collective responsibilities and duties, that is, a conflict central to the developing system of democracy, the rule of the collective. The aesthetic form of tragedy for Vernant is thus integrally related to its historical moment.

Perhaps of most importance, however, is the way Vernant articulates an insight of Gernet's on the working of tragic language within these agonistic frames. For Vernant sees the mobilisation of different and shifting senses of words as a fundamental dynamic of tragedy: 'in the language of the tragic writers there is a multiplicity of different levels' that informs each *agōn*: 'the dialogue exchanged and lived through by the heroes of the drama undergoes shifts in meaning as it is interpreted and commented upon by the chorus and taken in and understood by the spectators ... Words take on opposed meanings depending on who utters them.'[28] Thus exchanges on stage often demonstrate the failure of communication between characters and display the difficulty and opacity of the language of the city to the city, its audience. The most positivistic element of the philological tradition aims to delimit the meanings of words to unambiguous and clear usage – to 'solve the problem' of uncertain sense – and so it is not surprising that there has often been a fierce debate between Vernant (and his followers) and more traditional philologists about the necessary ambiguity of tragic language.[29]

Vernant and Vidal-Naquet also stressed a different side of tragedy's connection with ritual, one which several earlier scholars had developed. Models of different rituals – sacrifice, the scapegoat, ephebic initiation – are seen as fundamental elements of tragic narrative. That is, tragedy is viewed as manipulating and exploring ritual patterns to express a sense of order and disorder in the world.[30] Thus when the killing of Agamemnon is staged as a corrupt sacrifice in the *Oresteia*, the imagery articulates how Clytemnestra has corrupted a nexus of normative relations between humans, between humans and animals, and between humans and gods.[31] In this view, the action of tragedy is represented and needs to be analysed through

---

[28] Vernant and Vidal-Naquet (1988) 42.   [29] See Ch. 6 above.

[30] So Vernant uses the scapegoat ritual to analyse *Oedipus the King* (Vernant and Vidal-Naquet (1988) 113–40) and Vidal-Naquet uses the myth and ritual of the ephebeia to analyse *Philoctetes* (Vernant and Vidal-Naquet (1988) 161–79).

[31] Zeitlin (1965).

specific ritual patterns. Tragedy does not simply function as a ritual but, as it does with myth, it represents, redeploys, and comments on ritual. This approach has led to several readings of plays by a range of critics to show how widely diffused culturally specific rituals and other social models are in Greek dramatic narratives.[32]

Structuralist anthropology has been particularly influential in this type of analysis. One version of structuralism claims that polarities – binary oppositions such as male/female, up/down, raw/cooked – are the basic building blocks of a culture's mental landscape, and that myth works to mediate such polarities.[33] Since Greek writing is particularly fond of such polarised expressions, it has been particularly open to such analysis. Because tragedy is so often concerned with threats to civilised order, the categories in which civilised order is represented are particularly highlighted. So there have been many readings of tragedy that focus on how its texts manipulate such polarities.[34]

At their best, anthropologically based critiques have helped uncover ways in which the polarising tendency of Greek language can be related to the rituals staged in drama (and as drama) and tragedy's concern with social order and disorder. At its worst, such anthropologically based criticism has mechanistically catalogued polarities or tried to fit tragedy's complex narratives too simply into a grid of rituals. In the analysis of the religion and the ritual and cultural practices of other societies, however, the discipline of anthropology has provided fundamental insights. Since tragedy has increasingly been viewed not under the discrete rubric of 'literature' but rather as a cultural event of the polis, and since the importance of understanding a different culture's different categories of representation has been increasingly emphasised, so the techniques of anthropology have proved indispensable, as well as a source of turbulent disagreement, for the study of ancient theatre and its texts.

STAGECRAFT AND PERFORMANCE CRITICISM

The studies that grow out of anthropologically based perceptions of theatre as social drama are often self-consciously and explicitly opposed to the traditions of criticism which place tragedy narrowly within the category 'literature'. In the last twenty years there has also been a striking move towards viewing the tragic texts as scripts for dramatic performance in the theatre (and a notable increase in the number of performances of Greek

[32] See e.g. Foley (1985); Segal (1981), (1982); Seaford (1981), (1994); Zeitlin (1965).
[33] For introductions to structuralism, see Leach (1970); Culler (1975); Lévi-Strauss (1977).
[34] See e.g. Segal (1982); Whitlock-Blundell (1989); Goldhill (1986).

tragedy in Western theatre). Although Fraenkel could write (on *Ag.* 613–14) 'For Greek tragedy there exists also something like a grammar of dramatic technique', there is relatively little discussion of such technique in his monumental edition of the *Agamemnon*. The growth of studies of stage-craft, however, has been so rapid that one of Fraenkel's pupils can – with a certain overstatement – claim that 'these days all but a lunatic fringe of students of Greek drama would accept the primacy of performance'.[35]

There are many difficulties that at first sight face a stagecraft critic of ancient theatre, particularly in comparison with the archives of the Renaissance stage, which have been so tellingly explored for Renaissance performance studies.[36] First, the texts we have contain almost no stage directions, and the few that survive concern mainly off-stage noises only. Even the attribution of speeches to particular characters can be doubtfully transmitted in our manuscript tradition. Second, our knowledge of the possibilities of staging – the techniques of scene-painting, set construction, mechanical devices – is at best rudimentary and often constructed from the bare scripts or from late sources, which regularly (and wrongly) assume that contemporary resources were necessarily available to an earlier period. It is deeply important, for example, that there was a *theologeion*, a 'god-walk' above the house; that cranes could be used; that a dancing area was separate from a stage; but detailed evidence, from the question of dating to questions of their varied use and significance, is wholly lacking. Although we know that Sophocles wrote a book on the chorus, for example, and that scene-painting and other aspects of theatre were the subject of technical and academic discussion, all but the barest fragments of such material is now lost. Third, our evidence for costuming comes from the texts themselves or from vase-painting (as discussed by Taplin in Ch. 4 above). Vase-paintings are most certainly not documentary records of performance; and to read from their manipulations and imaginings back to particular stagings is extremely hard, although many scholars feel that a general picture at least may be gleaned from this body of representation. For later periods we have some discussion of the technical aspects of masking and costume, which have been profitably analysed especially for Greek comedy.[37] Fourth, music and dance are integral elements of Greek drama. We have next to no information on the performance of either, and while the theoretical pronouncements of ancient writers from Plato to Lucian may help with a sociological understanding of the role of these arts in Greek culture, they

[35] Taplin (1977) 2.
[36] See Orgel (1975); Sinfield (1983); Tennenhouse (1986); Berry (1989). Taplin (1995) stresses a more positive view of the comparison.
[37] See Wiles (1991).

337

SIMON GOLDHILL

cannot help reconstruct a movement or a sound.[38] For example, although Lucian, centuries later, can talk of dance as a form of mimetic communication, which tells a story as a mime does, we do not know even in general whether choruses in fifth-century tragedy ever used such representational illustration of the songs they were singing. Fifth, we have no audience reports from the period of the type that have been so instructive for later drama and ritual in Europe. Plato and Aristotle offer our most extensive audience response to theatre, but they are concerned with the emotional, moral, and sociological effect of theatre and only very rarely with details of performance. Indeed, Aristotle in the *Poetics* (1450b17–19) notoriously rejects *opsis*, 'spectacle', as an integral part of tragedy. Sixth, although we know that in many cases the playwright was actively involved in the production of his plays as 'director' and even as actor, and that a prominent individual funded the chorus of each production and may have had some influence over the production, we have no detailed evidence of how these arrangements functioned and we have no contemporary accounts of production of the sort which are so illuminating for Renaissance masques, say. This dearth of evidence has not, however, proved an insuperable barrier.

Archaeology in particular has given a good, if very general, picture of the space of Athenian theatre and its arrangement, and several studies have utilised this material in a striking way. Oliver Taplin, for example, has focused on the 'grammar' of exits and entrances in Aeschylean drama, making use of our knowledge of the two long entrance ways on each side of the stage and the development of a stage building with central doors. His long and influential study takes the form of a scene-by-scene reading of all of Aeschylus' plays that attempts to clarify how the fundamental dramatic device of entering and leaving the stage space is handled by Aeschylus, which not only goes some way towards the recovery of at least basic stage directions, but also helps explore the possibilities of staging, even of such technical aspects as the *ekkuklēma*, the trolley for revealing a scene from inside the central doors of the house. He notes properly that a stagecraft critic 'seldom deals in certainties, usually in possibilities, or at best probabilities', but proceeds by a careful sifting of such possibilities towards a general view of Aeschylus' stage action, a view informed by the 'practical aspects of staging'.[39] Most importantly, Taplin is explicit that for him 'the staging of Greek tragedy ... is ancillary to literary criticism': 'any clarifica-

---

[38] On dance in ancient culture, see Mullen (1982); Winkler (1990b) 50–8; Lonsdale (1993); on music, see most recently West (1992). Despite Taplin's optimism (1995) 100–1, we cannot confidently say anything of a single note of tragic music.

[39] Taplin (1977) 19.

338

tion of theatrical or dramatic technique', he writes, 'may help, given a critical framework, towards constructive interpretation'.[40] The discussion of 'significant action' – Taplin's object of enquiry – depends on and contributes to an understanding of the play's significance. This means that stagecraft criticism for Taplin can never properly be a separate sphere from literary interpretation. Many critics who have followed Taplin's lead into stagecraft have not followed this recognition, and where at its best stagecraft criticism can explore the conventions and possibilities of staging to illumine the nature of theatrical representation and its production of meaning, at its worst stagecraft criticism has descended into critics saying how they would direct plays, or the mere listing of entrances and exits. Indeed, there is still much room for the consideration of the most basic principles by which stagecraft criticism operates. For Taplin, it is a crucial starting-point that 'all significant action' is 'implicit in' or 'sanctioned by' or 'indicated in the words' of the play.[41] Wiles writes, however: 'a good dramatist does not use language to duplicate information available to the eye'.[42] These two statements of principle are not necessarily opposed to each other, but do mark what remains a constitutive and highly problematic issue of stagecraft criticism: *how* to move from a script to a performance. For all the advances of stagecraft criticism, the central questions of what a script can be said to represent are still hotly contested.

Two particular areas of stagecraft have provoked especial interest, the mask and the organisation of stage space. The convention of masking has been much discussed with regard to what it might imply or deny about a concern with characterisation.[43] Some critics have read an increasingly self-conscious awareness of the mask as a convention in fifth-century drama. As ever, Euripides is seen as the avant-garde exposer of convention as convention because of his focus on a tension between surface appearance and inwardness (though such an interest is also typical of much contemporary writing: the contrast between reality and illusion, mental states and verbal utterances, physical form and moral worth are all standard elements of fifth-century intellectual activity). Although there have also been interesting discussions of the use of masks in other ritual aspects of Greek culture,[44] there has not yet been a full and adequate treatment that brings together these different uses of masking in Greek culture.

The stage space itself also shows an important dynamic of inside and outside. The formal development of a set to include regularly a building with doors at the centre and rear of the stage places a focus on the boundary

---

[40] Taplin (1978) 4.   [41] Taplin (1977) 30–1.
[42] Wiles (1991) 137.   [43] See e.g. Jones (1962); Foley (1980).
[44] See e.g. Frontisi-Ducroux (1991) and (1995).

of the door, the hidden secrets of the inside of the house, and the public space of the stage. The *ekkuklēma*, a platform which rolls through the door, and can carry a tableau from the inside, formalises the transition from inside to outside.[45] Since many tragedies are concerned both with intrafamilial secrets and horrors, and with a tension between the world of the family and the world of the polis, the organisation of stage space and the thematic interests of the drama develop hand in hand.[46] So, Taplin shows well how in the *Oresteia* Clytemnestra's entrances and exits dramatise the theme of the control of the house by controlling the point of entrance to the house.[47]

That plays are 'written for performance' is a starting-point for a discussion that engages both the anthropologically based study of the social drama of theatre and the study of stagecraft: they are two necessary responses to the event of tragedy.

PSYCHOANALYSIS AND GREEK TRAGEDY

Psychoanalytic criticism, which has been so influential in twentieth-century literary study, has had an impact on the criticism of Greek tragedy in an explicit and implicit way. There are several critics who have read widely in psychoanalytic writing and used the models of mind, desire and the unconscious developed by Freud and his epigones to explain both the effect of tragedy and tragedy's narrative patterns. Orthodox Freudian analysis has been particularly evident, with Lacan rarely invoked.[48] Tragedy's power is explained as the pleasure and horror of observing the staged enactment of its audience's subconscious desires. Oedipus, that Freudian talisman, fulfils his audience's desire to kill the father and to marry the mother (hence his blinding – a symbolic castration – as the return via punishment of the rule of repression[49]). This develops a long tradition of the psychological interpretation of tragedy's effect, started for us by Plato, into a modern theoretical model of pleasure and the subconscious. Tragedy's narrative is also expressed in terms of the predetermined pattern of psychological development outlined in Freudian theory. So Segal glosses the *Bacchae* as follows:

---

[45] The date of the introduction of the *ekkuklēma* is unclear. See Taplin (1977) 442–3, who thinks it might postdate Aeschylus. It is, however, possible that it was utilised in the *Oresteia*.

[46] See e.g. Easterling (1988); Foley (1982); Padel (1990).

[47] Taplin (1978) 340–57.

[48] See e.g. Simon (1978); Devereux (1976); Caldwell (1974); Slater (1968); Segal (1982); for a more Lacanian version see Green (1979); Pucci (1992); duBois (1988).

[49] See e.g. Devereux (1973), criticised by Buxton (1980).

The *Bacchae* presents a son's fantasy-solution to his oedipal rivalry with his father. The threatening, vigorous, biological and sexual father is absent. The paternal figure who replaces him, the aged grandfather, Cadmus, is old and weak and has relinquished his (royal) power or *kratos* to his son. The mother is left to concern herself entirely with the son who is offered infantile dependence on her, the 'luxury' of being held once more, like a baby, in her arms.[50]

The inverted commas around the term 'luxury' are needed because Pentheus – the son – is at this point being dismembered by his mother, who fails even to recognise him – which is seen as 'the reassertion of the reality principle' against the fantasy-solution to the family story. This translation of tragic narrative into psychoanalytic narrative depends on three debatable assumptions. First that there is a universal pattern of psychological development, a cross-cultural transhistorical 'human nature' – so that Pentheus, a son, will always be an exemplification of 'the son'. Second, that the Freudian description of human nature – its family romance – is universally valid. Third, that a dramatic narrative in a culture which does not know of psychoanalysis, can be (best) expressed as if it were an account of psychological development, so that tragedy can only confirm what – for the twentieth century – is already known about such a development. Similar assumptions are at work in psychoanalytic readings of Greek society as a whole. The danger of a distorting appropriation of ancient culture to a modern model – a worry relevant to all modern criticism of ancient texts – is, in other words, very strongly marked in such psychoanalytic readings. Or as Žižek wittily faces the problem: '*Richard II* proves beyond any doubt that Shakespeare had read Lacan, for...'[51]

It will not do, however, simply to ignore the questions which pychoanalysis has placed on the agenda. First, there is, as I have mentioned, a long tradition of attempting to explain the uncanny emotional power of tragedy. Some sort of psychological theory is *necessarily* involved in such a project. Ancient theory – Aristotle and Plato disagree on the psychology of tragedy and offer different ways of linking a theory of mind to the experience of tragedy – is now beginning to be studied in detail,[52] but there is no reason to assume that the very particular theories offered by Plato and Aristotle are normative for the ancient world in general or beyond modern critique. And it is hard to imagine a modern account which simply bypassed Freud's writing. Second, Greek tragedy itself is much concerned with what can be called psychology, not merely in the representation of the mental states of its famous women and madmen, but also and more commonly in the

[50] Segal (1982) 283.   [51] Žižek (1991) 9.   [52] See e.g. Belfiore (1992).

discussion of the sets of attitudes that lead to and help explain the sexual and social transgressions of tragic narrative.[53] The problem – particularly well articulated by historians and anthropologists – of reading another culture's categories of mind and mental attitudes is especially difficult with these literary representations of normal and abnormal attitudes. An orthodox Freudian reading may seem to translate Greek narrative into an anachronistic model, but can any modern reading wholly escape such charges of appropriation and distortion – the lures of its own tacit knowledge? If tragedy contributes to a history of the self – as critics from Nietzsche to Snell to Vernant have differently argued – what language, what techniques should be used for an exploration of that history?

It is indeed easy to see how often an *implicit* psychological model – sometimes influenced at least indirectly by Freud – can inform readings of tragedy, especially where there is no explicit commitment to any formal theory. The *Bacchae* is a particularly interesting case. We have already seen something of an explicitly orthodox Freudian account of the play. Dodds, in what is the standard critical edition of the play, offers no explicit affiliation to a body of theoretical material (although I have already mentioned the importance of his studies on the irrational for his commentary); the edition is, however, full of talk of the dangers of repressing desire: 'To resist Dionysus', he writes, 'is to resist the elemental in one's own nature.'[54] Dionysus is seen as touching 'a hidden spring in Pentheus' mind'[55] when he offers the chance to watch the women in the hills, a spring that allows him to act out what Winnington-Ingram calls 'his unconscious desire'.[56] Even Kitto sees the play as 'a sharp contrast of one mind and another'[57] – two psychological constitutions that he goes on to sketch in detail. It is indeed hard to discuss Pentheus, his attitude to Dionysus, and Dionysus' effect on him, without touching on such issues of mind and mental stability. To describe Pentheus' willingness to go to the mountain as the releasing of 'his unconscious desire' – rather than a god-sent madness, say – is to imply a model of mind, a model of desire, and a model of divine influence, not to mention a theory of characterisation and representation. Indeed, there is much contemporary study of how such common critical terms as 'character', 'role', 'persona' can be applied to Greek drama, a discussion where theories of representation necessarily overlap with psychological concerns.[58] As the historical construction of the 'concept of the self' remains firmly on

---

[53] See e.g. Goldhill (1986) 168–98; Padel (1992), (1995).

[54] Dodds (1960a) xiv.   [55] Dodds (1960a) 166.

[56] Winnington-Ingram (1948a) 103.   [57] Kitto (1961) 379.

[58] See e.g. Jones (1962); Gould (1978); Easterling (1990); Goldhill (1990b); each with further bibliography.

the agenda in many areas of the humanities, so too in Greek culture and Greek drama the central categories of dramatic representation – which necessarily involve psychological models – need careful and continuing analysis.

The seductions of the Freudian model will no doubt continue to be felt in the criticism of tragedy. It remains to be seen whether critics who work with such a methodological commitment can also engage with the problems of cultural appropriation that historians and anthropologists have raised with regard to understanding other cultures' mental categories and categories of mind. Since the description of character necessarily involves the mobilisation of (at least) implicit psychological models, it is unlikely that the criticism of Greek tragedy can expect wholly to avoid an engagement with psychological and psychoanalytic theory.

THE HISTORY AND POLITICS OF READING

Structuralist interpretations of Greek tragedy, and of Greek literature and ritual in general, have been very widely absorbed into the mainstream of criticism, often without acknowledgement as such. Key structuralist analyses – for example, of the scene of sacrifice as a way of categorising men, beasts, gods; of the importance of the raw and the cooked; of marriage as the exchange of women between men – are widely taken for granted, and provide an excellent example of the way a methodological approach can be diffused through many different types of work on tragedy. Post-structuralist critiques, however, have, as yet, been less evident. Although the self-reflexivity of tragedy is debated in many ways and although the collapse of binary oppositions into more complex relations has been traced in Greek tragedy, the challenge of post-structuralism to consider the theories of language and representation involved in any critical enterprise has been all too rarely explored – despite Derrida's evident engagement with Greek culture and with Plato in particular.[59] Rather, much recent controversy has focused on the political discourse of tragedy and on the politics of reading tragedy.

Since tragedy is a performance for and before the assembled polis, there have been repeated attempts to understand it as a historico-political event, and, especially, to locate the didactic message of tragedy.[60] The anthro-

---

[59] Derrida (1981) is the *locus classicus*; see also Derrida (1992). Specifically on tragedy, see Goldhill (1984); Goff (1990); Pucci (1980). See also in general Goldhill (1994b). Euben (1986) and Hexter & Selden (1992) show only a few signs of novelty in this direction.

[60] For tragedy as a didactic genre, see Croally (1994), and (with less sophistication) Gregory (1991).

pologically based readings I have already discussed are one important response to this project. Since Engels took the *Oresteia* as a key text for his analysis of the origin of the family, private property and the State, tragedy has often been seen, particularly by Marxist writers, as an exploration or demonstration of power relations within the polis.[61] There have also been, however, repeated attempts to link the plays and their funding very closely to more narrowly defined political events. Since the *Oresteia* was performed shortly after Ephialtes, the proposer of major democratic legal reforms, was assassinated, and since the *Eumenides* has Athena address the issue of the establishment of the legal system in Athens, the *Oresteia* has been seen as speaking very directly to these issues – so that, for example, one surprisingly precise message that critics have extracted from the *Eumenides* is an Aeschylean comment on which classes of citizens should be admitted to the role of *archōn* and hence to sit in the court of the Areopagus.[62] In a similar fashion, Aeschylus' *Persians* has been seen as a statement of passionate support for Themistocles – which, conjoined with the fact that Pericles was the funder (*chorēgos*) of the play, has led critics to attempt to construct an elaborate political positioning for the playwright.[63] The lack of any explicit reference to contemporary political figures in tragedy (as opposed to comedy) makes such political allegorising – especially when dependent on modern ideas of political process – highly speculative.

More promising has been the understanding of how tragedy adopts, manipulates and discusses contemporary political and legal language and ideology. So, for example, the dramatic figure of the tyrant has been carefully analysed as a contributory factor in the fifth-century representation of that bugbear of democracy,[64] and the conflicts of tragedy have been seen as analogous to – and commenting on – the conflicts of the legal and political arena.[65] In particular the study of myth and of gender has been instrumental in uncovering the political force of tragedy. Although there are many fine scholars who are feminists, the fact that tragedy is written by citizens – adult, enfranchised males – performed by citizens, and watched almost exclusively by citizens, means that some of the routes taken by feminist scholarship for other periods, e.g. to discuss women writers, female subjectivity, strategies of social and intellectual repression, have not been

[61] E.g. Thomson (1941); di Benedetto (1978); Citti (1978); Rose (1992); see also Hall (Ch. 5 above).

[62] See for the argument on 'zeugite admission to the archonship', Dover (1957) and Dodds (1960b), and, more sophisticatedly, Macleod (1982). For overviews of the problem see Conacher (1987) 195–212; Sommerstein (1989) 216–18; Goldhill (1986) 33–56.

[63] See e.g. Podlecki (1966b).

[64] See e.g. Cerri (1975); di Benedetto (1978); Saïd (1985); Lanza (1977).

[65] See e.g. Meier (1990), (1993); Eden (1986); Euben (1990); Farrar (1988).

widely followed in the study of Greek tragedy (and much work remains to be done in a field that has been and is dominated by male scholars). Rather, many scholars – often stimulated and well informed by feminist work – have explored both the representation of gender relations (often focused on the representation of female roles within the male frame of tragedy) and the explicit discussion of gender issues that many tragedies stage (cf. Ch. 5 above for bibliography and further discussion). This has led to a particularly intense investigation of the connection between a discourse of gender and a discourse of citizenship and the mythical narratives of tragedy.[66] Critics have articulated, for example, how a myth like that of autochthony – birth from the soil itself – becomes in tragedy a topic that speaks to issues of gender (and) politics.[67] All myths of origin have evident ideological force. But the myth of autochthony, which implies an inherent link to the land and a bypassing of women's role in generation, becomes especially significant in Athenian patriarchal society, as the rules of citizenship and the practice of state imperialism become major issues. So, a work like the *Oresteia*, so important in the history of gender relations, has been read and re-read as a drama that speaks to the polis through a closely woven nexus of ideas of myth, gender, politics:[68] a text both for the politics of Athens and for the politics of the present. Not only does such a history of a play's readings, a history of its *reception*,[69] deepen our sense of the historically contingent nature of critical understanding, but also the different levels on which the trial scene of the *Eumenides* expresses a message to the citizens – its mythic narrative of gods and heroes, its political discourse addressed to the city, its discussion of gender roles – shows well the complexities of the public rhetoric of tragedy, and the variety of approaches required to understand such a multilayered cultural event.

Much of the most recent work on tragedy has tried to explore this political rhetoric of tragedy – without seeing particular policies or personages allegorised in each aspect of the drama, as much earlier political analysis of tragedy had attempted. The way in which such work utilises a methodologically sophisticated understanding of how myth works within culture, of how a dramatic performance communicates, and of how the language of tragedy functions, shows how the different strands of criticism I

---

[66] See e.g. Loraux (1993) e.g. 197–253; Winkler & Zeitlin (1990) esp. chs. 2–6; Zeitlin (1978); Merck (1978); Segal (1981); Goff (1990); Goldhill (1986) esp. chs. 3 and 6; and it is worth noting Winnington-Ingram (1948b) as a remarkable early contribution.

[67] See Loraux (1993) 197–253; Zeitlin (1982), (1989).

[68] Goldhill (1986) 51–6 traces some of these readings.

[69] There has been surprisingly little work on reception theory and classical drama. See, though, Steiner (1984); Michelini (1987) 1–51; and Chs. 9–12 of this volume.

have outlined in the previous sections continue to interact in the contemporary debates on Greek tragedy. Indeed, the contemporary debate is particularly hard to characterise except as an explosive combination of elements of these diverse and interrelated traditions of criticism, and it is in general far from easy to construct simple affiliations. This sense of contemporary critical multiformity is not necessarily just a product of that critical blindness or sensitivity which results from too great a closeness to a subject, but also a result of the changing institutional position of Classics in the academy, where it can no longer be assumed that Classics has the privileged position of the nineteenth century, and where the boundaries of the field have become less clearly determined (and thus, on occasion, more vigorously policed, more passionately transgressed).

'The history and politics of reading', however, was chosen as a title for this last brief section also so that I could (finally) re-emphasise that in the preceding pages my critical approach to critical approaches has been all too self-consciously selective and polemical – partial in all senses. This is not only because of the restrictions of space, of course, distorting though such a frame for such a wide range of material must be. It is also because it is not possible – however judicious and responsible a critic may be – to offer a neutral version of such a teleological project as a history of modern critical approaches to tragedy. As a modern literary critic I am part of what I am meant to be describing. There is a more important point to stress here, however, than an apologetic or sly recognition that I may have stood on some (friends') toes. Classical literary criticism has often resisted discussion of theoretical matters. In this book, too, this is the final chapter, a final consideration. Yet methodology is not a supplement to reading; theory is not opposed to practice. A methodology is what makes reading – any reading – possible. Each of the preceding chapters of this book has been the instantiation of a methodological position, more or less explicitly considered. Critical theory – the discussion of such methodology – is a necessary factor in any critical understanding of Greek tragedy. Since this book is dedicated to helping readers develop such a critical understanding, 'modern critical approaches' is inevitably our shared and unending project.

BIBLIOGRAPHICAL NOTE

There is no adequate study of the development of critical approaches to Greek tragedy in English. On Victorian classicism, see F. M. Turner, *The Greek Heritage in Victorian Britain* (New Haven 1981); G. W. Clarke, ed., *Rediscovering Hellenism: the Hellenic Inheritance and the English Imagination* (Cambridge 1989); M. Bernal, *Black Athena* (New Brunswick 1987) – but none of these has anything specific on tragedy. On the history of classical scholarship, see Pfeiffer (1968); Lloyd-Jones (1982). There are many histories of literary criticism focusing on the nineteenth and twentieth centuries, but few pay due attention to the role of Classics: an exception is Baldick (1983). There are excellent accounts of individual thinkers and tragedy: see e.g. Silk & Stern (1981), A. & H. Paolucci, *Hegel on Tragedy* (New York 1962), and innumerable books on 'Tragedy and the tragic' (a subject which tends to attract the grand theoretical sweep) – most recently Silk (1996) – but no adequate survey of the changing response to tragedy as an idea or institution from the nineteenth to the twentieth century.

GLOSSARY

agora   the market-place or civic centre (lit. 'gathering-place') of a Greek city

agōn   contest (in athletics or battle)/ argument

agōnia   contest, anguish

aition   an explanation through myth

aitios   responsible, guilty, the cause of

anagnōrisis   recognition in drama

andreia   the Greek concept of 'manliness'

antistrophē   metrically identical stanza (lit. the 'counterturn') to the preceding *strophē* (lit. the 'turn') in the choral ode

archōn   one of 9 officials appointed each year

aulos/oi   double pipe played by the musician in tragedy

bia   force, violence

boulē   executive council of 500 citizens who prepared and enacted the business of the policy-making Assembly

bouleutikon   block of seats in the theatre reserved for members of the *boulē*

chorēgia   the role of a *chorēgos*

chorēgos/oi   wealthy citizen(s) called upon by the state to fund choruses for each of the tragedians, comic dramatists and dithyrambic poets at the City Dionysia

choreia   combination of song and dance performed by a *choros*

choreutai   members of the chorus

choros   group in performance

daimon   superhuman/power

deixis   an exhibition/demonstration

deme/*dēmos* village/ward of Attica

deus ex machina a god who appears at the end of a tragedy suspended by the *mēchanē*/crane (lit. 'god from the machine') to solve an otherwise intractable ending

didaskalia record of dramatic productions

dikē justice, law, right/penalty

ekkuklēma trolley/platform which wheels out to reveal a scene from inside the central doors of the stage building (*skēnē*)

eleutheria freedom

embolima choral songs (lit. 'things thrown in') that could be used as entr'actes

ephebe adolescent on the verge of manhood

epideictic usu. 'epideictic rhetoric' – highly rhetorical speeches designed for maximum flourish and display in delivery

epode a free-standing stanza usually following the *strophē* and *antistrophē* in the choral ode

Erinyes Furies

genos a small (aristocratic) grouping of families within the **phratry**

hamartia mistake / tragic error (not, as often claimed, 'tragic flaw')

hupokrisis rhetorical debate (non-theatrical)

hupokritēs actor (lit. 'answerer')

hypothesis/hupothesis ancient scholar's introduction to a play

isēgoria equal freedom with regard to public speaking

katharsis Aristotle's much debated term (lit. 'a purging') to explain tragedy's effect on the audience's emotions

kerkides wedges of seats in the Greek theatre

kleos glory/fame for heroic achievement

kommos lament, sometimes used of lyric (i.e. sung) dialogue between actor and chorus

kōmos celebratory revel

koruphaios leader of the chorus

kothornos/oi decorated boots worn by tragic actors

kurios male guardian of an Athenian woman

metic resident alien in Athens

muthos story/plot of a play

nostos/oi return journey(s) to the home

orchēstra 'dancing-floor' in the Greek theatre, often circular

ostrakon potsherd on which names of candidates for ostracism (10 years' exile by majority vote of 6,000-plus Athenians casting ballots in the *agora*) were written down

paidagōgos/oi tutor(s), i.e. slave(s) who accompanied schoolboys

parodos entrance song of the chorus

parrhēsia equal freedom with regard to expressing opinion

parthenos/oi virgin(s)

peithō persuasion

peripeteia unexpected turn of events in tragedy identified by Aristotle in the *Poetics*

philos/oi friend(s)/allies

phorbeia cheek-band worn by pipes-player

phratry/ies group(s) to which only Athenian citizens could belong

phronimos the wise citizen

pompē ceremonial procession

proagōn the preliminary event before the dramatic contest at which the dramatists advertised their plays

prohedriai honorific seats in the front rows of each block in the theatre, reserved particularly for priests, notably the priest of Dionysus, and dignitaries

prosōpon mask/face

rhēsis/eis formal set-speech(es) in tragedy

rhētōr/ores public speaker(s) in the Assembly

sikinnis special dance of the satyrs involving kicking and jumping

skēnē/ai stage building(s)

sparagmos tearing apart of the flesh of the quarry in Dionysiac ritual

stasimon/a choral ode(s)

stasis civil strife and civil war

stēlē   monument

stichomythia   rapid exchange of one- or two-line utterances between two or more characters

strophē   the first major stanza in the choral ode (lit. the 'turn') metrically identical to the *antistrophē* (lit. the 'counterturn')

technē   art, skill

theātēs/ai   spectator(s)

thelxis   enchantment

thete   dependent labourer/serf

thiasos   Dionysus' band of followers

thorubos   hubbub in the theatre

thumelē   the altar in the middle of the *orchēstra* in the Greek theatre

tragōidos/oi   tragic actor(s)

xenos/oi   foreigner(s)

CHRONOLOGY

c. 534	According to tradition, Thespis wins prize for tragedy at the City Dionysia
525/4?	Birth of Aeschylus
508/7	Cleisthenes' Reforms
497/6 *or*	
496/5	Birth of Sophocles
494	Persian annihilation of Miletus
493/2	Phrynichus' *Capture of Miletus*
490	First Persian invasion: Battle of Marathon
486	Comic drama introduced at the City Dionysia
484	Aeschylus' first victory in dramatic contest
c. 480	Birth of Euripides
480	Second Persian invasion: Battles of Artemisium, Thermopylae, Salamis
479	Battle of Plataea
478	Formation of Delian League
476?	Phrynichus' *Phoenician Women*
472	Aeschylus' *Persians* wins first prize
c. 470	Birth of Socrates
468	Sophocles' first victory in dramatic contest, with *Triptolemus*
467	Aeschylus' *Seven against Thebes* wins first prize with *Laius*, *Oedipus*, *Sphinx* (satyr play)
c. 460s	Aeschylus' *Suppliant Women* wins first prize
462	Ephialtes' reform of the Areopagus Council
	Alliance of Athens with Argos
461	Ephialtes' assassination
458	Aeschylus' *Oresteia* wins first prize with *Proteus* (satyr play)
456	Death of Aeschylus
455	Euripides' first entry in dramatic contest, with *Peliades*
451	Pericles' citizenship law
449	Institution of prize for the best tragic actor
c. 445	Birth of Aristophanes
442?	Sophocles' *Antigone*
441	Euripides' first victory in dramatic competition

438	Euripides' *Alcestis* wins second prize as part of tetralogy with *Cretan Women, Alcmaeon in Psophis, Telephus*
431	Euripides' *Medea* wins third prize with *Philoctetes, Dictys, Theristai* (satyr play)
431–404	Peloponnesian War between Athens and Sparta
430	Plague breaks out in Athens
430–428?	Sophocles' *Oedipus the King*
	Euripides' *Children of Heracles*
429	Death of Pericles
c. 429	Birth of Plato
428	Euripides' *Hippolytus* (revised version) wins first prize
425	Aristophanes' *Acharnians*
	?Euripides' *Andromache*
424	Aristophanes' *Knights*
pre-423?	Euripides' *Hecuba*
423	Aristophanes' *Clouds*
	?Euripides' *Suppliant Women*
422	Aristophanes' *Wasps*
421	Aristophanes' *Peace*
pre-415	?Euripides' *Electra*
	?Euripides' *Heracles*
415–13	Sicilian Expedition
415	Euripides' *Trojan Women* wins second prize with *Alexander, Palamedes, Sisyphus* (satyr play)
414	Aristophanes' *Birds*
c. 413	Euripides' *Iphigeneia among the Taurians*
	?Sophocles' *Electra*
412	Euripides' *Helen* with *Andromeda* and ?*Cyclops* (satyr play)
411	Overthrow of democracy by Oligarchs (Revolution of the Four Hundred)
	Aristophanes' *Lysistrata* and *Women Celebrating the Thesmophoria*
409	Sophocles' *Philoctetes* wins first prize
	?Euripides' *Phoenician Women* with *Antiope* and *Hypsipyle*
408	Euripides' *Orestes*
406	Battle of Arginusae
406/5	Death of Euripides
	Death of Sophocles
after 406	Euripides' *Bacchae* wins first prize ⎫
	Euripides' *Iphigeneia at Aulis* ⎭ (posthumously produced)
405	Aristophanes' *Frogs*
404	Peace between Athens and Sparta
	Thirty Tyrants rule at Athens
403	Civil War in Athens
	Restoration of democracy

401	Sophocles' *Oedipus at Colonus* (posthumously produced)
399	Death of Socrates
393/2	Aristophanes' *Women in Assembly*
388	Aristophanes' *Wealth*
c. 387	Plato starts Academy
386	'Old tragedy' introduced at the City Dionysia
386/0	Death of Aristophanes
384	Birth of Aristotle and Demosthenes
367	Aristotle joins the Academy
358	Theatre of Epidaurus built
347	Death of Plato
342/1	Birth of Menander
339	'Old comedy' introduced at the City Dionysia
322	Deaths of Aristotle and Demosthenes
321	Menander's *Anger* wins first prize
c. 320s	Aristotle's *Poetics*

AESCHYLUS

Texts of the surviving plays: D. Page, Oxford 1972
M. L. West, Stuttgart 1990
Fragments: S. Radt, *Tragicorum Graecorum Fragmenta*, vol. 3, Göttingen 1985
Discussion of the text: M. L. West, *Studies in Aeschylus*, Stuttgart 1990

Commentaries:

Agamemnon (Ag.)	E. Fraenkel, 3 vols., Oxford 1950
	J. D. Denniston and D. Page, Oxford 1957
	J. Bollack and P. Judet de la Combe, 4 vols., Lille 1981–2
Libation-Bearers (Cho.)	A. F. Garvie, Oxford 1986
	A. Bowen, Bristol 1986
Eumenides (Eum.)	A. J. Podlecki, Warminster 1989, corr. 1992
	A. H. Sommerstein, Cambridge 1989
Persians (Pers.)	H. D. Broadhead, Cambridge 1960
	E. M. Hall, Warminster 1996
Prometheus Bound (P.V.)	M. Griffith, Cambridge 1983
Seven against Thebes (Sept.)	L. Lupaş and Z. Petre, Paris 1981
	G. O. Hutchinson, Oxford 1985
Suppliant Women (Suppl.)	H. Friis Johansen and E. W. Whittle, Copenhagen 1980

Translations:

Oresteia	H. Lloyd-Jones, 2nd edn, London 1979
	R. Fagles, Harmondsworth 1977
	T. Harrison, London 1981
Persians	A. J. Podlecki, Bristol 1991
All seven plays:	D. Grene and R. Lattimore, Chicago 1953
	M. Ewans, 2 vols., London 1995, 1996

SOPHOCLES

Texts of the surviving plays: R. D. Dawe, 7 vols., 3rd edn, Stuttgart and Leipzig
1996
H. Lloyd-Jones and N. G. Wilson, Oxford 1990 (corr.
edn, 1992)
Fragments: S. Radt, *Tragicorum Graecorum Fragmenta*, vol. iv, Göttingen 1977
H. Lloyd-Jones, Loeb Classical Library, vol. iii, Cambridge, MA, 1996
Discussion of the text: R. D. Dawe, *Studies on the Text of Sophocles*, 3 vols.,
Leiden 1973–8
H. Lloyd-Jones and N. G. Wilson, *Sophoclea: Studies on the
Text of Sophocles*, Oxford 1990

Commentaries:
On all seven tragedies: R. C. Jebb, Cambridge 1883–1900
J. C. Kamerbeek, Leiden 1953–84
Ajax (Aj.)   W. B. Stanford, London 1963
Antigone (Ant.)   G. Müller, Heidelberg 1967
A. L. Brown, Warminster 1987
Electra (El.)   J. H. Kells, Cambridge 1973
Oedipus the King (O.T.)   R. D. Dawe, Cambridge 1982
J. Rusten, Bryn Mawr 1990
J. Bollack, 4 vols., Lille 1990
Philoctetes (Phil.)   T. B. L. Webster, Cambridge 1970
R. G. Ussher, Warminster 1990
Women of Trachis (Trach.)   P. E. Easterling, Cambridge 1982
M. Davies, Oxford 1991
Fragments: A. C. Pearson, 3 vols., Cambridge 1917

Translations:
All seven tragedies: D. Grene and R. Lattimore, Chicago 1959
H. Lloyd-Jones, 2 vols., Loeb Classical
Library, Cambridge, MA, 1994
The Theban plays: R. Fagles and B. M. W. Knox,
Harmondsworth 1984
D. Taylor, London 1986
T. Wertenbaker, London 1992
Antigone, Oedipus the King, Electra   H. D. F. Kitto and E. M. Hall, Oxford 1994
Oedipus at Colonus (O.C.)   M. Whitlock-Blundell, Newburyport, MA,
1990
Philoctetes (The Cure at Troy)   S. Heaney, London 1991
Fragments: H. Lloyd-Jones, Loeb Classical Library,
Cambridge, MA, vol. iii, 1996

EURIPIDES

Text of the surviving plays: J. Diggle, 3 vols., Oxford 1982–94
Discussion of the text: J. Diggle, *Euripidea*, Oxford 1994

Fragments: A. Nauck, *Tragicorum Graecorum Fragmenta*, 2nd edn, Leipzig 1889
A new edition by R. Kannicht (= vol. v of *Tragicorum Graecorum Fragmenta*, Göttingen) is forthcoming
C. Austin, *Nova fragmenta Euripidea in papyris reperta*, Berlin 1968
C. Collard, M. Cropp, K. H. Lee, *Euripides, Selected Fragmentary Plays*, vol. i, Warminster 1995

Commentaries:

Alcestis (Alc.)	A. M. Dale, Oxford 1954
	D. Conacher, Warminster 1988
Andromache (Andr.)	P. T. Stevens, Oxford 1971
	M. Lloyd, Warminster 1995
Bacchae (Ba.)	E. R. Dodds, 2nd edn, Oxford 1960
	R. Seaford, Warminster 1996
Cyclops (Cycl.)	R. G. Ussher, Rome 1978
	R. Seaford, Oxford 1984
Children of Heracles (Hcld.)	J. Wilkins, Oxford 1993
Electra (El.)	J. D. Denniston, Oxford 1939
	M. J. Cropp, Warminster 1988
Hecuba (Hec.)	M. Tierney, Bristol 1979
	C. Collard, Warminster 1991
Helen (Hel.)	A. M. Dale, Oxford 1967
	R. Kannicht, 2 vols., Heidelberg 1969
Heracles (Her.)	G. W. Bond, Oxford 1981
	S. A. Barlow, Warminster 1996
Heracleidae (Hcld.)	see *Children of Heracles*
Hippolytus (Hipp.)	W. S. Barrett, Oxford 1964
	M. J. Halleran, Warminster 1996
Ion	A. S. Owen, Oxford 1939, repr. Bristol 1987
Iphigeneia at Aulis (I.A.)	W. Stockert, Vienna 1992
Iphigeneia among the Taurians (I.T.)	M. Platnauer, Oxford 1938
Medea (Med.)	D. L. Page, Oxford 1938
	A. Elliott, Oxford 1969
Orestes (Or.)	C. W. Willink, Oxford 1986
	M. L. West, Warminster 1987
Phoenician Women (Phoen.)	E. Craik, Warminster 1988
	D. J. Mastronade, Cambridge 1994
Suppliant Women (Suppl.)	C. Collard, 2 vols., Groningen 1975
Trojan Women (Tro.)	K. H. Lee, London 1976
	S. A. Barlow, Warminster 1986

Fragments: C. Collard, M. Cropp, K. H. Lee, vol. 1,
Warminster 1995

Translations: D. Grene and R. Lattimore, Chicago 1953–72
ed. W. Arrowsmith, *The Greek Tragedy in New Translations*,
Oxford 1973–
K. McLeish, *After the Trojan War* (*Tro.*, *Hec.*, *Helen*) Bath 1995

New translations are in progress as follows:
Loeb Classical Library, D. Kovacs, vol. 1 (*Cyclops*, *Alc.*, *Med.*),
Cambridge, MA, 1994; vol. 11 (*Children of Her.*, *Hipp.*, *Andr.*,
Hec.), 1995
Penguin Classics, J. Davie and R. Rutherford, vol. 1 (*Alc.*, *Med.*,
Children of Her., *Hipp.*), Harmondsworth 1996

WORKS CITED

The following abbreviations are used:

CHCL   *Cambridge History of Classical Literature*, vol. 1
       Greek Literature, eds. P. E. Easterling & B. M. W. Knox. Cambridge
       1985
LIMC   *Lexicon Iconographicum Mythologiae Classicae*. Zurich 1981–
Nauck² A. Nauck, *Tragicorum Graecorum Fragmenta*, 2nd edn. Leipzig 1889
TrGF   *Tragicorum Graecorum Fragmenta*, eds. B. Snell, S. Radt & R. Kannicht.
       Göttingen 1971–

Ackerman, R. (1987) *J. G. Frazer, his Life and Work*. Cambridge
Albini, U. (1991) *Nel Nome di Dioniso. Vita teatrale nell'Atene classica*. Milan
Alexander, D. M. (1953) 'Psychological fate in *Mourning Becomes Electra*', *PMLA*
   68: 923–34
Altman, J. B. (1978) *The Tudor Play of Mind*. Berkeley
Arkins, B. (1990) *Builders of My Soul: Greek and Roman Themes in Yeats*. Gerrards
   Cross
Arnott, P. D. (1962) *Greek Scenic Conventions in the Fifth Century BC*. Oxford
   (1989) *Public and Performance in the Greek Theatre*. London & New York
Arrowsmith, W. (1963) 'A Greek theater of ideas', *Arion* 2: 32–56
Ashton, G. (1992) *Catalogue of Paintings at the Theatre Museum, London*.
   London
Astley, N., ed. (1991) *Tony Harrison* (Bloodaxe Critical Anthologies I). Newcastle
   upon Tyne
Austin, C. (1968) *Nova fragmenta Euripidea in papyris reperta*. Berlin
Babcock, B., ed. (1978) *The Reversible World*. Ithaca
Bain, D. (1977) *Actors and Audiences: a Study of Asides and Related Conventions in
   Greek Drama*. Oxford
   (1987) 'Some reflections on the illusion in Greek tragedy', *BICS* 34: 1–14
Baldick, C. (1983) *The Social Mission of English Criticism 1848–1932*. Oxford
Baldry, H. C. (1971) *The Greek Tragic Theatre*. London
Barlow, S. A. (1986) *Euripides. Trojan Women*. Warminster
Barrett, W. S. (1964) *Euripides. Hippolytos*. Oxford
Bartsch, S. (1994) *Actors in the Audience*. Cambridge, MA, & London
Bassi, D. (1942–3) 'Nutrici e pedagogi nella tragedia greca', *Dioniso* 9: 80–7

Beacham, R. C. (1987) 'Revivals: Europe', in J. M. Walton, ed., *Living Greek Theatre: a Handbook of Classical Performances and Modern Productions*, 304–14. New York & Westport, CT

(1991) *The Roman Theatre and its Audience*. London

Beard, W. M. (1992) 'Frazer, Leach and Virgil: the popularity (and unpopularity) of *The Golden Bough*', *Comparative Studies in Society and History* 34: 203–24

Beauvoir, S. de (1962) *The Prime of Life*. Cleveland, OH (French original 1960)

Beazley, J. D. (1955) 'Hydria-fragments in Corinth', *Hesperia* 24: 305–19

Beck, F. A. (1975) *Album of Greek Education*. Sydney

Belfiore, E. (1992) *Tragic Pleasures: Aristotle on Plot and Emotion*. Princeton

di Benedetto, V. (1971) *Euripide: teatro e società*. Turin

(1978) *L'Ideologia del Potere e la Tragedia Greca*. Turin

Bérard, C., & C. Bron (1989) 'Satyric revels', in C. Bérard et al., eds., *A City of Images*, 131–49. Princeton (French original 1984)

Berry, P. (1989) *On Chastity and Power*. London

Bers, V. (1994) 'Tragedy and rhetoric', in I. Worthington, ed. *Persuasion. Greek Rhetoric in Action*, 176–95. London & New York

Bieber, M. (1961) *The History of the Greek and Roman Theater*, 2nd edn. Princeton

Bierl, A. F. H. (1991) *Dionysos und die griechische Tragödie* (Classica Monacensia Band 1). Tübingen

Boardman, J. (1989) *Attic Red-Figure Vases – the Classical Period*. London

Boegehold, A. (1994) 'Perikles' citizenship law of 451/0 BC', in Boegehold & Scafuro (1994) 57–66

Boegehold, A., & A. Scafuro, eds. (1994) *Athenian Identity and Civic Ideology*. Baltimore & London

Bolgar, R. R. (1954) *The Classical Heritage and its Beneficiaries*. Cambridge

Bond, G. W. (1988) *Euripides. Heracles*. Oxford

Bonner, R. (1905) *Evidence in Athenian Courts*. Chicago

Bouvrie, S. des (1990) *Women in Greek Tragedy: an Anthropological Approach*. Oslo

Bowersock, G. W. (1994) *Fiction as History: Nero to Julian*. Berkeley

Bowie, A. M. (1993) 'Religion and politics in Aeschylus' *Oresteia*', *CQ* 43: 10–31

Bowra, C. M. (1944) *Sophoclean Tragedy*. Oxford

Bremer, J.-M. (1969) *Hamartia: Tragic Error in the Poetics of Aristotle and in Greek Tragedy*. Amsterdam

(1976) 'Why messenger-speeches?', in J.-M. Bremer et al., eds., *Miscellanea tragica in honorem J. C. Kamerbeek*, 29–48. Amsterdam

Bremmer, J. (1994) *Greek Religion* (*Greece & Rome* New Surveys in the Classics 24). Oxford

Brommer, F. (1959) *Satyrspiele*, 2nd edn. Berlin

Brook, P. (1988) *The Shifting Point. Forty Years of Theatrical Exploration 1946–1987*. London

Brower, R. (1959) 'Seven Agamemnons' in R. A. Brower, ed. (1959) *On Translation*, 173–95, Harvard Studies in Comparative Literature 23. Cambridge, MA (= Brower (1974) 159–80)

(1974) *Mirror on Mirror: Translation, Imitation, Parody*. Cambridge, MA

Bruit, L. (1992) 'Daughters of Pandora and rituals in Grecian cities', in P. Schmitt Pantel, ed., *A History of Women in the West*, vol. 1 *From Ancient Goddesses to Christian Saints*, 338–76. Cambridge, MA

Bruit Zaidman, L., & P. Schmitt Pantel (1992) *Religion in the Ancient Greek City*. Cambridge (French original 1989)

Buchanan, J. J. (1962) *THEORIKA. A Study of Monetary Distributions to the Athenian Citizenry during the Fifth and Fourth Centuries B.C.* New York

Burgaud, A. (1984) 'L'Expérience du Groupe de Théâtre Antique de la Sorbonne', in *Le Théâtre Antique de Nos Jours: Symposium International à Delphes 18–22 Août 1981*, 67–82. Athens

Burian, P. (1974) 'Suppliant and savior: Oedipus at Colonus', *Phoenix* 28: 408–29
    ed. (1985) *Directions in Euripidean Criticism*. Durham, NC

Burkert, W. (1966) 'Greek tragedy and sacrificial ritual', *GRBS* 7: 87–121
    (1983) *Homo Necans*. Berkeley (German original 1972)
    (1987) *Ancient Mystery Cults*. Cambridge, MA
    (1990) 'Ein Datum für Euripides' *Elektra*: Dionysia 420 v. Ch.', *Museum Helveticum* 47: 65–9

Burnett, A. P. (1971) *Catastrophe Survived: Euripides' Plays of Mixed Reversal*. Oxford

Buschor, E. (1943) *Satyrtänze und frühes Drama*. Munich

Butts, H. R. (1942) *The Glorification of Athens in Greek Drama* (Iowa Studies in Classical Philology 11). Ann Arbor

Buxton, R. G. A. (1980) 'Blindness and limits: Sophocles and the logic of myth', *JHS* 100: 22–37
    (1982) *Persuasion in Greek Tragedy: a Study of 'Peitho'*. Cambridge
    (1994) *Imaginary Greece: the Contexts of Mythology*. Cambridge

Calame, C. (1986) 'Facing otherness: the tragic mask in ancient Greece', *History of Religions* 26: 125–41
    (1995) *The Craft of Poetic Speech in Ancient Greece* (French original 1989)

Calder, W. M. (1969) 'The date of Euripides' *Erechtheus*', *GRBS* 10: 147–56
    ed. (1991) *The Cambridge Ritualists Reconsidered*. Atlanta

Caldwell, R. S. (1974) 'The psychology of Aeschylus' *Suppliants*', *Arethusa* 7: 45–70

Cameron, A. (1968) *The Identity of Oedipus the King*. New York & London

Cameron, A., & A. Kuhrt (1983, rev. edn 1993) *Images of Women in Antiquity*. London & Sydney

Campbell, D. A. (1991) *Greek Lyric*, vol. III (Loeb Classical Library). Cambridge, MA

Campbell, L. (1891) *A Guide to Greek Tragedy for English Readers*. London

Carpenter, T. H., & C. A. Faraone, eds. (1993) *Masks of Dionysus*. Ithaca & London

Carrière, J.-C. 'La tragédie grecque, auxiliaire de la justice et de la politique', *StudClas* 15: 13–21

Cartledge, P. A. (1979) *Sparta and Lakonia: a Regional History 1300–362 BC*. London
    (1985) 'The Greek religious festivals', in P. E. Easterling & J. V. Muir, eds., *Greek Religion and Society*, 98–127. Cambridge
    (1990) 'Fowl play: a curious lawsuit in Classical Athens (Antiphon frr. 57–9 Thalheim)', in Cartledge, Millett & Todd (1990) 41–61
    (1993) *The Greeks. A Portrait of Self and Others*. Oxford (rev. edn 1997)
    (1995) *Aristophanes and his Theatre of the Absurd*, 3rd edn. Bristol & London

Cartledge, P. A., P. Millett & S. Todd, eds. (1990) *Nomos. Essays in Athenian Law, Politics and Society*. Cambridge

Cerri, G. (1975) *Il Linguaggio Politico nel Prometeo di Eschilo*. Rome

Chamay, J., & A. Cambitoglou (1980) 'La folie d'Athamas par le Peintre de Darius', *Antike Kunst* 23: 35–43

Chaniotis, A. (1993) 'Watching a lawsuit: a new curse tablet from Southern Russia', *GRBS* 34: 69–73

Charlton, H. B. (1946) *The Senecan Tradition in Renaissance Tragedy*. Manchester (originally published 1921)

Chiari, J. (1959) *The Contemporary French Theatre*. New York

Citti, V. (1978) *Tragedia e lotta di classi in Grecia*. Naples

Clark, D. R., & J. B. McGuire (1989) *W. B. Yeats: the Writing of Sophocles' King Oedipus*. Philadelphia

Classen, C. J., ed. (1976) *Sophistik*. Darmstadt

Cohen, D. (1991) *Law, Sexuality, and Society: the Enforcement of Morals in Classical Athens*. Cambridge

Cole, S. G. (1993) 'Procession and celebration at the Dionysia', in Scodel (1993) 25–38

Collard, C., M. Cropp & K. H. Lee (1995) *Euripides. Selected Fragmentary Plays*, vol. 1. Warminster

Conacher, D. J. (1987) *Aeschylus' Oresteia: a Literary Commentary*. Toronto

Connor, W. R. (1985) 'The razing of the house in Greek society', *TAPA* 115: 79–102

   (1987) 'Tribes, festivals, and processions: civic ceremonial and political manipulation in archaic Greece', *JHS* 107: 40–50

   (1989) 'City Dionysia and Athenian democracy', *Classica & Mediaevalia* 40: 7–32

Corsini, E., ed. (1986) *La Polis e il suo teatro*. Padua

Coward, R., & J. Ellis (1977) *Language and Materialism*. New York & London

Cremante, R., ed. (1988) *Teatro de Cinquecento*, vol. 1 *La Tragedia*. Milan & Naples

Croally, N. (1994) *Euripidean Polemic: the Trojan Women and the Function of Tragedy*. Cambridge

Cropp, M., E. Fantham & S. E. Scully, eds. (1986) *Greek Tragedy and its Legacy. Essays Presented to D. J. Conacher*. Calgary

Csapo, E. (1993) 'Deep ambivalence: notes on a Greek cockfight', *Phoenix* 47: 1–28, 115–24

Csapo, E., & W. J. Slater (1995) *The Context of Ancient Drama*. Ann Arbor

Culler, J. (1975) *Structuralist Poetics*. Ithaca

   (1988) *Framing the Sign*. Oxford

Dabdab Trabulsi, J. A. (1990) *Dionysisme. Pouvoir et société en Grèce jusqu'à la fin de l'époque classique*. Paris

Dale, A. M. (1968) *The Lyric Metres of Greek Drama*, 2nd edn. Cambridge

Damen, M. (1989) 'Actor and character in Greek tragedy', *Theatre Journal* 41: 316–40

Davie, D. (1964) *Ezra Pound: Poet as Sculptor*. Oxford

Davies, J. K. (1967) 'Demosthenes on liturgies: a note', *JHS* 87: 33–40

   (1971) *Athenian Propertied Families 600–300 B.C.* Oxford

   (1981) *Wealth and the Power of Wealth in Classical Athens*. New York

Dean, W. (1969) *Handel and the Opera Seria*. Berkeley

Dean-Jones, L. (1994) *Women's Bodies in Classical Greek Science*. Oxford

Delebecque, E. (1951) *Euripide et la guerre du Péloponnèse*. Paris

Derrida, J. (1981) *Dissemination*. Chicago (French original 1972)

    (1992) ' "Nous autres Grecs" ', in B. Cassin, ed., *Nos Grecs et leurs modernes*. Paris

Detienne, M. (1979) *Dionysos Slain*. Baltimore (French original 1977)

    (1981) *L'Invention de la mythologie*. Paris

    (1989) *Dionysus at Large*. Cambridge, MA (French original 1986)

Detienne, M., & J.-P. Vernant, eds. (1989) *The Cuisine of Sacrifice among the Greeks*. Chicago (French original 1979)

Develin, R. (1989) *Athenian Officials 684–321 B.C.* Cambridge

Devereux, G. (1973) 'The self-blinding of Oedipus', *JHS* 93: 36–49

    (1976) *Dreams in Greek Tragedy: an Ethno-Psycho-Analytical Study*. Oxford

Diggle, J. (1984) 'The manuscripts and text of *Medea*: II. The text', *CQ* 34 (= *Euripidea: Collected Essays*, 279–81. Oxford 1994)

Di Gregorio, L. (1976) 'Plutarco e la tragedia greca', *Prometheus* 2: 151–74

Dobrée, B. (1963) *Restoration Tragedy 1660–1720*. Oxford (originally published 1929)

Dodds, E. R. (1960a) *Euripides. Bacchae*, 2nd edn. Oxford

    (1960b) 'Morals and politics in the *Oresteia*', *PCPS* 6: 19–31 (= Dodds (1973a) 45–63)

    (1966) 'On misunderstanding the *Oedipus Rex*', *G&R* 13: 37–49 (= Dodds (1973) 64–78)

    (1973a) *The Ancient Concept of Progress and Other Essays*. Oxford

    (1973b) 'The religion of the ordinary man in Classical Greece', in Dodds (1973a) 140–55. Oxford

Donlan, W. (1980) *The Aristocratic Ideal in Ancient Greece*. Kansas

Dover, K. J. (1957) 'The political aspect of Aeschylus' *Eumenides*', *JHS* 77: 230–7

    (1974) *Greek Popular Morality in the Time of Plato and Aristotle*. Oxford

duBois, P. (1988) *Sowing the Body: Psychoanalysis and Ancient Representations of Women*. Chicago

    (1991) *Torture and Truth*. New York & London

Duchemin, J. (1968) *L'Agon dans la tragédie grecque*. Paris

Eagleton, T. (1983) *Literary Theory: an Introduction*. Oxford

Easterling, P. E. (1967) 'Oedipus and Polynices', *PCPS* 13: 1–13

    (1982) *Sophocles. Trachiniae*. Cambridge

    (1984a) 'Kings in Greek tragedy', in J. Coy & J. de Hoz, eds., *Estudios sobre los géneros literarios*, 33–45. Salamanca

    (1984b) 'Greek plays at Cambridge', in *Le Théâtre Antique de Nos Jours: Symposium International à Delphes 18–22 Août 1981*, 89–94. Athens

    (1984c) 'The tragic Homer', *BICS* 31: 1–8

    (1985) 'Anachronism in Greek tragedy', *JHS* 105: 1–10

    (1987a) 'Notes on tragedy and epic', in L. Rodley, ed., *Papers given at a Colloquium on Greek Drama in Honour of R. P. Winnington-Ingram* (Hell. Soc. Supp. 15) 52–61. London

    (1987b) 'Women in tragic space', *BICS* 34: 15–26

    (1988) 'Tragedy and ritual. "Cry 'Woe, woe', but may the good prevail" ', *Métis* 3: 87–109

(1989) 'City settings in Greek poetry', *PCA* 86: 5–17

(1990) 'Constructing character in Greek tragedy', in Pelling (1990) 83–99

(1993a) 'The end of an era? Tragedy in the early fourth century', in Sommerstein et al. (1993) 559–69

(1993b) 'Tragedy and ritual' in Scodel (1993) 7–23

(1994) 'Euripides outside Athens: a speculative note', *ICS* 19: 73–80

Eden, K. (1986) *Poetic and Legal Fiction in the Aristotelian Tradition*. Princeton

Ehrenberg, V. (1954) *Sophocles and Pericles*. Oxford

Eliot, T. S. (1951) 'Euripides and Professor Murray', in *Selected Essays*, 2nd edn, 59–64. London

(1957) 'Poetry and drama', in *On Poetry and Poets*, 72–88. London

Else, G. F. (1967) *The Origin and Early Form of Greek Tragedy*. Cambridge, MA

Euben, J. P., ed. (1986) *Greek Tragedy and Political Theory*. Los Angeles & London

(1990) *The Tragedy of Greek Political Theory. The Road not Taken*. Princeton

Evans, A. (1988) *The God of Ecstasy: Sex Roles and the Madness of Dionysos*. New York

Ewans, M. C. (1982) *Wagner and Aeschylus: the Ring and the Oresteia*. London

Faraone, C. A. (1991) 'The agonistic context of early Greek binding spells', in C. A. Faraone & D. Obbink, eds., *Magika Hiera. Ancient Greek Magic and Religion*, 3–32. New York & Oxford

Farrar, C. (1988) *The Origins of Democratic Thinking*. Cambridge

Finley, J. H. (1967) *Three Essays on Thucydides*. Cambridge, MA

Finley, M. I. (1977a) *Aspects of Antiquity*, 2nd edn. Harmondsworth

(1977b) 'Plato and practical politics' in Finley (1977a) 74–87

(1980) *The Idea of a Theatre*. London (BM lecture)

(1985) *Democracy Ancient and Modern*, 2nd edn. London

Finneran, R. J., G. Mill Harper & W. M. Murphy, eds. (1977) *Letters to W. B. Yeats*. London

Fish, S. (1980) *Is there a Text in this Class?* Cambridge, MA

Fisher, N. R. E. (1992) *Hybris. A Study in the Values of Honour and Shame in Ancient Greece*. Warminster

Flashar, H. (1991) *Inszenierung der Antike: Das griechische Drama auf der Bühne der Neuzeit 1585–1990*. Munich

Flickinger, R. (1918) *The Greek Theater and its Drama*. Chicago

Foley, H. P. (1980) 'The masque of Dionysus', *TAPA* 110: 107–33

(1981) 'The conception of women in Athenian drama', in H. P. Foley, ed., *Reflections of Women in Antiquity*, 127–68. New York, London & Paris

(1982) 'The "female intruder" reconsidered: women in Aristophanes' *Lysistrata* and *Ecclesiazusae*', *CP* 77: 1–21

(1985) *Ritual Irony: Poetry and Sacrifice in Euripides*. Ithaca

(1992) '*Anodos* dramas: Euripides' *Alcestis* and *Helen*', in Hexter & Selden (1992) 133–60

Fornara, C. W. (1983) *Archaic Times to the End of the Peloponnesian War*, 2nd edn. Cambridge

Foxhall, L. & A. Lewis, eds. (1996) *Greek Law in its Political Setting*. Oxford

Fraenkel, E. (1950) *Aeschylus. Agamemnon*, 3 vols. Oxford

(1965) Review of Ritchie (1964), *Gnomon* 37: 228–41

Fraser, P. M. (1972) *Ptolemaic Alexandria*, 3 vols. Oxford

Fraser, R. (1990) *The Making of The Golden Bough*. London

Friedrich, W. H. (1967) *Vorbild und Neugestaltung*. Göttingen

Fritz, K. von (1962) *Antike und moderne Tragödie*. Berlin

Frontisi-Ducroux, F. (1989) 'In the mirror of the mask', in C. Bérard et al., eds., *A City of Images*, 150–69. Princeton (French original 1984)

(1991) *Le dieu-masque: une figure du Dionysos d'Athènes*. Paris

(1995) *Du masque au visage*. Paris

Frontisi-Ducroux, F., & J.-P. Vernant (1983) 'Figures du masque en Grèce ancienne', *Journal de Psychologie* 76: 53–69 repr. in trans. in Vernant & Vidal-Naquet (1988) 189–206

Frye, N. (1965) *A Natural Perspective: the Development of Shakespearean Comedy and Romance*. New York & London

Gabrielsen, V. (1994) *Financing the Athenian Fleet*. Baltimore & London

Gager, J., ed. (1992) *Curse Tablets and Binding Spells from the Ancient World*. New York

Garner, R. (1987) *Law and Society in Classical Athens*. London & Sydney

(1990) *From Homer to Tragedy: the Art of Allusion in Greek Poetry*. London

Garnsey, P. (1988) *Famine and Food-Supply in the Graeco-Roman World*. Cambridge

Garvie, A. F. (1969) *Aeschylus' Supplices: Play and Trilogy*. Cambridge

Geertz, C. (1973) 'Deep plays: notes on the Balinese cockfight', repr. in *The Interpretation of Cultures*, 412–53. New York

(1980) *Negara: the Theater State in Nineteenth-Century Bali*. New York

Gellrich, M. (1988) *Tragedy and Theory: the Problem of Conflict since Aristotle*. Princeton

Gernet, L. (1981) *The Anthropology of Ancient Greece*. Baltimore (French original 1968)

Ghiron-Bistagne, P. (1976) *Recherches sur les acteurs dans la Grèce antique*. Paris

Gigante, M. (1983) *Ricerche Filodemee*, 2nd edn. Naples

Girard, R. (1977) *Violence and the Sacred*. Baltimore (French original 1972)

Goff, B. (1990) *The Noose of Words: Readings of Desire, Violence and Language*. Cambridge

Gogos, S. (1983) 'Bühnenarchitektur und Bühnenmalerei', *JOeAI* 54: 59–86

Golden, M. (1985) 'Pais, "child", and "slave"', *L'Ant. Class.* 54: 91–104

(1990) *Children and Childhood in Classical Athens*. Baltimore

Goldhill, S. (1984) *Language, Sexuality, Narrative: the Oresteia*. Cambridge

(1986) *Reading Greek Tragedy*. Cambridge

(1990a) 'The Great Dionysia and civic ideology', in Winkler & Zeitlin (1990) 97–129

(1990b) 'Character and action, representation and reading: Greek Tragedy and its critics', in Pelling (1990) 100–27

(1991) *The Poet's Voice: Essays on Poetics and Greek Literature*. Cambridge

(1992) *Aeschylus. The Oresteia*. Cambridge

(1994a) 'Representing democracy: women at the Great Dionysia', in Osborne & Hornblower (1994) 347–69

(1994b) 'The failure of exemplarity' in I. de Jong & J. P. Sullivan, eds., *Modern Critical Theory and Classical Literature*, 51–73. Leiden

Gordon, R. L. (1979) 'Reason and ritual in Greek tragedy: on René Girard *Violence and the Sacred* and Marcel Detienne *The Gardens of Adonis*', *Comparative Criticism Yearbook* 1: 279–310

Gould, J. P. A. (1973) 'Hiketeia', *JHS* 93: 74–103

(1978) 'Dramatic character and "human intelligibility" in Greek tragedy', *PCPS* 24: 43–67

(1980) 'Law, custom and myth: aspects of the social position of women in classical Athens', *JHS* 100: 38–59

(1985) 'Tragedy in performance', in *CHCL*, 263–81

(1987) 'Mothers' Day. A note on Euripides' *Bacchae*', in L. Rodley, ed. *Papers given at a Colloquium on Greek Drama in Honour of R. P. Winnington-Ingram* (Hell. Soc. Supp. 15) 32–9. London

Gouldner, A. W. (1965) *Enter Plato. Classical Greece and the Origins of Social Theory*. New York

Green, A. (1979) *The Tragic Effect*. London (French original 1969)

Green, J. R. (1982) 'Dedication of masks', *RevArch* 2: 237–48

(1989) 'Theatre production: 1971–1986', *Lustrum* 31: 7–71

(1991) 'On seeing and depicting the theatre in classical Athens', *GRBS* 32: 15–50

(1994) *Theatre in Ancient Greek Society*. London

(1995) 'Theatrical motifs in non-theatrical contexts on vases of the late fifth and fourth centuries', in A. Griffiths, ed., *Stage Directions: Essays in Ancient Drama in Honour of E. W. Handley* (BICS Suppl. 66) 193–220

Green, J. R., & E. W. Handley (1995) *Images of the Greek Theatre*. London

Green, P. (1960) 'Some versions of Aeschylus', in *Essays in Antiquity*, 185–215. London

Greenblatt, S. (1985) 'Invisible bullets: renaissance authority and its subversion', in J. Dollimore and A. Sinfield, eds., *Political Shakespeare: New Essays in Cultural Materialism*, 18–47. Manchester

Gregory, J. (1991) *Euripides and the Instruction of the Athenians*. Ann Arbor

Griffith, M. (1995) 'Brilliant dynasts: power and politics in the *Oresteia*', *Classical Antiquity* 14: 62–129

Grove, G. (1880) *A Dictionary of Music and Musicians*, 4 vols. London

Guicharnaud, J. (1967) *Modern French Theatre: from Giraudoux to Beckett*. New Haven

Hall, E. (1989a) *Inventing the Barbarian: Greek Self-Definition through Tragedy*. Oxford

(1989b) 'The archer scene in Aristophanes' *Thesmophoriazusae*', *Philologus* 13: 38–54

(1990) 'The changing face of Oedipus and the mask of Dionysus', *Cambridge Review*, 70–4

(1993a) 'Asia unmanned: images of victory in classical Athens' in J. Rich & G. Shipley, eds., *War and Society in the Greek World*, 108–33. London

(1993b) 'Political and cosmic turbulence in Euripides' *Orestes*', in Sommerstein et al. (1993) 263–85

(1995) 'Lawcourt dramas: the power of performance in Greek forensic oratory', *BICS* 40: 39–58

(1996) *Aeschylus' Persians*. Warminster

Halliwell, S. (1987) *The Poetics of Aristotle: Translation and Commentary*. London

(1993) 'The function and aesthetics of the Greek tragic mask', *Drama* 2: 195–211

Halperin, D. M., J. J. Winkler & F. Zeitlin, eds. (1990) *Before Sexuality: The Construction of Erotic Experience in the Ancient Greek World.* Princeton

Hamburger, K. (1969) *From Sophocles to Sartre: Figures from Greek Tragedy, Classical and Modern.* New York (German original 1962)

Hamilton, R. (1974) 'Objective evidence for actors' interpolations in Greek tragedy', *GRBS* 15: 387–402

Handley, E. W., & J. Rea (1957) *The Telephus of Euripides (BICS* Suppl. 5). London

Hansen, M. H. (1987) *The Athenian Assembly in the Age of Demosthenes.* Oxford
(1991) *The Athenian Democracy in the Age of Demosthenes.* Oxford

Hanson, A. E. (1990) 'The medical writers' woman', in Halperin, Winkler & Zeitlin (1990) 309–37

Hanson, V. D. (1989) *The Western Way of War.* New York
ed. (1991) *Hoplites. The Classical Greek Battlefield Experience.* London & New York
(1995) *The Other Greeks. The Family Farm and the Agrarian Roots of Western Civilization.* New York

Harder, R. E. (1993) *Die Frauenrollen bei Euripides.* Stuttgart

Harris, W. V. (1989) *Ancient Literacy.* Cambridge, MA

Harrison, J. (1912) *Themis.* Cambridge

Harrison, T. (1991) *The Trackers of Oxyrhynchus,* 2nd edn. London

Hartigan, K. V. (1995) *Greek Tragedy on the American Stage: Ancient Drama in the Commercial Theater, 1882–1994.* Westport, CT, & London

Harvey, F. D. (1966) 'Literacy in the Athenian democracy', *REG* 79: 585–635

Hatzopoulos, M., & L. D. Loukopoulos, eds. (1981) *Philip of Macedon.* London

Havelock, E. A. (1982) *The Literate Revolution and its Cultural Consequences.* Princeton

Hearnshaw, F. J. C. (1929) *The Centenary History of King's College London 1828–1928.* London

Hedreen, G. (1994) 'Silens, nymphs and maenads', *JHS* 114: 47–69

Henderson, J. J. (1990) 'The *demos* and the comic competition', in Winkler and Zeitlin (1990) 271–313
(1991) 'Women and the Athenian dramatic festivals', *TAPA* 121: 133–47
(1993) 'Comic hero versus political elite', in Sommerstein et al. (1993) 321–40

Henrichs, A. (1978) 'Greek maenadism from Olympias to Messalina', *HSCP* 82: 121–60
(1982) 'Changing Dionysiac identities', in B. F. Meyer & E. P. Sanders, eds., *Jewish and Christian Self-Definition,* vol. III *Self-Definition in the Graeco-Roman World,* 137–60, 213–36. London
(1984) 'Loss of self, suffering, violence: the modern view of Dionysus from Nietzsche to Girard', *HSCP* 88: 205–40
(1990) 'Between city and country: cultic dimensions of Dionysus in Athens and Attica', in M. Griffith & D. J. Mastronarde, eds., *Cabinet of the Muses. Festschr. T. Rosenmeyer,* 255–77. Lanham
(1993) ' "He has a God in Him": human and divine in the modern perception of Dionysus', in Carpenter & Faraone (1993) 13–43. Ithaca & London
(1994) 'Der rasende Gott: zur Psychologie des Dionysos und der Dionysischen in Mythos und Literatur', *Antike und Abendland* 40: 31–58

(1995) 'Why should I dance?', *Arion* 3: 56–111

(1996) Entry on 'Dionysus' in *The Oxford Classical Dictionary*, 3rd edn. Oxford

Herington, J. (1985) *Poetry into Drama. Early Tragedy and the Greek Poetic Tradition*. Berkeley

Hexter, R., & D. Selden, eds. (1992) *Innovations of Antiquity*. London & New York

Hoffmann, H. (1974) 'Hahnenkampf in Athen', *RA*: 195–220

Hoffmann, R. J. (1989) 'Ritual license and the cult of Dionysus', *Athenaeum* 67: 91–115

Hornblower, S. (1991) *The Greek World 479–323 BC*, 3rd edn. London & New York

Humphreys, S. C. (1978) *Anthropology and the Greeks*. London

(1985a) 'Lycurgus of Butadae: an Athenian aristocrat', in J. W. Eadie and J. Ober, eds. *The Craft of the Ancient Historian. Festschr. C. G. Starr*, 199–252. Lanham & London

(1985b) 'Social relations on stage: witnesses in classical Athens', *History and Anthropology* 1: 313–69

Hunter, V. (1994) *Policing Athens: Social Control in the Attic Lawsuits, 420–320 BC*. Princeton

Jameson, F. (1981) *The Political Unconscious*. Ithaca

Jameson, M. H. (1994) 'The ritual of the Athena Nike parapet', in Osborne & Hornblower (1994) 307–24

Jeanson, F. (1955) *Sartre par lui-même*. Paris

Jebb, R. C. (1883–96) *Sophocles: the Plays and Fragments*, 7 vols. Cambridge

(1890) *Sophocles, Antigone*, 3rd edn. Cambridge

Jocelyn, H. D. (1969) *The Tragedies of Ennius*. Cambridge

Jondorf, G. (1969) *Robert Garnier and the Themes of Political Tragedy in the Sixteenth Century*. Cambridge

Jones, A. H. M. (1957) *Athenian Democracy*. Oxford

Jones, C. P. (1991) 'Dinner Theater', in W. J. Slater, ed., *Dining in a Classical Context*, 185–98. Ann Arbor

(1993) 'Greek drama in the Roman Empire', in Scodel, (1993) 39–52

Jones, E. (1953) *Sigmund Freud: Life and Work*, vol. 1 *The Young Freud 1856–1900*. London

Jones, J. (1962) *On Aristotle and Greek Tragedy*. London (repr. 1983)

Jones, P. V. et al. (1984) *The World of Athens*. Cambridge

de Jong, I. J. F. (1991) *Narrative in Drama: The Art of the Euripidean Messenger-Speech*. Leiden

Just, R. (1989) *Women in Athenian Law and Life*. London & New York

Kaimio, M. (1970) *The Chorus of Greek Drama within the Light of the Person and Number Used*. Helsinki

(1988) *Physical Contact in Greek Tragedy: a Study of Stage Conventions*. Helsinki

(1993) 'The protagonist in Greek tragedy', *Arctos* 27: 19–33

Kamerbeek, J. C. (1978) *The Plays of Sophocles*, part III *The Antigone*. Leiden

Katrak, K. H. (1986) *Wole Soyinka and Modern Tragedy* (Contributions in Afro-American and African Studies 96). New York

Katz, M. (1994) 'The character of tragedy: women and the Greek imagination', *Arethusa* 27: 81–103

Kelly, H. A. (1993) *Ideas and Forms of Tragedy from Aristotle to the Middle Ages.* Cambridge

Kennedy, D. (1985) *Granville Barker and the Dream of Theatre.* Cambridge

Kerferd, G. (1981) *The Sophistic Movement.* Cambridge

Kerman, J. (1988) *Opera as Drama*, 2nd edn. New York

Keuls, E. (1985) *The Reign of the Phallus. Sexual Politics in Ancient Athens.* Berkeley (rev. edn 1993)

Kierkegaard, S. (1987) 'The tragic in ancient drama reflected in the tragic in modern drama', in *Either/Or*, part I, 139–64. Princeton (Danish original 1843)

Kindermann, H. (1979) *Das Theaterpublikum der Antike.* Salzburg

King, H. (1983) 'Bound to bleed: Artemis and Greek women', in Cameron & Kuhrt (1983) 109–27

Kitto, H. D. F. (1956) *Form and Meaning in Drama.* London

(1961) *Greek Tragedy*, 3rd edn. London (originally published 1936)

Knight, R. (1974) *Racine et la Grèce.* Paris (originally published 1951)

Knox, B. M. W. (1952a) 'The lion in the house', *CP* 47: 17–25 (repr. in Knox (1979) 27–38)

(1952b) 'The *Hippolytus* of Euripides', *YCS* 13: 1–31 (repr. in Knox (1979) 205–30)

(1957) *Oedipus at Thebes.* New Haven

(1961) 'The *Ajax* of Sophocles', *HSCP* 65: 1–37

(1964) *The Heroic Temper: Studies in Sophoclean Tragedy.* Berkeley

(1977) 'The *Medea* of Euripides', *YCS* 25: 193–225 (repr. in Knox (1979) 295–322)

(1979) *Word and Action. Essays on the Ancient Theater.* Baltimore & London

(1992) 'Athenian religion and literature', *The Cambridge Ancient History*, vol. v, 2nd edn, 272–82. Cambridge

Kokolakis, M. (1959) 'Pantomimus and the treatise περὶ ὀρχήσεως', *Platon* 11: 1–56

Kolb, F. (1979) 'Theater und Polis', in G. A. Seeck, ed., *Das griechische Drama*, 504–45. Darmstadt

(1981) *Agora und Theater, Volks- und Festversammlung.* Berlin

(1989) 'Theaterpublikum, Volksversammlung und Gesellschaft in der griechischen Welt', *Dioniso* 59: 345–51

Kraut, R., ed. (1992) *The Cambridge Companion to Plato.* Cambridge

Krentz, P. (1982) *The Thirty at Athens.* Ithaca

Kuch, H. (1974) *Kriegsgefangenschaft und Sklaverei bei Euripides.* Berlin

ed. (1983) *Die griechische Tragödie in ihre gesellschaftlichen Funktion.* Berlin

Kurke, L. (1991) *The Traffic in Praise: Pindar and the Poetics of Social Economy.* Ithaca

Kyle, D. G. (1987) *Athletics in Ancient Athens.* Leiden

(1992) 'The Panathenaic games: sacred and civic athletics', in Neils et al. (1992) 77–101

Kyrtatas, D., ed. (1993) *Opsis Enypniou.* Herakleion

de Lacy, P. (1952) 'Biography and tragedy in Plutarch', *AJP* 73: 159–71

Lane Fox, R. (1980) *The Search for Alexander.* New York & London

(1994) 'Aeschines and Athenian democracy', in Osborne & Hornblower (1994) 135–55

Lanza, D. (1977) *Il Tiranno e il suo Pubblico*. Turin
(1979) *Lingua e discorso nell'Atene delle professioni*. Naples
(1983) 'Lo spettacolo', in M. Vegetti, ed., *Oralità, Scrittura, Spettacolo*, 107–26. Turin
Lattimore, R. (1964) *Story Patterns in Greek Tragedy*. London & Ann Arbor
Leach, E. (1970) *Lévi-Strauss*. London
Lefkowitz, M. R. (1981) *The Lives of the Greek Poets*. London
Lefkowitz, M. R., & M. B. Fant (1992) *Women's Life in Greece and Rome: a Source Book in Translation*, 2nd edn. London
Lentricchia, F. (1980) *After the New Criticism*. London
Lesky, A. (1983) *Greek Tragic Poetry*. New Haven (German original 1972)
Lévêque, P., & P. Vidal-Naquet (1996) *Cleisthenes the Athenian. An Essay on the Representation of Space and Time in Greek Political Thought*. Atlantic Highlands, NJ (French original 1964)
Lévi-Strauss, C. (1963) *Structural Anthropology*. New York (French original 1958; 2nd edn 1977)
Lintott, A. W. (1982) *Violence, Civil Strife and Revolution in the Classical City 750–330 BC*. London
Lissarrague, F. (1990) 'Why satyrs are good to represent', in Winkler & Zeitlin (1990) 228–36
Lloyd, G. E. R. (1983) *Science, Folklore and Ideology*. Cambridge
Lloyd, M. (1992) *The Agon in Euripides*. Oxford
Lloyd-Jones, H. (1982) *Blood for the Ghosts*. London
Longo, O. (1990) 'The theater of the polis', in Winkler & Zeitlin (1990) 12–19
Lonsdale, S. H. (1993) *Dance and Ritual Play in Greek Religion*. Baltimore & London
(1995) '*Homeric Hymn to Apollo*: prototype and paradigm of choral performance', *Arion* 3: 25–40
Loraux, N. (1986) *The Invention of Athens. The Funeral Oration in the Classical City*. Cambridge, MA (French original 1981)
(1987) *Tragic Ways of Killing a Woman*. Cambridge, MA (French original 1985)
(1993) *The Children of Athena. Athenian Ideas about Citizenship & the Division between the Sexes*. Princeton (French original 1984)
Maas, P. (1962) *Greek Metre*, transl. and revised by H. Lloyd-Jones, Oxford (German original 1923)
MacDowell, D. (1978) *The Law in Classical Athens*. London
(1985) 'Athenian laws about choruses', *Symposion (1982). Vorträge zur griechischen und hellenistischen Rechtsgeschichte*, 65–77. Cologne
Macintosh, F. (1994) *Dying Acts: Death in Ancient Greek and Modern Irish Tragic Drama*. Cork & New York
(1995) 'Under the blue pencil: Greek tragedy and the British Censor', *Dialogos* 2: 54–70
Mackinnon, A. (1910) *The Oxford Amateurs: a Short History of Theatricals at the University*. London
MacKinnon, K. (1986) *Greek Tragedy into Film*. London & Sydney
Macleod, C. W. (1982) 'Politics and the *Oresteia*', *JHS* 102: 124–44 (= Macleod (1983) ch. 3)

(1983) *Collected Essays*, ed. O. Taplin. Oxford

Malcolm, N. (1990) *George Enescu: his Life and Music*. London

Manasse, E. M. (1952) 'Iphigenie und die Götter', *Modern Language Quarterly* 13: 377–91

Markle, M. M. (1985) 'Jury pay and Assembly pay in Athens', in P. Cartledge & D. Harvey, eds., *CRUX. Festschr. G. de Ste. Croix*, 265–97. Exeter & London

Martin, R. P. (1989) *The Language of Heroes: Speech and Performance in the Iliad*. Ithaca

Martin-Harvey, J. (1933) *The Autobiography of Sir John Martin-Harvey*. London

Mason, H. A. (1969) 'The *Women of Trachis* and creative translation', *Cambridge Quarterly* 4: 244–72 (repr. in J. P. Sullivan, ed., *Ezra Pound: a Critical Anthology*, 279–310. Harmondsworth 1970)

McCall, D. (1969) *The Theatre of Jean-Paul Sartre*. New York

McDonald, M. (1983) *Euripides in Cinema: the Heart Made Visible*. Philadelphia

McDonald, M., & K. MacKinnon (1993) 'Cacoyannis vs. Euripides: from tragedy to melodrama', in N. W. Slater & B. Zimmermann, eds., *Intertextualität in der griechisch-römischen Komödie*. Stuttgart

Meier, C. (1990) *The Greek Discovery of Politics*. Cambridge, MA (German original 1980)

(1993) *The Political Art of Greek Tragedy*. Cambridge (German original 1988)

Merck, M. (1978) 'The city's achievement: the patriotic Amazonomachy and ancient Athens', in S. Lipshitz, ed., *Tearing the Veil*, 95–115. London

Mette, H.-J. (1977) *Urkunden dramatischer Aufführungen in Griechenland*. Berlin

Michelini, A. (1987) *Euripides and the Tragic Tradition*. Wisconsin

Mikalson, J. D. (1975) *The Sacred and Civil Calendar of Athens*. Ann Arbor

(1982) 'The heorte of heortology', *GRBS* 23: 213–21

(1991) *Honor Thy Gods. Popular Religion in Greek Tragedy*. Chapel Hill & London

Mitchell, R. (1991) 'Miasma, mimesis, and scapegoating in Euripides' *Hippolytus*', *CA* 10: 97–122

Morrison, J. S., & J. F. Coates (1986) *The Athenian Trireme*. Cambridge

Mossman, J. M. (1988) 'Tragedy and epic in Plutarch's Alexander', *JHS* 108: 83–93

Mueller, M. (1980) *Children of Oedipus and Other Essays on the Imitation of Greek Tragedy 1550–1800*. Toronto

Muir, L. R. (1995) *The Biblical Drama of Medieval Europe*. Cambridge

Muller, W. (1982) *Choreia: Pindar and Dance*. Princeton

Müller, A. (1909) 'Das Bühnenwesen in der Zeit von Constantin d. gr. bis Justinian', *Neue Jahrbücher* 12: 36–55

Murray, G. (1913) *Euripides and his Age*. London

Murray, O., ed. (1990) *Sympotica. A Symposium on the Symposion*. Oxford

Nagy, G. (1990) *Pindar's Homer. The Lyric Possession of an Epic Past*. Baltimore

(1996) *Poetry in Performance*. Cambridge

Neils, J. et al. (1992) *Goddess and Polis. The Panathenaic Festival in Ancient Athens*. Princeton

Newiger, H.-J. (1961) 'Elektra in Aristophanes' *Wolken*', *Hermes* 89: 422–50

Norrish, P. (1988) *New Tragedy and Comedy in France 1945–70*. Totowa, NJ

Nugent, S. G. (1988) 'Masking becomes Electra: O'Neill, Freud, and the feminine', *Comparative Drama* 22: 37–55

Nüssbaum, M. C. (1986) *The Fragility of Goodness. Luck and Ethics in Greek Tragedy and Philosophy*. Cambridge

Ober, J. (1989) *Mass and Elite in Democratic Athens. Rhetoric, Ideology, and the Power of the People*. Princeton

Ober, J., & B. S. Strauss (1990) 'Drama, political rhetoric, and the discourse of Athenian democracy', in Winkler & Zeitlin (1990) 237–70

O'Brien, J. (1953) *Portrait of André Gide*. New York

O'Regan, D. E. (1992) *Rhetoric, Comedy and the Violence of Language in Aristophanes' Clouds*. New York

Orgel, S. (1975) *The Illusion of Power: Political Theater in the English Renaissance*. Berkeley

Ortner, S. B. (1974) 'Is female to male as nature is to culture?', in M. Z. Rosaldo & L. Lamphere, eds., *Women, Culture and Society*, 66–87. Stanford

Osborne, R. (1985) 'Law in action in classical Athens', *JHS* 105: 40–58
  (1987) 'Viewing and obscuring the Parthenon frieze', *JHS* 107: 98–105
  (1993) 'Competitive festivals and the polis: a context for dramatic festivals at Athens', in Sommerstein et al. (1993) 21–37

Osborne, R., & S. Hornblower, eds. (1994) *Ritual, Finance, Politics, Festschr. D. M. Lewis*. Oxford

Østerud, S. (1973) 'The intermezzo with the false merchant in Sophocles' *Philoctetes* 542–627', *C&M* 9: 10–26

Ostwald, M. (1988) 'The reform of the Athenian state by Cleisthenes', *The Cambridge Ancient History*, vol. IV, 2nd edn, 303–46. Cambridge
  (1992) 'Athens as a cultural centre', *The Cambridge Ancient History*, vol. V, 2nd edn, 306–69. Cambridge

Padel, R. (1983) 'Women: model for possession by Greek daemons', in Cameron & Kuhrt (1983) 3–19
  (1990) 'Making space speak' in Winkler & Zeitlin (1990) 336–65
  (1992) *In and Out of the Mind. Greek Images of the Tragic Self*. Princeton
  (1995) *Whom Gods Destroy*. Princeton

Parke, H. W. (1977) *Festivals of the Athenians*. London & New York

Parker, R. (1987) 'Festivals of the Attic demes', *Boreas* 15: 137–47
  (1996) *Athenian Religion*. Oxford

Patterson, C. B. (1981) *Pericles' Citizenship Law of 451–450 BC*. New York
  (1986) 'Hai Attikai. The other Athenians', *Helios* 13: 49–67

Paul, G. (1991) 'Symposia and deipna in Plutarch's Lives and other historical writings', in W. J. Slater, ed., *Dining in a Classical Context*, 157–69. Ann Arbor

Pelling, C., ed. (1990) *Characterization and Individuality in Greek Literature*. Oxford

Pfeiffer, R. (1968) *History of Classical Scholarship*. Oxford

Pickard-Cambridge, A. W. (1927) *Dithyramb, Tragedy and Comedy*. Oxford
  (1946) *The Theatre of Dionysus in Athens*. Oxford
  (1962) *Dithyramb, Tragedy and Comedy*, rev. edn. Oxford
  (1988) *The Dramatic Festivals of Athens*, 2nd edn rev. J. Gould & D. M. Lewis. Oxford

Plathhy, J. (1985) *The Mythical Poets of Greece*. Washington, DC

Pocock, G. (1973) *Corneille and Racine: Problems of Tragic Form*. Cambridge

Podlecki, A. J. (1966a) 'The power of the word in Sophocles' *Philoctetes*', *GRBS* 7: 233–75

(1966b) *The Political Background of Aeschylean Tragedy*. Ann Arbor

(1990) 'Could women attend the theater in ancient Athens? A collection of testimonia', *AncWorld* 21: 27–43

Polacco, J. (1990) *Il teatro di Dioniso Eleutereo ad Atene*. Rome

Poliakoff, M. B. (1987) *Combat Sports in the Ancient World: Competition, Violence, and Culture*. New Haven

Pomeroy, S. (1975) *Goddesses, Whores, Wives and Slaves. Women in Classical Antiquity*. New York

Poole, A. (1976) 'Total disaster: Euripides' *Trojan Women*', *Arion* 3: 257–87

Pope, M. (1986) 'Athenian festival judges – seven, five or however many', *CQ* 36: 322–6

Popp, H. (1971) 'Das Amoibaion' in W. Jens, ed., *Die Bauformen der Tragödie*, 221–75. Munich

Powell, A., ed. (1991) *Euripides, Women and Sexuality*. London & New York

Prag, A. J. N. W. (1985) *The Oresteia: Iconographic and Narrative Tradition*. Warminster

Privitera, G. A. (1991) 'Origini della tragedia e ruolo del ditirambo', *Studi Italiani di Filologia Classica* 84: 184–95

Pucci, P. (1980) *The Violence of Pity in Euripides' Medea*. Ithaca

(1992) *Oedipus and the Fabrication of the Father*. Baltimore

Puffett, D., ed. (1989) *Richard Strauss's Elektra* (Cambridge Opera Handbooks). Cambridge

Purdom, C. B. (1955) *Harley Granville Barker*. London

Rabinowitz, N. S. (1992) 'Tragedy and the politics of containment', in Richlin (1992) 36–52

(1993) *Anxiety Veiled: Euripides and the Traffic in Women*. Ithaca & London

Rawson, E. (1985) 'Theatrical life in Republican Rome and Italy', *Papers of the British School at Rome* 53: 97–113 (repr. in Rawson (1991) 468–87)

(1987) 'Discrimina Ordinum: the Lex Julia Theatralis', *Papers of the British School at Rome* 55: 83–114 (repr. in Rawson (1991) 508–45)

(1991) *Roman Culture and Society. Collected Papers*. Oxford

Reckford, K. J. (1972) 'Phaethon, Hippolytus, Aphrodite', *TAPA* 103: 405–32

(1974) 'Phaedra and Pasiphae: the pull backwards', *TAPA* 104: 307–28

Rehm, R. (1992) *Greek Tragic Theatre*. London & New York

(1994) *Marriage to Death: the Conflation of Wedding and Funeral Rituals in Greek Tragedy*. Princeton

Reinhardt, K. (1979) *Sophocles*. Oxford (German original 1933)

Reynolds, L., & N. Wilson (1991) *Scribes and Scholars*, 3rd edn. Oxford

Richlin, A., ed. (1992) *Pornography and Representation in Greece and Rome*. New York

Ritchie, W. (1964) *The Authenticity of the Rhesus of Euripides*. Cambridge

Roberts, J. T. (1994) *Athens on Trial. The Antidemocratic Tradition in Western Thought*. Princeton

Romilly, J. de (1982) 'Le thème de la liberté et l'évolution de la tragédie grecque', in J. Polacco, ed., *Théâtre et spectacles dans l'antiquité. Actes du colloque de Strasbourg 5–7 novembre 1981*, 215–26. Strasbourg

(1995) *Tragédies grecques au fil des ans*. Paris

Rose, P. W. (1992) *Sons of the Gods, Children of Earth: Ideology and Literary Form in Ancient Greece*. Ithaca & London

Rosivach, V. J. (1987) 'Autochthony and the Athenians', *CQ* 37: 294–306

Rösler, W. (1980) *Polis und Tragödie. Funktionsgeschichtliche Betrachtungen zu einer antiken Literaturgattung*. Konstanz

Roueché, C. M. (1993) *Performers and Partisans at Aphrodisias in the Roman and Late Roman periods* (*JRS* Monograph 6). London

Ryan, K. (1989) *Shakespeare*. New York & London

Saïd, S. (1985) *Sophiste et tyran, ou le problème du Prométhée enchaîné*. Paris

Ste Croix, G. E. M. de (1981) *The Class Struggle in the Ancient Greek World*. London & Ithaca (corr. impr. 1983)

Sartre, J.-P. (1976) *Sartre on Theater*, eds. M. Contat & M. Rybalka. New York

Schadewaldt, W. (1970) 'Der "Zerbrochene Krug" und "König Ödipus"', in *Hellas und Hesperien. Gesammelte Schriften zur Antike und zur neueren Literatur*, vol. II, 333–40 (=*Schweizer Monatshefte* 37 (1957) 311–18)

Schaps, D. M. (1977) 'The woman least mentioned: etiquette and women's names', *CQ* 27: 232–30

Schlesier, R. (1993) 'Maenads as tragic models', in Carpenter & Faraone (1993) 89–114

Schmidt, M. (1967) 'Dionysien', *Antike Kunst* 10: 70–81

(1982) 'Oidipus und Teiresias', in *Praestant Interna. Festschr. U. Hausmann*, 236–43. Tübingen

Schrade, L. (1960) *La Représentation d'Edipo Tiranno au Teatro Olimpico (Vicence 1585)*. Paris

(1964) *Tragedy in the Art of Music*. Cambridge, MA

Scodel, R., ed. (1993) *Theater and Society in the Classical World*. Ann Arbor

Seaford, R. (1984) *Euripides. Cyclops*. Oxford

(1981) 'Dionysiac drama and the Dionysiac mysteries', *CQ* 31: 252–75

(1987) 'The tragic wedding', *JHS* 107: 106–30

(1993) 'Dionysus as destroyer of the household: Homer, tragedy and the polis', in Carpenter & Faraone (1993) 115–46

(1994) *Reciprocity and Ritual. Homer and Tragedy in the Developing City-State*. Oxford

Segal, C. (1965) 'The tragedy of Hippolytus: the waters of Ocean and the untouched meadow', *HSCP* 70: 117–69 (= Segal (1986a) 165–221)

(1981) *Tragedy and Civilization. An Interpretation of Sophocles*. Cambridge, MA

(1982) *Dionysiac Poetics and Euripides' Bacchae*. Princeton

(1983) 'Greek myth as a semiotic system and the problem of tragedy', *Arethusa* 16: 173–98 (= Segal (1986a) 48–74)

(1986a) *Interpreting Greek Tragedy: Myth, Poetry, Texts*. Ithaca & London

(1986b) 'Greek tragedy and society: a structuralist perspective', in Segal (1986a) 21–47 (= Euben (1986)) 43–75

(1990) 'Dionysus and the gold tablets from Pelinna', *GRBS* 31: 411–19

(1993a) *Oedipus Tyrannus. Tragic Heroism and the Limits of Knowledge*. New York & Don Mills, Ontario

(1993b) *Euripides and the Poetics of Sorrow*. Durham, NC, & London

(1995) 'Spectator and listener' in J.-P. Vernant, ed., *The Greeks*, 184–217. Chicago

(1996) 'Catharsis, audience and closure in Greek tragedy', in Silk (1996) 149–72

Seidensticker, B. (1971) 'Stichomuthia', in W. Jens, ed., *Die Bauformen der Tragödie*. Munich

(1979) 'Sacrificial ritual in the *Bacchae*', in G. W. Bowersock et al., eds., *Arktouros. Hellenic Studies Presented to Bernard M. W. Knox*, 181–90. Berlin

(1992) 'The political use of antiquity in the literature of the German Democratic Republic', *ICS* 17: 347–67

Shapiro, H. A. (1989) *Art and Cult under the Tyrants in Athens*. Mainz

(1992) '*Mousikoi Agones*: music and poetry at the Panathenaia', in Neils et al. (1992) 53–75

Sifakis, G. M. (1995) 'The one-actor rule in Greek tragedy', in A. Griffiths, ed., *Stage Directions: Essays in Ancient Drama in Honour of E. W. Handley* (= *BICS* Suppl. 66) 13–24. London

Silk, M. S., ed. (1996) *Tragedy and the Tragic*. Oxford

Silk, M. S., & J. P. Stern (1981) *Nietzsche on Tragedy*. Cambridge

Simon, B. (1978) *Mind and Madness in Ancient Greece: the Classical Roots of Modern Psychiatry*. Ithaca, NY

Simon, E. (1954) 'Die Typen der Medeadarstellung in der antiken Kunst', *Gymnasium* 61: 203–27

(1982a) *The Ancient Theatre*. London & New York (German original 1972)

(1982b) 'Satyr-plays on vases in the time of Aeschylus', in D. Kurtz & B. Sparkes, eds., *The Eye of Greece*. Cambridge

(1983) *Festivals of Attica. An Archaeological Commentary*. Madison & London

Sinclair, R. K. (1988) *Democracy and Participation in Athens*. Cambridge

Sinfield, A. (1983) *Literature in Protestant England 1560–1660*. London

Sissa, G. (1990a) *Greek Virginity*. Cambridge, MA (French original 1987)

(1990b) 'Maidenhood without maidenhead: the female body in ancient Greece', in Halperin, Winkler & Zeitlin (1990) 339–64

Slater, P. (1968) *The Glory of Hera*. Boston

Smethurst, M. J. (1989) *The Artistry of Zeami: a Comparative Study of Greek Tragedy and Nō*. Princeton

Snell, B. (1953) *The Discovery of the Mind. The Greek Origins of European Thought*. Oxford (German original 1948)

(1986) *Tragicorum Graecorum Fragmenta*, vol. 1 *Didascaliae, Catalogi, Testimonia et Fragmenta Tragicorum minorum*, 1st edn corrected and augmented by R. Kannicht. Göttingen

Sommerstein, A. H. (1989) *Aeschylus. Eumenides*. Cambridge

Sommerstein, A. H., S. Halliwell, J. Henderson, & B. Zimmermann, eds. (1993) *Tragedy, Comedy and the Polis. Papers from the Greek Drama Conference, Nottingham 18–20 July 1990*. Bari

Sourvinou-Inwood, C. 'Something to do with Athens: Tragedy and Ritual', in Osborne & Hornblower (1994) 269–89. Oxford

Soyinka, W. (1976) *Myth, Literature and the African World*. Cambridge

Stallybrass, P., & A. White (1986) *The Politics and Poetics of Transgression*. London

Steinberg, M. P. (1991) 'The incidental politics to Mendelssohn's Antigone', in R. L. Todd, ed., *Mendelssohn and His World*, 137–57. Princeton

Steiner, G. (1961) *The Death of Tragedy*. New York
  (1984) *Antigones*. Oxford
  (1992) *After Babel: Aspects of Language and Translation*, 2nd edn. Oxford
Stephanis, I. E. (1988) *Dionysiakoi Technitai. Symboles sten Prosopographia tou Theatrou kai tes Mousikes ton Archaion Ellenon*. Heraklion
Stoltzfus, B. (1969) *Gide's Eagles*, Carbondale & Edwardsville, IL
Stone, D. (1974) *French Humanist Tragedy: a Reassessment*. Manchester
Storr, A. (1992) *Music and the Mind*. London
Strauss, B. S. (1985) 'Ritual, social drama and politics in classical Athens', *AJAH* 10: 67–83
Stravinsky, I. (1970) *The Poetics of Music in the Form of Six Lessons*. Cambridge, MA (Russian original 1947)
Strohm, H. (1957) *Euripides. Interpretation zur dramatischen Form (Zetemata 15)*. Munich
Strunk, O. (1952) *Source Readings in Music History: from Classical Antiquity to the Romantic Era*. London
Styan, J. L. (1975) *Drama, Stage and Audience*. Cambridge
Sutton, D. F. (1987) 'The theatrical families of Athens', *AJP* 108: 9–26
Synodinou, K. (1977) *On the Concept of Slavery in Euripides*. Ioannina
Taplin, O. P. (1977) *The Stagecraft of Aeschylus*. Oxford
  (1978) *Greek Tragedy in Action*. London
  (1986) 'Fifth-century tragedy and comedy: a *synkrisis*', *JHS* 106: 163–74
  (1989) *Greek Fire*. London
  (1992) 'The new Khoregos vase', *Pallas* 38: 139–50
  (1993) *Comic Angels and Other Approaches to Greek Drama through Vase-Painting*. Oxford
  (1995) 'Opening performance: closing texts?', *Essays in Criticism* 45: 93–120
Taplin, O. P., & P. J. Wilson (1993) 'The "aetiology" of tragedy', *PCPS* 39: 169–80
Taylor, R. (1976) *The Drama of W. B. Yeats: Irish Myth and the Japanese Nō*. New Haven & London
Tennenhouse, L. (1986) *Power on Display: the Politics of Shakespeare's Genres*. New York & London
Thomas, R. (1992) *Literacy and Orality in Ancient Greece*. Cambridge
Thomson, G. (1941) *Aeschylus and Athens*. London
Thorndike, S. (1960) 'The theatre and Gilbert Murray', in J. Smith & A. Toynbee, eds., *Gilbert Murray; an Unfinished Autobiography*. London
Todd, S. (1990) 'The purpose of evidence in Athenian courts', in Cartledge, Millett, & Todd (1990) 19–39
Too, Y. L. (1995) *The Rhetoric of Identity in Isocrates: Text, Power, Pedagogy*. Cambridge
Trendall, A. D. (1988) 'Masks on Apulian red-figured vases' in J. Betts, J. Hooker, & J. R. Green, *Studies in Honour of T. B. L. Webster*, vol. II, 137–54. Bristol
  (1989) *Red Figure Vases of South Italy and Sicily*. London
  (1991) 'Farce and tragedy in South Italian vase-painting', in T. Rasmussen & N. Spivey, eds., *Looking at Greek Vases*, 151–82. Cambridge
Trendall, A. D., & A. Cambitoglou (1978) *The Red-Figured Vases of Apulia*. 3 vols. Oxford

(1983) *First Supplement to the Red-Figured Vases of Apulia* = BICS Suppl. 42. London.

(1992) *Second Supplement to the Red-Figured Vases of Apulia* = BICS Suppl. 60. London.

Trendall, A. D., & T. B. L. Webster (1971) *Illustrations of Greek Drama*. London

Treu, K. (1983) 'Griechische Tragödie und Theaterpraxis' in H. Kuch, ed., *Die griechische Tragödie in ihre gesellschaftlichen Funktion*, 141–59. Berlin

Trevelyan, H. (1941) *Goethe and the Greeks*. Cambridge

Turner, E. G. (1963) 'Dramatic representations in Graeco-Roman Egypt: how long do they continue?', *Ant. Class.* 32: 120–8

Turner, V. (1969) *The Ritual Process. Structure and Anti-Structure*. Chicago & London

(1973) *The Forest of Symbols. Aspects of Ndembu Ritual*. Ithaca

(1974) *Drama, Fields, and Metaphors. Symbolic Action in Human Society*. Ithaca & London

(1982) *From Ritual to Theatre. The Human Seriousness of Play*. New York

Vanderpool, E. (1970) *Ostracism at Athens*. Princeton

Vegetti, M., ed. (1983) *Oralità, Scrittura, Spettacolo*. Turin

Vernant, J.-P. (1991) *Mortals and Immortals: Collected Essays*, ed. F. I. Zeitlin. Princeton

Vernant, J.-P., & P. Vidal-Naquet (1988) *Myth and Tragedy in Ancient Greece*, 2 vols. in 1. Cambridge, MA (French original 1973, 1986)

Versnel, H. S. (1990) 'What's sauce for the goose is sauce for the gander: myth and ritual, new and old', in L. Edmunds, ed., *Approaches to Greek Myth*, 23–90. Baltimore

Vickers, B. F. (1973) *Towards Greek Tragedy*. London

Vidal-Naquet, P. (1981) *Le chasseur noir: formes de pensée et formes de société dans le monde grec*. Paris

(1992) 'Note sur la place et le statut des étrangers dans la tragédie grecque', in R. Lonis, ed., *L'Etranger dans le monde grec*, vol. II, 297–313. Nancy

Walcot, P. (1976) *Greek Drama in its Theatrical and Social Context*. Cardiff

Walder, D. (1984) *Athol Fugard*. Houndsmills & London

Walton, J. M., ed. (1987) *Living Greek Theatre: a Handbook of Classical Performance and Modern Production*. New York & Westport, CT

Waters, K. H. (1985) *Herodotus the Historian*. London

Webster, T. B. L. (1967) *The Tragedies of Euripides*. London

Weinberg, B. (1961) *History of Literary Criticism in the Italian Renaissance*. Chicago

West, F. (1984) *Gilbert Murray: a Life*. London

West, M. L. (1992) *Ancient Greek Music*. Oxford

(1994) 'Reginald Pepys Winnington-Ingram 1904–1993', *ProcBritAcad* 84: 579–97

Whitehead, D. (1986a) *The Demes of Attica 508/7 – ca 250 BC*. Princeton

(1986b) 'Festival liturgies in Thorikos', *ZPE* 62: 213–20

(1995) 'Monumental political architecture in Archaic and Classical Greek *Poleis*', in D. Whitehead, ed., *From Political Architecture to Stephanus Byzantinus*. Stuttgart

Whitlock-Blundell, M. (1989) *Helping Friends and Harming Enemies*. Cambridge
Whitman, C. (1951) *Sophocles: a Study in Heroic Humanism*. Cambridge, MA
Wiles, D. (1991) *The Masks of Menander*. Cambridge
Wilkins, J. (1993) *Euripides. Heraclidae*. Oxford
Williams, B. (1993) *Shame and Necessity*. Berkeley, Los Angeles & Oxford
Wilson, D. (1987) *Gilbert Murray OM 1866–1957*. Oxford
Wilson, P. J. (1991) 'Demosthenes 21 (*Against Meidias*): democratic abuse', *PCPS* 37: 164–95
  (1993) 'The representation and rhetoric of the collective: Athenian tragic choroi in their social context', diss. Cambridge
  (forthcoming) *Tragedy and Democracy: the Athenian Choregia*. Cambridge
Winkler, J. J. (1990a) *The Constraints of Desire*. London & New York
  (1990b) 'The Ephebes' Song: *tragoidia* and *polis*', in Winkler & Zeitlin (1990) 20–62
Winkler, J. J., & F. Zeitlin, eds. (1990) *Nothing to do with Dionysos? Athenian Drama in its Social Context*. Princeton
Winnington-Ingram, R. P. (1948a) *Euripides and Dionysus: an Interpretation of the Bacchae*. Cambridge (repr. Amsterdam 1969)
  (1948b) 'Clytemnestra and the vote of Athena', *JHS* 68: 130–47 (repr. (1983) in *Studies in Aeschylus*. Cambridge)
  (1980) *Sophocles: an Interpretation*. Cambridge
  (1985) 'The origins of tragedy', in *CHCL*, 258–63
Witt, M. A. F. (1993) 'Fascist ideology and theatre under the Occupation: the case of Jean Anouilh', *Journal of European Studies* 23: 49–69
Wycherley, R. E. (1978) *The Stones of Athens*. Princeton
Xanthakis-Karamanos, G. (1979) 'The influence of rhetoric on fourth-century tragedy', *CQ* 29: 6–76
  (1980) *Studies in Fourth-century Tragedy*. Athens
Yarrow, P. J. (1978) *Racine*. Totowa, NJ
Yunis, H. (1988) *A New Creed: Fundamental Religious Beliefs in the Athenian Polis and Euripidean Drama*. Göttingen
Zeitlin, F. I. (1965) 'The motif of the corrupted sacrifice in Aeschylus' *Oresteia*', *TAPA* 96: 463–505
  (1978) 'Dynamics of misogyny in the *Oresteia*', *Arethusa* 11: 149–84 (= Zeitlin (1996) 87–119)
  (1980) 'The closet of masks: role-playing and myth-making in the *Orestes* of Euripides', *Ramus* 9: 51–77
  (1982) *Under the Sign of the Shield: Semiotics and Aeschylus' Seven against Thebes*. Rome
  (1984) 'The dynamics of misogyny: myth and myth-making in the *Oresteia*', in J. Peradotto & J. P. Sullivan, eds., *Women in the Ancient World: the Arethusa Papers*, 149–84. Albany
  (1985) 'The power of Aphrodite: Eros and the boundaries of self in the *Hippolytus*', in P. Burian, ed., *Directions in Euripidean Criticism*, 144–97. Durham, NC (= Zeitlin (1996) 219–84)
  (1986) 'Thebes: theater of self and society in Athenian drama', in Euben (1986) 101–41. Berkeley, Los Angeles & London (= Winkler & Zeitlin (1990) 130–67)

(1989) 'Mysteries of identity and designs of the self in Euripides' *Ion*', *PCPS* 35: 144–97 (=Zeitlin (1996) 285–338)

(1990) 'Playing the other: theater, theatricality and the feminine in Greek drama', in Winkler & Zeitlin (1990) 63–96 (=Zeitlin (1996) 341–74

(1992) 'The politics of Eros in the *Danaid* trilogy of Aeschylus', in Hexter & Selden (1992) 203–52 (=Zeitlin (1996) 123–71

(1993) 'Staging Dionysus between Thebes and Athens', in Carpenter & Faraone (1993) 147–82

(1996) *Playing the Other. Gender and Society in Classical Greek Literature.* Chicago

Zimmermann, B. (1991) *Greek Tragedy. An Introduction.* Baltimore & London (German original 1985)

(1992) *Dithyrambos: Geschichte einer Gattung (Hypomnemata 98)*. Göttingen

Žižek, S. (1991) *Looking Awry: an Introduction to Lacan through Popular Culture.* Cambridge, MA, & London

Zuntz, G. (1963) *The Political Plays of Euripides.* Manchester (1st edn 1955)

INDEX

Note: Illustration references are in italics.

Accius 226
Acestor 4
Achaeus 4
Achilles Tatius 105
actors 14, 18; civic status 17, 18, 95;
    diplomacy 217; male monopoly 8, 26;
    Neoptolemus' career 214, 215, 217–20;
    number of speaking 152–3, 205, 231;
    payment 26, 152, 217; primacy in Japanese
    theatre 313; prizes 26, 153, 352;
    professionalisation and influence 35, 119,
    153–4, 156, 207, 215–16, 220, 224;
    repertoire development 40, 213, 215, 220;
    Rome 223; solo performances 156, 158,
    220; Tegean inscription 212n6, 222,
    224; see also vase painting
Actors' Touring Company 320n56
adaptations, modern theatrical: film and
    television 276–82; French
    neoclassical 234–8, 240–5; Goethe
    238–40; Oedipus 240–53; opera 261–71;
    Orestes and Electra 254–61; recent
    stage 282–3; Renaissance 229–34
Aeschines 15, 34, 56, 59, 62, 216
Aeschylus 5, 352; family see Astydamas; and
    Herodotus 11; on Homer 185;
    innovation 20; number of actors 153,
    205; and Pericles 10, 25; political
    attitude 22; religious language 20; in
    Syracuse 5, 213
    Agamemnon: chorus 158, 163, 164, 165,
        200; Fraenkel's edition 326, 327, 337;
        gender issues 107, 122, 140; language
        131, 139–40, 164; lower class
        perspective 123; modern performances
        285, 290–1, 319; off-stage action 154;
        opening 119, 167; plot patterns 107–8,

113, 119, 122; religious ritual 131, 335;
    slaves 113, 119; translations 272, 273–4;
    on war 13, 98, 111
    Bassarids 120
    Eleusinians 101
    Eumenides: and Athenian polis 26, 102,
        167, 192; chorus 199n37; courtroom
        scene 15, 20, 102, 132, 135, 167, 192,
        344, 345; Furies 63, 96, 192; T. S. Eliot
        and 256; final procession 138, 139;
        language 20, 132, 138, 140, 192
    Libation-Bearers: chorus 111, 140;
        dikē 138; nineteenth-century production
        289; nurse 115, 124; plot patterns 107–8,
        115, 188, 189; Sophocles' and Euripides'
        references 168–9, 179–80, 185, 196; vase
        painting 72, 72; on war 98
    Net-Fishers 97
    Oresteia: chronology 352; Engels and 344;
        gender issue 139, 192; on justice 21–2;
        language 131, 132, 137–40; modern
        performances 281, 301, 305, 308, 311,
        314–18, 319, 320; plot patterns 97, 192,
        196; translations 276, 301, 308; see also
        individual plays above
    Persians 96, 100, 352; battle of Salamis 17,
        25, 99; modern productions 308, 309,
        321; opening 166, 167; plot patterns
        107–8, 186, 187–8; and recent
        events 17, 19, 25, 186, 344
    Philoctetes 180n7
    Prometheus Bound 96–7, 188, 272, 276;
        modern production 277, 305–6, 307
    Prometheus the Fire-Kindler 44
    Seven against Thebes 30, 98, 195–6, 198,
        306, 352; plot patterns 182, 188
    Supplicant Women 111n46, 188, 305;

chronology 151–2, 352; chorus 97, 163;
democratic voting 20–1, 132;
language 136–7
Thamyris 120
Theoroi or *Isthmiastae* 49
aetiology 100, 102–3, 167–8, 348
African adaptations 282–3
Agamemnon see Aeschylus
Agathon 5, 55, 155, 208; *Antheus* 98, 185
agōn (type of scene) 127, 135, 348
agōnia see competitive ethos
agōnothetēs (official) 212
aitia see aetiology
aitios, aitiasthai 132–3, 348
Aixone, inscription from 6, 7
Ajax see Sophocles
Alamanni, Luigi 230n8
Alcestis see Euripides
Alcibiades 57
Aldus Manutius 229n5
Alexander III, the Great, of Macedon 4, 54
Alexandria, Egypt 4, 35, 224, 225, 325
Alexis 59, 65, 107
aliens, resident 18–19, 61, 350
ambiguity *see* language
Anderson, Judith 275, 312
andreia 13, 54, 348
Andromache see Euripides
Anguillara, Giovanni Andrea del' 230n8
Anouilh, Jean 253
Anthesteria 62
anthropology 253, 327, 331–6, 343–4
Antigone see Euripides; Sophocles
Antiphanes 183
Antiphon 14–15, 32, 118–19
antistrophē 128, 348
Aphareus 214
Aphrodisias, Asia Minor 225–6
Apollo 224, 268, 269–71, 299
Arashi, Tokusaburo 314
Archelaus, king of Macedon 5
Archestratus 212n6
Archilochus 48
archives, Athenian public 15–16, 35
archons 18, 32, 152, 348
Areopagus 102, 167, 344
Arginusae, Battle of 11, 353
Argos, Heraia at 224
Aristion 4
aristocrats 98–9, 111, 112, 123, 124, 172
Aristodemus of Metapontum 217
Aristophanes: assemblies 27–8, 132;
chronology 352–4; courtroom

scene 132; direct address to audience
166; heroes 98; on Lenaea 60–1; on
tragedy 93, 95–6, 125, 127; and women
27–8, 63, 66, 65, 93, 106
Acharnians 60–61, 132; *Clouds* 12, 98,
134, 166; *Frogs* 21, 93, 125, 212;
Lysistrata 27, 106, 298; *Peace* 9, 63, 65,
98, 127; *Wasps* 132; *Women in
Assembly* 27–8, 98, 132; *Women
Celebrating the Thesmophoria* 27, 28,
95–6
Aristotle: on actors' influence 154, 207, 220;
chronology 354; on citizenship 16; on
fourth century tragedians 212, 216; on
iambic metre 127; influence in modern era
228–9n3; on *Oedipus the King* 88, 230,
240; on plot structure 88, 178, 180–1; on
private and political content 104, 207; on
psychology of tragedy 67, 171, 333, 341;
on slaves 118; on origins of tragedy 39,
45–6, 155; on rhetoric in tragedy 207; and
transmission of texts 225; on universal
significance of tragedy 94; and women 26,
27
Arrowsmith, William 276
art, visual *see* painting
Artavasdes, king of Armenia 221–2
Artists of Dionysus (*technitai Dionusou*) 216,
224
Aschieri, Pietro 306
Assembly, Athenian 17, 21, 24, 33, 54, 58;
Aristophanes' parodies 27–8, 132;
excluded groups 27–8, 65, 93; language
influences tragedy 118, 132–3
Astydamas the younger 205, 212n6, 214,
215, 216
Athenodorus (actor) 214
Athens 4, 22–35; Acropolis 19, 58, 101;
Agora 23; Artists of Dionysus 224n42;
class divisions 16; critiques in tragedy 120;
history 22–35; modern festivals 309;
Painted Stoa 94; performance culture 5–6,
54; superiority asserted in tragedy 100–3;
theatres, (earliest) 23, (of Dionysus, all-
stone) 15–16, 35, 57, (of Herodes Atticus)
288, 309; and Thebes 23, 101, 102–3;
tragedy specifically located in 94; *see also*
archives; Areopagus; Assembly; *boulē*;
citizenship; civic life; democracy; People's
Court
athletics 13–14, 54, 308
Attica: dialect 4, 127–8; *see also* demes; vase
painting

Auden, W. H. 269
audience 54–68; chorus's guidance to 163–5;
  as citizen body 57–66, 67, 95; collusion
  with 167–71, 179, 195; of comedy 165,
  166, 167; direct address 165, 166–7;
  education of 15, 19–20, 66–7; reminded
  of theatricality of event 158, 165–72, 177;
  seating 58–60; size 57; *see also*
  participation
aulos 12, 71, 71, 73, 73, 348
autochthony myth 30–1, 101, 345

Bacchae see Euripides
barbarians 22, 97
Bardi, Count Giovanni de' 262
Barton, John 314
Bebst, H. 230n7
Benson, Frank 290–91
Berkoff, Steven 271n74
Berlin 298–9, 308, 309, 316, 318
Berlioz, Hector 266
birth (low/high) 99, 111
Birtwistle, Harrison 316
Blanchard, E. L. 288
Böckh, August 286
Boeotia 8, 23, 101, 102–3
boots, actors' 71, 73, 74, 76, 80, 223, 349
Boswell, Laurence 320n56
Bouhélier, Saint-Georges de 308
boulē, Athenian 58–9, 61, 348
Bowra, Maurice 330
Bradfield College, Berks. 291
Brecht, Bertolt 318
Breuer, Lee 281
Brooke, J. 313n51
Browne, Maurice 302–3
Browning, Robert 273–4, 291
Bruce, Hon. W. N. 290–1
Buchanan, George 229, 231n13
Burgess, Anthony 311n47
Burkert, Walter 332, 333
Burne-Jones, Edward Coley 291

Cacoyannis, Michael 277, 277, 282
Caldarone, Maria 313n51
Calzabigi, Ranieri de' 264
Cambelotti, Duilio 306
Cambridge Greek Plays 292, 293, 294–5,
  305
Cambridge Ritualists 331–2, 333
Camerata 262, 285
Campbell, Douglas 311
Campbell, Lewis 289, 290

canon of tragic texts 212, 225
Carcinus 212n6
Casson, Lewis 302
Casteldine, Annie 321n58
Catselli, Electra 277
Cavalli, Francesco 262
Ceausescu family 320
censorship, British 285, 295–8, 302, 320
Chaeremon 212n6
Charpentier, Marc-Antoine 263–4
Chaucer, Geoffrey 178
Cherubini, Luigi 265
Chicago Little Theatre 302–3
childlessness 104, 110
Children of Heracles see Euripides
Choerilus 184
chorēgoi, chorēgia 10–11, 18, 57, 152, 348;
  citizens and metics 18–19, 95;
  Demosthenes 34, 57; fourth century 156,
  212; Pericles 10, 25; Themistocles 24
choreia see dance; song
chorus 42–4, 155–7, 157–8, 163–5, 348;
  choice of 163, 176, 198; citizen status 95;
  declining role? 207; deixis 161, 162–3;
  intervention in action 140, 198n36;
  leader 128; leaving stage 199; modern 231,
  234, 302, 304–5, 309, 319; odes 128, 199;
  satyr plays 157; self-referentiality 42–4,
  182, 196; size 157; vase painting 69–70,
  70; as witnesses 163–5; *see also* dance;
  dithyramb; song
chronological perspective 22–35
Cinyras (anon.) 220, 221
citizenship 16; law of double descent 28–9,
  30, 104, 352; participants in festivals 18,
  57–66, 67, 95, 213
Citti, Franco 280
civic life 3–35; agonistic nature 20–1;
  chronological perspective 22–35;
  individual/collective tension 16, 60, 104,
  335; language 20–1, 128, 132–3, 135; and
  religion 6, 334; theatrical nature of power
  217–20, 221; tragedy as part of 3, 18–22,
  89–90, 206, 207, (audience as civic body)
  57–66, 67, 95, (citizenship of participants)
  18, 57–66, 67, 95, 213, (and civic identity)
  17, 45, 48, 55, 56, 95, 97, (education
  through tragedy) 15, 19–20, 66–7, (plots
  involve community) 182, 185, 192–3,
  233–4; *see also* citizenship; current events;
  democracy; lawcourts; liturgies; oligarchy;
  participation; pay, public; *stasis*
civilisation 97, 141–5

class, social 16, 31, 110–18, 122–3, 124; *see also* aristocrats; slaves; thetes
Cleisthenes 22, 23, 25, 29, 352
Cleon (demagogue) 20, 54
Clever, Edith 318
cocks 12–13, 50
Cocteau, Jean 248, 251–2, 268
comedy: audience contact 165, 166, 167; chorus 157; civic function declines 207; critical/affirmative stance 191; death not mentioned 97; Dionysiac conception 52; at Great Dionysia 26, 37, 352, 354; at Lenaea 26; New Comedy 35; non-terrestrial settings 96; self-referentiality 196; vase-paintings 75, 76, 82
competitive ethos 11–16, 54, 127, 133, 145–9
concubines 122
conflict 181–3, 187
Constitution of the Athenians 10
contests, verbal 14, 20–1, 118–19, 127, 145–9
controversy 21–2, 120, 182, 191, 206
conventions, performance 152–5, 196
Corinth 224n42
Corneille, Pierre 240, 241–3, 285
Corneille, Thomas 263
costumes 73, 73, 74, 76, 197, 337
Council (*boulē*) 58–9, 61, 348
Courtney, W.L. 290–1, 297, 301
Craig, Gordon 294, 305
crane, stage 337
Crane, Walter 294
Crassus Dives, M. Licinius 221–2
criticism, modern 324–47; anthropological 253, 327, 331–6, 343–4; cultural appropriation 341, 342, 343; and form 329; history and politics of reading 343–6; multiple approaches 330–1; New Criticism 328–9; philology 324–31; post-structuralist 343; psychoanalysis and 340–3; on Sophocles 329–31; stagecraft and performance criticism 336–40; structuralist 333, 334, 336, 343
current events, reference to 17, 24–5, 31–2, 173, 185, 186; supposed direct 94, 344
Cyclops see Euripides

Dacier, André 246n39
dance 42, 45, 52, 128, 156–7, 158, 220–1, 337–8
Dassin, Jules 278, 278–9

Davoli, Ninetto 280
death 52, 53, 97; on- and off-stage 154, 199, 219–20, 222; quasi-sacrificial killings 188, 192, 193, 335
debate, antagonistic 14, 20–1, 118–19, 127, 145–9
deception 141–5, 169–70, 196–8
deixis 154, 161–3, 348
Delos, Dionysiac sculpture on 49, 50
Delphi 224, 277, 305–6, 307
demes 67, 349; theatres 3, 6, 7, 23–4
Demeter 51
democracy, Athenian: and aristocratic subjects 172; collective/individual tension 16, 60, 335; critiques 120–1; demise (322 BC) 35, 212; and participation 33; reformers, *see* Cleisthenes; Ephialtes; Pericles; and religion 45, 334; sources' attitudes to 8–9, 16; tragedy and development of 3, 15, 19–20, 66–7, 93, 124–6, 334–5
Demosthenes 15, 56, 104, 127, 217, 354; and theatrical language 34, 56–7, 127
Derrida, Jacques 343
deus ex machina 349
dialects 127–8
didaskaliai 183, 214–17, 349
dikē 137–9, 349
Dio Chrysostom 180n7
Diodorus of Sicily 11, 226
Diomedes (grammarian) 232
Dionysia, Great (City) 8, 14, 17, 55–7; actors' prize 26, 153, 352; Assembly reviews conduct 24; as civic function 18, 55–66, 67, 95, 213; comedy 26, 37, 352, 354; dithyrambic choruses 37, 57, 59; early history 39–40; and Eleutherae 8, 23, 55; in fourth century 33, 213, 214–17; international nature 19, 56, 59, 60–1; officers 18, 212, (*see also* archons); *pompē*, procession 48, 55, 61, 63, 65; records, see *didaskaliai*; revivals 40, 154, 156, 213, 215, 354; rules of competition 152; sacrifice 3–4, 6, 17, 34, 55; satyr plays 37–44, 214, 215, 216; slaves and 56, 61–2; third century 224; women's participation 55, 62–6
Dionysia, Rural 6, 8, 24, 48, 206n44; revivals 156, 213
Dionysus 7, 36–53, 130, 206; and afterlife 45, 52; ambiguous nature 22, 36, 37, 45, 48, 51, 53; and Apollo 268, 269–71, 299; Artists of 216, 224; *Bacchae* as staged by 197–8, 203; and civic identity 45, 48;

and dithyramb 37, 52; emblems 45, 48–9, 50; and masks 8, 37, 45, 49, 51, 52–3; multiplicity of aspects 44–5, 47–8, 53; mystery cult 23, 36, 37, 45, 51, 52, 131; Nietzsche on 36, 52; otherness 45, 95; and origins of drama 45–7; as outsider 8, 37; and plot patterns 37, 46–7, 52; uniqueness, reasons for connection with tragedy 44–53, 224; as year spirit 332

disguise 45, 53, 196–8

dissemination of tragedy 76, 213–14

distancing 158, 165–72

dithyramb 37, 39, 47, 52, 90n26, 157; at Great Dionysia 37, 57, 59

Dodds, E. R. 332, 342

Dodona 224

Dolce, Lodovico 272

Donatus 232

Donner, Johann Jakob Christian 286

Doolittle, Hilda ('H. D.') 274–5

Doric dialect 128

Dryden, John 240, 243–5, 301

Dublin, Abbey Theatre 296–7, 304–5

Durkheim, Emile 332, 334

Edinburgh 288, 289–90, 292, 313–14

education: civic, through tragedy 15, 19–20, 66–7; school texts 129, 225

ekkuklēma (stage machinery) 338, 340, 349

Electra see Euripides; Sophocles

Electra myth, modern plays on 254–61, 285

Eleusinian mysteries 51

Eleutherae 8, 23, 55

Eliot, T. S. 273, 276, 304, 328; The Family Reunion 254, 256–8, 261

embolima (insert songs) 155, 207, 349

Enescu, George 268–9

Engels, Friedrich 344

eniautos daimon theory 331

Enlightenment 238–40, 253, 265

Ennius 226

ephebes 19–20, 55, 56, 59, 335, 349; adolescence 20, 191–3

Ephialtes 25, 26, 344, 352

Epic Cycle 107–8, 129, 169–70, 174

epic tradition 135, 171; see also Epic Cycle; Homer

Epidaurus 308–9, 316, 354

epodes 128, 349

Erasmus, Desiderius 229

Erigone, myth of 48

Euaretus 214, 215

Eumenides see Aeschylus

Eunapius of Sardis 222–3

Euripides: Aeschylean references 168–9, 179–80, 185, 195–6, 258; chronology 352, 353; and expectations 185, 190, 195–6, 202; lower-class perspective 93, 119, 123–4; in Macedon 5, 213; and masks 198n34, 339; Nietzsche on 145, 206; number of actors 153; plots 107–8, 119, 185, 188, 189–90, 195–6, 202; political stance 20, 32; popularity 5, 212n6, 215, 225, 232; translations 229–30, 271–2, 274–5, 302; and women 29–30, 93, 98, 108–9, 111, 119

Alcestis 40, 154, 188, 199n37, 229, 353

Alexander 112

Andromache 105, 108, 113, 122, 123, 124, 353; Andromache's situation 98, 111, 112, 119, 122; plot patterns 107–8, 188

Antigone 21, 184–5

Antiope 112, 120

Archelaus 213

Bacchae: chorus 163; chronology 353; costuming 197; Dionysus 22, 47, 131, 197–8, 203; Dodds' edition 332; gender 197–8; language 131; messengers 115, 124; metatheatre 197–8, 203; modern versions 36, 269, 270, 271, 282–3, 302, 311n47, 313; in Armenia, with Crassus' head 221–2; Pentheus 45, 192–3, 197–8, 200; plot 107–8, 108–9, 188, 192–3; psychoanalytic criticism 340–1, 342

Children of Heracles 97, 99, 112, 120–1, 188, 353

Cyclops 41, 43, 48, 353

Electra 16, 97, 110, 112, 114–15, 166; Aeschylean references 168–9, 179–80, 185, 196, 258; modern versions 277, 277, 302; plot patterns 97, 179–80, 188, 189

Erechtheus 16, 19, 101

fr. 189 119

Hecuba 20, 97, 111, 188, 229, 353; Polymestor's blinding 154–5, 158; on war 13, 98

Helen 18, 111, 122, 124, 197, 353; chorus 199n37; plot patterns 97, 107–8, 189; women and slaves 119, 124

Heracles 102, 105, 106, 111, 273, 353; plot patterns 107–8, 182, 188, 190

Hippolytus 353; chorus 158, 165; deixis 161n22; ephebic theme 20, 203–4; first version 201–2; gender-blurring 203; gods 173, 203, 205; *hypothesis* 202; language 204–5; metatheatricality 173, 203; modern versions 234–7, 278, 278–9, 285, 296, 302; nurse 116, 117–18, 202, 235; on-stage death 154; plot 107–8, 116, 182, 188, 201–5; setting 103; vase painting 82, 83; on women 30, 108, 116, 117–18, 204

Hypsipyle 120

Ion 103, 104, 122; modern versions 274–5, 286, 320; patriotic myths 30–1, 101; plot 182, 187, 189; slaves 112, 115–16

Iphigeneia at Aulis 107, 108, 111, 188, 319, 353; translations 229, 230n7, 272

Iphigeneia among the Taurians 97, 100, 189, 353; modern versions 238–40, 303; vase painting 76–8, 77

Medea 353; Aegeus 103, 104; chorus 161, 162, 163, 165; expectations overturned 195; formal signals of rhythm and delivery 158–61; Medea 18, 22, 108, 109; modern versions 279, 298, 302, 311n47, 312, 313–14, 314, 320; plot patterns 97, 107–8, 119, 120, 188, 189; setting 103; slaves 114, 115, 119; translations 229, 275, 302; vase paintings 78–80, 78, 79, 81; women's voice 18, 121

Melanippe Captive 122

Orestes 111n46, 214, 230n8, 320, 353; plot 97, 107–8, 185, 188, 190, 192; political aspects 32, 132

Philoctetes 180n7

Phoenician Women 20, 166, 232, 272, 353; modern productions 320, 321n58; plot 110, 188, 195–6; Thrasybulus' dream 11

Stheneboea 118

Suppliant Women 11, 154, 188, 190, 353; political aspects 97, 101, 120

Telephus 112

Trojan Women: chorus 161n22, 163, 176–7; chronology 353; deixis 161n22, 173–7; gods' role 173–4; Hecuba 111, 174–6; Helen–Hecuba debate 145–9, 175; historical setting 31–2; language 134–5, 137, 145–9; manipulation of myth 148–9; modern versions 277, 282, 302, 313, 319, 320, 321n58; panegyric of Athens 100; plot 105, 108, 181; ritual enacted 175;

theatricality 177; translation 302–4; on war 13, 98

Europe, Eastern 318, 320, 321

Ezekiel, *Exagoge* 211n2

exile 97–8

existentialism 254

exits and entrances 338–9, 340

expectations *see* plot

Fagles, Robert 276

family 104–5, 110; actors' and dramatists' 216–17

Farr, Florence 302

fascism 36, 306, 308

fate 182–3, 253

feminism 313, 344–5

Fenollosa, Ernest 312

Festival Fund *see* Theoric Fund

festivals, ancient: civic function 5–11, 95, 185, 333; *see also* Dionysia, Great *and* Rural; Lenaea

festivals, modern 305–9

fictional plots 185–6, 208

films 277–81, 282, 312

fleet, Athenian 16, 17, 32

Fleg, Edmond 269

Florence 262, 285

foreigners (non-Athenians): characters in tragedy 93, 95, 100–3, 111n46, 122–3, 124–6; at Great Dionysia 19, 56, 59, 60–61; playwrights and actors 4, 213; theatres 213–14, 224; *see also* aliens, resident

Fotopoulos, Dionysis 316

foundling plot 186–7

Four Hundred, Revolution of the 32, 353

fourth century 33–5, 40, 207, 208, 212–20; *see also* revivals

Fraenkel, Eduard 326, 327, 337

freedom: Dionysus and 23, 45, 48; of expression 125; loss, as theme 111, 112, 123; Sartre on 258, 259, 260

Freud, Sigmund, and Freudianism 240, 254, 255, 289, 311, 340–3

Friedrich Wilhelm IV, Kaiser 286, 288

Frohman, Daniel 292

Fugard, Athol 283

Gabrieli, Andrea 230, 261

Gaius, Emperor 219–20

Gargallo, Count Mario Tomas 306

Garnier, Robert 233–4, 235

Gascoigne, George 272

Gémier, Firmin 308
gender: blurring and reversal 106, 197–8, 203; politics of 66, 103–10, 139, 140, 192, 344–5; *see also* women
Gernet, Louis 333–4
ghosts 96
Gide, André 248–51
Gielgud, John 312
Girard, René 332–3
Giraudoux, Jean 253
Giustiniani, Orsatto 230
Gladstone, William Ewart 292
Gluck, Christoph Wilibald 264–5
gods: epiphanies 96, 337; language 205; man's relationship 96–7, 135, 206, 330; quasi-'directorial' role 173, 197–8, 203; reconciliation by 181; and retribution-pattern plots 187–8
Godwin, E. W. 294
Goethe, Johann Wolfgang von 238–40, 276, 286
Goodwin, Professor W. W., of Harvard 291
Gorgias 119, 134, 145, 146–7
Gospel at Colonus, The (musical) 281
Granville-Barker, Harley 299, 303–4
Gray, Revd Herbert Branston 291
Gray, Terence 305
Grotius 232
Guarini, Giovanni Battista 262
guest-friendship (*xenia*) 216
Gulf War 321
Guthrie, Tyrone 310–11, 311, 312

'H. D.' (Hilda Doolittle) 274–5
Hall, Peter 276, 314, 316, 317
Holiday, Henry 294
hamartia 181, 349
Handel, George Frideric 264
Harcourt, Robert 297
Harrison, Jane Ellen 294, 332
Harrison, Tony 38, 39, 276, 316
Harvard University 291–2, 304
Hays, Bill 281
Heaney, Seamus 282
Hecuba see Euripides
Hegel, Georg Wilhelm Friedrich 181, 286–7
Helen see Euripides
Heliodorus (novelist) 226
'Hellenic spirit' 94
Henze, Hans Werner 269, 270, 271
Heracles see Euripides
Heraclitus of Ephesus 13
Herculaneum 69

hero cult 131
Herodotus 11
Hiero of Syracuse 213
Hippias (tragic poet) 4
Hippocratic corpus 109–10
Hippolytus see Euripides
historical events in tragedy 17, 24–5, 31–2, 94, 173, 185, 186, 344
Hitler, Adolf 36
Hoffmann, François Benoit 265
Hofmannsthal, Hugo von 267, 298–301
Hölderlin, Johann Christoph Friedrich 268
Homer 107–8, 129–30, 172, 176, 185, 194
Honegger, Arthur 268
hoplites 16, 17–18
Horace 5, 39–40
household 104–5, 110
hubris (overweening pride) 181
humanist drama 229–34
hupothesis/hypothesis 151–2, 202, 349

imagination 99–100, 121, 122–3, 125–6
individual: /collective tension 16, 60, 335; modern focus on 234–5, 237, 255
Ingegneri, Angiolo 230
initiation: ephebic 20–1, 335; mystic 45, 53
innovation 20, 154–5, 178–80, 183, 184–5, 206–7
inscriptions: Aphrodisias 225–6; deme 6, 7; *see also didaskaliai*; *Marmor Parium*; Tegea
intertextuality 168–9, 179, 193–5, 195–8
Ion see Euripides
Ion of Chios 4, 40
Iphigeneia at Aulis see Euripides
Iphigeneia among the Taurians see Euripides
isēgoria 126, 349
Isocrates 15, 34
Italy, South 5; satyr plays 41n23; vases 74–88, 75, 78, 79, 81, 83, 84, 86, 89, 90

Jaffrey, Madhur 313n51
Japan 312–14, 314
Jason of Tralles 221–2
Jebb, Richard 330
Jeffers, Robinson 275, 312
Jenkin, Fleeming 289–90
Jones, Henry Arthur 296, 296
Josephus 219–20
Jowett, Benjamin 290
juries 58, 65
justice 21–2, 95, 137–9; *see also* lawcourts

Kabuki theatre 313, 319

Kallman, Chester 269
Kani, John 283
Kathakali theatre 319
katharsis 333, 349
Keats, John 276
Kent, Jonathan 320
kerkides (sectors of theatre) 58, 349
Kierkegaard, Søren 94
Kinwelmersh, Francis 272
Kitto, H. D. F. 329, 330, 342
Kleist, Heinrich von 247–8
Knox, B. M.W. 330
kommos (ritual) 131, 349
kōmos (revel) 55, 349
kothornoi (boots) 71, 73, 74, 76, 80, 349
Koun, Karolos 309, 314, 315, 316
Koundouros, Nikos 321
kratos 136–7
kurios (guardian) 99, 106–9, 349

Lacan, Jacques 340
Lacroix, Jules 289, 290, 296
language 127–50; ambiguity and
    polysemy 136–50, 335; contests of words
    14, 20–1, 118–19, 127, 145–9; dialects
    127–8; epic 129–30, 135; and gender 140;
    heightened 122–3, 127, 128, 171–2;
    misunderstandings 136, 335;
    paradox 133–4, 146; powers 139–40,
    200–1; tragedy as drama of words
    199–200, 204–5, 302; word/deed
    opposition 142, 144, 149, 204; *see also*
    rhetoric; *and under* civic life; lawcourts;
    religion; *and individual dramatists and
    plays*
Lattimore, Richmond 276
lawcourts 14–16, 54, 58, 65, 93;
    Aristophanes' mock 132; in *Eumenides* 15,
    20, 102, 132, 135, 167, 192, 344, 345;
    language of 118–19, 132–3, 137–9
laws 32; citizenship 28–9, 30, 104, 352; clash
    of divine and man-made 22, 95
League of Nations 304
Lee, Nathaniel 240, 243–5, 301
Leighton, Frederick, Lord 294
Lenaea 8, 14, 18–19, 26, 33, 60–1; satyr
    plays 40, 216
Libation-Bearers see Aeschylus
libations 56, 131
life, interaction of drama with 217–20, 221,
    222
London productions: Covent Garden 287,
    287–8, 299, 300, 301; Gate Theatre

313n51; Hengler's Circus 294, 295; Lyric,
    Hammersmith 313n51; Old Vic 304, 309,
    310; Queen's Theatre 288; Young Vic
    313n51
Longianus, C. Julius 225–6
Los Angeles Olympic Games 313
Louis XIV of France 262
Lowell, Robert 276
Lucian 105, 226, 338
Lully, Jean Baptiste 263
Lumley, Lady Jane 272
Lycurgus (Athenian politician) 15–16, 33, 35,
    57

McCarthy, Lillah 301, 303, 304
Macedon 33, 34, 35, 212, 217; Athenian
    playwrights in 5, 213; Philip II 217,
    218–20, 223
McLeish, Kenneth 281
McMurray, Mary 313n51
MacNeice, Louis 274
maenads 45, 48, 49, 106
Magna Graecia *see* Italy, South
Mantua 263
manuscript tradition 15–16, 35, 216–17,
    224–6, 229, 325, 326
Marmor Parium 216
Martin-Harvey, John 297, 301
Marxism 344
masks: comic 7; Dionysus and 8, 37, 45, 49,
    51, 52–3; Euripides' awareness of 198n34,
    339; modern criticism on 339; modern
    productions 305, 311, 311, 316, 317; and
    number of actors 153; Roman 223; vase-
    paintings 45, 49, 69, 70, 70, 71, 73, 73, 74,
    75, 88–9
Mauss, Marcel 332, 334
Medea see Euripides
medicine 109–10
Melos, massacre at 31–2, 173
Menander 35, 354
Mendelssohn-Bartholdy, Felix 286–8, 289
Mercouri, Melina 278
messengers 113, 115, 124, 154, 199; vase-
    paintings 80, 81, 82, 83, 85, 86–7, 87, 88,
    113
metatheatricality 193–8, 203
metics 18–19, 61, 350
metres 157–61, 171, 198; anapaests 157,
    158, 159; iambic 127, 157, 158, 159, 160;
    lyric 111, 128, 156, 157, 158, 171
Midas and Silenus 52–3
Miletus, Persian sack of 24, 32, 352

Milhaud, Darius 267–8
Miller, Arthur 276
Milton, John 229
Minneapolis, USA 311
Mitchell, Katie 320n56, 321n58
Mnester (*pantomimus*) 219, 220
Mnouchkine, Ariane 319
Moisewitsch, Tanya 311
Monteverdi, Claudio 262, 263
Moore, Albert Joseph 288
Morell, Thomas 272
Moscow 288, 320
Mounet-Sully, Jean 269, 289, 290, 296, 297
Mule, Giuseppe 306
Müller, Heiner 318
Murray, Gilbert 291n12, 297–8, 302, 332;
    translations 272–3, 296, 299, 301, 302–4
Muses 157
music 128, 156–7, 224, 337–8; see also *aulos*;
    dance; song
Mussolini, Benito 36, 306
Müthel, Lothar 308
mystery cults 23, 36, 37, 45, 51, 52, 131
myth 180–93; Athens appropriates other
    cities' 101–3, 120; autochthony 30–1, 101,
    345; fourth-century use 208, 215;
    intertextuality 193–5; lack of orthodox
    versions 184–5; manipulation 148–9, 179;
    megatext 190–3; modern use 231–2,
    234–7; multivalence 173, 221, 231–2;
    norm validation 191; patriotic 30–1, 101,
    120, 345; and plots 180–93, 208, 215;
    poets in 119–20; story patterns adapted
    to 186, 189

naturalism 161, 298–301
Nazism 308, 318
neoclassicism, seventeenth-century 234,
    240–47, 285, 286
Neoptolemus (actor) 214, 215, 217–20
Nero, Emperor 223
New York 281, 292, 304, 312, 319, 320
Nietzsche, Friedrich Wilhelm 36, 52, 145,
    206, 299; and Wilamowitz 284, 324–5
Nigeria 282–3
Ninagawa, Yukio 313–14, 314
Noble, Adrian 318–19
Noh drama 312, 319
Nostoi (Epic Cycle) 107–8, 174
Notre Dame University, USA 291, 296
Ntshona, Winston 283
nurses 112, 114–15, 116, 117–18, 123–4,
    202, 235

odes, choral 128, 199
Oedipus at Colonus see Sophocles
Oedipus the King see Sophocles
Oligarch, Old 10
oligarchy 32, 35, 212, 353
Olivier, Laurence 309, 310
Olympic Games, modern 308, 313
O'Neill, Eugene 254–6, 261, 276
openings of plays 119, 166–7
opera 261–71, 285
oracles 120–1, 164
orators, forensic 14–15, 17; see also rhetoric
Oresteia see Aeschylus
Orestes see Euripides
Orestes myth 184, 254–61
Orff, Carl 268
Origen 119
origins of tragedy 3–4, 20–1, 22–3, 39, 45–7,
    51
ostracism 25, 350
otherness 45, 93–126
outsiders 8, 18, 22, 37, 93
Oxford University 290–1, 292, 304

paidagōgoi 114–15, 350
painting 69, 90; see also vase painting
Palladio, Andrea 230, 231
Palmer (Sikelianou), Eva 305–6
Panathenaea, Great 13, 58, 61, 64, 65, 129
pantomimi 220–1
Papas, Irene 277
papyri 225, 326
paradox 133–4, 146
Paris 287, 308, 319
parodos 128
Parratt, Walter 291
parrhēsia 126, 350
Parthia 221–2
participation 16–18, 33, 54, 55–7, 67, 167;
    spectating as 8, 51, 54
Pasolini, Pier Paolo 279–81, 280
pastoral drama, fifteenth/sixteenth-century
    262
Patrici, Francesco 261n61
pay, public 9–10, 17, 26, 33
Peisistratus 3, 22
Peloponnesian War 4, 5, 11, 31–2, 173, 205,
    353
People's Court 14, 16, 21, 26; see also
    Areopagus
performance: conscious theatricality 158,
    165–72, 177; Dionysiac 37–44, 52–3;
    evidence of form 151–77, (chorus's

indications) 163–5, (deixis) 161–3, (metres) 157–61, (*Trojan Women* as example) 173–7; evocation of previous 168–9, 195–8; rules and conventions 152–5; and scholarship 284; and spectating 51; stagecraft 336–40; *see also individual aspects*

performance criticism 336–40

performance culture 5–6, 54

performances, modern 284–323, 336–7; nineteenth-century 285–94; turn of century, *Oedipus* 294–301; World War era 302–9; post-war era 309–21; *see also* adaptations; political commentary

Peri, Jacopo 262

Pericles 9, 10, 25, 26, 133, 353; citizenship law 28–9, 30, 104, 352

peripeteia 111, 181, 200–1, 350

Persians see Aeschylus

Persian Wars 17, 19, 24, 352

persuasion 20, 139–40, 141–5, 148, 192, 206

phallus 45, 48–9, 50, 55

Philip II of Macedon 217, 218–20, 223

Philoctetes see Sophocles

philology 324–31, 332, 335

Phoenician Women see Euripides

Phrynichus 184; *Capture of Miletus* 24, 32, 352; *Phoenician Women* 24, 167, 352

pictorial record 69–90; *see also* vase painting

Piraeus; theatre 14

Plague, Great Athenian 31, 353

Plataea, Battle of 173, 352

Plato 9, 67, 127, 338, 354; on Great Dionysia 5, 55, 57–8; on psychology of tragedy 333, 340, 341; on women 26–7, 63–4, 119

Gorgias 61–2; *Laws* 9, 63–4; *Republic* 26–7, 119, 127; *Symposium* 5, 55, 57–8

pleasure of tragedy 171, 182, 340

plot- and narrative patterns 93–126, 178–9, 180–93; basic 94–5; conflict 181–3, 187; Dionysiac 37, 46–7, 52; and expectations 179, 187, 190, 195–6, 202, 212; fate and 182–3; and foreigners 93, 95, 100–3, 125; *Hippolytus* analysed 201–5; historical events 185, 186; invented tales 185–6, 208; multivocal form challenges ideologies expressed in 118–24; myth 183–6; and slaves 93, 110–18, 125; story patterns 186–90; and women 93, 95, 103–10, 124

plots 178–208; form and 198–201; innovation 178–80, 183, 184–5; and

metatheatre 193–8; modern adaptations 228, 231–2; and myth 180–93, 208; repetition 178–80, 206; *see also* plot- and narrative patterns

Plutarch 40, 119, 221–2, 226

Poel, William 302

Poland 318

polis and political life, *see* civic life

political commentary in modern productions 254, 258–9, 318, 319–20, 320–1

political discourse of tragedy 343–6

polyphony of tragedy 93, 118–26, 191

pompai (processions) 350; Panathenaea 58, 64, 65; *see also under* Dionysia, Great

Pompeii 69

positivism 327, 328, 335

possession, ecstatic 37, 45, 48

post-structuralism 343

Potsdam 286–7, 288

Potter, Robert 272

pottery *see* vase painting

Pound, Ezra 312

Poynter, Sir E. 294

Pratinas 4, 44, 184

pride, overweening (*hubris*) 181

priestesses 28, 122

processions *see pompai*

productions, modern *see* performances, modern

Prometheus Bound see Aeschylus

Protagoras 97, 133

Psachos, K. 305, 306

psychoanalysis 253, 340–3

Racine, Jean 234–7, 285

Rameau, Jean-Philippe 264

Rangabis (translator) 288

Raphael, Frederic 281

rebirth 45, 53, 331

reception 209–347; ancient world 211–27; *see also* adaptations; criticism; performances, modern

recognition, conventions of 196

reconciliation 181–2, 256

redemption 52, 258, 261

reference to other plays *see* intertextuality

Reinhardt, Karl 328, 329, 330

Reinhardt, Max 298–301, 300, 308, 309

release, emotional 39, 333

religion: and civic life 6, 334; cultic origins of tragedy 3–4; fourth-century change 223–4; language of 20, 130–1, 135, 164; slaves' participation 62; song and dance in 157;

women's role 27, 28, 64, 65, 106, 122; *see also* Dionysus
Renaissance 229–34, 326
repertoire 40, 213, 220
reversals: gender 106; paradoxical 133–4, 146; rituals of 333
revivals of plays 40, 154, 156, 212n6, 213, 215, 225, 354
rhēseis (speeches) 127–8, 134–5, 350
Rhesus (anon.) 33, 123, 156, 199n37, 211n2
rhetoric 34, 56–7, 225, 232–3; epideictic 134, 349; in tragedy 118–19, 133–5, 143, 145–9, 207, 208, 345
Richmond, Professor W. B. 291
Rigg, Diana 320
Rinuccini, Ottavio 262
rites de passage 186–7, 191–3, 203–4
ritual 175, 335–6; apotropaic 332–3, 335; interpretation of tragedy 331–2; language of 130–1, 135; *see also* Dionysus
Robben Island, South Africa 283
Robertson, Toby 313n51
Romagnoli, Ettore 306
Romania 319–20
Rome, ancient 5, 18, 35, 219–23, 226
Rondiris, Dimitris 309
Rotrou, Jean de 234
Royal Shakespeare Company 318–19, 320n56, 321n58
Rucellai, Giovanni 230n8, 231n14
rules of performance 152–5
rural festivals *see* Dionysia, Rural

sacrifice 332–3, 335, 343; at festivals 3–4, 6, 17, 34, 55; in tragedy 188, 192, 193, 335
Saint-Denis, Michael 309
Salamis, Battle of 17, 25, 99, 352
salvation 52, 258, 261
Sartre, Jean-Paul 254, 258–61, 282
satyr plays 37–44, 52; Astydamas' 216; chorus 42–4, 157; Euripides' 41, 43, 48, 353; fourth-century 40, 214, 215, 216; at Great Dionysia 37–44; at Lenaea 40; same performers as tragic trilogy 38, 39, 42, 51, 153, 172; settings 97; Sophocles' 43–4, 48, 97; vase paintings 38, 41, 73, 73, 90n26
satyrs 7, 44n31, 45, 49
Saxe-Meiningen Company 289
Scaliger, Joseph Justus 233
scapegoats 203, 332–3, 335
scenes 127–8
Schlegel, August 286

scholarship, ancient 35, 151, 225, 284, 325, 326; see also *hupothesis/hypothesis*
scholia 225, 326
Scione, defeat of 173
seating in theatre 58–60, 63
Sellars, Peter 321
Seneca 226, 228, 233, 235n22, 240n33, 243, 285
Serban, Andrei 319–20
settings 96–7, 103–4, 141, 333
Seven against Thebes see Aeschylus
Shelley, Percy Bysshe, *The Cenci* 295, 296
Shirley, William 285
Sicily 5, 32, 353; vase-paintings 41n23, 87
Sikelianos, Angelos 305–6
Silenus 52–3
singing *see* song
skēnē 75, 82, 103–4, 338–9, 339–40, 350
slaves 110–18, 123–4; 'assistants to the Council' 61; at Great Dionysia 56, 61–2; old, in vase paintings 78–9, 78, 79, 80, 81, 82, 83, 85, 86–7, 87, 88, 113; plot patterns express inferiority 93, 110–18, 123, 125; tragedy gives voice 93, 119, 124–6; *see also* nurses; *paidagōgoi*
sociology of tragedy 93–126; *see also* foreigners; slaves; women
Socrates 206, 208, 352, 354
soliloquy 199
song 220, 261–2; choral 42–4, 128, 156–7, 157–8; insert (*embolima*) 155, 207, 349; solo 158, 220
Sophists 133
Sophocles: chronology 33, 352, 353; language 131, 135, 137, 141–5; modern criticism 329–31; number of actors 153; political stance 32; satyr plays 43–4, 48, 97; vase paintings 84–8, 84, 86, 87; and women's view-point 29, 30, 119, 121
Ajax 13, 97, 111, 162, 181, 188, 200; chorus 17, 199; literary allusions 130, 194; modern productions 292, 293, 306; on-stage death 154
Andromeda 72
Antigone 15, 85, 100, 352; chorus 163, 198; Creon 104, 124, 133, 182; deixis 162–3; laws of gods and men 21, 22, 95; modern adaptations and productions 233, 268, 283, 285–8, 289, 306, 318–19, 321; plot patterns 97, 184–5, 189; translations 230n8, 268, 288; women in 30, 99, 105, 109, 119
Dionysiscus 48

INDEX

Electra 106, 110, 114–15, 169, 353;
intertextuality 130, 168–9; plot 97,
107–8, 112, 179–80, 188, 189; Serban's
version 320
Oedipus at Colonus 131, 153n6, 162, 199;
first peformance 33, 216–17, 354;
modern adaptations and productions
281, 288, 304–5, 318–19; patriotism 19,
100, 102–3; plot patterns 97, 188, 189;
translations 274; vase painting *84*, *84*,
85
Oedipus the King: Aristotle on 88, 230,
240; and British censorship 285, 295–8,
302, 320; chorus 165, 182; community
tragedy 182; deixis 161, 162; first
production 33, 353; Freud and 240, 340;
modern adaptations 240–53, 268–9;
modern productions 289, 290, 302,
(Vicenza, 1585) 228, 230–1, 261, 285,
(nineteenth-century) 269, 289, 290,
291–2, 294–5, 296, 297, (Edwardian)
294–301, 302, 320, (World War era)
297, 304, 308, 310–11, *311*, 312, (post-
war) 309–12, 318–19, (film and
television) 279–81, *280*, 312;
peripeteia 200–1; plot patterns 187, 189,
192; power of words 200–1; sacrifice
332–3; slaves in 112, 113–14;
translations 230n8, 274, 289, 296, 298,
299, 301, 304, 309
Philoctetes 19–20, 162, 180n7, 181, 190,
353; cast 17, 105; on civilisation 97,
141–5; deception 141–5, 169–70,
196–7; language 137, 141–5; modern
adaptation 282; opening lines 129–30
Tereus 121
Thamyris 120
Trackers 43–4, 97
Triptolemus 352
Women of Trachis 161–2, 164–5,
194n30; modern versions 275, 290;
plot patterns 97, 107–8, 111, 112, 122,
188; women's viewpoint 119, 121
South Africa 283
Soyinka, Wole 282–3
Sparta 23, 32
spectating 8, 51, 54, 165–72, 333, 340
speeches 127–8, 134–5, 199, 350
Spender, Stephen 276
Spintharus 4
stage buildings, *see skēnē*
stagecraft 336–40
Stanislavsky 288, 289

Stanley, Professor David 304
stasima (choral odes) 128, 350
stasis 25–6, 31, 99, 350
Stein, Peter 314, 316, 318, 320
stēlē, honorific 6
Stiblinus 232
stichomythia 127–8, 158, 351
Stobaeus (John of Stobi), *Florilegium* 219
Stratford, Ontario 310–11, *311*
Strauss, Richard 267
Stravinsky, Igor 268
strife, civil, *see stasis*
strophē 128, 351
Stroux, Karl Heinz 309
structuralism 333, 334, 336, 343
Suetonius 219
Suppliant Women see Aeschylus; Euripides
Suzuki, Tadashi 313
Sydney, University of 292
symposia 54, 131
Syracuse 5, 213, 224, 306, 308
Szymanowski, Karol 269n73

Tanayev, Sergei Ivanovich 267
Taplin, Oliver 337, 338–9, 340
Taylor, Don 281
technitai Dionusou ('Artists of Dionysus')
216, 224
Tegea, inscription from 212n6, 222, 224
television 277, 281
Telson, Bob 281
texts 15–16, 35, 216–17, 224–6, 229, 325,
326
Théâtre du Soleil 319
theatres 5, 338; deme 3, 6, 7, 23–4; outside
Attica 213–14, 224; Piraeus 14;
seating 58–60; *skēnai* 75, 82, 103–4,
338–9, 339–40, 350; *see also under* Athens
theatricality, reminders of 158, 165–72, 177
Theatro Technis 309, 314, *315*, 316
Thebes, Athens and 23, 101, 102–3
Themistocles 24, 25, 344
Theodectes 212n6
Theodorus (actor) 119
Theophrastus, *Characters* 62, 118
Theoric Fund 9–10, 33–4, 62–3, 66–7
Thesmophoria 28
Thespiae 224n42
Thespis 22, 23, 24, 183–4, 352
thetes 16, 351
Thettalus (actor) 214, 215, 217
Thirty Tyrants 32, 353
Thomson, James 285

Thorikos 6
Thorndike, Sybil 309
Thrasybulus (admiral) 11, 14
Thucydides 9, 11, 15, 20, 54, 133
Thurii 11, 74n9, 89
tickets, theatre 59
Tieck, Ludwig 286
time, past and present 167, 182, 206
time-span of Athenian tragedy 46, 205–8
Timocles 214, 215
Timotheus of Zacynthus (actor) 222
Todhunter, John 294, 295
Togamura, Japan 313
Toho Company 313
tokens, lead 59
Tokyo University 312
trade union (Artists of Dionysus) 216, 224
translation 229–30, 271–6; see also
    adaptations; performances, modern
    theatrical; and under individual
    tragedians
Tree, Sir Herbert Beerbohm 294, 296, 297
Trench, Herbert 297, 299
tribes 57, 59–60
tribute, Athenian imperial 56, 60
Trissino, Giangiorgio 231
Trojan Women see Euripides
Turnage, Mark-Anthony 271n74
tyrant, figure of 344

universality of Greek tragedy 94
university productions 289–94, 304, 312,
    319

Valois, Ninette de 305
Vandenhoff, George and daughter 288
vase painting 69–90, 213; Attic 12, 69–74,
    70, 71, 73, 77, 88–90; aulos-players 12,
    71, 71; Basle Dancers 69–70, 70;
    Capodarso Painter 85–8, 87; Choregos
    Vase 75, 76; of comedy 75, 76, 82;
    Corinth pyre fragments 70–1, 71, 88; of
    dithyramb 90n26; political subjects 89–90;
    Pronomos Vase 73, 73–4; satyrs and satyr
    plays 38, 41, 44n31, 73, 73, 90n26;
    Sicilian 41n23, 87; South Italian 5, 74–88,
    75, 78, 79, 81, 83, 84, 86, 89, 90; 'X is
    handsome' type 71–2, 89; see also under
    masks; messengers; slaves; and individual
    tragedians
Vellacott, Philip 313n51
Venice 263
Vernant, Jean-Pierre 136–7, 334–6

Vicenza 228, 230–1, 261, 285
Vidal-Naquet, Pierre 334, 335
Vietnam War 282
violence 154, 199, 219–20, 222
virility 13, 54, 348
Volmoeller, Karl 301
Voltaire, François Marie Arouet de 240,
    245–6

Wagner, Richard 266–7, 284, 289
Wajda, Andrej 318
warfare 13, 14, 16, 56, 59, 97–8; criticism of
    militarism 13, 18, 121
Warr, George 292, 294
Weimar, Goethe at 286
Weinstock, Heinrich 309
Wenckstern, A. 267
Werfel, Franz 282
Wertenbaker, Timberlake 318–19
Whitman, Cedric 330
Wilamowitz-Moellendorff, Ulrich von 284,
    308, 324–5
Wiles, D. 313n51
wine 41, 45, 48, 53
Winnington-Ingram, R. P. 330, 342
women 26–31, 103–10; in absence of
    husband or kurios 106–9, 116;
    autochthony myth devalues 30–1, 101,
    345; concubines 122; displaced 97–8, 111;
    disruptive 30, 95, 99, 106–9, 116;
    feminism 313, 344–5; and festivals 8, 28,
    55, 62–6; heightened language 119, 122–3;
    Hippolytus' invective against 30, 117–18,
    204; invisibility 64, 105; male/female
    confrontation 22, 206; marriage 121–2,
    193, 343; medical ideas on 109–10; plot
    patterns express inferiority 93, 95, 103–10,
    125; as psychologically frail 106, 109,
    115–18; religious role 27, 28, 64, 65, 106,
    122; tragedy gives voice 29–30, 93, 119,
    121–2, 124–6; see also gender, politics of
    and under individual dramatists
Women of Trachis see Sophocles
Women's Peace Party 303
words see language
World Wars, era of 282, 302–9
Wright, Nicholas 320n56

xenia (guest-friendship) 216

year spirit 331
Yeats, W. B. 274, 296–7, 304–5, 309, 312
Yugoslavia, former 321